Communications
in Computer and Information Science 916

Commenced Publication in 2007
Founding and Former Series Editors:
Phoebe Chen, Alfredo Cuzzocrea, Xiaoyong Du, Orhun Kara, Ting Liu,
Dominik Ślęzak, and Xiaokang Yang

More information about this series at http://www.springer.com/series/7899

Juan Carlos Figueroa-García
Juan G. Villegas · Juan Rafael Orozco-Arroyave
Pablo Andres Maya Duque (Eds.)

Applied Computer Sciences in Engineering

5th Workshop on Engineering Applications, WEA 2018
Medellín, Colombia, October 17–19, 2018
Proceedings, Part II

 Springer

Editors
Juan Carlos Figueroa-García ⓘ
Department of Industrial Engineering
Universidad Distrital Francisco José de
 Caldas
Bogotá
Colombia

Juan Rafael Orozco-Arroyave ⓘ
Department of Electronics
 and Telecomunications Engineering
University of Antioquia
Medellín
Colombia

Juan G. Villegas ⓘ
Department of Industrial Engineering
University of Antioquia
Medellín
Colombia

Pablo Andres Maya Duque ⓘ
Department of Industrial Engineering
University of Antioquia
Medellín
Colombia

ISSN 1865-0929   ISSN 1865-0937   (electronic)
Communications in Computer and Information Science
ISBN 978-3-030-00352-4   ISBN 978-3-030-00353-1   (eBook)
https://doi.org/10.1007/978-3-030-00353-1

Library of Congress Control Number: 2018953754

This Springer imprint is published by the registered company Springer Nature Switzerland AG
The registered company address is: Gewerbestrasse 11, 6330 Cham, Switzerland

Preface

The fifth edition of the Workshop on Engineering Applications (WEA 2018) focused on computer science, simulation, the Internet of Things (IoT), logistics, as well as computational intelligence and its applications. This is a big step, since WEA has become consolidated as a scientific forum for engineering and applied sciences in academia and industry.

WEA 2018 was held during October 17–19, 2018, at the Universidad de Antioquia in Medellín, Colombia. The workshop was a parallel event in the framework of Expoingenieria 2018. This latter event was a broad forum for the interchange of knowledge between academia, industry, and the state, organized to commemorate the 75th anniversary of the Engineering School of the Universidad de Antioquia.

We received more than 200 submissions covering topics such as computer science, IoT, logistics, operations research, simulation systems, systems dynamics, systems modeling, power and electrical applications, software engineering, computer informatics, computational intelligence, intelligent computing and others. All submissions were rigorously peer–reviewed using EasyChair and 97 papers were accepted for presentation at WEA 2018. The Program Committee divided all submissions into two volumes. In this second volume, the proceedings focus on applied optimization to different engineering fields, IoT, signal processing, networks and some miscellaneous applications including bioinformatics and pattern recognition, robotics, and others.

The Faculty of Engineering of the Universidad Distrital Francisco José de Caldas, the School of Engineering of the Universidad de Antioquia, the Corporación Unificada Nacional (CUN), the Faculty of Engineering of the National University of Colombia, and the Infantry School of the National Colombian Army made significant efforts to guarantee the success of the conference. We would like to thank all members of the Program Committee and the referees for their commitment to help in the review process and for spreading our call for papers. We would like to thank Alfred Hofmann and Jorge Nakahara from Springer for their helpful advice, guidance, and their continuous support in publishing the proceedings. Moreover, we would like to thank all the authors for supporting WEA 2018 — without all their high–quality submissions the conference would not have been possible.

Finally, we are especially grateful to the University of Antioquia for supporting the organization of the event, particularly to the professors and students of the research groups INCAS and GITA, the Department of Industrial Engineering, Expoingeniería, the Universidad de Antioquia Foundation, the IEEE Universidad Distrital Francisco José de Caldas Student branch, the Institute of Industrial and Systems Engineers Chapter 985 (IISE) of the Universidad Distrital Francisco José de Caldas, the Laboratory for Automation and Computational Intelligence (LAMIC), the Acquisition and Representation of Knowledge Expert Systems and Simulation (ARCOSES) research groups of the Universidad Distrital Francisco José de Caldas, and the Algorithms and Combinatory (ALGOS) research group of the National University of Colombia.

October 2018   Pablo Andres Maya Duque
                                                   Juan Rafael Orozco-Arroyave
                                                          Juan G. Villegas
                                                   Juan Carlos Figueroa-García

Organization

General Chair

Juan Carlos Figueroa–García   Universidad Distrital Francisco José de Caldas, Colombia

Finance Chair/Treasurer

Pablo Andres Maya Duque   Universidad de Antioquia, Colombia

Technical Chairs

Juan G. Villegas   Universidad de Antioquia, Colombia
Carlos Montenegro Marín   Universidad Distrital Francisco José de Caldas, Colombia

Publication Chair

Eduyn López–Santana   Universidad Distrital Francisco José de Caldas, Colombia

Track Chairs

Edwin Rivas   Universidad Distrital Francisco José de Caldas, Colombia
German Mendez–Giraldo   Universidad Distrital Francisco José de Caldas, Colombia
Juan G. Villegas   Universidad de Antioquia, Colombia
Juan Rafael Orozco–Arroyave   Universidad de Antioquia, Colombia

Logistics Chairs

Pablo Andres Maya Duque   Universidad de Antioquia, Colombia
Yesid Díaz   Corporación Unificada Nacional de Educación Superior (CUN), Colombia

Plenary Speakers

Vladik Kreinovich   The University of Texas at El Paso (UTEP), USA
Juan J. Merelo Guervoz   Universidad de Granada, Spain
Roberto Murphy   INAOE, Mexico
Carlos Cabrera   Miami Dade College, USA

Program Committee

Abdellah Kacha	University of Jijel, Algeria
Adil Usman	Indian Institute of Technology at Mandi, India
Adolfo Jaramillo–Matta	Universidad Distrital Francisco José de Caldas, Colombia
Alvaro D. Orjuela–Cañon	Universidad Antonio Nariño, Colombia
Alvaro Jaramillo	Universidad de Antioquia, Colombia
Andres M. Alvarez Mesa	Universidad Nacional de Colombia
Aydee Lopez	Universidade Estadual de Campinas (UNICAMP), Brazil
Carlos Franco–Franco	Universidad del Rosario, Colombia
Carlos Osorio–Ramírez	Universidad Nacional de Colombia
Christopher Mejía	MIT, USA
DeShuang Huang	Tongji University, China
Diana Ovalle	Universidad Distrital Francisco José de Caldas, Colombia
Diana P. Tobón Vallejo	Universidad del Valle, Colombia
Diego Botia	Universidad de Antioquia, Colombia
Eduyn López–Santana	Universidad Distrital Francisco Jose de Caldas, Colombia
Edwin Rivas	Universidad Distrital Francisco José de Caldas, Colombia
Eliana M. Toro	Universidad Tecnológica de Pereira, Colombia
Elmar Nöth	University of Erlangen–Nuremberg, Germany
Elvis Eduardo Gaona	Universidad Distrital Francisco José de Caldas, Colombia
Eugenio Yime	Universidad del Atlántico, Colombia
Feizar Javier Rueda–Velazco	Universidad Distrital Francisco José de Caldas, Colombia
Francisco Ramis	Universidad del Bío Bío, Chile
Germán Hernández–Pérez	Universidad Nacional de Colombia, Colombia
Giovanny Tarazona	Universidad Distrital Francisco José de Caldas, Colombia
Gonzalo Mejía	Universidad C. Valparaiso, Chile
Guadalupe González	Universidad Tecnológica de Panamá, Panama
Guillermo Cabrera	Universidad C. Valparaiso, Chile
Gustavo Gatica	Universidad de Santiago de Chile/Universidad Andrés Bello, Chile
Gustavo Puerto L.	Universidad Distrital Francisco José de Caldas, Colombia
Henry Diosa	Universidad Distrital Francisco José de Caldas, Colombia
Heriberto Román–Flores	Universidad de Tarapacá, Chile
I–Hsien Ting	National University of Kaohsiung, Taiwan
Isabel Agudelo	Logyca, Colombia

Ivan Santelices Manfalti	Universidad del Bío–Bío, Chile
Jair Cervantes–Canales	Universidad Autónoma de México, Mexico
Jairo R. Montoya–Torres	Universidad de La Sabana, Colombia
Jairo Serrano	Universidad Tecnológica de Bolívar, Colombia
Jairo Soriano–Mendez	Universidad Distrital Francisco José de Caldas, Colombia
Jan Rusz	CTU, Czech Republic
Javier Arturo Orjuela–Castro	Universidad Nacional de Colombia, Colombia
Javier F. Botia–Valderrama	Universidad de Antioquia, Colombia
Jesus Lopez	Universidad de Antioquia, Colombia
Jhon James Granada Torres	Universidad de Antioquia, Colombia
Jose Ignacio Rodríguez Molano	Universidad Distrital Francisco José de Caldas, Colombia
Jose Luis González–Velarde	Instituto Tecnológico de Monterrey, Mexico
Jose Luis Villa	Universidad Tecnológica de Bolívar, Colombia
Juan Carlos Figueroa–García	Universidad Distrital Francisco José de Caldas, Colombia
Juan Camilo Vásquez	Universidad de Antioquia, Colombia
Juan Carlos Rivera	Universidad EAFIT, Colombia
Juan Felipe Botero–Vega	Universidad de Antioquia, Colombia
Juan G. Villegas	Universidad de Antioquia, Colombia
Juan Rafael Orozco–Arroyave	Universidad de Antioquia, Colombia
Laura Lotero	UPB, Colombia
Laura Lotero	Universidad Pontificia Bolivariana, Colombia
Lindsay Alvarez	Universidad Distrital Francisco José de Caldas, Colombia
Luis J. Morantes Guzmán	Instituto Tecnológico Metropolitano, Colombia
Mabel Frías	Universidad de las Villas Marta Abreu, Cuba
Mario Chong	Universidad del Pacífico, Peru
Martha Centeno	University of Turabo, Puerto Rico
Martin Pilat	Charles University, Czech Republic
Mauricio Pardo Gonzalez	Universidad del Norte, Colombia
Michael Till Beck	LMU, Germany
Miguel Melgarejo	Universidad Distrital Francisco José de Caldas, Colombia
Milton Herrera	Universidad Piloto de Colombia, Colombia
Milton Orlando Sarria Paja	Universidad Santiago de Cali, Colombia
Nelson L. Diaz Aldana	Universidad Distrital Francisco José de Caldas, Colombia
Nicanor García	Universidad de Antioquia, Colombia
Nicolas Clavijo	Universidad Javeriana Cali, Colombia
Oscar Acevedo	Universidad Tecnológica de Bolívar, Colombia
Oswaldo Lopez Santos	Universidad de Ibagué, Colombia
Pablo Andres Maya Duque	Universidad de Antioquia, Colombia
Pablo Manyoma Colombia	Universidad del Valle, Colombia

Paulo Alonso Gaona	Universidad Distrital Francisco José de Caldas, Colombia
Rafael Bello–Pérez	Universidad de las Villas Marta Abreu, Cuba
Roberto Ferro	Universidad Distrital Francisco José de Caldas, Colombia
Rodrigo Linfati	Universidad del Bío–Bío, Chile
Roman Neruda	Charles University, Czech Academy of Sciences
Santiago Murillo Rendón	Universidad Nacional de Colombia, Colombia
Sergio Rojas–Galeano	Universidad Distrital Francisco José de Caldas, Colombia
Steven Latré	University of Antwerp, The Netherlands
Tomás Arias	Universidad de Antioquia, Colombia
Victor Cantillo	Universidad del Norte, Colombia
Victor Medina García	Universidad Distrital Francisco José de Caldas, Colombia
William Camilo Rodríguez	Universidad Distrital Francisco José de Caldas, Colombia
William Sarache	Universidad Nacional de Colombia, Colombia
Xavier Hesselbach	Universitat Politècnica de Catalunya, Spain
Yesid Díaz	Corporación Unificada Nacional de Educación Superior (CUN), Colombia
Yurilev Chalco–Cano	Universidad de Tarapacá, Chile

Contents – Part II

Internet of Things (IoT)

Digital Signal Processing (DSP)

Network Applications

Miscellaneous Applications

Contents – Part I

Computational Intelligence

Simulation Systems

Software Engineering

Power and Energy Applications

Green Logistics and Optimization

Optimal Location of Protective Devices Using Multi-objective Approach

Oscar D. Montoya[1], Ricardo A. Hincapie[2], and Mauricio Granada[2]($\boxtimes$) (iD)

[1] Department of Electrical and Electronic Engineering,
Technological University of Bolivar (Universidad Tecnológica de Bolívar),
Cartagena, Colombia
odmontoya@utb.edu.co

[2] Department of Electrical Engineering,
Technological University of Pereira (Universidad Tecnológica de Pereira),
Risaralda, Colombia
{ricardohincapie,magra}@utp.edu.co

Abstract. In this paper a multi-objective model for the problem of optimal location of reclosers and fuses in power electric distribution systems is presented, considering the possibility of fuse rescue through the coordinated operation with reclosers and continuous operation with fuses of repetition. The problem is presented based on a mixed integer non-linear programming model with four objectives of minimization: Average System Interruption Frequency Index (ASIFI), System Average Interruption Frequency Index (SAIFI), Momentary Average Interruption Frequency Index (MAIFI) and the cost of the protective elements, and a set of non-linear technical and economic constraints. A Non-dominated Sorted Genetic Algorithm (NSGA II) is used as solution technique. In addition to this, the mathematical model presented for the MAIFI and SAIFI indices, is evaluated in the commercial optimization package of GAMS, in order to meet a global optimum from the one-objective point of view. The methodology proposed is assessed in two test systems from the literature highlight the efficiency of the presented model in improving system reliability while reducing associated costs.

Keywords: Distribution protection design · MAIFI · SAIFI · NSGA II

1 Introduction

Due the electric sector has a fundamental roll in many aspects, the entities in charged of the regulation, establish more strict politics around quality subjects in the energy service delivery. In the case of distribution systems, utilities are subjected to three possible conditions. First of all, they can be benefited with economic and commercial incentives regarding the quality and reliability of service delivery. Under these conditions it is clear that the power electric utilities are always looking for benefits since the economic point of view, for which it is

© Springer Nature Switzerland AG 2018
J. C. Figueroa-García et al. (Eds.): WEA 2018, CCIS 916, pp. 3–15, 2018.
https://doi.org/10.1007/978-3-030-00353-1_1

necessary to pose strategies, that permit to enhance their quality and reliability indices, through operation schemes under the concept of optimal network, that means, *"a distribution system is efficient, if it is able to deliver power quality to the customers, with the minimum possible physical resource"*. In 2010 Ferreira et al. in [7] develop a multi-objective methodology for location of reclosers, sectionalizers, fuses and switching keys in power electric distribution systems through a mathematical formulation that minimizes three objectives simultaneously SAIFI, SAIDI and MAIFI. In 2012 Pulgarín et al. in [13] develop a methodology for optimal location of normally open reclosers to transfer load between medium-voltage circuits using the concept of operative areas. The mathematical model is mixed integer non-linear, and the NSGA II algorithm is used as solution technique. The methodology is validated in a Colombian distribution system belonging to Empresa de Energía del Quindio. In the same year Tio et al. present at [14] a mixed binary non-linear programming model for optimal location of reclosers and fuses, through the application of coordination strategies *"fuse blow scheme"* and *"fuse saving scheme"*. In 2012, Penuela in his doctoral thesis [12] presents different mathematical models for the expansion and operation of power electric systems, considering different protection devices (reclosers, sectionalizers, fuses and relays) and distributed generation sources. In 2014 Montoya et al. in [10] present a multi-objective model, considering as objective functions the investment cost and the non served energy level of the network, using the concept denominated as operative areas of constant energy. Recently, Bretas et al. in [2] present a multi-objective mixed integer linear programing model for distribution systems reliability optimization. Karpov and Akimov in [9] present a genetic algorithm to find a recloser placement corresponding to the optimal value of SAIFI index.

Because the distribution systems reliability optimization problem is though inherently multi-objective, in this paper, we use a binary programming models for ASIFI, SAIFI, and MAIFI to propose a multiobjective approach for distribution systems reliability optimization, considering the simultaneous minimization of reliability indices and associated costs. We adapt the NSGA II algorithm and propose a simple coding scheme, to obtain the best trade-off between the three objective functions. This approach introduces new feasible solutions in the solution space, which may lead to optimal solutions better than those that can be found otherwise.

2   Problem Description

In this work, frequency indices for temporary failures are used in function of customers and load connected (SAIFI and ASIFI), and for temporary failures in function of customers connected (MAIFI) [8,14]. In the Fig. 1, a typical configuration is presented [6].

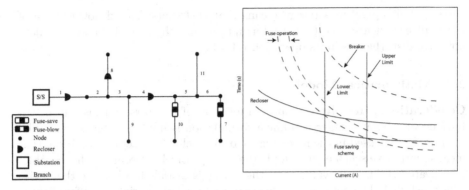

Fig. 1. Distribution system configuration

Fig. 2. Fuse and recloser operation curves

2.1 Protective Devices

A common practice in the utilities, is using reclosers and fuses under diverse coordination schemes to safeguard the network from failure phenomenons [12]. In this context, it is assumed the possibility of location of two equipments in the system. The first of them is the recloser, which is able to interrupt short-circuit currents and isolate the system in case of a permanent failure, in addition to this, it is able to re-close automatically a default number of times, to remove temporary failures of the system. The second device is the fuse, which operates in a failure, independent of its nature, if the short-circuit current overcomes its threshold. Once this happens, the device is destroyed and it is necessary to replace it [12].

2.2 Coordination Schemes

Fuse-Save Scheme is a strategy that permits to safeguard and/or protect the fuses from non desired activations, caused by temporary failures; this strategy is based on the fast and slow operation curves of the recloser. A basic idea of its operation is shown in the Fig. 2, where the upper limit of the save strip implies that for lower failure currents the recloser upstream will operate faster than the fuse, preventing its destruction. This process is repeated as many times as the number of programmed slow curves it has; if the failure has not been isolated, the recloser operates by slow curve, providing enough time to the fuse to clear the failure [11,14]. It is important to point out that for failure events with short-circuit currents higher than the given currents by the fuse-save, the fuse will operate first and for currents lower than the currents contained in the save zone, the fuse will never be in operation.

Fuse-Blow Scheme corresponds to the autonomous operation of the fuse in the presence of a failure of any nature, that means, the principle of this scheme is the activation of the fuse at any event, when the failure current surpasses the starting current. This operative strategy means that customers located downstream of the fault experience a sustained interruption, and the rest of the system does not have disturbances in its operation [11,14].

2.3   Mathematical Model

Cosiderations. To solve the optimal location of reclosers and fuses in distribution systems, an integer non-linear formulation is used. The binary variables x_i, y_i and z_i are used in the modeling to locate reclosers, fuses of repetition, that means, with save scheme and simple fuses, respectively. If some of the variables is activated (taking the value of 1) the device is installed, otherwise the device is not installed. The notation employed to represent the variables, differ slightly, respect to the model in the papers [3–14]. To elaborate the complete model the following aspects are taken into account: (i) the protection devices are in perfect status, (ii) the failure rate of the protection devices equals zero (0), (iii)the protection devices are three-phase, (iv) the distribution system is always radial and (v) the failures are mutually exclusive and independent.

Nomenclature

Sets and functions

Ω_s: Set of sections of the feeder.

Ω_{sn}:   Subset of Ω_S that contains those sections that require a protection device

$F(i)$:   Function that contains the set of sections from the substation until the section i, excluding the section i and including the section situated immediately after the substation.

$F'(i)$:   Function that contains the set of sections from the substation until the section i, including the section situated immediately after the substation.

$G(j, i)$: Function that returns the set of sections in the way from the section j until section i, excluding the section j and including the section i.

$G'(j,i)$: Function that returns the set of sections in the way from the section j until section i, excluding both sections.

$h(j, i)$: Function that contains the section located immediately after the section j towards section i.

$M(j,i)$:Function that returns the set of sections j downstream the section i.

Variables

x_i: Binary decision variable of installation ($x_i = 1$) or not ($x_i = 0$) of a recloser in section i.

y_i: Binary decision variable of installation ($y_i = 1$) or not ($y_i = 0$) of a fuse of repetition in section i.

z_i: Binary decision variable of installation ($x_i = 1$) or not ($x_i = 0$) of a simple fuse in section i.

Parameters and sub-indices

γ_i: Permanent failure rate in section i in [failures/year-km].

λ_i: Temporary failure rate in section i in [failures/year-km].

C_x: Fixed cost installation of a recloser.

C_y: Fixed cost installation of a fuse of repetition.

C_z: Fixed cost installation of a simple fuse.

i, j, k: Indices associated to the sections.

L_i: Total load supplied by section i in [kW].
L_i':   Load attended downstream the section i in [kW].
L_T: Total load of the feeder in [kW]
N_i: Number of customers attended by section i.
N_i':   Number of customers connected downstream the section i.
N_T: Total number of customers of the feeder.
M_f: Maximum number of fuses that can be installed.
M_r: Maximum number of reclosers that can be installed.
$N_c^{\max}$: Maximum number of cascaded devices.
$n_s^{\max}$:   Total number of sections.

Objective Functions: the indices ASIFI, SAIFI, MAIFI and the installation costs of the protection devices are considered as objective functions.

   ASIFI Model: The reliability index is defined for a distribution feeder as:

$$ASIFI = \sum_{i \in \Omega_S} \lambda_i * L_i / L_T = A_{qa}/L_T \tag{1}$$

   To take into account the incidence of the location of the protection devices in the distribution network, the numerator of (1) can be rewritten as:

$$A_{qa} = \sum_{i \in \Omega_S} \left\{ \begin{array}{l} \lambda_i L_i' + \gamma_i y_i L_i' + \lambda_i \left[\sum_{j \in F(i)} \left(L_j' - L_{h(j,i)}' \right) \left[\prod_{k \in G(j,i)} (1 - x_k)(1 - y_k)(1 - z_k) \right] \right] \\ + \gamma_i \left[\sum_{j \in F(i)} (1 - y_j) L_j' \left[\prod_{k \in G(j,i)} (1 - x_k)(1 - y_k) \right] \right] \end{array} \right\} \tag{2}$$

   SAIFI Model: The reliability index is defined for a distribution feeder as:

$$SAIFI = \sum_{i \in S} \lambda_i * N_i / N_T = A_{qs}/N_T \tag{3}$$

   By using the formulation of the numerator A_{qs} in function of the binary decision variables, it is obtained (4).

$$A_{qs} = \sum_{i \in \Omega_S} \left\{ \begin{array}{l} \lambda_i N_i' + \gamma_i y_i N_i' \lambda_i \left[\sum_{j \in F(i)} \left(N_j' - N_{h(j,i)}' \right) \left[\prod_{k \in G(j,i)} (1 - x_k)(1 - y_k)(1 - z_k) \right] \right] \\ + \gamma_i \left[\sum_{j \in F(i)} (1 - y_j) N_j' \left[\prod_{k \in G(j,i)} (1 - x_k)(1 - y_k) \right] \right] \end{array} \right\} \tag{4}$$

   When the models ASIFI (2) and SAIFI (4) are compared, it is possible to notice that the only existing variation, is the way to quantify the frequency of the failures in the system, since the perspectives of the load connected and the quantity of the customers connected respectively. Both models are mathematically similar. By the other hand, the first and third term in (2) and (4), correspond to the influence of the permanent failures. Additionally, the customers upstream the section i, in the surroundings of the closest recloser or fuse, could experience a sustained interruption. The second and forth term in (2) and (4), represent the contribution of the temporary failures in the frequency indices.

MAIFI Model: The index for a distribution feeder is typically represented as:

$$MAIFI = \sum_{i \in S} \gamma_i * N_i / N_T = A_m / N_T \tag{5}$$

the numerator of (5) can be rewritten as:

$$A_m = \sum_{i \in \Omega_s} \begin{bmatrix} \gamma_i x_i N_i' + \gamma_i \left[\sum_{j \in F(i)} x_j N_j' \left[\prod_{k \in G(i,j)} (1 - x_k)(1 - y_k) \right] \right] \\ + \lambda_i z_i \left[\sum_{j \in F(i)} x_j \left(N_j' - N_i' \right) \left[\prod_{k \in G'(i,j)} (1 - x_k)(1 - y_k) \right] \right] \\ + \lambda_i \left[\sum_{j \in F(i)} x_j \left[\begin{array}{c} \sum_{k \in G'(i,j)} z_k * \left(N_j' - N_k' \right) \\ \prod_{m \in G(k,i)} (1 - x_k)(1 - y_k)(1 - z_k) \\ \prod_{m \in G(k,i)} (1 - x_k)(1 - y_k) \end{array} \right] \right] \end{bmatrix} \tag{6}$$

For the MAIFI model, the first two terms in (6), represent the contribution of a temporary failure in section i, because the closest recloser upstream the failure makes the customers connected downstream of the recloser experience temporary interruptions of the service. In the quantification of the reliability indices for the distribution system through the mathematical models presented in (2), (4) and (6), some aspects are considered: if the sets evaluated by the sums or the products are null, the neutral elements are added to the operations, that means, in the case of the sum it is added zero (0) and in the case of the multiplication it is added one (1) to the operation.

Cost Model: To quantify the total cost of installation of the protection devices, it is formulated an expression in function of the decision variables which adds the costs of each device installed as:

$$ICOST = \sum_{i \in \Omega_s} [C_x * x_i + C_y * y_i + C_z * z_i] \tag{7}$$

In this model, it is assumed that the installation costs of the protection devices do not depend on the place of installation, this is the reason why the costs coefficients are assumed constants.

Constraints: In (8) it is restricted the existence of an only protection device in each section. Sometimes it is essential that protection devices are installed at any specific location of the distribution system, in (9) it is presented a constraint that corresponds to the need of a recloser or a fuse [3–14].

$$x_i + y_i + z_i \leq 1 \quad \forall_i \in \Omega_s \tag{8} \qquad x_i + y_i + z_i = 1 \quad \forall_i \in \Omega_{sn} \tag{9}$$

It is usual to find operation conditions that do not require to exceed a specific quantity of protection devices in the network, for which the constraints of fuses and reclosers are defined as (10) and (11).

$$\sum_{i \in \Omega_s} y_i + z_i \leq M_f \qquad (10) \qquad\qquad \sum_{i \in \Omega_s} x_i \leq M_r \qquad (11)$$

In order to warranty the correct operation of the save schemes and continuous operation of fuses, two conditions are required: (i) the non-existence of reclosers downstream of a fuse, and (ii) the non-existence of a fuse of repetition downstream of a simple fuse. The above can be expressed according to (12) and (13).

$$y_i + z_i + x_j \leq 1 \quad \forall \, (j,i) \in M \quad (12) \qquad y_i + z_j \leq 1 \quad \forall \, (j,i) \in M \qquad (13)$$

To warranty an adequate coordination between the different protection devices installed in the network, sometimes it is convenient to establish a constraint that shows the maximum number of devices that can be connected cascade, which can be defined as (14).

$$\sum_{i \in F(i)} y_i + z_i + x_i \leq N_c^{\max} \qquad (14)$$

3   Proposed Methodology

The mathematical model presented in the above section, shows four (4) objective functions, three of which present a conflictive behaviour. In this work two possible sets of objective functions are considered, the first of them has the objective functions SAIFI, MAIFI and ICOST, and the second set corresponds to the objective functions ASIFI, MAIFI and ICOST.

3.1   Multi-objective Optimization Algorithm NSGA II

The basic idea of this algorithm is that during the evolutionary step t, the set of descendants Q_t of size N is generated from the set of parents P_t of the same size, using the genetic operators of selection, crossing and mutation [5]. In function of the above two populations (P_t, Q_t) a population R_t of size $2N$ is conformed. After this, by using a sorting, the population is classified in Pareto fronts, which consists in determining for each individual a dominance level in relation to the other solutions; according to this, only the best N solutions will be part of the population P_{t+1}, where the process starts again [4]. This process is repeated until a number generational cycles elapse without evolution or until a predefined number of iterations is reached [5,13].

3.2   Proposed Codification

To represent appropriately a possible location of protection devices in the distribution system and taking the advantage that the model is binary, a codification through a $3 * n_s$ matrix is proposed, in which each row corresponds to a type of protection device. The first row corresponds to the possible location of reclosers; the second row represents the possibility of location of fuses of repetition for the coordination scheme *fuse-blow* and the last row contains the possibilities of location of simple fuses for implementation of save strategies. To be illustrative, if it is considered that the possible configuration of a radial feeder as presented in Fig. 1, for this system the codification that represents the location of protections is shown in Fig. 3.

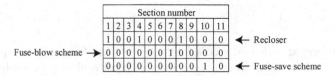

Fig. 3. Proposed codification

3.3   Generate Inicial Population

To generate the initial population, a three-layer constructive heuristic algorithm is used. The first layer is in charge of generating a random set of individuals similar to the set presented in Fig. 3 of size N. The second stage consists in a routing through all the elements of the distribution network, in which it is verified whether or not it is possible to locate an element belonging the position i of the individual j in the network segment i. In the third layer the individual is accepted if it complies with all the constraints given by the mathematical model. Otherwise, this stage makes a local improvement of the individual, until this complies with the constraints, and it is accepted if it is different from the elements already stored at the population. The final set corresponding to the output of the above process, is the initial population of the NSGA II algorithm.

4   Test Systems and Results

In order to validate the methodology proposed, two test systems are used from the specialized literature, with different dimensions, which are available in [1,14].

4.1   System 1

The first system is taken from reference [14]. This is a 9-section network, 5000 customers and a load connected of 7500 kVA. In the Table 1 the system data is presented and the configuration is shown in Fig. 4. For this system the following aspects are considered: (i) at the exit of the substation there is a main protection, (ii) the maximum number of reclosers to install is three, (iii) there is no limit in the number of fuses, (iv) there is no limit in the number of fuses, (v) fuses cannot be installed in the main section (network segments 1, 2, 3 and 4), (vi) in sections 5, 7, 8 and 9 a protection device has to be installed, (vii) it is not possible the coordination between reclosers installed in Sects. 2 and 3, and (viii) a maximum of 4 elements connected cascade is permitted.

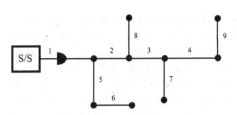

Fig. 4. Configuration of test system 1

Table 1. Dates of test system 1

$Section_i$	λ_i	γ_i	N_i	L_i
1	0,8	1,2	800	1500
2	0,8	1,4	1200	700
3	0,9	1,6	800	600
4	0,7	1,0	600	350
5	0,9	2,0	500	2250
6	0,7	1,7	300	350
7	0,8	2,8	400	300
8	1,0	3,2	200	1000
9	0,5	0,7	200	450

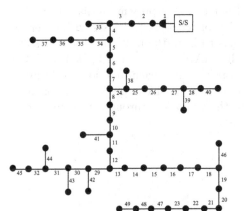

Fig. 5. Configuration of test system 2

Table 2. Data of test system 2

$Sect_i$	λ_i	γ_i	N_i	L_i	$Sect_i$	λ_i	γ_i	N_i	L_i
1	0,43	0,68	3	465	26	0,66	2,29	210	300
2	0,37	1,28	120	375	27	1,13	3,92	21	51
3	0,26	0,41	0	0	28	0,39	1,34	0	0
4	0,47	0,73	3	315	29	0,28	0,45	6	730
5	0,24	0,38	0	0	30	0,13	0,21	1	50
6	0,26	0,41	1	25	31	0,12	0,19	3	275
7	0,39	0,61	1	50	32	0,21	0,33	3	125
8	0,25	0,39	1	25	33	0,14	0,22	30	160
9	0,28	0,44	0	0	34	0,62	0,98	90	125
10	0,34	0,53	3	275	35	0,6	2,09	0	0
11	0,08	0,13	51	100	36	0,53	0,84	0	0
12	0,17	0,27	200	765	37	0,7	2,43	100	300
13	0,35	0,56	155	315	38	1,2	4,16	50	125
14	0,25	0,40	1	100	39	0,54	1,86	50	150
15	0,48	1,66	50	125	40	1,26	4,38	645	1530
16	0,21	0,33	0	0	41	0,73	1,15	19	100
17	0,74	1,17	451	1280	42	1,04	3,63	35	225
18	0,54	1,88	54	225	43	0,11	0,17	101	515
19	0,38	1,33	1	50	44	0,5	0,78	10	1400
20	0,42	1,47	174	400	45	0,93	1,47	60	425
21	0,8	2,78	1	50	46	0,96	1,50	30	160
22	0,48	0,75	234	550	47	0,66	1,04	0	0
23	0,61	0,96	0	0	48	0,94	3,27	216	650
24	0,96	3,34	141	200	49	0,56	0,88	87	225
25	0,56	1,95	1	25	–	–	–	–	–

4.2   System 2

The second system is taken from reference [1] and is shown in the Fig. 5. This medium-sized system belongs the utility Qazvin in Iran with 49 sections, with a total of 3413 customers and a load connected of 13336 kVA. In the Table 2 the data of the system is presented.

The following aspects are considered for this system: At the exit of the substation there is a main protection. The maximum number of reclosers to be installed is three. There is no limit in the number of fuses. In the main section (network segments 1, 2, 3 and 4) fuses cannot be installed. In section 5, 7, 8 and 9 there must be a protection device. It is not possible the coordination between the reclosers installed in Sects. 2 and 3. A maximum of 4 elements connected cascade is permitted.

4.3   Implementation of the Proposed Methodology

The metaheuristic optimization technique NSGA II used for solving the optimal location of protection devices, to improve the reliability indices, was implemented in a computer *Intel Core 2 Duo* with *4 GB* of *RAM* and operative system *Windows*® *7 Professional* employing the software *MATLAB*® *2010a*.

The costs associated to the reclosers, simple fuses and fuses of repetition are *US*$12.000, *US*$100 and *US*$400, respectively. In order to verify the efficiency of the proposed methodology the objective functions SAIFI (4), MAIFI (6) and ICOST (7) are considered, however, in the Tables 1 and 2 it is presented the information needed for the implementation of the index ASIFI (2).

Analysis of System 1: The Pareto front of Fig. 6 presents a discrete multi-objective behaviour of the optimal location of reclosers and fuses with different coordination schemes. In the Pareto front of Fig. 6, the best one-objective solutions for each problem are: SAIFI = 2,346, MAIFI = 3,336 and ICOST = 12.400 US$. These solutions correspond to the optimums of each function, performing a one-objective analysis, which was checked through the implementation of a genetic algorithm of *Chu & Beasley* and the validation through the commercial optimizer GAMS with the solver KNITRO.

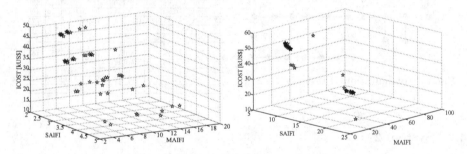

Fig. 6. Optimal front for system 1   **Fig. 7.** Optimal front for system 2

Table 3 presents a reduced non-dominated set of solutions, obtained from the Pareto front of Fig. 6. It is necessary to clarify that after the evolutionary process of the NSGA II, the final front contains 50 non-dominated individuals. Nevertheless the reduced set shown in Table 3 is obtained through a random selection of points along the complete set which is done to show a general scheme of the result, highlighting the minimums associated to each objective function. For the set of solutions already presented in Table 3, the set of elements corresponding to each solution are presented in Table 4.

Analysis of System 2: Figure 7 presents the Pareto optimal front corresponding to the location of reclosers and fuses in the 49-network segments system.

Table 3. Optimal front (system 1)

Number	SAIFI	MAIFI	ICOST [kUS$]
1	2,3460	9,1780	48,4000
2	3,5100	19,1900	12,5000
3	2,4860	14,0700	24,5000
4	3,1480	3,3360	38,0000
5	2,6400	5,5720	48,6000
6	2,9080	4,5400	36,9000
7	2,8120	8,1760	25,1000
8	2,9920	3,6360	49,3000
9	3,1600	3,6640	37,6000
10	3,1480	8,9560	24,7000

Table 4. Set of devices installed

Number	Reclosers	FBF	FSF
1	[1,3,4,5]	0	[6,7,8,9]
2	1	0	[5,6,7,8,9]
3	[1,3]	0	[5,6,7,8,9]
4	[1,3,4]	[5,6,7,8,9]	0
5	[1,3,4,5]	7	[8,9]
6	[1,3,5]	[7,8]	9
7	[1,3]	[6,7]	[5,8,9]
8	[1,3,4,8]	[5,6,7]	9
9	[1,3,8]	[5,6,7,9]	0
10	[1,3]	5	[7,8,9]

As in the 9-network segments system, in this system it is possible to find the one-objective solutions in the extreme points of the Pareto front, the best one-objective solutions for each problem are: SAIFI = 3,7222, MAIFI = 6,0606 and ICOST = 12.900 US$.

In the Figs. 6 and 7 the behaviour of the Pareto fronts for both test systems is presented and the discrete characteristic in its solution is clearly observable. First of all, the cost function presents a progressive escalation, that means, there are regions where clusters of points and empty regions are presented, this condition is presented because those clusters are located in zones where a determined number of reclosers are proposed, that means, each scale in cost in ascending way, increases in one the number of reclosers located in the system. Secondly, the dispersion around each cluster of solutions, represents the variation in the selection of the fuses to be installed in each configuration.

From the results obtained for test system 1, in Table 3 it can be seen that the solution with the best SAIFI indicator is solution 1. Verifying in Table 4 the devices installed in this solution it can be seen that it was not installed no simple fuse (FBS). For the MAIFI indicator the best value was found by solution 4. When verifying in Table 4 the devices installed in this solution, it is observed that no fuse with fuse-save scheme (FSF) was installed. These two solutions represent the extreme points of the Pareto optimal front. Thus, in general it is observed that the SAIFI indicator improves if a combination of reclosers and fuses is made with a fuse-save scheme. The MAIFI indicator improves if there is a combination of reclosers with simple fuses.

5   Conclusions

A multi-objective methodology was developed that allows the optimal location of reclosers and fuses with two coordination schemes in distribution systems to improve the reliability indices. The mathematical model used gathers the coordination characteristics mentioned before. In addition to this, a cost function was included, which provides sensitivity to the selection of the best solutions inside its solution space.

A highly discrete behaviour was evidenced in the set of non-dominated solutions belonging the Pareto fronts for each test systems. From what it was mentioned before, it is possible to confirm that the efficiency of the methodology proposed is strongly related to the selection of the initial population; because a discrete space generates multiple infeasible solutions and makes the evolutionary process of the algorithm more difficult.

From the Pareto fronts obtained, it is clear that the behaviour of the reliability indices SAIFI and MAIFI are in conflict, that means, their quality is highly dependent on the type of coordination scheme chosen, for which it is impossible to find a protections scheme that enhances both indices simultaneously. The SAIFI indicator improves if a combination of reclosers and fuses is made with a fuse-save scheme. The MAIFI indicator improves if there is a combination of reclosers with simple fuses.

In the mathematical formulation of the problem, the coordination scheme known as *"fuse blow scheme"* through the insertion of a new device called fuse of repetition was considered, which improves the economic performance for the utility, because a temporary failure is removed by that element and the operation is reset automatically without human intervention, minimizing in this manner the times of unavailability of service supply.

References

1. Abdi, S., Afshar, K., Ahmadi, S., Bigdeli, N., Abdi, M.: Optimal recloser and auto-sectionalizer allocation in distribution networks using IPSO-Monte Carlo approach. Int. J. Electr. Power Energy Syst. **55**, 602–611 (2014)
2. Bretas, A.S., Cabral, R.J., Leborgne, R.C., Ferreira, G.D., Morales, J.A.: Multi-objective milp model for distribution systems reliability optimization: a lightning protection system design approach. Int. J. Electr. Power Energy Syst. **98**, 256–268 (2018)
3. Bupasiri, R., Wattanapongsakorn, N., Hokierti, J., Coit, D.W.: Optimal electric power distribution system reliability indices using binary programming. In: Proceedings Annual Reliability and Maintanability Symposium (2003)
4. Coello, C.C., Veldhuizen, D.V., Lamont, G.B.: Evolutionary Algorithms for Solving Multi-objective Problems. Kluwer Academic, Dordrecht (2002)
5. Deb, K., Pratap, A., Agarwal, S., Meyarivan, T.: A fast and elitist multi-objetive genetic algorithm: NSGA-II. IEEE Trans. Evol. Comput. **6**, 182–197 (2002)
6. Ferreira, G., Bretas, A.: A nonlinear binary programming model for electric distribution systems reliability optimization. Electr. Power Energy Syst. **43**, 384–392 (2012)
7. Ferreira, G.D., Bretas, A.S., Cardoso Jr., G.: Optimal distribution protection design considering momentary and sustained reliability indices. In: Modern Electric Power Systems (2010)
8. Group, I.W.: IEEE trial-use guide for electric power distribution reliability indices. Technical report, Institute of Electrical and Electronics Engineers (1998)
9. Karpov, A.I., Akimov, D.A.: Integral indicators improvement (SAIFI) of power supply reliability in electric distribution systems based on reclosers placement optimization. In: 2018 IEEE Conference of Russian Young Researchers in Electrical and Electronic Engineering (EIConRus), pp. 663–666. IEEE (2018)
10. Montoya, O.D., Arias, A., Granada, M., Hincapié, R.A.: Optimal location of reclosers by using MOEA SPEA II. In: Simpósio Brasileiro de Sistemas Eétricos (2014)

11. O'Meally, C.A., Burke, J.: A fuse blow-scheme: its impact on overhead distribution system reliability and power quality. IEEE Ind. Appl. Mag. **16**, 37–42 (2010)
12. Penuela, C.A.: Desenvolvimento de técnicas e modelos matemáticos para solução do problema de planejamento da expansão e operação de sistemas de distribuição de energia eléctrica com geradores distribuidos. Ph.D. thesis, Universidad Estadual Paulista "Julio de Mesquita Filho", Facultade de Engenharia, Capus de Ilha Solteira (2012)
13. Pulgarín, C.A., Rios, M.A., Acosta, C.A., Hincapié, R.A., Granada, M., Gallego, R.A.: Localización óptima de reconectadores normalmente abiertos para transferencia de carga. Mundo Eléctrico **50**, 38–44 (2012)
14. Tio, A.E.D.C., Cruz, I.B.N.C., Malquisto, B.M., del Mundo, R.D.: A binary programming model for reliability optimization considering fuse-blow and fuse-save schemes. In: IEEE Conference TENCON (2012)

Adaptive Energy Management System for Self-consumption in Productive Processes

Jorge Barrientos[1], José David López[1(✉)], and Felipe Valencia[2]

[1] SISTEMIC, Engineering Faculty, Universidad de Antioquia UDEA,
Calle 70 No. 52-21, Medellín, Colombia
jabarrientosg@gmail.com, josedavid@udea.edu.co
[2] Solar Energy Research Center SERC-Chile, Department of Electrical Engineering,
University of Chile, Santiago, Chile
felipe.valencia@sercchile.cl

Abstract. Productive processes are the largest consumers in power systems. The energy required by these processes is usually supplied by the power grid with its associated high operative costs. In this work, we propose a methodology to design energy management systems for self-consumption in productive processes with non-conventional local energy resources. Our goal is to maximize the use of the local energy resources to reduce the amount of energy contracted with the service supplier, and consequently to reduce production costs of the process. This methodology includes a robust-optimization-based energy management strategy to include power variability through the generation of a finite number of possible future scenarios of uncertain variables such as power demand and power from non-conventional energy sources. It allows improving the performance of the power supplies as our simulation results show.

Keywords: Non-conventional energy sources
Energy management system · Stochastic programming
Industrial processes

1 Introduction

According to the International Energy Agency, the world industrial sector consumes 42% of the total demanded energy around the world [5]. Furthermore, industry is the most pollutant end-user sector [4]. Then, in the near future the industry sector will face the dual challenge of implementing low energy and low pollution technologies while simultaneously maintaining its competitiveness [4]. Non-Conventional Energy Sources (NCES) are a suitable opportunity for industries to reduce their environmental impacts and to increase profitability. However, when NCES are integrated in productive processes, technical issues might arise due to their variability. Thus, the grid support and the dispatchable local energy sources must be coordinated through an energy management system (EMS) in such a way that a reliable supply of electric energy is achieved, despite of the unexpected power variations of the NCES and demand.

© Springer Nature Switzerland AG 2018
J. C. Figueroa-García et al. (Eds.): WEA 2018, CCIS 916, pp. 16–27, 2018.
https://doi.org/10.1007/978-3-030-00353-1_2

Several EMS-based approaches have been presented in the literature to deal with the uncertainty associated with these power variations. Some examples of prediction-based EMS are reported in [7,9]. The main idea of these predictive strategies is to anticipate the performance of both NCES and power demand to maintain a suitable performance of the power system during power fluctuation. However, these strategies do not include the uncertainty directly in the EMS problem formulation, and single predictions are not enough to improve the robustness of the system. For this reason, some strategies such as those in [8,11] focus on this problem. In these works, authors represent uncertainty through prediction scenarios, but selecting them is still a research challenge. Furthermore, these methodologies have not clear strategies to determine a suitable number of scenarios to represent uncertainty, and they do not improve the uncertainty representation in real-time. In addition, all above applications are oriented to energy management in microgrids to supply energy on communities.

Particularly for productive processes, some EMS approaches with NCES integration have been proposed. In [2], the authors proposed a NCES integration based on a phenomenological process model. But they did not implement control actions over the local energy sources to correct any low performance in real-time. [10] presented a solar and wind source integration in a water desalination process through a model predictive control strategy. In this approach, the controller managed both sources and process. Nevertheless, it required a specific process model making it problem specific. In [3], a fuzzy controller was presented to manage a generation system with multiple types of sources and an experimental variable load. They did not implement an optimal control strategy in order to reduce the computational cost of the controllers.

In this work, we propose to tackle above mentioned drawbacks with an EMS design methodology based on the robust optimization strategy presented in [1]. Our goal is to include uncertainties as part of the energy management problem formulation in productive processes with NCES penetration. With this new approach, we expect to improve robustness of the energy supplied to the industrial process by reducing the possibility of collapse caused by unexpected variations associated with the NCES and power demanded by the process, which is basically the definition of robustness in this frame.

The proposed methodology consists of the following stages: Characterization of power demand and generation of available NCES; stochastic modeling of the power demand and power from the non-conventional resources (with the stochastic model, multiple possible future scenarios or realizations of the uncertain variables are computed in order to represent the future power variations); and design of a robust EMS to maximize the use of the available NCES. Realizations are included to improve the power system performance along the day. In this formulation, an additional constraint is included to avoid the energy surpluses injection into the main grid, and then to promote the self-consumption in countries where energy injection into the grid is not regulated.

The main advantages of the proposed methodology are: (i) it does not require an specific process model, i.e., it can be applied in any productive process; (ii) uncertainties are explicitly included in the proposed EMS through multiple scenarios in order to improve the robustness of the local power system under unexpected power flows variations; (iii) it is simple to implement because it only requires historical time series of the power demand and power from NCES to be designed; and finally, (iv) the parameters of the stochastic models are updated every sample time with the new measurements from the system; it allows improving the dynamic performance and the adaptive capabilities of the EMS.

This work is organized as follows: in Sect. 2 we present a methodology to manage energy in productive process where NCES are integrated. In Sect. 3, the proposed methodology is applied to design an EMS in a typical cooper extraction process, which is partially supplied with wind energy. In Sect. 4, simulations results are presented and discussed. Finally, conclusions are presented in Sect. 5.

2   Proposed EMS Design Methodology

The optimization problem with multiple scenarios presented in [1] can be written as an expected value minimization problem:

$$\min_{X} \quad \mathbf{E}(F(X, \bar{a} + u)) \tag{1}$$
$$\text{subject to:} \quad G(X, \bar{a} + u) \leq b$$

Where X is the set of decision variables, which are calculated such that $F(X, \bar{a} + u)$ is minimum. $F(X, \bar{a} + u)$ is an objective function and $G(X, \bar{a} + u)$ represents a group of physical and operative constraints of the process. b is commonly expressed as a fixed parameter and a is an uncertain parameter. To consider uncertainties explicitly in the problem, a is expressed such as $a = \bar{a} + u$, where $\bar{a}$ and u are the mean and uncertainty components of a, respectively. However, this problem could not be mathematically tractable since the expected value of $F(X, \bar{a} + u)$ might not be differentiable. Nevertheless, it can be solved when a takes a finite number of values that represent the original population. Then, the problem can be reformulated as:

$$\min_{X} \quad p_1 * F(X, a_1) + \ldots + p_K * F(X, a_K) \tag{2}$$
$$\text{subject to:} \quad G(X, a_i) \leq b; \quad i = 1, \ldots, K$$

Where K is a finite number of chosen scenarios for a and $p_i, \ldots, p_K$ are the occurrence probabilities of each scenario. The goal with this formulation is to find a value of X such that $F(X, a)$ can be minimized, whereas all constraints imposed by the a_i scenarios are simultaneously satisfied.

2.1   Generating and Selecting Scenarios

Power from NCES and power demand scenarios can be obtained from forecasting. An EMS with power forecasting models can achieve better planning of the power sources and improve the dynamic response of the system. We use a set of possible future scenarios obtained from a set of probability density functions (PDF), which are fitted via previous analysis of the historical time series of the uncertain variables, and their parameters are updated in every sample time to include the new measurements into the uncertainty representation process. The advantage of this method is that a suitable uncertainty representation can be achieved without the need of a complex model. In addition, this method allows updating historical information with every new measurement to update the parameters of the PDFs. The drawback of this method is that it is not possible to include exogenous variables in the process of the generation of the future scenarios, in other words, it is not possible to include the influence of exogenous variables on the uncertain variables. However, according to our simulations, it is a suitable strategy for average renewable NCES and demand conditions.

First, we combine historical time series from all uncertain variables to obtain only one time series. For example, the general form of the power balance with a renewable NCES is $P_G + P_R = P_D$, where P_G, P_R, and P_D are the power from grid, from the renewable NCES and demanded power respectively. Uncertain variables in this case are P_R and P_D, if we combine them in only one uncertain variable P_C we obtain, $P_C = P_D - P_R$, and then, power balance can be rewritten such as $P_G = P_C$, where now, there is only one uncertain variable, which is the combination of the two original ones. This process allows finding easily a PDF to represent the variability of the problem, and to reduce the computational effort of the final problem.

Then, possible future scenarios are generated using a method for uncertainty representation which is proposed based on [1, 7, 9]. Thereafter, we need to select those scenarios that represent the uncertainty of the historical data. Our goal is to represent uncertainties in the historical information through a finite number of possible future variations of the variable in order to improve the robustness of our EMS as follows:

1. Classifying historical information: Combined initial time series is disaggregated according to their resolution; then, we obtain a time series for every sample time along a day. For example, a time series of 365 days with 1 h resolution provides 24 disaggregated time series, each with 365 points.
2. Fitting time series: Disaggregated time series are fitted through a PDF; then, parameters of every time series are calculated. From the example of step 1, we obtain parameters of 24 PDFs for the 24 time series.
3. Generating scenarios: With the parameters of all PDFs, a finite number of realizations or future scenarios are generated for every sampling time. On our example, K scenarios are generated for each hour according to the respective PDFs.
4. Estimating the minimum number of scenarios: The goal with the generated scenarios is to represent uncertainties in the historical information, which will allow to the EMS having into account the K possible variations that the uncertain variables could have in the future, in other words, the control actions of the EMS will satisfy all the operational conditions that could impose each of those K possible future variations; achieving in this way to improve the robustness of the EMS. In this regard, K scenarios must be

selected such that the PDF parameters calculated from the generated scenarios and from the original disaggregated time series are as close as possible. In this work, the maximum allowed difference was 5%. Finally, minimum number of scenarios can be determined through a plot of K vs. PDF parameters difference as we show in the next section. This step is only performed once in the EMS design stage. When the EMS is in operation mode, only steps 1 to 3 are executed every sample time to update PDF parameters with new measurements.

2.2 Robust EMS Formulation

Based on the selected realizations, a robust EMS is proposed to maximize the use of NCES and to improve robustness of the power system when unexpected variations occur. The objective of the multiple scenarios explained in Subsect. 2.1 is to anticipate the future behavior of the NCES and demand and to improve the robustness of the whole power system in the long term, even under unexpected power flow variations.

Since we promote the self-consumption in productive processes, our EMS approach is formulated as an uni-nodal problem, i.e., we assume that all loads and sources are connected to the same connection point. In other words, the transmission constrain is not included. In (3) the formulation of the problem in an uni-nodal form and including single prediction is presented according to [7,9]:

$$\min_{P_{gi}^{(r)}, P_{ns}^{(r)}, P_{lo}^{(r)}} \sum_{r=1}^{N_p} \left(\sum_{i=1}^{M} (C_{gi} P_{gi}^{(r)}) + (C_{ns} P_{ns}^{(r)}) + (C_{lo} P_{lo}^{(r)}) \right) \tag{3}$$

subject to $r = 1, \ldots, N_p$ constraints:

$$\sum_{i=1}^{M} P_{gi}^{(r)} + P_{ns}^{(r)} - P_{lo}^{(r)} - \sum_{j=1}^{N} P_{dj}^{(r)} + \sum_{m=1}^{O} P_{Rm}^{(r)} = 0$$

$$P_{gi}^{\min}, P_{ns}^{\min}, P_{lo}^{\min} \leq P_{gi}^{(r)}, P_{ns}^{(r)}, P_{lo}^{(r)} \leq P_{gi}^{\max}, P_{ns}^{\max}, P_{lo}^{\max}$$

with $i = 1, \ldots, M$. P_{gi} is the power from the i-th controllable energy source. C_{gi} is the cost associated with the i-th energy source. P_{ns} and C_{ns} are the non-supplied power and their associated cost, respectively. P_{lo} and C_{lo} are the lost power and their associated cost, respectively. P_{Rm} is the power from the m-th renewable energy source. P_{dj} is the demanded power of the j-th load. $P_{gi}^{\min}$, $P_{ns}^{\min}$, $P_{lo}^{\min}$, $P_{gi}^{\max}$, $P_{ns}^{\max}$ and $P_{lo}^{\max}$ are the minimum and maximum physical constraints of the decision variables. M, N and O are the number of dispatchable energy sources, loads, and renewable sources respectively. Superscript $\bullet^{(r)}$ refers to the number of the step along to the prediction horizon of the variable $\bullet$. And N_P is the prediction horizon.

The optimization problem formulation (3) includes the single prediction of the available energy from the NCES and the demand to improve the performance of the system in the long term via anticipation of the possible variations.

However, predictions are not enough to improve the robustness of the system under unexpected future power variations. For this reason, we directly include uncertainties in the optimization problem formulation [1]. This inclusion is performed through the generation of a finite number of possible future scenarios with their respective occurrence probability. But first, we define uncertain sets for every renewable energy source P_{Rm} and power demand P_{dj}:

$$[P_{Rm}^{(1)}, \ldots, P_{Rm}^{(N_P)}] \in := \{(P_{Rm(1)}^{(1)}, \ldots, P_{Rm(1)}^{(N_P)}), \ldots, (P_{Rm(K)}^{(1)}, \ldots, P_{Rm(K)}^{(N_P)})\}$$

$$[P_{dj}^{(1)}, \ldots, P_{dj}^{(N_P)}] \in := \{(P_{dj(1)}^{(1)}, \ldots, P_{dj(1)}^{(N_P)}), \ldots, (P_{dj(K)}^{(1)}, \ldots, P_{dj(K)}^{(N_P)})\}$$

Here, $m = 1, \ldots, O$ and $j = 1, \ldots, N$, where O and N are the amount of NCESs and power demands respectively. Now, every scenario can be defined as follows considering all NCES and demands (contraction Scen means Scenario):

$$\text{Scen\#}s = \{(P_{Rm(s)}^{(1)}, \ldots, P_{Rm(s)}^{(N_P)}), (P_{dj(s)}^{(1)}, \ldots, P_{dj(s)}^{(N_P)})\}$$

for $s = 1, \ldots, K$ generated scenarios. Finally, we formulate an optimization problem for the robust EMS where uncertainties are included through the inclusion of above scenarios in form of K sets of constraints, one set per considered scenario. Every step time of every realization or scenario has an occurrence probability. However, the numerical tractability of the problem can be affected when the number of constraints increases. Therefore, following the procedure presented in [1], the expected value optimization problem is reformulated in its equivalent epigraph form:

$$\min_{P_{gi}^{(r)}, P_{ns}^{(r)}, P_{lo}^{(r)}, t_{(s)}^{(r)}} \sum_{r=1}^{N_p} \left(\sum_{i=1}^{M} (C_{gi} P_{gi}^{(r)}) + (C_{ns} P_{ns}^{(r)}) + (C_{lo} P_{lo}^{(r)}) \right) + \sum_{s=1}^{K} \left(\sum_{r=1}^{N_p} p_{(s)}^{(r)} t_{(s)}^{(r)} \right)$$

subject to:

$$\text{set\#}s \begin{cases} \sum_{i=1}^{M} P_{gi}^{(1)} + P_{ns}^{(1)} - P_{lo}^{(1)} + \sum_{m=1}^{O} P_{Rm(s)}^{(1)} - \sum_{j=1}^{N} P_{dj(s)}^{(1)} \leq t_{(s)}^{(1)} \\ \vdots \\ \sum_{i=1}^{M} P_{gi}^{(N_P)} + P_{ns}^{(N_P)} - P_{lo}^{(N_P)} + \sum_{m=1}^{O} P_{Rm(s)}^{(N_P)} - \sum_{j=1}^{N} P_{dj(s)}^{(N_P)} \leq t_{(s)}^{(N_P)} \end{cases}$$

$$P_{ns}^{(r)}, P_{lo}^{(r)} \geq 0; \quad P_{gi}^{\min} \leq P_{gi}^{(r)} \leq P_{gi}^{\max}; \quad t_{(s)}^{(r)} >= 0$$

with $s = 1, \ldots, K$, $i = 1, \ldots, M$, and $r = 1, \ldots, N_p$. Here, subscript $\bullet_{(s)}$ is the counter of the selected scenarios. p is the probability of each step in every scenario, and t is the additional decision variable that appears because of the epigraph form transformation. The selection of the number of scenarios is carried out according to the procedure proposed on Subsect. 2.1.

3 Simulation Set-Up

We tested our proposed methodology via simulation with a robust EMS for a typical copper extraction process supplied from the bulk grid, a local conventional generator, and a NCES (a wind generator in this case). In general, mining process is considered as an intensive energy process because it consumes around 700 kWh/tone mined [6]. Simulations were performed with power curves of a real process and real historical information of wind speed in the same location. The EMS controls the amount of power imported from the main grid and the local generator, so that they can compensate power fluctuations from the NCES and the demanded power.

IEEE benchmark of nine nodes and three generators was used to represent the electric grid of the selected productive process. Mathematical nomenclature is defined as: **g2** is the energy source in node 2 and it represents power from main grid; **g3** is the energy source in node 3 and it represents the local generator; **w** is the energy source in node 1 and it represents a NCES, a wind energy source for this case; **L5, L6, L8** are the system loads connected in nodes 5, 6 and 8 respectively, and they represent the total power demand of the copper extraction process.

3.1 Robust Energy Management System Formulation

The efficiency of generators and loads of the power system when exchanging power among them mainly depends on the management of those power flows through the EMS. Then, in (4), the proposed robust EMS for the power system of the copper process is presented. In this robust problem formulation, uncertainties are included through the inclusion of K possible future scenarios of the uncertain variables, which are expressed as K constraints:

$$\min_{t^{(r)}_{(s)}, P^{(r)}_{g2}, P^{(r)}_{g3}, P^{(r)}_{ns}, Plo^{(r)}} (C_{g2}P^{(1)}_{g2} + C_{g3}P^{(1)}_{g3} + C_{ns}P^{(1)}_{ns}$$

$$\vdots$$

$$+C_{g2}P^{(N_P)}_{g2} + C_{g3}P^{(N_P)}_{g3} + C_{ns}P^{(N_P)}_{ns} + C_{lo}P^{(N_P)}_{lo}) + (p^{(1)}_{(1)}t^{(1)}_{(1)} + \ldots + p^{(N_P)}_{(1)}t^{(N_P)}_{(1)}$$

$$\vdots$$

$$+p^{(1)}_{(K)}t^{(1)}_{(K)} + \ldots + p^{(N_P)}_{(K)}t^{(N_P)}_{(K)})$$

$$(4)$$

subject to $s = 1, \ldots, K$ sets:

$$\text{set}\#s \begin{cases} P^{(1)}_{g2} + P^{(1)}_{g3} + P^{(1)}_{ns} - P^{(1)}_{lo} + P^{(1)}_{w(s)} - P^{(1)}_{d5(s)} - P^{(1)}_{d6(s)} - P^{(1)}_{d8(s)} \leq t^{(1)}_{(s)} \\ \vdots \\ P^{(N_P)}_{g2} + P^{(N_P)}_{g3} + P^{(N_P)}_{ns} - P^{(N_P)}_{lo} + P^{(N_P)}_{w(s)} - P^{(N_P)}_{d5(s)} - P^{(N_P)}_{d6(s)} - P^{(N_P)}_{d8(s)} \leq t^{(N_P)}_{(s)} \end{cases}$$

and to the following constraints:

$$P^{\min}_{g2} \leq P^{(r)}_{g2} \leq P^{\max}_{g2} \qquad P^{\min}_{g3} \leq P^{(r)}_{g3} \leq P^{\max}_{g3}$$

$$P^{(r)}_{ns}, P^{(r)}_{lo} \geq 0; \qquad t^{(r)}_{(s)} >= 0; \quad r = 1, \cdots, N_p$$

where P_{g2} and P_{g3} are the two power flows from the two controllable energy sources, grid and local generator respectively for this case. C_{g2} and C_{g3} are the costs associated with the controllable energy sources mentioned above. P_{ns} and C_{ns} are the non-supplied power and its associated cost. P_{lo} and C_{lo} are the lost power and its associated cost. P_w is the power from wind energy source. P_{d5}, P_{d6}, P_{d8} are the demanded power of the three loads of the test system. $P_{g2}^{\min}$, $P_{g3}^{\min}, P_{ns}^{\min}, P_{lo}^{\min}, P_{g2}^{\max}, P_{g3}^{\max}$ $P_{ns}^{\max}$ and $P_{lo}^{\max}$ are the minimum and maximum physical constraints of the decision variables. Finally, $\{\text{set}\#1, \cdots, \text{set}\#K\}$ are the power balance constraints that need to be satisfied for each $s = 1, \ldots, K$ scenario.

The robust solution obtained with this formulation reduces the possibility of the power system to collapse when an unexpected power variation occurs. Thereby, our robust energy management strategy helps to improve the dynamical performance of the system during unexpected power flow variations.

4   Simulation Results

The minimum number of scenarios was selected through the procedure presented in Sect. 2.1. Figure 1 shows the relation between the number of considered scenarios and the error of the statistical parameters. In this case, a normal distribution was used to represent the uncertainty of the historical time series (it is only one time series because of the combination of all uncertain variables that we presented in Sect. 2.1). We found that 1500 is a suitable number of scenarios to reduce the error of the mean (μ) and standard deviation (σ) to around 5%. It means that the uncertainty on the historical data is represented by this amount of scenarios with 95% representation percentage.

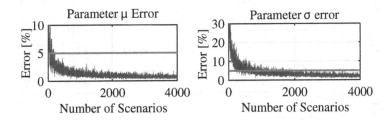

Fig. 1. Error of the statistical parameters vs. Number of considered scenarios. For this example, the error goes below 5% (red lines) with 1500 scenarios. (Color figure online)

We carried out simulation experiments with different EMS strategies during one day. All experiments were executed with conditions presented in Fig. 2. The figure shows a situation where the total power demand is always greater than the wind power, except in some intervals where the wind power is greater than the power demand. These mismatches have some consequences, which were analyzed.

Historical time series used for simulation was measured from the power consumed by a real copper mining process, and from a wind power plant (close to the place where power demand data were obtained). The sampling time of all tested controllers was 15 min.

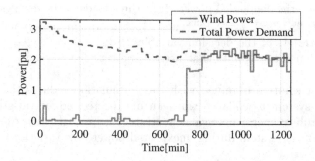

Fig. 2. Power delivered by the wind turbine and the total power demand of the system. The simulations were performed under these conditions.

The power system was tested on a typical situation to analyze its dynamic behavior with the proposed robust EMS and a non-robust EMS. In minute 1000 and along the 30 following minutes, wind speed decreased unexpectedly to zero. Although this is a totally unpredictable event, the controller had to react and try to compensate it. Figure 3 shows the dynamic performance of the power on the dispatchable sources, it means, grid and conventional local generator.

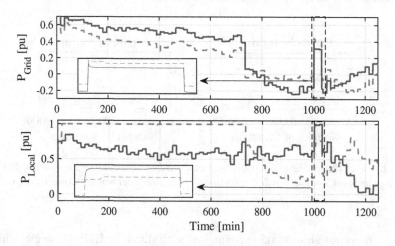

Fig. 3. Power from grid (top panel) and from local generator (bottom panel) under an unexpected absence of wind power. Proposed robust EMS (solid blue line). Non-robust EMS (dash red line) (Color figure online)

Table 1. Maximum variation of the delivered power from the dispatchable sources with the proposed robust EMS and a non-robust EMS caused by a wind event.

Max. power change		
Source	EMS	Max ΔP [MW]
Grid	Non-robust	10.7
	Robust	1.3
Local generator	Non-robust	9.6
	Robust	1.4

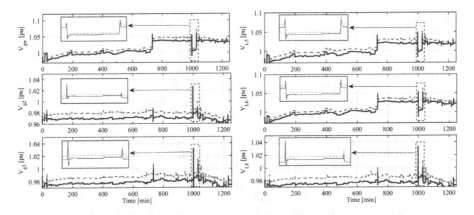

Fig. 4. Voltages in the main nodes of the power system under unexpected reduction of the wind power. Proposed robust EMS (solid blue line). Non-robust EMS (dash red line). (Color figure online)

When the wind turbine stopped producing energy, the grid and the local generator increased their delivered power to compensate this event. However, according to the used EMS, the dynamical performance was different. Figure 3 shows that the changes in the delivered power from the controllable energy sources with the proposed robust EMS are smaller than in the non-robust EMS during the unexpected outage of the wind generator. In the case of the local generator, it means that the energy consumption efficiency was improved, suggesting that the useful life of the machine was extended. The magnitudes of these changes are presented in Table 1.

Regarding the voltage performance, Fig. 4 and Table 2 show a faster response when the proposed EMS was used. In addition, the overshoot voltage magnitude was also reduced. In general, the stability of the power system was improved with the proposed EMS. Furthermore, the figure shows that voltages are always lower when the robust EMS was used, i.e., there is a wider range to regulate reactive power through the voltage manipulation in the case of considering voltage as a control variable.

Table 2. Numerical differences between a non-robust EMS and the proposed robust EMS under an unexpected wind power reduction*.

Voltages in unexpected wind event					
Node	EMS	IST [s]	FST [s]	Iovsh [%]	Fovsh [%]
1	Non-robust	90	90	−2.2	2.5
	Robust	60	45	−1.7	2.3
2	Non-robust	90	75	3.6	2.1
	Robust	60	45	4.9	1.8
3	Non-robust	90	90	3.5	2.7
	Robust	60	45	4.6	2.5
5	Non-robust	90	90	−2.1	2.4
	Robust	60	45	−1.6	2.2
6	Non-robust	90	90	−2.4	2.6
	Robust	60	45	−1.9	2.4
8	Non-robust	90	90	3.5	2.4
	Robust	60	45	4.8	2.2

*Here, **IST** and **FST** are the initial (min 1000) and final (min 1030) stabilization times respectively, **Iovsh** and **Fovsh** are initial (min 1000) and final (min 1030) overshoot respectively. The wind turbine is connected to Node 1. Nodes 2 and 3 are the connections of the bulk grid and the local generator, respectively. Nodes 5, 6, and 8 are the loads L5, L6 and L8 connections, respectively.

5   Conclusions

In this work, we proposed a methodology to manage energy in productive processes with NCES penetration via a robust EMS. Unlike other works in the literature [7–9, 11, 12], our methodology is manly oriented to promote self-consumption in productive processes in countries where it is not possible to sell energy surpluses to the main grid. The EMS includes a method to consider uncertainties in the NCES and power demand using historical information updated on real-time, with the objective of minimizing the operative costs. Our methodology allows avoiding large power variations in the local generator. A desirable characteristic in systems with NCES, because in productive processes it is a common practice to use thermal generation units to supply part of the power consumption of the process and they show a slow power response by nature. Furthermore, the proposed robust EMS ensures a suitable dynamical performance of the power system, which is not the case with a non-robust EMS.

A typical industrial process includes sensitive voltage devices, i.e., the dynamic behavior of the voltage is a critical aspect in power systems. Thereby, the proposed EMS has several advantages because it reduces the time response and voltage overshoot during abrupt unexpected power variations. In addition, our approach reduces the voltage level in all nodes of the power system (inside the permissible limits), which allows increasing the span to control the reactive power of the system.

Although a non-robust EMS allows having lower operative costs of the system, the proposed approach improves several dynamic aspects of an industrial power system such as the energy efficiency, the useful life of its components, and economic savings in the long term.

References

1. Boyd, S., Vandenberghe, L.: Convex Optimization, 7th edn. Cambridge University Press, Cambridge (2009)
2. Chu, K.C., Kaifuku, K., Saitou, K.: Optimal integration of alternative energy sources in production systems for minimum grid dependency and outage risk. In: CASE, pp. 640–645 (2014)
3. Erdinc, O., et al.: Experimental performance assessment of an online energy management strategy for varying renewable power production suppression. Int. J. Hydrog. Energy **37**(6), 4737–4748 (2012). Optimization Approaches to Hydrogen Logistics
4. Fais, B., Sabio, N., Strachan, N.: The critical role of the industrial sector in reaching long-term emission reduction, energy efficiency and renewable targets. Appl. Energy **162**, 699–712 (2016)
5. International Energy Agency: Key world energy statistics (2014)
6. Millar, D., Levesque, M., Lyle, G., Bullock, K.: Enabling advanced energy management practice for mineral operations. In: Annual General Meeting of the Canadian Institute of Mining, Montreal, PQ, Canada, pp. 22–25 (2011)
7. Olivares, D.E., Cañizares, C.A., Kazerani, M.: A centralized energy management system for isolated microgrids. IEEE Trans. Smart Grid **5**(4), 1864–1875 (2014)
8. Olivares, D.E., Lara, J.D., Cañizares, C.A., Kazerani, M.: Stochastic-predictive energy management system for isolated microgrids. IEEE Trans. Smart Grid **6**(6), 2681–2693 (2015)
9. Parisio, A., Rikos, E., Glielmo, L.: A model predictive control approach to microgrid operation optimization. IEEE Trans. Control Syst. Technol. **22**(5), 1813–1827 (2014)
10. Qi, W., Liu, J., Christofides, P.: Supervisory predictive control for long-term scheduling of an integrated wind/solar energy generation and water desalination system. IEEE Trans. Control Syst. Technol. **20**(2), 504–512 (2012)
11. Valencia, F., Collado, J., Sáez, D., Marín, L.G.: Robust energy management system for a microgrid based on a fuzzy prediction interval model. IEEE Trans. Smart Grid **7**(3), 1486–1494 (2016)
12. Zhang, Y., Gatsis, N., Giannakis, G.B.: Robust energy management for microgrids with high-penetration renewables. IEEE Trans. Sustain. Energy **4**(4), 944–953 (2013)

A Traffic Flows Scheme for User-BS Association in Green HetNets

Luis A. Fletscher[1]($\boxtimes$), José M. Maestre[2], and Catalina Valencia Peroni[3]

[1] Departamento de Ingeniería Electrónica y Telecomunicaciones,
Facultad de Ingeniería, Universidad de Antioquia UdeA, Medellín, Colombia
luis.fletscher@udea.edu.co
[2] System Engineering and Automation Department, School of Engineering,
Universidad de Sevilla, Seville, Spain
pepemaestre@us.es
[3] Process and Energy Department, Universidad Nacional de Colombia,
Medellín, Colombia
cavalenciapa@unal.edu.co

Abstract. Energy efficiency in the next-generation of cellular networks is an important topic due to the expected increase in the number of nodes. Previous research has shown the relationship between the number of users connected to a cellular network base station (BS) and its energy consumption. For this reason, the study of optimal mechanisms that balance the load of users over the available base stations is a key element in the field of energy efficiency in cellular networks. However, the user-BS association process is not trivial because the problem explodes combinatorially. For this reason, it is necessary to explore mechanisms able to be executed in the order of milliseconds. In this paper, we compare two different user - BS association policies and their impact on grid consumption in a heterogeneous cellular network (HetNet) powered by hybrid energy sources (grid and renewable energy). The first proposal is based on a discrete optimization problem and the second is a relaxation that uses traffic flows. These schemes are compared to the traditional best-signal-level mechanism and evaluated in a realistic simulation scenario to study the impact on grid consumption, number of users served, and computation time. The new proposed user allocation policies result in lower grid electricity consumption and lower average unserved users compared to the traditional association scheme.

Keywords: Energy efficiency · Green networks · HetNets

1 Introduction

Green cellular networks are a field of great interest today, especially when we consider that mobile communications networks consume about 0.5% of the global energy supply [1,2]. For this reason, different projects have studied the energy behavior of a cellular network and ways to reduce its consumption, e.g., ICT-EARTH [3] and Trend [4].

© Springer Nature Switzerland AG 2018
J. C. Figueroa-García et al. (Eds.): WEA 2018, CCIS 916, pp. 28–39, 2018.
https://doi.org/10.1007/978-3-030-00353-1_3

The main energy consumption in a cellular network is produced by base stations (BSs), and it depends on the number of active users in a given time slot [5]. For this reason, a balance of downlink traffic loads among BSs by an appropriate user-BS association mechanism is needed to minimize on-grid consumption. Hence, renewable energies are a good option to deploy infrastructure in scenarios with connection limits or without grid connection (off-grid), e.g., in developing countries. However, integrating renewable energy in next-generation cellular networks has various challenges related to network architecture and energy sources [6].

In the literature, it is possible to find several approximations to solve the load-balancing problem in HetNets. Andrews *et al.* present a survey of different technical approaches to HetNet load-balancing [7]. Here it is possible to observe the need to explore new load balancing mechanism different to traditional optimization techniques because the problem of associating users to base stations is NP-hard and not computable even for small-sized HetNets. From the optimization viewpoint, several load-balance approaches to increase energy efficiency in cellular networks have been proposed in recent years. In [8], Han and Ansari presented a virtually distributed algorithm named vGALA to reach a balance between network utilities and green energy utilization in software-defined radio access networks powered by hybrid energy sources. Likewise, Zhou *et al.* proposed a heuristic algorithm for target cell selection combined with a power control algorithm for coverage optimization to guide users towards BSs with a renewable energy supply [9]. Ye *et al.* present a low-complexity distributed algorithm to solve the association problem jointly with resource allocation in an on-grid HetNet. They assume that users can be associated with more than one BS at the same time, as a relaxation of the NP-hard problem. Silva et al., use the classic optimal transportation approach to study the mobile association problem in cellular networks [10]. Game theory has also been used to solve the user-BS association problem. In [11] authors present a scheme based on a game of two players moving between a macro base station and a small cell, with both BS connected to the grid. To take the association decision, players use a distribute algorithm trying to maximize their payoffs independently.

Also, to reach energy efficiency in cellular networks, other approximations have been proposed [12], with one of them being the utilization of renewable power sources [13]. According to the International Energy Agency (IEA), the 14% of the global population (1.1 billion people) live without electricity in 2017 [14].

In this work, three different alternatives are evaluated to analyze energy consumption on a given case study. The first of the three alternatives is a traditional scheme where users select the BS with a better signal level [15]. The second uses a discrete branch-and-bound optimizer to assign users to BS. Our final proposal uses a traffic-flow perspective to relax the discrete optimization problem and improve computational time [16]. The success of the proposed schemes is considered from an energy-efficiency perspective, which means a reduction of on-grid consumption. An extended analysis of these and other techniques can be found in [17].

To evaluate the proposed mechanisms, we use two-tier HetNet such as that of Fig. 1, which is composed of one macro base station (MBS) and multiple small cells base stations (SCBSs). On-grid energy powers the MBS, and SCBSs are powered exclusively by wind. The MBS provides basic coverage while the SCBSs are deployed in its coverage area to enhance network capacity and absorb traffic load. Note that the proposed system does not include batteries to reduce maintenance, environmental, and production costs. Our proposal differs from previous works because our target is energy efficiency through grid consumption reduction, which is a different perspective in this research field. Also, our off-grid SCBSs are assumed not to have batteries support, making more demanding the control strategies to guarantee QoS levels. Finally, we test different alternatives in a complex scenario (37 BS-750 users), including an original approach based on traffic flows.

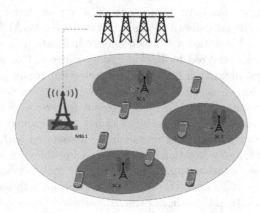

Fig. 1. Scenario: a HetNet powered by hybrid energy sources.

The outline of the rest of the article is as follows: Sect. 2 presents the proposed user-BS connections schemes. Section 3 describes the simulation scenario. In Sect. 4, the performance of the proposed schemes is evaluated, including the analysis of results. Finally, in Sect. 5 the conclusions are provided.

2   Cell Selection Schemes

Our goal is to minimize on-grid consumption by balancing downlink traffic loads among BSs using an adequate user association scheme. To this end, let us define a geographical area $L \subset R^2$ that contains B base stations and U users. Let $x \in L$ denote a location, and $j \in B$ be the BS index, where $j = 1$ represents the MBS. Time is divided into T time slots of length τ seconds and $t \in T$ denotes the $t - th$ time slot. Each SCBS updates its cell size every τ seconds by changing the transmission power according to the amount of renewable energy available at its location. For simplicity, we drop the time slot index t for the rest of the paper.

Each small cell can only serve U_M users simultaneously; although the MBS has not limit for the amount of associated users for simplicity. The number of active users in a time slot is given by U_A. Assuming that mobile users are uniformly distributed in the geographical area [18], the traffic load of the $j - th$ BS in the $t - th$ time slot can be expressed as

$$\rho_1 = \frac{\sum_{i=1}^{U} y_{i,1}}{U_A} \tag{1}$$

$$\rho_j = \frac{\sum_{i=1}^{U} y_{i,j}}{U_M}, \tag{2}$$

where $y_{i,j}$ is the user association indicator. If user i is associated with BS j in the $t - th$ time slot, $y_{i,j} = 1$, otherwise $y_{i,j} = 0$. Note that $0 \le \rho_j \le 1$ for all j.

It is also assumed that at each time slot a user can be associated with the $j - th$ BS if the signal level received $s_{i,j}$ is greater than a threshold φ.

Finally, U_S is the amount of users using the systems in a time slot and it will be a Quality of Service (QoS) objective. It is expressed as

$$U_S = \frac{\sum_{j=1}^{B} \sum_{i=1}^{U} y_{i,j}}{U_A} \tag{3}$$

The energy consumption model is based on the results of project EARTH [5]. The EARTH model states that energy consumption of a BS consists of two parts: the static power consumption and the dynamic power consumption. It can be expressed as

$$C_j = \Delta_j \rho_j P_j \tau + E_j^S \tag{4}$$

where Δ_j is the slope of load-dependent energy consumption of BS j, P_j is the transmission power of BS j at the $t - th$ time slot, ρ_j is the traffic load of BS j at the $t - th$ time slot and E_j^S is the static energy consumption of BS j in each time slot. Static power consumption is related to the energy required for the normal operation of a BS, and the dynamic power consumption is the additional energy demand caused by the traffic load, which is approximated by a linear function of the load.

Here, the total energy consumption of the network scenario in a given time slot is the sum of the grid consumption (due to MBS) and the green consumption (due to SCBSs). Hence, the reduction of consumption in BS 1 (MBS) is the key to increasing energy efficiency.

To reduce the consumption from the grid in the HetNet, different user-BS connection policies are proposed. As stated previously, three different mechanisms are presented and compared here. The first is the standard better-signal-level mechanism, which is used to compare the performance of the alternatives. The second is based on traditional discrete optimization techniques, and, finally, a flow relaxation of the discrete problem is implemented.

2.1 Best-Signal-Level Policy

In traditional cellular networks, mobile users connect to the BS that offers the best signal-to-interference-plus-noise ratio (SINR), which depends on BS power transmission, path loss, and interference from other BSs. However, this mechanism is not entirely adequate for HetNets, because SCBSs with available resources can be ignored by users when receiving a stronger signal from an MBS [19]. We will refer to this procedure as traditional policy, and it will be the baseline for evaluating the performance of proposed mechanisms. Note that, for simplicity, we used only path loss to determine the user's best received signal.

2.2 Optimization Method

Given that the objective is to reduce the overall system grid consumption, it is possible to formulate the following optimization problem

$$\min_{y} \sum_{i=1}^{U} y_{i,1} \tag{5}$$

s.t.

$$\sum_{i=1}^{U} y_{i,j} \leq U_M \qquad j = 2,3,\ldots,B \tag{6}$$

$$y_{i,j}.s_{i,j} \geq \varphi \tag{7}$$

$$U_S = \frac{\sum_{j=1}^{B} \sum_{i=1}^{U} y_{i,j}}{U_A} \geq \varepsilon \tag{8}$$

$$\sum_{j \in B} y_{i,j} \leq 1 \qquad \forall i \in U \tag{9}$$

$$y_{i,j} \in \{0,1\} \qquad \forall i, \forall j \tag{10}$$

where (5) is the objective function, which focuses on minimizing consumption from the grid with an optimal assignment of active users to available BS over each time slot. Equations (6)–(10) are the problem constraints: (6) establishes that a small cell j can serve a maximum of U_M users simultaneously; (7) is the user's received signal level constraint, where $s_{i,j}$ is the signal level received by user i from BS j and φ is the minimum signal level required by an user to have service; (8) stands for the minimum percentage of users served (U_S), which is a QoS constraint; (9) requires that an user is served only by one BS in a time slot; and (10) establishes that $y_{i,j}$ is a binary variable.

The optimal connection policy is attained solving (5) by means of an integer linear optimization problem. To find a solution, a branch-and-bound method is used. Information preprocessing and previous knowledge of the problem are also helpful to reduce the computational burden. In particular, the following preprocessing was applied to the data given to the optimizer:

1. *Reduction of space search.* The matrix $S_{i,j}$ was simplified according to the number of active BSs (b), to reduce the search space from $U \times B$ to $U \times b$ where $b \leq B$, with B being the number of BSs in the network.
2. *Time slot adjustment.* Since the optimization is performed in each time slot, it is important that its length is sufficient to perform the calculations, but not too much, thus avoiding changes in the system being ignored.

2.3   Traffic Flow Approximation

Approximation based on traffic flows was also considered to solve the computation burden issues of integer optimization and it was originally presented in [17]. This perspective uses a relaxation of the discrete problem and generates a solution with the optimal flows exchanged between BSs. This approach has been successfully applied to problems such as traffic management [20] and supply chains [21]. Figure 2 presents an illustration of this perspective. The incorporation of a new virtual BS ($B + 1$) can be observed, which is used to discard traffic according to the defined QoS level.

The mechanism uses input information from a matrix with the potential flows that can be exchanged between BSs ($F_{i,j}$) in each time slot. This matrix is built from the received signal level of each user from each BS, the active BSs according to the wind speed, the BS adjacency matrix, and the number of users connected to each BS. The potential matrix flow, the number of resource blocks (RBs) available in each BS, and the QoS level are used as constraints of a linear optimization problem that minimizes the sum of flows from any base station to the MBS (BS 1). Equations (11)–(16) present the formal description of the optimization problem.

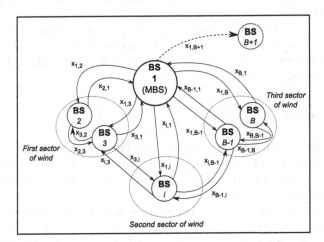

Fig. 2. Traffic flow approximation.

$$\min_x \sum_{i=1}^{B+1} x_{i,1} \tag{11}$$

s.t.

$$\sum_{i=1}^{B+1} x_{i,j} \leq F_{i,j} \qquad j = 1,2,3,\ldots,B+1 \tag{12}$$

$$\frac{\sum_{j=1}^{B} \sum_{i=1}^{B} x_{i,j}}{U_A} \geq \varepsilon \times U_A \tag{13}$$

$$\sum_{i=1}^{B+1} x_{i,j} \leq U_j^M \qquad j = 1,2,\ldots,B+1 \tag{14}$$

$$\sum_{j \in B} x_{i,j} = x_i \qquad \forall i \tag{15}$$

$$0 \leq x_{i,j} \qquad \forall i, \forall j \tag{16}$$

where $x_{i,j}$ is the traffic flow from BS i to BS j in a time slot and x_i is the total traffic of the BS i in a time slot. Equation (11) is the objective function, which seeks to minimize the flows to the MBS and hence reduce the overall consumption from the grid of the cellular network. The constraint (12) specifies that the flow between two BSs cannot exceed the limits established by the potential flows matrix. Equation (13) defines the QoS level, and guarantees that the sum of all flows is higher than the desired percentage of users served ε. Constraint (14) establishes the limit in the number of users to be received by a BS. This limit is defined by the number of RB available in the destination BS in each time slot. Constraint (15) imposes flow conservation. This means that all users will be served, even by the $B+1$ BS or the same BS that originated the flow. Finally, (16) defines that flows must be positive.

Once the solution to this problem is found, a rounding process is executed to obtain integer values and assign users to BS according to these values. Finally, a remarkable feature of this approach is that it can be implemented easily in a distributed fashion [22,23].

3   Simulation Scenario

In the next generation cellular networks, deployments with a 2-tier downlink HetNet will be common. One MBS and multiple SCBS powered with hybrid energy supply will be a valid option to face both the growing users demand and the energy consumption problem.

The scenario described in Sect. 1 was implemented to evaluate the proposed alternatives regarding their consumption of energy. The case study considered is composed of one MBS and 36 overlapping SCBSs. This is the minimum number of SCBSs needed to cover the MBS area. In this scenario, the MBS is powered by on-grid energy, and it is always on, ensuring constant coverage over the area. Each BS has one sector, and only large-scale loss is considered in the simulation.

The technical parameters of the simulation are defined according to an LTE system with a geographical area of $3.5\,\mathrm{km}^2$ [24], with uniform inter-site distance between BSs of 500 m and the environmental parameters from Medellín (Colombia). Also, given the population density of this city ($2500\,\mathrm{hab/km}^2$) and the mobile internet penetration in Colombia (10%), 750 users are considered in the experiments. The users are moving according to a random walk point model. Table 1 summarizes the parameters used in the simulation. As mentioned previously, small cells are powered only by green energy. In this way, to reduce the deployment cost and to mitigate the environmental impact, each SCBS has a micro-turbine that provides green energy without a battery system. The goal of each SCBS is to receive users from the MBS and therefore reduce its consumption from the grid.

Table 1. Simulation parameters

Parameter	Value
Coverage area	$3.5\,\mathrm{km}^2$
Number of users	750
System	LTE
BW LTE	20 MHz
RB per BS	100
N. macro base station	1
N. MBS sectors	1
N. SCBS	36
Inter site distance	500 m
Tx power MBS	43 dBm
Tx power SCBS	22 dBm
Static power cons. MBS	130 w
Static power cons. SCBS	6.8 w
Consumption slope MBS	4.7
Consumption slope SCBS	4.0
Pathloss model	cost 231 model
Antenna gain	15 dBi
Receiver sensitivity	$-107.5\,\mathrm{dBm}$
Size of request file	500 Kb
Time slot	2 s
Users mobility model	random walk point
Mobility speed	4 km/h

3.1 Renewable Power Potential

Introducing renewable energy (RE) power sources in a cellular network requires understanding RE dynamics and their relationship with energy consumption at BS. In this work, we consider that wind is the source of the renewable power. In particular, real data is used to define a Weibull probability distribution that represents the expected wind speed at a specific location and a time interval. From this prediction, it is possible to determine the amount of energy produced by a micro-turbine in a period.

The simulation considers the behavior of the wind in Medellín, based on 3-year data provided by weather stations of SIATA [25]. Using @Risk7 [26], it was possible to define three sectors with different wind behaviours in the simulation area. It was found that sector one presents mean wind speed of 1.787 m/s, sector two has a mean wind speed of 1.880 m/s, and in sector three has a mean wind speed of 2.238 m/s.

According to the average wind speed, a micro-turbine was selected for the SCBSs with a start-up wind speed of 2 m/s. The power potential of microturbine is 26 w when wind speed is between 2 m/s and 3 m/s, and 35 w when wind speed is higher than 3 m/s.

The simulation is configured with different average wind speeds in the sectors under the coverage area of the MBS. Wind dynamics vary every minute. Therefore, there are three possible green energy scenarios: no SCBS has sufficient green energy, the SCBSs of only one sector have green energy to work, and more than one sector has green energy (this case could be even when all SCBS have energy in the same period).

Traffic requests are modeled as an inhomogeneous Poisson point process. The arrival rate per area $\lambda(x)$ and the traffic size are independently distributed with mean $\mu(x)$ to capture the spatial traffic variability [27].

4 Results

Using MATLAB®and IBM Cplex Optimizer, it was possible to evaluate the different connection schemes and their impact on grid power consumption. The temporal variability of traffic on the cellular network was not considered. For this reason, a simulation time of 15 min was used to observe the behavior of the proposed solutions. The active BSs along the corresponding 450 time slots define the $S_{i,j}$ matrix and the search space in each optimization.

To compare the performance of the mechanisms with the traditional best-signal-level scheme, six key performance indicators (KPI) are proposed: average grid consumption (watts/min), percentage of users served, average transmission rate (Mbps), percentage of consumption reduction compared to the traditional scheme, transmitted bits per grid-consumed watts, and simulation time. Table 2 shows the KPI results for each scheme. The optimizer policy was implemented for two different QoS objectives, being equivalent to 85% of the baseline defined by the traditional scheme. We found a reduction in consumption with respect to the traditional connection scheme. In particular, the optimizer of 85% has good

Table 2. Association schemes comparison

User association scheme	Aver. grid consump. (watts/min)	Grid consump. reduct. (%)	Users served (%)
Signal level policy	6055	-	85.8
Optimizer 85%	5733	5.3	85.5
Optimizer 90%	5903	2.5	90.2
Traffic flows 85%	5765	4.8	86.1

grid energy savings of 5.3% compared to the signal-level policy. Only when $U_S = 90\%$ do we observe that the optimizer grid consumption is close to the traditional scheme. Therefore, if the best signal level is not the main criteria for selecting a base station, a reduction in the average rate can be achieved. It is important to remember that the optimizer does not have constraints or incentives related to the transmission rate.

Regarding the computational time required for the simulations, Table 3 shows a comparison of the results of implementing the different policies when different amounts of users are present in the network. It can be observed that the optimizer increases its computational time markedly when the number of users grows.

With traffic flows, it is possible to observe a reduction of the consumption from the grid to levels comparable to those of the discrete optimizer (4.8%). This result is very important because the discrete optimizer delivers the optimum consumption of the system according to a QoS level. The other key element is the quality of service (U_S) in the system, which presents a small improvement if the traditional scheme is compared to the traffic flow. The processing time of the traffic flows is lower than the discrete optimizer's and remain practically constant with the growth of users, thus representing a good option for improving the consumption and maintaining QoS levels in scenarios with a large number of users.

Table 3. Computation time for the simulations [s]

User association scheme	500 users	750 users	1000 users
Signal level policy	211	287	261
Optimizer 85%	507	1158	2077
Traffic flows 85%	392	554	507

5   Conclusions and Future Work

Three different user-BS association schemes for HetNet hybrid cellular networks were compared in this paper. Our simulations allow observing that the optimization-based schemes result in lower power grid consumption.

It is important to emphasize the good response of the traffic flow approximation, despite being a relaxation of the original optimization problem. It reaches KPI values closer to those of the discrete optimization in suitable computational time. The possibility of implementing the traffic flow mechanism in a distributed scenario is another advantage, with it being difficult in discrete optimization-based schemes. Future work in this line can consider exploring alternatives to improve average transmission rates.

The next stage in the study of alternatives for improving the energy consumption of these kinds of networks should include analysis of delays in the user association process and their impact on the quality of service of the system. In the same way, to achieve complete energy management, it is necessary to consider storage systems to support the off grid BSs.

Finally, it was demonstrated that by using mechanisms with low computation times it is possible to reach levels of energy saving and QoS similar to those obtained with discrete optimization-based methods.

References

1. Lubritto, C., et al.: Energy and environmental aspects of mobile communication systems. Energy **36**(2), 1109–1114 (2011)
2. Hasan, Z., Boostanimehr, H., BhargavaGhazzai, V.: Green cellular networks: a survey, some research issues and challenges. IEEE Commun. Surv. Tutor. **13**(4), 524–540 (2011)
3. ICT-EARTH. ICT-EARTH. https://www.ict-earth.eu
4. TREND. Towards real energy-efficient network design. http://www.fp7-trend.eu/
5. Auer, G., et al.: How much energy is needed to run a wireless network? IEEE Wirel. Commun. **18**(5), 40–49 (2011)
6. Hassan, H., Nuaymi, L., Pelov, A.: Classification of renewable energy scenarios and objectives for cellular networks. In: IEEE International Symposium on Personal, Indoor and Mobile Radio Communications, PIMRC, London, pp. 2967–2972 (2013)
7. Andrews, J.G., Singh, S., Ye, Q., Lin, X., Dhillon, H.: An overview of load balancing in HetNets: old myths and open problems. IEEE Wirel. Commun. **21**(2), 18–25 (2014)
8. Han, T., Ansari, N.: A traffic load balancing framework for software-defined radio access networks powered by hybrid energy sources. IEEE/ACM Trans. Netw. **99**, 1–14 (2015)
9. Zhou, J., Li, M., Liu, L., She, X., Chen, L.: Energy source aware target cell selection and coverage optimization for power saving in cellular networks. In: IEEE/ACM International Conference on Green Computing and Communications & International Conference on Cyber, Physical and Social Computing, Hangzhou, pp. 1–8 (2010)
10. Silva, A., Tembine, H., Altman, E., Debbah, M.: Optimum and equilibrium in assignment problems with congestion: mobile terminals association to base stations. IEEE Trans. Autom. Control **58**(8), 2018–2031 (2013)
11. Chekroun, S., Sabir, E., Kobbane, A., Tembine, H., Bouyakhf, E., Ibrahimi, K.: A distributed open-close access for Small-Cell networks: a random matrix game analysis. In: Wireless Communications and Mobile Computing Conference (IWCMC) (2015)

12. Suarez, L., Nuaymi, L., Bonnin, J.: An overview and classification of research approaches in green wireless networks. EURASIP J. Wirel. Commun. Netw. **2012**, 142 (2012)

13. Dhillon, H., Li, Y., Nuggehalli, P., Pi, Z., Andrews, J.: Fundamentals of heterogeneous cellular networks with energy harvesting. IEEE Trans. Wirel. Commun. **13**(5), 2782–2797 (2014)

14. International Energy Agency: World energy outlook 2017, Paris (2017). https://www.iea.org/access2017/

15. ETSI. LTE, General packet radio service (GPRS) enhancements for evolved universal terrestrial radio access network (E-UTRAN). http://www.etsi.org/

16. Orlin, J., Magnanti, T., Ahuja, R.: Network Flows: Theory, Algorithms, and Applications. Pearson, London (1993)

17. Fletscher, L., Maestre, J., Valencia, C.: An assessment of different user-BS association policies for green HetNets in off-grid environments. Trans. Emerg. Telecommun. Technol. **28**(12), 1–15 (2017)

18. Liu, D., Chen, Y., Chai, K., Zhang, T., Elkashlan, M.: Two dimensional optimization on user association and green energy allocation for HetNets with hybrid energy sources. IEEE Trans. Commun. **63**(11), 4111–4124 (2015)

19. Andrews, J.: Seven ways that hetnets are a cellular paradigm shift. IEEE Commun. Mag. **51**(3), 136–144 (2013)

20. Smulders, S.: Control of freeway traffic flow by variable speed signs. Transp. Res. Part B: Methodol. **24**(2), 111–132 (1990)

21. Sarimveis, H., Patrinos, P., Tarantilis, C., Kiranoudis, C.: Dynamic modeling and control of supply chain systems: a review. Comput. Oper. Res. **35**(11), 3530–3561 (2008)

22. Camponogara, E., Scherer, H.: Distributed optimization for model predictive control of linear dynamic networks with control-input and output constraints. IEEE Trans. Autom. Sci. Eng. **8**(1), 233–242 (2011)

23. Maestre, J., Negenborn, R.: Distributed Model Predictive Control Made Easy. Springer, Heidelberg (2014). https://doi.org/10.1007/978-94-007-7006-5

24. 3GPP: LTE Evolved Universal Terrestrial Radio Access Network (E-UTRAN); self-configuring and self-optimizing network (SON) use cases and solutions (2014). http://www.3gpp.org/dynareport/36902.htm

25. SIATA: Medellín and Aburrá Valley early warning system, a project of the Aburrá Valley metropolitan area and the city of Medellín. SIATA - Sistema de Alertas Tempranas. http://www.siata.gov.co/

26. Palisade Corporation. @Risk 7. http://www.palisade.com/risk/

27. Kim, H., de Veciana, G., Yang, X., Venkatachalam, M.: Distributed α-optimal user association and cell load balancing in wireless networks. IEEE/ACM Trans. Netw. **20**(1), 177–190 (2012)

Logistics IRP Model for the Supply Chain of Perishable Food

Javier Arturo Orjuela-Castro[1]($\boxtimes$), Diego Batero-Manso[1],
and Juan Pablo Orejuela-Cabrera[2]

[1] Faculty of Engineering, Industrial Engineering Department,
Universidad Distrital, Francisco José de Caldas, 110231 Bogotá, D.C., Colombia
jorjuela@udistrital.edu.co, diegoindustrial@gmail.com
[2] Faculty of Engineering, School of Industrial Engineering,
Universidad del Valle, Cali (Valle), Colombia
juan.orejuela@correounivalle.edu.co

Abstract. The joint management of routing and inventories has become a field of particular importance for the academic community in recent years. However, there were no models identified in the literature review that contemplate the characteristics of the supply chain of fresh food. The authors of this paper propose an IRP (Inventory Routing Problem), multi-objective, multi-product and multi-echelon model of mixed linear programming which considers the shelf life of the food. The model is applied to the supply chain of perishable fruits. The two scenarios evaluated constitute the base for a strategy proposal to reduce costs, maximize the contribution margin and diminish the losses of fruit.

1 Introduction

The Inventory Routing Problem (IRP) in the Supply Chain of Perishable Food (SCPF), has become relevant for the academic community in recent years [1]. The simultaneous study of routing and inventories, although complex, has a positive impact on the overall performance of the Chain [2, 3]. However, inventory management, distribution and routing, produces high losses and logistics costs [4].

Fruits produced in Colombia, compared to other subtropical countries, have a better quality of their organoleptic characteristics: color, flavor, aroma, higher content of soluble solids and degrees Brix [5]. This paper presents a multi-objective mathematical model of the SCPF applied to 5 fruits: mango, blackberry, strawberry, orange and mandarin from a region in Colombia [6].

The SCPF is made up of six echelons: producers, the supply central, wholesalers, hypermarkets, agro-industrial and retailers, the last echelon in turn made up of marketplaces and shopkeepers. The model allows the establishment of the Distribution Plan and inventories for each fruit as well as: the capacities required in each echelon of the chain, the total cost of the chain, the contribution margin and the impact of losses. The model surpasses previous models for considering the reduction from post-harvest losses in more than two fruits.

© Springer Nature Switzerland AG 2018
J. C. Figueroa-García et al. (Eds.): WEA 2018, CCIS 916, pp. 40–52, 2018.
https://doi.org/10.1007/978-3-030-00353-1_4

The article begins with a literature review, methodology and proposed mathematical model, based on the papers [7–10] and continues with the case study through two scenarios and the strategies formulated in order to reduce the level of losses in the SCPF.

2 Literature on IRP Models for Perishables

The first article that was identified as IRP for perishables included the allocation and distribution of the product from a regional collection center to a defined set of retailers with random demands [11]. There are several methods of solution when the IRP is NP-hard. Chen et al. [12] applied quality time windows for a perishable product with a limited shelf life in order to control the deterioration. Propose a two-stage heuristic to solve the multi-product version of the IRP with multiple clients. Another two-stage heuristic for a linear programming model was proposed by Mirzaei and Seifi [13].

Another IRP for perishable foods assuming uncertain demands, including seasonality factors, was proposed by Sivakumar [14], studied indicators such as gas emissions from transport vehicles, levels of food waste, transport times and the final quality of the distribution chain.

Amorim et al. [15] also propose an IRP for perishable food. They distinguish between two classes: fresh and mature, based on shelf life. The product is discarded at the maximum age in the inventory. They then study the impact of perishability on the IRP models for a perishable product with a fixed shelf life [1]. In both studies they restrict the storage time in the facilities without considering deterioration. Coelho and Laporte [16] include lifecycle monitoring of a perishable product with a fixed shelf life in an IRP. Jia et al. [17] propose an integrated IRP in which a supplier with a limited production capacity distributes a single item to a set of retailers using homogenous vehicles and considering a fixed deterioration of the food. The assumption of an unlimited shelf life of the product in the IRP models does not allow for the consideration of the decay in food quality, an obstacle for the application of the basic models of the IRP on the supply chain of perishable food (SCFP) [18]. These considerations have brought new objectives such as the ability to control quality and reduce waste in the SCPF as well as environmental and social impacts [2].

Al Shamsi et al. [19] propose a model with two chain echelons. Suppliers send products with a fixed shelf life and storage time to retailers. The model includes CO_2 emissions. Soysal et al. [2] show a multi-period IRP model. It includes the level of service to meet an uncertain demand applied on the distribution of fresh tomatoes to supermarkets. Mirzaei and Seifi [13] consider a two-echelon SC. The shelf life is a linear or exponentially decreasing function, the model considers any unit that is still in inventory at the time of the next delivery as lost. Rahimi et al. [20] present a multi-objective IRP model composed of three parts; one associated to economic cost, one to the level of customer satisfaction and one to environmental aspects. Hiassat et al. [21] propose a location, inventory and routing model for perishable foods. The model determines the number and location of required deposits, they develop a genetic algorithm and a heuristic for local search to solve the problem. The work of Azadeh et al. [22] presents an IRP model with transshipment for a single perishable food item. It is solved with a genetic algorithm, calculating the parameters using a Taguchi design.

Future Work in IRP should include the characteristics of SCPF [23], which could include stochastic and dynamic conditions. The solution models and methods should take into account factors such as cold chain, hygiene standards, air pollution, greenhouse gas emissions, waste generation, road occupation and other aspects related to City Logistics [24] and Green Logistics [25].

3   IRP Mathematical Models for Perishable Foods

In this section the IRP mathematical model for perishable foods is formulated.

3.1   Sets

V_a = Producers, where a = {1, 2, ..., A}
V_b = Wholesalers, where b = {1, 2, ..., B}
V_0 = Collection center
V_c = Hypermarkets, where c = {1, 2, ..., C}
V_d = Agroindustry, where d = {1, 2, ..., D}
V_e = Retailers markets, where e = {1, 2, ..., E}
V_f = Retailers shopkeepers, where f = {1, 2, ..., F}
V = All nodes, where $V = V_a \cup V_b \cup V_c \cup V_d \cup V_e \cup V_f \cup V_0$
V' = All nodes without producers $V' = V_b \cup V_c \cup V_d \cup V_e \cup V_f \cup V_0$
V_{dem} = delivery nodes $V_{dem} = V_c \cup V_d \cup V_e \cup V_f$
V_{int} = intermediate delivery and reception nodes $V_{int} = V_b \cup V_0$
$A = AllarcsA = \{(i,j) : i, j \in V, i \neq j\}$
T = Time periods in weeks, t = {1, 2, ..., T}
P = Food products, p = {1, 2, ..., P}
K = Vehicles, k = {1, 2, ..., K}

3.2   Parameters

$d_{p,t}^i$ = Demand by node $i \in V'$ of food type p, in the time period t, in kg.
m_p = Maximum shelf life of the type of food p, in days.
ca_k = Capacity of a vehicle in entities of 20 kg.
$a_{i,j}$ = Distance between the node i.e. j, $(i,j) \in A$, in km.
r_p = Penaltycost for lost food type p, in \$/kg.
$Co_{i,jk}$ = Variable Transport cost per kg*kl, for arc $(i, j) \in A$, the type of truck k, in \$/kg*kl.
$Cf_{i,jk}$ = fixed Transport cost per kilometer, for arc $(i, j) \in A$ the type of truck k, in \$/kl.
$h_{i,p}$ = Cost of maintaining inventory in the node type $i \in V'$, of food type p.
$mc_{i,p}$ = Contribution margin in the node type $i \in V$, for the food type p, in \$/kg.

3.3 Decision Variables

$I_{p,t}^i$ = Quantity of inventory in node type $i \in V'$, of food type p, at the end of the period $t \in T$. Where $I_{p,0}^i = 0, \forall i \in V_e \cup V_f \, \forall p \in P$.

$B_{p,t}^{i,k}$ = Quantity picked up in node type $i \in V'$, of food $p \in P$, by vehicle $k \in K$, at the beginning of period t, in kg.

$Q_{p,t}^{i,k}$ = Quantity delivered at node type $i \in V'$, of food $p \in P$, by vehicle $k \in K$, at the beginning the period t, in kg.

$$X_{k,t}^{i,j} = \begin{cases} 1, \text{ if the flow is from origin to destination } i \in V \text{ to } j \in V, \\ \qquad \text{in vehicle } k \in K, \text{ in period } t \in T \\ 0, \text{ otherwise.} \end{cases}$$

$F_{k,p,t}^{i,j}$ = Flow between node i and node j, of food p, by vehicle k y, in the period t i, in kg.

$W_{p,t}^i$ = Quantity of loss in node $i \in V'$, of food $p \in$, in the time period $t \in T$, in kg.

$U_{k,t}^i$ = position in the node path io $V/\{0\}$, in vehicle k ve, in the period $t \in T$.

3.4 Objectives

The mathematical model includes two objectives. The first objective function (1) is composed of inventory, routing, and costs from losses.

$$\text{Min } F_1 = \sum_{i \in V'} \sum_{p \in P} \sum_{t \in T} I_{p,t}^i h_{i,p}$$

$$+ \sum_{(i,j) \in A} \sum_{k \in K} \sum_{t \in T} \left[X_{k,t}^{i,j} Cf_{i,j} a_{ij} + \sum_{p \in P} Co_{i,j} a_{ij} F_{k,p,t}^{i,j} \right] + \sum_{i \in V'} \sum_{p \in P} \sum_{t \in T} W_{p,t}^i r_p. \tag{1}$$

The second objective function (2) maximizes the contribution margin of the chain. It differentiates between the quantity delivered and the food losses per echelon, multiplied by the unitary contribution margin in pesos per kilogram (subtraction between the selling price and the cost). This objective maximization function has not been found in the revised literature, it was designed based on the considerations of cost from fruit losses.

$$\text{Max } F_2 = \sum_{i \in V'} \sum_{p \in P} \sum_{t \in T} \left(d_{p,t}^i - W_{p,t}^i \right) mc_{i,p} \tag{2}$$

3.5 Constraints

The constraint number (3) and (4) allows to calculate the inventory levels for each node per period, based on the total cargo delivered, picked and the expected demand, losses are added to the proposal by Soysal et al. [26]. It is assumed that the inventory at the beginning of the planning period is zero.

$$I_{p,t}^i = I_{p,t-1}^i + \sum_{k \in K} Q_{p,t}^{i,k} - d_{p,t}^i - W_{p,t}^i \ \forall i \in V_{dem}, p \in P, t \in T. \tag{3}$$

$$I_{p,t}^i = I_{p,t-1}^i + \sum_{k \in K} Q_{p,t}^{i,k} - \sum_{k \in K} B_{p,t}^{i,k} - d_{p,t}^i - W_{p,t}^i \forall i \in V_{int}, p \in P, t \in T. \tag{4}$$

The constraint number (5) and (6) establishes that the amount of food losses will depend on the inventory of the period, discounting the days of the maximum useful life of the product, also considering the demand and losses of the previous period.

$$I_{p,t}^i - \sum_{a=t}^{t+m_p} d_{p,a}^i \le \sum_{a=t}^{t+m_p} W_{p,a}^i \forall i \in V_{dem}, p \in P, t \in T \mid \{t \le |T| - m_p\} \tag{5}$$

$$\sum_{i \in (V_{int})} I_{p,t}^i - \sum_{j \in V'} \sum_{a=t}^{t+m_p} d_{p,a}^j \le \sum_{i \in (V_{int})} \sum_{a=t}^{t+m_p} W_{p,a}^i \forall p \in P, t \in T \mid \{t \le |T| - m_p\} \tag{6}$$

The constraint number (7) and (8) suggested by [27, 28], guarantees that each vehicle can cover one route at most for a given period of time, and guarantee the continuity of the route.

$$\sum_{i \in V, i \ne j} X_{k,t}^{i,j} = \sum_{i \in V, i \ne j} X_{k,t}^{j,i}, \forall j \in V \backslash \{0\}, k \in K, t \in T. \tag{7}$$

$$\sum_{j \in V, i \ne j} X_{k,t}^{i,j} \le 1, \forall i \in V, k \in K, t \in T. \tag{8}$$

The constraint number (9) and (10) restrict the direct flows from producer to retailers and vice versa

$$X_{k,t}^{i,j} = 0, \forall i \in (V_a), j \in (V_e \cup V_j), k \in K, t \in T. \tag{9}$$

$$X_{k,t}^{j,i} = 0, \forall i \in (V_a), j \in (V_e \cup V_j), k \in K, t \in T. \tag{10}$$

The constraint number (11) they guarantee the behavior of the flows and their relationship with deliveries and collections.

$$\sum_{j \in V, i \ne j} F_{k,p,t}^{j,i} - \sum_{j \in V, i \ne j} F_{k,p,t}^{i,j} = Q_{p,t}^{i,k} \\ - B_{p,t}^{i,k} \forall i \in V', k \in K, p \in P, t \in T. \tag{11}$$

The restriction number (12) guarantees that only flows are given in the arcs that are chosen, and that the flow does not exceed the capacity of the vehicle

$$F^{i,j}_{k,p,t} \leq ca_k X^{i,j}_{k,t} \quad \forall (i, j) \in A, \, k \in K, \, p \in P, \, t \in T. \tag{12}$$

The constraint number (13) ensure that vehicles cannot pick up product from a node that does not have that product.

$$\sum_{k \in K} B^{i,k}_{p,t} \leq I^i_{p,t-1} + \sum_{k \in K} Q^{i,k}_{p,t} - d^i_{p,t} - W^i_{p,t} - I^i_{p,t} \, \forall i \in V_{int}, \, p \in P, \, t \in T. \tag{13}$$

The constraint number (14) guarantees the elimination of subtours. It relates the position variable of the node in the route, with respect to the binary variable, which indicates whether the vehicle travels the arc iteratively to complete all the origin destination.

$$U^i_{k,t} + 1 \leq U^j_{k,t} + |V|\left(1 - X^{i,j}_{k,t}\right), \quad \forall (i,j) \in A(V\backslash\{0\}), \, k \in K, \, t \in T. \tag{14}$$

The constraints numbers (15) to (20) are associated with the non-negativity and the conditions of the decision variables.

$$X^{i,j}_{k,t}, \in \{0, 1\}, \forall (i, j) \in A, k \in K, t \in T. \tag{15}$$

$$F^{i,j}_{k,p,t} \geq 0, \forall (i, j) \in A, k \in K, p \in P, t \in T. \tag{16}$$

$$I^i_{p,t} \geq 0, \forall i \in V', p \in P, t \in T. \tag{17}$$

$$W^i_{p,t} \geq 0, \quad \forall i \in V', p \in P, t \in T. \tag{18}$$

$$U^i_{k,t} \geq 0, \forall i \in V\backslash\{0\}, \, k \in K, \, t \in T. \tag{19}$$

$$Q^{i,k}_{p,t}, \, B^{i,k}_{p,t} \geq 0, \quad \forall i \in V', \, k \in K, \, p \in, \, t \in T. \tag{20}$$

4 Supply Chain of Perishable Fruit Products, Case Study

The multi-echelon and multi-objective model of mixed linear programming is applied to the SC of perishable fruit, having as reference the models [2, 13, 26]. In Fig. 1 a complete directed graph is presented $G = (N, E)$, where N represents the source nodes and E the target nodes.

4.1 Input Information

Based on 74 surveys, filled by the agents of the chain and complemented with secondary information [29], the supply was determined for each type of fruit in the following 10 municipalities selected from the department of Cundinamarca - Colombia:

La Palma, Topaipí, Tena, Arbeláez, Anolaima, La Mesa, Villapinzón, Suesca, Cogua, Ubalá. Demand was calculated per node for a 4-week planning time frame, in Bogotá D.C, Capital of Colombia with 10 million inhabitants. Distances were determined from the source nodes to the destination nodes. Inventory maintenance costs were determined based on the survey; they are equivalent to 15% of the average selling price of the fruit.

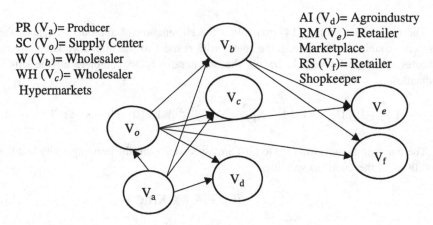

Fig. 1. Echelons of the fruit SC identified for the model.

4.2   Assumptions of the Model

Several fruits are offered by the Supply Center, each type with a fixed shelf life. Fruits can be sent to any node of the graph except to producers. Two scenarios were considered. The first one is the direct application of the IRP model to the current fruit SC. In the second scenario the Supply Central is proposed as the node that centralizes the reception of food from the producers and dispatch it to the other nodes. In the literature review it was determined that for IRP models of perishable foods this is a convenient arrangement [30]. The quantity of fruit available at the level of the wholesaler is limited by its shelf life in the time-horizon planning. Each vehicle covers at most one route per day. Each retailer can be serviced by more than one vehicle as the total cargo assigned to each can be divided into two or more vehicles. The demand for fruit is known through the time-horizon planning. For each retailer there is a cost to keep inventory in each period. However, if the fruit is kept in inventory more than indicated, it is calculated as food loss. The first operation that takes place in a day is the delivery, then the consumption and finally, the inventory level is recalculated.

4.3 Results

The proposed multi-objective mathematical model was applied to SC of perishable fruit. It allows calculating the use of transport capacities, costs, analysis of losses as well as routing aspects. The fruit IRP model was programmed in the GAMS *(General Algebraic Modeling System)*.

Analysis of Total Cost and Contribution Margin. To solve the proposed algorithms, the Epsilon Restriction *(ε-constraint)* method was used. For this purpose, an objective function that minimizes cost was chosen, and the objective function 2 was included as a constraint. By applying the mathematical model, minimizing the total cost and maximizing the contribution margin for scenarios 1 and 2, the result obtained was that scenario 1 exceeds the contribution margin of scenario 2 by 9.4%. With respect to the total cost scenario 2 had a 4.19% lower cost than scenario 1. As for the total losses, it is clear that in scenario 2 they are 8.24% lower than scenario 1. In Fig. 2 the minimum cost for each level of contribution margin is shown for each scenario.

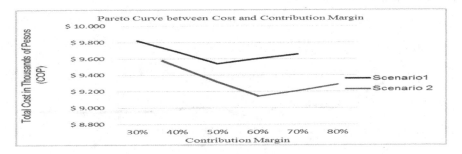

Fig. 2. Pareto curve comparison, scenario 1 and 2, between (Total cost) and (Contribution margin).

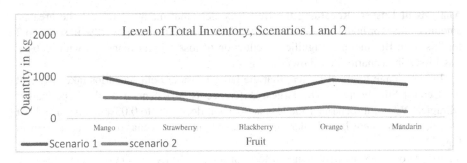

Fig. 3. Level of final average inventory *(quantity in kg)* per *(fruit)* for scenario 1 and 2.

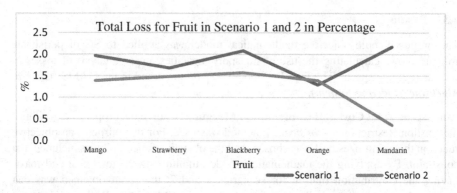

Fig. 4. Level of *(total loss per fruit)* consolidated from all the nodes *(quantity in kg)* for both scenarios.

Inventory Management. A final average inventory was obtained based on demand, storage capacity and type of fruit. As shown in Fig. 3, scenario 2 has an inventory of 43, 24% less than scenario 1.

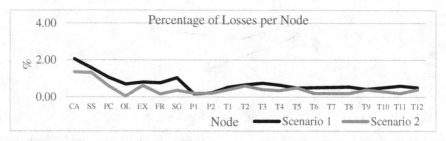

Fig. 5. *(Percentage of losses per node), (losses in %). Where (CA) is the Central supply, (SS) is Surtifruver in la Sabana, (PC) is the Placita Campesina, (OL) is Olímpica, (EX) is warehouses Éxito, (FR) is Agroindustria Frutisima, (SG) is Agroindustria San Gregorio, (P1) is market 1, (P2) is market 2, and (T1) to (T12) the respective 12 shopkeepers.*

Analysis of Losses. Regarding the fruit it is clear that mango produces the greatest amount of loss for both scenarios. However there is a reduction of 59.12% in scenario 2 for this fruit. But the most significant reduction of losses is for mandarin with 95.64% less losses in scenario 2 as shown in Fig. 4.

In percentage terms, it is clear that the largest loss in both scenarios takes place at the Central Supply node. The largest difference is in the node of the hypermarket Olímpica. While in scenario 1 the loss is 0.53% it decreases to 0.03% in scenario 2. At the retail level, there is a similar amount of loss in both scenarios as can be seen in Fig. 5.

Figure 6 shows the percentage of loss for the five fruits and the two scenarios with respect to the quantity demanded. The fruit with the lowest loss is orange and the greatest is blackberry. Although a similar behavior can be observed for each fruit scenario 1 is only better for orange.

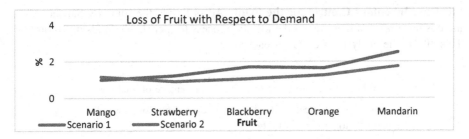

Fig. 6. Percentage of *(fruit loss with respect to demand)*, for each *(fruit)* scenario 1 and 2.

4.4 Formulation of Strategies

The centralized scenario with the Supply Center reduces the total cost by 4.19% compared with the first scenario. The distribution and inventory plans obtained suggest that it is better to centralize collection and distribution operations [20]. However, this finding can be expanded considering that the city can have such nodes at strategic locations and not exclusively in Supply Centers [21]. The results show that the cost of routing is the most representative as it exceeds 70% of the total costs in both scenarios. Inventory costs are above 20% and the costs of losses do not exceed 2%. Therefore, if the current routing conditions are improved, the total cost may be significantly reduced.

With respect to the losses and according to the results obtained, it can be observed that they increase as a function of the number of nodes and distribution routes at the end of the supply chain, the retailers. Given the central analysis that determines an IRP model and considering the results obtained, the proposed strategies for the fruit chain in Bogotá D.C is as follows:

Strategy: Use a Heterogeneous Fleet of Vehicles. As the mathematical model shows, the use of vehicle capacity is fundamental for the reduction of costs and losses. Currently the transport in Bogotá DC is carried out in vehicles that are not suitable for cargo and not even transporting fruits exclusively. This increases the risks for mechanical damages and damages from handling the cargo. A heterogeneous fleet, as shown in Table 1, will improve deliveries, as well as the capacity available for the system, which, in conjunction with the inventory plan, would reduce the expected costs.

The use of vehicles of different capacity as proposed would allow a reduction in routing costs by 10.3%, and the contribution margin could increase by 4.6%, with a minimum impact on the level of losses.

Table 1. Types of vehicles proposed.

Type of vehicle	Capacity (Ton)	%
Simple (truck)	1.4	25
Truck	3.5	35
Turbo C2	4.5	25
Simple C2	8	15

Strategy: Inventory Control for the Fruit. According to the study by Sánchez [30] there is no control of the costs of the logistic process for perishable foods in Colombia. This affects the analysis of costs for each fruit.

Table 2. Comparison of scenarios in percentage of total cost.

Scenario	Routing cost	Inventory cost	Costs from food loss	Total
Scenario 1	80.52%	18.8%	1.40%	100%
Scenario 2	77.65%	21.24%	1.11%	100%

As for cost discrimination, the second scenario is better, as shown in Table 2. The total cost is higher in scenario 1 given that it does not consider a collection center for fruits. Therefore, the sensitivity analysis of the model shows that the routing costs are inversely proportional to the inventory costs for the fruits analyzed. The strategy proposed is to implement systems that prolong the shelf life of the food in order to increase the quantities that can be delivered.

Strategy: Define a Distribution Plan and Inventory of Fruits According to Demand. The study presented by [31] shows that most of the production of perishables is not made with a technical analysis of the demand, generating an imbalance between supply and demand. In areas like Bogotá even street vendors hence observe the supply, the importance of applying logistical knowledge to agriculture. The second scenario has the lowest cost and the best margin, with a total loss of 8.20% fruit, derived from transportation (30%), storage (25%), poor demand planning and unsold fruit (15%).

5   Conclusions

The proposed multi-objective, multi-product and multi-echelon IRP mathematical model contributes to the literature of this type of problem, bringing it closer to the real behavior and complexity of the SCPF. The reviewed models have a cost approach, while the presented model allows the analysis and reduction of losses given the inclusion of the shelf life in the model. The objective function relates the losses to the margin of contribution in the studied echelons.

The IRP model validated in the SC of perishable fruits, allows the planning of inventories and routing simultaneously and thus the reduction of post-harvest losses. The experimentation with the mathematical model and analysis of results allowed an evaluation of two scenarios and a proposition of strategies for SC in Cundinamarca - Bogotá D.C, reducing costs, maximizing contribution margin and reducing losses. The analysis of the model determined the minimum cost for the routing and inventory of each fruit and the losses of each agent of the chain, the margin of contribution as well as the losses with respect to demand.

6   Future Work

The multi-objective, multi-echelon, multiproduct mathematical model proposed can be extended to a model that is integrated in Inventory Routing Problem with Production Decisions, in order to establish the most appropriate time and place for sowing fruits. Another model to develop may be Location Inventory Routing, which takes into account the location of collection centers in rural municipalities and distribution centers for urban logistics in the mega-city.

A future model could include heterogeneous vehicle fleets, assessing vehicle speed, fuel consumption and emissions of CO_2 as well as sustainable management aspects for SCPFs. Given the perishability of food over time, the development of a dynamic model it required, with stochastic variables for a probabilistic analysis.

References

1. Amorim, P., Almada Lobo, B.: The impact of food perishability issues in the vehicle routing problem. Comput. Ind. Eng. **67**, 223–233 (2014)
2. Soysal, M., Bloemhof-Ruwaard, J.M., Haijema, R., Van Der Vorst, J.G.A.J.: Modeling an inventory routing problem for perishable products with environmental considerations and demand uncertainty. Int. J. Prod. Econ. **164**, 118–133 (2015)
3. Rahimi, M., Baboli, A.: A bi-objective inventory routing problem by considering customer satisfaction level in context of perishable product. In: Computational Intelligence in Production and Logistics Systems, pp. 1–7. IEEE, Orlando, FL, USA (2014)
4. Orjuela-Castro, J.A., Diaz Gamez, G.L., Bernal Celemín, M.P.: Model for logistics capacity in the perishable food supply chain. In: Figueroa-García, J.C., López-Santana, E.R., Villa-Ramírez, J.L., Ferro-Escobar, R. (eds.) WEA 2017. CCIS, vol. 742, pp. 225–237. Springer, Cham (2017). https://doi.org/10.1007/978-3-319-66963-2_21
5. Orjuela Castro, J.A., Calderón, M.E., Buitrago Hernandez, S.P.: La cadena agroindustrial de frutas. Uchuva y tomate de árbol. Fondo De Publicaciones Universidad Distrital, Bogotá D. C (2006)
6. Orjuela-Castro, J.A., Morales-Aguilar, F.S., Mejía-Flórez, L.F.: Which is the best supply chain for perishable fruits, Lean or Agile? Rev. Colomb. Cienc. Hortícolas **11**, 294–305 (2017)
7. Orjuela-Castro, J.A., Herrera-Ramírez, M.M., Adarme-Jaimes, W.: Warehousing and transportation logistics of mango in Colombia: a system dynamics model. Fac. Ing. **26**, 73–86 (2017)
8. Orjuela-Castro, J.A., Casilimas, W., Herrera-Ramírez, M.M.: Impact analysis of transport capacity and food safety in Bogota. In: 2015 Workshop on Engineering Applications - International Congress on Engineering (WEA), pp. 1–7 (2015)
9. Orjuela-Castro, J.A., Sepulveda-Garcia, D.A., Ospina-Contreras, I.D.: Effects of using multimodal transport over the logistics performance of the food chain of uchuva. In: Figueroa-García, J.C., López-Santana, E.R., Ferro-Escobar, R. (eds.) WEA 2016. CCIS, vol. 657, pp. 165–177. Springer, Cham (2016). https://doi.org/10.1007/978-3-319-50880-1_15
10. Orjuela-Castro, J.A., Sanabria-Coronado, L.A., Peralta-Lozano, A.M.: Coupling facility location models in the supply chain of perishable fruits. Res. Transp. Bus. Manag. **24**, 73–80 (2017)
11. Federgruen, A., Zipkin, P.: A combined vehicle routing and inventory allocation problem. Oper. Res. **32**, 1019–1037 (1985)

12. Chen, H.K., Hsueh, C.F., Chang, M.S.: Production scheduling and vehicle routing with time windows for perishable food products. Comput. Oper. Res. **36**, 2311–2319 (2009)
13. Mirzaei, S., Seifi, A.: Considering lost sale in inventory routing problems for perishable goods. Comput. Ind. Eng. **87**, 213–227 (2015)
14. Sivakumar, B.: A perishable inventory system with retrial demands and a finite population. J. Comput. Appl. Math. **224**, 29–38 (2009)
15. Amorim, P., Parragh, S.N., Sperandio, F., Almada-Lobo, B.: A rich vehicle routing problem dealing with perishable food: a case study. TOP **22**, 489–508 (2014)
16. Coelho, L.C., Laporte, G.: Optimal joint replenishment, delivery and inventory management policies for perishable products. Comput. Oper. Res. **47**, 42–52 (2014)
17. Jia, T., Li, X., Wang, N., Li, R.: Integrated inventory routing problem with quality time windows and loading cost for deteriorating items under discrete time. Math. Probl. Eng. **2014**, 1–14 (2014)
18. Lahyani, R., Khemakhem, M., Semet, F.: Rich vehicle routing problems: from a taxonomy to a definition. Eur. J. Oper. Res. **241**, 1–14 (2015)
19. Al Shamsi, A., Al Raisi, A., Aftab, M.: Pollution-inventory routing problem with perishable goods. In: Golinska, P. (ed.) Logistics Operations, Supply Chain Management and Sustainability. E, pp. 585–596. Springer, Cham (2014). https://doi.org/10.1007/978-3-319-07287-6_42
20. Rahimi, M., Baboli, A., Rekik, Y.: Inventory routing problem for perishable products by considering customer satisfaction and green criteria. In: Freitag, M., Kotzab, H., Pannek, J. (eds.) Dynamics in Logistics. LNL, pp. 445–455. Springer, Cham (2017). https://doi.org/10.1007/978-3-319-45117-6_39
21. Hiassat, A., Diabat, A., Rahwan, I.: A genetic algorithm approach for location-inventory-routing problem with perishable products. J. Manuf. Syst. **42**, 93–103 (2017)
22. Azadeh, A., Elahi, S., Farahani, M.H., Nasirian, B.: A genetic algorithm-Taguchi based approach to inventory routing problem of a single perishable product with transshipment. Comput. Ind. Eng. **104**, 124–133 (2017)
23. Castro, J.A.O., Jaimes, W.A.: Dynamic impact of the structure of the supply chain of perishable foods on logistics performance and food security. J. Ind. Eng. Manag. **10**, 687–710 (2017)
24. Morganti, E., Gonzalez-Feliu, J.: City logistics for perishable products. The case of the Parma's Food Hub. Case Stud. Transp. Policy **3**, 120–128 (2015)
25. Jedliński, M.: The position of green logistics in sustainable development of a smart green city. Procedia - Soc. Behav. Sci. **151**, 102–111 (2014)
26. Soysal, M., Bloemhof-Ruwaard, J.M., Haijema, R., Van Der Vorst, J.G.A.J.: Modeling a green inventory routing problem for perishable products with horizontal collaboration. Comput. Oper. Res. **89**, 168–182 (2016)
27. Park, Y.B., Yoo, J.S., Park, H.S.: A genetic algorithm for the vendor-managed inventory routing problem with lost sales. Expert Syst. Appl. **53**, 149–159 (2016)
28. Liu, S.-C., Chen, A.-Z.: Variable neighborhood search for the inventory routing and scheduling problem in a supply chain. Expert Syst. Appl. **39**, 4149–4159 (2012)
29. Castañeda, I., Canal, L., Orjuela Castro, J.A.: Caracterización de la logística de la cadena de abastecimiento agroindustrial Frutícola en Colombia (2012)
30. Vianchá Sánchez, H.Z.: Modelos y configuraciones de cadenas de suministro en productos perecederos Models and configurations of supply chains in perishable goods. Ing. y Desarro. **32**, 138–154 (2014)
31. Paredes, A.M., Salazar, A.F.: Visión sistémica del análisis de la flexibilidad en cadenas de suministro de productos perecederos. Rev. S&T **12**, 63–86 (2014)

A Mathematical Model Under Uncertainty for Optimizing Medicine Logistics in Hospitals

Carlos Franco[1](✉), Eduyn Ramiro López-Santana[2],
and Juan Carlos Figueroa-García[2]

[1] Universidad del Rosario, Bogotá, Colombia
carlosa.franco@urosario.edu.co
[2] Universidad Distrital Francisco José de Caldas, Bogotá, Colombia
{erlopezs, jcfigueroa}@udistrital.edu.co

Abstract. Managing resources in hospitals is one of the most challenging duties in healthcare. The complexity of supply chain management in hospitals is high due to different factors such as life cycle of medicines, demand uncertainty, variation of prices, monetary resources, space constraints, among others. The main important factor of the supply chain in hospitals is the welfare of patients which depends of the correct management and administration of medicines, in this way backorders or stockouts are not allowed. In this paper we propose a mathematical model to make real planning over a health care supply chain considering real factors face by decision makers. For testing results we have used real data considering different sources of uncertainty. We have choose 5 different types of medicines and run the optimization model to determine the optimal solution over a set of scenarios generated for modeling uncertainty. For testing the results, we have compare over a year planning the results obtained by our policy and the results obtained by the hospital, improving the results in terms of costs.

Keywords: Optimization · Robust optimization · Optimization under scenarios
Hospital planning · Pharmaceutical logistics

1 Introduction

Pharmaceutical costs are representative expenses in hospitals. It can vary between 25 to 30% of the total costs [1], also logistic costs associate to moving, conditioning, handling and dispatching medicines are a very big portion of the total logistic costs, they can vary between 35 to 40% of the total logistic costs [2]. Pharmaceutical expenses are one of the most important global issues for planning because in the world can be estimated that medicines consume 20%–30% of global health spending [3]. However, pharmaceutical supply chain management is more difficult than typical applications within industrial companies since medicines and surgical supplies must be available for use always and methods are not developed for this type of industries [4].

The managing of medicines in hospitals represents considerable challenges like the needs to store medicines and surgical supplies that required to be of sufficient quantity and availability for the staff to use when necessary, inventory policies and service levels among others.

© Springer Nature Switzerland AG 2018
J. C. Figueroa-García et al. (Eds.): WEA 2018, CCIS 916, pp. 53–60, 2018.
https://doi.org/10.1007/978-3-030-00353-1_5

To model uncertainty in any situation, it can be adjusted by a distribution function but in some cases these values of uncertainty cannot be adjusted by a specific distribution function. In this study we have model the uncertainty generating scenarios that allow to model the real behavior of the random parameters. In the managing of medicines two types of different risks can occur: stockouts or surplus inventories [5].

In this paper we have developed and optimization model that consider some random aspects to model the real aspects of decision makers in hospitals that allows to obtain robust solutions that improve the performance of management the medicines. The paper is organized as follows: Sect. 2 introduce some literature review, in Sect. 3 the mathematical model is presented and in Sect. 4 some results are analyzed. Finally, in Sect. 5 the conclusions are presented.

2   Overview of Related Literature

A review of different models about pharmaceutical supply chain is introduced in [6] where the proposed taxonomy is made by differentiated different echelons of the chain and different levels. The proposed literature is divided into network optimization, inventory models and optimization of distribution of medicines. A first conclusion is that in inventory models the most source of uncertainty is the demand and it has been deeply studied but some other sources has not been included in these studies. A first approximation of inventory models with medicines was proposed in [7] where an extension of the periodic review model is proposed, they implement space constraints in the model, but it is included in the objective function. Also, in [4], a space constraint is used. The proposal considers the volume of the medicines to include as a constraint of space limitation. Some other models have developed approximations to the same problem, but these models are not developed for medicines or the management of hospitals [8–12].

A stochastic and periodic review model is presented in [13]. Objective function is formulated in terms of stock-out and budget. Also, in [14] a Markov chain model is proposed using the order up to level policies and considering stochastic demand, batching, emergency deliveries, and service levels, also a heuristic is proposed to reduce the computational complexity. Little and Coughlan [4] develop a constraint-based model for determining stock levels for all products at a storage location with space constraints, which considers the criticality of medicines. This model is an extension of a previous article presented by [7].

In [15] an extension of the (R, s, S) model is proposed. It is denoted as the (R, s, c, S) model based on the classic EOQ model. Another inventory model has been developed in [16]. Two models are proposed, one based on (s, S) model and the second one is formulated in terms of optimal allocation. Also, an approximation via simulation is presented in [17]. Two stages are considered, a Markov decision process to represent medicine demand and the use of simulation to evaluate the inventory policies characterized in the first phase. Another approximation using system dynamics was developed by Wang et al. [18].

Also, some approaches use RFID systems as those presented in [19, 20]. A different objective function is used in [21] the maximization of the total net profit is considered. A mixed integer linear programming is used. Also, a proposal for testing inventory policies by considering characteristics of medicines is developed in [1] where for testing the policies, a simulation model is developed.

3 Problem Definition

The objective of the mathematical model is to ensure that decisions of purchasing medicines consider the costs associated with prices of medicines, purchases not planed, also the problem considers constraints associated to human resources capacities, satisfaction of demand and availability of medicines in the market.

3.1 Mathematical Model

The proposed mathematical model is as follows:

Sets

- T = Time periods in the planning horizon
- P = Set of type of medicines
- S = Set of suppliers
- L = Set of medicine's life cycle
- K = Set of scenarios

Parameters

- d_{ptk} = Demand of each type of medicine in each scenario
- lt_{spk} = Lead time of each supplier for each medicine in each scenario
- c_{psk} = Cost of each medicine in each scenario
- ls_p = Lot size of each medicine
- av_{sp} = Availability of each medicine by each supplier
- ut_p = Unit doses time for each type of medicine
- lc_p = Life cycle for each medicine
- ec_p = Cost of each medicine for avoid unsatisfied demand
- cap = Availability of human resources in hours
- mna = Number allowed for making supplies, this parameter implies that there is a limitation in the number of orders because of administrative capacity

Variables

- Q^s_{pt} = Number of lots of medicines for each period required to each supplier

$$y^s_{pt} = \left\{ \begin{array}{c} 1\ if\ the\ requirement\ of\ medicine\ p\ to\ supplier\ is\ made \\ 0\ otherwise \end{array} \right\}$$

- IP^{lk}_{pt} = Inventory level for each medicine with specific life cycle in each time in each scenario

- I_{pt}^k = Net Inventory level of medicines for each time period and each scenario, this variable totalized the previous variable per period time
- RP_{pt}^{lk} = Amount of medicine distributed for each period time for each scenario
- R_{pt}^k = Net amount of medicine distributed
- EQ_{pt} = Number of lots purchased in emergency cases for each period time

$$MinZ = \left(\sum_{k \in K} \sum_{t \in T} \sum_{s \in S} \sum_{p \in P} c_{spt} * Q_{pt}^{sk} + \sum_{t \in T} \sum_{p \in P} ec_p * EQ_{pt} \right.$$
$$\left. + \sum_{s \in S} \sum_{k \in K} \sum_{t \in T} \sum_{p \in P} \sum_{l \in L|(t-l)\rangle lt_{spk}-1} c_{psk} * IP_{pt}^{lk} \right) / |K| \tag{1}$$

$$IP_{pt}^{lk} = IP_{pt-1}^{l-1k} - RP_{pt}^{lk} \quad \forall t, \forall p, \forall l | l \leq t \text{ and } t - l \leq lc_p - 1, \forall k \tag{2}$$

$$IP_{pt}^{lk} = \sum_{s \in S} ls_p * Q_{pt-lt_{spk}}^s - RP_{pt}^{lk} \quad \forall t, \forall p, \forall l = 1, \forall k \tag{3}$$

$$I_{pt}^k = \sum_{l \in 1..t} IP_{pt}^{lk} \quad \forall t, \forall p, \forall k \tag{4}$$

$$R_{pt}^k = \sum_{l \in 1..t} RP_{pt}^{lk} \quad \forall t, \forall p, \forall k \tag{5}$$

$$Q_{pt}^s \leq M * y_{pt}^s \quad \forall t, \forall p, \forall s \tag{6}$$

$$y_{pt}^s \leq av_{sp} \quad \forall t, \forall p, \forall s \tag{7}$$

$$\sum_{p \in P} \sum_{s \in S} ut_p * ls_p * Q_{pt}^s \leq cap \quad \forall t \tag{8}$$

$$R_{pt}^k + ls_p * EQ_{pt} = d_{Ptk} \quad \forall t, \forall p, \forall k \tag{9}$$

$$\sum_{p \in P} \sum_{s \in S} y_{pt}^s \leq mna \quad \forall t, \forall k \tag{10}$$

$$RP_{pt}^{lk} = 0 \quad \forall t, \forall p, \forall l | t - l > lc_p - 1, \forall k \tag{11}$$

$$\begin{array}{c} Q_{pt}^s \geq 0, y_{pt}^s \geq 0 \quad \forall t, \forall p, \forall s \\ IP_{pt}^{lk} \geq 0, RP_{pt}^{lk} \geq 0 \quad \forall t, \forall p, \forall l, \forall k \\ R_{,pt}^k I_{pt}^k \geq 0 \quad \forall t, \forall p, \forall k \\ EQ_{pt} \geq 0 \quad \forall t, \forall p \end{array} \tag{12}$$

The objective function consists in minimizing the average expected total costs overall scenarios. It contains the costs of regular purchases, the costs of emergency purchases and the costs of loss of medicines, Eq. (1).

For modeling the inventory levels of medicines considering life cycle we proposed two different types of constraints, in Eq. (2) we define the inventory level for each type of medicine for each scenario in the corresponding age of life, this means that in a specific period of time for a specific medicine there are amounts of the medicine that bellows to a different age, for example in period 2 for medicine 1 can be medicines with age 1 and/or age 2. In this way, the constraints for an specific medicine in an specific period time in a specific age is equal to the amount of medicine in the previous period that has the one year less of life minus the amount of medicine given to satisfy the demand in an specific cycle life, this means that it can be selected which age of medicine it is going to satisfy the demand.

Equation (3) is complementary to Eq. (2) because it models the age of medicines, when a purchase is made the age of medicines in inventory are 1, in this way we can model the age of medicines when they increase the period of life. Finally, the amount of medicines with age one given to satisfy the demand is subtracted. Constraints (4) contains the net inventory for a specific type of medicine in every period time in each scenario as the total amount of medicines in a specific period time in a specific scenario for each type of medicine.

Similarly to Eq. (4), in Eq. (5) the amount of medicines distributed to satisfy the demand is totalized. Equation (6) guarantees that only it is possible to purchase medicines if the binary variable is activated. The availability of medicines is modeled as the relationship between the binary variable that defines if a specific amount of medicine is supply by a specific company and the parameter that indicates if the company has in its portfolio a specific medicine, this constraint is modeled in Eq. (7).

By regulation every medicine must be put in unit-doses packages, so people for pharmacy are involved in this task. Human resource capacity is modeled in Eq. (8).

The amount of medicines given to satisfy the demand must be the exactly demand because patients cannot wait until suppliers provide medicines and this is because of the health of patients. The maximum number of orders allowed to made in a month is modeled in Eq. (10) and it is not allowed to distribute medicines out of the life cycle as presented in Eq. (11). Finally, the types of variables are modeled with Eq. (12).

4   Results

4.1   Instances Description

For testing the proposed model, we have used real data for a hospital that allowed us to analyze and generate different types of scenarios considering real life conditions that can not be modeled with the traditional models. Some random parameters were generated for generating scenarios and provide robustness to the solution. We have selected 5 types of different medicines to generate scenarios and analyze the results of the application of our model and the solution generated by the hospital. For each type of medicine, we have generated 30 different scenarios varying the selling price of suppliers, lead times and demand where we consider a full year divided into months. For analyzing the results also, we have run our model in a year planning to compare the results of the optimal solution provided by our approach and the solution made by the hospital.

4.2   Results and Analysis

For analyzing the results, we first summarize the gap between the solutions. These results are summarized in Table 1 as follows: column one contains the type of medicine, column two shows the worst scenario in costs over the total scenarios (in Colombian pesos), column three presents the best scenario in costs over the 30 scenarios (in Colombian pesos), and finally the gap as a percentage and the average results are presented.

Table 1. Scenario results

Medicine	Worst scenario	Best scenario	Gap	Average scenario
1	$ 6,202,767	$ 6,100,822	1.67%	$ 6,151,239
2	$ 5,603,429	$ 4,967,355	12.81%	$ 5,570,349
3	$ 3,522,535	$ 3,512,620	0.28%	$ 3,518,658
4	$ 12,173,578	$ 12,156,288	0.14%	$ 12,164,385
5	$ 26,502	$ 23,814	11.29%	$ 25,097
Average	$ 1,304,395,581	$ 1,295,714,056	0.67%	$ 5,485,946

In Table 1, it can be concluded that the average distance between solutions doesn't exceed 1%, in that case we can say that our method hasn't a big variation between the results, therefore the method obtain a good quality solution for the real case application. Now for comparing the results to see the differences between the real situation and the results obtained by our model, we have run our model with different data and we have compared our solution generated without consider the new data and the decisions taken by the hospital's manager. These results are summarized in Fig. 1. Where the real policy is presented in costs (by color blue) and the optimal policy obtained by our model is presented in color orange. Results of real values are not presented because of internal policies of the hospital.

The improvement of the planning for each medicine is 3.71%, 99.63%, 10.20%, 0.26% and 12.97% respectively. This means that in average in 25% is improved the policy of managing medicines in the hospital. Also it can be concluded that for 4 of the 5 medicines the improvement is at least 10% except for medicine 1 and 4, also for medicine 2 the improvement is over 90% presented a big reduction of the total costs if the model were implemented.

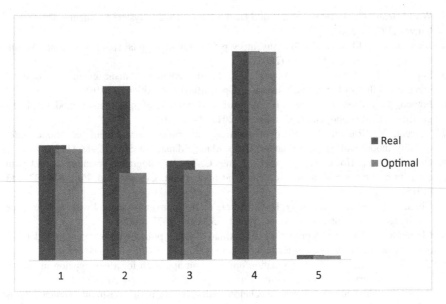

Fig. 1. Comparison between optimal policy and real policy (Color figure online)

5 Conclusions

In this paper we have studied the problem of planning medicines in the case of a hospital. Some sources of uncertainty were considered considering real situation presented in the planning of resources such as demand, lead times and life cycle. 30 different scenarios were considered for modeling uncertainty and for each parameter these scenarios were adapted for considering different variations of values. A total of five medicines were considered for testing the results obtaining improvements in the total costs.

Future works will consider development of different approaches as stochastic optimization, simulation optimization and also other sources of uncertainty. Also, testing the model over a big number of medicines for considering the real case of application in the decision making.

Acknowledgments. We thank Fair Isaac Corporation (FICO) for providing us with Xpress-MP licenses under the Academic Partner Program subscribed with Universidad Distrital Francisco Jose de Caldas (Colombia).

References

1. Gebicki, M., Mooney, E., Chen, S.-J., Mazur, L.M.: Evaluation of hospital medication inventory policies. Health Care Manag. Sci. **17**(3), 215–229 (2014)
2. McKone-Sweet, K.E., Hamilton, P., Willis, S.B.: The ailing healthcare supply chain: a prescription for change. J. Supply Chain Manag. **41**(1), 4–17 (2005)

3. World Health Organization. The World Health Report Health System Financing: The Path to Universal Coverage (2010)
4. Little, J., Coughlan, B.: Optimal inventory policy within hospital space constraints. Health Care Manag. Sci. **11**, 117–183 (2008)
5. Zepeda, E.D., Nyaga, G.N., Young, G.J.: Supply chain risk management and hospital inventory: effects of system affiliation. J. Oper. Manag. **44**, 30–47 (2016)
6. Franco, C., Alfonso-Lizarazo, E.: A structured review of quantitative models of the pharmaceutical supply chain. Complexity **2017**, 1–13 (2017)
7. Vincent, V., Ranton, M.: Hospital pharmacy inventory management: economic order quantity model with space limitation. Hosp. Mater. Manag. Q. **5**(3), 82–86 (1984)
8. Ouyang, L.-Y., Ho, C.-H., Su, C.-H., Yang, C.-T.: An integrated inventory model with capacity constraint and order-size dependent trade credit. Comput. Ind. Eng. **84**, 133–143 (2015)
9. Chou, S.-Y., Julian, P.C., Hung, K.-C.: A note on fuzzy inventory model with storage space and budget constraints. Appl. Math. Model. **33**, 4069–4077 (2009)
10. Chung, K.-J.: The correct proofs for the optimal ordering policy with trade credit under two different payment methods in a supply chain system. TOP **20**(3), 768–776 (2012)
11. Tsai, S.C., Zheng, Y.-X.: A simulation optimization approach for a two-echelon inventory system with service level constraints. Eur. J. Oper. Res. **229**, 364–374 (2013)
12. Priyan, S., Uthayakumar, R.: Two-echelon multi-product multi-constraint product returns inventory model with permissible delay in payments and variable lead time. J. Manuf. Syst. **36**, 244–262 (2015)
13. Şatir, A., Cengiz, D.: Medicinal inventory control in a university health centre. J. Oper. Res. Soc. **38**(5), 387–395 (1987)
14. Guerrero, W.J., Yeung, T., Guéret, C.: Joint-optimization of inventory policies on a multi-product multi-echelon pharmaceutical system with batching and ordering constraints. Eur. J. Oper. Res. **231**, 98–108 (2013)
15. Dellaert, N., Van De Poel, E.: Global inventory control in an academic hospital. Int. J. Prod. Econ. **46–47**, 277–284 (1996)
16. Kelle, P., Woosley, J., Schneider, H.: Pharmaceutical supply chain specifics and inventory solutions for a hospital case. Oper. Res. Health Care **1**(2–3), 54–63 (2012)
17. Vila-Parrish, A.R., Ivy, J.S., King, R.E., Fitts, E.P.: A simulation-based approach for inventory modeling of perishable pharmaceuticals. In: Winter Simulation Conference, pp. 7–15 (2008)
18. Wang, L.-C., Cheng, C.-Y., Tseng, Y.-T., Liu, Y.-F.: Demand-pull replenishment model for hospital inventory management: a dynamic buffer-adjustment approach. Int. J. Prod. Res. **53** (24), 7533–7546 (2015)
19. Çakıcı, Ö.E., Groenevelt, H., Seidmann, A., Simon, W.E.: Using RFID for the management of pharmaceutical inventory—system optimization and shrinkage control. Decis. Support Syst. **51**(4), 842–852 (2011)
20. Schapranow, M.-P., Mu¨ller, J., Zeier, A., Hasso, P.: Costs of authentic pharmaceuticals: research on qualitative and quantitative aspects of enabling anti-counterfeiting in RFID-aided supply chains. Pers. Ubiquit. Comput. **16**, 271–289 (2012)
21. Gökçe, C., Harun, Y.R.: A novel approach for inventory problem in the pharmaceutical supply chain. J. Pharm. Sci. **24**(4), 1–16 (2016)

Hybrid PSO-TS-CHR Algorithm Applied to the Vehicle Routing Problem for Multiple Perishable Products Delivery

Jesus David Galarcio Noguera[(✉)] [iD],
Helman Enrique Hernández Riaño[iD],
and Jorge Mario López Pereira[iD]

Universidad de Córdoba, Carrera 6 N 76 - 103, Montería, Colombia
jgalarcionoguera04@correo.unicordoba.edu.co

Abstract. In this paper, we dealt with the routing of refrigerated and non-refrigerated vehicles for the delivery of multiple perishable products, with known demands, the capacity of vehicles in the heterogeneous fleet, and a number of available vehicles of both types. We propose a mathematical model that seeks to minimize the loss of freshness by perishable products, considering the time they remain in the vehicles and the vehicles' storage door openings on the route, from the moment they leave the depot until they arrive at the final customer. The most important contribution of this work is the implementation of the hybrid PSO-TS-CHR algorithm to solve this problem, which is compared with a Genetic Algorithm (GA). The results showed that the metaheuristic that gives the greatest quality solutions for the stated problem of both is the hybrid algorithm.

Keywords: Metaheuristics · Vehicle routing problem
Multiple perishable products delivery · Heterogeneous fleet

1 Introduction

In recent years, many variants of the vehicle routing problem have emerged from practical application needs in multiple scenarios. These particular cases usually depend on customer requirements (time windows, multiple planning periods, etc.), network and vehicle characteristics (multiple depots, traffic, heterogeneous fleet, etc.), driving restrictions (regulation of working hours, breaks for lunch, etc.), or improved decision-making in tactical or strategic planning (inventory or location routing) [26].

The difficulty in solving vehicle routing problems is that most of them are classified as NP-hard combinatorial optimization problems—that is, they are difficult to solve, which has led to the development and implementation of a wide number of heuristic and metaheuristics techniques in order to find high-quality solutions in a reasonable computational time [4].

The research that has focused on the supply chain planning of perishable products has been limited. Among them, we highlight the programming and vehicle routing with a heterogeneous fleet for distribution of fresh milk [25], the development of a logistics

© Springer Nature Switzerland AG 2018
J. C. Figueroa-García et al. (Eds.): WEA 2018, CCIS 916, pp. 61–72, 2018.
https://doi.org/10.1007/978-3-030-00353-1_6

distribution service provider based on metaheuristic techniques for food plants that sell and distribute fresh food products [20], and the construction of an algorithm for the distribution of fresh vegetables [19]. Similarly, Galarcio [6] present a new metaheuristic and a mathematical model for the distribution of perishable products that aims to minimize the total travel time and tardiness in the delivery of transported products. Also, Song and Ko [24] formulated a VRP with refrigerated and general-type vehicles for multiple perishable products delivery in order to maximize the total sum of customer satisfaction, which depended on the freshness at the time of delivery, however, the mathematical model presented in this paper – VRP with refrigerated and general-type vehicles managing freshness - has not yet been approached using metaheuristics.

In this work, we addressed the VRP of multiple perishable products with refrigerated and general-type vehicles, including aspects such as heterogeneous fleet, customer service times and freshness as a critical factor. It was possible to introduce simplicity to the model formulated in [24], presenting it as a vehicle routing problem (VRP) variant, with the vehicle type as an assigned attribute and an objective function designed to minimize the loss of freshness according to the categories presented by Vidal et al. [26]. As a novelty, multiple products were considered and a new hybrid algorithm was applied to solve the stated problem.

This work is structured as follows: First, we describe related concepts to the products' freshness, classify the products according to their perishability level, and describe the conditions that must be given for products of this type to be transported by a non-refrigerated vehicle. Next, the formulation of the mathematical model to optimize the freshness in the delivered products is shown. Later, we explain in detail the characteristics of the applied algorithms to solve the proposed problem. Finally, we present an analysis that allows us to determine which of the algorithms is the most adequate to solve the stated problem.

2 General Considerations of the Problem

When a perishable product is delivered to a large number of customers, it is difficult to maintain its freshness because of long travel times and frequent stops. To reduce the deterioration of products with a short shelf life, it is important that these products be delivered in as timely a manner as possible [14]. This type of products are included in the meta-category of deterioration by Goyal and Giri [10] and it is possible to classify them in highly perishable, moderately and non-perishable.

We have developed a mathematical model that seeks to minimize the loss of freshness of multiple products through the inclusion of this factor in route planning. The products only can be moderately perishable with a fixed lifetime, taking into account that the use of both vehicle types is allowed. In refrigerated vehicles, the freshness of the product can be mainly affected by the vehicle door openings during the route and, to a lesser extent, by the elapsed time from the moment the vehicle leaves the depot until it reaches the final customer. For non-refrigerated vehicles, the product freshness is slightly affected by the door openings, given that for these vehicles a fully closed storage is not assumed.

3 Mathematical Model

3.1 Problem Description

We present a mathematical model, based on the concept of the CCVRP, to measure the time it takes a vehicle to travel from the depot to a specific customer [18]; we also consider the restrictions and rates presented in Song and Ko [24] that are related to the number of door openings from the moment a vehicle leaves the depot until it reaches a customer. To formulate the objective function, a relation between freshness and customer satisfaction is used, taking into account both the number of door openings and the travel time from the depot to the customers. The rates of freshness reduction may be related to the vehicle type traveling the route, the perishability level of products, and the conditions under which the product is transported. In this work, the freshness reduction rates are randomly generated between 0 and 1, considering ranges according to the type of vehicle. The demand in the objective function is included to prioritize the delivery according to the volume of product. If an initial product freshness value that decreases along the route is considered, the objective function that maximizes freshness may include a reduction that considers the mentioned rates. However, setting the objective function to minimize the reduction of freshness instead of maximizing this variable renders an initial freshness value unnecessary.

3.2 Notation

Sets

- V: Set of nodes $(i, j \in \{0, \ldots, n\})$
- V': Set of customers $(i, j \in V \setminus \{0\})$
- R: Set of vehicles $(k \in \{1, \ldots, K\})$
- P: Set of products $(p \in \{1, \ldots, m\})$

Parameters

- t_{ij}: Travel times matrix between nodes i and j. $(i, j \in V)$
- d_{jp} : Demand of customer j of product p. $(j \in V', p \in P)$
- s_i : Service time for the customer i. $(i \in V')$
- C_k : Capacity in volume of vehicle k. $(k \in R)$
- V_p : Product volume p. $(p \in P)$
- θ_p^k : Freshness reduction rate of product p per traveled time unit when the product is transported by a vehicle k. $(p \in P, k \in R)$
- ψ_p^k : Freshness reduction rate associated with the door openings when the product p is transported by a vehicle k. $(p \in P, k \in R)$
- K : Fleet size
- M: Large positive number

Variables

- Z : Total freshness loss
- t_i^k : Travel time of vehicle k from the depot to the customer i.

- na_{ik} : Number of door openings of the vehicle k's storage from the depot to customer i.
- x_{ijk} : Binary decision variable that takes the value of 1 if vehicle k travels from node i to node j.
- y_{ik} : Binary decision variable that takes the value of 1 if vehicle k visits node i.

3.3   Mathematical Model

Given the previous notation, the mathematical model for the problem can be stated as follows:

$$Min(Z) = \sum_{k \in R} \sum_{i \in V} \sum_{j \in V'} x_{ijk} \sum_{p \in P} d_{jp} \left(t_j^k \theta_p^k + na_{jk} \psi_p^k \right) \qquad (1)$$

Subject to:

$$\sum_{j \in V} x_{jik} = \sum_{j \in V} x_{ijk}, \forall i \in V, k \in R \qquad (2)$$

$$\sum_{k \in R} \sum_{j \in V} x_{0jk} = \sum_{k \in R} \sum_{i \in V} x_{i0k} \qquad (3)$$

$$\sum_{k \in R} \sum_{i \in V} x_{i0k} \leq K \qquad (4)$$

$$\sum_{j \in V} x_{jik} = y_{ik}, \forall i \in V, k \in R \qquad (5)$$

$$\sum_{k \in R} y_{ik} = 1, \forall i \in V' \qquad (6)$$

$$1 - na_{jk} \leq M\left(1 - x_{0jk}\right), \forall j \in V', k \in R \qquad (7)$$

$$na_{ik} + 1 - M\left(1 - x_{ijk}\right) \leq na_{jk}, \forall i, j \in V', k \in R \qquad (8)$$

$$t_{0j} - t_j^k \leq M\left(1 - x_{0jk}\right), \forall j \in V', k \in R \qquad (9)$$

$$t_i^k + s_i + t_{ij} - M\left(1 - x_{ijk}\right) \leq t_j^k, \forall i, j \in V', k \in R \qquad (10)$$

$$\sum_{j \in V'} \left(\sum_{p \in P} d_{jp} V_p\right) y_{jk} \leq C_k, \forall k \in R \qquad (11)$$

$$na_{ik} \geq 0, integer, \forall i \in V', k \in R \qquad (12)$$

$$t_i^k \geq 0, \forall i \in V', k \in R \qquad (13)$$

$$x_{ijk} \in \{0, 1\}, \forall i, j \in V, i \neq j, k \in R \qquad (14)$$

$$y_{ik} \in \{0, 1\}, \forall i \in V, k \in R \qquad (15)$$

In the objective function (1), the expression that accompanies the sum of θ_p^k calculates the sum of the elapsed times from the depot to each of the customers, whereas in the expression on the right, the sum of ψ_p^k calculates the cumulative number of door openings up to the target customer of each product. Equations (2) to (6) guarantee the flow conservation through the network to the maximum number of available vehicles of both types and the allocation of vehicles per customer. The expressions (7) and (8) calculate and control the cumulative count of door openings per customer. Constraints (9) and (10) calculate the time elapsed from the depot to the customers and additionally prohibit the formation of subtours [18]. Finally, (11) is the capacity constraint, and Eqs. (12) to (15) define integrality and nonnegativity constraints of variables in the problem.

4 Metaheuristics

Among the most popular metaheuristics are those inspired by nature, which are based on methods that represent the success of animal behaviors and microorganisms that work in groups; these metaheuristics have been adapted to carry out optimization tasks in complex domains of data or information [16]. Some of them are particle swarm, inspired by flocks of birds or shoals [15]; the ant colony optimization, based on the behavior of forage ants [3]; and the genetic algorithms, inspired by natural phenomena such as mutation and reproduction [9, 12]. To solve the proposed model, we have used genetic algorithm and a hybrid PSO-TS-CHR algorithm.

4.1 Genetic Algorithm

For this metaheuristic, it is common to find the following steps: the generation of the initial population, parent selection, crossover, mutation, and update of each generation [16]. The used evolutionary algorithm has been adapted to enhance its performance by applying the improved SB2OX crossover operator [21].

The crossover and mutation probabilities, *Cp* and *Mp*, have been adjusted from a reasonable number of tests with randomly proposed percentages. Figure 1 shows a flowchart describing how this metaheuristic operates.

First, the problem and algorithm parameters (stop criterion, crossing probability, mutation probability and population size) are checked. Then, an initial population is created, where each individual represents a solution in permuted encoding, each number is a specific client, and its order is the sequence in which they are assigned to the vehicles. The population is evaluated according to the objective function of the problem and the defined parameters.

To make the selection, four individuals are chosen randomly from the population to participate in a tournament taking into account its evaluation. Multiple tournaments are required to select a population for the crossing with the same size as the initial population. Afterwards, two parents cross using the SB2OX [21] if the crossover probability is fulfilled. In case of the solution is infeasible, a repair function is applied. Otherwise, the mutation is carried out through the selection and random exchange of

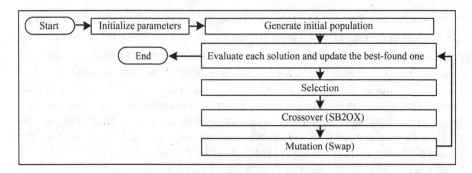

Fig. 1. Genetic algorithm flowchart.

two elements of an individual if a random number between zero and one is less or equal than the mutation probability. Finally, the loop is repeated until the algorithm stop criterion is met.

4.2   Hybrid PSO-TS-CHR Algorithm

The PSO-TS-CHR is a hybrid metaheuristic algorithm developed by Galarcio [5] that has been applied to solve VRP for perishable products [5, 6]. For efficiency, it combines the chromatic algorithm [22], particle swarm optimization [2, 15], and the tabu search (TS) [1, 7, 8]. In this algorithm, the solutions are particles. These particles are divided in two parts: a permuted vector of customers and a non-permuted vector of vehicles; in this way, the customers are assigned to a vehicle in a specific position as shown below in Fig. 2.

Fig. 2. Representation of a particle.

Each particle is obtained through the generation of $Ngen_n$ random particles, afterwards, the particle with the best objective function value is selected and it is created a swarm with N particles.

Once the particle swarm X is created, each particle Xi from the swarm is evaluated and its objective function value is stored in variable Fi. Thereafter, variable $pBesti$ is used to store the best position of particle Xi over the search, and the evaluation result of $pBesti$ is stored in a variable $FpBesti$. In addition, the best particle found during the search, G, and its evaluating value, Fg, are stored analogically. The variables stated before are updated throughout the search.

Every particle has the possibility of being transformed by one of three operators - *use of the best particle, particle fusion, and rotation of particle elements* - according to the value of a randomly generated number between zero and one for each particle by iteration. This transformation is only carried out if the resulting particle obtains an improvement in the objective function with regard to its particle of origin; otherwise, the particle *Xi* is replaced by its corresponding *pBesti*, that is to say, *Xi* becomes to its best position found, *pBesti*. After this procedure, a tabu search operator is applied by ranges for each particle with the help of the parameter *pran*, defined as the percentage of neighbors to be generated within the total range of neighbors [6].

After a number of iterations determined by the parameter *ARRAM*, a multiple start is made, which implies cleaning the individual memory of all the particles and create a new swarm.

Use of the Best Particle. This operator was taken from the chromatic algorithm [11, 22], and adapted to this algorithm [5, 6]. The operator is particularly used to take the values placed in each position *j* of the particle G_j and insert it in the same position of a particle *Xi*. For a better understanding, Fig. 3 is shown below.

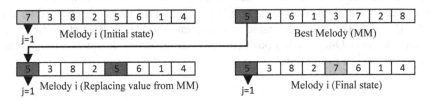

Fig. 3. Use of the best particle

Particle Fusion. In the particle fusion operator two particles are randomly taken from the swarm. At the first particle, it is assigned the letter *S* and the number one; at the second particle, it is assigned the letter *P* and the number two, then, it is generated a vector with random numbers between one and two, and a new particle is built from this vector. This task is carried out assigning the values of the position *j* from the particles *S* or *P* (depending on the vector already generated) to the new particle from left to right. Finally, when a value is already assigned in a position of the new particle, it proceeds to assign a new value of the same particle (*S* or *P*) but in a new position. This operator was taken and adapted from the chromatic algorithm [11, 22]. Look Fig. 4 for an example.

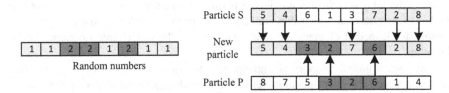

Fig. 4. Particle fusion process

Rotation of Particle Elements. This operator, taken from the chromatic algorithm, is based on the analogy of the musical process in which, for a note, the basic and most important melodic changes are those in its first, fourth, fifth, and octave notes of the musical scale. To perform this melody variation, a minimum of eight variables (in this case, customers) is required, taking into account that the movements to be performed, need to meet certain distances, which are simplified in the general scale of musical notes [22]. Thus, the corresponding elements will be the first, the fourth, the fifth and the eighth. The rotation of particles can be in two ways: descending and ascending rotation particles.

For the descending rotation particles, a key position is selected generating a random number j between eight and the k elements of the particle to be the eighth of the corresponding elements. From this, the fifth, the fourth, and the first are obtained, and the corresponding movements are made from left to right, thus changing the order and positions of each elements. Each element rotates forward in order to be located next to the closest key position, as shown in Fig. 5(a).

This procedure is similar to the descending rotation particles; however, the elements rotation is performed from right to left. Here, a random number j between one and the $(k - 8)$ elements of the particles is generated to obtain the first of the corresponding elements. Once, the key positions have been selected, the rotation movements are made, as shown in Fig. 5(b).

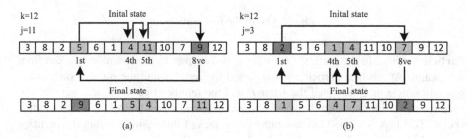

Fig. 5. Descending and ascending rotation particles

Tabu Search Operator. In the tabu search by ranges of a particle, a percentage of its neighbors is generated by swap and evaluated. Also, an average permanence rate is calculated for each one. Here, an individual memory allows storing the exchanges made by the tabu search operator in the particle, then, a parameter t determines the number of iterations in which they will be stored in the tabu list of that particle. This memory is cleaned if changes are made when using the other three operators in the algorithm.

Likewise, a global memory is implemented to allow having a history of the frequency in which the client-position-vehicle relationship is repeated during the search, creating an average permanence rate, *Tmperm*, to the generated neighbors. This rate seeks to move away the search from those solutions that have been very recurrent throughout the entire search. Moreover, it is used as an indicator for the selection of the exchange to be performed for a particle in the tabu search process.

Next, a movement value, *Vm*, is calculated to be used in the selecting of the exchange about to make in the particle. To obtain *Vm*, it has to take into account three aspects: the fitness of the particle, the fitness and the average permanence rate of the generated neighbors. Thereafter, the neighbors are organized using *Vm* and the individual memory (or individual tabu list) of the particle and it is selected the neighbor with the best *Vm*. In exceptional cases in which a neighbor has the best fitness of the search, we can also use the aspiration criteria which allows to make exchanges violating the tabu list.

For a better understanding, a flowchart is shown in Fig. 6.

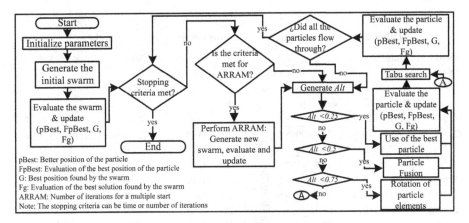

Fig. 6. Hybrid PSO-TS-CHR flowchart.

5   Results and Analysis

A comparative experiment was performed for the two algorithms with 10 different instances: 5 of each for 50 and 100 customers. The sample size was calculated according to the work of Montgomery [17], who showed the need to perform 10 replicates for this experiment.

Thus, to solve the 10 instances 10 times with two different algorithms, a total of 200 runs were performed and a time of 30 min was set for each run. For the implemented algorithms, the parameter settings shown in Table 1 were used.

Table 1. Parameters used for each of the algorithms

Genetic algorithm			Hybrid PSO-TS-CHR algorithm				
Population size	Cp	Mp	N	Ngen_n	t	pran	ARRAM
2000	0.95	0.05	10	1500	30	0.07 (7%)	100

To build the instances, we used 10 Solomon instances [13, 23] for the vehicle routing problem with time windows of 50, and 100 customers, adding the respective parameters of this variant of the vehicle routing problem and using service times and removing the time windows. The modified instances are publicly available at https://goo.gl/UJbJoR.

The results of the experiment are summarized in Table 2, which highlights the best average (underlined with a line) and the best value obtained (underlined with two lines) by the algorithms in each instance. In addition, the general standard deviation (*std*), the general average (*Avg*) and the deviation by algorithm are shown for each instance.

From the perspective of frequency of better averages and better results, the outcomes favored the PSO-TS-CHR.

Table 2. Overall summary of the results obtained by the algorithms

Instance (i,# of customers)	Algorithm						Min. avg. for the instance i	Min F for the instance i	Avg	Std
	GA			PSO-TS-CHR						
	Avg (F)	Min (F)	Std. dev	Avg (F)	Min (F)	Std. dev				
(1, 50)	2149.1	2105.8	24.9	2115.5	2102.1	8.3	2115.5	2102.1	2205.9	108.7
(2, 50)	3040.0	3009.2	25.6	2995.5	2990.0	5.6	2995.5	2990.0	3118.6	152.4
(3, 50)	2057.4	2031.8	21.7	2017.1	1999.0	11.9	2017.1	1999.0	2204.7	245.0
(4, 50)	6524.0	6510.7	6.8	6508.7	6502.6	3.7	6508.7	6502.6	6635.6	179.7
(5, 50)	1416.5	1292.1	96.1	1196.2	1189.6	5.4	1196.2	1189.6	1454.2	239.6
(1, 100)	9903.0	9524.5	160.1	7816.5	7754.1	44.2	7816.5	7754.1	9120.9	953.9
(2, 100)	7367.9	7215.2	68.1	6051.3	6007.2	25.6	6051.3	6007.2	6919.9	632.4
(3, 100)	3892.9	3813.9	60.0	2780.3	2743.2	25.1	2780.3	2743.2	3554.2	564.7
(4, 100)	5796.7	5621.8	107.4	4225.1	4132.6	46.0	4225.1	4132.6	5441.3	904.2
(5, 100)	7614.7	7493.5	64.1	5539.2	5467.6	38.8	5539.2	5467.6	6943.8	1034.1

To compare the results from different instances, we changed them to a standard distribution using Eq. (16). It should be noted that for each of the 10 instances, the mean and standard deviation were calculated. We used statistical software to analyze the data.

$$Z = \frac{x_i - \bar{x}}{\sigma} \tag{16}$$

At this point, the corresponding assumptions to execute an analysis of variance were verified to the variable Z; however, normality assumption was not satisfied for the residuals. Thus, it was necessary to use Mood's median test, a nonparametric method on which it is possible to base an analysis.

In this test was evaluated the hypothesis that the medians of the samples for each algorithm are equal. Because the P value for the chi-square test is less than 0.05, the medians of the samples are significantly different with a confidence level of 95.0%. The algorithm with the best performance is the one which its confidence interval is towards the left. It can be observed that the confidence intervals do not overlap. From Mood's median test, it can be inferred that the hybrid PSO-TS-CHR presents the best performance in terms of quality solutions of the compared algorithms.

6 Conclusions

One of the main contributions of this work is the implementation of the hybrid PSO-TS-CHR algorithm to solve the stated problem. In this context, the results showed that this algorithm can provide the best results in terms of quality solutions, with a confidence level of 95%, compared to the genetic algorithm. Also, for the time selected (30 min), it proved to be efficient in terms of execution times for both instance sizes.

Another relevant contribution is the developed mathematical model for the vehicle routing problem of refrigerated and general-type vehicles for the delivery of multiple perishable products. It is innovation lies in simplicity and the significant decrease in the quantity of restrictions with respect to other similar models presented in the literature.

In future work, the calculation of the values for the θ_p^k and ψ_p^k parameters according to the characteristics of the products to be transported can be studied. Finally, this model type could be used to improve the quality of perishable products at the time of delivery in the distribution process.

References

1. Batista, B.M., Glover, F.: Introducción a la Búsqueda Tabú. Rev. Electrón. Comun. Trab. ASEPUMA **03**, 1–36 (2007)
2. Clerc, M.: Discrete particle swarm optimization, illustrated by the traveling salesman problem. In: Clerc, M. (ed.) New Optimization Techniques in Engineering. STUDFUZZ, vol. 141, pp. 219–239. Springer, Berlin (2004). https://doi.org/10.1007/978-3-540-39930-8_8
3. Dorigo, M., Stützle, T.: Ant Colony Optmization. Massachusetts Institute of Technology, Cambridge (2004)
4. Dyer, M., Stougie, L.: Computational complexity of stochastic programming problems. Math. Program. **106**, 423–432 (2006)
5. Galarcio, J.: Ruteo de vehiculos refrigerantes y de tipo general para la entrega de multiples productos perecederos. Universidad de Cordoba (CO) (2018)
6. Galarcio, J.D., Buelvas, M.P., Nisperuza, P.A., López, J.M., Hernández, H.E.: A New Metaheuristic Applied to the Capacited Vehicle Routing Problem (CVRP) for the Distribution of Perishable Products. Ing e innov. **5**(1) (2017)
7. Glover, F.: Tabu search part I. ORSA J. Comput. **1**, 190–206 (1989). https://doi.org/10.1287/ijoc.1.3.190
8. Glover, F.: Tabu search, part II. ORSA J. Comput. **2**, 4–32 (1990). https://doi.org/10.1287/ijoc.2.1.4
9. Goldberg, D.E.: Genetic Algorithms in Search Optimization and Machine Learning. Addison-Wesley, Reading and Menlo Park (1989)
10. Goyal, S.K., Giri, B.C.: Recent trends in modeling of deteriorating inventory. Eur. J. Oper. Res. **134**, 1–16 (2001). https://doi.org/10.1016/S0377-2217(00)00248-4
11. Hernández, F., Poveda, J.: Aplicación de la metaheurística cromática al problema de secueciación de proyectos con recursos limitados (RCPSP). Universidad de Córdoba (2014)
12. Holland, J.H.: Adaptation in Natural and Artificial Systems: An Introductory Analysis with Applications to Biology, Control, and Artificial Intelligence. University of Michigan Press, Oxford (1975)

13. Homberger, J., Gehring, H.: Extended Solomon's VRPTW instances (1999). http://www. fernuni-hagen.de/WINF/touren/menuefrm/probinst.htm
14. Hsu, C.-I., Hung, S.-F., Li, H.-C.: Vehicle routing problem with time-windows for perishable food delivery. J. Food Eng. **80**, 465–475 (2007)
15. Kennedy, J.F., Eberhart, R.C., Shi, Y.: Swarm Intelligence. Morgan Kaufmann, Los Altos (2001)
16. Marinakis, Y., Marinaki, M.: A hybrid genetic - particle swarm optimization algorithm for the vehicle routing problem. Expert Syst. Appl. **37**, 1446–1455 (2010). https://doi.org/10. 1016/j.eswa.2009.06.085
17. Montgomery, D.C.: Diseño Y Análisis De Experimentos, pp. 21–692. Limusa Wiley, London (2004)
18. Ngueveu, S.U., Prins, C., Wolfler Calvo, R.: An effective memetic algorithm for the cumulative capacitated vehicle routing problem. Comput. Oper. Res. **37**, 1877–1885 (2010). https://doi.org/10.1016/j.cor.2009.06.014
19. Osvald, A., Stirn, L.Z.: A vehicle routing algorithm for the distribution of fresh vegetables and similar perishable food. J. Food Eng. **85**, 285–295 (2008). https://doi.org/10.1016/j. jfoodeng.2007.07.008
20. Prindezis, N., Kiranoudis, C.T., Marinos-Kouris, D.: A business-to-business fleet management service provider for central food market enterprises. J. Food Eng. **60**, 203–210 (2003). https://doi.org/10.1016/S0260-8774(03)00041-4
21. Ruiz, R., Maroto, C., Alcaraz, J.: Solving the flowshop scheduling problem with sequence dependent setup times using advanced metaheuristics. Eur. J. Oper. Res. **165**, 34–54 (2005)
22. Sabie, R., Mestra, A.: Un nuevo método de optimización que se fundamenta a través de un algoritmo de búsqueda basado en la escala cromática de las notas musicales. Universidad de Córdoba (2011)
23. Solomon, M.M.: Algorithms for the vehicle routing and scheduling problems with time window constraints. Oper. Res. **35**, 254–265 (1987)
24. Song, B.D., Ko, Y.D.: A vehicle routing problem of both refrigerated - and general-type vehicles for perishable food products delivery. J. Food Eng. **169**, 61–71 (2016). https://doi. org/10.1016/j.jfoodeng.2015.08.027
25. Tarantilis, C.D., Kiranoudis, C.T.: A meta-heuristic algorithm for the efficient distribution of perishable foods. J. Food Eng. **50**, 1–9 (2001). https://doi.org/10.1016/S0260-8774(00) 00187-4
26. Vidal, T., Crainic, T.G., Gendreau, M., Prins, C.: A unified solution framework for multi-attribute vehicle routing problems. Eur. J. Oper. Res. **234**, 658–673 (2014)

Districting Decisions in Home Health Care Services: Modeling and Case Study

Sebastian Cortés[1]([✉]), Elena Valentina Gutiérrez[1], Juan D. Palacio[2], and Juan G. Villegas[1]

[1] Departamento de Ingeniería Industrial, Facultad de Ingeniería,
Universidad de Antioquia, Medellín, Colombia
{sebastian.cortes,elena.gutierrez,juan.villegas}@udea.edu.co
[2] Departamento de Ciencias Matemáticas, Escuela de Ciencias,
Universidad EAFIT, Medellín, Colombia
jpalac26@eafit.edu.co

Abstract. Home health care (HHC) services are a growing segment in the global health care industry in which patients receive coordinated medical care at their homes. When designing the service, HHC providers face a set of logistics decisions that include the districting configuration of the coverage area. In HHC, the districting problem seeks to group small geographic basic units-BUs (i.e., city quarters) into districts with balanced workloads. In this work, we present a modeling approach for the problem that includes a mixed integer linear programming (MILP) formulation and a greedy randomized adaptive search procedure (GRASP). The MILP formulation solves instances up to 44 BUs, while the GRASP allows to solve instances up to 484 BUs in less than 2.52 min. Computational experiments performed with a set of real instances from a Colombian HHC provider, show that the GRASP can reduce workload imbalances in a 57%.

Keywords: Home health care · Districting
Mixed integer linear programming
Greedy randomized adaptive search procedure

1 Introduction

Social and economic factors, such as accessibility to food, primary health care, potable water, antibiotics and other medicines, have generated increases in population and life expectancy [23]. These phenomena have lead to a substantial increase in demand for home health care (HHC) services worldwide. In the U.S., 12,200 HHC providers were registered in 2011, and more than 4.7 million patients received HHC services [14]. In Europe, between 1% and 5% of the total public health budget is spent on HHC services [8,9]. In Colombia, registered HHC providers, which are mainly private companies, have increased from 482 as of December 2013, to 1,644 as of April 2018 [6].

© Springer Nature Switzerland AG 2018
J. C. Figueroa-García et al. (Eds.): WEA 2018, CCIS 916, pp. 73–84, 2018.
https://doi.org/10.1007/978-3-030-00353-1_7

One of the decisions that HHC providers face when designing the service is the districting configuration of the coverage urban area [10]. The districting problem (DP) consists of defining districts made up of several territorial basic units-BUs (i.e., city quarters), allocating to each district the available resources, so that the workload of the staff and the quality of services provided to patients are equitable [1]. The DP is critical in HHC and the impact of a districting configuration goes beyond network design and customer service considerations. The capacity of each medical staff is limited in each period, and their productivity is influenced by the size of the area in which the assigned patients are located [2]. If an urban area is divided into few large districts, medical staff will spend a significant proportion of their shifts travelling long distances among patients' homes, thus quality of care can be affected and possibly increased risk of complications and death could ensue. On the other hand, if districts are too many and too small, the coordination of patient's assignments and service delivery becomes more complex and less efficient [11]. Therefore, the districting configuration influences the quality of decisions at operative levels.

The DP arises from the political field since the 60's, and its applications include logistics transportation, school districting, commercial or design of sales territories, emergency services, police districting, disaster management, and electricity supply [17]. In this work we are interested in DP in HHC. To the best of our knowledge, four works have addressed the DP in HHC. In [4], the authors solved a DP in the management of public HHC services for a local community health clinic in Montreal, Canada. They modeled the situation as a multi-criteria optimization problem and solved it with a tabu search heuristic. Two criteria were considered in the objective function: the mobility of visiting staff and the workload equilibrium among districts. Authors were able to solve instances up to 32 BUs with six districts. The author in [2], studied a HHC districting problem through a set partitioning model, which was solved by a column generation heuristic that integrated ideas from optimization and local search. This approached allowed to solve instances up to 156 BUs with 32 districts. Authors in [3], modelled the DP in HHC through mixed-integer programming with two models: the first one aimed to equitably distribute medical staff workloads, while the second aimed to minimize a measure of compactness, i.e., the maximum distance between two BUs assigned to the same district. These models were able to solve instances from 10 to 100 BUs and districts from one to four. In [12], the authors studied the DP considering three factors: geographical distribution of the population, security conditions to access BUs, and trends in the demand for HHC services. They presented a bi-objective mathematical model. The first objective was to minimize the total travel workload, and the second one was to minimize the total workload deviations across all districts. Authors carried out a case study in the city of Cali, Colombia, and they solved instances up to 22 BUs and districts from one to 12, following a lexicographic approach.

Our contribution in this work is three-fold. First, we present a modeling approach for the problem based on a mixed integer linear programming (MILP) formulation. Second, we implemented a greedy randomized adaptive search procedure (GRASP) to solve the problem. Third, we present a case study of a HHC provider which delivers services within the Aburrá Valley, in Antioquia, Colombia. The modeling approach allows to solve real large-scale instances for the DP in HHC, in suitable computational times. Furthermore, to the best of our knowledge, we are able to solve HHC instances with sizes up to three times the ones reported in the literature, while improving current districting configurations. The remainder of this paper is structured as follows. Section 2 presents the MILP model for the DP in HHC. Section 3 describes the proposed GRASP metaheuristic. Section 4 presents the comparison of the solution methods and the results of the case study. Finally, Sect. 5 summarizes the main findings and concludes the paper outlining future work opportunities.

2 Mathematical Model

In this section, we present a mixed integer linear programming model for the DP in the HHC context. This MILP is based on the *p-regions* formulation proposed by [7]. This kind of formulation, known as *flow p-regions model* (Flow^{PRM}) includes a group of decisions variables called flow variables which contribute to model contiguity conditions between BUs in the problem. This approach is initially inspired by [22], where contiguity is accomplished by assigning a flow unit from each BU of a region (district), to a previously selected sink for the district. The flows represent a graph which starting node is the sink defined and the flows are guided by arcs between the selected nodes (BUs). Each district has a BU as its sink and the network of flows is defined as arcs connecting adjacent BUs. If a BU is assigned to a district, then, that BU must provide a flow unit that goes to the sink of the district. Moreover, a flow can not be shared by more than one district.

We define the set of BU, $\mathcal{I}$ ($i \in \mathcal{I}$) and therefore, it is possible to consider the sets $\mathcal{N}_i$ which represent the set of BU adjacent to the basic unit i (i.e., the BUs that share at least one geographical point or line with i). Each BU i has a known workload denoted by c_i. Without loss of generality, c_i is measured in hours. Additionally, we define $\mathcal{K}$ as the set of districts. To make decisions with the Flow^{PRM}, we define the binary variable y_{ik} that takes the value of one if BU i is included in district k where $i \in \mathcal{I}$ and $k \in \mathcal{K}$. The variable t_{ij} is also binary and take the value of one if BU i and BU j are assigned to the same district. t_{ij} takes the value of zero, otherwise. To measure the flow that goes from BU i to BU j in a district k, we define the variable f_{ijk}. The binary variable w_{ik} takes the value of one if BU i is selected as sink; and w_{ik} is fixed to zero, otherwise. Finally, variable λ_k denotes the workload of the district k while variables λ_{max} and λ_{min} represent the maximum and minimum workload over the districts.

The proposed MILP inspired on the Flow^{PRM} follows:

$$\min z = \lambda_{max} - \lambda_{min} \tag{1}$$

subject to,

$$\sum_{k \in \mathcal{K}} y_{ik} = 1 \qquad\qquad \forall\, i \in \mathcal{I} \tag{2}$$

$$w_{ik} \leq y_{ik} \qquad\qquad \forall\, i \in \mathcal{I}, k \in \mathcal{K} \qquad (3)$$

$$\sum_{i \in I} w_{ik} = 1 \qquad\qquad \forall\, k \in \mathcal{K} \qquad (4)$$

$$f_{ijk} \leq y_{ik} \cdot (|\mathcal{I}| - |\mathcal{K}|) \qquad\qquad \forall\, i \in \mathcal{I}, j \in \mathcal{N}_i, k \in \mathcal{K} \qquad (5)$$

$$f_{ijk} \leq y_{jk} \cdot (|\mathcal{I}| - |\mathcal{K}|) \qquad\qquad \forall\, i \in \mathcal{I}, j \in \mathcal{N}_i, k \in \mathcal{K} \qquad (6)$$

$$\sum_{j \in \mathcal{N}_i} f_{ijk} - \sum_{j \in \mathcal{N}_i} f_{jik} \geq y_{ik} - (|\mathcal{I}| - |\mathcal{K}|) \cdot w_{ik} \quad \forall\, i \in \mathcal{I}, j \in \mathcal{N}_i, k \in \mathcal{K} \qquad (7)$$

$$t_{ij} \geq y_{ik} + y_{jk} - 1 \qquad\qquad \forall i, j \in \mathcal{I} : i < j, k \in \mathcal{K} \qquad (8)$$

$$\lambda_k = \sum_{i \in \mathcal{I}} c_i \cdot y_{ik} \qquad\qquad \forall k \in \mathcal{K} \qquad (9)$$

$$\lambda_{max} \geq \lambda_k \qquad\qquad \forall\, k \in \mathcal{K} \qquad (10)$$

$$\lambda_{min} \leq \lambda_k \qquad\qquad \forall\, k \in \mathcal{K} \qquad (11)$$

$$\lambda_k \geq \lambda_{k-1} \qquad\qquad \forall k \in \mathcal{K} : k \geq 2 \qquad (12)$$

$$y_{ik} \in \{0, 1\} \qquad\qquad \forall\, i \in \mathcal{I}, k \in \mathcal{K} \qquad (13)$$

$$w_{ik} \in \{0, 1\} \qquad\qquad \forall\, i \in \mathcal{I}, k \in \mathcal{K} \qquad (14)$$

$$t_{ij} \in \{0, 1\} \qquad\qquad \forall i, j \in \mathcal{I} : i < j \qquad (15)$$

$$f_{ijk} \geq 0 \qquad\qquad \forall\, i \in \mathcal{I}, j \in \mathcal{N}_i, k \in \mathcal{K} \qquad (16)$$

$$\lambda_k \geq 0 \qquad\qquad \forall k \in \mathcal{K} \qquad (17)$$

$$\lambda_{max}, \lambda_{min} \geq 0 \qquad\qquad (18)$$

The objective function (1) minimizes the workload imbalance measure as the difference between the maximum and minimum workload among all districts (i.e., the range of the workload). As pointed in [20], balance can be obtained in different activity measures (number of customers/patients, product/service demand, and workload), our formulation is flexible enough to handle any of these three measures. Constraints in (2) ensure that each BU is assigned to a single district k. Expressions in (3) assign one sink in a district k only to BUs that compose such district while equations in (4) force the model to fix only one sink to each district. The group of constraints (5) and (6) allow a flow between BUs i and j, only if both units are assigned to district k and also if i and j are contiguous. Inequalities in (7) force each BU i to supply at least one flow unit. If that BU is not a sink, then a net flow greater or equal to one is fixed for i. On the other hand, for BUs that represent sinks, these constraints allow a negative net flow of $|\mathcal{I}|-|\mathcal{K}|-1$ units since sinks do not have outflow. The expressions (8) set variables t_{ij} equal to one if BUs i and j are assigned to the same district k. Constraints (9) calculate in variables λ_k the total workload of each district. Inequalities in (10) and (11) define respectively the maximum (λ_{max}) and minimum workload (λ_{min}) included in the objective function (1). Constraints in (12) are valid inequalities that order the districts by non-decreasing workloads. These valid inequalities reduce the number of alternative symmetric solutions, and therefore decrease the computational effort required in the branch-and-bound procedure [21]. Finally, expressions (13) to (18) define the domain of the decisions variables.

As a graphical example of a solution of the $Flow^{PRM}$ model. Figure 1 shows the value of decision variables for a districting configuration. In this case BUs D, E G, and H form the district 1 so variables $y_{D,1}$, $y_{E,1}$, $y_{G,1}$ and $y_{H,1}$ take the value of one. Note also that E is assigned as the district sink, therefore three units of flow go to E (one unit per BU assigned to district 1).

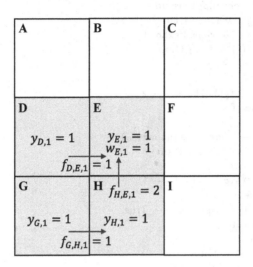

Fig. 1. Example of a solution of $Flow^{PRM}$ MILP

3 A GRASP to Solve the DP

To solve large instances of the DP, we rely on a GRASP metaheuristic. GRASP design provides a simple approach to solve efficiently a wide range of combinatorial optimization problems [16]. Particularly, in [18–20] the authors have shown that GRASP based heuristics are suitable for the solution of large-scale DPs. The proposed GRASP generates DP solutions in two phases, Algorithm 1 summarizes its main structure. In the first phase, we build an initial solution with $|\mathcal{K}|$ districts using procedure BuildDistrictsRand (line 4). The second improvement phase (lines 6–26) is a variable neighborhood descent (VND) procedure [13] that explores sequentially neighborhoods DecreaseMaxLoad and IncreaseMinLoad to improve the initial solution. The greedy randomized construction and VND cycle repeats for MaxIterations and the best solution found during the search is reported (line 28).

Greedy Randomized Construction. The greedy randomized construction phase (procedure BuildDistrictsRand) initializes the solution by selecting randomly $|\mathcal{K}|$ BUs as seeds of the districts to be created. Then, the procedure adds sequentially an adjacent BU to each one of the districts. To select the BU that

---

Algorithm 1. GRASP for the districting problem: general structure

---

1: **function** GRASP(DP,r,MaxIterations)
2:    $z^* \longleftarrow \infty$, $s^* \longleftarrow \emptyset$
3:    **for** r = 1 to MaxIterations **do**
4:        $s_0 \longleftarrow$ BuildDistrictsRand($|\mathcal{K}|$,r)
5:        LocalOptimum $\longleftarrow$ false, Neighborhood $\longleftarrow$ 1
6:        **while** not LocalOptimum **do**
7:            **if** Neighborhood=1 **then**
8:                $s \longleftarrow$ DecreaseMaxLoad(s_0)
9:                **if** $f(s) \leq f(s_0)$ **then**
10:                   $s_0 \longleftarrow s$
11:               **else**
12:                   Neighborhood $\longleftarrow$ 2
13:               **end if**
14:           **else**
15:               $s \longleftarrow$ IncreaseMinLoad(s_0)
16:               **if** $f(s) \leq f(s_0)$ **then**
17:                   $s_0 \longleftarrow s$
18:                   Neighborhood $\longleftarrow$ 1
19:               **else**
20:                   LocalOptimum $\longleftarrow$ True
21:               **end if**
22:           **end if**
23:           **if** $f(s) \leq z^*$ **then**
24:               $s^* \longleftarrow s$, $z^* \longleftarrow f(s)$
25:           **end if**
26:       **end while**
27:   **end for**
28:   **return** s^*
29: **end function**

---

will be added to a given district, we build a restricted candidate list ($\mathcal{RCL}$) with the adjacent BUs having the r smallest workloads. Then, the procedure picks randomly one BU from the $\mathcal{RCL}$ and adds it to the district. The randomized construction procedure iterates until all BUs belong to a district.

Variable Neighborhood Descent–VND. A VND is a deterministic variant of variable neighborhood search that explores sequentially several neighborhoods [13]. To solve the DP we embedded two neighborhoods within the VND. The first one, DecreaseMaxLoad (line 8 of Algorithm 1) selects the district of solution s_0 with the maximum load and evaluates if transferring one of its BUs to another adjacent district improves the objective function by reducing λ_{max}. By contrast, the second neighborhood, IncreaseMinLoad (line 15 of Algorithm 1) selects the district in s_0 with the minimum load and evaluates if adding a BU from its neighboring districts improves the objective function by increasing λ_{min}. If one of the neighborhoods improves the solution, VND restarts the search from the new improved solution using neighborhood `DecreaseMaxLoad`. On the other hand, if none of the neighborhoods improves the solution the search stops at a local optimum (line 20 of Algorithm 1). In our implementation, VND explores both neighborhoods using a best improvement strategy, i.e. it analyzes all the BUs of the district under consideration and selects the one that generates the maximum improvement of the objective function.

As pointed out in [20] some BUs cannot be removed from one district if their removal destroys the connectivity of the district. Formally, let $G(\mathcal{T})$ be the graph induced by the adjacency matrix of district $\mathcal{T}$. If $G(\mathcal{T} \setminus \{i\})$ $(i \in \mathcal{T})$ is not connected, then BU i cannot be removed from district $\mathcal{T}$. This definition coincides with the notion of *cut vertices* in graph theory [5]. Therefore, while exploring the neighborhoods in the VND we forbid the removal of any BU that is a cut vertex in the induced graph of its district.

4 Results

Initially, we analyze and compare Flow^{PRM} and GRASP in terms of the quality of the solutions obtained with both approaches and their efficiency to solve the DP in the HHC context. To compare the solution methods, we use four test instances based on the Home Health Care Program (Programa de Atención Domiciliaria–PAD, for its acronym in Spanish) offered by a Colombian health care provider in the Aburrá Valley (Antioquia). To analyze the impact of the size of the problem, we included instances with increasing number of BUs from 16 to 60. Moreover, we tested six different number of districts per instance, namely $|\mathcal{K}| = \{2, 3, 4, 0.25|\mathcal{I}|, 0.5|\mathcal{I}|, 0.75|\mathcal{I}|\}$.

The Flow^{PRM} formulation was solved with FICO's Xpress 8.1 optimizer. We report the best upper and lower bound found by the optimizer after a maximum solution time of one hour. The GRASP metaheuristic was implemented in Java using the Eclipse development environment. Moreover, to find the cut vertices of a given district we rely on the `jgrapht` package [15]. We set the parameters of GRASP to $r = 3$ and `MaxIterations`= 5000 after a detailed fine tuning process. Single runs of both methods were performed on a computer with an Intel core-i7 processor (6GB of RAM) running under Windows 7 64-bit.

Table 1 compares the results of Flow^{PRM} and GRASP. This table reports the objective function of the best interger solution (*Imb.*) and best lower bound (*Best LB*) obtained by the optimizer, the corresponding optimallity gap (*Gap*). For the GRASP this table include the objective found of the best solution found during the search (*Imb.*). We also report the running times (in seconds) of both methods. The table also reports the best-known solution (BKS) for each instance, values in bold indicate that a given method matched the BKS. Additionally, proven optima are underlined.

As it can be seen in the table, the MILP formulation reported optimal solutions in 10 out of 23 instances. All of them with less than 60 BUs. In the remaining instances, at least a feasible solution was found within the time limit. For the test instances with 60 BUs, no optimal solution was found for any of the values

Table 1. Comparison of Flow^{PRM} and GRASP for small DP instances

Instance				Flow PRM					GRASP	
Id	$|\mathcal{I}|$	$|\mathcal{K}|$	BKS	Imb.	Time (s)	Best LB	Gap (%)	Imb.	Time (s)
1	16	2	2.05	**2.05**	4.42	2.05	0.00	**2.05**	8.33
		3	136.77	**136.77**	68.83	136.77	0.00	**136.77**	2.92
		4	442.69	**442.69**	76.31	442.69	0.00	**442.69**	1.97
		8	1137.90	**1137.90**	3599.85	349.35	225.72	1137.96	0.86
		12	2772.58	**2772.58**	3600.15	2281.41	21.53	**2772.58**	0.73
2	29	2	0.22	**0.22**	3.84	0.22	0.00	0.33	14.99
		3	4.82	**4.82**	13.20	4.82	0.00	**4.82**	13.16
		4	20.06	**20.06**	307.14	20.06	0.00	28.60	6.58
		7	123.00	**123.00**	31.98	123.00	0.00	**123.00**	2.62
		15	255.98	**255.98**	3600.13	216.95	17.99	**255.98**	0.79
		22	255.98	**255.98**	3602.50	227.70	12.42	**255.98**	0.70
3	44	2	2.20	**2.20**	2.89	2.20	0.00	**2.20**	35.26
		3	104.14	**104.14**	3600.29	104.04	0.10	**104.14**	36.68
		4	182.40	**182.40**	7.28	182.40	0.00	190.86	16.11
		11	336.00	**336.00**	3600.32	304.83	10.23	**336.00**	1.38
		22	336.00	**336.00**	3600.92	327.28	2.66	**336.00**	0.98
		33	336.00	**336.00**	30.57	336.00	0.00	**336.00**	1.06
4	60	2	0.01	**0.01**	3600.26	0.00	100.00	0.04	145.17
		3	0.28	17.41	3599.97	0.00	100.00	**0.28**	111.90
		4	2.84	900.58	3600.41	0.00	100.00	**2.84**	44.94
		15	316.17	396.00	3605.50	260.01	52.30	**316.17**	3.27
		30	396.00	**396.00**	3602.26	318.99	24.14	**396.00**	1.90
		45	396.00	**396.00**	3601.23	374.06	5.87	**396.00**	1.49
Avg Time (s)					2059.14				19.73

considered for $|\mathcal{K}|$. This shows that the DP becomes harder to solve as the number of BUs grows. Likewise, instances with few districts seem easier to solve for the optimizer, since most of the optimal solution come from instances with 2 to 4 districs. On the other hand, the GRASP matched the optimal solution in 7 out of 10 instances and matched the upper bound found by Flow^{PRM} in another 8 instances. Remarkably, in the instances with 60 BUs (where the optimizer always stopped due to the time limit), GRASP results improve the solution of Flow^{PRM} in 3 out of 6 instances and matched the upper bound in another 2. Furthermore, the average running time of GRASP (19.73 s) is far below the one of Flow^{PRM} (2059.14 s). In summary, these results evidence the need to resort to approximate approaches such as GRASP in larger DP instances.

4.1 Case Study

The data of the case study is based on the information of the PAD operation for 2015. During this year, the HHC provider served 1349 acute patients located in the urban area of the Aburrá Valley (Antioquia). The coverage area of the service includes 484 BUs (city quarters). Figure 2(a) shows a heat map according

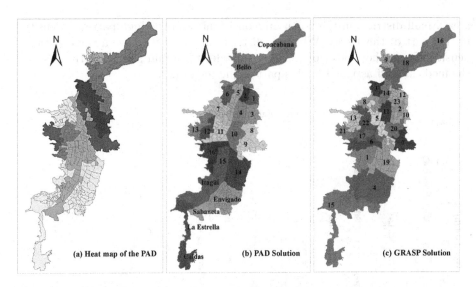

Fig. 2. Heat map of workload in the Aburrá Valley (a), current districting decisions (b), and GRASP solution for the case study (c)

to the workload in these quarters. The PAD used as districting solution the political division of the territory: the 16 communes of Medellín (capital city of Antioquia) and the other 7 municipalities of the Aburrá Valley (depicted in Fig. 2(b)). Therefore, the coverage area was divided into 23 districts. However, as it can be seen in Fig. 3, using this type of districting solution in practice does not guarantee a workload balance between the medical staff.

Service demands for HHC services of the PAD, and therefore workloads, were estimated in hours. Other works in the literature estimate HHC demands and workloads in hours [3,4,12], and only one considers demand as number of home visits [2]. Measuring such estimations in hours allows to include the variability in demand for HHC services derived from the diversity of medical procedures and types of patients. Consequently, we calculated demand estimations considering the type of medical procedure, the epidemiological profile of the covered population, and the frequencies of home visits.

To improve the districting decisions of the PAD, we ran several times the GRASP method for the DP instance with 484 BUs using a rook contiguity measure (i.e., two BUs are considered as adjacent if they share a segment in the map). The best solution found by GRASP (depicted in Fig. 2(c)) has an objective function of 2298.17 hours of workload imbalance. This result represents a 57% reduction of the workload imbalance obtained with the districting operated in 2015 (with an imbalance of 5317.85 hours). Figure 3 compares the workload of the new 23 districts of the solution proposed by GRASP against those of the previous PAD solution. As it can be seen in this figure, GRASP generates solutions with a more even workload distribution. This can be accomplished because the GRASP districts adapt to the patient's distribution in the coverage area. Small districts in the north are consistent with the high patient's density in this part of the Valley. Whereas, districts in the south have a small patient density. Then, they have to be larger in order to obtain similar workloads for the medical staff assigned to this part of the territory.

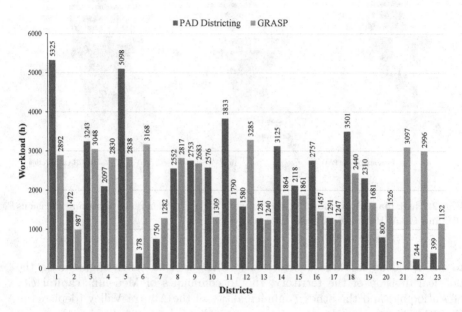

Fig. 3. Comparison of the workload of the 23 districts for the PAD and GRASP solutions

5   Conclusions

In this work, we proposed a modeling approach for the districting problem in HHC, based on two strategies. First, we adapted a MILP model based on a *p-regions* formulation, called Flow^{PRM}. The model ensures contiguity through a set of flow variables that represent a graph, and minimizes workload imbalance. For the second strategy, we implemented a GRASP metaheuristic which consists of a greedy randomized phase that designs feasible initial solutions in parallel, from a set of random seeds, and a local search that improves initial solutions by exploring two neighborhoods. We evaluated and compared the Flow^{PRM} and the GRASP in terms of the quality of the solutions, and their efficiency to solve the DP in HHC. Furthermore, we carried out a case study with a HHC provider from Antioquia, Colombia. The case study allowed to evaluate the modeling approach with real large-scale instances, and to evidence improvement opportunities in the districting configuration for HHC services.

According to the results, the Flow^{PRM} reported optimal solutions for 44% of the test evaluated, all of them of less than 60 BUs. For the remaining 56%, the model found at least one feasible solution within one hour. For instances with

60 BUs, no optimal solution was found, which evidenced the need for more efficient approximate solution methods. The GRASP matched the proven optimal solutions in 74% of the cases, and it improved 13% of the solutions found by the Flow^{PRM}, in instances with more than 60 BUs. These improvements were achieved within an average computational time far below from the ones of the Flow^{PRM}. The modeling approach was also evaluated through a case study with a real HHC provider, which delivers these service in a coverage area with 484 BUs. The approach found solutions in reasonable computation times (2.52 min on average), and results evidenced that the current districting configuration can be improved by 57%. Moreover, and to the best of our knowledge, the approach proposed is the first to solve large-scale instances up to 484 BUs for the districting problem in the HHC context.

As a future research opportunity, the inclusion of travel times within the modeling approach can provide better districting configurations. The time that medical staff spends on travelling between patients' homes is a large proportion of their working time, and therefore modeling the problem considering such factor will give a better representation of districting decisions. This inclusion generates challenges in terms of mathematical modeling and solution methods.

Acknowledgments. The authors are grateful to Universidad of Antioquia, specifically to the *Vicerrectoría de Investigación*, for their partial funding in the research project PRV16-1-03. We also thank the *IPS Universitaria* and their HHC program (PAD) for providing the information used in this work.

References

1. Bashir, B., Chabrol, M., Caux, C.: Literature review in home care. In: 9th International Conference on Modeling, Optimization & Simulation (2012)
2. Bennett, A.R.: Home Health Care Logistics Planning. Doctoral dissertation, Georgia Institute of Technology (2010)
3. Benzarti, E., Sahin, E., Dallery, Y.: Operations management applied to home care services : analysis of the districting problem. Decis. Support. Syst. **55**(2), 587–598 (2013). https://doi.org/10.1016/j.dss.2012.10.015
4. Blais, M., Lapierre, S.D., Laporte, G.: Solving a home-care districting problem in an urban setting. J. Oper. Res. Soc. **54**(11), 1141–1147 (2003). http://www.palgrave-journals.com/doifinder/10.1057/palgrave.jors.2601625
5. Bondy, J.A., Murty, U.S.R.: Graph Theory with Applications. Macmillan, London (1976)
6. Colombia, Ministerio de Salud y Protección Social: Registro Especial de Prestadores de Servicios de Salud (2018). https://prestadores.minsalud.gov.co/habilitacion/
7. Duque, J.C., Church, R.L., Middleton, R.S.: The p-regions problem. Geogr. Anal. **43**(1), 104–126 (2011)
8. Fikar, C., Hirsch, P.: Home health care routing and scheduling: a review. Comput. Oper. Res. **77**, 86–95 (2017)
9. Genet, N., Boerma, W., Kroneman, M., Hutchinson, A., Saltman, R.: Home care across Europe: case studies (2013)

10. Gutiérrez, E.V., Vidal, C.J.: Home health care logistics management: framework and research perspectives. Int. J. Ind. Eng. Manag. (IJIEM) **4**(3), 173–182 (2013)
11. Gutierrez, E.V.: Home Health Care Logistics Management Problems: An Integrated Approach to support Decisions with Hierarchical Interdependencies. Doctoral dissertation, Universidad del Valle (2014)
12. Gutiérrez, E.V., Vidal, C.J.: A home health care districting problem in a rapid-growing city. Revista Ingenieria y Universidad **19**(1), 87–113 (2015)
13. Hansen, P., Mladenović, N., Todosijević, R., Hanafi, S.: Variable neighborhood search: basics and variants. EURO J. Comput. Optim. **5**(3), 423–454 (2017)
14. Harris-Kojetin, L., Sengupta, M., Park-Lee, E., Valverde, R.: Long-term care services in the United States: 2013 overview. Vital Health Stat. Ser. 3, Anal. Epidemiol. Stud. **37**, 1–107 (2013)
15. Naveh, B.: JGraphT - a free Java graph library (2018). https://github.com/jgrapht/jgrapht
16. Resende, M.G., Ribeiro, C.C.: Optimization by GRASP: Greedy Randomized Adaptive Search Procedures. Springer, New York (2016). https://doi.org/10.1007/978-1-4939-6530-4
17. Ricca, F., Scozzari, A., Simeone, B.: Political districting: from classical models to recent approaches. Ann. Oper. Res. **204**(1), 271–299 (2013)
18. Ríos-Mercado, R.Z.: Assessing a metaheuristic for large-scale commercial districting. Cybern. Syst. **47**(4), 321–338 (2016)
19. Rios-Mercado, R.Z., Escalante, H.J.: GRASP with path relinking for commercial districting. Expert Syst. Appl. **44**, 102–113 (2016)
20. Ríos-Mercado, R.Z., Fernández, E.: A reactive GRASP for a commercial territory design problem with multiple balancing requirements. Comput. Oper. Res. **36**(3), 755–776 (2009)
21. Sherali, H.D., Smith, J.C.: Improving discrete model representations via symmetry considerations. Manag. Sci. **47**(10), 1396–1407 (2001)
22. Shirabe, T.: A model of contiguity for spatial unit allocation. Geogr. Anal. **37**(1), 2–16 (2005)
23. World Bank: Life expectancy learning module (2011). http://www.worldbank.org/depweb/english/modules/social/life/

Modeling Strategy for Supply Chain Design Considering Multiple Periods and Backlogging

César Amilcar López Bello[1,2], William J. Guerrero[2(✉)],
and José Ignacio Rodríguez Molano[1]

[1] Universidad Distrital Francisco José de Caldas, Bogotá, Colombia
clopezb@udistrital.edu.co
[2] Faculty of Engineering, Universidad de La Sabana, Chía, Colombia
williamguru@unisabana.edu.co

Abstract. This paper presents a mathematical model to optimize the supply chain design considering a planning horizon with multiple periods and backlogging. The objective function aims to minimize the sum of transportation, inventory holding and backlogging costs. The model is represented in a graph, generalizing a minimum cost flow problem. A study case for a manufacturing company is presented and results are analyzed.

Keywords: Optimization · Logistics · Inventory management
Transportation · Mathematical programming

1 Introduction

The objective of the mathematical model presented in this paper is to determine the flow with minimum cost (of a good) over a distribution network in order to satisfy a product demand over a multi-period planning horizon. The company that motivated the study has four factories and distributes them to four distribution centers, where it is distributed to five consumption centers. The optimization of transportation and inventory management decisions is required by the company for the forthcoming weeks.

Thus, in the scientific literature the use of transportation and distribution models is broad and useful to solve supply chain design problems over distribution networks which involves the interconnection of facilities such as factories, collection centers, warehouses, and consumption centers, among others. These facilities produce, demand, or store different goods. Different contexts are studied in the literature, for example, Ng and Lo [1] study the case of a robust design of a supply chain using ferries, and Cleophas et al. study urban transportation [2]. Król [3] uses artificial intelligence to optimize a transportation network development. Stathopoulos et al. [4] presents a recent review on innovative models for

© Springer Nature Switzerland AG 2018
J. C. Figueroa-García et al. (Eds.): WEA 2018, CCIS 916, pp. 85–95, 2018.
https://doi.org/10.1007/978-3-030-00353-1_8

transportation science and Mejjaouli and Babiceanu [5] study the Cold supply chain implementing an RFID monitoring system.

The supply chain design problem has been widely studied in the literature. García and You [6] present a recent literature review finding that enterprise-wide optimization methods are one of the main challenges for future research, together with research opportunities on supply chain design for energy and sustainability. A review on sustainable supply chain design problems is presented by Eskandarpour et al. [7]. Govindan et al. [8] focus their literature review on closed-loop supply chain design models. Also, Farahani et al. [9] present a survey of more than 200 articles on supply chain design considering a competitive market. Bloemhof and Soysal [10] study the supply chain literature for the food industry.

Nevertheless, relatively few real-case studies are published in the literature. Varsei and Polyakovskiy [11] present a real application for the wine industry in Australia, considering a single period from a strategic standpoint. Jabbarzadeh et al. [12] present an emergency blood supply chain design model implementation using real data, where backlogging is not allowed. Hasani and Khosrojerdi [13] present a robust global supply network design under demand and procurement cost uncertainties for a real case. Finally, for the health care setting, Pishvaee et al. [14] develop a model to design a sustainable medical supply chain for needles and syringes.

Most supply chain design problems consider models for a single moment of time, and the temporal aspect of the decisions is not contemplated. This assumes that the supply chain is not capable of covering the demand with inventory or with backlogging (pending orders) in later periods. In this paper we include these aspects in the supply chain design. Nonetheless, in our modeling approach, backlogging is allowed to satisfy past demand in cases where production or transportation capacity is not enough. Still, since backlogging usually means poor customer service levels, it is penalized in the objective function.

Decision-making regarding the solution of supply chain design considering transportation and distribution problems can be classified as strategic decisions, where it is intended to cover long-term needs and involves the evaluation of decisions such as the opening of supply facilities, transshipment or retailer opening, as well as the development of new routes or the sizing of the fleet of vehicles. The tactical level in which it is sought to establish distribution policies and are planned in the medium term. Finally the operational level in which it is sought to determine the resources and operations required to meet the requirements demanded in a distribution network, such as in the vehicle routing models [15].

The main contribution of the article is to show a versatile mathematical modeling of transportation and production planning decisions, when optimizing a supply chain design with significant variations in the levels of supply capacity and demand over a multi-period planning horizon, by allowing to increase inventory levels, and backlogging.

In Sect. 2 the mathematical model is detailed to optimize the supply chain design. Section 3 presents the case of study that motivates this work. Section 4 presents the analysis of the results. Conclusions and the future research are presented in Sect. 5.

2 Mathematical Model

Consider a supply chain with multiple echelons such as the producers, distribution centers, warehouses and retailers. A single commodity is considered in this case, such as boxes or pallets, which may contain several references of products. Assume that each echelon is capable of storing a maximum amount of product. Further, customers have known demand for a set of periods in the future. The objective of the logistic operations to optimize is to determine the flow of products from producers to the final consumer using the distribution centers and warehouses, which allow to store product and change the transportation modes to reach more customers at minimum costs.

To model the problem mathematically, consider a directed graph $G = \{N, A\}$, where the set of nodes N represents copies of the set of production centers, distribution centers, warehouses, retailers, and customers. Each node representing a facility is replicated for each period in the time-horizon. These copies allow us to plan inventory and transport operations in multiple periods of the planning horizon.

The set of arcs A represent the flows of products. Three types of arcs are considered: First, the arcs connecting two nodes in the same period between two different facilities represent transportation decisions. Second, the arcs connecting copies of nodes of the same facility for consecutive periods represent inventory holding decisions, from period t to period $t + 1$. Third, arcs connecting copies of nodes of the final echelon backward represent backlogging flow, for example from period t to period $t-1$. Thus, the problem is modeled with the following sets and decision variables:

Referential Sets

- i: Index representing the nodes origins $i = \{1, 2, \dots, m\}$
- j: Index representing the destination nodes $j = \{1, 2, \dots, m\}$
- t: Index that represents the periods $t = \{1, 2, \dots, u\}$.

Decision Variables

- X_{ijt}: Amount of flow to be transported from node "i" to node "j" in period "t"
- $I_{it}^{(+)}$: Available inventory level of the product in node "i" at the end of period "t"
- $I_{it}^{(-)}$: Level of pending orders in node "i" at the end of period "t".

An example of the graph G is presented in Fig. 1. The objective function of the problem is expressed in Eq. 1 and indicates that the total transportation,

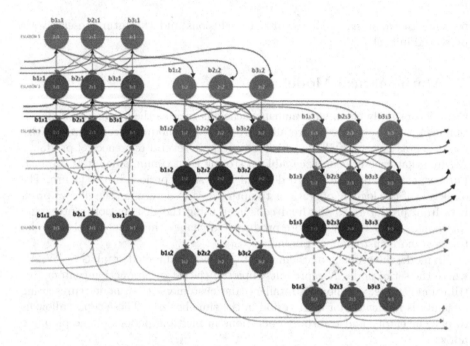

Fig. 1. Example of the graph G to model transportation and inventory decisions for a supply chain design problem

inventory holding, and backlogging costs for the supply chain, which is computed as the sum of the flow costs in each period of time in the graph.

$$F = f(X_{ijt}, I_{it}^{(+)}, I_{it}^{(-)}, i = j = 1, 2, \ldots, m, \wedge t = 1, 2, \ldots, u) \tag{1}$$

Model parameters

- b_{it} : Capacity in node "i" in period "t"
  - If $b_{it} > 0 \longrightarrow$ It is a supply node.
  - If $b_{it} < 0 \longrightarrow$ It is a demand node.
  - If $b_{it} = 0 \longrightarrow$ It is an intermediate or transshipment node.
- C_{ijt}: Cost per unit of flow from node "i" to node "j" at instant "t"
- h_t: Cost of inventory maintenance per unit of product in period "t"
- π_t: Penalty cost per pending unit in period "t"
- L_{ijt}: Minimum amount of flow over the arch$(i, j) \in A$ in the period "t"
- U_{ijt}: Maximum allowed amount of flow over the arch$(i, j) \in A$ in the period "t"
- L_{it}: Minimum inventory level in node "i" in period "t"
- U_{it}: Maximum inventory level in node "i" in period "t".

The mathematical model is as follows:

Formulation

$$Minimize \quad F = \sum_{i=1}^{m}\sum_{j=1}^{m}\sum_{t=1}^{u} C_{ijt}X_{ijt} + \sum_{i=1}^{m}\sum_{t=1}^{u} h_t I_{it}^{(+)} + \sum_{i=1}^{m}\sum_{t=1}^{u} \pi_t I_{it}^{(-)} \quad (2)$$

Subject to:

Balance Constraints

$$\sum_{j=1}^{m} X_{ijt} + I_{it}^{(+)} - I_{it}^{(-)} - \sum_{r=1}^{m} X_{rit} - I_{it-1}^{(+)} + I_{it-1}^{(-)} = b_{it} \quad \forall i, \quad and \quad \forall t \quad (3)$$

Flow Capacity Constraints

$$L_{ijt} \leq X_{ijt} \leq U_{ijt} \quad for \quad each \quad arc\,(i,j,t) \in A \quad (4)$$

$$L_{it} \leq I_{it} \leq U_{it} \quad para \quad cada \quad arco \quad (i,t,t+1) \in A \quad (5)$$

Logical Conditions

$$X_{ijt}, I_{it}^{(+)}, I_{it}^{(-)} \geq 0 \quad \forall i, \forall j, \wedge \forall t \quad (6)$$

Balance constraints

The Eq. 3 represent the balance of material or nodal equilibrium, which expresses the conditions that occur in each node of the network of the supply chain, and indicates that the outgoing or divergent flow from a particular node is equal to the ingoing flow to the node, plus the inventory required to cover later period demand. Stock level and pending orders that converge to that node is less or equal to the capacity of the node over the distribution network.

Flow capacity constraints

Equation 4 expresses the condition that the flow of transport and distribution over the distribution network is limited between a lower limit and an upper limit for each period in a time horizon. Equation 5 states that the inventory levels will be limited by a policy of safety stock and storage capacity. Finally, Eq. 6 state the nature of the decision variables.

3   Study Case

The case that motivated this study is a manufacturing company which produces in four geographically dispersed factories and distributes them to four distribution centers, where it is distributed to five consumption centers as shown in Fig. 2.

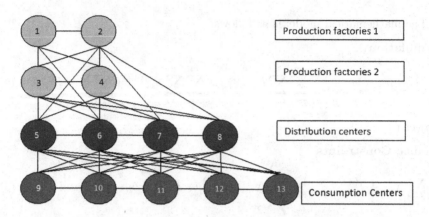

Fig. 2. Representation of the supply chain under study

Table 1. Capacity and forecast of demand at each node in the network for the case of study.

Node	Week 1	Week 2	Week 3	Week 4
Node 1	1450	1450	1460	1420
Node 2	1520	1520	1530	1500
Node 3	1633	1633	1643	1600
Node 4	1432	1432	1460	1480
Node 5	−250	−252	−120	−180
Node 6	−233	−253	−230	−230
Node 7	0	−300	−190	−195
Node 8	−180	0	−250	−270
Node 9	−920	−940	−1100	−1050
Node 10	−1180	−1020	−995	−995
Node 11	−760	−980	−1100	−1100
Node 12	−1045	−1015	−980	−980
Node 13	−1370	−1290	−1100	−1110

The capacity of supply and demand required in each production factory, in each collection point and in each consumption center is shown in Table 1, where the quantities offered is represented by the positive numbers associated with the origin nodes and the demands required by the negative numbers associated to the consumption nodes. It is easy to show that the problem is balanced by computing the total capacity of the nodes to 24163 units and the total expected demand is also 24163 units.

The unitary transportation costs are expressed in \$/kilogram of load between vertices (locations), which are shown in Table 2. The cost of keeping inventory per week has been calculated at \$ 20/kg stored per week. The flow capacity between locations is 800 kg. These costs are computed using historical data from recent months. The arcs denoted by "-" are forbidden arcs since transportation of product is not possible or decisions are not logical for the model. For example, sending product from a consumption node to a factory is forbidden since we do not consider returns or a closed-loop supply chain.

Table 2. Unitary transportation costs

	1	2	3	4	5	6	7	8	9	10	11	12	13
1	-	20	25	23	-	27	-	-	-	-	-	-	-
2	20	-	18	19	25	-	28	27	-	-	-	-	-
3	25	18	-	8	13	11	10	14	-	-	-	-	-
4	23	19	8	-	10	13	11	10	-	-	-	-	-
5	-	25	13	10	-	4	-	-	13	18	16	15	14
6	27	-	11	13	4	-	3	-	16	13	15	16	12
7	-	28	10	11	-	3	-	2	11	10	14	12	18
8	-	27	14	10	-	-	2	-	15	13	18	16	14
9	-	-	-	-	13	16	11	15	-	5	-	-	-
10	-	-	-	-	18	13	10	13	5	-	4	-	-
11	-	-	-	-	16	15	14	18	-	4	-	6	-
12	-	-	-	-	15	16	12	16	-	-	6	-	3
13	-	-	-	-	14	12	18	14	-	-	-	3	-

Considering the case presented before, the corresponding graph is presented in Fig. 3. In this graph, a copy of each facility is created to represent each period in the time horizon of the problem.

4   Results

The model is implemented in CPLEX 12.1. These results correspond to a Laptop with a Intel Core i7 with 2.60 GHz processor, 8 GB of RAM and running on Windows 10Pro. Optimal results are provided in Tables 3 and 4. The computation time is less than 1s. Thus, the company may evaluate different scenarios and changes in the supply chain features. In detail, Table 3 presents the transportation decisions between each pair of facilities. Table 4 presents the inventory-on-hand to stock at each facility each week. The optimal objective function value is $733.433. Figure 4 depicts the flows on the network of the optimal solution, presenting simultaneously transportation and inventory management decisions. This results show that backlogging is not an optimal decision for this case.

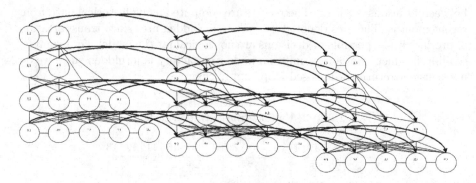

Fig. 3. graph of the problem with multiple copies of the facilities to observe the temporality of the decisions

Table 3. Variable X_{ijt}: Amount of flow from node "i" to node "j" in period "t"

	Week 1	Week 2	Week 3	Week 4
N1.N4	553.000	665.000	742.000	620.000
N1.N6	800.000	800.000	800.000	800.000
N2.N5	800.000	800.000	800.000	800.000
N2.N7	720.000	720.000	730.000	700.000
N3.N5	33.000	33.000	43.000	
N3.N6	800.000	800.000	800.000	800.000
N3.N7	800.000	800.000	800.000	800.000
N4.N5	545.000	587.000	800.000	500.000
N4.N7	800.000	800.000	800.000	800.000
N4.N8	640.000	710.000	602.000	800.000
N5.N9	120.000	800.000	403.000	250.000
N5.N11	193.000	153.000	640.000	420.000
N5.N12	245.000	215.000	180.000	180.000
N5.N13	570.000		300.000	270.000
N6.N11	567.000	547.000	460.000	680.000
N6.N13	800.000	800.000	800.000	800.000
N7.N9	800.000	140.000	697.000	800.000
N7.N10	800.000	800.000	800.000	800.000
N7.N11		280.000		
N7.N12	800.000	800.000	800.000	800.000
N8.N7	80.000		157.000	295.000
N8.N10	380.000	220.000	195.000	195.000
N8.N13		490.000		40.000

Table 4. Variable I_{it}: Inventory available in node "i" in period "t"

	Week 1	Week 2	Week 3
N1	97.000	82.000	
N6			110.000

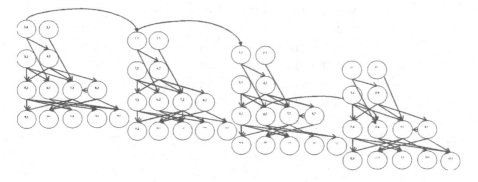

Fig. 4. Solution graph presenting the optimal solution for the flows in the network of the case of study.

4.1 Sensitivity Analysis

A sensitivity analysis is performed in this setting. First by analyzing the optimal dual variable values associated to Eq. 3 that are depicted in Table 5. These results allow us to conclude that supply quantities in nodes 1–4 for week 1 are critical. These means that production in these factories for week 1 must be guaranteed in order to avoid significant increases in costs. Thus, node 1 (factory 1) has the largest dual variable value. That is, it is recommended to invest in increasing the capacity at factory 3 and 4 and reduce capacity in factory 1 in the long term.

As for the retail side of the supply chain (consumption centers), it can be seen that reducing the satisfied demand in weeks 1 and 2 will increase the cost by ($19-$22) due to larger inventory levels. In weeks 3 and 4, reducing the satisfied demand by one unit may decrease costs by ($18-$41). In fact, it is clear for the company now that sales at node 11 (consumption center 11) are the least profitable for week 4, and prices should be increased in this retailer. Therefore, it is concluded that in the short term, the planning decisions are more sensitive to demand at nodes 9 and 10. For weeks 3 and 4, the planning decisions are more sensitive to demand at nodes 11 and 12, were changes in 1 demanded unit modify the cost by ($20-$41).

Sensitivity analysis is also performed over the arc capacity. Results indicate that by increasing capacity by one unit, operational costs may be reduced by ($7). The company is studying the option of buying larger trucks for the long run. Currently the expected benefit is not significant enough.

Table 5. Optimal dual variable values for Eq. 3 for the case of study.

Node	Week 1	Week 2	Week 3	Week 4
Node 1	68	48	28	8
Node 2	61	41	21	1
Node 3	48	28	8	−12
Node 4	45	25	5	−15
Node 5	35	15	−5	−25
Node 6	34	14	−6	−26
Node 7	33	13	−7	−27
Node 8	35	15	−5	−25
Node 9	22	2	−18	−38
Node 10	22	2	−18	−38
Node 11	19	−1	−21	−41
Node 12	20	0	−20	−40
Node 13	21	1	−19	−39

5   Conclusions and Future Research

We have studied a supply chain design problem in which transportation and inventory management decisions are made, considering multiple echelons and the possibility of performing backlogging. In this case, the problem is represented with a graph were nodes represent a copy of a facility, replicated as many times as periods in the planning horizon. The numerical instance is provided and the optimal solution shows how the product flows through the network. The optimal points were inventory should be held are also identified.

Future research includes the modeling of a supply chain facing stochastic demand, costs, and/or transportation times, with multiple products and multiple objectives such as the minimization of environmental and social impacts, and the minimization of risks such as the risks associated with the transport of hazardous materials, stock-out risks, or the risk that the product is stolen in transportation could be studied (see [16]). Further, a closed loop supply chain setting in which some products may be recovered to be recycled could be analyzed.

References

1. Ng, M., Lo, H.K.: Robust models for transportation service network design. Transp. Res. Part B: Methodol. **94**, 378–386 (2016)
2. Cleophas, C., Cottrill, C., Ehmke, J.F., Tierney, K.: Collaborative urban transportation: recent advances in theory and practice. Eur. J. Oper. Res. (2018, in press). https://doi.org/10.1016/j.ejor.2018.04.037
3. Król, A.: The application of the artificial intelligence methods for planning of the development of the transportation network. Transp. Res. Procedia **14**, 4532–4541 (2016). Transport Research Arena TRA2016

4. Stathopoulos, A., Cirillo, C., Cherchi, E., Ben-Elia, E., Li, Y.-T., Schmöcker, J.-D.: Innovation adoption modeling in transportation: New models and data. J. Choice Model. **25**, 61–68 (2017). IATBR 2015–14th International Conference on Travel Behaviour Research (IATBR)
5. Mejjaouli, S., Babiceanu, R.F.: Cold supply chain logistics: system optimization for real-time rerouting transportation solutions. Comput. Ind. **95**, 68–80 (2018)
6. Garcia, D.J., You, F.: Supply chain design and optimization: challenges and opportunities. Comput. Chem. Eng. **81**, 153–170 (2015)
7. Eskandarpour, M., Dejax, P., Miemczyk, J., Péton, O.: Sustainable supply chain network design: an optimization-oriented review. Omega **54**, 11–32 (2015)
8. Govindan, K., Soleimani, H., Kannan, D.: Reverse logistics and closed-loop supply chain: a comprehensive review to explore the future. Eur. J. Oper. Res. **240**(3), 603–626 (2015)
9. Farahani, R.Z., Rezapour, S., Drezner, T., Fallah, S.: Competitive supply chain network design: an overview of classifications, models, solution techniques and applications. Omega **45**, 92–118 (2014)
10. Bloemhof, J.M., Soysal, M.: Sustainable food supply chain design. In: Bouchery, Y., Corbett, C.J., Fransoo, J.C., Tan, T. (eds.) Sustainable Supply Chains. SSSCM, vol. 4, pp. 395–412. Springer, Cham (2017). https://doi.org/10.1007/978-3-319-29791-0_18
11. Varsei, M., Polyakovskiy, S.: Sustainable supply chain network design: a case of the wine industry in Australia. Omega **66**, 236–247 (2017)
12. Jabbarzadeh, A., Fahimnia, B., Seuring, S.: Dynamic supply chain network design for the supply of blood in disasters: a robust model with real world application. Transp. Res. Part E: Logist. Transp. Rev. **70**, 225–244 (2014)
13. Hasani, A., Khosrojerdi, A.: Robust global supply chain network design under disruption and uncertainty considering resilience strategies: a parallel memetic algorithm for a real-life case study. Transp. Res. Part E: Logist. Transp. Rev. **87**, 20–52 (2016)
14. Pishvaee, M., Razmi, J., Torabi, S.: An accelerated benders decomposition algorithm for sustainable supply chain network design under uncertainty: a case study of medical needle and syringe supply chain. Transp. Res. Part E: Logist. Transp. Rev. **67**, 14–38 (2014)
15. Kaligari, E.P., Guerrero, W.J.: Métodos de optimización para el problema de ruteo de vehículos con inventarios y ventanas de tiempo duras. Revista Ingeniería Industrial **14**(3), 31–49 (2015)
16. Bullock, J.A., Haddow, G.D., Coppola, D.P.: Transportation safety and security. In: Bullock, J.A., Haddow, G.D., Coppola, D.P. (eds.) Homeland Security, 2nd edn., pp. 169–188. Butterworth-Heinemann (2018)

A Metaheuristic Approach
for the Cumulative Capacitated Arc
Routing Problem

Sergio Andrés Lenis[ID] and Juan Carlos Rivera[(✉)][ID]

Mathematical Modeling Research Group, Department of Mathematical Sciences,
Universidad EAFIT, Medellín, Colombia
{slenis,jrivera6}@eafit.edu.co

Abstract. In this paper we propose a new variant of the capacitated
arc routing problem (CARP). In this new problem the objective function becomes a cumulative objective computed as the traveled distance
multiplied by the vehicle load. A metaheuristic approach is proposed
which is based on the hybridization of three known procedures: GRASP,
VND and Set covering model. The metaheuristic is tested with some
benchmark instances from CARP. The results allow to evaluate the performance with the different metaheuristic components and to compare
the solutions with the classical objective function.

Keywords: Capacitated arc routing problem · Cumulative objective
GRASP · Set covering based post-optimization · VND
Hybrid metaheuristic

1 Introduction

The *Capacitated Arc Routing Problem* (CARP), first proposed by [12], is a distribution (or collecting) problem which consists of finding a set of minimum cost
routes for a fleet of identical capacitated vehicles while serving the required arcs.

The solution methods developed to solve the CARP can be applied to
problems related to: the routing of street sweepers, garbage trucks, school buses,
electric meter readers, etc. [3]. Getting to know this problem and its applications
is of great importance because it deals with real-life day-to-day problems that
can improve services.

The *Cumulative Capacitated Arc Routing Problem* (CCARP) is a new
variant of the CARP in which the objective function becomes a flow-
based function, i.e. energy consumption minimization. [15] argue that the
real cost of a vehicle traveling between two nodes depends on several conditions like the load of the vehicle, fuel consumption per mile (kilometer), fuel price, time spent or distance traveled to a given node, depreciation of the tires and the vehicle, maintenance, driver wages, time spent
on visiting all customers, total distance traveled, etc. Even though most

© Springer Nature Switzerland AG 2018
J. C. Figueroa-García et al. (Eds.): WEA 2018, CCIS 916, pp. 96–107, 2018.
https://doi.org/10.1007/978-3-030-00353-1_9

of those attributes can be represented by a distance measure, others cannot, i.e. load of the vehicle, fuel consumption per mile (kilometer), maintenance, depreciation of the tires and the vehicle. The latter can be represented by the flow (i.e. weight, load or number of items in the vehicle) on the corresponding arc. Additionally, these functions are also related to service-based objectives, customer satisfaction, and CO_2 and pollutant emissions [7,18]. [15] propose a mathematical model for the *Cumulative Vehicle Routing Problem* (CumVRP) which includes a flow-based objective for the *Capacitated Vehicle Routing Problem* (CVRP). In this paper we extend the same idea for arc routing models.

The CCARP can be defined on an undirected connected graph $G = (V, E)$. The set $E = \{1, \ldots, m\}$ is composed by m edges and $V = \{1, \ldots, n\}$ is the set of n nodes. The nodes represent transition points between two consecutive edges. Each edge $e \in E$ is associated with a demand $q_e \geq 0$ and a cost of traversing $c_e \geq 0$. A fleet K of identical vehicles, each with capacity W, is based at the depot (a special node). Every vehicle must perform a route which must start and finish at the depot and it must be guaranteed that the demand of each route does not exceed the vehicle capacity W. The objective function becomes the flow minimization, where the flow on an arc is the vehicle load as it traverses that arc.

It is important to note that in the classical CARP each route can be performed in any direction without changing the travel distance or travel time. On the contrary, the direction in which every route is traversed in the CCARP has an enormous impact because a large distance at the end of the route has a higher cost than this distance at the beginning when the load is lower.

The remaining of this paper is organized as follows: Sect. 2 summarizes the state of the art on related problems. The metaheuristic approach is depicted on Sect. 3, while Sect. 4 describes the computational experiments performed as well as the main results. Section 5 closes the paper with concluding remarks and future research directions.

2 Literature Review

To the best of our knowledge, this is the first research that defines and solves the CCARP. Nevertheless, some related problems have been studied.

Several researchers have addressed the CARP, where the objective function is to minimize the total traveled distance. [3] propose a cutting plane algorithm which improves previous lower bounds. These improved lower bounds allow to prove optimality on some previously found solutions when the new lower bound is equal to a heuristic solution. This algorithm is based on the aggregated variables for the CARP proposed by [2]. [13] propose exact algorithms for the CARP based on Branch & Bound strategies.

Given that the CARP belongs to NP-hard class of problems, heuristic algorithms have been proposed for problems of this kind. The most simple heuristic algorithms are called constructive methods. According to [21], constructive heuristics for the CVRP and the CARP can be partitioned into four categories: (a.) insertion methods, (b.) merge methods, (c.) cluster-first route-second heuristics, and (d.) route-first cluster-second or tour splitting heuristics.

[21] focus on improving the splitting principle in order to obtain a more efficient algorithm given that they are seldom used because of poor reputation due to its performance. They also propose a greedy randomized adaptive search procedure (GRASP) and an iterated local search (ILS) which outperform classical constructive heuristics. A guided local search is described by [4] while [6] use a tabu search metaheuristic to solve the CARP. [17] have proposed the first genetic algorithm for the CARP. They have also proposed some realistic extensions of the problem. Literature reviews have been presented by [8,9,24].

Cumulative objective functions have already been studied for the *traveling salesman problem* (TSP) and the *vehicle routing problem* (VRP). When the TSP deals with minimizing the sum of arrival times, it is known as the *traveling repairman problem* (TRP) [23], the *minimum latency problem* (MLP) [1,5], or the *delivery man problem* (DMP) [10]. The k-TRP extends the TRP to the case where k agents are available to visit the required nodes [14].

The capacitated version of the k-TRP is in fact a VRP variant called *cumulative capacitated vehicle routing problem* (CCVRP). A memetic algorithm is proposed by [20] to solve the CCVRP. [22] improve some results with an ALNS metaheuristic and [16] develop a very efficient two-phase metaheuristic. [19] propose an exact method based on branch-and-cut-and-price algorithm.

[7] compare three different objective functions, i.e. total traveled distance, maximal arrival time, and average arrival time, for the VRP and the TSP. [15] propose the *cumulative vehicle routing problem* (CumVRP) using an objective function similar to ours, where instead of considering the sum of arrival times, the sum of arrival times multiplied by the vehicle load at each node is minimized.

Our model combines both concepts, arc routing and cumulative objective, to define a new CARP variant. In the following section we propose a metaheuristic approach to deal with this problem.

3   Metaheuristic Approach

Our metaheuristic approach is a hybrid GRASP $\times$ VND algorithm which uses multiple starts by using randomized constructive solutions, four local search moves and a post-optimization procedure based on a set covering model. Next, we depict each algorithm component.

3.1   Objective Function Computation

Before describing the metaheuristic components, it is important to understand how the objective function is computed. Let us suppose that $s = \{e_1, \ldots, e_t\}$ is a single-route solution composed by t edges, and the distance of the edge i and its demand are d_i and q_i, respectively. Here we assume that the demand of an edge is uniformly distributed along the edge. Now, the objective function can be computed by Eq. (1).

Table 1. Example of computation of the objective function over a route (cumulated values).

	e_0	e_7	e_{20}	e_{18}	e_{17}	e_{21}	e_{20}^*	e_7^*	e_0^*
Distance (D_i)	13	15	29	39	42	54	68	70	83
Demand (W_i)	1	2	3	4	4	5	5	5	5
Objective function (C_i)	0	2	30	60	72	120	190	200	265

$$Z(w) = \sum_{i=1}^{n} \frac{d_i \cdot q_i}{2} + \sum_{j=1}^{n} \sum_{i=1}^{j-1} d_j \cdot q_i + w \cdot \sum_{i=1}^{n} d_i \qquad (1)$$

The first term in Eq. (1) represents the cost related to the demand on the edge which is being traversed. The second term corresponds to the cost related to the load of the vehicle due to previously traversed edges. The last term is the vehicle weight w times the total distance traveled. It can be seen that the first term is constant. It does not depend on the edge order, so we do not use it in our comparisons and following examples. The vehicle weight w is also constant during the whole route, nevertheless, different values are considered in Sect. 4 in order to analyze its impact on the solution.

The computation of the objective function is easily understood with the help of Table 1, where an example corresponding to a route is shown. Each column shows the cumulated distance, cumulated demand and the partial objective function after crossing the corresponding edge, assuming the vehicle weight is equal to zero. For instance, after crossing the third edge, e_{20}, the cumulated distance is $D_i = 29$, the cumulated demand is $W_i = 3$, and the cost is computed as $C_i = C_{i-1} + (D_i - D_{i-1}) \cdot W_{i-1} = 2 + (29 - 15) \cdot 2 = 30$.

In Table 1, edges e_0 and e_0^* are the same, except that through e_0^* the vehicle does not distribute (nor collect) on that edge, it only traverses the edge.

3.2 Constructive Solutions

Two constructive algorithms have been designed for this problem. We describe both algorithms and how they are modified to generate multiple initial solutions.

The first constructive algorithm is based on the idea of the route-first cluster-second heuristics. At the beginning, the algorithm constructs a route that spans through all the required edges without considering capacity constraints. The initial node is the depot and the route leaving from there must contain each edge at least one time in order to guarantee that a vehicle is going to supply its demand. The decision criteria to pick the next edge is to pick the shortest one that is adjacent to the current node. When all incident edges have been traversed, the route continues to the closer node incident to a non-traversed edge. After that, the algorithm scans the route taking into account the capacity, given that every time the vehicle is at its full capacity it has to return back to the depot. The next vehicle continues the route at the node where the last vehicle reached its full capacity in order to guarantee that all the edges are traversed in the predefined order.

The need to return back to where the last vehicle had left off could lead to a vehicle traversing a long distance to continue the route. Therefore, we propose a second constructive algorithm that intends to mitigate this problem. Now, the same decision criteria for previous routes is applied, but every time the vehicle reaches its capacity it returns back to the depot and the process starts again with a new vehicle.

Finally, the decision criteria of the shortest edge is dropped out and replaced by a randomized selection between the set of nearest edges. This way we are able to generate a set of good quality solutions.

3.3 Local Search Moves

Pick up in last repeated edge: This move is useful when a route traverses an edge more than once. In such cases, as the objective function considers the load of the vehicle, it is always better to pick up the demand during the last crossing. For instance, when this move is applied to the edge e_0 in the example in Table 1, the cost of the solution decreases from 265 to 195. It can be noted that this move does not have any impact on the total traveled distance or time.

Reverse loops: The orientation in which each route is traversed is a main source of energy consumption. This leads to the question of whether or not the current orientation is the optimal one. This local search move looks for each loop and tries both orientations, staying with the one that gives a better objective function.

Edge exchange between routes: This procedure interchanges edges between routes. Unlike previous moves, this is performed between two routes, so it is necessary to guarantee capacity constraints before applying it. In order to take this move into consideration, it is necessary that both routes have common edges and one of them serves that edge. Once again, this move does not impact the traveled distance.

Path reconstruction between required edges: None of the proposed local search moves improve total distance. In this move we isolate the served edges in a route and reconstruct the solution by ensuring minimum distances between those edges. During the reconstruction process, the algorithm can choose to preserve or not the original orientation of each edge. If it is chosen to preserve the original orientation of the edges, then it is necessary to find the minimum distance to the required node in order to achieve this goal. Otherwise, the algorithm does not care about the original orientation and chooses a path to the nearest node in order to cover that edge.

3.4 Post-optimization Procedure

After a number of iterations is executed and a collection of solutions is obtained, a post-optimization process based on a set covering formulation can be performed. It is basically a mathematical model that takes information from routes in local optima solutions and intends to configure the best possible solution. The mathematical model is described by Eq. (2) to (5) where binary decision variables x_i indicate if a route is in the solution. We assume that R routes are available with cost c_i. The parameter λ_{ie} indicates if route i serves the edge e. The model minimizes the total cost (Eq. (2)), subject to that $|K|$ routes must be selected (Eq. (3)) and all edges must be served (Eq. (4)). Note that in Eq. (4) a task can be performed several times, which allows for a wider range of solutions.

$$\min \ Z = \sum_{i=1}^{R} c_i \cdot x_i \tag{2}$$

$$\sum_{i=1}^{R} x_i = |K| \tag{3}$$

$$\sum_{i=1}^{R} \lambda_{ie} \cdot x_i \geq 1, \quad \forall \, e \in E \tag{4}$$

$$x_i \in \{0,1\}, \quad \forall \, i \in \{1,\ldots,R\} \tag{5}$$

4   Computational Results

The proposed metaheuristic is implemented in Python 3.6.5. It has been tested on a Intel Core i7-6700HQ CPU 2.6GHz computer with 16 GB of RAM and Ubuntu 18.04 LTS. As benchmark instances, we use gdb instances for the CARP from [11]. Note that our proposed model and objective function does not need any adaptation because the same instances for the CARP are useful for the CCARP.

The results can be divided into four groups. The first one compares the performance of different constructive solutions (see Subsect. 4.1). The second set of experiments compares the different local search moves (see Subsect. 4.2). The post-optimization procedure is evaluated in the third set of experiments (see Subsect. 4.3). The last set of experiments in Subsect. 4.4 compares CARP and CCARP solutions.

4.1   Constructive Algorithm Performance

Here, the two constructive solutions and the randomized version (only one solution) are compared. Four criteria are used to compare the three methods: distance minimization and flow minimization with three values for the vehicle weight w. When $w = 0$ we consider an extreme case where distance has no direct effect on the objective function. When $w = W$ we suppose that the load capacity W and the vehicle have the same weight. Finally, $w = 0.5W$ is an intermediate value for comparison. Table 2 shows the objective function reached for each constructive method and each instance. The best solutions appear in bold.

Table 2. Comparison between solutions from different proposed constructive methods.

Ins	Distance			$w = 0$			$w = 0.5\ W$			$w = W$		
	Const$_1$	Const$_2$	Const$_R$	Const$_1$	Const$_2$	Const$_R$	Const$_1$	Const$_2$	Const$_R$	Const$_1$	Const$_2$	Const$_R$
1	411	381	**367**	**829**	898	922	**1035**	1089	1106	**1240**	1279	1289
2	454	**407**	429	**922**	924	1018	1149	**1128**	1233	1376	**1331**	1447
3	396	371	**348**	**764**	848	771	962	1034	**945**	1160	1219	**1119**
4	364	357	**353**	**783**	883	846	**965**	1062	1023	**1147**	1240	1199
5	492	474	**471**	**994**	1193	1116	**1240**	1430	1352	**1486**	1667	1587
6	408	375	**370**	846	955	**827**	1050	1143	**1012**	1254	1330	**1197**
7	410	**365**	395	**811**	877	966	**1016**	1060	1164	**1221**	1242	1361
8	491	**448**	476	5514	**5240**	5768	5760	**5464**	6006	6005	**5688**	6244
9	418	**366**	374	4621	4427	**4319**	4830	4610	**4506**	5039	4793	**4693**
10	341	**317**	324	**1436**	1626	1565	**1607**	1785	1727	**1777**	1943	1889
11	493	**443**	461	10173	**9898**	11481	10420	**10120**	11712	10666	**10341**	11942
12	610	618	**596**	**8992**	9139	11041	**9297**	9448	11339	**9602**	9757	11637
13	651	**570**	579	10017	**9874**	10870	10343	**10159**	11160	10668	**10444**	11449
14	128	118	**118**	**1037**	1065	1083	**1101**	1124	1142	**1165**	1183	1201
15	66	62	**62**	866	**783**	978	899	**814**	1009	932	**845**	1040
16	139	139	**133**	1293	1355	**1029**	1363	1425	**1096**	1432	1494	**1162**
17	99	95	**93**	1452	1519	**1334**	1502	1567	**1381**	1551	1614	**1427**
18	194	194	**191**	**3042**	3209	3216	**3139**	3306	3312	**3236**	3403	3407
19	69	**63**	65	682	726	**665**	717	758	**698**	751	789	**730**
20	133	**131**	132	**1407**	1473	1814	**1474**	1539	1880	**1540**	1604	1946
21	180	**178**	180	2002	1967	**1591**	2092	2056	**1681**	2182	2145	**1771**
22	218	215	**210**	2233	2275	**2222**	2342	2383	**2327**	2451	2490	**2432**
23	255	255	**245**	2515	3098	**2395**	2643	3226	**2518**	2770	3353	**2640**

It can be seen that there is not a dominant method for any criterion. In general, the first algorithm performs better than the others, nevertheless it does not reach any best solution for the distance criterion. The latter shows the great difference between both objectives. It is also important to note that a randomized solution is in general better than the second constructive method.

4.2 Local Search Moves Comparison

Table 3 allows to compare the performance between local search moves. The improvements in the objective function are compared for the first three moves against the results with the constructive method 1 in column 2. In addition, two comparisons are made with three or four moves together. For each comparison, the objective function value Z and the percentage deviation respect the constructive solution are reported. In the last row we compute the average percentage improvement.

It can be seen in Table 3 that moves 1 and 3 have less impact than move 2. Move 2 gets 6 out of 23 best solutions and an average improvement of 31.6%.

Table 3. Different combinations of the local search moves.

Ins	Const$_1$	Move 1		Move 2		Move 3		Moves 1 to 3		Moves 1 to 4	
		Z	%	Z	%	Z	%	Z	%	Z	%
1	829	810	2.29	608	26.66	829	0.00	608	26.66	**578**	30.28
2	922	889	3.58	**671**	27.22	922	0.00	**671**	27.22	**671**	27.22
3	764	732	4.19	543	28.93	739	3.27	**543**	28.93	**538**	29.58
4	783	734	6.26	**545**	30.40	612	21.84	**545**	30.40	**545**	30.40
5	994	994	0.00	762	23.34	793	20.22	671	32.49	**651**	34.51
6	846	754	10.87	**556**	34.28	846	0.00	**556**	34.28	**556**	34.28
7	811	771	4.93	623	23.18	689	15.04	**561**	30.83	**561**	30.83
8	5514	4689	14.96	3861	29.98	5322	3.48	**3831**	30.52	**3831**	30.52
9	4621	4371	5.41	3157	31.68	4357	5.71	3028	34.47	**2994**	35.21
10	1436	1383	3.69	1102	23.26	1381	3.83	**1063**	25.97	**1063**	25.97
11	10173	9997	1.73	7384	27.42	9712	4.53	**7231**	28.92	**7231**	28.92
12	8992	8905	0.97	5426	39.66	8522	5.23	**5352**	40.48	**5352**	40.48
13	10017	7860	21.53	4240	57.67	8979	10.36	4240	57.67	**3992**	60.15
14	1037	1022	1.45	604	41.76	1022	1.45	**599**	42.24	**599**	42.24
15	866	860	0.69	618	28.64	832	3.93	**584**	32.56	**584**	32.56
16	1293	1245	3.71	901	30.32	1193	7.73	**866**	33.02	**866**	33.02
17	1452	1426	1.79	**1159**	20.18	1321	9.02	**1159**	20.18	**1159**	20.18
18	3042	3011	1.02	1938	36.29	3007	1.15	**1901**	37.51	**1901**	37.51
19	682	552	19.06	**460**	32.55	592	13.20	**460**	32.55	**460**	32.55
20	1407	1173	16.63	706	49.82	1236	12.15	**695**	50.60	**695**	50.60
21	2002	1950	2.60	1320	34.07	1815	9.34	1231	38.51	**1213**	39.41
22	2233	2219	0.63	1568	29.78	2161	3.22	**1555**	30.36	**1555**	30.36
23	2515	2501	0.56	**2016**	19.84	2511	0.16	**2016**	19.84	**2016**	19.84
			5.59		31.60		6.73		33.31		33.77

Nevertheless, when the three moves are performed together, an additional improvement can be reached, getting 18 out of 23 best solutions. When the path reconstruction move is applied, some solutions are improved and 5 additional best solutions are found.

4.3   Post-optimization Procedure Performance

In this set of experiments we compare the best solution found by the metaheuristic (Sol$_M$), including the four local search moves, with the solution found after the post-optimization procedure (Sol$_{SC}$). The columns "Dev" in Table 4 indicate the percentage deviation between both solutions. As it is made in Table 2, comparisons include four different cases of the objective function: total distance

Table 4. Comparison between the best found solution (between 3000 solutions from metaheuristic) and the solution with the set covering model.

Ins	Distance			$w = 0$			$w = 0.5W$			$w = W$			Time
	Sol_M	Sol_{SC}	Dev	Sol_M	Sol_{SC}	Dev	Sol_M	Sol_{SC}	Dev	Sol_M	Sol_{SC}	Dev	(s)
1	316	316	0.00	403	309	23.32	1374	1323	3.71	2020	1988	1.58	11.6
2	345	339	1.73	462	372	19.48	1530	1473	3.72	2224	2163	2.74	14.4
3	275	275	0.00	367	282	23.16	1244	1202	3.37	1807	1759	2.65	11.1
4	287	287	0.00	408	327	19.85	1270	1270	0.00	1844	1844	0.00	8.2
5	383	383	0.00	502	397	20.91	1698	1637	3.59	2464	2404	2.43	15.5
6	298	298	0.00	400	308	23.00	1373	1297	5.53	1992	1916	3.81	11.6
7	325	325	0.00	427	322	24.59	1406	1381	1.77	2056	2031	1.21	9.4
8	363	350	3.58	2665	2438	08.51	8097	7676	5.19	12904	12268	4.92	65.9
9	337	305	9.49	2215	1962	11.42	7201	6606	8.26	11582	10649	8.05	73.2
10	275	275	0.00	767	591	22.94	2221	2063	7.11	3596	3478	3.28	9.6
11	406	395	2.70	5610	4162	25.81	16080	14920	7.21	26530	25367	4.38	27.4
12	502	458	8.76	3233	3047	05.75	12941	12469	3.64	21475	20359	5.19	20.5
13	544	536	1.47	2877	1773	38.37	14827	13764	7.16	25917	24884	3.98	10.8
14	100	100	0.00	420	284	32.38	1619	1477	8.77	2639	2548	3.44	7.0
15	58	58	0.00	478	355	25.73	1618	1505	6.98	2694	2585	4.04	7.2
16	129	127	1.55	611	449	26.51	2226	2057	7.59	3774	3649	3.31	12.2
17	91	91	0.00	880	648	26.36	2791	2559	8.31	4611	4379	5.03	11.2
18	164	164	0.00	1536	1208	21.35	4883	4520	7.43	7845	7580	3.37	15.5
19	55	55	0.00	289	183	36.67	1059	1059	0.00	1774	1774	0.00	4.9
20	121	121	0.00	573	413	27.92	2336	2184	6.50	3948	3809	3.52	12.5
21	158	156	1.26	781	550	29.57	3131	2823	9.83	5185	4903	5.43	13.6
22	202	200	0.99	1065	790	25.82	4033	3655	9.37	6746	6307	6.50	21.4
23	235	233	0.85	1258	880	30.04	4744	4270	9.99	7927	7377	6.93	24.3
Avg			1.41			23.89			5.87			3.73	18.22

and cumulative objective with three values of vehicle weight. The last column indicates the computing time (in seconds) to perform the metaheuristic (without including the post-optimization process).

It is important to mention that for each objective the set covering is adapted by changing the cost parameter c_i to the corresponding objective computed on every route. Other components of the metaheuristic are the same.

The results allow to see the great impact of set covering post-optimization process on metaheuristic solutions. The average improvement is 1.41% for distance objective and 10 out of 23 instances have been improved. The higher impact occurs for the cumulated objective when $w = 0$ where all instances have been improved and the average improvement is 23.89%. When $w = 0.5W$ and $w = W$, 21 out of 23 instances are improved and the average improvements are 5.87% and 3.73% respectively. The computing time ranges between 4.9 and 73.2 seconds with an average of 18.22.

Table 5. Comparison between the best solution for the CARP problem (evaluated under different objective functions) and the set partitioning problem solution (combination of 3000 solutions).

Ins	Distance		$w = 0$		$w = 0.5\,W$		$w = W$		$w = 1.5\,W$		Time
	Sol_L	Sol_{SC}	Sol_L	Sol_{SC}	Sol_L	Sol_{SC}	Sol_L	Sol_{SC}	Sol_L	Sol_{SC}	(s)
1	**316**	**316**	469	**309**	1417	**1323**	2049	**1988**	2997	**2936**	8.7
2	**339**	**339**	600	**372**	1617	**1469**	2295	**2159**	3312	**3194**	10.7
3	**275**	**275**	439	**282**	1264	**1202**	1814	**1759**	2639	**2584**	7.4
4	**287**	**287**	446	**327**	1307	**1270**	1881	**1844**	2742	**2705**	4.9
5	**377**	383	718	**403**	1849	**1638**	2603	**2404**	3734	**3553**	12.2
6	**298**	**298**	497	**308**	1391	**1297**	1987	**1916**	2881	**2810**	6.2
7	**325**	**325**	450	**322**	1425	**1381**	2075	**2031**	3050	**3006**	9.1
8	**348**	350	2961	**2438**	7833	**7685**	12357	**12327**	**17229**	17255	25.9
9	**303**	305	2889	**1961**	7131	**6618**	11070	**10661**	15312	**15015**	27.4
10	**275**	**275**	938	**577**	2313	**2039**	3688	**3454**	5063	**4869**	7.8
11	**395**	**395**	7060	**4034**	16935	**15044**	26810	**25234**	36685	**35109**	59.6
12	**458**	**458**	4687	**3047**	12931	**12469**	20717	**20359**	28961	**28603**	8.8
13	**536**	**536**	7936	**1769**	19276	**13799**	30076	**24919**	41416	**36420**	10.7
14	**100**	**100**	586	**281**	1686	**1477**	2686	**2548**	3786	**3691**	6.1
15	**58**	**58**	587	**350**	1689	**1497**	2733	**2577**	3835	**3717**	9.6
16	**127**	**127**	1052	**443**	2576	**2059**	4100	**3648**	5624	**5220**	14.9
17	**91**	**91**	683	**654**	2594	**2565**	4414	**4385**	6325	**6296**	21.7
18	**164**	**164**	1864	**1215**	4980	**4483**	7932	**7579**	11048	**10699**	183.1
19	**55**	**55**	289	**183**	1059	1059	1774	1774	2544	2544	2.8
20	**121**	**121**	1012	**413**	2706	**2184**	4279	**3809**	5973	**5559**	7.1
21	**156**	**156**	1344	**551**	3528	**2821**	5556	**4901**	7740	**7141**	13.0
22	**200**	**200**	1568	**788**	4368	**3654**	6968	**6306**	9768	**9162**	28.1
23	**233**	**233**	1778	**878**	5040	**4272**	8069	**7379**	11331	**10725**	31.6

4.4 Comparison Between CARP and CCARP Solutions

In this section, as there are not other methods in the literature to compare our solutions, we compare them against the best known solutions for the CARP. Table 5 shows, for every objective, the value of CARP solution (Sol_L) and our algorithm for CCARP (Sol_{SC}) taken from Table 4. The computing time here includes all the components of the metaheuristic.

To compare the proposed objective function, the values are recomputed for the literature solutions. In order to have a fair comparison, we apply our local search moves to those solutions. As we explained before, the order in which the arcs are served affects the proposed objective function and CARP solutions do not take this into account.

From Table 5 we can see that our metaheuristic finds 20 out 23 best known solutions for the classical CARP, with an average deviation of 0.12%. For the other cases, our methods finds almost all best known solutions. It only fails to reach the best solution for instance 8 where $w = 1.5W$. The best CARP solutions also find 4 best known solutions for our proposed objective. Note that when the weight of the vehicle increases in comparison to its load the total distance has a greater impact on the objective function.

When the vehicle weight increases, the percentage deviation between both solutions decreases. These values vary from 40.58% for $w = 0$ to 3.64% for $w = 1.5W$.

5   Conclusions

In this paper we proposed a new capacitated arc routing variant, called the cumulative capacitated arc routing problem, in which the objective function becomes to minimize the flow over arcs, i.e. traveled distance multiplied by vehicle load. This problem has applications in contexts when energy or fuel consumption, reduction of emissions, maintenance costs, or service quality becomes more important than the total travel distance or time.

An effective GRASP × VND metaheuristic with a post-optimization procedure based on set covering mathematical formulation is proposed. Three of the moves performed by the proposed VND are specific for this objective function given that they do not improve traveled distance.

The results prove the importance of developing new and specific solutions methods for the CCARP. They also allow to identify effective moves to improve solutions within a local search procedure. The post-optimization procedure based on set covering formulation also shows a positive impact on the final solution.

Multiobjective approaches can be addressed as a future research direction given that total traveled distance and flow objectives are relevant in real-life applications. Other objectives can also be considered.

References

1. Archer, A., Williamson, D.P.: Faster approximation algorithms for the minimum latency problem. In: Proceedings of the Fourteenth Annual ACM-SIAM Symposium on Discrete Algorithms (SODA) (2003)
2. Belenguer, J.M., Benavent, E.: The capacitated arc routing problem: valid inequalities and facets. Comput. Optim. Appl. **10**(2), 165–187 (1998)
3. Belenguer, J.M., Benavent, E.: A cutting plane algorithm for the capacitated arc routing problem. Comput. Oper. Res. **30**(5), 705–728 (2003)
4. Beullens, P., Muyldermans, L., Cattrysse, D., Oudheusden, D.V.: A guided local search heuristic for the capacitated arc routing problem. Eur. J. Oper. Res. **147**(3), 629–643 (2003). https://doi.org/10.1016/S0377-2217(02)00334-X. http://www.sciencedirect.com/science/article/pii/S037722170200334X
5. Blum, A., Chalasani, P., Coppersmith, D., Pulleyblank, B., Raghavan, P., Sudan, M.: The minimum latency problem. In: Proceedings of the Twenty-Sixth Annual ACM Symposium on Theory of Computing, STOC 1994, pp. 163–171. ACM, New York (1994)

6. Brandao, J., Eglese, R.: A deterministic tabu search algorithm for the capacitated arc routing problem. Comput. Oper. Res. **35**(4), 1112–1126 (2008). https://doi.org/10.1016/j.cor.2006.07.007. http://www.sciencedirect.com/science/article/pii/S0305054806001535
7. Campbell, A.M., Vandenbussche, D., Hermann, W.: Routing for relief efforts. Transp. Sci. **42**(2), 127–145 (2008). https://doi.org/10.1287/trsc.1070.0209
8. Corberán, A., Laporte, G.: Arc routing: problem, methods, and applications. In: SIAM (2014)
9. Dror, M.: Arc Routing. Theory, Solutions and Applications. Springer, Boston (2000). https://doi.org/10.1007/978-1-4615-4495-1
10. Fischetti, M., Laporte, G., Martello, S.: The delivery man problem and cumulative matroids. Oper. Res. **41**(6), 1055–1064 (1993)
11. Golden, B., Dearmon, J., Baker, E.: Computational experiments with algorithms for a class of routing problems. Comput. Oper. Res. **10**(1), 47–59 (1983). https://doi.org/10.1016/0305-0548(83)90026-6. http://www.sciencedirect.com/science/article/pii/0305054883900266
12. Golden, B.L., Wong, R.T.: Capacitated arc routing problems. Networks **11**(3), 305–315 (1981)
13. Hirabayashi, R., Saruwatari, Y., Nishida, N.: Tour construction algorithm for the capacitated arc routing problem. Asia-Pac. J. Oper. Res. **9**, 155–175 (1992)
14. Jothi, R., Raghavachari, B.: Minimum latency tours and the k-traveling repairmen problem. In: Farach-Colton, M. (ed.) LATIN 2004. LNCS, vol. 2976, pp. 423–433. Springer, Heidelberg (2004). https://doi.org/10.1007/978-3-540-24698-5_46
15. Kara, I., Kara, B., Kadri, M.: Cumulative vehicle routing problems, pp. 85–98 (2008)
16. Ke, L., Feng, Z.: A two-phase metaheuristic for the cumulative capacitated vehicle routing problem. Comput. Oper. Res. **40**, 633–638 (2013)
17. Lacomme, P., Prins, C., Ramdane-Chérif, W.: A genetic algorithm for the capacitated arc routing problem and its extensions. In: Boers, E.J.W. (ed.) EvoWorkshops 2001. LNCS, vol. 2037, pp. 473–483. Springer, Heidelberg (2001). https://doi.org/10.1007/3-540-45365-2_49
18. Lin, C., Choy, K., Ho, G., Chung, S., Lam, H.: Survey of green vehicle routing problem: past and future trends. Expert. Syst. Appl. **41**(4), 1118–1138 (2014). https://doi.org/10.1016/j.eswa.2013.07.107. http://www.sciencedirect.com/science/article/pii/S095741741300609X
19. Lysgaard, J., Wøhlk, S.: A branch-and-cut-and-price algorithm for the cumulative capacitated vehicle routing problem. Eur. J. Oper. Res. **236**(3), 800–810 (2014)
20. Ngueveu, S.U., Prins, C., Calvo, R.W.: An effective memetic algorithm for the cumulative capacitated vehicle routing problem. Comput. Oper. Res. **37**(11), 1877–1885 (2010)
21. Prins, C., Labadi, N., Reghioui, M.: Tour splitting algorithms for vehicle routing problems. Int. J. Prod. Res. **47**(2), 507–535 (2009)
22. Ribeiro, G.M., Laporte, G.: An adaptive large neighborhood search heuristic for the cumulative capacitated vehicle routing problem. Comput. Oper. Res. **39**(3), 728–735 (2012)
23. Tsitsiklis, J.N.: Special cases of traveling salesman and repairman problems with time windows. Networks **22**, 263–282 (1992)
24. Wøhlk, S.: A decade of capacitated arc routing. In: Wasil, E. (ed.) The Vehicle Routing Problem: Latest Advances and New Challenges. Operations Research/Computer Science Interfaces Series, vol. 43, pp. 29–48. Springer, Boston (2008). https://doi.org/10.1007/978-0-387-77778-8_2

A Mixed-Integer Linear Programming Model for a Selective Vehicle Routing Problem

Andrea Posada, Juan Carlos Rivera$^{(\boxtimes)}$ (iD), and Juan D. Palacio

Departamento de Ciencias Matemáticas, Escuela de Ciencias, Universidad EAFIT,
Medellín, Colombia
{aposad31,jrivera6,jpalac26}@eafit.edu.co

Abstract. In this paper, we propose a new vehicle routing problem variant. The new problem is a type of selective vehicle routing model in which it is not necessary to visit all nodes, but to visit enough nodes in such a way that all clusters are visited and from which it is possible to cover all nodes. Here, a mixed-integer linear programming formulation (MILP) is proposed in order to model the problem. The MILP is tested by using adapted instances from the generalized vehicle routing problem (GVRP). The model is also tested on small size GVRP instances as a special case of our proposed model. The results allow to evaluate the impact of clusters configuration in solver efficacy.

Keywords: Combinatorial optimization
Mixed-integer linear programming · Selective vehicle routing problem

1 Introduction

In operations research and logistics, one of the main studied problems is the *vehicle routing problem* (VRP). VRP is a family of problems which aims to find a set of routes, one for each vehicle, such that each client is visited by one vehicle exactly once while the total traveled distance is minimized. Specific conditions imposed on routes, vehicles, required nodes, resources, etc., are used to define different models and applications.

In this paper, we propose a new VRP variant based on *selective vehicle routing problems* (SVRP). In the proposed problem, a fixed size fleet of homogeneous capacitated vehicles based at a depot needs to visit a set of nodes. Nodes are grouped by clusters in such a way that each node can belong to one or several clusters. As main feature of SVRP, not all nodes need to be visited; nevertheless all clusters do. Each node has a known demand which must be satisfied: nodes can be visited by vehicles or their demand can be covered by a visited node within the same cluster. The objective function is to minimize the total traveled distance. Note that this problem can be seen as a generalization of the *generalized vehicle routing problem* (GVRP) when each node belongs to only one cluster. Figure 1(a) depicts an example of the SVRP where 38 nodes are

J. C. Figueroa-García et al. (Eds.): WEA 2018, CCIS 916, pp. 108–119, 2018.
https://doi.org/10.1007/978-3-030-00353-1_10

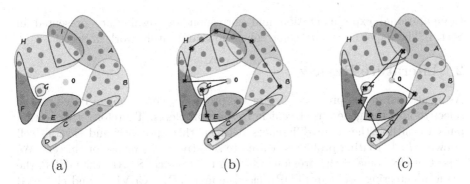

Fig. 1. Illustration of the SVRP and Examples of feasible solutions.

scattered on nine clusters represented by letter from A to H. The figure shows that the depot belongs to a single-node cluster, and several conditions can be found for required nodes: (a.) single-nodes clusters, i.e. clusters with only one node (see cluster G), (b.) clusters which are subsets of other larger clusters (see clusters D and C), (c.) clusters without intersections (see cluster E), and (d.) clusters with non-empty intersection (see clusters H, I and A). Two examples of feasible solutions are shown in Fig. 1(b) and (c).

As mentioned in [2], applications of this kind of models can be found in response operations in the humanitarian logistics context in which relief aid can be delivered on any close-enough node in order to cover a wider disaster region in a shorter period of time. They can also be found in commercial applications where some customers can be represented by several nodes (not necessarily close) but only one of them is required to be visited. Another use can be found as a subproblem of other vehicle routing models when heuristic concentration strategies are used. In [15] other applications of generalized routing problems are also described; for instance, location-routing decisions as post-box location contexts in which a minimum length tour for a postal vehicle is designed for visiting selected locations. A particular application called the Traveling Circus Problem is also mentioned since circus managers aim to design a tour at minimum cost covering a set of villages within a maximum distance limit from each one of them. [6,15] also describe material flow systems design applications for block layout of productions plants as generalized routing problems. Authors in [18] describe briefly how a post-optimization procedure for examination timetabling problems are tackled as routing problem with clusters. In this case, constraints for the maximum number of exams to write in each day are imposed by fixing each slot of time as a vertex and each day as a cluster. Urban transport routes design can be also modeled as a selective vehicle routing problem where a subset of potential bus stops must be selected to be visited and demand from non-visited sites must get to near visited stops.

The remaining of the paper is organized as follows: Sect. 2 summarizes the state of the art about related problems. A mathematical definition and a mixed integer linear programming (MILP) formulation is presented in Sect. 3.

Computational experimentation and corresponding results are presented in Sect. 4. The paper ends with some conclusions and future work in Sect. 5.

2 Literature Review

As mentioned in the previous section, we propose a new problem based on the selective and the generalized vehicle routing problems. Therefore, this section aims to outline the main differences between this approach and several well known vehicle routing problems related to selective visits or use of clusters. We report briefly some of the previous work on the classical SVRP, the GVRP, the team orienteering problem (TOP), close-enough VRP (CEVRP) and clustered VRP (CluVRP).

The SVRP is a group of problems characterized by total cover of nodes but not necessarily by visiting them. Some of the problems inside this group are: the min-max selective vehicle routing problem (MMSVRP), with the objective to minimize the longest route and not need to visit all clients by using a close enough definition instead [25]; the SVRP with integrated tours, composed by two routing problems: the first one builds routes and the second fixes the length of each stop [3]. In [25], an integer programming formulation and a branch and cut framework are presented for the MMSVRP. The min-max nature of the objective function and the fact that not all the vertices need to be visited make it harder to solve. On the other hand, heuristic methods that rely on GRASP and on the solution of a restricted integer program based on a set covering reformulation for the problem are presented in the same paper. They found out that the heuristic is able to significantly improve the best upper bounds provided by exact methods within a limited running time. [10] implements an exact method based on branch and bound techniques, while a parallel genetic algorithm [4] and constructive methods [10] represent heuristic techniques.

Recently, some research on stochastic selective vehicle routing problem was also done [4]. Three formulations are proposed to account for different optimization strategies under uncertain demand level: reliable, robust and fuzzy selective vehicle routing problems.

Although our model and SVRP versions in the literature visit a set of selected nodes in order to cover all nodes, ours differs by grouping nodes into clusters.

The generalized vehicle routing problem (GVRP), introduced by [11], is an extension of the classical VRP in which customers are partitioned into clusters and the depot forms its own cluster. The objective is to design a minimum length collection of routes for the fleet of vehicles, originating and terminating at the depot, while visiting exactly one customer from each cluster, subject to capacity constraints. Some integer programming formulations can be found in [8,14,20]. In [14], an integer programming formulation with polynomial increasing number of binary variables and constraints is presented. More recently, [8] proposed four integer programming formulations: two of them based on multicommodity flow and the others based on exponential sets of inequalities. Lastly, [20] describe two novel models and their extensions for the case in which vertices of any cluster of each tour are contiguous.

Several solution methods have been proposed: a solution by transforming the GVRP into a capacitated arc routing problem (CARP) [11], a hybrid heuristic algorithm obtained by combination of a genetic algorithm with a local-global approach to the problem and a local search [21], an ant colony algorithm (ACO) for the dynamic GVRP [19], a branch and cut algorithm [20] and an incremental neighbourhood tabu search for the GVRP with time windows [17]. Exact methods are also proposed to deal with the GVRP. In [2], authors design a column generation (CG) algorithm to provide competitive lower bounds for instances with up to 101 nodes and 24 clusters. On the other hand, they also include an iterated local search (ILS) able to find solutions with a small gap.

Despite the similarities between our model and GVRP, ours allows to have non-empty intersections between clusters.

Our model also differs significantly from the TOP since the family of orienteering problems includes a limited route length (or time) and their main objective is to maximize the total collected profit. After the orienteering problems were introduced in [12,24], many papers have addressed this family of problems. For instance, [5] propose an MILP based on packing formulations. The authors design a branch and price strategy which outperforms best known solutions for benchmark instances with up to 200 nodes. [1] also formulate an MILP for a TOP when profit of each node as a decreasing function of time. They design a Dantzig-Wolfe decomposition to compute lower bounds as well as a evolutionary local search to find upper bounds on instances up to 102 nodes.

A well-known application of vehicle routing and traveling salesman problems is the meter reading to record electricity, water and gas consumption. Nowadays, it is not necessary for utility companies to visit each customer since radio frequency identification technology (RFID) may be used. When RFID is available, it is possible to get close-enough to customers but not necessarily visit them. These problems are known as close-enough TSP (CETSP) and close-enough VRP (CEVRP). A first approach to the CETSP is presented in [13] with six different heuristics and defining the concept of close-enough as a neighborhood of points for each node (e.g., a disc of radius r). [16] address the CETSP and its multi-vehicle extension, the CEVRP, via non-linear mathematical programming and also with heuristic approaches based on graph reduction strategies. [23] present heuristic algorithms and an integer programming model for the CETSP. The heuristics are designed to deal with the problem in two stages. Firstly, the algorithm selects a set of street segments to be traversed based on the neighborhood for each node. Then, in the second stage, a route is finally designed based on the selected streets in stage one. Recently, [9] compute new benchmarks for upper and lower bounds and also present a new graph reduction algorithm outperforming previous applications for the CETSP. As in CETSP and CEVRP vehicles are not forced to visit any node, these models differ significantly from ours since we must ensure that one node per cluster is visited.

The CluVRP is a variant in which nodes are grouped into predefined clusters, all clusters are visited and all the nodes in each cluster must be served before the vehicle leaves the cluster. The CluVRP differs from our approach since we only require a served node in each cluster, this is, not all the nodes in a cluster must be visited. The CluVRP has been addressed by [22] where an MILP able to find optimal Hamiltonian path between each pair of vertices in each cluster is proposed. [20] also presents a MILP for a special CluVRP case: the clustered generalized vehicle routing problem (CGVRP). The CGVRP aims to find a set of routes starting and ending at the depot, visiting all the nodes and finding a Hamiltonian path between clusters. As a variant of the GVRP, the CGVRP also consider clusters as mutually exclusive and exhaustive subsets of nodes. [7] proposes an integer programming formulation for the CluVRP and two exact solution strategies based on branch and cut, and branch and cut and price. The solution strategies are tested on instances with up to 483 nodes, 97 clusters and cluster sizes that vary from one to 71 nodes. [26] tackle the CluVRP via metaheuristic algorithms. The first one is based on an iterated local search and the second is a unified hybrid genetic search. Given the heuristic nature of the solution strategies, [26] deal with instances up to 1200 nodes and 240 clusters.

3   Mathematical Definition and Mixed Integer Linear Programming Formulation

Our SVRP can be mathematically defined as follows: Let $\mathcal{G} = (\mathcal{V}, \mathcal{E})$ be an undirected graph. The set $\mathcal{V} = \{0, 1, \ldots, n\}$ contains the origin (depot), labeled as 0, and the set of n required nodes. The set $\mathcal{E}$ is composed by all edges or arcs (i, j), i.e. $\mathcal{E} = \{(i, j) \mid i, j \in \mathcal{V}, i \neq j\}$. Each vertex $i \in \mathcal{V}$ has associated a certain amount of demand q_i and a spatial coordinate (x, y), and each arc $(i, j) \in \mathcal{E}$ a distance d_{ij}, which is the euclidean distance between nodes i and j. The set of vertices $\mathcal{V}$ is partitioned into $m + 1$ non-empty subsets, called clusters, i.e. $\mathcal{V}_0, \mathcal{V}_1, \ldots, \mathcal{V}_m$, such that $\bigcup_{c \in \mathcal{C}} \mathcal{V}_c = \mathcal{V}$ being $\mathcal{C} = \{0, 1, 2, \ldots, m\}$ the set of clusters. For modeling purposes, we define the parameter λ_{ic} which indicates if the node $i \in \mathcal{V}$ belongs to cluster $c \in \mathcal{C}$ ($\lambda_{ic} = 1$) or not ($\lambda_{ic} = 0$). The total demand for each cluster can be satisfy via any of its nodes. A fleet $\mathcal{K}$ of identical vehicles (homogeneous fleet) with individual capacity Q are based at the depot. It can be assumed, without loss of generality, that $|\mathcal{K}| \leq |\mathcal{C}|$.

A solution for the problem in $\mathcal{G}$ is a collection of $|\mathcal{K}|$ constrained routes, one for each vehicle. Each vehicle $k \in \mathcal{K}$ must perform a route which starts at the depot 0, spans a set $\mathcal{V}^k \setminus \{0\}$ of selected nodes and ends at the depot 0, while its total load must not exceed to capacity Q and all clusters are visited. The objective is to minimize the total traveled distance. As nodes can belong to several clusters (see Figs. 1(b) and (c)) and each cluster must be visited, we define the parameter $w_i = \frac{1}{\sum_{c \in \mathcal{C}} \lambda_{ic}}$ for each node $i \in \mathcal{V}$, which avoids to over-count the demand of nodes when computing the demand of clusters.

As vertices are grouped by clusters, there are some cases of special attention. In Fig. 1, two possible special situations could be seen. There is a vertex that belongs to three different clusters A, I and H, so if it is visited, all nodes in any of the three clusters are covered. On the other hand, a cluster could be a subset of another one, as D in Fig. 1. Now, if the vertex that forms D is visited, not only is cluster D covered, but also cluster C. However, as any cluster only can be visited once, D cannot be covered if another vertex in C, different from the one mentioned before, is visited. Therefore, vertices belonging to several clusters or to clusters that are subsets of others are vertices of interest.

The proposed mathematical model uses three types of decision variables. Binary decision variables x_{ij}^k become equal to one ($x_{ij}^k = 1$) if vehicle $k \in \mathcal{K}$ traverses the arc $(i,j) \in \mathcal{E}$, and zero ($x_{ij}^k = 0$) otherwise. Binary decision variables y_c^k are equal to one ($y_c^k = 1$) if cluster $c \in \mathcal{C}$ is spanned by route $k \in \mathcal{K}$, zero ($y_c^k = 0$) otherwise. Finally, auxiliary variables u_{ij} are related to the order of arcs in each route and are used to avoid subtours.

The mathematical formulation, henceforth called MILP$_1$, is described by the model (1) to (13).

$$\min Z = \sum_{i \in \mathcal{V}} \sum_{j \in \mathcal{V}} \sum_{k \in \mathcal{K}} d_{ij} \cdot x_{ij}^k \tag{1}$$

$$\text{s.t.} \quad \sum_{\substack{i \in \mathcal{V} \\ i \neq j}} \sum_{k \in \mathcal{K}} x_{ij}^k \leq 1, \quad \forall\, j \in \mathcal{V} \setminus \{0\} \tag{2}$$

$$\sum_{\substack{i \in \mathcal{V} \\ i \neq j}} \left(x_{ij}^k - x_{ji}^k \right) = 0, \quad \forall\, j \in \mathcal{V},\ k \in \mathcal{K} \tag{3}$$

$$\sum_{k \in \mathcal{K}} y_c^k = 1, \quad \forall\, c \in \mathcal{C} \setminus \{0\} \tag{4}$$

$$\sum_{k \in \mathcal{K}} x_{ji}^k \leq 1 - \lambda_{ic} \cdot \lambda_{jc}, \quad \forall\, i,j \in \mathcal{V},\ c \in \mathcal{C},\ i \neq j \tag{5}$$

$$\sum_{i \in \mathcal{V}} \sum_{\substack{j \in \mathcal{V} \\ i \neq j}} \sum_{k \in \mathcal{K}} x_{ij}^k \cdot \lambda_{jc} = 1, \quad \forall\, c \in \mathcal{C} \tag{6}$$

$$\sum_{i \in \mathcal{V}} \sum_{\substack{j \in \mathcal{V} \\ i \neq j}} x_{ij}^k \cdot \lambda_{jc} = y_c^k, \quad \forall\, k \in \mathcal{K},\ c \in \mathcal{C} \tag{7}$$

$$\sum_{i \in \mathcal{V}} \sum_{c \in \mathcal{C}} w_i \cdot q_i \cdot \lambda_{ic} \cdot y_c^k \leq Q, \quad \forall\, k \in \mathcal{K} \tag{8}$$

$$n \cdot \sum_{k \in \mathcal{K}} x_{ij}^k \geq u_{ij}, \quad \forall\, i,j \in \mathcal{V},\ i \neq j \tag{9}$$

$$\sum_{\substack{j \in \mathcal{V} \\ i \neq j}} (u_{ij} - u_{ji}) = \sum_{\substack{j \in \mathcal{V} \\ i \neq j}} \sum_{k \in \mathcal{K}} x_{ij}^k, \quad \forall\, i \in \mathcal{V} \setminus \{0\} \tag{10}$$

$$x_{ij}^k \in \{0,1\}, \quad \forall\, i,j \in \mathcal{V},\ k \in \mathcal{K} \tag{11}$$

$$y_c^k \in \{0,1\}, \quad \forall\, c \in \mathcal{C},\ k \in \mathcal{K} \tag{12}$$

$$u_{ij} \geq 0, \quad \forall\, i,j \in \mathcal{V} \tag{13}$$

In this formulation, the objective function (1) is the total traveled distance minimization. Constraints (2) assure that any node can be visited at most once.

Note that, as the main feature of the proposed problem is that not all nodes need to be visited, these equations can be equal to zero. Equations (3) indicate that if a vehicle arrives to a node, it must leave it. Equations (4) guarantee that all clusters are visited, that means all nodes are covered by at least one route. Constraints in (5) prevent arcs from being traversed between nodes in the same cluster. In a similar way, constraints (6) force to visit every cluster exactly once. Variables x_{ij}^k and y_c^k are linked by Eq. (7). Vehicle capacity is limited by equations (8). Subtours elimination constraints are represented by equations (9) and (10). Equations (9) oblige variables u_{ij} to take the value zero if the arc (i, j) is not traversed ($x_{ij}^k = 0, \ \forall \ k \in \mathcal{K}$), and limit their maximum value to n. Equations (10) induce decreasing values on variables u_{ij} across a route for traversed arcs. Finally, constraints (11) to (13) define the domain of the decision variables.

In an alternative way, constraints (6) and (7) can be rewritten as (14) and (15). In Sect. 4, the computational experiments allow to compare the performance of the model by using the different versions of these equations. To do so, let us define $MILP_2$, $MILP_3$ and $MILP_4$ as new mathematical models. For $MILP_2$, equations in (6) are replaced by constraints in (14). $MILP_3$ includes (14) and (15) (equations in (6) and (7) are omitted). Finally, for $MILP_4$ equations in (7) are replaced by constraints in (15).

$$\sum_{\substack{i \in \mathcal{V}}} \sum_{\substack{j \in \mathcal{V} \\ j \neq i}} \sum_{k \in \mathcal{K}} x_{ij}^k \cdot \lambda_{jc} \leq 1, \qquad \forall \, c \in \mathcal{C} \tag{14}$$

$$\sum_{\substack{i \in \mathcal{V}}} \sum_{\substack{j \in \mathcal{V} \\ j \neq i}} x_{ij}^k \cdot \lambda_{jc} \geq y_c^k, \qquad \forall \, k \in \mathcal{K}, \ c \in \mathcal{C} \tag{15}$$

In Sect. 4 the mathematical model is tested, and different combinations using Eqs. (14) and (15) are compared. Some GVRP instances have are also tested in order to analyze the performance of the model on that special case.

4   Computational Experiments

The proposed mathematical models are implemented in CPLEX 12.7. They have been tested on a 2.40 GHz Intel Core i7 computer with 8 GB of RAM and Windows 10 Professional. Two sets of experiments are reported. The first one compares the resolution of the MILP for 36 SVRP instances (see Subsect. 4.2). The second set of experiments applies the same MILP model for 12 instances of the special case where no overlapping is presented, the GVRP (see Subsect. 4.3).

Subsection 4.1 describes the benchmark instances we use to evaluate the mathematical model performance.

4.1   Problem Instances

For the GVRP tests we use the instances from [8] available in the literature. As MILP can only be used on small size instances, we selected 12 instances up to 63 nodes. Nevertheless, there are not instances for our proposed SVRP. Therefore, we modified the GVRP instances by adding some random chosen nodes on the predefined clusters. Some times this procedure produces unfeasible instances, so we manually checked and adapted them in order to get feasible instances. For each GVRP instance we have generated three SVRP instances, with three levels of complexity. Here we refer as complexity the maximum number of clusters per node (MNCN). As a result we have $12 \cdot 3 = 36$ SVRP instances. Given the randomness when including nodes in each cluster, note that $\sum_{i \in \mathcal{V}} \sum_{c \in \mathcal{C}} \lambda_{ic}$ may vary for each instance. To provide a measure of complexity that describe a single instance, we propose an average cluster density (ACD) ratio, computed as follows:

$$ACD = \frac{|\mathcal{V}|}{\sum_{i \in \mathcal{V}} \sum_{c \in \mathcal{C}} \lambda_{ic}} \tag{16}$$

For GVRP instances the ratio ACD is equal to 1. Note that when a node belongs to several clusters, it becomes easier to cover a wider area by visiting that node.

4.2   Results on SVRP Instances

Table 1 summarizes the computational experiments performed for the SVRP and GVRP instances. The first column indicates the mathematical model. The second one shows the average gap. The third column corresponds to the average computing time in seconds. Fourth column stores the number of optimal solution found. Columns five to seven show the same indicators for the GVRP model.

It can be seen that model $MILP_3$ presents the lower average gap, the shortest running time and the largest number of optimal solutions found. The average gap does not present a significant difference for models $MILP_1$, $MILP_2$ and $MILP_4$. Models $MILP_1$ and $MILP_4$ also present very close results for average time and number of optimal solutions.

Table 1. Summary results - SVRP and GVRP

Model	SVRP			GVRP		
	Average gap	Average time (s)	Number of optimal solutions	Average gap	Average time (s)	Number of optimal solutions
$MILP_1$	21.26%	1848.22	19	33.90%	2742.76	3
$MILP_2$	21.38%	1663.40	20	29.19%	2505.06	4
$MILP_3$	19.51%	1602.86	22	29.83%	2555.15	4
$MILP_4$	21.46%	1848.88	19	33.91%	2978.26	3

4.3   Results on GVRP Instances

As it is mention in previous sections, GVRP is a special case of our SVRP where each node belongs to only one cluster. In Table 1 can be found a summary of

Table 2. General results for best performed MILP

$|V|$	$|K|$	$|C|$	GVRP MNCN=1			SVRP MNCN=2				MNCN=3				MNCN=4			
			Z	Gap	Time	ACD	Z	Gap	Time	ACD	Z	Gap	Time	ACD	Z	Gap	Time
16	8	9	238.82	0.00%	5.76	0.67	449.84	22.71%	3600.00	0.64	407.10	0.00%	37.78	0.40	477.26	0.00%	1.90
22	2	12	161.82	0.00%	111.75	0.71	558.12	55.11%	3600.00	0.51	566.59	0.00%	98.40	0.39	600.78	0.00%	11.31
22	8	12	314.00	0.00%	195.48	0.71	778.38	72.47%	3600.00	0.55	639.42	72.44%	3600.00	0.47	612.32	63.53%	3600.00
23	8	13	314.38	0.00%	947.38	0.66	332.37	18.38%	3600.00	0.49	304.03	0.00%	811.59	0.38	309.65	0.00%	852.48
32	5	17	508.95	16.80%	3600.00	0.65	247.77	0.00%	0.73	0.49	238.30	0.00%	0.69	0.38	265.45	0.00%	0.72
45	7	24	721.56	43.50%	3600.00	0.61	123.48	0.00%	10.34	0.46	154.37	0.00%	15.04	0.43	123.58	0.00%	0.20
45	5	16	411.14	22.910%	3600.00	0.68	287.60	0.00%	4.51	0.58	285.74	0.00%	0.91	0.43	256.02	0.00%	0.72
50	8	26	406.89	35.80%	3600.00	0.65	265.34	0.00%	2.24	0.53	299.25	0.00%	2.50	0.39	273.13	0.00%	3.99
55	15	29	629.50	58.90%	3600.00	0.76	362.50	46.69%	3600.00	0.52	303.44	29.28%	3600.00	0.42	312.30	0.00%	3211.44
60	10	31	553.33	50.10%	3600.00	0.69	561.58	62.15%	3600.00	0.53	480.24	40.68%	3600.00	0.39	503.32	0.00%	1976.46
60	15	31	738.69	61.20%	3600.00	0.67	435.67	52.07%	3600.00	0.51	385.87	52.71%	3600.00	0.39	365.39	0.00%	138.70
63	9	22	861.62	61.10%	3600.00	0.71	578.63	56.59%	3600.00	0.50	575.24	57.38%	3600.00	0.41	227.60	0.00%	120.17
Average				29.19%	2505.06	0.68		32.18%	2401.48	0.53		21.04%	1580.58	0.41		5.29%	826.51

Table 3. MILP performance for ACD ratio values

	ACD < 0.5	$0.5 \leq$ ACD ≤ 0.65	ACD > 0.65
Number of instances	15	15	9
Instances with Gap 0.00%	14	7	1
Average Gap	7.05%	22.86%	37.66%
Average Time (s)	923.81	1611.22	3000.75

the results by using the four proposed MILP models for the GVRP selected instances.

Similarly to results for the SVRP, the models $MILP_1$ and $MILP_4$ present the poorer results: higher average gap and running time, and less number of optimal solutions. Nevertheless, the best average gap and average running time are obtained by the model $MILP_2$. $MILP_2$ and $MILP_3$ reach the same number of optimal solutions.

Table 2 shows, for each instance, the performance of the best model on each problem: model $MILP_2$ on GVRP and model $MILP_3$ on SVRP. For the generalized version, $MILP_3$ is able to deliver optimal solutions for instances with up to 23 nodes in less than 1382 seconds. For instances with more than 50 nodes, note that gap values increase when the number of vehicles ($|\mathcal{K}|$) also increases. For selective problems, values of MNCN influences the performance of the MILP since the number of optimal solutions increase as more clusters per node are allowed. In this case, if MNCN is equal to 2, 3 and 4, then the number of optimal solutions is 4, 7 and 11 respectively. Given the relation between MNCN and the ratio ACD, the smaller value for ACD, the tighter average gap. The average CPU time also decreases for small values of ratio ACD. Table 3 summarizes these performance issues showing that if the ACD< 0.5, it is possible to find gaps equal to 0% except for one instance (in which $|\mathcal{V}| = 22$, $|\mathcal{K}| = 8$ and ACD $= 0.47$). For values of $0.5 \leq$ ACD ≤ 0.65 the percentage of guaranteed optimal solutions decreases to 46.67% (seven out of 15 instances). Finally, harder instances are grouped with an ACD>0.65; for this family of instances, just one optimal solution is reported.

5   Concluding Remarks

In this paper, we present a new type of selective vehicle routing problem and we also formulate a MILP able to deal with small instances. The proposed MILP is tested on instances of the GVRP and adapted instances of the SVRP. We also rewrite some of the constraints in the MILP in order to compare the efficiency of four different models. The model with best performance on GVRP ($MILP_2$) is able to deliver 4 optimal solutions for 12 instances with up to 23 nodes. For the SVRP, the model with best performance ($MILP_3$) finds 22 optimal solution out of 36 instances. The average cluster density ratio (ACD) and the maximum number of clusters per node (MNCN) have a great impact on the models performance; when ACD decreases or MNCN increases, instances become easier.

Finally, we propose some future research directions. Firstly, to enhance the performance of our MILPs it is possible to study different valid inequalities and their behavior on solution times and quality (gap). Secondly, design (meta) heuristic approaches; these algorithms can provide good quality solutions while the required computation time is significantly reduced. On the other hand, there are opportunities about applications with different vehicle routing features. New formulations based on cumulative objectives, split deliveries, time windows, multiple trips per vehicle, among others can also be addressed. In addition, our formulations can be combined within a matheuristic approach based on heuristic concentration to solve different VRP applications.

References

1. Afsar, H.M., Labadie, N.: Team orienteering problem with decreasing profits. Electron. Notes Discret. Math. **41**, 285–293 (2013)
2. Afsar, H.M., Prins, C., Santos, A.C.: Exact and heuristic algorithms for solving the generalized vehicle routing problem with flexible fleet size. Int. Trans. Oper. Res. **21**(1), 153–175 (2014)
3. Şahinyazan, F.G., Kara, B.Y., Taner, M.R.: Selective vehicle routing for a mobile blood donation system. Eur. J. Oper. Res. **245**(1), 22–34 (2015)
4. Allahviranloo, M., Chow, J.Y., Recker, W.W.: Selective vehicle routing problems under uncertainty without recourse. Transp. Res. Part E: Logist. Transp. Rev. **62**, 68–88 (2014)
5. Archetti, C., Bianchessi, N., Speranza, M.G.: Optimal solutions for routing problems with profits. Discret. Appl. Math. **161**(4–5), 547–557 (2013)
6. Baldacci, R., Bartolini, E., Laporte, G.: Some applications of the generalized vehicle routing problem. J. Oper. Res. Soc. **61**(7), 1072–1077 (2010)
7. Battarra, M., Erdoğan, G., Vigo, D.: Exact algorithms for the clustered vehicle routing problem. Oper. Res. **62**(1), 58–71 (2014)
8. Bektaş, T., Erdoğan, G., Røpke, S.: Formulations and branch-and-cut algorithms for the generalized vehicle routing problem. Transp. Sci. **45**(3), 299–316 (2011)
9. Carrabs, F., Cerrone, C., Cerulli, R., Gaudioso, M.: A novel discretization scheme for the close enough traveling salesman problem. Comput. Oper. Res. **78**, 163–171 (2017)
10. Doerner, K.F., Gronalt, M., Hartl, R.F., Kiechle, G., Reimann, M.: Exact and heuristic algorithms for the vehicle routing problem with multiple interdependent time windows. Comput. Oper. Res. **35**(9), 3034–3048 (2008)
11. Ghiani, G., Improta, G.: An efficient transformation of the generalized vehicle routing problem. Eur. J. Oper. Res. **122**(1), 11–17 (2000)
12. Golden, B.L., Levy, L., Vohra, R.: The orienteering problem. Nav. Res. Logist. **34**(3), 307–318 (1987)
13. Gulczynski, D.J., Heath, J.W., Price, C.C.: The close enough traveling salesman problem: a discussion of several heuristics. In: Alt, F.B., Fu, M.C., Golden, B.L. (eds.) Perspectives in Operations Research. Operations Research/Computer Science Interfaces, vol. 36, pp. 271–283. Springer, Boston (2006). https://doi.org/10.1007/978-0-387-39934-8_16

14. Kara, I., Bektaş, T.: Integer linear programming formulation of the generalized vehicle routing problem. In: Proceedings of the 5th EURO/INFORMS Joint International Meeting (2003)
15. Laporte, G., Asef-Vaziri, A., Sriskandarajah, C.: Some applications of the generalized travelling salesman problem. J. Oper. Res. Soc. **47**(12), 1461–1467 (1996)
16. Mennell, W.K.: Heuristics for solving three routing problems: Close-enough traveling salesman problem, close-enough vehicle routing problem, sequence-dependent team orienteering problem. Ph.D. thesis, University of Maryland (2009)
17. Moccia, L., Cordeau, J.-F., Laporte, G.: An incremental tabu search heuristic for the generalized vehicle routing problem with time windows. J. Oper. Res. Soc. **63**(2), 232–244 (2012)
18. Palekar, U., Laporte, G.: Some applications of the clustered travelling salesman problem. J. Oper. Res. Soc. **53**(9), 972–976 (2002)
19. Pop, P., Pintea, C., Dumitrescu, D.: An ant colony algorithm for solving the dynamic generalized vehicle routing problem. Ovidius University Annals of Constanta. Series of Civil Engineering, vol. 1, pp. 373–382 (2009)
20. Pop, P.C., Kara, I., Marc, A.H.: New mathematical models of the generalized vehicle routing problem and extensions. Appl. Math. Model. **36**(1), 97–107 (2012)
21. Pop, P.C., Matei, O., Sitar, C.P.: An improved hybrid algorithm for solving the generalized vehicle routing problem. Neurocomputing **109**, 76–83 (2013)
22. Sevaux, M., Sörensen, K., et al.: Hamiltonian paths in large clustered routing problems. In: Proceedings of the EU/MEeting 2008 Workshop on Metaheuristics for Logistics and Vehicle Routing, EU/ME, vol. 8, pp. 411–417 (2008)
23. Shuttleworth, R., Golden, B.L., Smith, S., Wasil, E.: Advances in meter reading: heuristic solution of the close enough traveling salesman problem over a street network. In: Golden, B., Raghavan, S., Wasil, E. (eds.) The Vehicle Routing Problem: Latest Advances and New Challenges. Operations Research/Computer Science Interfaces, vol. 43, pp. 487–501. Springer, Boston (2008). https://doi.org/10.1007/978-0-387-77778-8_2
24. Tsiligirides, T.: Heuristic methods applied to orienteering. J. Oper. Res. Soc **35**(9), 797–809 (1984)
25. Valle, C.A., Martinez, L.C., da Cunha, A.S., Mateus, G.R.: Heuristic and exact algorithms for a min-max selective vehicle routing problem. Comput. Oper. Res. **38**(7), 1054–1065 (2011)
26. Vidal, T., Battarra, M., Subramanian, A., Erdogan, G.: Hybrid metaheuristics for the clustered vehicle routing problem. Comput. Oper. Res. **58**, 87–99 (2015)

Internet of Things (IoT)

Voltage Quality in Distribution Systems for Smart Cities Using Energy Internet

Alvaro Espinel[(⊠)] and Adriana Marcela Vega

Universidad Distrital Francisco José de Caldas, Bogotá, Colombia
{aespinel, avegae}@udistrital.edu.co

Abstract. This paper shows the design of a prototype to measure voltage in a distribution system by means of the quality indicators established by energy regulation in Colombia. The design is proposed according to the new context where smart energy systems require energy internet, that is their real time manipulation with databases located in the cloud, in order to locate them in intelligent spaces such as the future cities. Therefore, the quality of the voltage in these environments is of vital importance to guarantee an adequate service in the different sectors in a city.

Keywords: Smart cities · Energy internet · Smart energy · Voltage quality

1 Introduction

The main characteristics of a smart city include information and communication technologies (ICT), devices, services and intelligent administration. Internet of Things (IoT) is used for this, which connects devices with internet through specific communication protocols for the exchange of information to achieve aspects such as location, tracing, monitoring and administration in order to provide information to users and actions of massive data flow in real time [1].

Energy Internet promotes the interaction between the exchange and personalization of the electric power value chain, since it is no longer just a type of service but it is becoming a technological support platform and a generalized resource, which can transform the lifestyle of consumers and the commercial operation of the companies providing the service.

The penetration of renewable energy within Smart cities in the electrical grid requires the voltage quality, since possible disturbances such as flickers, harmonics, etc., can spread and degrade the performance of loads [2]. The development of meters minimizes costs because they record the energy service continuity allowing the location and detection of faults, besides providing information of possible compensation by the service providers, if the maximum admissible values of duration and frequency of interruptions have been exceeded [3].

© Springer Nature Switzerland AG 2018
J. C. Figueroa-García et al. (Eds.): WEA 2018, CCIS 916, pp. 123–135, 2018.
https://doi.org/10.1007/978-3-030-00353-1_11

2 Theoretical Framework

In recent years, the term "Smart cities", has contemplated different analysis approaches, Fig. 1 shows how it integrates with the Smart energy and Energy Internet. In the following section each of the treated concepts is explained.

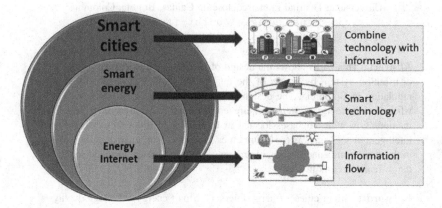

Fig. 1. Smart cities integration with smart energy and energy internet, Source: Authors

2.1 Smart Cities

Smart cities require a robust communication infrastructure in the face of the changes proposed with the use of energy on both the supply and demand aspects, however, energy management is still restricted by closed information environments, so as the architecture of transmission networks was developed with centralized generation standards, without taking into account the further integration it required with distributed generation, making this situation a technical complexity [4].

Energy management is one of the most demanding issues within a Smart city, as it provides life quality to inhabitants through the optimal management of their resources, which adds complexity to energy systems [5].

2.2 Smart Energy

Smart energy is the development of future energy systems, through integration with information and communication technologies, they will be multi-energy sustainable systems that will require the optimal administration of energy through planning, control and management of resources with the help of an Energy hub or energy center for various consumption sectors [6].

Smart Energy includes sectors such as electricity, heating, cooling, industry, buildings, transport, etc. It also allows to identify affordable energy solutions for the transformation towards the renewable and sustainable future [7].

2.3 Energy Internet

Energy generation systems have evolved in four stages: decentralized, centralized, distributed and finally smart. The latest ones are the innovative representation of energy management that is also known as Energy internet, which means that the business and service electric power model becomes more innovative every day, since the flow of information required by the Smart cities is integrated [8].

The collected data becomes vulnerable because it is stored in the cloud, this is why the security in the transmission and storage of them to preserve them in the ICT infrastructure is important. In addition, records and alerts can help prevent problems such as potential theft of energy, detect anomalies, etc. [9].

The development of Smart grids facilitates the flow of bidirectional energy and the information flows of small power generators such as electric vehicles (EV). The actual current grid infrastructure cannot guarantee the maximum benefits of these devices, it is necessary that they have connectivity with distributed energy resources in the context of energy internet [10].

2.4 Voltage Quality

The quality of the energy is very important for Smart cities and depends on the power delivered by the power supply, the supply of voltage is of good quality if the RMS (Root Mean Square) value it has remains within the specified variation range, which means that it is stable and does not suffer distortions.

Due to the rapid penetration of distributed energy, operators must maintain voltage levels within operational limits in the grid and ensure the provision of voltage quality [11], especially for sensitive loads, as in the industrial sector because they mainly include voltage drops and disturbances in harmonics caused by sudden short circuits or non-linear load fluctuations [12].

3 Metodology and Analysis Approach

The methodology that will be followed for the development of this investigation consists in the next four points and will be discussed through the current section:

(1) Regulatory framework in Colombia.
(2) Prototype design to determine DES (Duration Equivalent of Service interruptions), FES (Frequency Equivalent of service interruptions) and Voltage Quality indicators.
(3) Web application model.
(4) Pilot Tests.

3.1 Electric Power Regulation

The regulatory framework for quality in regional transmission and local distribution systems is contained in the Energy and Gas Regulation Commission Resolution (CREG) 070 of 1998, which has been supplemented by the CREG Resolutions, some of which are: 025 and 089 of 1999, 096 of 2000, 159 of 2001, 084 of 2002, 113 of 2003, 016 of 2007, 097 of 2008. However, according to resolution 024, the quality of the Electrical Power, is the set of qualifiers of phenomena inherent to the voltage waveform, which allow to judge the value of the deviations of the instantaneous voltage according to the standard form and frequency of the wave [13].

There are two types of service quality indicators in the regulation: The first one have to do with the quality of the power supplied, such as the regulation of voltage, waveform and power factor, called DES or the sum of the time in hours of service interruptions, and calculated according to Eq. 1:

$$DES = \sum_{i=1}^{NTI} t(i) \tag{1}$$

where NTI is the total number of interruptions in the circuit, i means interruption and $t(i)$ denotes time in hours of the interruption.

The second one is the quality indicator of the service provided related to the continuity in the service provision called FES [14], or the sum of the number of times the service is interrupted, calculated as shown in Eq. 2:

$$FES = NTI \tag{2}$$

3.2 Prototype Design to Determine DES, FES and Voltage Quality Indicators

The proposed prototype includes two components: (1) a data collection system for measuring the voltage, in order to determine the ranges in which it varies, the time and date of the disconnections and their frequency and (2) a web-based software management system with multilayer architecture and a database management system that allows storage on the web, in order to carry out the statistical analysis for the determination of voltage variations and the DES and FES indicators.

Data Acquisition System. The system for data acquisition is made up of six (6) stages that are observed as a whole in Fig. 2 by means of a block diagram of the System, which operates as follows:

(1) The voltage measurement is made through the measurement transformer that reduces the voltage signal from 120 to 12 V of alternating current, primary tension 120 V, secondary tension 12 V ac, dielectric rigidity between 3600 V, protection IP00, frequency 60 Hz.
(2) The resistive divider reduces the entering 12 V to 2.4 V which is the output voltage of the resistive divider that enters to the digital analog converter. The voltage of 2.4 V has been selected because it enables the system so that it can operate with supply voltages of up to 240 V, in which case the output voltage of the divider would be 4.8 V, voltage admissible without risks by the digital analog converter,

(3) Analog to Digital Converter, which allows having 65535 possible values for the readings of the 2.4 V,

(4) The signal output of the digitized voltage in 16 bits, is serialized and communicated to the ATM 328 processor, by means of the I2C [15] communication protocol, which uses two bits to make transfer data.

(5) The data signal containing the voltage value is processed in the microprocessor according to the algorithms that recover the value of the measurement and status of the energy service that is monitored. The code that implements the web server is also implemented in the processor, the MAC (Media Access Control address), IP (Internet Protocol) address and communications port of the device are defined, finally,

(6) The integrated circuit W5100 receives the processor data through Serial protocol Peripheral Interface-SPI, in order to transmit them to the Web.

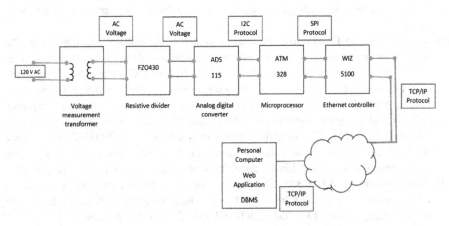

Fig. 2. Block diagram of the prototype design

The structure described above conforms the voltage meter and the monitor of the operation status of the network that allows measuring the interruptions to determine the DES and FES indicators, object of the present investigation. The meter is invoked through a high-level HTTP protocol of the OSI (Open System Interconnection) model, using the following line in the browser:

http://192.168.0.5:8080

This address is required from the web application that is located on the personal computer where it is kept with the database management system.

(a) **Transformer for voltage measurement.** The purpose of this stage is to adapt the voltage signal that reaches the measuring point with a reference value of 120 V to the measuring system that accepts an input of 12 V of alternating current. The transformer that is used for the measurement is of low cost and reduced size, in such a way that it does not affect the size of the measurement equipment. For this case a transformer from an old mobile phone charger was used.

(b) **Resistive divider to adapt voltage signal.** Because the voltage level of 12 V is still too high for the analog input of the ATM328 microprocessor, the voltage divider that commercially identifies with the FZ0430 is used [16]. This resistive divider allows measuring voltages up to 25 V, and has resistors of 30kOhm and 7.5kOhm, which means that the voltage perceived after the module is a division with a factor of 5 (7.5/(30 + 7.5)). This module is based on resistance and it can make the input voltage of red terminal reduce 5 times of original voltage, the max ATM328 input voltage is 5 V, so the input voltage of this module should be not more than 5 V x 5 = 25 V, in this case is 12 V. Because the ATM328 AVR chip have 10 bit ADC, so this module simulation resolution is 0.00489 V equal (5 V/1023), and the input voltage of this module should be more than 2.4 V, that corresponding to 491 binary code. The 10 bits offered by the ATM328, with an internal converter, are not enough to make an adequate measurement for this instrument class, which is why it was decided to implement an analog to digital conversion process with greater precision, for which a converter of 16 bits was selected.

(c) **Digital Analog Convertor.** In order to improve the voltage reading process, a digital analogue converter commercially known as ADS115 was selected. The ADS1115 device is precision, low-power, 16-bit, I2C-compatible, analog-to-digital converters (ADCs) offered in an ultra-small, leadless, X2QFN-10 package, and a VSSOP-10 package. Also incorporates a programmable gain amplifier (PGA) and a digital comparator. These features, along with a wide operating supply range [17]. This module simulation resolution is 0.0000762940 V equal (5 V/65535), and the input voltage of this module should be more than 2.4 V, that corresponding to 31.457 binary code. This resolution y best for this proposed.

(d) **Microprocessor ATM 328.** The high-performance Microchip 8-bit AVR RISC-based microcontroller combines 32 KB ISP flash memory with read-while-write capabilities, 1 KB EEPROM, 2 KB SRAM, 23 general purpose I/O lines, 32 general purpose working registers, three flexible timer/counters with compare modes, internal and external interrupts, serial programmable USART, a byte-oriented 2-wire serial interface, SPI serial port, 6-channel 10-bit A/D converter (8-channels in TQFP and QFN/MLF packages), programmable watchdog timer with internal oscillator, and five software selectable power saving modes. The device operates between 1.8–5.5 V [18]. The Atmega328 is a high performance integrated circuit based on a RISC microcontroller (Reduced Instruction Set Computer), with a flach memory with the read-while-write ability, 1 KB of EEPROM memory, 2 KB of SRAM, 23 lines of E/S [18].

(e) **Ethernet Controller.** The W5100 is a single-chip Internet-enabled 10/100 Ethernet controller designed for embedded applications where ease of integration, stability, performance, area and system cost control are required. The 5100 has been designed to facilitate easy implementation of Internet connectivity. The W5100 is IEEE 802.3 10BASE-T and 802.3u 100BASE-TX compliant [19]. The W5100 chip is a Hardwired TCP/IP embedded Ethernet controller that enables easier Internet connection for embedded systems. W5100 suits users in need of stable Internet connectivity best, using a single chip to implement TCP/IP Stack, 10/100 Ethernet MAC and PHY. Hardwired TCP/IP stack supports TCP, UDP,

IPv4, ICMP, ARP, IGMP, and PPPoE, which has been proven through various applications over many years. W5100 uses a 16ytes internal buffer as its data communication memory [20].

4   Web Application Model to Determine Indicators

The model of the web application for processing the data obtained by the measurement system on a personal computer is implemented as a three-layer application, separating the presentation layer or graphical user interface from the application logic and persistence (database), as shown in Fig. 3 [21]. Isolation from one layer to another allows the application to migrate or operate on multiple platforms, including mobile devices in the future.

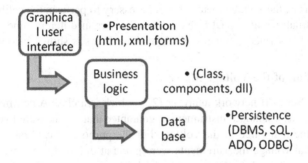

Fig. 3. Layer architectonic model

4.1   Presentation Layer (Graphical User Interface)

It will be developed in Web type forms (Aspx), with C# programming languages. This layer corresponds to the user interface and allows to visualize in real time the measured data of voltage and based on them to establish the cuts in the service of energy based on the level of voltage equal to zero volts. The data history and the real-time voltage measurements can be visualized in analog and digital form.

4.2   Application Logic Layer (Classes and Components)

It will be developed in class library projects with C# programming languages. These components implement the logic of the application to perform the process of taking data from the meter and store them in the database. This component performs the reading process using *http request* commands, requesting to the measuring device only the measured voltage data, the date and time the system takes where the application is installed. The packages and classes that implement the application logic are left in the component named: *LogicaMedidasDesFes.dll.*

4.3 Persistance Layer (DataBase)

The persistence or data storage layer was implemented with the SQL SERVER Database Server 2016. In the database stores one (1) minute intervals, three (3) fields, one with the value of the voltage, another called TimeStamp that contains date and time with seconds of the moment in which the data is recorded and a third field that registers the disconnections called Service Status. In this last field a zero (0) is stored when in the voltage reading presents a change in the nominal voltage reading to zero (0) V, that is, a service cut is detected. Otherwise, Number 1 is stored in this field. The name of the database that was implemented is: MedidasDesFes.mdf and the table that stores the data is named: *MedidaVoltajes*, where the fields are: *IdLectura, VoltajeMedido, FechaHoraLectura* and *EstadoServicio*.

5   Results and Discussion

To perform tests of the voltage meter, it was necessary to perform the calibration of the device, the estimations of the DES and FES indicators in different time intervals and finally analyze the service estimator. Each of these items is shown below.

5.1   Calibration of the Voltage Meter

The Fluke 430 Series II network analyzer [22], which is a class A certified measuring device, was used as a standard instrument to guarantee that the measured voltage can be considered as the real value of the voltage. For the purpose of calibrating the voltage meter, residential voltage measurements were made at different time intervals and the technique described in the GUM (Guide to the Expression of Uncertainty in Measurement) was used, endorsed by organizations such as: BIPM, IEC, IFFC, ISO, IUPAC, IUPAP and OIML [23].

Evaluation of the Voltage Measurement Uncertainty: Uncertainties evaluated to calibrate the voltage meter are Type A and are determined by the statistical analysis of the taken measurements. The typical uncertainty is the experimental standard deviation of the measures taken as the basis for the average of the V measured values, according to Eq. 3 [24]:

$$\bar{V} = \frac{1}{n}\sum_{j=1}^{n} Vj \qquad (3)$$

where $\bar{V}$ is the verage voltage, Vj is the voltage through time and n is the sample size.

Subsequently, the standard uncertainty $u(vj)$ is evaluated, which is obtained by calculating the experimental standard deviation of the sample (v) and sample size, with the Eqs. 4 and 5:

$$S(v) = \sqrt{\frac{1}{n-1} \sum_{j=1}^{n} (vj - \bar{v})^2} \qquad (4)$$

where $S(v)$ is the sample standard deviation and

$$u(Vj) = \frac{S(v)}{\sqrt{n}} \qquad (5)$$

where $u(Vj)$ is the typical uncertainty.

The sample size n must be big enough to ensure a good estimator of uncertainty. Additionally, in order to guarantee the central tendency, four (4) tests were developed where 200 measurements were taken in each of them, after averaging the values in volts (V) are shown in Table 1.

Table 1. Experimental tests

Test 1	Test 2	Test 3	Test 4
V	V	V	V
119.1	120.8	120.0	119.3

Based on the fact that the value of the standard meter voltage was V = 120 V, and the average voltage measured in the experiment of: $\bar{v}$ = 119.8 V, it was proceeded to calculate the Error and the uncertainty of the instrument that is being calibrated according to the equations previously shown, resulting in an Error incorporating the uncertainty of E = −0.2 ± 0.90 volts, Instrument Class = (Maximum Error/Scale)* (100), Class = (0.29/120)*100 = 0.24. The previous confirms that it is a precision tool with certification possibilities for commercial or residential use.

5.2 Estimator of the DES and FES Indicators

The measured data is stored in the database as shown in Fig. 4:

SQLQuery4.sql ..esFes.mdf (sa (59))*		MedidasDesFe...bo.MedidaVoltajes	
IdLectura	VoltajeMedido	FechaHoraLectura	EstadoServicio
3	120,5000	2018-01-01 07:01:02.000	0
4	121,5677	2018-01-01 07:02:03.000	0
5	119,1262	2018-01-01 07:03:06.000	1

Fig. 4. Data base storage

During the operation of the measurement system, readings are made at programmable intervals that were established in one (1) minute, i.e. 60 measurements per hour and 1440 per day, this amount of data allows the database to have a storage projection of long term.

For the determination of the DES indicator, which corresponds to the total time of disconnection in a range of dates, the number of values in which the voltage is zero (0) were counted by means of an SQL statement, as the time interval measured corresponds to one (1) minute the total time will be given in minutes, for the requested date time interval. This means that the system is configurable from the graphical user interface, where the query form allows changing the initial date and the final date for which the indicator is to be determined, as follows:

SELECT COUNT(VoltajeMedido) AS DES FROM [MedidasDesFes.mdf].[dbo].[MedidaVoltajes] WHERE VoltajeMedido=0 AND FechaHoraLectura>=@mFechaInicial AND FechaHoraLectura<=@mFechafinal.

The real-time execution statement provides the following results:

SELECT count(VoltajeMedido) AS DES FROM [MedidasDes-Fes.mdf].[dbo].[MedidaVoltajes] WHERE VoltajeMedido=0 AND FechaHoraLectura>='16/02/2018'AND FechaHoraLectura<='16/03/2018'

This leads to a DES = 0 min, which corresponds to the days between February 16 and March 16 of 2018, according to CODENSA Invoice No. 3548908-7, of the property where the test was conducted. For the determination of the FES Indicator, which corresponds to the total number of service cuts during a range of dates, the sum of all ones stored in the Service Status field is made as mentioned in Sect. 4.3. Each value of one (1) stored in this field corresponds to a cut of the service therefore the total is obtained from the sum of the cuts for the interval of date that is required.

SELECT SUM(EstadoServicio) AS FES FROM FROM MedidasDes-Fes.mdf].[dbo].[MedidaVoltajes]WHERE FechaHoraLectura =@mFechaInicial AND FechaHoraLectura =@mFechafinal SELECT SUM(EstadoServicio) AS FES FROM [MedidasDesFes.mdf].[dbo].[MedidaVoltajes] WHERE FechaHoraLectura>'16/02/2018'AND FechaHoraLectura<'16/03/2018'

For this case, the result shows FES = 0 INTERRUPCION.

The previous one is the test performed on the system in real operation contrasted with a grid operator invoice. For the purposes of verifying the operation of the system under cut conditions, simulated cuts were made and the system managed to detect the interruptions in a precise and trustable manner.

5.3   QoS Service Quality Estimator

The estimation of the service quality established by the regulation focuses on the DES and FES indicators, which for the previous case in the time interval between February 16 and March 16, resulted in DES = 0 and FES = 0, however, this is not a reliable indicator of quality of service because the voltage variations could put at risk the electrical equipment that is connected to the installation. For this reason, the system was designed in such a way that voltage graphs and tables with statistics can be obtained to establish the following values:

- **Maximum Voltage per Period**

SELECT MAX(VoltajeMedido) AS MaximoVotaje   FROM MedidasDes-Fes.mdf].[dbo].[MedidaVoltajes] WHERE VoltajeMedido=0 AND FechaHoraLectura>'16/02/2018'AND FechaHoraLectura<'16/03/2018'

For this case, the result was: 123.5698 Volts

- **Minimum Voltage per Period**

SELECT MAX(VoltajeMedido) AS MaximoVotaje   FROM MedidasDes-Fes.mdf].[dbo].[MedidaVoltajes] WHERE VoltajeMedido=0 AND FechaHoraLectura>'16/02/2018'AND FechaHoraLectura<'16/03/2018'

For this case, the result was: 117.5698 Volts

- **Average Voltage per Period**

*SELECT AVG(VoltajeMedido) AS MaximoVotaje
FROM [MedidasDesFes.mdf].[dbo].[MedidaVoltajes] WHERE VoltajeMedido=0
AND FechaHoraLectura>'16/02/2018'AND FechaHoraLectura<'16/03/2018'*

For this case, the result was: 119.5698 Volts.

The system in this initial stage only reports the related indicators and the source code of the queries in the database are provided so that the simplicity with which a system incorporating different technologies can be useful for the benefit of the users of the energy service and in accordance with the existing regulatory framework and the most important at low cost built with easily achievable elements in the market.

5.4   Communication Tests

The results coming from all measurements and the implementation of the system in a web environment, make infer that the communication protocols used between the different devices including I2C, SPI, TCP/IP and high-level protocol http, have reached a degree of maturity and reliability that can practically be considered as components of the system that guarantee the operation of the system as a whole.

6   Conclusions

The design and implementation of the system to establish the indicators DES, FES and voltage quality, it could be classified as a precision instrument, with the option of carrying out the certification process to be used in commercial applications. Of course, the above will require more tests and above all a construction process where the elements that were used can be integrated in a reduced space.

The presented device can be very useful for grid operators to be integrated into its distribution system, been able to perform remote monitoring of voltage quality and share information to the switch DES and FES indicators at a detailed level of its different sectors. Currently, it can be observed that these indicators are obtained only by feeders that cover large sectors, which leaves out small groups of users when they fail to occur in smaller circuits such as those corresponding to a distribution transformer.

From a technical point of view, the system allows bidirectional communication data, which can be classified as a device for measuring the quality of the voltage (Smart energy), allowing to have knowledge on how the voltage reaches the users of the network, it is also a good option because it allows detecting possible service failures to protect the system, also to start the process towards where the networks migrate, which is to operate in real time, a strategy that has been called energy internet.

Finally, with the increase in the penetration of renewable energy sources in the distribution grid, it is necessary to have mechanisms to monitor the quality of the voltage and the service, therefore a device such as the one built in the near future will be a standard element, which should be included in the bidirectional energy meter, as part of the modernization of the sector, which will aim to have the best indicators in terms of DES and FES in accordance with the law.

Acknowledgments. The authors would like to thank to Universidad Distrital Francisco Jose de Caldas and GESETIC Research Group and his students who made this study possible.

References

1. Kim, T.-H., Ramos, C., Mohammed, S.: Smart city and IoT. Futur. Gener. Comput. Syst. **76**, 159–162 (2017)
2. Hrishikesan, V.M., Kumar, C., Liserre, M.: Voltage quality improvement in smart transformer integrated distribution grid. In: The 43rd Annual Conference of the IEEE Industrial Electronics Society, Beijing (2017)
3. Gómez, V., Hernandez, C.: Diseño y construcción de un prototipo de medición de los indicadores de calidad del servicio de energía eléctrica (DES y FES) para usuario residencial. Revista Lasallista de Investigación, 94–101 (2010)
4. Song, Y., Lin, J., Tang, M., Dong, S.: An internet of energy things based on wireless LPWAN. Engineering **3**, 460–466 (2017)
5. Calvillo, C.F., Sánchez Miralles, A., Villar, J.: Energy management and planning in smart cities. Renew. Sustain. Energy Rev. **55**, 273–287 (2016)
6. Mohammadia, M., Noorollahi, Y., Mohammadiivatloo, B., Hosseinzadeh, M., Yousefi, H., Khorasani, S.T.: Optimal management of energy hubs and smart energy hubs–a review. Renew. Sustain. Energy Rev. **89**, 33–50 (2018)
7. Lund, H., Østergaard, P.A., Connolly, D., Mathiesen, B.V.: Smart energy and smart energy systems. Energy **137**, 556–565 (2017)
8. Zhou, K., Yang, S., Shao, Z.: Energy internet: the business perspective. Appl. Energy **178**, 212–222 (2016)

9. Baig, Z.A., et al.: Future challenges for smart cities: cyber-security and digital forensics. Digit. Investig. **22**, 3–13 (2017)
10. Mahmud, K., Town, G.E., Morsalin, S., Hossain, M.: Integration of electric vehicles and management in the internet of energy. Renew. Sustain. Energy Rev. **82**, 4179–4203 (2018)
11. Vilman, A., Jerele, M.: Voltage quality provision in low-voltage networks with high penetration of renewable production. IET J. 2053–2056 (2017)
12. Zheng, Z., Xiao, X., Chen, X.Y., Huang, C., Zhao, L., Li, C.-S.: Performance evaluation of a MW-Class SMES-BES DVR system for mitigation of voltage quality disturbances. IEEE Trans. Ind. Appl. (2018)
13. Com. de Reg. de En. y Gas. Res. 024 2005. http://apolo.creg.gov.co/Publicac.nsf/Indice01/Resoluci%C3%B3n-2005-CREG024-2005
14. Comisión de Regulación de Energía y Gas. Indicadores de Calidad para la Continuidad en la Prestación del Servicio de Energía Eléctrical (2004). http://apolo.creg.gov.co/Publicac.nsf/2b8fb06f012cc9c245256b7b00789b0c/e1a28dced41bcc8f0525785a007a6b12/$FILE/D-20CALIDAD%20DEL%20SERVICIO.pdf
15. T-Bem. http://learn.teslabem.com, http://learn.teslabem.com/fundamentos-del-protocolo-i2c-aprende/2/. Accessed 01 Jan 2016
16. Tinkbox. http://tinkbox.ph, http://tinkbox.ph/store/modules/voltage-sensor-module-arduino-dc0-25v-code-fz0430. Accessed 01 Jan 2015
17. Texas Inst. ADS1115. http://www.ti.com/lit/ds/symlink/ads1115.pdf
18. Microchip. ATmega328. https://www.microchip.com/wwwproducts/en/ATmega328
19. W5100 Datasheet. Datasheet. https://www.sparkfun.com/datasheets/DevTools/Arduino/W5100_Datasheet_v1_1_6.pdf
20. WIZNET. http://www.wiznet.io, http://www.wiznet.io/product-item/w5100/. Accessed 01 Jan 2016
21. Xia, Y., Xu, K., Li, Y., Xu, G., Xiang, X.: Modeling and three-layer adaptive diving control of a cable-driven underwater parallel platform. IEEE Access **6**, 24016–24034 (2018)
22. Fluke Corporation, Fluke Europe. http://solutions.fluke.com, http://solutions.fluke.com/eses/fluke-430. Accessed 01 Jan 2014
23. Red Nacional de Metrología, Red Nacional de Metrología Chile. http://www.metrologia.cl, http://www.metrologia.cl/link.cgi/Noticias/66. Accessed 01 Jan 2011
24. Bonilla, L., Echeverría, D., Cepeda, J.: Metodología para Identificar Áreas de Control de Voltaje en un Sistema Eléctrico de Potencia Aplicando Simulación Monte Carlo. Revista Técnica Energía, **14**, 72–79 (2018)
25. Triola, M.: Estadística. Pearson, London (2014)
26. Cronos Electrónica. Sensor de Voltaje. https://www.cronoselectronica.com/sensores/47-fz0430.html
27. Microchip Corporation. https://www.microchip.com, https://www.microchip.com/wwwproducts/en/ATmega328. Accessed 01 Jan 1988

Failures Monitoring in Refrigeration Equipment

Oscar de Jesús Ballestas Ortega and José Luis Villa[✉]

Centro de Excelencia y Apropiación en Internet de las Cosas (CEA-IoT),
Universidad Tecnológica de Bolívar, Cartagena, Colombia
oballestas25@gmail.com, jvilla@utb.edu.co

Abstract. The refrigerators are the responsible to assure the temperature and humidity conditions for perishable products stored in it. In this sense, it is necessary to guarantee its good performance at all times in order to preserve the products. In this article We propose a failures monitoring system for refrigeration equipment using Internet of Things (IoT) technologies. The aim of the solution is to manage preventive and corrective maintenance programs and, in this way, We look for assuring the conditions of the consigned products that are distributed along an entire country. We present the conceptualization, the design of the system and the results of the proof of concept.

Keywords: Industrial internet of things · Asset management
Refrigeration equipment

1 Introduction

The machines involved in industrial processes present failures that make them less efficient and, in the worst case inhibit its performance completely, forcing to stop the process unexpectedly. It is necessary to identify the failures opportunely and define maintenance programs, not only according to the dates set by the manufacturers but also according to the conditions that the machine has been exposed [13]. This concept extends to the industries dedicates to manufacturing equipment, since they must ensure an optimal performance after it has been delivered to the client then send the technical personnel on time before the damage becomes a complex problem.

In the specific case of the food and vaccines industries, the failures in refrigeration equipment prevent guarantee the necessaries temperature conditions for the preservation of perishables products, during the distribution and storing process [5]. This brings it to expire before the scheduled date and as result the product is lost, the demand can not be met and the company is economically affected. The case proposed in this work is focused on the point of sale of the product where it is in consignment, what implies that its loss affects in most part to the company and not to the seller. The company deliver a refrigerator

© Springer Nature Switzerland AG 2018
J. C. Figueroa-García et al. (Eds.): WEA 2018, CCIS 916, pp. 136–146, 2018.
https://doi.org/10.1007/978-3-030-00353-1_12

for the conservation of the product but requires information about the equipment performance for its maintenance.

This kind of problems can be addressed using Internet of Thing technologies. In this paper, We propose a general solution for this kind of problems and study their implementation through a prototype. The results shows a positive feasibility of the proposed solution and exhibit the challenges faced by this kind of solutions.

This paper is structured as follows. In Sect. 2 is described the problem in detail, in Sect. 3 is shown the related work, in Sects. 4 and 5 are presented the proposed architecture and some results for the implementation of the monitoring system. The conclusions and considerations of future work are indicated in Sect. 6.

2   Problem Description

Refrigeration equipment in the point of final distribution of the cold chain, are in the hands of a staff who are attentive to the product as such, but not to the refrigerator. In this way, the equipment sometimes is not working in its optimal conditions and the staff only see the problem until they observe that the perishable is not cooling properly, and only until this moment the failure is notified to the technical personnel. But, the refrigerator has been working certain time outside of ideal conditions. The lack of information for the cooling process prevents guarantee the efficient performance of the equipment because the failures have not been detected in time, and the maintenance is not managed correctly.

In [7] are identified the main causes of failures in refrigerators as are described below: Cooling unit fault, refrigerant leak, improper thermostat adjustment and power outage. In consequence, it is necessary to define some criteria that let define which parts are not working properly, and identify certain failures pattern according to historical data for the performance of the equipment.

To solve the lack of information, we propose a solution using Internet of Thing - IoT technologies. Should be considered the fact that it is not possible to assure a continuous and stable connection to the internet in all the places where the refrigerator is.

3   Related Work

In the food industry there exist systems oriented for monitoring of the perishables products throughout the cold chain process. In [16] is presented a system to monitor temperature and humidity of a container using RFID technologies, the information is only available when track is inside of the range of the RFID reader. A similar work [11], includes sensor for gas measurements, and additionally, integrates GPRS communication to collect the data on a server, and Bluetooth capabilities to send the information to the driver; in this way, it is possible manage the delivery of the product correctly.

Other solutions are deployed using Wireless Sensor Networks (WSN) considering the temperature conditions, e.g. [2,3]. Some works are focused in the tracking of the product along of the cold chain [8]. Other applications are presented for medical products [9], reading data of temperature and location of the product in real time, including a mobile application to connect a cellphone to the refrigerator via BLE.

For the maintenance of the industrial equipment, in [12] is proposed an IoT system for monitoring of industrial motor conditions, taking into account data of vibration, voltage, current, and bearing and winding temperatures, of the motor; the data are sent to the cloud via Wi-Fi, and it is possible to access them remotely. In [1] is presented a Big Data application for renewable energy, including a predictive maintenance system for wind turbines. These predictions estimate the performance for the next hour; this process is carried out every ten minutes. In [6] the failures forecast is obtained from machine learning techniques for a Slitting machine, and so avoid quality defects.

Another predictive maintenance tool is proposed in [13] to anticipate failures in medical equipment and schedule corrective and preventive maintenance efficiently based on data services. Similarly, in [15] is presented a predictive maintenance system using machine learning. In [7] a study is presented to determine the main causes of failure of the refrigeration equipment to improve the maintenance practices, but the data are not available remotely as an IoT monitoring system. In [10] is proposed an intelligent refrigerator for food management based in RFID technology, this checks the conditions inside the refrigerator and with a cloud data service platform, gives information about the shelf life and the availability of the food.

The aim of the work proposed in this document it is not only check the temperature conditions of the product but rather supervise the conditions of the equipment responsible for its conservation in the point of sale. With the data collected would be able to manage a predictive maintenance of the refrigerator.

4   Proposed Architecture

The proposed solution is based on a monitoring system of the source voltage and refrigeration temperature of the equipment, each variable is continuously checked, but the logged values only correspond to the data that are outside of the established work limits, and the values when it returns to normal conditions.

The main communication is performed through Wi-Fi to send data to the cloud and manage alarm messages. Nevertheless, as mentioned above, is not possible assure a continuous and stable connection to Internet, therefore is included the option to send data via GPRS, from which is possible generate SMS messages for mobile devices through of a cellphone operator. In Fig. 1 is shown the architecture developed from the reference architectures proposed in [4,17,18] which is described below.

– **Perception Layer.** The purpose of this layer is to perceive the physical properties of the objects by sensors to convert the information in digital

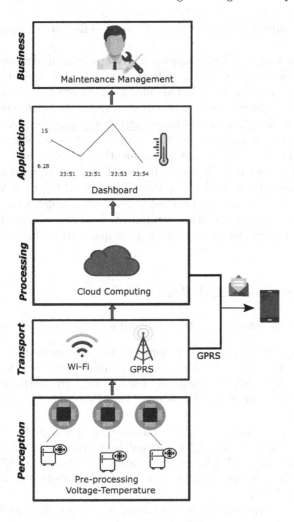

Fig. 1. Proposed architecture for failures monitoring

signals for the data transmission in the network. In this layer are present the sensors and the circuits for the temperature and voltage measurements, connected to a device - microcontroller to process the signals.

- **Transport Layer.** The main task of this layer also called the Network Layer, is the data transmission received from the perception layer to the processing center, for the proposed case, the microcontroller sends the information to the next layer via Wi-Fi, or GPRS considering the availability of the internet network.
- **Processing Layer.** This layer is the responsible for storing, analyzing and processing the information of the objects from the transport layer. The technologies involved are the database, intelligent processing, cloud computing,

ubiquitous computing among others. Here are collected all the sensor data of every refrigerator.

- **Application Layer.** Its objective is the IoT applications development for the diverse field of interest from the data of the processing layer. In this layer is possible to visualize all the collected data in a dashboard. It is possible manage alarm messages which are sent from the server. For the GPRS communication these are sent directly from the microcontroller to a cellphone.
- **Business.** This corresponds to the management layer of the Internet of Things. In this layer take place the applications management and the business models, considering that the success of the IoT technologies does not depend only on the technology by itself, but also of the innovation and the appropriate business models. This last layer is responsible for the maintenance management of the refrigeration equipment, from the information obtained, identifying the damaged parts and the principal sectors affected of the country.

5 Implementation and Results

The devices chosen according to the proposed architecture are described below:

- In the perception layer, for the temperature measurement was selected a *thermistor 10K NTC 3950*; for the voltage measurement was implemented a circuit rectifier without a regulation stage, with the purpose of detecting the voltage source changes. The acquisition of the sensed data was done by *Arduino UNO*.
- For the transport layer, the GPRS communication was performed by a *SIM 900 module* which receives AT command from Arduino to send the data to the mobile device. For Wi-Fi communication was chosen a *ESP8266 module* to send the values to the cloud, both devices are controlled by serial communication with Arduino.
- For the processing and application layer was used the cloud services of *Ubidots*, to collect and visualize the data, and generate SMS or Telegram alarm messages.
- The businesses layer has not been included in the prototype presented and correspond to future work.

5.1 Sensors Calibration

Temperature Sensing

For temperature sensing, the thermistor NTC 10 $K\Omega$ is connected in series with a 10 $K\Omega$ resistor. According to the resistance value of the thermistor is determined the temperature value from Steinhart - Hart equation (Eq. 1) proposed in [14].

$$T = \frac{1}{A + B\,ln(R) + C\,(ln(R))^3} \tag{1}$$

The A, B and C values correspond to Steinhart-Hart coefficients, which depends of characteristic of each thermistor, for this case they are equivalent to $A = 1.26012 \times 10^{-3}$, $B = 2.11343 \times 10^{-4}$ and $C = 1.88590 \times 10^{-7}$. This values were determined by solving a 3 × 3 equation system with reference data of temperature-resistance, given in tables for the thermistor NTC 10K. With this values was performed a test in four different temperature conditions as described below:

– Condition 1. Room temperature.
– Condition 2. Room temperature and presence of heat source.
– Condition 3. Zone of lower cooling of a refrigerator for domestic use.
– Condition 4. Zone of higher cooling of a refrigerator for domestic use (freezer).

The results of the test are shown in the Table 1, these represent the mean data taken every ten seconds for one minute. The values for the thermistor are compared to the measurement of a temperature and humidity datalogger USB DT-171, which is taken as a reference and was subjected at the same time to the same conditions of the thermistor.

Table 1. Mean values and percentage errors for temperature

Condition	Datalogger (°C)	Thermistor (°C)	%Error
1	29.52	27.13	8.09
2	34.00	32.41	4.67
3	19.65	19.50	0.79
4	9.51	11.38	−19.56

The percentage errors obtained for the first three conditions were lower than 10%. It means a good performance for the implementation of the thermistor in relation to the datalogger. For the last condition the error is greater, nevertheless, it is necessary to highlight the precision of $\pm 2.5\,°C$ of the datalogger. This indicates that the sensed value is inside of the reference temperature range.

Voltage Sensing

For the voltage variable were performed some test for the rectifier circuit with the following equipment: Variac Tech # TR610, GW DC source and Fluke 17 multimeter. The output of the circuit corresponds to a DC signal, therefore, were registered the DC values for different levels of the AC input signal using a variable autotransformer. In the Table 2 is shown the results of the test with the simulation data for the circuit.

The variable of interest for the circuit is the RMS value of the supply voltage, so it was necessary to define an expression to relates the DC voltage of the output with the input signal. For this, it was realized an adjustment of the data

Table 2. Output and input voltages for voltage sensing

v_{in} rms	V_{out} DC simulation	V_{out} DC multimeter	% error V_{out}
20	0.322	0.312	3.11
40	0.644	0.634	1.55
60	0.967	0.948	1.96
90	1.453	1.428	1.72
110	1.776	1.745	1.75
120	1.938	1.902	1.86
140	2.261	2.223	1.68
160	2.585	2.544	1.59
180	2.909	2.876	1.13
220	3.556	3.518	1.07
240	3.880	3.829	1.31
250	4.042	3.960	2.03

to straight line from a linear regression model with the data of the Table 2. As result, for a correlation coefficient of 1, it was obtained the following equation:

$$V_{out} = 0.0160\, v_{in} - 0.0074 \tag{2}$$

The results for a new test are shown in Table 3. The two columns are the input voltage measurements from the multimeter and Arduino. The data indicate a good performance of the implementation for the voltage measurements, according to a maximum percentage error of 2.05%.

5.2 Test for Temperature and Voltage

The system is considered in a state of failure when the variable is not inside of minimum and maximum limits established. The measurement is realized every 30 s when three conditions of failures are satisfied the data is sent to the cloud and the alarms messages are managed.

The data are only sent when the failure is registered, once in this state, is generated a new message only when the conditions of the system have returned to normal, and similarly to the failure this is validated when it completes three acceptable measures and so all the counters are reset to zero. The results shown below correspond to temperature and voltage tests carried out individually and the integration of both variables.

In the test performed, it is defined a maximum value of 10 °C for the temperature variable, which depends on the refrigeration requirements of the product. For the voltage is considered a 110 Vrms value for normal operating conditions, the adequate work range is between 100 Vrms and 125 Vrms, which differ about 10% from the nominal value. For the system test, the temperature sensor is

Table 3. Multimeter and Arduino voltage measurements

v_{in}rms Multimeter	v_{in}rms Arduino	% error
20	19.59	2.05
40	39.47	1.33
60	59.97	0.05
90	89.57	0.48
110	110.65	−0.59
120	120.94	−0.78
140	141.13	−0.81
160	161.6	−1.00
180	181.36	−0.76
220	222.3	−1.05
240	241.42	−0.59
250	251.84	−0.74

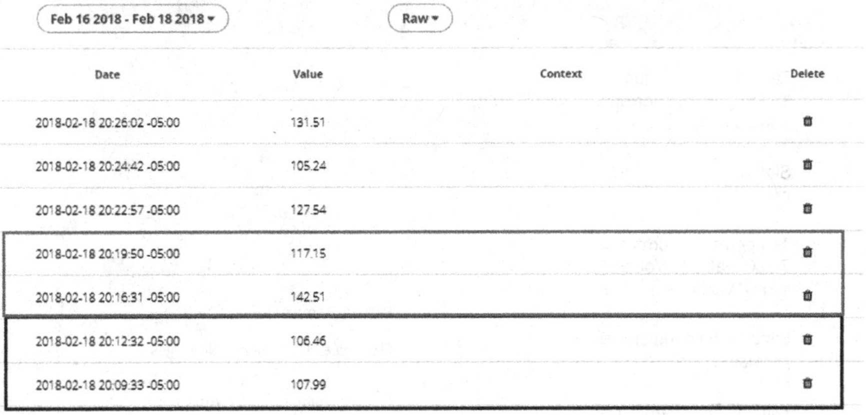

Feb 16 2018 - Feb 18 2018 ▾		Raw ▾	
Date	**Value**	**Context**	**Delete**
2018-02-18 20:26:02 -05:00	131.51		🗑
2018-02-18 20:24:42 -05:00	105.24		🗑
2018-02-18 20:22:57 -05:00	127.54		🗑
2018-02-18 20:19:50 -05:00	117.15		🗑
2018-02-18 20:16:31 -05:00	142.51		🗑
2018-02-18 20:12:32 -05:00	106.46		🗑
2018-02-18 20:09:33 -05:00	107.99		🗑

Fig. 2. Voltage datalog (Vrms) (Color figure online)

introduced in a refrigerator for domestic use, after some time is removed and finally is placed again, this lets us force the system to pass from normal conditions to failure state and later return to the normal state. The source voltage was controlled using a variable autotransformer Tech model # TR610 to represent the low supply and over-voltage conditions.

Independently but in a similar experiment, temperature and voltage tests were performed, sending data to the cloud using the Wi-Fi ESP8266 module and with the GPRS SIM900 module. In the first case, once the data on the cloud, a Telegram message to a mobile device is sent and, in this way, it is not necessary to use GPRS communication to send SMS messages.

Date	Value	Context	Delete
2018-02-18 20:25:59 -05:00	17.55		🗑
2018-02-18 20:24:38 -05:00	8.69		🗑
2018-02-18 20:22:51 -05:00	13.50		🗑
2018-02-18 20:19:47 -05:00	5.79		🗑
2018-02-18 20:16:28 -05:00	5.69		🗑
2018-02-18 20:12:28 -05:00	7.06		🗑
2018-02-18 20:09:30 -05:00	13.14		🗑

Feb 16 2018 - Feb 18 2018 ▾   Raw ▾

Fig. 3. Temperature datalog (°C) (Color figure online)

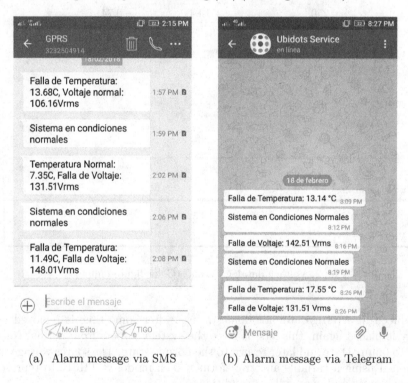

(a) Alarm message via SMS   (b) Alarm message via Telegram

Fig. 4. Temperature and voltage failures

After performing some tests with two variables independently, those are integrated into one system that is in normal conditions when both the temperature and voltage are inside the desired range. Additionally is added a "Normality" variable which is equal to 1 when the system satisfies the condition and otherwise is 0. The results are shown in Figs. 2 and 3. In the Fig. 2 the voltage values are presented consecutively inside the work limits adequate (blue box). This is because there were failures in the temperature variable at the same time of these measurements that can be checked in Fig. 3. Similarly, this happens for the normal temperature data in the red box. The Fig. 4a and b show the alarms messages sent via GPRS and telegram respectively.

6   Conclusions and Future Work

The proposed architecture, the selected devices and the circuits implemented respond appropriately to the need for failures monitoring for the voltage and temperature variables allowing the sending of data to the cloud and manage alarm messages to mobile devices. With a GPRS module the sending of information even when there is not a Wi-Fi network available for the internet connection is guaranteed. The tests realized were carried out for only one node, nevertheless, the architecture is easily scalable considering that Ubidots let us work with multiple devices and for this case, each node doted with an ESP8266 and SIM900 modules. It implies an independent work and therefore they are not affected by the new devices added to the system.

As indicated above, this document presents the design and the proof of concept of the solution. For this reason, it is necessary to work in some aspects to ensure a completely functional system such as establish failures criteria based on historical data from test for several equipment, and in this way, manage the predictive maintenance of the refrigerator.

Acknowledgement. The authors would like to acknowledge the cooperation of all partners within the *Centro de Excelencia y Apropiación en Internet de las Cosas (CEA-IoT)* project. The authors would also like to thank all the institutions that supported this work: the Colombian Ministry for the Information and Communications Technology (*Ministerio de Tecnologías de la Información y las Comunicaciones - MinTIC*) and the Colombian Administrative Department of Science, Technology and Innovation (*Departamento Administrativo de Ciencia, Tecnología e Innovación - Colciencias*) through the *Fondo Nacional de Financiamiento para la Ciencia, la Tecnología y la Innovación Francisco José de Caldas* (Project ID: FP44842-502-2015).

References

1. Canizo, M., Onieva, E., Conde, A., Charramendieta, S., Trujillo, S.: Real-time predictive maintenance for wind turbines using big data frameworks. arXiv preprint arXiv:1709.07250 (2017)
2. Chandra, A.A., Lee, S.R.: A method of wsn and sensor cloud system to monitor cold chain logistics as part of the iot technology. Int. J. Multimedia Ubiquit. Eng. **9**(10), 145–152 (2014)

3. Dittmer, P., Veigt, M., Scholz-Reiter, B., Heidmann, N., Paul, S.: The intelligent container as a part of the internet of things. In: 2012 IEEE International Conference on Cyber Technology in Automation, Control, and Intelligent Systems (CYBER), pp. 209–214. IEEE (2012)
4. Fremantle, P.: A reference architecture for the internet of things. WSO2 White Paper (2015)
5. Hatchett, R.: The medicines refrigerator and the importance of the cold chain in the safe storage of medicines. Nurs. Stand. (2014+) **32**(6), 53 (2017)
6. Kanawaday, A., Sane, A.: Machine learning for predictive maintenance of industrial machines using iot sensor data. In: 2017 8th IEEE International Conference on Software Engineering and Service Science (ICSESS), pp. 87–90. IEEE (2017)
7. Lennon, P., et al.: Root cause analysis underscores the importance of understanding, addressing, and communicating cold chain equipment failures to improve equipment performance. Vaccine **35**(17), 2198–2202 (2017)
8. Lin, J.Y., Do, T.A., Yang, B.K., Huang, Y.F.: Design of refrigerated cargo tracking systems. In: 2013 International Joint Conference on Awareness Science and Technology and Ubi-Media Computing (iCAST-UMEDIA), pp. 400–406. IEEE (2013)
9. Palacio, M.G., et al.: A novel ubiquitous system to monitor medicinal cold chains in transportation. In: 2017 12th Iberian Conference on Information Systems and Technologies (CISTI), pp. 1–6. IEEE (2017)
10. Qiao, S., Zhu, H., Zheng, L., Ding, J.: Intelligent refrigerator based on internet of things. In: 2017 IEEE International Conference on Computational Science and Engineering (CSE) and IEEE International Conference on Embedded and Ubiquitous Computing (EUC), vol. 2, pp. 406–409, July 2017. https://doi.org/10.1109/CSE-EUC.2017.262
11. Schumacher, I., Wollenstein, J., Kalbitzer, J.: Low-power UHF-RFID sensor tags for a complete monitoring and traceability of the cold chain. In: Proceedings of 2012 European Conference on Smart Objects, Systems and Technologies (SmartSysTech), pp. 1–6. VDE (2012)
12. Shyamala, D., Swathi, D., Prasanna, J.L., Ajitha, A.: Iot platform for condition monitoring of industrial motors. In: 2017 2nd International Conference on Communication and Electronics Systems (ICCES), pp. 260–265. IEEE (2017)
13. Sipos, R., Fradkin, D., Moerchen, F., Wang, Z.: Log-based predictive maintenance. In: Proceedings of the 20th ACM SIGKDD International Conference on Knowledge Discovery and Data Mining, pp. 1867–1876. ACM (2014)
14. Steinhart, J.S., Hart, S.R.: Calibration curves for thermistors. In: Deep Sea Research and Oceanographic Abstracts, vol. 15, pp. 497–503. Elsevier (1968)
15. Susto, G.A., Schirru, A., Pampuri, S., McLoone, S., Beghi, A.: Machine learning for predictive maintenance: a multiple classifier approach. IEEE Trans. Ind. Inform. **11**(3), 812–820 (2015). https://doi.org/10.1109/TII.2014.2349359
16. Todorovic, V., Neag, M., Lazarevic, M.: On the usage of RFID tags for tracking and monitoring of shipped perishable goods. Procedia Eng. **69**, 1345–1349 (2014)
17. Weyrich, M., Ebert, C.: Reference architectures for the internet of things. IEEE Softw. **33**(1), 112–116 (2016)
18. Wu, M., Lu, T.J., Ling, F.Y., Sun, J., Du, H.Y.: Research on the architecture of internet of things. In: 2010 3rd International Conference on Advanced Computer Theory and Engineering (ICACTE), vol. 5, pp. V5–484. IEEE (2010)

From SDL Modeling to WSN Simulation for IoT Solutions

Andres Felipe Fuentes Vasquez$^{(\boxtimes)}$ ⓘ and Eugenio Tamura ⓘ

Pontificia Universidad Javeriana – Cali, Calle 18 No 118-250, Cali, Colombia
{affuentes,tek}@javerianacali.edu.co

Abstract. Both the Internet of Things (IoT) and Wireless Sensor Networks (WSN) are technologies characterized by integrating heterogeneous devices with low processing and storage capabilities and power consumption efficiency. The increasing number of operating systems and hardware platforms available for IoT applications suggests the need of developing a simple and agile approach which allows that specifications can be easily converted into executable code for simulation and implementation thus easing validation and verification of requirements. This involves the design, development, testing, and deployment phases. This paper proposes an integration scheme through which IoT solutions based on WSN can be designed using Specification and Description Language (SDL), and then translated directly into code for IoT-oriented operating systems like Contiki. The main goals are to quickly adjust the designs, and execute tests on different hardware-software configurations, thus reducing errors along the life cycle.

Keywords: Specification and Description Language (SDL) ·
Wireless Sensor Networks (WSN) · Internet of Things (IoT) ·
Modeling · Simulation · PragmaDev Studio · Contiki · Cooja

1 Introduction

The fast development of IoT and WSN applications and its associated growth of connected devices, which is predicted to be in the order of billions for the coming years [13], make necessary to take advantage of simulation tools and mechanisms that facilitate the transition from the design to the implementation of a WSN project [16], before making investments in hundreds of devices for testing purposes.

Therefore, a direct integration between modeling languages such as Specification and Description Language [12] (SDL henceforth) with development languages becomes relevant. Hence, the method for IoT solutions development based on WSN proposed in this paper would allow to go quickly from a descriptive design to the implementation and simulation of a prototype.

The proposed method includes an integration scheme which takes a system specified in SDL using PragmaDev Studio 5.x [15], and translate it to executable

© Springer Nature Switzerland AG 2018
J. C. Figueroa-García et al. (Eds.): WEA 2018, CCIS 916, pp. 147–160, 2018.
https://doi.org/10.1007/978-3-030-00353-1_13

code for operating systems such as Contiki [9], in order to be simulated in Cooja [10], which is a simulation tool for WSN. Cooja allows analyzing features such as power consumption and connectivity issues among others in a WSN. A proposal of this kind for IoT solutions that use a WSN to gather data, will lead to shorter development times and lower costs in its life cycle, due to the possibility to detect flaws and mistakes early before the production of the prototype starts. This becomes relevant, since it is more cost-effective to identify potential problems before a system turns into a commercial product [17].

2   Related Work

Since WSN has become a subject of research and development, new fields of application for domains such as health, mobility, agriculture or smart cities [16,19] have been increasing in an exponential manner. Hence, the demand for deploying this kind of systems has being grown lately. This trend implies a faster yet robust development of WSN-based systems in scenarios where different needs are constrained by hardware and software resources.

A WSN could be composed of thousands of sensors with limited resources. Having in mind this aspect, one of the most efficient ways to obtain a preliminary idea of the behavior of a WSN is to perform a simulation. Having tools that allow both easy modeling and quick testing by simulating the different solution alternatives [5] becomes necessary, as well as tools that offer advantages to developers to move from specification to implementation of a given prototype.

Several works had been carried out to determine which simulation methods are more efficient and how it is possible to have specification tools with the capacity of simulating and generating code for WSN motes.

In [2] a simulation scheme is developed, in which the authors use SysML for the specification and design of the WSN model; for future work they conclude about the necessity of creating an integration scheme between the specification and code generation for the system. In [18] an approach for modeling WSN from system specification using the Unified Modeling Language (UML) is presented; authors also propose a procedure for automatic code generation from UML models to SystemC.

On the other hand, works like [7,14] explain how simulating a WSN is extremely useful since deploying a massive network could be expensive. Both works expose the relevance of a scheme for automated code generation during the development of WSN and IoT projects.

All of the above works argue that an integration scheme between specification and code generation is of great help for rapidly implementing and simulating WSN-based IoT applications to estimate their performance before deployment.

3   A Method for WSN-Based IoT Solutions Development

Going from specification to implementation of a system involves a coding phase, which takes the designs, previously validated, to code them for execution in the deployment infrastructure. Figure 1 depicts a method proposed for IoT solutions development based on WSN.

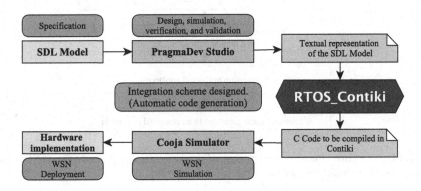

Fig. 1. Proposed method for WSN-based IoT solutions development

First, a model is specified using SDL graphical symbols via PragmaDev Studio. This framework also allows injecting events to the model to test its functionality from a logical viewpoint, including message exchange between agents. Once the model has been debugged and adjusted, it can be exported to a textual representation. This intermediate representation can be C code to be executed in a variety of Operating System (OS). To the best of the authors' knowledge, currently there is no support for Contiki. Therefore, the inclusion of an integration scheme for automatic code generation for Contiki would bring a mechanism to bridge the SDL models with the simulation provided by Cooja. Since Cooja provides a network simulator and hardware emulators for several chipsets, WSN solutions can then be tested and debugged before its deployment. Furthermore, once the solution has been debugged, there is no need to change the code for deployment purposes. The integration scheme, called RTOS_Contiki, would also allow checking non-functional aspects of a WSN such as power consumption, via Cooja.

4 Proposed Integration Scheme

Figure 2 depicts a diagram with the required steps for the development of the proposed integration scheme. Its input is an SDL model described using PragmaDev Studio (step 1). Then, a pivot language needs to be chosen. It allows representing the graphical SDL symbols into a textual language (step 2). The textual representation obtained by using the pivot language is translated to the target language; in this case, C language for Contiki, by using a script which applies translation rules in order to generate a C program (step 3), that can be compiled and executed in Contiki and simulated in Cooja (step 4).

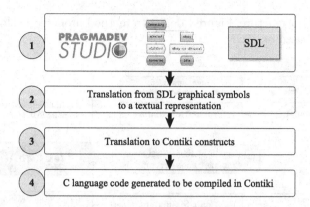

Fig. 2. Steps required for the development of the integration scheme between SDL and C language for Contiki development.

When analyzing the steps of the diagram in Fig. 2, the first task is to identify the salient features of SDL as an specification language as well as the characteristics of Contiki as the translation target. Therefore, it is necessary to introduce the nature of SDL and Contiki.

SDL. Is a language used for the description and specification of systems that has proved its merits for the design of complex systems [6]. Every SDL system is built by using four fundamental elements. The first one is the System Architecture, where a system is described through functional blocks. The second one is the Communication Structure, which illustrates how the processes inside the SDL system communicate to each other, via messages that flow through communication channels. The third one is the Behavioral Structure, where the behavior of the processes is graphically described by using extended finite state machines, which are triggered when a message arrives. The last one is the Data Structure, in which the variables used in the SDL system are defined as abstract data types, using specific concepts and notations.

For the development of the integration scheme, the more relevant SDL elements are the Behavioral Structure (Fig. 3) and the Data Structure, since the diagrams that represent the behavior of the processes, including the variables and data, are the ones that need to be translated to C code for Contiki.

For the specification, testing and simulation of SDL models in this work, PragmaDev Studio is used. It is also capable of translating an SDL specification to C language for a given OS target, such as VxWorks or FreeRTOS which are Real-Time OS (RTOS), using a translation procedure of its own. It is important to mention that currently PragmaDev Studio does not support Contiki as a target OS.

Contiki. Is a modular OS, with a multi-layer structure. Contiki programming is based on an event-management model, where tasks are executed within the

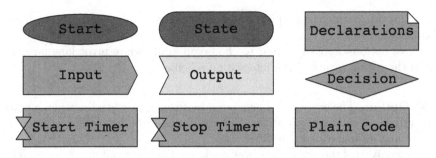

Fig. 3. Key SDL symbols to describe the behavior of processes [15].

same context. Contiki offers support for multiple processes (the so-called pro-tothreads).

Contiki OS was written using the C language, and the development of appli-cations and programs is done in C language as well. Contiki allows compiling applications developed in the C language, within a structure that contains the definition of the OS own constructs, through which the application processes are defined, as well as the threads and events. Listing 1.1 shows the basic layout of a program written in the C language for Contiki. It contains the declaration of a process (line 2), a sentence to start executing the process (line 3), as well as the definition of the process (lines 5–13). Typically, for IoT solutions, each process has an infinite loop whose body defines the state machine that describes the logic of the process. A WSN has several instances of a process or even several instances of different processes.

Listing 1.1. Basic layout of a program written in C language for Contiki.

```
1  /*-----------------------------------------------------*/
2  PROCESS ( pName , "processName" );
3  AUTOSTART_PROCESSES ( &pName );
4  /*-----------------------------------------------------*/
5  PROCESS_THREAD ( pName , event , data )
6  {
7    /* Resource allocation and variable definition */
8    PROCESS_BEGIN ();
9    for ( ; ; ){ /* Infinite loop */
10     /* Process body */
11     }
12   PROCESS_END ();
13 }
```

4.1 Translation from SDL Graphical Symbols to a Textual Representation

As can be inferred from Fig. 2, it is necessary to select a pivot language, which shall be used as a bridge between a graphical language such as SDL and a textual language that allows representing the graphical model. Then, the pivot language is used for translating the graphical SDL symbols to C code for Contiki by means of translation rules.

Three options were evaluated to choose an appropriate pivot language that fulfills the requirements of the integration scheme.

First Option. The output files generated by PragmaDev Studio, when a model is described, were examined at first. These files describe both the system architecture and its behavior using XML tags.

The analysis of the output files was made for different versions of PragmaDev, including versions 4.x and 5.x. The result of this revision showed that the XML structure of the output files changes depending on the version. This fact implies that by using the XML output files as input, the integration scheme would depend on the version of PragmaDev Studio on which the model was developed.

Second Option. PragmaDev Studio allows exporting the model to languages developed by third parties for formal design verification. Currently, these languages are: IF [4], created by VERIMAG laboratories, FIACRE [3], and xLIA [8], created by CEA (Laboratory for Integration of Systems and Technology).

IF, FIACRE y xLIA allow representing almost every SDL primitive [15] in a textual language. This representation is very precise, but its structure is more appropriate to convey information for verification purposes. Thus, it becomes harder to derive the translation rules required by the objective language of the proposed integration scheme (C code for Contiki).

Third Option. A translation procedure included in PragmaDev Studio allows code generation from a SDL specification to C language for several target OS; most of them are oriented towards single processor systems. This procedure generates a representation of the SDL concurrent behavior, using a sequential language like C, representing the SDL graphical symbols with macros, which are easily identified inside the code generated because they start with the prefix RTDS_.

Via this option, it was possible to characterize how PragmaDev derives a textual representation (C code) targeted to a particular OS. The code embodies the representation of the process definitions, variables and state machines of an SDL system.

Table 1 shows the translation from relevant SDL graphical symbols to RTDS_ macros in C language.

Table 1. Translation from SDL graphical symbols to RTDS_ macros in C language as generated by the translation procedure of PragmaDev Studio.

SDL graphical symbol	PragmaDev textual representation
signal (value)	RTDS_MSG_RECEIVE_*signal* (*value*);
signal (value) TO pName	RTDS_MSG_SEND_*signal*_TO_NAME ("pName", RTDS_process_*pName*, *value*);
SET (1000, T1)	RTDS_SET_TIMER (*T1*, *1000*);
RESET (T1)	RTDS_RESET_TIMER (*T1*);

4.2   Translation to Contiki Constructs

According to the findings of the third option, the input to the proposed integration scheme is a C program, generated by PragmaDev Studio translation procedure, that represents the SDL system. PragmaDev provides two types of integration schemes: one for RTOS and other for POSIX/Windows. Since the structure of Contiki is more akin to that of an RTOS, this will be the choice to use, and hence, the integration scheme will be called RTOS_Contiki. This scheme was developed by following the next steps:

1. Setting up a RTOS_Contiki directory, which includes the necessary support files for the correct generation of C code for Contiki.
2. Developing a translation script, which defines the translation rules from RTDS_ macros to C code for Contiki.
3. Developing an automatic execution method for RTOS_Contiki within PragmaDev Studio.

4.3   RTOS_Contiki

Figure 4 depicts the same steps shown in Fig. 2, but with steps 2 and 3 modified to work using the chosen pivot language and the integration scheme designed for C code generation for Contiki (RTOS_Contiki).

Step 2 takes as input the diagram representing an SDL system created in step 1 using PragmaDev Studio. Then, the translation procedure is executed; the resulting output uses the RTDS_ macros to represent the process structure.

The input of step 3 takes the C code files generated by the translation procedure of PragmaDev Studio. These files are translated by a script written in Python (Contiki.py), generating the C code files in which the Contiki constructs represent the SDL system.

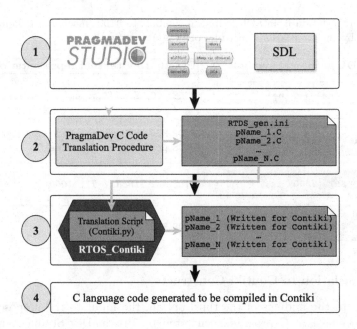

Fig. 4. Final diagram detailing the required steps for the RTOS_Contiki integration scheme developed for translating SDL designs to C language for Contiki.

Setting up the RTOS_Contiki Directory. The RTOS_Contiki integration scheme is derived from the VxWorks RTOS integration, which is recommended by PragmaDev Studio developers, as a good departing point to create a new RTOS integration, since this OS supports almost all the SDL graphical symbols implemented in PragmaDev Studio [15]. The creation of RTOS_Contiki requires putting all the support files that PragmaDev Studio needs for the translation procedure inside a directory named RTOS_Contiki. The required files are listed in Table 2.

The RTOS_Contiki directory must be created in the **share/ccg** path, located in the PragmaDev Studio installation directory.

Translation Script. For the translation of the macros defined in the RTDS_MACRO.h file, a translation script written in Python 3.0, called Contiki.py was developed and included in the RTOS_Contiki directory. The script should run after the translation procedure of PragmaDev Studio has finished.

The translation procedure generates a file called RTDS_gen.ini. This file contains the names of the signals, processes, and states of the SDL system. The translation script iterates over this file in order to use the very same names to define new types for the signals and states using C enumerations. These type definitions are written in a header file named definition.h.

Table 2. Required files for creating a new RTOS integration for PragmaDev Studio.

File	Description
Bricks	Defines static code fragments that are used to generate the C code by PragmaDev Studio. The code fragments are target specific and include such things as header files. For further information see the PragmaDev Reference Manual [15]
RTDS_BasicTypes.h	Defines the C data types used by PragmaDev Studio for basic RTOS concepts such as message queues, tasks, and processes
RTDS_MACRO.h	Defines the macro names used by PragmaDev Studio for basic RTOS concepts such as message queues, tasks, and processes. This file also contains the macro definitions that represent the Behavioral Structure of the SDL language
RTDS_Env.c	For simulation purposes, PragmaDev makes use of an external process that represent the system environment. This file describes the behavior of a default environment process
addrules.mak	References optional rules and files that should be used and included during the building procedure
DefaultOptions.ini	Contains a set of options for the integration and the compilation procedure

The translation procedure also generates an additional file for each SDL process. Each file describes an extended finite state machine that represents the structure of the related SDL process. The base name of the file corresponds to the name of the SDL process. Thus, once the names of these files are identified, the script opens one file at a time and iterates over it, identifying every RTDS_ macro that represents a given SDL graphical symbol, and then applies the appropriate translation rule for the target OS; in this case, a C language construct for Contiki (see Table 3).

Automating Code Generation Using RTOS_Contiki. PragmaDev provides a file called WizardConfig.ini that was edited as shown in Listing 1.2 in order to embed the RTOS_Contiki integration scheme into PragmaDev Studio (see line 2). The file is also included into the RTOS_Contiki directory. Note that the file includes a command line to execute the Python script; see line 5. RTDS_HOME defines the PragmaDev Studio installation directory.

Table 3. Translation rules defined for the RTOS_Contiki script.

PragmaDev textual representation	Contiki translation
RTDS_MSG_RECEIVE_*signal* (*value*);	uint8_t InValue; InValue = *value*;
RTDS_MSG_SEND_*signal*_TO_NAME ("pName", RTDS_process_*pName*, *value*);	uint8_t OutSignal, OutValue; OutSignal = (uint8_t) *signal*; OutValue = *((uint8_t *) data); process_post (& *pName*, OutSignal, & OutValue);
RTDS_SET_TIMER (*T1*, *1000*);	static struct etimer timer_*T1*; etimer_set (& *T1*, *1000*);
RTDS_RESET_TIMER (*T1*);	etimer_stop (& *T1*);

Listing 1.2. WizardConfigwork.ini file to embed the RTOS_Contiki integration scheme into PragmaDev Studio.

```
1  [COMMON]
2  tmpldir=${RTDS_HOME}/share/ccg/RTOS_Contiki
3  beforebuildcmd=
4  cp ${RTDS_HOME}/share/ccg/RTOS_Contiki/Contiki.py Contiki.py;
5  Python3 Contiki.py;
```

5 A Simple Example of Code Generation and Simulation

In order to test the proposed integration scheme, the SDL example systems included with PragmaDev were successfully translated. On the other hand, in general, it is hard to establish a development time using the proposed approach, since it depends on problem complexity and familiarity with SDL. Nevertheless, we strongly believe that using SDL provides a simple manner to model, document and maintain a solution. Besides, by automatically translating the solution to code, there is no need to know all of the details of the target OS used and, by doing the translation that way, it is less likely to make mistakes compared to manually writing the code.

To illustrate the usage of the proposed method, a simple system designed in SDL will be translated into C language for Contiki, by applying the developed RTOS_Contiki integration scheme.

Once the C code for Contiki that represents the SDL system is obtained, it will be simulated in Cooja and some simulation results will be shown.

The example SDL system, which will be named Contiki_Motes, is shown in Fig. 5.

For development purposes a MacBook Pro (Intel i5 running at 2 GHz, 8 GIB RAM, macOS v10.12) was used. Drawing the model using PragmaDev Studio took around 30 min; simulating it needed 5 min. Translating the SDL model into Contiki code using RTOS_Contiki took less than a minute.

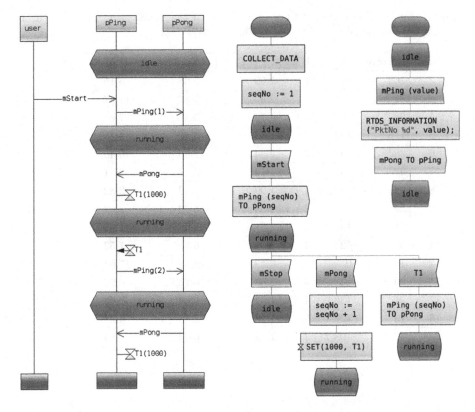

Fig. 5. The SDL sample system `Contiki_Motes`, designed using PragmaDev Studio, has two processes that communicate to each other to exchange a simple message.

For simulation purposes, a 20 SkyMote [1] motes WSN was laid out in a 5x4 mesh. The distance between motes is 30 m and there are no speed limitations in data transmission. The WSN operates on a 2,480 MHz frequency, which corresponds to channel 26 of standard 802.15.4 [11]. The simulation executes the code translated from SDL to C by running the `Contiki_Motes` test system on each mote by emulating a SkyMote.

Configuring the WSN into Cooja took another 10 min. Compiling the Contiki code for a SkyMote took another minute. The simulation of the WSN into Cooja was executed for 30 min to get information about the WSN behavior.

The SDL `COLLECT_DATA` task in the start transition, when parsed by the script, enables the creation of a Contiki process that collects performance information from each mote and sends it to a sink mote, through which the overall performance of the network can be collected.

In this way, Cooja's Sensor Data Collect functionality is able to gather information from the entire network to illustrate aspects of power consumption, average use of the radio transmitter, as well as number of network hops for each message as shown in Table 4 for some of the motes.

Table 4. Information collected from some nodes of the WSN, using Cooja's Sensor Data Collect functionality and the SDL COLLECT_DATA task.

Node	Received	Lost	Hops	CPU Power	Listen power	Transmit power
2	169	21	1	1.69	6.68	5.16
3	61	117	2	2.45	7.89	11.47
4	28	152	3	1.72	5.35	7.04
5	176	11	1	1.43	5.40	4.18
6	38	141	2	2.34	7.86	10.46
7	9	141	3	1.14	3.54	3.77
8	29	144	4	1.09	3.12	3.82
9	59	115	2	2.05	6.79	9.08
10	21	156	3	2.51	8.68	11.68
11	5	62	4	2.02	6.80	7.52
12	1	0	5	3.49	12.35	17.64
13	39	133	3	2.08	6.75	9.20
17	21	133	4	1.67	5.47	7.09
18	13	126	5	1.16	3.48	4.25
Avg	47.79	103.71	3	1.92	6.44	8.03

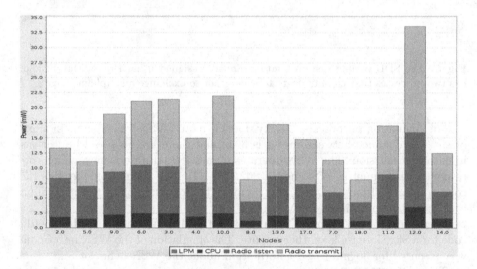

Fig. 6. Average power consumption for the motes in the Contiki_Motes WSN, estimated using Cooja Sensor Data Collect functionality.

To transmit data across the WSN, the COLLECT_DATA process uses the Contiki MAC Radio Duty Cycling Protocol, which is simulated by Cooja. In Fig. 6, power consumption of the WSN is shown in the Cooja interface.

6   Concluding Remarks

This paper presents a method for IoT solutions development based on WSN that involves a codification phase to go from specification to implementation of a design. In order to speed up the codification phase, an integration scheme, called RTOS_Contiki was developed, through which, an SDL model developed in PragmaDev Studio is translated directly to C code using defined translation rules, to be compiled in Contiki and simulated in Cooja.

For the development of the integration schema, it was necessary to identify a pivot language that represents, in textual form, the SDL graphical symbols. Furthermore, by designing target-specific translation rules, the pivot language was used for generating code for Contiki OS, and it could be used as a vehicle for generating code for other RTOS (e.g., RIOT).

Cooja simulator offers features that allow simulating a WSN and the behavior of each node of a network, in both its functional and non-functional aspects. Furthermore, it is possible to measure characteristics of the entire network, such as power consumption, network traffic, among others. A system with these characteristics gives project developers the ability to evaluate designs quickly at low cost.

The proposed method offers to IoT developers the possibility of simulating their designs in Cooja, starting from a graphical SDL design, with no need to manually translate the SDL design in C language, thanks to the RTOS_Contiki integration scheme. Therefore, this feature provides an agile development mechanism, which represents a contribution for the development of IoT solutions based on WSN that eases the deployment of real applications, by introducing a productivity advantage.

Acknowledgement. The authors would like to acknowledge the cooperation of the team at *Centro de Excelencia y Apropiación en Internet de las Cosas – Nodo Occidente*. The CEA-IoT (www.cea-iot.org) is supported by the following institutions: the Colombian Ministry for the Information and Communications Technology (*Ministerio de Tecnologías de la Información y las Comunicaciones - MinTIC*) and the Colombian Administrative Department of Science, Technology and Innovation (*Departamento Administrativo de Ciencia, Tecnología e Innovación - Colciencias*) through the *Fondo Nacional de Financiamiento para la Ciencia, la Tecnología y la Innovación Francisco José de Caldas* (Project ID: FP44842-502-2015).

References

1. Advanticsys: MTM-CM5000-MSP. https://www.advanticsys.com/shop/mtmcm 5000msp-p-14.html
2. Ammar, N., Chaieb, H.: From modeling with SysML to simulation with Contiki Cooja simulator of wireless sensor networks. In: 30th International Conference on Advanced Information Networking and Applications Workshops, pp. 760–765 (2016)
3. Berthomieu, B., Bodeveix, J.P.: Fiacre: an intermediate language for model verification in the topcased environment. In: ERTS (2008)

4. Bozga, M., Graf, S., Mounier, L.: IF-2.0: a validation environment for component-based real-time systems. In: Brinksma, E., Larsen, K.G. (eds.) CAV 2002. LNCS, vol. 2404, pp. 343–348. Springer, Heidelberg (2002). https://doi.org/10.1007/3-540-45657-0_26

5. Braun, T., Christmann, D., Gotzhein, R., Mater, A.: SDL implementations for wireless sensor networks – incorporation of PragmaDev's RTDS into the deterministic protocol stack BiPS. In: Amyot, D., Fonseca i Casas, P., Mussbacher, G. (eds.) SAM 2014. LNCS, vol. 8769, pp. 271–286. Springer, Cham (2014). https://doi.org/10.1007/978-3-319-11743-0_19

6. Chaparadza, R., Prakash, A.: The role of SDL in the design, simulation, validation of system models, and code-generation, in the recently emerged and growing domain of autonomic systems engineering. In: IEEE Globecom, pp. 1013–1018 (2013)

7. Cheong, E., Lee, E.A.: Joint modeling and design of wireless networks and sensor node software. EECS Department, University of California (2006)

8. Deltour, J., Faivre, A., Gaudin, E., Lapitre, A.: Model-based testing: an approach with SDL/RTDS and DIVERSITY. In: Amyot, D., Fonseca i Casas, P., Mussbacher, G. (eds.) SAM 2014. LNCS, vol. 8769, pp. 198–206. Springer, Cham (2014). https://doi.org/10.1007/978-3-319-11743-0_14

9. Dunkels, A., Gronvall, B.: Contiki - a lightweight and flexible operating system for tiny networked sensors. In: 29th Annual IEEE International Conference on Local Computer Networks, pp. 455–462 (2004)

10. Eriksson, J., Österlind, F.: COOJA/MSPSim: interoperability testing for wireless sensor networks. In: Proceedings of the 2nd International Conference on Simulation Tools and Techniques (2009)

11. IEEE: IEEE Std 802.15.4 - IEEE Standard for Low-Rate Wireless Networks. https://standards.ieee.org/findstds/standard/802.15.4-2015.html

12. International Telecommunication Union: Specification and Description Language, Recommendation Z.100. https://www.itu.int/rec/T-REC-Z.100/en

13. Lucero, S., et al.: IoT platforms: enabling the Internet of Things. IHS Technology white paper (2016)

14. Mozumdar, M.M.R., Gregoretti, F.: A framework for modeling, simulation and automatic code generation of sensor network application. In: Sensor, Mesh and Ad Hoc Communications and Networks, pp. 515–522. IEEE (2008)

15. PragmaDev: PragmaDev Studio Reference Manual. www.pragmadev.com/downloads/Manuals/RefManual.pdf

16. Seungjun, Y., Hyojung, J.: Issues and implementation strategies of the IoT industry. In: 10th International Conference on Innovative Mobile and Internet Services in Ubiquitous Computing, pp. 503–508 (2016)

17. Stecklein, J.M., Dabney, J., Dick, B., Haskins, B., Lovell, R., Moroney, G.: Error cost escalation through the project life cycle (2004)

18. Villa, J., Serna, D., Aedo, J.: System-C code generation from UML for wireless sensor networks design. In: International Conference on Modeling, Simulation and Visualization Methods, MSV, vol. 11, pp. 53–60 (2011)

19. Wan, J., Tang, S.: Software-defined industrial internet of things in the context of industry 4.0. IEEE Sens. J. **16**(20), 7373–7380 (2016)

Design and Implementation of a Laboratory Sample Collection System Using an Unmanned Aerial Vehicle (UAV)

Edgar Krejci Garzon[✉], Yesid Diaz Gutiérrez, Manuel Alberto Salgado Alba, and Fernando Agusto Celis Florez

Corporación Unificada Nacional de Educación Superior CUN, Bogotá, Colombia
{edgar_krejci,yesid_Diaz,manuel_Salgado,fernando.Celis}@cun.edu.co

Abstract. The use of innovative technology is available to apply in many ways and in different fields of knowledge, the Horus research group, has focused its efforts implementing solutions, integrating unmanned aerial vehicles known as drones in different areas. The use of drones to perform different tasks is not new, but from the point of view of the Horus research group, it was established that this technology can be applied to analyze different water systems with possible contamination quickly and efficiently, otherwise to collect samples in places where access is difficult it would take more time and money in the process. For that, a system was designed using a drone assembled by the research group with a pumping system, to collect samples for further analysis in laboratory in a way that they are not contaminated using technical standards according to the regulations of the area where they are collect.

Keywords: Drone · Samples · Protocol · UAV

1 Introduction

The use of drones in our society every day is very common, in commercial applications have the potential to dramatically alter several industries, and, in the process, change our attitudes and behaviors and impact our daily lives. The proponents of late modern war argue that it has become surgical, sensitive and scrupulous, and remotely operated Unmanned Aerial Vehicles or 'drones' have become diagnostic instruments in contemporary debates over the conjunction of virtual and 'virtuous' war [1] the implementation of these equipment managed and piloted by certified professionals are essential to solve different problems, where access by land is very difficult, the group research found a problem of water pollution generated in a stream that is located in south of Bogota city called Chiguaza, [2] it causing serious health problems to the student community of a public school, for this reason it is vital to take samples of this water

© Springer Nature Switzerland AG 2018
J. C. Figueroa-García et al. (Eds.): WEA 2018, CCIS 916, pp. 161–172, 2018.
https://doi.org/10.1007/978-3-030-00353-1_14

source to maintain control and prevent pollution affecting the students of the sector.

According to Alenna Otto Many industries can potentially benefit from pilotless technology because it can reduce labor cost. Drones can operate in dangerous environments that would be inaccessible to humans. Furthermore, pilotless technology lowers the weight of theaircraft, and thus its energy consumption, by making the cockpit and environmental systems, which provide air supply, thermalcontrol, and cabin pressurization, unnecessary. Drones do not require roads and can, thus, access locations that are difficult to reach by roads [3].

The project provides information in two areas, first the collection of samples in sterile bottles used according to technical standards of laboratory, during transport recommended refrigeration at 4°C and protection of the Light, especially if it is suspected that the water is contaminated with pathogenic organisms. It is necessary when refrigerating the samples take precautions and necessary measures to prevent any contamination coming from the melted ice [4], so that in a time no more than six hours those samples arrive at the laboratory and could be analyzed, with the purpose of determining the level of contamination existing, After using a web application the data can be sent quickly to the competent authorities so that they take the pertinent actions and prevent this water source from contamination and affect the community that is close to this water tributary.

It is important to highlight that the project intends to provide information for the analysis of the level of toxicity of this water source, where the amount of foam, level of chemical elements harmful to human health, and to be able to give early warnings to the relevant authorities, see Fig. 1.

Fig. 1. Evidence, Chiguaza stream and its level of contamination present in the water source.

The stream descends from the southeastern hills to flow to the river Tunjuelito the hand of man has contributed to the pollution of this water source, adding to it industrial waters, chemical pollution, lead residues, mercury, copper, sand, gravel and other materials coming from the exploitation of subsoil [5].

Along the stream it can be observed that it crosses the Colombia viva school and the Molinos sports center, where the people of this community are affected by bad smells, in addition to respiratory annoyances. Each time rainfall occurs and the flow of the stream increases, mosquito proliferation is generated, which requires constant monitoring and sampling of water in different places with difficult access, for which the use of a Drone it is vital to achieve this goal.

To make this type of sampling, it must be fixed different points in the water tributary to analyze which factors are contributing to regenerate pollutants up to the location point of the living district of Colombia. The Fig. 2 shows the location of this stream and its respective distance.

Fig. 2. Broken path Chiguaza stream source Google Maps, latitude = 4.5, longitude = −74

2   Use of Drones in the Field of Water Sampling

Because of its great versatility in access to bodies of water whose quality control represents some degree of difficulty, unmanned aerial vehicles called drones are a very useful tool during the sampling operation, as the first stage of the chain of custody of samples for the quality control of a body of water. However, the nature of the equipment required for sampling and the drone's load capacity limit the hydrological scenario of operation and, consequently, the type of sampling that can be carried out through said equipment.

Hydrological monitoring is fundamental for the knowledge of the water resource based on which the decisions for its administration and management are supported, according to the criteria of the National Plan for the Integral Management of the Water Resource - PNGIRH. In this sense, the Institute of Hydrology, Meteorology and Environmental Studies, IDEAM, is in charge of establishing the protocols and procedures for quality monitoring of the national water resource as one of its scientist support functions to the Environmental Information System [6].

The IDEAM has made available a Protocol for the Monitoring and Monitoring of Water based on whose types of sampling it is possible to establish the use and potential of a drone for taking water samples from certain water bodies [7]. In this sense, the utility of the equipment is given to the extent that the sample of water taken through the drone represents the quality of the water body from which it comes, as a basis for the validity in the measurement of physicochemical or microbiological parameters whose analysis obtains information to infer possible affectations of natural or anthropic origin on the hydric body. Checking the characteristics of stationary flight and the carrying capacity of a drone, it is feasible to use it for the following types of sampling in accordance with the Protocol for Water Monitoring and Monitoring:

Punctual sample. It is possible to make discrete point intakes of both surface and depth in stationary surface water bodies whose composition does not vary with time, as well as in quasi-stationary surface water bodies whose composition may vary slightly with time, but which are likely to be stabilized or homogenized for a period of 24 h or less through a treatment.

Point sampling allows to obtain water quality status characterizations at a certain geographical point and time, based on which it is possible to configure water body quality histories. Integrated sampling It is possible to integrate several point samples obtained at a geographical point and at a specific moment, but at different depths in the same water column.

Sequential composite sample. It is also possible to obtain a water sample that represents an average quality in a specific period of time, based on the mixture of constant and continuous samples obtained by pumping, or of the mixture of equal volumes of water collected at regular intervals.

Although composite sampling is economical because it requires less samples, it compromises the level of detection of variability of the measurement parameters during the sampling time.

Basic principles for measuring through a drone. The usefulness of an unmanned aerial vehicle (drone) in the field of water analysis from water bodies is only sustainable insofar as the analysis of the samples obtained with this equipment permit measurement values of physicochemical parameters and microbiological statistics equivalent to the results of the analysis of samples taken in identical geographic point conditions and time period by certified personnel in water sampling, in accordance with the Protocol for Water Monitoring and Monitoring.

The validity of the statistical process of homologation of the results of analysis of samples obtained by the drone in comparison with the results obtained by certified personnel, is determined by factors such as the impossibility of completely eliminating errors (spurious and systematic) of measurement in water bodies, which by their nature present considerable fluctuations in the values of the parameters measured in a given period of time, which introduces uncertainty in the calculation of dispersion measures that are the basis for the calculation of probabilities. This implies an estimation of the uncertainty based on the study of the sources of error associated with the measurement when the point samples are independent of each other. However, hydrological observations are not usually independent random variables.

3 Description of the Problem

The procedures for taking water samples require a strict protocol where the sample that is taken must not have any type of contaminant, before and after the procedure, to make these samples requires certified and trained personnel to carry out the process, the times they are critical and to have reliable samples several shots must be taken at different points, that is why it needs to have a system that is easy to use and reliable so that the samples are taken as much as possible on the same day, since a water affluent to be in constant movement the samples tend to change constantly, a typical example is one of the most polluted rivers in the world, the Bogota river one of the most studied, for the process of data collection, is an extensive process and expensive, so the main problem is the delay in these samples and the cost that the process has. The Fig. 3 shows the factor of affectation due to organic contamination of the Bogota River, that

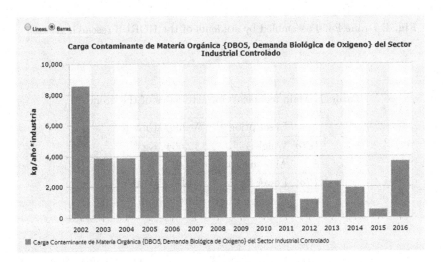

Fig. 3. Polluting load river Bogotá (National observatory source of Bogota).

is why the importance of having more efficient systems of sample collection for faster and more effective results.

4   Design Model Sample Collector

4.1   Unmanned Aerial Vehicle to Be Used

The equipment that was used to make the samples is a DJI F450 kit see Fig. 4, DJI is known mainly for its high-end drones line but it also has a very economical kit that serves to implement prototypes, to mount sensors, the chassis allows mounting all the necessary electronics, autopilot, GPS, brushless motors, [8] which was assembled by the Horus research group, this chassis and equipment has the advantage that can be modified and work to implement any electronic device, to perform Actual tests of the water sample collection device [9].

The great advantage of this equipment is that it serves as the basis for calculating the efficiency of the water collection system, depending on the amount of liquid that needs to be collected, we can implement another drone that supports more payload.

Fig. 4. Drone F450 assembled by students of the HORUS research group.

Table 1. Main technical characteristics of the drone

	Description	Value	Unit
Wto	Weight	12,054	Kg
S	Alar surface	0,749	m^2
Pto	Power	3147	Watt
Lb	Fuselage length	1400	mm

4.2   Characteristics of the Drone

The preliminary calculation of the size is obtained from the study of similar aircraft, and adapting the calculation theory of manned aircraft to the UAV (batteries fixed weight, without crew without life maintenance systems, etc. ...), the weight, and fuselage length, Table 1. And the design point that satisfies the most restrictive actions of the UAV is defined [10].

4.3   Assembly System Sample Collector with Arduino Nano and Mini Brushless Water Pump for DIY Agriculture Drone Spray Gimbal 5 L 10L

According to the advantages we have with the drone, we can assemble a device to operate by radio frequency the mini pump remotely, see Fig. 5. The technical characteristics of the mini pump are in Table 2, using an Arduino nano device to activate the pump. performs programming, to activate the mini pump remotely using a relay to activate the entire device, making previous calculations with the pump is activated 30 s accurate time to fill a sterile collector jar of water samples of 500 Ml.

Table 2. Mini pump technical characteristics

Name: Agricultural drone brushless Water Pump spray/white
Model: 12-420
Weight: 294g
Power: 16W
Operating voltage: 12V
Maximum current: 1.3A
Maximum pressure: 0.45Mpa
Flow: 3L / min
Agricultural drone model:5L/10L
Size: 110 * 90 * 65mm

4.4   Implementation Used to Send a Radio Frequency Signal to the FS-IA6 Device Keeping Un Mind the Radio Electric Spectrum Used in Aeronautics

The FS-IA6 module is a signal receiving device that operates the whole system so that the drone works without problem, using the radio control of the brand FlySky FS-I6 to 2.4 GHz according to the publication drones cheap "If we want Therefore, we must seek a more powerful control which will surely have a greater value, another option is also to look for a remote control that works in the standard frequency of 2.4 GHz, the controls normally used have lower frequencies, can achieve greater range and greater penetration through obstacles. These controls use frequencies in the UHF band, however they are being banned".

water collection prototype

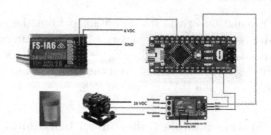

Fig. 5. Receiver connections FS-IA6, to the Arduino nano module, with a relay for activating the pump remotely.

To activate the sample collection system, the available channel 6 is used to activate the sample collection device that is mounted on the drone, for which calculations were made, keeping in mind the current regulations, and the efficiency of the system was determined using the 2.4 GHz frequency.

Using the following equation, which measures the power loss in the free space, it is determined that the most efficient means of transmission with the remote system to activate the collector device is by radio waves.

$$PEA(dB) = 20 \log 10(d) + 20 \log 10(f) + K$$

The formula is interpreted in the following way, the Loss in Free Space is proportional to the square of the distance and also proportional to the square of the frequency [11].

4.5   Process Model 1

The system works in an efficient way for the collection of samples, so that it is not contaminated by external factors while the drone collects them, see Fig. 6; the phases of the process are:

1. Flight Route is programmed.
2. The drone pilot uses Channel 9 of the radio control to activate the device when it reaches the fixed point on the route.
3. The sample is collected according to the calculation of time to fill the container where the sample is stored.
4. The drone returns to the starting point.
5. The technician collects the samples in the container with all the rules to avoid contaminating them.
6. They are sent to the laboratory to process the sample.

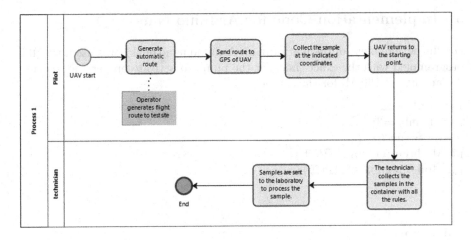

Fig. 6. Process model 1 implementation.

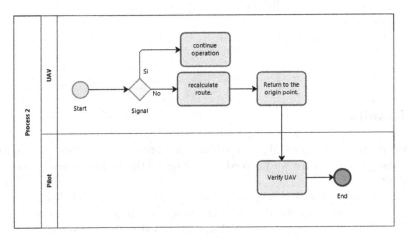

Fig. 7. Process model 2 implementation.

4.6   Process Model 2

In case of loss of signal by the operator, the automatic system of the drone detects that the signal, with the radio control was lost, cancels the mission and returns to the starting point, see Fig. 7.

1. Flight route schedule.
2. It is detected that the signal was lost with the drone.
3. The drone detects communication loss.
4. Automatically the drone return to the starting point.

5 Implementation Code for Arduino Nano

For the development of the platform, an Arduino nano device was used, which is programmed with the exact times for the pump to activate properly and collect the amount of 500 Ml for the sample.

```
int entrada=1;
int bomba=3;
void setup() {
pinMode(entrada ,INPUT);
pinMode(bomba ,OUTPUT);
}


void loop() {
if (digitalRead(entrada)>0){
digitalWrite(bomba ,HIGH);
delay(30000);
digitalWrite(bomba ,LOW);
}
}
```

6 Results

Taking reference to the Chiguaza stream, we proceed to collect the samples using the system, where we proceed according to the technical parameters for sampling.

If it is possible to collect, the 500 Ml of the water system is labeled and stored taking into account the standards for sampling. At the same time a specialized technician collects other samples with the standard procedure used, to be later compared in a laboratory.

It is determined that the efficiency and rapidity in taking samples improves times and, most importantly, being able to collect samples in places where access is very difficult, using drones and the pump system streamlines processes.

According to the data collected, it is evident that, with the collection system, the times for sampling are better than the time used by an environmental technician.

7 Conclusions and Recommendations

The use of unmanned aerial vehicles, facilitates work in places where data collection is very difficult for human personnel, the design of devices using hardware components for the Arduino platform, is very practical and economical for multiple uses, not only for the case that this article deals with if not for different ideas that can help the collection of data in an effective, safe and fast way.

In this sense it is important to consider the current regulation for the use of unmanned aerial vehicles, in the case of Colombia this regulation limits the use of these vehicles, in certain areas of the country, especially in the cities, that is why the solutions are. They must be routed in areas where this regulation allows the use of this technology. In another countries for example Europe the regulation says in a Law Library of Congress text titled Regulation of Drones surveys the rules that apply to the operation of civilian drones in twelve countries, as well as the European Union. The report includes individual country studies on Australia, Canada, China, France, Germany, Israel, Japan, New Zealand, Poland, South Africa, Sweden, Ukraine, and the United Kingdom. It also contains a comparative summary that provides information about the International Civil Aviation Organization's 2011 circular titled Unmanned Aircraft Systems (UAS) (CIR328). The report notes the criteria selected by the surveyed countries and by the EU for implementing a number of operational requirements. Such criteria often include the weight and/or type of use of drones [12].

The research work resulting from this article leads us to make the comparisons of the samples taken by the Drone and by the environmental technician, in this process some data will come out, which will show us if the system does not contaminate the samples taken, and be able to have reliable results to be processed in software platforms.

References

1. Gregory, D.: From a view to a kill: drones and late modern war. Theory Cult. Soc. **28**(7–8), 188–215 (2011). https://doi.org/10.1177/0263276411423027
2. María, A., Velásquez, T.: Lineamientos ambientales para la recuperación de la quebrada Chiguaza en su recorrido por la localidad Rafael Uribe Uribe Bogotá. Universidad de Bogotá Jorge Tadeo Lozano (UJTL), Bogotá D.C. (2010)
3. Otto, A., Agatz, N., Campbell, J., Golden, B., Pesch, E.: Optimization approaches for civil applications of unmanned aerial vehicles (UAVs) or aerial drones: a survey. Networks (2018). https://doi.org/10.1002/net.21818
4. Varón, J.E.: Manual de Instrucciones para la toma, Preservacion y transporte de muestras de agua de consumo humano para muestras de laboratorio, Bogota (2011)
5. Periódico El tiempo, p. e., www.eltiempo.com. Recuperado el 14 de 02 de 2018, de. http://www.eltiempo.com/archivo/documento/MAM-50381. Accessed 21 Feb 1994
6. Guía de Prácticas Hidrológicas, Volumen I, Hidrología - De la medición a la información hidrológica, OMM-N 168, Capítulo 7, p I, 7–6. Métodos de Observación
7. Protocolo para el Monitoreo y Seguimiento del Agua, Instituto de Hidrología, Meteorología y Estudios Ambientales - IDEAM 2007, Capitulos 2 y 3
8. Santana, E.: www.xdrones.es. http://www.xdrones.es/kit-drone/. Accessed 15 Feb 2018
9. Futuro, M.D.: Tomas muestras Hidricas quebrada Chiguaza. Bogota. Obtenido de. https://www.youtube.com/watch?v=3oFlQuQm85E. Accessed 22 June 2017
10. GRUPO UAx UPV. http://uaxupv.blogs.upv.es/diseno-y-fabricacion-de-un-uav-de-diez-kilogramos-de-carga-paga/. Accessed 08 Feb 2018

11. Meléndez, J.E.: http://repositorio.urp.edu.pe. Recuperado el 23 de 3 de 2018, de http://repositorio.urp.edu.pe/bitstream/handle/urp/77/ojeda_je.pdf? sequence=1. Accessed 03 Feb 2008
12. Levush, R.: The Law Library of Congress (2016)

Internet of Things Proposal for Measuring Wind Variables in a Smart Home Environment

Jairo Fernando Gutiérrez, Alvaro David Orjuela-Cañón[(⊠)] [iD],
and Juan Mauricio Garcia

Universidad Antonio Nariño, Bogotá D.C., Colombia
{jaguitierrez, alvorjuela, jm.garcia}@uan.edu.co

Abstract. This work presents a proposal to implement an appliance to get information from wind variables as renewable resource in electrical energy generation. The device is supported on an Arduino application and ThingSpeak tools to obtain important mount of data for future studies of the wind resource. The implemented device is presented from the smart home concepts explained as layers of an Internet of Things approach. Results show as easily this proposition can be developed as an alternative in a smart home environment, where each house can be employed to measure its own wind renewable resources.

Keywords: Internet of Things · Wind speed · Wind direction
Acquisition system

1 Introduction

In the last years, when different alternatives for obtaining electrical energy from clean generation, the photovoltaic and wind sources are though as first options [1, 2]. This has made that for 2015, renewable energy provided an estimated of 19.3% of global final energy consumption and increased the installed capacity in developing countries, according with the Renewable Energy Policy Network for the 21st Century (REN 21) [3]. Thus, new proposals including possibilities of generation inside the urban centers, where the consumption is higher, are promising topics of interest. Applications based on new approaches of hardware and software have augmented the use of technologies for the smart grids. In spite of this, in Colombia electrical energy generation is obtained through hydroelectric plants with a 70%, but with an increment of photovoltaic systems due to new technologies and tendencies [4].

On another hand, currently a new technologic trend called Internet of Things (IoT) is known as a network of physical devices or appliances, which use electronic, software, sensors, actuators and connectivity domains. This has expanded the number of applications inside the cities addressed to smart grids based on IoT [5, 6]. Explanation of this advancement is related with the necessity of getting knowledge about available resources and its importance to manage the generated energy versus consumption, and improve the efficiency of potential sources. The information with this objective is enough useful when

© Springer Nature Switzerland AG 2018
J. C. Figueroa-García et al. (Eds.): WEA 2018, CCIS 916, pp. 173–182, 2018.
https://doi.org/10.1007/978-3-030-00353-1_15

the variables depend on meteorological parameters, as speed wind or solar radiation, which can show a behavior unknown and intermittent [2].

For the improvement of smart grid in terms of getting information, novelty devices and specialized applications demand, more and new technologies to perform the mentioned tasks are exhibited each year. Examples of this can be found in smart metering systems, modern sensing techniques, and advances in information and communication systems [7, 8]. These aspects are relevant and known as demand response management (DRM) for smart grids, where more information is employed to enhance the behavior of the system, based on resources information obtained through data mining techniques.

Based on the exposed motivation, the present proposal introduces a device to collect information from four variables with information of the wind and, in a wireless mode, send the data to a repository in the cloud. Appliance was thought as a application in a home environment, where local connectivity resources can be exploited to implement the system. In this way, each residence can become to know how the behavior of the wind resource helps to generate electricity, and thereby, make a decision about how to project the use of aerogenerators to supply the local power consumption.

Similar works have been employed with comparable proposals and techniques. For example, Rathore *et al.* used a real-time environment monitor in an urban area to analyze meteorological variables [9], but their work had as focus the visualization of multiple sensors and data, having differences with the present proposal in the mode to attempt a home appliance with information in real-time. Also, Guzman *et al.* implemented a weather station to obtain environment information [10]. That study differs of the present proposal in the storage system, which was based on a memory card without a feedback in real-time mode. Saini *et al.* built a system to visualize and generate alerts based on measure from meteorological data [11]. For accomplishing the objective that system was based on Zigbee wireless technology, an Arduino platform and LabView software. Therefore, to develop all operation the device works on personal computer. Finally, Partha *et al.* developed a similar application to measure humidity and temperature in an indoor location based on IoT but, in spite of similarities with the proposal performed here, the objective of the authors was different to the present proposal [6].

This document was divided into four sections. Section two shows the methodology used to elaborate the appliance, which is based on concepts given by Talari to expose the IoT systems [12]. Results are discussed in section three, where physical aspects of the device and obtained data are visualized. Finally, section four presents some conclusions and future work to improve and take advantage of the exhibited implementation.

2 Methodology

According with Talari *et al.* [12], IoT systems can be represented as a structure of three layers (see Fig. 1). First layer represents the sensors that acquire data, then, a network layer, where the communication is described, and finally, an application layer with information about the development can be used. These three layers are described next for developing the description of this proposal.

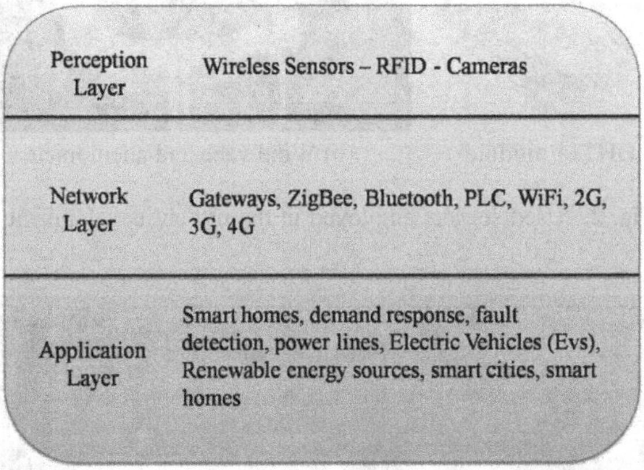

Fig. 1. Three layer for the IoT development according with [12].

2.1 Perception Layer

The perception layer includes a group of devices that allow to perceive, detect objects, obtain or exchange information, providing new opportunities and challenges for smart grid applications [13]. For our case, this layer was settled by four sensors, which capture wind speed, wind direction, temperature and humidity data, located in the Universidad Antonio Nariño – Circunvalar Campus (latitude and longitude 4°38'07.6" N - 74°03'26.3"W) in the eastern hills in Bogota, Colombia. An acquisition system was implemented, based on Arduino MEGA © technology configured to obtain the mentioned variables in a terrace of the highest building, where there is airstream presence.

For capturing the information, an anemometer encodes the wind speed by simply closing a switch with each rotation and a wind vane reports the wind direction as a voltage produced by the resistors combination inside the sensors. This vane holds a magnet allowing up to 16 different positions to be determined. The DHT11 sensor module was used to obtain a calibrated digital output form humidity and temperature. This sensor employs a resistive type component for humidity and NTC type component for temperature, with an 8-bit microcontroller that ensures high reliability, long term stability and fast response. Compatibility with Arduino was the main motivation to make a decision about its employment [6]. All sensors were conditioning to acquire data to a sample period of 15 s (see Fig. 2). This because future studies with data demand this sample rate, according with a previous work related with solar resource [14]. Sensors were connected to the Arduino MEGA (see Fig. 3) to do the acquisition and communication with a server where the data will be stored.

Also, a unit of power supply was implemented for autonomy of the appliance. For this, a solar panel of 20 W was connected to a battery 12v-5Ah charger to warranty that a long period of time for acquisition.

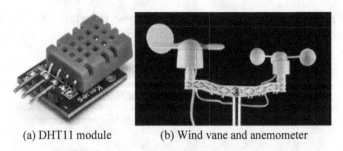

(a) DHT11 module   (b) Wind vane and anemometer

Fig. 2. Used sensors employed in the present development.

Fig. 3. Arduino MEGA employed in the present development.

2.2 Network Layer

Wi-Fi was the technology adopted to develop the communication between perception layer and the server in the present work. The ESP8266 Wi-Fi module, from Espressif Systems was employed for this objective (see Fig. 4). This module is part of different devices designed for IoT, also its capacity to be directly connected to Arduino board was the main reason for use it, which can be programmed to work with or without an additional board.

Home Area Network (HAN) was operated to connect the appliance, which use short-range standard Wi-Fi. In this way, the device can be aggregated to a current network available in an easy mode, where all monitoring and control components in a home are connected by the HAN. This can be used in a home context, according with the objective of this work [15].

Programming of the ESP module was developed using AT commands, where the information was sent to the HAN access point and then to the internet cloud. For this, the communication was established through the Arduino WiFi library with pre-built configuration into the Arduino IDE. IEEE 802.11b/g/n protocol was utilized according with its easy installation, compatibility, and mobility advantages. The protocol defines a frequency of 2.4 GHz with a radius of connectivity around 100 m, appropriated for this work.

Fig. 4. ESP8266 module employed in the present development.

2.3 Application Layer

This layer is related with where the information will be received and visualized. In this way, depends on how is manipulated the information and who is involved with this. Then, this front end could be a smart home, a smart city, a power monitoring system or an integrated of renewable energy system. According with the objective of this work, an application for smart home must de considered. For this, Thingspeak is a web based open Application Programming Interface (API) IoT source information platform [16, 17], that allows to store the sensor data for different IoT applications, at the same time permits a visualization of data as an output in a graphical form at the web level.

Thingspeak employs a communication system based on internet, which allows to establish a connection acting as data packet. Data are stored in the cloud, permitting to process and visualize the information through MATLAB © functions and toolboxes. This tool works with Arduino through the ThingSpeak communication library with pre-built functions that accelerate the process of its implementation. For this, it is necessary to create an API key specific for the user and then, it is possible to build the layout with a particular number of variables to exhibit.

3 Results

The entire system was installed in a plastic shield with resistance to the environment conditions. Figure 5 shows the subsystems placed in the shield. Battery can be seen at the bottom and a regulator connected to the solar panel is at the top. On the left side the Arduino board and an auxiliary board for power supply subsystem connections can be observed. Finally, on the right side there is a battery charger that can be plugged to the electrical network. The appliance located and working is exhibit in Fig. 6. It is possible to see the physical implementation of the sensors and the center unit in the plastic shield.

Data obtained with the present proposal are available to the general public in the channel 440743 of the ThingSpeak tool (https://thingspeak.com/channels/440743). Figure 7 visualizes the layout of the data in the ThingSpeak web for the speed and direction of the wind, humidity and temperature.

Figure 8 shows the time series for an acquisition obtained during a week. It is possible to see the behavior or the wind through the mentioned variables. Temperature evidence the daily cycle, exhibiting the peak values at noon of each day. The humidity has a behavior up 50% most of the time, and for the speed and direction of the wind, its performance has stochastic movements. Analysis of the time series is out of the scope of the present work, for this reason deeper studies were not developed to understand the meteorological phenomena.

An analysis of the speed data was developed, where the time series was cleaned from outliers and missing values. For this, values outer than a maximum of 16 m/s approximately because higher estimates cannot be seen in the Bogota city. Also, the values were normalized into interval [0, 1], through the formula:

$$y_{normalized} = \frac{y_i - y_{min}}{y_{max} - y_{min}} \tag{1}$$

where y_i is the original value, y_{min} is the minimum and y_{max} is the maximum value of the time series. Figure 9 shows the normalized time series for a week horizon. This information will be useful to design forecasting models of this variable in analogous way to work developed in [14].

Fig. 5. Appliance in a plastic shield.

Fig. 6. Autonomous appliance located in measurement place.

Fig. 7. Visualization of the four variables in the ThingSpeak platform.

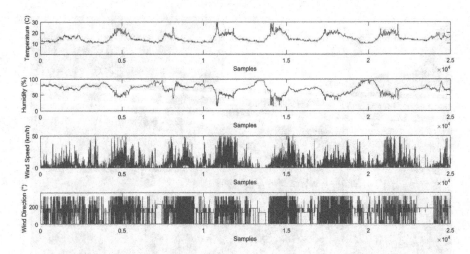

Fig. 8. Time series of the four variables acquisition during a week.

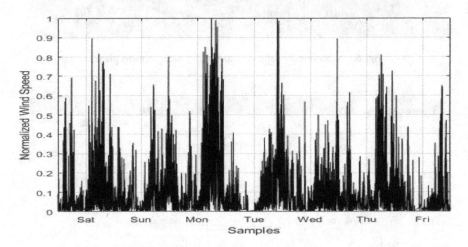

Fig. 9. Time series of the normalized wind speed.

4   Conclusions and Future Work

The result of the present proposal allowed to obtain a huge volume of data from information about temperature, humidity, wind speed and wind direction, that are useful for future analysis of this wind renewable resource. Processing and analyzing these data can reveal deeper insights to make a decision that an expert does to improve the projection of the use of aerogenerators for electrical energy supply for a home application.

The implemented appliance can be seen as a technology to collect massive amounts of data is available today, where process of efficient managing for information extraction is useful for making decisions.

Data acquisition was developed with periods of time in seconds. For this reason the Arduino platforms and tools were advantageous to complete the objective of getting data. Also, additional devices and sensors available in the market allow to develop the appliance, causing that the research activities can be centered in the analysis of data.

As future work and in the same direction of measure meteorological variables, radiation information can be added to the system to obtain a map of the resources most employed to generate electricity in our country.

Acknowledgments. Authors thank to Universidad Antonio Nariño, which through the entitled project "Design and implementation of a intelligent management system to optimize the resources of a microgrid" with code 2017211 was a financial support for this work.

References

1. Hakuta, K., Masaki, H., Nagura, M., Umeyama, N., Nagai, K.: Evaluation of various photovoltaic power generation systems. In: 2015 IEEE International Telecommunications Energy Conference (INTELEC), pp. 1–4 (2015)
2. Zhao, H., Wu, Q., Hu, S., Xu, H., Rasmussen, C.N.: Review of energy storage system for wind power integration support. Appl. Energy **137**, 545–553 (2015)
3. Sawin, J.L., et al.: Renewables 2017 Global Status Report (2017)
4. Olaya, Y., Arango-Aramburo, S., Larsen, E.R.: How capacity mechanisms drive technology choice in power generation: the case of Colombia. Renew. Sustain. Energy Rev. **56**, 563–571 (2016)
5. Rathore, M.M., Ahmad, A., Paul, A., Rho, S.: Urban planning and building smart cities based on the internet of things using big data analytics. Comput. Netw. **101**, 63–80 (2016)
6. Ray, P.P.: Internet of things cloud enabled MISSENARD index measurement for indoor occupants. Measurement **92**, 157–165 (2016)
7. Siano, P.: Demand response and smart grids: a survey. Renew. Sustain. Energy Rev. **30**, 461–478 (2014)
8. Gelazanskas, L., Gamage, K.A.A.: Demand side management in smart grid: a review and proposals for future direction. Sustain. Cities Soc. **11**, 22–30 (2014)
9. Rathore, P., Rao, A.S., Rajasegarar, S., Vanz, E., Gubbi, J., Palaniswami, M.: Real-time urban microclimate analysis using internet of things. IEEE Internet Things J. **5**(2), 500–511 (2017)
10. Guzman, B.Y.G., Ceron, M.F.R., Cubides, H.E.R., Patarroyo, D.J.R.: Design and implementation of a prototype of an automatic weather station for the measurement of Eolic and solar energy resource. In: Figueroa-García, J.C., López-Santana, E.R., Villa-Ramírez, J.L., Ferro-Escobar, R. (eds.) WEA 2017. CCIS, vol. 742, pp. 108–118. Springer, Cham (2017). https://doi.org/10.1007/978-3-319-66963-2_11
11. Saini, H., Thakur, A., Ahuja, S., Sabharwal, N., Kumar, N.: Arduino based automatic wireless weather station with remote graphical application and alerts. In: 2016 3rd International Conference on Signal Processing and Integrated Networks (SPIN), pp. 605–609 (2016)

12. Talari, S., Siano, P., Loia, V., Tommasetti, A., Catalão, J., et al.: A review of smart cities based on the internet of things concept. Energies **10**(4), 421 (2017)
13. Jaradat, M., Jarrah, M., Bousselham, A., Jararweh, Y., Al-Ayyoub, M.: The internet of energy: Smart sensor networks and big data management for smart grid. Procedia Comput. Sci. **56**, 592–597 (2015)
14. Orjuela-Cañón, A.D., Hernández, J., Rivero, C.R.: Very short term forecasting in global solar irradiance using linear and nonlinear models. In: 2017 IEEE Workshop on Power Electronics and Power Quality Applications (PEPQA), pp. 1–5 (2017)
15. Stojkoska, B.L.R., Trivodaliev, K.V.: A review of Internet of Things for smart home: challenges and solutions. J. Clean. Prod. **140**, 1454–1464 (2017)
16. Maureira, M.A.G., Oldenhof, D., Teernstra, L.: ThingSpeak–an API and Web Service for the Internet of Things. World WideWeb (2011). http://www.Mediat.chnology.leiden.edu/images/uploads/docs/wt2014_thingSpeak.pdf. Accessed 7 Nov 2015
17. Pasha, S.: ThingSpeak based sensing and monitoring system for IoT with matlab analysis. Int. J. New Technol. Res. **2**, 19–23 (2016)

Design of Urban Mobility Services for an Intermediate City in a Developing Country, Based on an Intelligent Transportation System Architecture

Ricardo Salazar-Cabrera[1](✉) ⓘ and Álvaro Pachón de la Cruz[2]

[1] University of Cauca, Popayán, Colombia
ricardosalazarc@unicauca.edu.co
[2] University ICESI, Cali, Colombia
alvaro@icesi.edu.co

Abstract. Problem: Services that use ICT (Information and Communications Technologies) have been developed to improve the mobility in cities; however, especially in developing countries, these services are not often based on adequate reference architectures, such as ITS (Intelligent Transport Systems) architectures, which prevent integration and interoperability. Objective: Propose a development process for the design of mobility services in an intermediate city of a developing country, based on an ITS architecture formulated particularly considering context. Methods: The reference ITS architectures and the particular context of a Colombian intermediate city are reviewed, in order to identify which is the best process to adapt an ITS architecture to these type of cities. With the process identified, the ITS architecture for *Popayán* (Colombian intermediate city) is designed and finally, the design of the services based on it, is carried out. Results: The methodology developed for the design of the ITS architecture and the architecture designed particularly for *Popayán* are summarized. Following, the design of two mobility services ("Public transport vehicle tracking" and "Traffic measurement") for that city based on architecture is detailed. Conclusions: The particular environment of an intermediate city and its priorities allows to determine the services to select for its ITS architecture from a reference architecture. ITS architecture development of a city allows the incremental development of services that really improve their mobility in a sustainable manner.

Keywords: Intelligent Transport Systems · Urban mobility · ITS architecture
Mobility services · Mobility in developing countries

1 Introduction

Traffic accidents are the most important causes of death in the world, and the main cause of death among people between 15 years and 29 years [1]. Besides, mortality rates in low-income countries are more than double compared to high-income countries [1].

© Springer Nature Switzerland AG 2018
J. C. Figueroa-García et al. (Eds.): WEA 2018, CCIS 916, pp. 183–195, 2018.
https://doi.org/10.1007/978-3-030-00353-1_16

Colombia has presented in the last 10 years, considerable problems in terms of the number of traffic accidents and deceased persons, which have a marked tendency to increase [2]. In addition, there is a marked difference between the death rates of some cities in the country. In some of the intermediate cities of the country (population between 100,000 and 1,000,000 inhabitants such as *Pasto, Popayán, Ibagué, Cúcuta, Armenia, Pereira, Santa Marta, and Neiva*) the average of death rates due to traffic accidents is almost 50% more than the values of the main cities.

In cases involving deaths, disobedience to traffic rules caused the greatest number of accidents in Colombia (42%), followed by speeding (32%) and possible mechanical failures (8%) [3].

In addition to the loss of lives caused by traffic accidents and the other harmful consequences these generate related to the road safety of the city, there are other problems related to mobility in cities such as high traffic congestion.

The data of traffic congestion in cities worldwide, are measured by different international organizations, among the most recognized are: "Tom Tom Traffic Index" [4] (which does not have data of Colombian cities) and "Inrix Global Traffic Score Card" [5]. The "Inrix Global Traffic Score Card" indicates that *Bogotá*, capital city of Colombia, is ranked sixth in the ranking, with a total of 75 annual hours that travelers spend in congestion. In same report, some intermediate Colombian cities are included, with values between 45 and 27 h that travelers spend in congestion.

In search of a solution for problems of road safety and high traffic in these cities, a large number of intelligent mobility services have been developed, however, very few of these services have been developed based on an adequate reference architecture, as Intelligent Transport System (ITS) architecture is for mobility services.

Intelligent Transportation Systems (ITS) are defined as: "the application of advanced technologies in sensors, computers, communications, and management strategies to improve the safety and efficiency of the land transportation system" [6].

An architecture defines a framework within which a system can be built. An architecture defines "what" should be done, not "how" it will be done [6]. An ITS architecture is a system architecture created for the ITS domain. It consists of several descriptions of the system, each one concentrating on specific sets of characteristics [7]. Once, the ITS architecture of the city is obtained, it is necessary to discuss the technologies that will be used for the design and develop of the mobility services.

When mobility services are developed in a city, without an adequate ITS architecture, it may be that the services meet well with the specific objective that these were created, however, it's very possible, their infrastructure and/or functionality is not adequately integrated, nor does it interoperates with other mobility services.

The main developed countries of the world (United States, European Union and Japan, among others) have taken initiative in development of ITS architectures. Many other countries (developing countries mainly), have created their own national ITS architectures based on these architectures. Although many developing countries have ITS architectures (including Colombia), the cities have not taken this architecture into account for the development of their services, very likely because the government entities do not promote their use adequately.

The purpose of this paper is to present a process for the design of mobility services in an intermediate city of a developing country, based on an ITS architecture that takes into account the particular context of the city and also using adequate enabling technology and standards of communication to provide these services. The proposal presented was applied to the city of *Popayán* (Colombian intermediate city), designing two mobility services that try to improve the identified problems of road safety and traffic management, trying to avoid the mentioned causes that generate them. The service "public transport vehicle tracking" will allow control of the speed of these vehicles and compliance with other traffic laws, in an attempt to minimize the number of accidents of these vehicles. The service "traffic measuring" will allow provide users and drivers with valuable information (speed on the route mainly) so that they can make travels more efficiently, additionally, they will be able to avoid increasing traffic at a certain crossroad, making use of said information.

In the following sections, related previous works are described; later, it is presented the process carried out to propose the methodology and the design of services; the document continues with description of results obtained, presenting a summary of the methodology designed for the development of ITS architecture, the ITS architecture of an intermediate city in particular (*Popayán*), and the design of services for this city; finally the discussion and conclusions are presented.

2 Related Works

2.1 ITS as a Solution for Problems of Road Safety and High Level of Traffic

ITS have contributed considerably in the development of solutions that improve road safety conditions and traffic worldwide. Since the 1970 s, countries such as the United States, Japan, European Union and South Korea have implemented solutions (in collaboration with vehicle manufacturers) that allow communication between vehicles and road infrastructure, or between vehicles, to try to improve traffic and safety [8].

In addition, ITS services have been developed for traffic analysis using computer vision techniques; this field on ITS allows automatic monitoring objectives such as congestion, traffic rule violation, and vehicle interaction [9].

The safety of cyclists and pedestrians on the road, who are some of the most vulnerable users, has also been an approach to developments in ITS. For this, systems have been used to allow interaction (through technology) between bicycles and vehicles, or the detection of pedestrians on the road [10].

2.2 Design of Regional ITS Architectures

Yokota and Weilland formulated a proposal to implement an ITS architecture in developing countries [11]. The authors presented four (4) criteria in the construction of architecture: affordability, regional compatibility, geopolitics and technical aspects.

The proposal was presented more than twelve years ago and versions of the architectures evaluated have been updated. In addition, although criteria are mentioned to be considered in the specification of the architecture and a basic process is proposed, a clear and detailed methodology for the design of the ITS architecture is not established. Nor is there an example of application of the criteria and the proposed process.

United States Department of Transportation presented a proposal in 2006 to "develop, use, and maintain a regional ITS architecture" [12]. In the document, six steps are established for these activities in ITS architecture. In [12], although some aspects are still valid for the development of a regional architecture, its application is limited exclusively to American architecture, excluding the possibility of incorporating other relevant aspects of other reference architectures.

FRAME architecture (European ITS architecture) is referenced for the development of a regional architecture [13]. The document proposes certain steps to get from the needs of the stakeholders to the views of the architecture. As mentioned with respect to [12], in [13] the regional ITS architecture that can be designed will be focused exclusively on the reference architecture (FRAME), additionally, the context of said reference architecture is very different from the context in this work.

With respect to the national reality, the country has an initiative called ITS Colombia national architecture [14]. The national architecture ITS is an adaptation (in 2010) of the American architecture, which unfortunately no updates have been made and no research work was found based on that architecture.

In a local project, a model for the development of ITS services for Colombian cities used the national ITS architecture and alternatives to the methodological support described in American architecture [15]. The work focused mainly on the development of a service model, however, it did not present a methodology for designing a particular ITS architecture for an intermediate city, as it is intended done in this work.

2.3   Implementation of Mobility Services Based on ITS Architectures

In a reviewed project was developed a prototype for ITS, which is useful to track a public service vehicle through GPS, receive payment of tickets, analyze crowds within said bus and finally, measure the environment inside the bus [16]. In the IoT (Internet of Things) infrastructure proposed in this project, the data collected from the sensors are sent through Internet and processed by the monitoring system to make useful decisions and send them to the visualization system. After defining the proposed system (for an intelligent bus) and its architecture, an ITS is proposed through the exploitation of the smart bus technology and the IoT infrastructure.

In [17] another development of an ITS, a system responsible for intelligent parking assistance based on IoT, is presented. Parking assistance, in the system proposed is provided by the following steps: sensors detect whether a parking space is occupied and transmit data to the central server. The smartphone app requests a parking space and guides drivers to that free space. The parking fee is paid directly through the smartphone application.

INTEL proposed the construction of another ITS, with the use of IoT [18]. The proposed architecture has three (3) main layers: sensing layer, communication layer and service layer. The sensing layer uses a "vehicle terminal" that interacts with the conductors and acts as a "gateway" for the technology inside the vehicle and the sensors. The communications layer ensures real-time, secure, and reliable transmission from a "vehicle terminal" to the service layer. The service layer supports various applications using various technologies such as "cloud computing", "data analytics", and information and data processing.

In the last documents presented [16–18], some ITS proposals based on enabling technology (mainly IoT) are presented, however, none of them is based on an ITS architecture that is taken as reference, which makes it difficult to develop related services in a sustainable way, integration and interoperability. In addition, the proposals (with the exception of [18]) are focused on solving a specific mobility problem, they do not present a proposal that can be applied to any of the smart mobility domains.

3   Methods

3.1   Development of a Methodology for the Design of an ITS Architecture

For this initial objective (ITS architecture for these cities), some activities were carried out, such as: the study of the most representative international reference ITS architectures (American, European, Asian, Colombian), the analysis of the environment of the city through the PESTLE tool (Politic, Economic, Social, Technological, Legal, and environment aspects) that is a business analysis technique [19], and the study of methodologies for the development of a regional ITS architecture.

In the design process of the ITS architecture, it was identified that it was convenient to integrate in a coherent, systemic, and orderly way, these non-articulated pieces, through a methodology for the formulation of the ITS architecture. Besides, it was determined by the authors that it was useful for similar works in other intermediate cities of the country (Colombia) or for intermediate cities in developing countries.

Therefore, the stages of the methodology were designed including: the inputs, the activities that must be developed; the techniques and tools that can be used to execute the activities of each stage; and finally, the outputs, which constitute the deliverables resulting of the execution of the activities of each stage. The use of inputs, tools and outputs, were taken as a good practice used in the description of project management methodologies of the PMI (Project Management Institute) and Scrum.

Once the aforementioned methodology was developed, its application was made for the final formulation of the ITS architecture for the city of *Popayán*.

3.2   Design of Services Based on the ITS Architecture Developed for *Popayán*

At this point, once the ITS architecture for the city has been designed, the technologies are evaluated, because the architecture was the "what" should be done, and the design and implementation are the "how".

We initially proceeded to identify the most appropriate enabling technologies for the implementation of ITS, for which the information collected in the previous related works was used. It was determined that the IoT is being considered in the proposed solutions for an "intelligent city" allowing the ITS architecture to materialize, guaranteeing that services are developed and provided to the citizen or the end user [20].

The IoT architectures of international reference were subsequently identified and different options for implementing a system using IoT technology were evaluated for the city. From the reviewed IoT architectures [21–26], it was established that the most complete architecture is that presented by the IoT- A (IoT Architecture [25]).

Once the appropriate IoT architecture was defined to implement a system in the city, we proceeded to validate whether this architecture fits well for the implementation of the ITS with the architecture determined for the city of *Popayán*. When validation was done, it was determined what mobility services would be implemented.

We determined as an adequate project scope, to design two mobility services. The following aspects (related with principal causes of traffic accidents in Colombia, reviewed before) were taken into account in the comparison and evaluation of services: improvement of road safety, relationship with traffic management, utility of the service for the end user (according to our concept), and complexity (in terms of hardware and software required, actors involved and development time).

As a result of service evaluation, selected services were: "public transport vehicle tracking" (identified with PT01) and "traffic measurement" (TM05). The design developed of the first service is presented in the following section of this report.

4   Results

4.1   Methodology for the Development of an ITS Architecture

A resume of the four stages of our methodology is presented below.

Review of the Reference ITS Architectures. In Fig. 1, the inputs, tools and outputs of the first stage are presented (as an example of what was done in each of the stages). At this stage it is necessary to carry out a systematic review of the updated versions of representative architectures at the international level, the standards, the national architecture of the assessed country and the regional (or city) architectures designed in the country. The review requires a critical comparative analysis of the service areas that each one covers, verifying that the services of interest to the city are included.

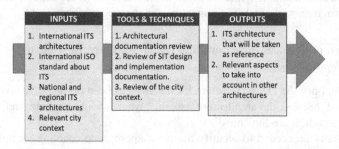

Fig. 1. Inputs, tools and techniques and outputs of stage 1.

Analysis of the Context of the City. The inputs of this stage are: methodologies for development of regional reference architectures and the context of the city in its broadest sense. As tool of the stage, in addition to the review of regional method-ologies, context analysis tool called PESTLE is used. As a result, special considerations of city context are obtained, which allow to determine the components of the ITS architecture.

Determination of Architecture Components. The specific components that allow to establish the ITS architecture of the city depend on the selected base architecture. The most commonly used international reference architectures (such as the American or European one) consider a set of components of the ITS architecture; stakeholders and processes in the functional view; physical objects and subsystems in the physical view.

Design of Views of the ITS Architecture. With components of the ITS architecture of the city and the identified objective services, this stage propose designing of the views that describe architecture. The functional and physical views are usually designed, although views considered necessary can be added to clarify as much as possible.

4.2   Development of the ITS Architecture for *Popayán*, Following Methodology

The methodology described was applied for the city of *Popayán* (Colombian inter-mediate city with problems in road safety and traffic) as a case for the project.

For the determination of the reference ITS architecture, a comparison was made between the American ITS architecture ARC-IT [6], the FRAME architecture [27], the architecture of Malaysia [28], the ISO proposal [29] and Colombian architecture [14]. Sixteen services areas were considered with respect to five ITS architectures. The architecture with largest number of covered areas was the American.

After reviewing documentation of the architectures and the context of the city, it was confirmed that the more suitable ITS architecture was the American architecture (2017). Two service areas of another architectures were added as complements.

The PESTLE tool was used to identify the particular conditions that were relevant in the design of the ITS architecture. In this analysis, aspects such as extension (512 km^2) and inhabitants (approximately 400,000) were taken into account to have an idea of the required ITS dimension; the economic activities of the city, to determine the type of companies (*Popayán* is no industrial city); the laws and regulations at the national and regional level regarding ITS; the traffic safety and traffic management statistics of the city; and the conditions of the current public transport system.

The tools suggested by the methodology were used to identify the most relevant stakeholders and their needs. Later, a priority analysis of their needs were done, reducing the number to 17 needs, among them: reduction of accident rate, compliance with traffic regulations by drivers and pedestrians, and traffic information at critical points.

For determination of service packages considered in the ITS architecture for *Popayán*, prioritized needs of stakeholders and special considerations identified in the context of the city were taken into account. Finally, 35 service packages (33 selected from more than 100 service of ITS American reference architecture and 2 more from other architectures) were taken into account for the ITS architecture for *Popayán*.

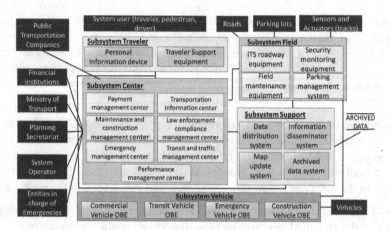

Fig. 2. Physical view, general ITS architecture of *Popayán* (adapted from ARC-IT [6]).

Then, each one of the components (functional and physical) of the architecture was identified. With these components, the views of the ITS architecture were designed. The functional view allows identify the selected processes and relationships between these processes. For general physical view of the architecture (obtained from functional view) presented in Fig. 2, the actors of the system, the subsystems, and the physical objects are taken into account. The general physical view (adapted from ARC-IT physical view) allows visualizing proposed "subsystems" and, within each subsystem, the physical objects that it includes. Through them, the selected services are provided.

The advantages of the proposed methodology and its application in the city of *Popayán*, with respect to the reference ITS architectures and their application methodologies, are presented in the discussion and conclusions of this document.

4.3   Design of Intelligent Mobility Services for the City of *Popayán*

As previously mentioned, for the design of mobility services, the facilitating technologies were first identified to implement the ITS architecture of the city of *Popayán* and it was determined that the IoT was the adequate technology to do so.

With the adequate IoT architecture to implement a system (based in [25] mainly), an ITS architecture adapted to the IoT technology was obtained (presented in Fig. 3).

As previously mentioned, two services were selected (PT01 and TM05) to perform its detailed design, according to the parameters previously indicated. To define the "detailed diagram" of each service, the architecture presented in Fig. 3 was taken into account, to determine which objects should be considered and what changes should be made. In addition, the diagrams of the physical architecture proposed by ARC-IT (main reference architecture) were reviewed (as presented in Fig. 4 for service PT01).

The "detailed diagram" for the service "PT01" is presented as an example in Fig. 5.

Next, physical and logical objects, from each "detailed diagram" of the services, were described, presenting the specific functionality to be developed. In addition, it was determined with what elements (hardware, software, communications, interactions) the service could be designed. With elements and functionality described, the "specific

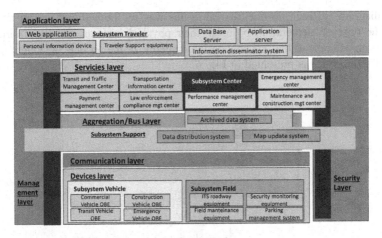

Fig. 3. ITS architecture adapted to IoT, developed using physical view (Fig. 2) adapted to [25].

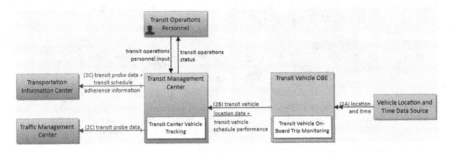

Fig. 4. Detailed physical architecture of PT01 service. Source: ARC-IT [6].

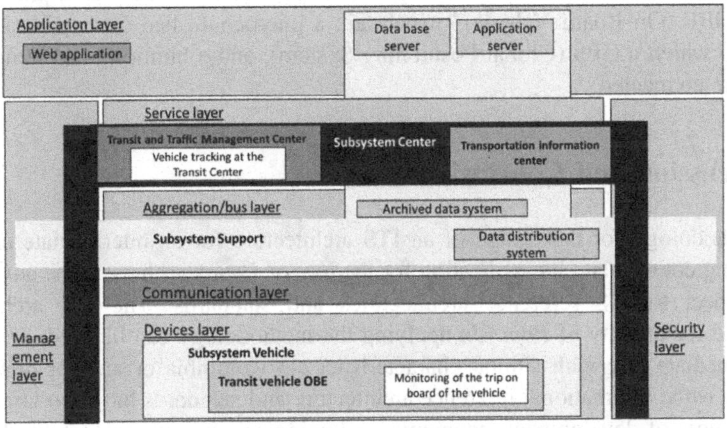

Fig. 5. "Detailed diagram" of the service "PT01".

design diagram" of each service (named in this way by the authors) was made, indicating the type of elements to be used, their physical location and the information
flows. As an example of the "specific design diagram" of the service, the diagram made
for the PT01 service is presented in Fig. 6.

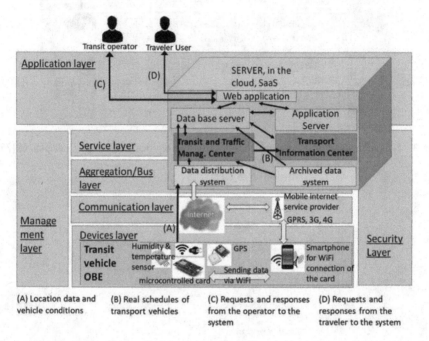

Fig. 6. "Specific design diagram" of the service "Public transport vehicle tracking". Developed
by authors using "detail diagram" (Fig. 5) and selected technology.

From Fig. 6 it is important to highlight the hardware elements used in the "Transit
vehicle OBE (On Board Vehicle)" which are: a microcontrolled card (with access to
Wi-Fi) to which a GPS (Global Positioning System), and a humidity and temperature
sensor are connected.

5   Discussion and Conclusions

Our methodology for the design of an ITS architecture for an intermediate city of a
developing country and its application for the city of *Popayán*, have some advantages
with respect to ITS reference architectures and standards. The ITS architecture
developed for the city of *Popayán* applying the methodology can be used directly for
an intermediate city with similar characteristics (in Colombia or another developing
country); while international reference architecture and standards have too large scope
and a context of development (economic, technological and cultural) totally different.

If the intermediate city (of a developing country), for which it is wanted to design an ITS architecture, has some characteristics that differ considerably from the city that is taken as an example (*Popayán*), it is possible use the proposed methodology to develop another version of ITS architecture that will be more adjusted to the context. The use of the methodology proposes the revision of several reference ITS architectures, not just one, which allows to use the best features of each one. Additionally, the detailed analysis of the city context allows an adequate and focused reduction of the services and components of the architecture.

The detailed process for the design of mobility services using the recommended IoT technology can be used starting from ITS architecture designed for *Popayán* (if it applies) or from another ITS architecture that is designed more precisely.

It should be considered that although the design of mobility services is a significant step, the development process of these services and operation tests is very important, to evaluate if the architecture developed for the city meets the requirements and allows obtaining services really integrated and interoperable.

As conclusions of the work we have that the identification and consideration of the particular conditions of an intermediate city of a developing country is a fundamental step to formulate an adequate ITS architecture, because it determines some important restrictions to be taken into account, among which are the selected services. Besides, a city that makes an incremental deployment of its portfolio of mobility services requires a reference architecture that allows the integration and interoperability of services.

The city of *Popayán* has a large number of challenges regarding mobility; among others, the road infrastructure is necessary to improve and expand it, the new means of public transport must be implemented, and compliance with traffic regulations to be improved. Some of these challenges can be achieved with help of mobility services, for which it is relevant to be able to continue with works related to the subject.

As future work is expected that a pilot of the services designed be developed, in a controlled environment. Besides, the collected data and results obtained must be presented with the aim of contributing to improvement of mobility of the city, which can result in the reduction of current traffic accident rates and an improvement of traffic.

References

1. World Health Organization, report on the world situation of road safety 2015. http://www.who.int/violence_injury_prevention/road_safety_status/. Accessed 12 July 2017
2. National Institute of Legal Medicine and Forensic Sciences, Comportamiento de muertes y lesiones en los accidentes de tránsito, Colombia (2015). http://www.medicinalegal.gov.co/documents/20143/49523/Accidentes+de+transporte+primera+parte.pdf. Accessed 10 Apr 2018
3. National Institute of Legal Medicine and Forensic Sciences, Muertes y lesiones no fatales en accidentes de tránsito, Colombia (2011). http://www.medicinalegal.gov.co/documents/20143/49511/Accidentes+De+Transito.pdf. Accessed 10 Apr 2018
4. Tom Tom Traffic Index. https://www.tomtom.com/. Accessed 12 Apr 2018
5. Inrix Global Traffic Score Card. http://inrix.com/scorecard/. Accessed 12 Apr 2018
6. National ITS Architecture. http://local.iteris.com/arc-it/. Accessed 28 Oct 2017

7. Jesty, P., Bossom, R.: Why do you need an ITS architecture? European and national perspectives. In: 4th European Congress on ITS and Services (2004)
8. An, S., Lee, B.-H., Shin, D.-R.: A survey of intelligent transportation systems. In: 2011 Third International Conference on Computational Intelligence, Communication Systems and Networks, pp. 332–337. IEEE (2011). https://doi.org/10.1109/cicsyn.2011.76
9. Buch, N., Velastin, S.A., Orwell, J.: A review of computer vision techniques for the analysis of urban traffic. IEEE Trans. ITS **12**, 920–939 (2011)
10. Silla, A., et al.: Can cyclist safety be improved with intelligent transport systems? Accid. Anal. Prev. **105**, 134–145 (2017)
11. Yokota, T., Weiland, R.: ITS System Architectures For Developing Countries (2004). http://siteresources.worldbank.org/EXTROADSHIGHWAYS/Resources/ITSNote5.pdf. Accessed 15 Mar 2018
12. U.S. Department of Transportation. Regional ITS architecture guidance: Developing, using, and maintaining an ITS architecture for your region (2006). https://ops.fhwa.dot.gov/publications/regitsarchguide/. Accessed 21 Nov 2017
13. Jesty, P.H., Bossom, R.A.P.: Using the FRAME architecture for planning integrated intelligent transport systems. In: 2011 IEEE Forum on Integrated and Sustainable Transportation Systems, pp. 370–375. IEEE (2011). https://doi.org/10.1109/fists.2011.5973610
14. Consensus Systems Technologies (ConSysTec). Arquitectura Nacional ITS de Colombia. http://www.consystec.com/colombia/web/. Accessed 13 Nov 2017
15. Pachón, Á., Liscano, T., Montoya, D.: Service development model in ITS for Colombian Cities. Sistemas Telemática **13**(34), 31–48 (2015)
16. Bojan, T., Kumar, U., Bojan, V.: An internet of things based intelligent transportation system. In: 2014 IEEE International Conference on Vehicular Electronics and Safety, pp. 174–179 (2014). https://doi.org/10.1109/icves.2014.7063743
17. Rajesh, A., Pavansai, D.V.: Internet of things based smart transportation systems. Int. J. Res. Appl. Sci. Eng. Technol. (IJRASET) **4**(XI) (2016). IC Value: 13.98 ISSN 2321-9653. https://www.ijraset.com/fileserve.php?FID=5897. Accessed 14 Sept 2017
18. INTEL Corporation, Building and Intelligent Transportation System with The Internet Of Things, Solution Blueprint, Internet Of Things (2014). https://www.intel.com/content/www/us/en/internet-of-things/blueprints/iot-building-intelligent-transport-system-blueprint.html. Accessed 08 Feb 2018
19. Bush, T.: PESTLE analysis: everything you need to know (2016). http://pestleanalysis.com/pestle-analysis-everything-you-need-know/internal-pdf://0.0.0.225/pestle-analysis-everything-you-need-know.html. Accessed 12 Aug 2017
20. ITU-T Focus Group on Smart Sustainable Cities. An overview of smart sustainable cities and the role of information and communication technologies. Focus Group Technical Report (2014). https://www.itu.int/en/ITU-T/focusgroups/ssc/Documents/Approved_Deliverables/TR-Overview-SSC.docx. Accessed 21 Oct 2017
21. Ji, Z., Ganchev, I., O'Droma, M.: A generic IoT architecture for smart cities. In: 25th IET Irish Signals & Systems Conference 2014 and 2014 China-Ireland International Conference on Information and Communities Technologies (ISSC 2014/CIICT 2014), pp. 196–199. Institution of Engineering and Technology (2014). https://doi.org/10.1049/cp.2014.0684
22. Fremantle, P.: A Reference Architecture for the Internet of Things. WSO2 White Paper (2014). https://doi.org/10.13140/RG.2.2.20158.89922
23. Green, J.: The Internet of Things Reference Model. IoT World Forum, pp. 1–12 (2014)
24. Infocomm Media Development Authority, Singapore Government, Internet Of Things. https://www.imda.gov.sg/-/media/imda/files/industry-development/infrastructure/technology/internetofthings.pdf?la=en. Accessed 20 Mar 2018

25. IoT-A Internet Of Things Architecture. Deliverable D1.5, Final architectural reference model for the IoT v3.0. http://www.meet-iot.eu/deliverables-IOTA/D1_5.pdf. Accessed 20 Mar 2018

26. Bahga, A., Madisseti, V.: Internet Of Things (A Hands-On-Approach), Book A Hands-On-Approach series, 446 p. (2014). ISBN-10 0996025510

27. European Intelligent Transport Systems (ITS) Framework Architecture. FRAME Architecture. http://frame-online.eu/. Accessed 10 Apr 2018

28. ITS Malaysia. Establishing the ITS System Architecture for Malaysia. http://www.itsmalaysia.com.my/content.php. Accessed 10 Apr 2018

29. ISO Online Browsing Platform. ISO 14813-1:2015 standard. https://www.iso.org/obp/ui/#iso:std:iso:14813:-1:ed-2:v1:en. Accessed 10 Apr 2018

Development of a WEB Prototype Based on JSON and REST Technology to Manage Progress in the Physical and Psychological Rehabilitation of People with Cognitive Disability

William Ruiz Martínez[1]([⊠]), Roberto Ferro Escobar[2]([⊠]), and Yesid Díaz[1]([⊠])

[1] Corporación Unificada Nacional CUN, Bogotá, Colombia
{william_ruizmar, yesid_diaz}@cun.edu.co
[2] Universidad Distrital Francisco Jose de Caldas, Bogotá, Colombia
robertoferro@hotmail.com

Abstract. The vulnerable population with motor and cognitive disabilities in our country confronts daily to endless number of situations that transgress its rights and possibilities to carry on a dignified life. This way we implement a prototype of a web application using Ajax, JSON and REST technologies with the aim to avoid overloads and response times in the remote server and allow to improve the reliability, speed and veracity of the information, beside to can integrate and store the basic information of the patients, treatments performed and progresses in the rehabilitation of population with different kind of motor and cognitive disabilities.

Keywords: Disabilities · Cognitive · Rehabilitation · Web · JSON
REST

1 Introduction

According to statistical data from the National Administrative Department of Statistics (Dane) [1], in Colombia there are 2'624,898 people with some type of disability, equivalent to 6.3% of the population.

However, the Register of Location and Characterization of Persons with Disabilities (RLCPD) created by the Ministry of Health and Social Protection presented in August 2014, that in the country only about 1'121.274 have been registered with a disability in banks of data. According to these governmental data on disability issues, it can be inferred that they are almost 50% far from reality and that they are far from reliable, since neither the same governmental entities of national and municipal nature know exactly how many people disabled exists in the country and much less in the city under study, in addition to factors of great importance such as: The conditions in which they are, recovery treatments they have received and progress made, for these factors is that the importance of the project is makes it so obvious, since it will allow to unify and

J. C. Figueroa-García et al. (Eds.): WEA 2018, CCIS 916, pp. 196–203, 2018.
https://doi.org/10.1007/978-3-030-00353-1_17

consolidate key information in an online system that can meet the search and query requirements of relevant information of the disabled population by governmental and private entities that allow to know the reality of these people and based on the results found design policies and programs for to improve their quality of life [2].

Complementing the above, to know the situation of people with cognitive disabilities through the prototype of a Web application using Ajax technologies, will optimize response times and avoid server overload, since only the requested information will be supplied without using non-essential resources such as all the load of the page, in addition the fact that the site is hosted in the cloud will allow its total availability at any time and day that a consultation is necessary.

Therefore, consulting updated, reliable and truthful information from public and private organizations is essential, since it would allow public and private policies focused on the disabled population to be more effective and allow them to have a better quality of life, from projects or strategies of inclusion and coverage in mobility, education, sports, work and health [3].

2   Research Methodology

2.1   Research Approach

This research work is based on two parts, the methodological or investigative part complemented with the disciplinary part. The first part is established under the following parameters:

1. Selection of the research topic
2. Design of information gathering tools
3. Application of information gathering tools
4. Processing of information
5. Description, analysis and interpretation of the data collected

Regarding the disciplinary part, we have the following stages or phases:

1. Analysis stage: Establish the functional and non-functional requirements of the prototype.
2. Design stage: Architectural design of the prototype
3. Stage of software development: Routines for programming modules and interfaces
4. Maintenance stage: Modification of components and correction of errors.

2.2   Compilation of Information

The development of the proposed prototype is carried out in the rehabilitation institution called "Reina Sofia Foundation" of the city of Ibagué (Tolima), where the institution works with patients with cognitive disabilities (especially patients with Down syndrome, autism and cerebral palsy). For the collection of information, the problem was addressed from several aspects, among which the following stand out:

- The psychological (Psychologist of the foundation)
- The cognitive (Special education graduate)
- The physical or motor (Physical Therapist)

Once the technical requirements have been determined, it is necessary to apply the criteria established by Wright [4], to obtain the "what", "how" and "why" of the proposed research in order to carry out the software application (Fig. 1).

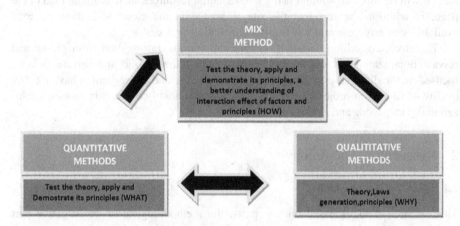

Fig. 1. Research methodology applied

2.3 Processing of Information

The development of this point will focus on the 3 aspects dealt with at the information collection point, since based on the information provided by the professionals interviewed, we have an information survey according to the planned objective.

Psychological Aspect: By conducting the interview with the psychologist of the foundation we could establish that the management of this type of population is quite complex, since there are different types and degrees of disabilities, often these pathologies are innate or acquired. The cognitive development of this type of people is slow and sometimes they regress, losing all the advanced terrain.

Cognitive Aspect: Through the interview conducted with the graduate in special education, we were able to determine that patients with Asperger syndrome are people who are too intelligent but who have difficulties communicating. There are three types of disability: low, medium and high.

Engine Aspect: By conducting the interview with the physical therapist we could establish that children with Down syndrome have spinal problems, their neck is very short and can be easily injured, they should handle activities such as: running, but not spinning or anything similar, and other pathologies such as hypermobility, which consists of the exaggerated increase in mobility in the joints, reaching this type of patients to a greater degree of flexibility than the rest of the population.

2.4   Application Architectural Design

In terms of software engineering, one of the most important and important phases is design because it allows answering the question of what is the system going to do?

Therefore, it is vital to develop a design methodology that allows us to visualize the interaction between the different components of the system, for this purpose we have opted for the object-oriented methodology [5], since it allows us to have a global vision of the system and in a more detailed way obtain a more specific view of key components of the system and the relationships between them.

The design have two phases:

Architectural: It focuses on the representation of the structure of the components, properties, relationships and interactions of the software.
Design data: Where we facilitate the representation of the data components of the architecture.

In addition, it is important to determine the advantages and importance of this phase in the software development process, as follows:

- Facilitate communication among stakeholders in the different stages of system development.
- Determine the first design decisions that will have a profound impact on all software engineering work.
- It is an integral model of how the system is structured and how its components work together.

The architectural design is an ideal scenario for the use of UML (Unified Modeling Language) [6], since among its main advantages we have: It is a standard language for building plan software, in addition to allowing us to visualize, specify, build and document the artifacts of the system.

2.5   Functional Requirements

Component Diagram. The definition of a component is "a modular, deployable and replaceable part of a system, which includes the implementation and exposes a set of interfaces" [8], the components form the architecture of the software and, consequently, play a role in the achievement of the objectives and the requirements of the system that is going to be built. As the components are found in the software architecture, they must communicate and collaborate with other components and with entities (other systems, devices, people, etc.) that exist outside the software's borders. Next, we present the component diagram of the proposed prototype (Table 1).

Table 1. Functional requirements of the prototype

No.	Requirement	Description
RF-1	Register users	The administrator of the system will be in charge of registering the different types or levels of users
RF-2	Modify and inactivate users	The system administrator can modify the level of access or restriction for a particular user
RF-3	Register patients	The system operator must register each of the patients with their respective basic data (names, surnames, registration date)
RF-4	Modify and inactivate patients	The system administrator should be able to modify or update patient information, as well as inactivate a patient if necessary
RF-5	Register disabilities	The system operator must enter the types of disabilities from two broad categories: Cognitive or motor
RF-6	Modification and inactivation of disabilities	The system administrator should be able to modify or update information on the types of disabilities recorded, as well as inactivate a particular disability
RF-7	Register treatments	The operator of the system must enter the different types of treatments applied to a patient, as well as the degree of progress or response to the treatment
RF-8	Modify and inactivate treatments	The system administrator must be able to modify or update information on the types of registered treatments, as well as inactivate a special treatment
RF-9	Generate reports	The operator must be able to generate a patient report that includes: Basic data, type of disability, response, and progress in treatments between certain dates ranges or through other parameters such as the patient's identity document or type of disability

Web Architecture. The term Representational State Transfer or REST was introduced and defined in the year 2000 by Roy Fielding in his doctoral thesis. Fielding is one of the main authors of the Protocol of hypertext transfer (HTTP) versions 1.0 and 1.1. For the development of the architecture of the proposed application a brief description of the components is made [9] (Figs. 2 and 3).

- PHP, as a server-side development language
- MYSQL, as a database engine, to store information.
- JSON, as a format for sending information.
- REST, as an architecture to manage the services and elements.

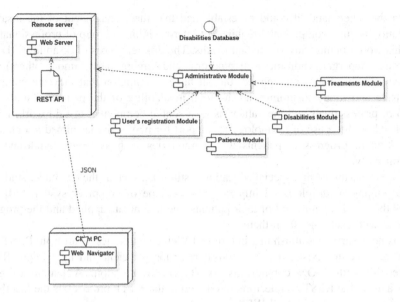

Fig. 2. Diagram of web prototype components

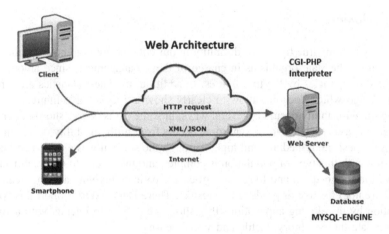

Fig. 3. Web architecture of the application

3 Results

The low efficiency of the state agencies in the handling of the figures on disability in the country was established, nor the agencies in charge really know the real figures on disability, this situation allows us to establish the clear abandonment and forgetting of the state for with the disabled population, which is reflected in the absence of programs and projects that support the disabled population.

On the other hand, it could be established that the management of the disabled population is quite complex and requires an interdisciplinary group of professionals so that this work obtains truly significant results. The different types of disabilities (Down syndrome, Asperger syndrome, Rett syndrome and cerebral palsy, among others) vary markedly in the treatments applied, but all have in common that they are complex, expensive and time-consuming and the total availability of the patient's family, the group of professionals and the patient as an essential component of said work. It was evidenced the little use of technology as support for play activities aimed at obtaining some kind of progress in patients with pathologies such as Down Syndrome and cerebral palsy.

It was determined that special education institutions such as the one under study are just beginning to develop and implement some type of computer system [10] that allows them to keep a record of their patients, the treatments applied and the progress obtained with each one, from them.

It is necessary to establish that in terms of Web technologies, apart from REST, the SOAP architecture exists, but it is considered more efficient and lightweight REST architecture with JSON components for it sent information. A feature of great importance in the REST architecture, in relation to the HTTP protocol, is the fact that it has a uniform interface for all WEB resources.

4 Conclusion

We can say that the true figures of disability in our country are not known in their true dimension by the state organisms in charge of their management, since among them there are discrepancies by the true figures. In addition, the latest statistics are three or four years ago which does not allow to clearly show a truly reliable figure.

Cognitive disability occurs in several ways, in some cases occurs shortly after birth or in certain cases such as Down syndrome occurs from birth, disability occurs in three phases or types: mild, medium and high, Through the study it was established that the interaction with this type of population is complex and the results of the treatments are perceived in the medium and long term, often the patients involute and the treatments applied are not effective or produce few results. There is a need to support this type of population by developing applications that allow the patient to interact with activities that stimulate their auditory, tactile and visual senses.

The use of the technologies that make up Ajax, allow to reduce considerably the overload of the servers and also load a page only the necessary information, becoming an excellent alternative for the development of lightweight and fast Web applications.

Acknowledgments. The authors wish to express their thanks to the students of the research group Kinect Club, the director of the "Reina Sofia" foundation of the city of Ibagué (Tolima), Luz Stella Castaño, to Dr. Sandra Cifuentes, and to the therapist. Physical Cristina Nieto of the IPS society of therapies of Tolima, without their valuable collaboration this project could not have been carried out, in the same way to the mayor of Ibagué and government of Tolima, for the information provided on the statistics of the disability in the city and the department.

References

1. DANE.   https://www.dane.gov.co/index.php/estadisticas-por-tema/demografia-y-poblacion/discapacidad
2. M.D.P.I. http://www.elnuevodia.com.co/nuevodia/opinion/columnistas/110171-las-cifras-de-la-poblacion-con-discapacidad-en-ibague-i
3. Wright, L.: Qualitative international management research. In: Handbook For International Management Research, Oxford (1995)
4. Silva, D., Mercerat, B.: Construyendo aplicaciones web con una metodologia de diseño orientada a objetos. Rev. Colomb. Comput. **2**, 50–61 (2001)
5. Booch, G., Jacobson, I.: El Lenguaje Unificado de Modelado. Addison-Wesley, Boston (1999)
6. Larman, C.: UML y Patrones. Prentice Hall, Madrid (2003)
7. Pressman, R.S.: Ingenieria del Software (Un enfoque practico). Mexico D.F., McGraw Hill (2010)
8. Perez, J.E.: Introduccion a Ajax. Creative Commons, Madrid (2008)
9. Kendall, K.E., Kendall, J.E.: Analisis y Diseño de Sistemas. Prentice Hall, Mexico D.F. (2011)

Automated Epileptic Seizure Detection System Based on a Wearable Prototype and Cloud Computing to Assist People with Epilepsy

Nicolas Escobar Cruz[1(✉)], Jhon Solarte[1(✉)],
and Andres Gonzalez-Vargas[1,2(✉)]

[1] Universidad Autónoma de Occidente, Santiago de Cali, Colombia
{juan_nic.escobar,john.solarte,
amgonzalezv}@uao.edu.co
[2] Grupo de investigación en ingeniería Biomédica G-BIO,
Santiago de Cali, Colombia

Abstract. Epilepsy is characterized by the recurrence of epileptic seizures that affect secondary physiological changes in the patient. This leads to a series of adverse events in the manifestation of convulsions in an uncontrolled environment and without medical help, resulting in risk to the patient, especially in people with refractory epilepsy where modern pharmacology is not able to control seizures. The traditional methods of detection based on wired hospital monitoring systems are not suitable for the detection of long-term monitoring in outdoors. For these reasons, this paper proposes a system that can detect generalized tonic-clonic seizures on patients to alert family members or medical personnel for prompt assistance, based on a wearable device (glove), a mobile application and a Support Vector Machine classifier deployed in a system based on cloud computing. In the proposed approach we use Accelerometry (ACC), Electromyography (ECG) as measurement signals for the development of the glove, a machine learning algorithm (SVM) is used to discriminate between simulated tonic-clonic seizures and non-seizure activities that may be confused with convulsions. In this paper, the high level architecture of the system and its implementation based on Cloud Computing are described. Considering the traditional methods of measurement, the detection system proposed in this paper could mean an alternative solution that allows a prompt response and assistance that could be lifesaving in many situations.

Keywords: Epileptic seizure detection · Wearable · Electromyography
Cloud computing · Accelerometry

1 Introduction

Epilepsy is considered one of the most common neurological disorders of the central nervous system and, according to the World Health Organization, it affects almost sixty-five million people worldwide [1]. One percent of the population of the world has epilepsy.

© Springer Nature Switzerland AG 2018
J. C. Figueroa-García et al. (Eds.): WEA 2018, CCIS 916, pp. 204–213, 2018.
https://doi.org/10.1007/978-3-030-00353-1_18

In countries where optimal treatments and adequate health conditions are available, it is estimated that 70% of patients respond to the medication to control the symptoms, and the remaining population have seizures that are not controlled by medications [2]. These patients diagnosed with pharmacoresistant epilepsy usually present a diminished life quality and an increased mortality rate. In Colombia, approximately 1.3% of the population suffers from epilepsy, a disease that represents 0.8% of the causes of mortality in the country [3]. One of the main symptoms of epilepsy symptoms are convulsions, which consist of compulsive repetitions of involuntary movements that can affect a part of the body (partial seizures) or its totality (generalized seizures), which leads to a series of adverse events that go from memory loss for a few seconds and wandering around, to falling to the ground and shaking abruptly [4]. 30% of the population with refractory epilepsy do not have a method to avoid or reduce epileptic seizures, which increases the risk of the patient in case of suffering a crisis in an uncontrolled environment during their daily life and without help from their caregivers.

For the reasons aforementioned, we believe that the implementation of an e-health system that allows family members and caregivers to know about the patient's condition [5], and be notified in time of the patient suffering a tonic-clonic crisis and his/her location, can help people with epilepsy to receive a quick response and assistance, improving the patient's care and, consequently, could be lifesaving for them. In this paper we present the prototype of a wearable device for epileptic (GTCS) episode detection. The device is based on a glove with two sensors measuring Accelerometry (ACC) and Electromyography (EMG). It also contains a Bluetooth module that allows communication with a smartphone, which is responsible for measuring the patient's biomedical data and processing it. The data is analyzed and processed online by a machine learning algorithm (SVM) working on a cloud computing service. This algorithm detects GTCS from other activities that may be confused with seizures. If a GTCS is detected the system sends a text message with the GPS coordinates of the patient to family members and caregivers. The rest of the paper is structured as follows: Sect. 2 reviews some previous works and different approaches proposed to detect epileptic seizures. Section 3 describes the design of the prototype and the training of the SVM algorithm. The cloud computing based software architecture of the system and mobile application are described in Sect. 4. Finally, conclusions and future works are exposed in Sect. 5.

2 Related Work

Conventionally, methods such as Electroencephalography (EEG) have been used to detect and diagnose epileptic seizures in patients. By analyzing the information on the recorded brain activity of the EEG signals, it is possible to detect epileptic seizures [6]. However, these types of procedures are exhaustive and complex, mainly carried out under appropriate clinical settings [7].

Today, there are also some companies that have developed commercial products with the objective of monitoring patients with epilepsy and notify the family and caregivers before the event of a convulsion activity.

For example, the Smartwatch Embrace [8] designed by scientists at the Massachusetts Institute of Technology (MIT) allows to monitor variables such as psychological stress status, as well as EDA measurement in the patient and notify the smartphone of the family and caregivers. Bioalert [9] is a mobile application developed by the Android Wear family of smartwatches, which is based on accelerometers for the detection of crises, it has the functionality of sound alert and notification if abnormal movements are detected. Emfit [10] is a monitoring system in bed, for the detection of patient movements during sleep at night. The device consists of two sensors that are located under the mattress. Other companies such as Bioserenity [11] have developed a vest and cap with a configuration with EDA, EEG and EMG sensors for the diagnosis and monitoring of patients, which provide a more elaborate solution for the analysis of epileptic crises in patients within a controlled medical environment.

Epileptic seizures are generally known to generate a series of repetitive and compulsive movements involuntarily in the patient. With the advancement of wearable sensors and protocols such as Wireless Body Area Networks (WBAN), many projects have been proposed focused on the development of viable solutions for the analysis of movements based on Accelerometry to identify epileptic seizures [8]. However, the main challenge is to differentiate convulsions from repetitive daily activities that the patient performs in different scenarios [6].

In this paper, we report the development of a wireless wearable system to detect generalized tonic-clonic seizures (GTCS). The key contributions of this work are 2 topics: (1) Our prototype focuses on long-term movement monitoring (ACC) and muscle activity (EMG); (2) the implementation of an epileptic seizure detection system using a machine learning SVM algorithm, which analyzes and processes in an ecosystem based on a Cloud computing platform.

3 System Description

In this section, we present the prototype design and construction, as well as the android application needed to send patient data and be able to make the preprocessing and feature extraction of epileptic information, then we describe the SVM algorithm with its cloud architecture.

3.1 Prototype Elaboration

Figure 1 shows the prototype and how the hardware components are embedded in a glove which the patient uses on the forearm. The garment was made with Elastane and Neoprene, materials that allow a life-long use in different environments of the patient's daily life, as well as being comfortable to use in conditions such as sweating.

Elastane contributes with humidity absorption [12] and protects the circuit from the user's sweat; besides, it is a material with highly elastic properties which allows it to be easily conditioned to the forearm of the user.

Neoprene is also elastic [13], and has electric and thermal insulation faculties that provide circuit protection from chemical agents. Additionally, Fig. 1 shows the two belts that were included for adjusting the glove to the measure of the forearm of each user.

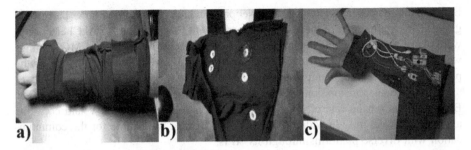

Fig. 1. Wearable sensor prototype. (a) View from outside. (b) EMG and EDA Electrodes. (c) Bitalino boards and electrodes inside the glove.

3.2 Hardware

Our system consists of a pair of sensors capable of collecting data on the muscular activity of the forearm and vibrations. To do this, we use Bitalino Freestyle BLE (r) evolution open source board, which includes a kit of biomedical sensors to work with. The Bitalino Freestyle board is based on the ATMega328 microcontroller which works at 20 MHz, we have 2 Kb of RAM memory, 1 Kb of ROM and 32 Kb of Flash memory. It is especially designed for development of wearable devices and smart fabrics [14]. This MCU can acquire and control up to 6 analog inputs, 1 analog output, 2 digital inputs channels up to 1 kHz of sampling rate. It is very light and has low energy consumption. It comes with a separate kit of components and sensors that can be integrated according to the project. For this project, the board is in charge of collecting the data from the sensors, and transmitting it to the smartphone via Bluetooth. We opted to use the Bluetooth LE module due to its low battery consumption, allowing the prototype's prolonged operation during the day.

The EMG and ACC sensors have their respective conditioning stages that allow the reduction of noise and deliver their output to the MCU. For the measurement of EMG we used a set of 3 Ag/AgCl electrodes for the measurement signal of the negative, positive and reference location in the forearm muscle. The conditioning stage of the EMG has a gain of 1009, a common mode rejection of 86 dB, this stage has a band pass filter of 25–480 MHz which is the bandwidth of the striated muscles. The EMG stage operates at 3.3 V and consumes an approximate 0.17 mA. The ACC sensor reacts to sudden movements, shock movements and progressive movements as well, it enables the measurement of these 3 axes and it works at a range of ± 3 g, as well as a low pass filter of 50 Hz. It consumes 1.8–3.6 V and about 0.35 mA. For the data transmission to the smartphone, we use a Bluetooth device.

The Bluetooth has a baud rate of up to 115200 Kbs, it consumes 2.4–3.6 V and approximately 18 mA. In addition, the module BLE is compatible for communication with diverse platforms through its APIs. Finally, the system needs a Li-Po battery of 3.7 V and 500 mAh.

The Fig. 1 (right) shows the prototype during its elaboration. As we can see, the elements have been assembled adjusting to the morphology of the forearm. The circuit component is composed by the power block supply, ACC and EMG sensor, and the

BLE module has been assembled with Neoprene which compose the inner part of the glove. The external part of the glove is covered with Elastane, the Ag/AgCl electrodes were placed for direct contact with the skin, based on areas where better EMG readings were obtained in the forearm [15] as we can see in Fig. 1 the On/Off switch of the prototype, so users can manipulate it.

For the data transmission to the smartphone, we use a Bluetooth device. The Bluetooth has a baud rate of up to 115200 Kbs, is fed with 2.4–3.6 V and consume approximately 18 mA. In addition, this module BLE is compatible for the communication with diverse platforms through its APIs.

Finally, the system needs a Li-Po battery of 3.7 Volts and 500 mAh

3.3   Software

Figure 2 shows the design of the architecture and the operation of the system in each of its stages. The software architecture starts with a mobile application that enables connection with the glove and capture patient data provided by sensors. The information is sent to an application web server that hosts an SVM machine learning algorithm, which classifies patient's data on-the-fly in order to predict whether or not a tonic-clonic seizure is occurring. In case that the patient is suffering a seizure attack, a request is sent to the text message server which integrates a database server where the numbers of the relatives and associated medical personnel are stored for each patient. Finally, a SMS message is sent to them with the patient's location.

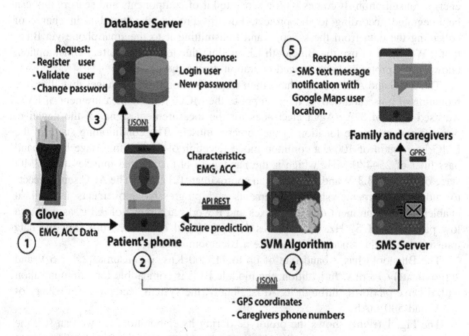

Fig. 2. System architecture

We developed an application on Android called "Seizure App", whose interface is shown in Fig. 3 where the patient can create an account in the system and connect with the glove (Fig. 3c). The application receives the data from sensors, sampled at a 1 kHz rate, then this information is stored in a data window of 5 s which is equivalent to 1750 samples of data. After that, a preprocessing stage is performed using the Android multithreading, making a feature extraction of data in order to send this to the SVM algorithm hosted in the cloud. Once the SVM classifies the patient's data, a message is returned to the application, if a convulsion is detected, the phone coordinates are captured and sent to the SMS server along with the patient's id to determine the telephone numbers of relatives and caregivers associated to this patient.

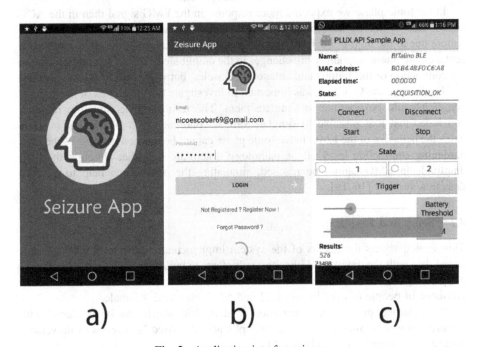

Fig. 3. Application interface views.

A Support Vector Machine (SVM) algorithm was developed using the Machine Learning Scikit-Learn library in Python with other scientific libraries given by Anaconda environment such as Numpy, Scipy for matrix operations. The algorithm receives the extracted characteristics from Seizure App, such as maximum, minimum, media and variance. This data is classified by SVM with a linear kernel which predicts between epileptic seizures and non-seizure activities. A cloud computing platform was used for the detection system. To this effect, a Docker container is used to provide the SVM with a Python ecosystem provided by Anaconda, and it is hosted by a web server with the Flask framework. The Linux container is executed 24/7 on a machine provided by the Heroku service.

4 Experimentation

4.1 Movement Patterns

Since we didn't have access to epileptic patients, the experimental phase was carried out with healthy people, who simulated the movements of a GTCS according to patterns reported in previous works. A GTCS includes a tonic phase and a clonic phase. In the first one, volunteers contracted and hardened the forearm muscles. In the second, they made repeated contractions of agonist and antagonist muscles of the same area. We used the forearm because literature reports that in a GTCS, the superior members of the body are a zone where the effects are greatly seen.

In the tonic phase we expected more response in the EMG signal than in the ACC signal. Due to muscle hardening, the EMG signal appears as a constant contraction pattern due to the high frequency contraction with little changes in the ACC amplitude. In the clonic phase we mainly big changes in the amplitude of the ACC are seen, due to the contraction of the agonist and antagonist muscles, but with slow EMG frequencies.

To simulate the GTCS, it was important to investigate the thresholds of the signals, and if it could be possible to simulate them. The results of the literature research concluded that it is possible to simulate similar conditions of a GTCS, but in some cases the behavior of the EMG in the tonic phase cannot be reached because of the high hardening contraction level of the pathology. Literature says that although the high amplitude in EMG cannot be reached, simulating the pattern can help to develop detection systems [16–19].

4.2 Setup and Results

This section shows the results of the system implementation and test. We have collected data with the device in 23 healthy volunteers to build a training dataset and used a separate group of 12 healthy volunteers to validate the system. The validation group consisted of people of ages between 22 and 54, 7 male and 4 female.

They carried out activities common in daily life which can be confused with seizures, as well as simulations of an epileptic activity based on a series of movement patterns characteristic of a GTCS [16].

Each type of task in Table 1 was repeated 5 times, indicated by n. For example, each volunteers repeated the tonic-clonic test up to 5 times during the construction of the dataset. The type of activity discriminates if the prototype should send an alarm or not. Positive activity is the type we wanted to detect (a GTCS) while negative activity is the one that could be a false alarm.

In the Table 2 is reported what activities generated a false alarm. We think is possible that the laterality could affect the results; we included the laterality of the subjects for posterior investigations that could use this project as a reference. The sensitivity and specificity rates were 100% and 60.4% respectively. We think is possible to have a higher specificity rate adding more subjects, trying with more characteristics and adding EDA to the detection system. In the Table 3 was included the rates of the test.

Table 1. False positive activities, and simulation of epileptic seizures.

Activity	Duration	Positive or Negative
Rubbing hands (n = 5)	10 s	Negative
Shake a drink (n = 5)	10 s	Negative
Brush teeth (n = 5)	10 s	Negative
Clean the shirt (n = 5)	10 s	Negative
Running, walking (n = 5)	20 s	Negative
Tonic-clonic phase (n = 5)	60 s	Positive

Table 2. Results of the test.

Laterality	Subject #	Sexuality (M: Male; F: Female)	GTC detected	False alarm activities (B: Brush teeth; C; Clean the shirt; R; Rubbing hands; S: Shake a drink;)
Left	1	M	Y	B
Left	2	M	Y	None
Left	3	M	Y	None
Right	4	M	Y	None
Right	5	M	Y	None
Left	6	M	Y	C
Right	7	M	Y	R, C, S, B
Right	8	F	Y	C, S, B
Right	9	F	Y	C, S, B
Right	10	F	Y	S
Right	11	F	Y	S, B
Right	12	F	Y	R, C, S, B

Table 3. Rates of the test.

		Classification			
		Positive	Negative		
Real	Positive	10	2	Sensitivity	83.3%
	Negative	19	41	Specificity	68.3%

Figure 4 shows the operation of the system in real conditions, where a seizure was simulated while traveling in a public vehicle and a SMS message is sent to a family member. It was also found that the maximum continuous operation time of the prototype was 19 h.

Fig. 4. SMS notification with the patient's location.

5 Conclusions

The system proposed in this document can detect specific seizure activity, namely generalized tonic clonic seizures, in patients with epilepsy. This work focused on two important areas: (1) the design of a long comfortable device and (2) the implementation of a cloud-based platform system for detection seizure attacks. The results obtained so far involve healthy volunteers simulating a GTCS movement pattern.

Therefore, further investigations require working with epileptic patients in order to improve the reliability and accuracy of the proposed seizure detection algorithm.

However, the limited results presented here indicate that the algorithm offers promising detection results. In addition, our proposed approach of a cloud-based system to record seizure data of various patients with epilepsy seems to be practical and efficient. According to our results the sensor can work continuously for a period of 19 h without charging the battery, and can extend its use with a Li-Po battery with more capacity.

Our next step is to perform tests in epileptic patients and include more frequency features that may improve the performance and accuracy of the seizure detection algorithm. Also, we intend to further integrate and miniaturize the wearable system. Moreover, we plan to develop a management system in which doctors can visualize storical seizure data from patients in order to improve their treatment.

References

1. Quet, F., Odermatt, P., Preux, P.-M.: Challenges of epidemiological research on epilepsy in resource-poor countries. Neuroepidemiology **30**(1), 3–5 (2008). https://doi.org/10.1159/000113299
2. Kobau, R., et al.: Epilepsy surveillance among adults-19 states, behavioral risk factor surveillance system 2008. MMWR Surveill Summ. **57**, 1–20 (2005)

3. Ministry of Health of Colombia. Press Release No 016 of 2017: Epilepsia: Mucho más que convulsiones, https://www.minsalud.gov.co/Paginas/Epilepsia-mucho-mas-que-convulsiones.aspx. Accessed 09 Jan 2017
4. Tzallas, T., et al.: Automated epileptic seizure detection methods: a review study. In: Chapter 4, pp. 75–98. InTech (2012)
5. Rodriguez, J.J.P.C., Compte, S.S., de la Torre Diez, I.: E-Health Systems: Theory and Technical Applications, 1st edn. Elsevier, New York City (2016)
6. Ulate-Campos, A., Coughlin, F., Gaínza-Lein, M., Fernández, I.S., Pearl, P.L., Loddenkemper, T.: Automated seizure detection systems and their effectiveness for each type of seizure. Seizure **40**, 88–101 (2016). Sciencedirect
7. Aghaei, H., Kiani, M.M., Aghajan, H.: Epileptic seizure detection based on video and EEG recordings. In: 2017 IEEE Biomedical Circuits and Systems Conference (BioCAS), Torino, Italy, pp. 1–4 (2017)
8. Embrace. https://www.empatica.com/product-embrace. Accessed Jan 23 2018
9. Biolert LTDA. https://bio-lert.com. Accesed 23 Jan 2018
10. Emfit. https://www.emfit.com. Accessed 23 Jan 2018
11. Bioserenity. http://bioserenity.com/fr. Accessed 23 Jan 2018
12. Senthilkumar, M., Anbunami, N., Hayavadana, J.: Elastane fabrics – a tool for stretch applications in sports. Indian J. Fibre Text. Res. **36**(3), 3 (2011)
13. dos Santos, K.B., Bento, P.C.B., Rodacki, A.L.F.: Efeito do uso do traje de neoprene sobre variáveis técnicas, fisiológicas e perceptivas de nadadores/Effects of a neoprene suit over technical, physiological and perceptive variables of swimmers. Revista Brasileira de Educação Física e Esporte, São Paulo, no. 2, p. 189 (2011)
14. Bitalino, http://bitalino.com/en/learn/documentation. Accessed 21 Apr 2018
15. Finneran, A., O'Sullivan, L.: Effects of grip type and wrist posture on forearm EMG activity, endurance time and movement accuracy. Int. J. Ind. Ergon. **43**(1), 91–99 (2013)
16. Ramgopal, S., et al.: Seizure detection, seizure prediction, and closed-loop warning systems in epilepsy. Epilepsy Behav. **37**, 291–307 (2014)
17. System public repository. https://github.com/nicolaxs69/SVM-Epilepsy–Machine-Learning-Classifier. Accessed 28 Apr 2018
18. Lasboo, A., Fisher, R.S.: Methods for measuring seizure frequency and severity. Neurol. Clin. **34**(2), 383–394 (2016). Mayo
19. Types of Seizures and Their Symptoms. WebMD. https://www.webmd.com/epilepsy/types-of-seizures-their-symptoms#1. Accessed 6 Sept 2017

Modeling and Implementation Data Architecture for the Internet of Things and Industry 4.0

José Ignacio Rodríguez-Molano[✉], Cesar Amilcar López-Bello, and Leonardo Emiro Contreras-Bravo

Universidad Distrital Francisco José de Caldas, Bogotá, Colombia
{jirodriguez, lecontrerasb}@udistrital.edu.co,
msccesar.lopez@gmail.com

Abstract. This paper analyzes Internet of Things (IoT), its use into manufacturing industry, its foundation principles, available elements and technologies for the man-things-software communication already developed in this area. And it proves how important its deployment is. Describes a proposal of data architecture of the Internet of things applied to the industry, a metamodel of integration (Internet of Things, Social Networks, Cloud and Industry 4.0) for generation of applications for the Industry 4.0, and the manufacturing monitoring prototype implemented with the Raspberry Pi microcomputer, a cloud storage server and a mobile device for controlling an online production.

Keywords: Industrial Internet of Things · Data mining · Modeling
Industry 4.0

1 Introduction

Thousands of millions of physical elements and objects will be equipped with different types of sensors and actuators, all of them connected in real-time to internet through heterogeneous networks. This will generate high amounts of data-flows [1] that have to be stored, processed and shown to be interpreted in an efficient and easy manner. Here is where IoT and Cloud computing integration permits that this huge amount of data can be stored in internet, keeping resources, services and data available and ready to use and for end-to-end service providing [2] both in the business and in the consumer field, from anywhere. It provides the virtual integration infrastructure for storage devices, analysis tools, monitoring and platform. The Internet of Things has been catalogued as heterogeneous and ubiquitous objects, all interconnected between them and communicating with each other via the Internet [3].

The Internet of Things counts on sensors or scattered objects to generate information from any accessible site or inside a machine. Thus, it requires the interconnection of these heterogeneous objects via the Internet [4, 5]. Here is found the importance of Smart Objects: physical objects with an embedded system that allows information processing and communication with other devices, and also the processes based on a certain action or event [6]. However, all of these complex systems present a

© Springer Nature Switzerland AG 2018
J. C. Figueroa-García et al. (Eds.): WEA 2018, CCIS 916, pp. 214–222, 2018.
https://doi.org/10.1007/978-3-030-00353-1_19

problem when connecting the Smart Objects due to the differences between software and hardware used for each process [7].

Due to the enlargement of the IoT and the Cloud Computing application development, technological problems decrease and an expansion of services is created in an industrial context [8]. This paper outlines the need to integrate the IoT, sensors, actuators, social networks and computing in the cloud. It will enable to build the Industrial Internet of Things (IIoT) up.

2   Architecture of Industrial Internet of Things IIoT

The different IoT architectures proposed have not converged to a reference model [9] or a common architecture. In current literature, several models can be found, as can be seen in Fig. 1 [10]. The basic model has three layers (layer application, network and perception). It was designed to address specific types of communication channels and does not cover all of the underlying technologies that transfer data to an IoT platform. Other models based on four layers (layer of sensors, network, services and interfaces) are designed in the context of industry 4.0 [11].

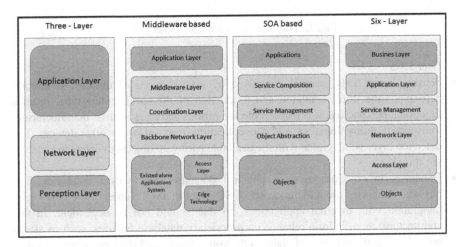

Fig. 1. IoT architectures [10].

2.1   Proposal for IIoT Architecture

In the context of Industry 4.0, a prototype of IIoT platform in 5 layers is presented pursuing the integration of sensors, actuators, networks, cloud computing and technologies of the Internet of Things (Fig. 2):

- Sensing layer
- Databases layer
- Network layer
- Data response layer

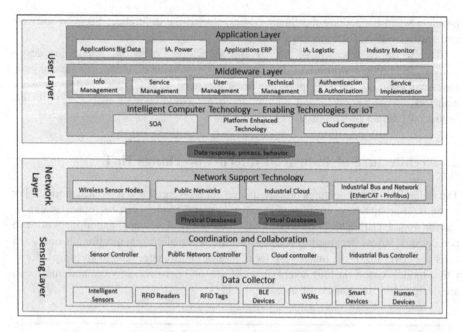

Fig. 2. Proposal of integration architecture

- User layer
- Sensing layer: This layer is composed by several types of devices. It directly determines the implementation and production of the specific data type. From a functional perspective, it is responsible for various activities such as manufacturing, transport, mobility, logistics, and data collection from sensors or other devices. The detection layer is integrated with the available hardware objects to detect the state of the things.
- Databases layer: Composed of physical databases and virtual databases. The physical databases use a common set of SQL and nonSQL (object). It enables easy integration with external applications, so that should not be dependent. In this architecture, there is little reliance on proprietary database features, such as stored procedures and triggers. IoT data come from sensors and devices, where the data can be collected and processed in real time.

Virtual data bases allow to expose schema and customized abstract data. Data abstraction approach provides logical link to the database in the network node, where the data are logically and physically separated and can be accessed from a single virtual schema. These abstract databases can be placed inside containers, based on the needs of the problem domain. Here, the acquired data are stored without processing (Figs. 3, 4 and 5).

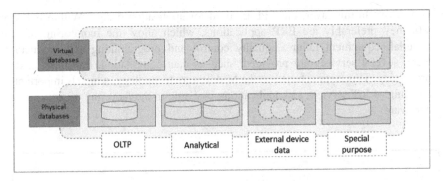

Fig. 3. Physical databases and virtual databases

- Network layer: The network layer is the infrastructure that supports connections between things through cable or wireless. IoT network layer, connects all things and enables them to know its environment. Through this layer all data are shared with all connected things. The network layer adds data from existing IT infrastructure. Here, the interaction between the Sensor layer and the User layer takes place. Also, it manages sensors and actuators and provides information to the next layer. In industry 4.0, the provided services are personalized according to the requirements of the application.
- Data response layer: This layer is a data set that can be assigned to devices and applications. It maintains the persistence of other layers. It focuses on providing automatic responses and it learns as it processes the response. Here, the processed data are maintained. Data are stored in a way that makes the physical database updated as stated by the user. All data received from the sensors are processed in the network node. The cloud-based components, the components near IoT devices and sensors are paired logically.

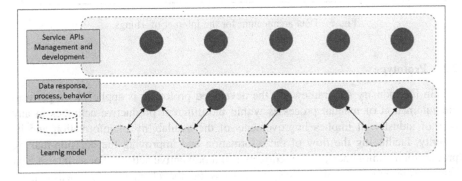

Fig. 4. Data response layer.

- User layer: In this layer, the API are used for application design. Within industry 4.0, they preferably are ERP applications, which allow the monitoring of raw material, equipment failures, quality control and programming and production. Here, several services are provided, such as data compilation, transmission data processing. This layer is based on the Middleware technology, which is important in enabling of IoT services and applications, assisting in the recycling of software and hardware.

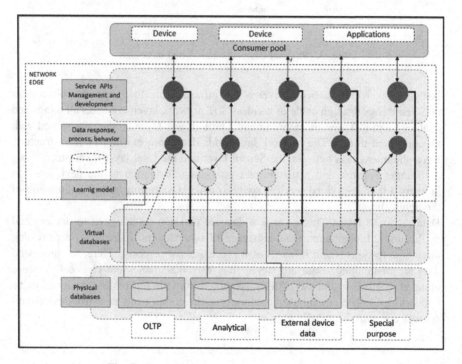

Fig. 5. Data architecture for the Internet of Things.

2.2 Prototype

Within the industry 4.0 framework, the developed prototype is applicable to perform the automation of manual processes within the different productive activities in any type of industry. It implies improvements of the availability of information and its security, facilitating the flow of the information and improving the decision-making process on the implementation of corrective and preventive actions. For an intermittent system (the activation of the system depends on the change in the measurement variable). The collection of slightly relevant information is almost zero and the presentation of the critical information is presented in an organized and systematic way, thereby improving data mining.

The advantages of deployment of this class of prototypes within productive processes or for tracking products [12] relates to the decrease in uncertainty and measurement errors. In addition, the possibility of implementing a measurement process has an advantage over an interrupted manual measurement. Also, by creating processes of traceability of data and information that did not previously exist (without the intervention of the human resource) given that the gathered information is continually pushed towards the Big Data or cloud computing for its consolidation.

The communication environment, subject of the surveillance system, allowed to monitor several variables. For this purpose, four sensors were used. They allowed to determine the flow of products in a production plant. The presence of gas in the complex, the alignment and stability of the equipment and the existence of contact between a person and the prototype. The information on changes in the status of sensors was processed in a microcomputer Raspberry Pi [13] (Fig. 6).

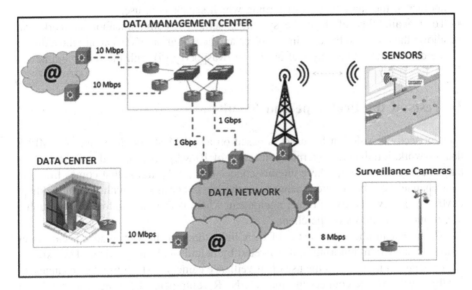

Fig. 6. Data flow in the proposed system

A communication object-object between the Raspberry Pi and a mobile device was deployed with the purpose of establishing the synchronization of data directly to the user via smartphone or tablet. It was achieved through the connection established between the Raspberry Pi and the storage server in the cloud. The prototype has the following features:

- Use of technologies of sensors: The prototype uses different sensors for the detection of "strange" elements in the working environment. Then it initiates capture and data communication. The sensor acts like a link between what happens in the process and the user.
- Data collection at any time: the prototype does not restrict the capture of images and is always aware of each movement in the area where the system is deployed.

- Data Transfer: it is possible to transfer data within the communication network that is composed by the user (via a mobile device) and the physical system (Raspberry Pi) through cloud computing.
- User interface: the prototype can communicate with the user through well-known platforms or server storage.
- Functional Independence: the prototype works automatically independently of the user, since the capture of data and their transfer functions are carried out only with the activation of a sensor and a wireless network.
- Communication with the mobile device: the system does not require direct intervention to the hardware or software to operate. The communication is conducted under the principles of communication machine-to-machine, in which the microcomputer Raspberry Pi and the sensors are the prototype and the mobile device is the terminal that enables communication with the user through a server and a communication network. The collected data are transferred from one machine to another in the same way, disregarding which sensor is in use.
- Total availability of data: the system generates a communication network that allows the access to the user in any place and consultation of data at any time, due to the connection of the physical prototype (Raspberry Pi) with the server online.

3   Tests of the Prototype and Results

The connectivity solution for users is based on a full Mesh topology over the MPLS data network, a redundant internet connection of 10 Mbps is proposed, a main 1 Gbps data channel and backup, these circuits concentrate all the traffic that comes from the data channels of the different sensors, each one is configured with a bandwidth of 8 Mbps. All services have a router equipment, which is responsible for directing traffic according to the needs of the client.

The user can check the status of their links through the web platform e-services through the basic monitoring tool delivered by default with the services. The external CCTV solution is based on the use of surveillance cameras, which use data channels of 8 Mbps each, to interconnect the four (4) NVR equipment, these are responsible for receiving and processing the images to be delivered to the user in the best conditions for handling them. It is proposed to maintain processing and storage capabilities capable of handling large amounts of data. The services are provided in common infrastructures, segmented and delivered separately to each user as a service.

- Virtual Servers: Virtualized servers for specific destination.
- Storage and Backup: Storage capacities decentralized platforms, and backup capabilities in centralized platforms defined by the user
- Networking: Both physical and virtual connection points are provided to interconnect the offered capacities.
- Security: IPS, Firewall, v DC capabilities in centralized platforms defined by the user.

The proposed solution is based on infrastructure as a service, which provides access to computing resources located in a virtualized environment, through a dedicated connection, the resources offered consist of virtualized hardware or processing infrastructure. The solution offered must meet with high availability (Figs. 7 and 8).

Fig. 7. Visualization of images by the data center

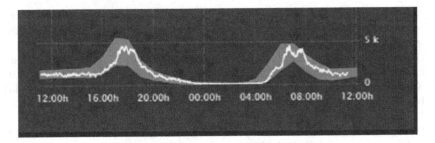

Fig. 8. Speed of data flow in the sensors

4   Conclusions and Future Work

The technology itself is not the main obstacle for the implementation of IIoT; the interfaces of interoperability of the systems belonging to different providers are, that hinders its adoption. The achievement of interoperability requires standardization of interfaces for interaction between different components of the system.

IIoT is the combination of computing technologies, communication and micro-electronics. Thus, there are many interfaces between hardware, software and network components. In the context of the industry 4.0, the proposed architecture let establish communication networks between objects and people that permit the flow of information in two ways, with minimal intervention in the network. Communication networks focus on direct and comprehensive transmission of data.

The change in the way of gathering and storing the information, as much as the use of sensors, requires a change in the technology. IIOT can register automatically, precisely and timely several parameters of the production process. The traditional industrial production performs the communication between machines via the M2M technology, but the IIOT can achieve connections between people, machines and physical objects. Nevertheless, in the IIOT environment, the function and the yield of communication devices are different. Some applications need a high performance in real-time, while others do not. Some application tasks are executed periodically while others are activated by events. These characteristics increase the complexity of the actual applications of the IIOT.

References

1. Wang, C., Daneshmand, M., Dohler, M., Hu, R.Q., Mao, X., Wang, H.: Guest editorial special issue on Internet of Things (IoT): architecture, protocols and services. IEEE Sens. J. **13**(10), 3505–3510 (2013)
2. Biswas, A.R., Giaffreda, R.: IoT and cloud convergence: opportunities and challenges. In: IEEE World Forum Internet Things, pp. 375–376 (2014)
3. Hao, L., Lei, X., Yan, Z., ChunLi, Y.: The application and implementation research of smart city in China. In: International Conference on System Science and Engineering, pp. 288–292 (2012)
4. Atzori, L., Iera, A., Morabito, G., Nitti, M.: The social Internet of Things (SIoT) – when social networks meet the internet of things: concept, architecture and network characterization. Comput. Netw. **56**(16), 3594–3608 (2012)
5. García, C.G., G-Bustelo, B.C.P., Espada, J.P., Cueva-Fernandez, G.: Midgar: generation of heterogeneous objects interconnecting applications. Comput. Networks **64**, 143–158 (2014)
6. Xu, B., Xu, L.D., Cai, H., Xie, C., Hu, J., Bu, F.: Ubiquitous data accessing method in IoT-based information system for emergency medical services. IEEE Trans. Ind. Inform. **10**, 1578–1586 (2014)
7. Gama, K., Touseau, L., Donsez, D.: Combining heterogeneous service technologies for building an Internet of Things middleware. Comput. Commun. **35**(4), 405–417 (2012)
8. Steiner, W., Poledna, S.: Fog computing as enabler for the industrial internet of things. e i Elektrotech. Informationstech. **133**, 310–314 (2016)
9. Krco, S., Pokric, B., Carrez, F.: Designing IoT architecture(s): a European perspective. In: 2014 IEEE World Forum on Internet of Things, pp. 79–84 (2014)
10. Fraga-lamas, P., Fernández-Caramés, T.M., Suárez-Albela, M., Castedo, L.: A review on Internet of Things for defense and public safety. Sensors, pp. 1–46 (2016)
11. Wan, J., et al.: Software-defined industrial Internet of Things in the context of industry 4.0. IEEE Sens. J. **16**, 7373–7380 (2016)
12. Lee, J., Bagheri, B., Kao, H.: A cyber-physical systems architecture for industry 4.0-based manufacturing systems. Manuf. Lett. **3**, 18–23 (2015)
13. Rodríguez Molano, J.I., Medina, V.H., Moncada Sánchez, J.F.: Industrial internet of things: an architecture prototype for monitoring in confined spaces using a Raspberry Pi. In: Tan, Y., Shi, Y. (eds.) Data Mining and Big Data, vol. 9714. Springer, Cham (2016). https://doi.org/10.1007/978-3-319-40973-3_53

Automatic Intelligibility Assessment of Parkinson's Disease with Diadochokinetic Exercises

L. Felipe Parra-Gallego[1(✉)], Tomás Arias-Vergara[1,2],
Juan Camilo Vásquez-Correa[1,2], Nicanor Garcia-Ospina[1],
Juan Rafael Orozco-Arroyave[1,2], and Elmar Nöth[2]

[1] Faculty of Engineering, Universidad de Antioquia UdeA, Calle 70 No. 52-21,
Medellín, Colombia
lfelipe.parra@udea.edu.co
[2] Pattern Recognition Lab, Friedrich-Alexander-Universität Erlangen-Nürnberg,
Erlangen, Germany

Abstract. This paper presents preliminary results for the analysis of intelligibility in the speech of Parkinson's Disease (PD) patients. An automatic speech recognition system is used to compute the word error rate (WER), the Levenshtein distance, and the similitude based dynamic time warping. The corpus of the speech recognizer is formed with speech recordings of three Diadochokinetic speech tasks: /pa-ta-ka/, /pa-ka-ta/, and /pe-ta-ka/. The data consist of 50 PD patients and 50 Healthy Controls. According to the results, the recognition error is lower for the healthy speakers (WER = 2.70%) respect to the PD patients (WER = 11.3%).

Keywords: Parkinson's disease · Intelligibility · Speech processing
Automatic speech recognition

1 Introduction

Parkinson's disease (PD) is a neurological disorder caused by the degeneration of neurons within the brain, resulting in the progressive loss of dopamine in the substantia nigra of the midbrain [1]. The primary motor symptoms include resting tremor, slowness of movement, postural instability, rigidity and several dimensions of speech are affected including phonation, articulation, prosody, and intelligibility [2,3]. These deficits reduce the communication ability of PD patients and make their normal interaction with other people difficult. The most outstanding disturbance is consonant imprecision [4]. In recent years, the research community has been developing systems that can diagnose and monitor PD in an objective and non-obtrusive way. As the speech production is one of the most complex processes in the brain, speech signals have been a focus in this research. Diadochokinetic (DDK) tasks are commonly included in speech

© Springer Nature Switzerland AG 2018
J. C. Figueroa-García et al. (Eds.): WEA 2018, CCIS 916, pp. 223–230, 2018.
https://doi.org/10.1007/978-3-030-00353-1_20

assessment protocols as they have shown to be useful in the differential diagnosis of dysarthria and even neurological disease. The sequential motion rate
diadochokinetic exercises involve the rapid repetition of syllable sequences, e.g.,
/pa-ta-ka/ [5]. There are different studies that considers DDK exercises analysis
to detect speech problems in PD patients. In [6] the authors present a portable
system for the automatic recognition of the syllables /pa-ta-ka/. The proposed
approach consists of a tablet and a headset to capture the speech signals. The
system was trained using speech recordings from two group of speakers: patients
with traumatic brain injuries and PD patients. The automatic recognition of
/pa-ta-ka/ is performed in the mobile device using an Automatic Speech Recognition (ASR)-based system. Speech impairments are assessed using the syllable
error rate (SER). Similarly, in [7] the authors presented an iOS application that
integrated a speech recognition system for the analysis of intelligibility problems
in PD patients. The corpus of the speech recognizer is formed with recordings of
the syllables /pa/-/ta/-/ka/. The syllable error rate was computed in two group
of speakers: healthy speakers and PD patients. According to the results, the SER
was lower for the healthy group (SER = 1.34%) respect to the patients (SER =
1.67%), however, the analysis of intelligibility is limited to one feature. In [8], the
authors modeled different articulatory deficits in PD patients in the rapid repetition of the syllables /pa-ta-ka/, and reported an accuracy of 88% discriminating
between PD patients and Healthy Controls (HC). In this work is presented a
ASR system trained with speech recordings of three DDK exercises: /pa-ta-ka/,
/pa-ka-ta/, and /pe-ta-ka/. Additionally, three different features based on the
word error rate (WER), the Levenshtein distance (LD), and the similitude based
dynamic time warping (sDTW) are considered. Furthermore, articulation and
intelligibility features are considered to train a classifier based on the support
vector machine (SVM) approach. Our main hypothesis is that the patients has
more difficulties to produce certain sound during speech, thus, it is possible to
detect those problems considering the DDK analysis.

2   Materials and Methods

2.1   Data

The PC-GITA database is considered for this study [9]. The data contain speech
utterances from 100 (50 PD, 50 HC) Colombian native speakers balanced in age
and gender. Speech signals were captured in a soundproof booth with a sampling
frequency of 44100 Hz and 16 bits resolution. All patients were diagnosed by an
expert neurologist a labeled according to the MDS-UPDRS-III (Movement Disorder Society-Unified Parkinson's Disease Rating Scale). Additional information
from the participants is shown in Table 1. Different DDK exercises were evaluated
in this study to assess the intelligibility of the patients. DDK tasks are based on
the rapid repetition of syllables that require the use of different speech articulators such as lips, larynx, or palate. These exercises increase motor and cognitive
activities in the patients, which make them suitable to assess the neurological
state and the speech impairments of the patients [10]. The DDK exercises used in

Table 1. Information of the participants from this study

	PD patients		HC subjects	
	Male	Female	Male	Female
Number of subjects	25	25	25	25
Age ($\mu \pm \sigma$)	61.3 ± 11.4	60.7 ± 7.3	60.5 ± 11.6	61.4 ± 7.0
Range of age	33–81	49–75	31–86	49–76
Duration of the disease ($\mu \pm \sigma$)	8.7 ± 5.8	12.6 ± 11.6	-	-
MDS-UDRS-III ($\mu \pm \sigma$)	37.8 ± 22.1	37.6 ± 14.1	-	-

this study consist of the rapid repetition of the syllables /pa-ta-ka/, /pa-ka-ta/, and /pe-ta-ka/. There is a special interest in the assessment of the phonemes included in these exercises to measure co-articulatory impairments in different muscles of the vocal tract. For instance, the phoneme /p/ is performed by pressing the lips together, the phoneme /t/ is produced by the interaction between the tongue and the bone obstruction behind the upper front tooth, while the phoneme /k/ is produced by the interaction between the soft palate and back of the tongue.

2.2 Feature Extraction

Articulation–These features are designed to model changes in the position of the tongue, lips, velum, and other articulators involved in the speech production process. The articulation impairment of the patients are modeled by extracting features from the voiced to unvoiced segment (offset) transitions, the unvoiced to the voiced segment (onset) transitions, and voiced segments. The set of features include the energy content distributed in 22 Bark bands, 12 Mel-frequency cepstral coefficients (MFCC) with their first and second derivatives, and the first two formant frequencies (F1 and F2) with their first and second derivatives. The total number of descriptors corresponds to 122. Four functionals are also computed, obtaining a 488-dimensional feature-vector per utterance. The complete description of the articulation features is available in [11], and the code is freely available[1].

Intelligibility–Intelligibility is related to the capability of a person to be understood by another person or by a system. This speech dimension causes loss of the communication abilities of the patients, producing social isolation especially at advanced stages of the disease [12,13]. Although extensively reported, impairments in speech intelligibility of PD patients have been analyzed through perceived intelligibility. We perform the intelligibility analysis based on an ASR, extracting several features to compare the recognized sentence with the real utterance produced by the speakers. The ASR is trained using the Kaldi framework [14]. The corpus of the ASR considers the words pataka, petaka, and

---

[1] https://github.com/jcvasquezc/DisVoice.

pakata; and several variations found in the recordings, e.g., bataka, patakam, badaga, among others. The acoustic model is created using a hidden Markov model (HMM), where each state corresponds to a phoneme. The HMM was trained with MFCCs with their first and second derivatives. In addition, a language model based on tri-grams was considered. An scheme of the ASR system is shown in Fig. 1. Specific ASRs are trained per DDK exercise. Then, we consider the transcrciptions obtained from the ASR to compute several features to assess the intelligibility impairments of the PD patients. The computed features include the WER, the LD, and the similitude based dynamic time warping sDTW, proposed previously [11].

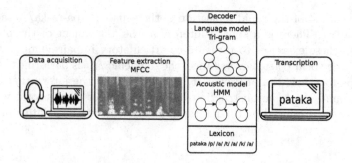

Fig. 1. Scheme of the automatic speech recognition system

The WER is the most common measure to evaluate the performance of ASR systems. We have the hypothesis that PD patients will produce more errors in the ASR than the HC subjects, producing larger WER. This feature is computed using the transcriptions generated by the ASR and the original transcription, according to Eq. 1, where S is the number of substitutions, B is the number of deletions, I is the number of insertions, and N is the total of words in the original transcription.

$$\mathrm{WER} = \frac{S + B + I}{N} \tag{1}$$

The LD is a metric used to measure the difference between text sequences. The LD between to text strings is obtained as the minimum number of single-character edits required to change one string into the other one. The main difference between WER and LD is that WER is computed at word level, while LD is computed as character-level, which may provide a more accurate estimation of the ASR evaluation. Finally the sDTW was introduced to analyse differences between two time–series that differ in time and number of samples. The dynamic time warping performs a time–alignment between two text sequences, then the euclidean distance is computed between the predicted and the original transcriptions. The distance measure is transformed into a similarity score using Eq. 2. If the original and recognized transcriptions are the same, the DTW_{dist} will be zero, and the sDTW will be 1.

$$\text{sDTW} = \frac{1}{1 + \text{DTW\_distance}} \tag{2}$$

2.3   Classification

The decision whether an speech utterance is from a PD patient or a HC subject is performed with a SVM with a Gaussian kernel with margin parameter C and bandwidth of the kernel γ. The parameters were optimized in a grid search with $10^{-3} < C < 10^4$ and $10^{-6} < \gamma < 10^3$. A 10-fold speaker independence cross-validation strategy is performed, where eight folds are used to train the SVM, one to optimize the hyper-parameters, and one for test.

3   Experiments and Results

3.1   Intelligibility Analysis

The WER, LD, and sDTW were computed per speakers (PD and HC), using the ASR system described in Sect. 2.2. Table 2 shows the obtained results for both patients and healthy speakers. It can be observed that the intelligibility of the patients is more affected than the HC. In particular, the WER and LD were lower in the HC group (WER $= 2.70\%$; LD $= 11.3 \times 10^{-2}$), compared to the other speech tasks. For the case of the sDTW, the highest distance was obtained for the HC (sDWT $= 79.1 \times 10^{-2}$), which means that there is higher similarity between the real and the estimated (ASR) transcriptions. These results support the hypothesis that the patients have more difficulties than the healthy speakers to produce rapid alternating sounds during the DDK exercises.

Table 2. Intelligibility features. **WER:** *Word Error Rate.* **LD:** *Levenshtein Distance.* **sDTW:** *Dynamic Time Warping.* **HC:** *Healthy Controls.* **PD:** *Parkinson's Diseases.*

Task	WER (%) HC	WER (%) PD	LD (10^{-2}) HC	LD (10^{-2}) PD	sDTW (10^{-2}) HC	sDTW (10^{-2}) PD
/pa-ka-ta/	4.90	11.7	1.71	9.92	76.3	69.3
/pa-ta-ka/	2.70	11.3	0.71	7.38	79.1	70.5
/pe-ta-ka/	2.90	7.10	1.26	2.97	78.8	73.8

3.2   Evaluation System

In order to evaluate the speech impairment of the patients, intelligibility and articulation features were extracted from each speech task and the combination of the three DDK exercises (Fusion). Additionally, both set of features were merged in order to test the suitability of the method to improved the detection speech problems in PD patients. Table 3 shows the performance of the SVM in terms of the accuracy (ACC), sensibility (SEN), specificity (SPE), and the area

Table 3. Performance of the SVM. *ACC: Accuracy. SEN: Sensibility. SPE: Specificity. AUC: Area Under the ROC Curve. Art+Int: Articulation and Intelligibility features. Fusion: Combination of the DDK speech tasks.*

Task	Feature	ACC (%)	SEN (%)	SPE (%)	AUC
/pa-ka-ta/	Articulation	75	81	73	0.78
	Intelligibility	56	53	64	0.54
	Art+Int	76	82	75	0.78
/pa-ta-ka/	Articulation	67	68	67	0.76
	Intelligibility	59	70	61	0.59
	Art+Int	73	74	74	0.78
/pe-ta-ka/	Articulation	68	72	69	0.74
	Intelligibility	61	68	63	0.61
	Art+Int	67	72	69	0.75
Fusion	Articulation	76	77	78	0.84
	Intelligibility	63	68	67	0.61
	Art+Int	72	72	75	0.82

under the ROC curve (AUC). In biomedical applications the AUC is interpreted as follows: AUC < 0.70 indicates poor performance, $0.70 \leq$ AUC < 0.80 is fair, $0.80 \leq$ AUC < 0.90 is good, and $0.90 \leq$ AUC < 1 is excellent [15]. Table 3 shows the results obtained for each speech tasks. The performance of the classifier is fair for the three DDK exercises (/pa-ka-ta/ $= 0.78$; /pa-ta-ka/ $= 0.76$; /pe-ta-ka/ $= 0.74$). When the articulation features are extracted from the combined DDKs the performance improved from fair to good (AUC $= 0.84$). When the intelligibility features are considered for training, the performance of the SVM is poor in all cases (/pa-ka-ta/ $= 0.54$; /pa-ta-ka/ $= 0.59$; /pe-ta-ka/ $= 0.61$; Fusion $= 0.61$). Figure 2 shows the ROC curves for each set of features on Fusion task. Figure 3 shows the distribution of the PD patients according to the WER and LD for the word /pa-ta-ka/. It can be observed that the PD patients are more dispersed than the healthy speakers, however, both group of speakers are very close to each other, which explain the low performance obtained for the intelligibility features.

Additional to the articulation and intelligibility features, the SVM was trained considering the combination of both set of features. From Table 3 it can be observed that the accuracies obtained are not significantly different from those obtained when only the articulation features are considered for training. These results are expected, since the DDK exercises are designed to assess articulation problems of the patients. Additionally, the corpus used to train the ASR is limited to the words /pa-ta-ka/, /pa-ka-ta/, and /pe-ta-ka/, thus, different miss-pronunciations produced by the speakers are not included, e.g., /ba-ta-ka/,/pa-pa-ka/.

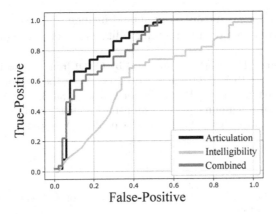

Fig. 2. ROC curve considering the Fusion of the three DDKs.

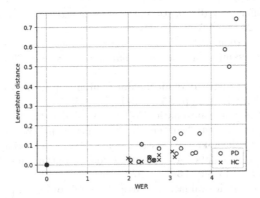

Fig. 3. Distribution of PD patients (O) and healthy speakers (X) considering two intelligibility features (LD vs. WER).

4 Conclusions

In this work is presented a methodology to model the intelligibility problems in the speech of PD patients. The ASR was trained considering speech recordings of the rapid repetition of the words /pa-ta-ka/, /pa-ka-ta/, and /pe-ta-ka/. According to the results, the recognition error in the ASR is lower in the healthy group respect to the patients, which, indicates that the patients have more problems to produce certain sounds during speech. Additionally, articulation, intelligibility, and the combination of both set of features were considered to train a SVM. In this case, the best results were obtained when the articulation features were considered to train the classifier. Furthermore, the results improved when the three DDK exercises were combined to train the SVM. This can be explained considering that the DDKs are exercises designed to detect articulation problems in pathological speech. Also, note that the corpus used to detect intelligibility problems is limited, thus, future work should include sentences, read texts, and monologues in order to model the intelligibility problem of the patients.

Acknowledgments. This work was financed by CODI from University of Antioquia by the grant Number PRV16-2-01 and 2015-7683. Also the authors thanks to the Training Network on Automatic Processing of PAthological Speech (TAPAS) funded by the Horizon 2020 programme of the European Commission. Tomás Arias-Vergara is under grants of Convocatoria Doctorado Nacional-785 financed by COLCIENCIAS.

References

1. Hornykiewicz, O.: Biochemical aspects of Parkinson's disease. Neurology **51**(2 Suppl 2), S2–S9 (1998)
2. Ho, A.K.: Speech impairment in a large sample of patients with parkinson's disease. Behav. Neurol. **11**(3), 131–137 (1999)
3. Darley, F.L.: Differential diagnostic patterns of dysarthria. J. Speech Lang. Hear. Res. **12**(2), 246–269 (1969)
4. Logemann, J.A.: Frequency and cooccurrence of vocal tract dysfunctions in the speech of a large sample of Parkinson patients. J. Speech Hear. Disord. **43**(1), 47–57 (1978)
5. Tjaden, K.: Characteristics of diadochokinesis in multiple sclerosis and Parkinson's disease. Folia Phoniatr. Logop. **55**(5), 241–259 (2003)
6. Tao, F., et al.: A portable automatic PA-TA-KA syllable detection system to derive biomarkers for neurological disorders. In: Interspeech, pp. 362–366 (2016)
7. Montaña, D.: A diadochokinesis-based expert system considering articulatory features of plosive consonants for early detection of Parkinson's disease. Comput. Methods Programs Biomed. **154**, 89–97 (2018)
8. Novotný, M.: Automatic evaluation of articulatory disorders in Parkinson's disease. IEEE/ACM Trans. Audio Speech Lang. Process. **22**(9), 1366–1378 (2014)
9. Orozco-Arroyave, J.R., et al.: New Spanish speech corpus database for the analysis of people suffering from Parkinson's disease. In: Language Resources and Evaluation Conference (LREC), pp. 342–347 (2014)
10. Yaruss, J.S.: Evaluating rate, accuracy, and fluency of young children's diadochokinetic productions: a preliminary investigation. J. Fluen. Disord. **27**(1), 65–86 (2002)
11. Orozco-Arroyave, J.R., et al.: NeuroSpeech: an open-source software for Parkinson's speech analysis. Digit. Signal Process. (2017, in Press)
12. De Letter, M.: The effects of levodopa on word intelligibility in Parkinson's disease. J. Commun. Disord. **38**(3), 187–196 (2005)
13. Miller, N.: Prevalence and pattern of perceived intelligibility changes in parkinson's disease. J. Neurol. Neurosurg. Psychiatry **78**(11), 1188–1190 (2007)
14. Povey, D., et al.: The Kaldi speech recognition toolkit. In: IEEE 2011 Workshop on Automatic Speech Recognition and Understanding, pp. 1–4 (2011)
15. Swets, J.A.: Psychological science can improve diagnostic decisions. Psychol. Sci. Public Interest **1**(1), 1–26 (2000)

Modeling and Simulation of Integration of Internet of Things and Manufacturing Industry 4.0

José Ignacio Rodríguez-Molano[1]([✉]), Jenny Alexandra Triana-Casallas[2], and Leonardo Emiro Contreras-Bravo[1]

[1] Universidad Distrital Francisco José de Caldas, Bogotá, Colombia
{jirodriguez, lecontrerasb}@udistrital.edu.co
[2] Universidad Santo Tomas, Villavicencio, Colombia
jennytriana@usantotomas.edu.co

Abstract. Internet of Things (IoT) is changing the processes in the manufacturing industry. It is creating new opportunities for both economies and society. The deployment of Internet of Things for the development of Industry 4.0 improves processes and manufacturing systems. In this type of systems, the information is related to the manufacturing status, trends in energy consumption by machinery, material logistics, customer orders, supply data and all data related to smart devices implemented in the processes. This paper describes an Internet of Things architecture applied to industry, a metamodel of integration in its phase II (Internet of things, social networks, cloud and industry 4.0) for the generation of applications for Industry 4.0.

Keywords: Industry 4.0 · Simulation · Manufacturing

1 Introduction

IoT has reached so much development and importance that several reports foresee it as one of the technologies of higher impact until 2025 [1]. Thousands of millions of physical elements and objects will be equipped with different types of sensors and actuators, all of them connected in real time to internet through heterogeneous networks. This will generate high amounts of data flows that have to be stored, processed and shown to be interpreted in an efficient and easy manner. Here is where IoT and Cloud computing integration permits that this huge amount of data can be stored in internet, keeping resources, services and data available and ready to use and for end-to-end service providing [2] both in the business and in the consumer field, from anywhere. It provides the virtual integration infrastructure for storage devices, analysis tools, monitoring and platform. Most interactions in internet are human-to-human (H2H).

The Internet of Things counts on sensors or scattered objects to generate information from any accessible site or inside a machine. Thus, it requires the interconnection of these heterogeneous objects via the Internet. This will lead to a future in which it is not only used for communication between people, but also between human

© Springer Nature Switzerland AG 2018
J. C. Figueroa-García et al. (Eds.): WEA 2018, CCIS 916, pp. 231–241, 2018.
https://doi.org/10.1007/978-3-030-00353-1_21

and machine, and even between different machines (M2M) [3]. Here is found the importance of Smart Objects: physical objects with an embedded system that allows information processing and communication with other devices, and also the processes based on a certain action or event. However, all of these complex systems present a problem when connecting the Smart Objects due to the differences between software and hardware used for each process.

Due to the enlargement of the IoT and the Cloud Computing application development, technological problems decrease and an expansion of services is created in an industrial context [4]. This paper outlines the need to integrate the IoT, sensors, actuators, social networks and computing in the cloud. It will enable to build the Industrial Internet of Things (IIoT) up. This article describes the conceptual characteristics of the elements to be taken into account in the integration proposal and presents the integration metamodel in its phase II.

2 State of the Art

2.1 Internet of Things

Internet of Things aims to connect millions of objects of any type to Internet. It will lead to potential great changes in our lives, providing a greater productivity, bettering our health, improving efficiency, reducing energy consumption and making comfortable our houses. These may be, as already proven in some researches such as the Arduino microcontrollers, microcomputers such as the Raspberry Pi, fridges, smartphones, sensors, actuators, Smart TVs, cars, smart tags as RFID, NFC and barcodes, QR (Quick Response Code, QR Code) codes, among many other types of objects.

IoT applications currently focus on the Smart Home, industry 4.0, so-called Industrial IoT (IIoT), municipalities or villages grouped in the concept Smart Town, cities also called Smart Cities [5] and the environment that sits under the concept Smart Earth. Each of these divisions has its own applications, although all are based on IoT. Smart homes seek to prioritize automation, industry to improve the manufacturing processes, towns and villages to preserve their cultural identity, the cities their livability and environmental communication with buildings and nature. Based on this, the purpose is to create a smart world, leading to the Smart World [6].

2.2 Cloud Computing

The use the cloud, has permitted to perform all the computing in it, without any need of own servers or mainframes. This has opened a new economic model in computing, the companies offer hardware, platforms and software as subscription services. They are housed in the cloud. All is packaged and on-demand, normally over the Internet. The services that are in the cloud can be managed, either to resupply them, modify them or release them with minimal effort thanks to the tools provided by the suppliers of such services. In addition, the services are offered in a robust, reliable and available way anytime and anywhere. Hence, the three basic components of Cloud Computing are the virtualization, the multi-tenancy and the web services [2].

2.3   Industrial Internet of Things: Industry 4.0

Industrial Internet of Things (IIoT), also known as industry 4.0, is the combination of Internet of Things with manufacturing. As an emerging technology is expected that IoT offers solutions to transform transportation and manufacturing systems, improving them to obtain greater efficiency, cost savings and time reduction in processes [7].

Industrial Internet of Things (IIoT) is connecting the machines together and with the physical world of sensors, increasingly more ubiquitous, increasing the speed of business and of industrial development exponentially. The IIoT goes beyond the M2M communication [8]. It includes the connection of industrial networks and service networks to different information storage infrastructure through the provision of software services and its autonomous control in the cloud. The Industrial Internet of Things is the new industrial revolution and the rise in the use of sensors, advanced data analysis and smart decision making is changing the world itself.

The continuous technological advances have enabled the development of new methods of communication between people and objects [9], which allow the exchange of information within the parameters of speed and security. Internet of them things has exploited these advances technological and the inclusion of new elements within them systems of information to allow the access remote and the control of the different systems. This technology is used to improve the efficiency of supply chains [10] and to improve the information obtained in real time throughout the process.

There is a large number of applications in the IIoT. Proof of it is a system to locate and monitor the transport [11], allowing to predict its future location and what traffic will be on the road. However, the main application of IIoT is in supply chains where RFID technology with greater intensity is used. Exactly because IoT has an important role in the logistics industries.

3   Metamodel of Integration

Here is shown the proposal for the creation of a system that generates applications for the industry 4.0 on various platforms or operating systems. They permits to connect objects of the Internet of Things through different networks, social networks included.

While defining a device, certain features of that device and the objects that it contains (sensors, actuators) must be defined as well. The device can include rules that grants some level of intelligence, unrelated to smart objects [12].

The system was designed applying MDE, which led to a flow of steps. First of all, is needed to define the problem domain to be resolved and which narrows the field of knowledge. In this proposal, the domain is the definition of devices that may connect to the different networks either for publishing data from its sensors or for control of their actuators by other users or devices that make use of the rules that allow to automate the processes.

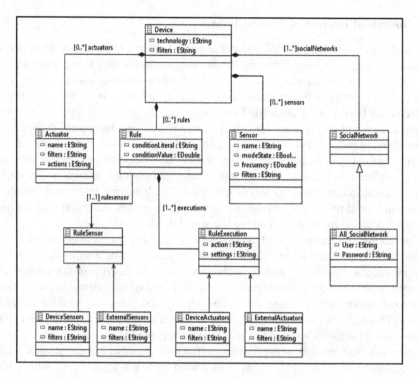

Fig. 1. Metamodel of the system. Phase I

Once the domain is bounded, the metamodel must be defined from a meta-metamodel, in this case Ecore (from Eclipse Foundation) (Fig. 1).

- The device: It is the main component and its definition is the target of the language. Its features are the technology that represents the device platform, in this particular case it is a Raspberry Pi, platform developed in one of the languages supported by Raspberry Pi; and the filters that represent the keywords necessary to identify the devices in the social networks. The device is shaped by other components: social networks, actuators, sensors and rules.
- Social Network (Social Internet of Things): A device may be associated to one or more social networks, at least one. Social networks are abstract components that another component must implement. I.e. a device can have social networks with different properties. However, all of them are social networks.
- Actuator: A device may be formed by actuators in addition to other components. By this component each one of the actuators of the device is defined. Their features are the name of the actuator, the actions that can be performed (at least one is required) and filters that might be used to identify the actuator in addition to the name.

- Sensor: A device may consist of sensors in addition to other components such as actuators. By using this component, each of the sensors available to the device is defined. Its features are the name of the sensor, which may be either in automatic or in manual operating mode (modeState), frequency of running if it is automated, and filters that can be used to identify the sensor in addition to the name.
- Rule: In addition to physical components such as sensors or actuators, a device may have rules that automate execution of the actions of its actuators, or invoke actions to actuators of other devices, being based on data from its sensors or from other sensors available in the social network. Their properties are the literal of the condition (conditionLiteral), for example "greater than", and the value that must fulfill the condition (conditionValue). In addition to these properties, a sensor has a rule (RuleSensor) and a series of executions to be performed if the condition is met (RuleExecution).
- RuleSensor: A sensor must have a rule that receives the value that will validate the condition to turn execution of actions automated. This component is an abstract component that implements two different components as there are two possibilities when selecting the rule of sensor: one or several sensors in the device itself (DeviceSensors), one or several sensors from external devices (ExternalSensors).

  1. One or several sensors in the device itself (DeviceSensors): The rules can be used to evaluate the condition. The value of one or several sensors in the same device still requires both its name and that they contain the indicated filters.
  2. One or several sensors from an external device (ExternalSensor): The rules can be used to evaluate the condition. The value of one or several sensors from an external device indicating the name of the sensor and the filters that identify the devices and/or sensors.

- Rule execution: A rule can have to perform several executions if the condition is correct or at least one execution to do. Rule execution is an abstract component that implements two different components as there are two possibilities as selecting the actuator which will make the implementation of an action: one or several actuators of the device itself (DeviceActuators), one or several actuators of external devices (ExternalActuators). This component has a number of properties shared by all the possibilities. These are the name of the action to perform and the parameters or settings that will use the action

  1. One or several actuators of the device itself (DeviceActuators): rules can perform an action of one or several actuators of the same device, yet requiring both its name (name) and that they contain the indicated filters.
  2. One or several actuators of an external device (ExternalActuators): rules can perform an action of an actuator of an external device indicating the name of the actuator and the filters that identify the devices and/or actuators (Fig. 2).

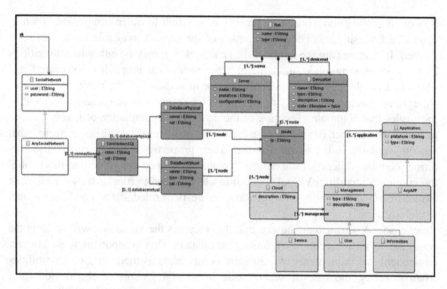

Fig. 2. Metamodel of the system. Phase II

3.1   Prototype

Within the industry 4.0 framework, the developed prototype is applicable to perform the automation of manual processes within the different productive activities in any type of industry. It implies improvements of the availability of information and its security, facilitating the flow of the information and improving the decision-making process on the implementation of corrective and preventive actions. The advantages of deployment of this class of prototypes within productive processes or for tracking products [13] relates to the decrease in uncertainty and measurement errors. In addition, the possibility of implementing a measurement process has an advantage over an interrupted manual measurement. Also, by creating processes of traceability of data and information that did not previously exist (without the intervention of the human resource) given that the gathered information is continually pushed towards the Big Data or cloud computing for its consolidation.

Based on the concepts of ubiquitous computing and communication M2M, implemented under the framework of the Internet of Things, the objective of this prototype is to capture data and provide access to them in real time and remotely. A communication environment-object and object-object was established to achieve the proposed objective. The communication environment, subject of the surveillance system, allowed to monitor several variables. For this purpose, four sensors were used. They allowed to determine the flow of products in a production plant. The presence of gas in the complex, the alignment and stability of the equipment and the existence of contact between a person and the prototype. The information on changes in the status of sensors was processed in a microcomputer Raspberry Pi.

A communication object-object between the Raspberry Pi and a mobile device was deployed with the purpose of establishing the synchronization of data directly to the user via smartphone or tablet. It was achieved through the connection established between the Raspberry Pi and the storage server in the cloud.

The prototype has the following features

- Use of technologies of sensors: the prototype uses different sensors for the detection of "strange" elements in the working environment. Then it initiates capture and data communication. The sensor acts like a link between what happens in the process and the user.
- Data collection at any time: the prototype allows capturing images and is always aware of each movement in the area where the system is deployed.
- Data Transfer: it is possible to transfer data within the communication network that is composed by the user (via a mobile device) and the physical system (Raspberry Pi) through cloud computing.
- User interface: the prototype can communicate with the user through well-known platforms or server storage.
- Functional Independence: the prototype works automatically independently of the user, since the capture of data and their transfer functions are carried out only with the activation of a sensor and a wireless network.
- Communication with the mobile device: the system does not require direct intervention to the hardware or software to operate. The communication is conducted under the principles of communication machine-to-machine, in which the microcomputer Raspberry Pi and the sensors are the prototype and the mobile device is the terminal that enables communication with the user through a server and a communication network. The collected data are transferred from one machine to another in the same way, disregarding which sensor is in use.
- Total availability of data: the system generates a communication network that allows users access in any place and request of data at any time, due to online connection of the physical prototype (Raspberry Pi) to the server (Fig. 3).

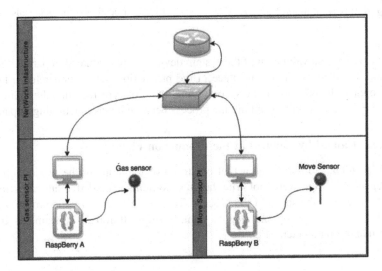

Fig. 3. Connection diagram of the prototype

4   Tests of the Prototype and Results

Tests to the monitoring system were performed with two sensors, making in each test the connection of each individual sensor to the Raspberry Pi. The tests were performed on a production line of ceramics in a period of 24 h of work (Figs. 4, 5, 6 and 7).

Fig. 4. Location humidity sensors.

Fig. 5. Location temperature sensors

Fig. 6. Location motion sensors

Fig. 7. Location of particle sensors

For the functional validation of the system devices were evaluated in parallel. In the first round, the devices already in place in the production line. It generated a failure report, stopping the process. In the second round the prototype recorded the failure and generated the report without stopping the process because it was functioning in parallel.

4.1   Stops Caused by Failures in the Production Flow

The data permitted to verify the actual condition of the stops in the production line. Some registered stops were not true failures, systems recorded them as a failure because a change in the speed of the process. The data generated by the prototype also recorded ordinary stops of and quality control stops. It forced adjustments in the decision making parameters (Fig. 8).

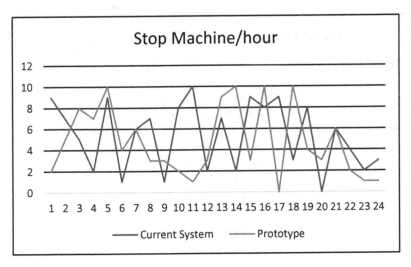

Fig. 8. Stops caused by failures in the production flow

4.2 Stops Caused by Misalignment and Instability of the Computer

The current computer does not count with this type of information, therefore it permits that the process generates failures, affecting the product. Also, it affects the equipment itself, because it subsequently generates a greater fault. The information provided by the prototype allowed to check and adjust the computer without generating any stop in the process.

The test of the monitoring system with the sensor of gas detection was carried out. Into the environment in which they were performed there was no presence of gases LP, methane or smoke. Consequently, signals sent by the sensor to the Raspberry Pi did not activate the collecting system nor synchronization (Figs. 9 and 10).

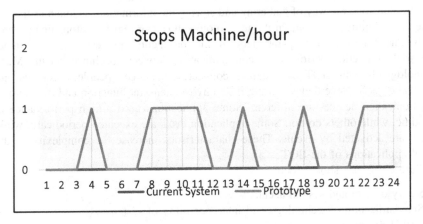

Fig. 9. Stops caused by misalignment and instability of the computer

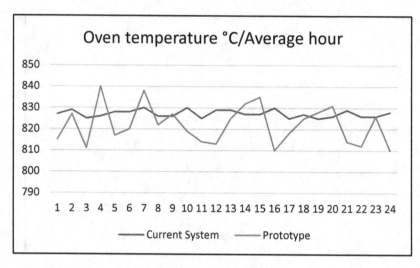

Fig. 10. Average temperature recorded

5 Conclusions and Future Work

The technology itself is not the main obstacle for the implementation of IIoT; the interfaces of interoperability of the systems belonging to different providers are, that hinders its adoption. The achievement of interoperability requires standardization of interfaces for interaction between different components of the system.

IIoT is the combination of computing technologies, communication and micro-electronics. Thus, there are many interfaces between hardware, software and network components. In the context of the industry 4.0, the proposed architecture let establish communication networks between objects and people that permit the flow of information in two ways, with minimal intervention in the network. Communication networks focus on direct and comprehensive transmission of data.

The change in the way of gathering and storing the information, as much as the use of sensors, requires a change in the technology. IIOT can register automatically, precisely and timely several parameters of the production process. The traditional industrial production performs the communication between machines via the M2M technology, but the IIOT can achieve connections between people, machines and physical objects. Nevertheless, in the IIOT environment, the function and the yield of communication devices are different. Some applications need a high performance in real-time, while others do not. Some application tasks are executed periodically while others are activated by events. These characteristics increase the complexity of the actual applications of the IIOT.

Future research should focus on:

- Safety of data and system accuracy
- Standardization of technology and interoperability of systems
- Actual deployments.

References

1. The US National Intelligence Council: Disruptive Civil Technologies: Six Technologies with Potential Impacts on US Interests out to 2025 (2008)
2. Biswas, A.R., Giaffreda, R.: IoT and cloud convergence : opportunities and challenges. In: 2014 IEEE World Forum Internet Things, pp. 375–376 (2014)
3. Roman, R., Zhou, J., Lopez, J.: On the features and challenges of security and privacy in distributed internet of things. Comput. Netw. **57**(10), 2266–2279 (2013)
4. Steiner, W., Poledna, S.: Fog computing as enabler for the industrial internet of things. e i Elektrotechnik und Informationstechnik **133**, 310–314 (2016)
5. Barriga, J.K.D., Romero, C.D.G., Molano, J.I.R.: Proposal of a standard architecture of IoT for smart cities. In: Uden, L., Liberona, D., Feldmann, B. (eds.) LTEC 2016. CCIS, vol. 620, pp. 77–89. Springer, Cham (2016). https://doi.org/10.1007/978-3-319-42147-6_7
6. Sanchez, L., et al.: SmartSantander: IoT experimentation over a smart city testbed. Comput. Netw. **61**, 217–238 (2014)
7. Anderl, R.: Industrie 4.0 - technological approaches, use cases, and implementation. At-Automatisierungstechnik **63**(10), 753–765 (2015)
8. Sanchez-Iborra, R., Cano, M.D.: State of the art in LP-WAN solutions for industrial IoT services. Sensors **16**(5), 708 (2016)
9. Baños-Gonzalez, V., Afaqui, M., Lopez-Aguilera, E., Garcia-Villegas, E.: IEEE 802.11ah: a technology to face the IoT challenge. Sensors **16**(11), 1960 (2016)
10. Ngai, E.W.T., Moon, K.K.L., Riggins, F.J., Yi, C.Y.: RFID research: an academic literature review (1995–2005) and future research directions. Int. J. Prod. Econ. **112**(2), 510–520 (2008)
11. Hao, L., Lei, X., Yan, Z., ChunLi, Y.: The application and implementation research of smart city in China. In: 2012 International Conference on System Science and Engineering (ICSSE), pp. 288–292 (2012)
12. García, C.G., Meana-Llorián, D., G-Bustelo, B.C.P., Lovelle, J.M.C.: A review about smart objects, sensors, and actuators. Int. J. Interact. Multimed. Artif. Intell. **4**(3), 7–10 (2017)
13. Lee, J., Bagheri, B., Kao, H.: A cyber-physical systems architecture for industry 4. 0-based manufacturing systems. Manuf. Lett. **3**, 18–23 (2015)

Digital Signal Processing (DSP)

Continuous Wavelet Transform for Muscle Activity Detection in Surface EMG Signals During Swallowing

Sebastian Roldan-Vasco[1,2(✉)], Estefania Perez-Giraldo[3],
and Andres Orozco-Duque[3]

[1] Grupo de Investigación en Materiales Avanzados y Energía, Facultad de
Ingenierías, Instituto Tecnológico Metropolitano, Medellín, Colombia
sebastianroldan@itm.edu.co
[2] Facultad de Ingeniería, Universidad de Antioquia, Medellín, Colombia
[3] Grupo de Investigación e Innovación Biomédica, Facultad de Ciencias Exactas y
Aplicadas, Instituto Tecnológico Metropolitano, Medellín, Colombia

Abstract. The surface electromyography (sEMG) has been used to
characterize normal and abnormal behavior of the swallowing related
muscles. One important activity in the analysis of the electromyographic
recordings, is the detection of bursts, indicators of muscle activations
but problematic in muscles with low signal-to-noise ratio (SNR). Most
of methods for burst detection are based on amplitude measures which
are signal-conditions dependent. We proposed a method to detect bursts
based on the continuous wavelet transform and thresholding over the
scalogram but not over amplitude. sEMG signals from 38 healthy subjects were recorded during swallowing tasks. We compared the proposed
method to the visual method as a reference, and a previous method based
on the Teager-Kaiser energy operator (TKEO). The proposed method
avoids detection of false negatives better than TKEO, and it is suitable
to apply in problems of burst detection in sEMG signals with low SNR.

Keywords: EMG · Surface electromyography
Continuous wavelet transform · Onset detection · Burst detection
Swallowing

1 Introduction

The swallowing mechanism is a sequential process with differentiated oral, pharyngeal, and esophageal phases that carry saliva, solids and fluids from the mouth
to the stomach. Alterations in this process is known as dysphagia. Normal swallowing involves the coordination of 30 pairs of muscles [5]. The infrahyoid muscles
and also another laryngeal and pharyngeal muscles, play an important role in
the pharyngeal phase behavior [8]. In special, the infrahyoid muscles descend
the hyolaryngeal complex toward the sternum [16]. Such displacement moves
the larynx under the base of the tongue and closes the laryngeal vestibule before

© Springer Nature Switzerland AG 2018
J. C. Figueroa-García et al. (Eds.): WEA 2018, CCIS 916, pp. 245–255, 2018.
https://doi.org/10.1007/978-3-030-00353-1_22

opening the upper esophageal sphincter [5]. Studies of surface electromyographic signal (sEMG) from infrahyoid muscles can help to determine alterations in swallowing, i.e. the presence of dysphagia [12,19,24]. However, these muscles have been relatively few investigated due to difficulty to assess them non-invasively [8].

Problems with sEMG acquisition from swallowing related muscles rely on the fact that they have small size and overlying fibers [5], producing low signal-to-noise ratio (SNR) and difficulties to detect the muscle activations (bursts). In the time elapsed between the end of a muscle burst and the beginning of the successive one, the muscle under study is silent. However, the electrode detects a background noise [13]. In order to evaluate the quality of the recorded signals, the background noise and SNR are usually estimated by manual or automatic segmentation of the signal in the time domain [1]. Signal processing and analysis methods can improve the SNR in the sEMG measurements from infrahyoid muscles [17]. Visual muscle onset determination by an expert examiner is considered to be the gold standard for detect the bursts [25]. However, this time-consuming method has moderate reproducibility and repeatability [4].

Automatic strategies for onset detection include the simple [7] and double-threshold [3], Teager-Kaiser energy operator (TKEO) [21]. Most of these methods are based on amplitude measures as well as they are oriented to analysis of the large muscles of limbs. It is well known that in sEMG signals, the amplitude depends on several uncontrolled variables such as: electrode-skin impedance, volume conductor, inter electrode distances, location of electrodes, etc. [6]. Furthermore, the heuristically chosen threshold has been shown to introduce errors into onset determination [7,23], specially in signals with low SNR. Some studies set the threshold by optimization, but this process can generate overfitting because the high variability of amplitude and SNR in sEMG recordings between trials and subjects.

In order to avoid the above mentioned problems, another strategies such as the maximum likelihood ratio [26] and gaussian-mixture models [10,15], have been implemented. These methods have the assumption that sEMG is generated by a Gaussian process - which is not exact - and need previous information about the distribution involved in the generation of sEMG signal.

In this study we propose a time-frequency method based on Continuous Wavelet transform (CWT) in order to detect bursts. This method is based on the scales-coefficients energies but not in amplitude measures. Our process includes a denoising step base on discrete wavelet transform (DWT) to improve the SNR. We tested the proposed method in a database with sEMG recorded in the right infrahyoid muscle during swallowing tasks. In order to make a comparison, we tested the signal with a previously reported threshold-based method which used amplitude based measures such as TKEO and RMS [17], instead measures of energy of the spectrogram. This is one of the first approaches aiming to characterize swallowing related signals in a automatic way, as a preliminary step to analyze muscle behavior in patients with swallowing disorders.

2   Materials and Methods

2.1   Subjects

We recruited 38 volunteers (16 males and 22 females), healthy subjects aged between 32 and 50 years old (41.16 ± 6.12). The following exclusion criteria were used for subject selection: dental braces, congenital oral malformations, active inflammatory processes (mouth, head or neck), strange elements in mouth (like piercing), diagnosed cognitive disorders (motor or sensorial), chronic obstructive pulmonary disease, head or neck cancer antecedents, or facial aesthetic surgery. All the males were well-shaved. A balanced sex ratio was not considered necessary. Informed consent was taken from each case and the study was approved from Ethics Committee of the Instituto Tecnológico Metropolitano.

2.2   Signal Acquisition

We analyzed right infrahyoid muscles during swallowing tasks. This muscle plays an important role in the oral and pharyngeal phases of the swallowing process. Myoelectrical activity was measured with a differential bioamplifier connected to the polygraph PowerLab 16/35 (AD Instruments Inc.). The sEMG signal was acquired with non-polarizable, bipolar, disposable and pre-gelled Ag/AgCl electrodes (Ref. 2228, 3M - $30\,mm \times 35\,mm$, $15\,mm$ diameter in gel area and interelectrode distance of $25\,mm$). The reference electrode was placed in the forehead. Figure 1 shows the placement of the sEMG electrodes.

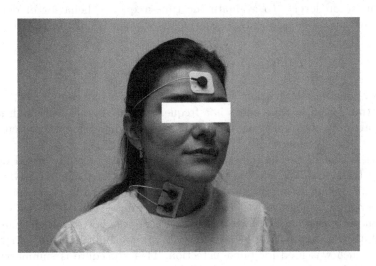

Fig. 1. Electrode placement for right infrahyoid sEMG acquisition.

The following boluses were taken by the subjects: thin liquid (water - 5, 10 and 20 mL), yogurt (3, 5 and 7 mL), and one saliva swallow; 266 sEMG recordings were used for analysis. The three consistencies have been used for assessment of penetration/aspiration in dysphagia [18]. Liquid and yogurt were delivered to the oral cavity via a 1.5 oz cup. Every task was video-recorded and initiated when the examiner require to swallow. Video frames were synchronized with the signal acquisition.

2.3   Signal Pre-processing

The sEMG signals were acquired with sampling frequency $F_s = 2\,\mathrm{kHz}$. The pre-processing, storage and visualization of the raw signals were carried out with LabChart Pro (AD Instruments Inc.). Offline analysis was performed using a custom program (Matlab, MathWorks Inc.). As the acquired signals have low signal-to-noise ratio (SNR) and are highly susceptible to crosstalk, another filter with narrow bandwidth was employed to improve the burst detection. The signals were filtered with a 5th order bandpass Butterworth filter between 90 and 250 Hz [17].

Each signal was visually inspected in the time domain in order to detect onset and offset of bursts. These times were saved for subsequent analysis and comparison with the automatic method proposed here.

2.4   Time-Frequency Method for Burst Detection

Every signal was denoised using a Discrete Wavelet Transform (DWT)-based algorithm, with soft minimax thresholding, symlet-8 as mother wavelet and 8 decomposition levels. To evaluate the time-frequency behavior of denoised sEMG, We applied subsequently a continuous wavelet transform (CWT) given by [20]:

$$CWT(s,\tau) = \frac{1}{\sqrt{s}} \int x(t)\psi^* \left(\frac{t-\tau}{s} \right) dt \qquad (1)$$

where $\psi(t)$ denotes the mother wavelet, the asterisk is the complex conjugate, τ is the translation in time and s is a frequency-related scale. Although initial signals have only one dimension, the CWT gives a bi-dimensional representation of scale vs. time (scalogram).

The selection of the mother wavelet must be done carefully based on the nature of the signal. We selected the Haar wavelet for analyzing sEMG signals since we are looking for amplitude changes in the signal and it has low complexity.

The original scalogram was rescaled in the range 1–255 ($CWT_{rs}(s_{rs},\tau)$). We sought for times τ with scales-coefficients energies above a background level E_{min}. With the information in ($CWT_{rs}(s_{rs},\tau)$), we built a projection vector $Proj(\tau)$ which was used for burst detection. This procedure is summarized in Algorithm 1. We defined a threshold for $Proj(\tau)$, denoted as Th_w, that define the points at which onset and offset points are detected. This procedure is detailed in the Algorithm 2. Both E_{min} and Th_w were optimized to get an accurate detection of bursts.

Algorithm 1. CWT-based algorithm for burst detection

1: **Input**: $CWT_{rs}(s_{rs}, \tau)$ - scalogram of EMG signal
2: **Input**: E_{min} - threshold of Energy defined by CWT coefficients.
3: **Input**: Th_w - threshold of CWT scales.
4: N = length of the signal.
5: **for** $j = 1, ..., N$ **do**
6:    $Proj(j) = f(CWT_{rs}(s_{rs}, j) \geq E_{min})$: $f(\bullet)$ counts the number of rows of j-th column of $CWT_{rs}(s_{rs}, \tau)$ greater than E_{min}
7: Calculate onset and offset for each burst using Algorithm 2.
8: **for** $j = 1, ...,$number of burst **do**
9:    **if** time between $offset_j$ and $onset_{j+1} \leq 250$ ms **then**
10:       Concatenate $offset_j$ and $onset_{j+1}$ in the same burst.
11: Remove all burst with a duration ≤ 100 ms.
12: Recalculate onset and offset using Algorithm 2
13: **Output**: onset and offset markers

If the difference between the offset of a burst and onset of the subsequent one was lesser than 250 ms, we unified both burst as only one. This was made to avoid the presence of consecutive bursts with non-physiological duration, and a false increasing of true positives.

Algorithm 2. Onset and offset marker

1: N = length of the signal.
2: **for** $i = 1, ..., N$ **do**
3:    **if** $Proj(i) \leq Th_w$ and $Proj(i+1) > Th_w$ **then**
4:       $i \leftarrow$ assign as onset
5:    **if** $Proj(i) > Th_w$ and $Proj(i+1) \leq Th_w$ **then**
6:       $i \leftarrow$ assign as offset

2.5 TKEO+RMS for Burst Detection

We compared the above mentioned method to a TKEO-based method for burst detection. This method has been reported for burst detection in signals with low SNR [21,27]. The TKEO of a discrete signal $x(t)$ is computed point-by-point follows:

$$TKEO\{x(t_i)\} = (x(t_i))^2 - x(t_{i-1})x(t_{i+1}) \tag{2}$$

We computed the RMS over the TKEO signal according to [17]. The resulting signal is denoted as $RMS_{TK}(t)$. We applied a fixed-size sliding window with length of 250 ms and steps of 100 ms. $RMS_{TK}(t)$ is decimated in time due to the windowing process. The burst detection was made using a threshold defined by the following expression:

$$Th_{TK} = \mu + h\sigma \tag{3}$$

where μ and σ are the mean and standard deviation of $RMS_{TK}(t)$, respectively, and h is a preset variable that defines the level of the threshold. The parameter h was fixed at 18 according to [17]. We applied a process similar to Algorithm 1 for burst detection through thresholding, but in this case $Proj(\tau)$ is changed by $RMS_{TK}(t)$.

2.6   Validation

A burst is limited by the time elapsed between the onset and the offset points. One trained person marked these points in order to avoid inter-expert variability and uncertainty. Every mark is done if and only if two conditions is accomplished: the laryngeal ascent is clearly identified in the video-recording and changes in amplitude and frequency are detected in the time-domain signal. The visual mark was used as reference for assessment of the proposed method.

We computed the true positives (TP), false positives (FP) and false negatives (FN) of burst detection process in the whole dataset. Both, the proposed CWT-detection based algorithm and TKEO-based algorithm were evaluated in comparison with the visual marks. Using TP, FP and FN, we computed the precision (Pr), recall (R) and F_1 score of the burst detection methods as follows:

$$Pr = \frac{TP}{TP+FP} \quad R = \frac{TP}{TP+FN} \quad F_1 = \frac{2 \times R \times Pr}{R + Pr}. \tag{4}$$

True negatives were not computed because they correspond to the identification of the background segments, which are not part of the interest of the current work. For the CWT-detection based algorithm, we compared different combination of parameters E_{min} and Th_w, and those that achieved the maximum value of the F_1 score were chosen as the optimal parameters. For the method based on TKEO, we varied Th_{TK} in order to maximize the F_1 score.

3   Results and Discussion

We propose a time-frequency method based on the CWT aiming to detect bursts in sEMG signals from infrahyoid muscles. The proposed method uses two thresholds: E_{min} and Th_w, which are applied to CWT scales but not to sEMG amplitude. We performed an exhaustive search to find the optimal parameters E_{min} and Th_w. E_{min} varied between 1 and 20 whereas Th_w varied between 1 and 30. Optimal parameters were found to be $E_{min} = 3$ and $Th_w = 18$. Left side of Fig. 2 shows the values generated by the F_1 score for variations of E_{min} when Th_w is fixed at the optimal value. In the same way, the right side of of Fig. 2 shows the values generated by the F_1 score for variations of Th_w when E_{min} is fixed at the optimal value. $E_{min} = 3$ means that, if energy for each scale is lesser or equal than 3 (in a scale between 1 and 255), that point of the scalogram is marked as noise. $Th_w = 18$ means that at less 18 scales - in a scalogram with

64 scales - contain energy components greater than E_{min}. It is clear that the energy threshold E_{min} is very small, which means that in our method, it is more important the scale-related threshold than the energy one. This finding avoids problems related to amplitude variability in the signals.

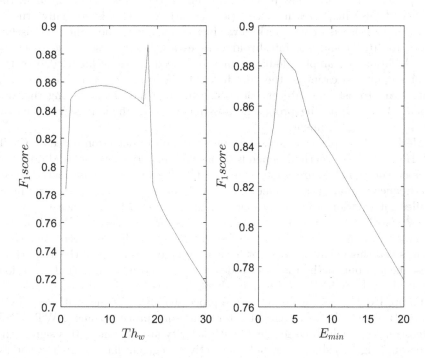

Fig. 2. Effect on F_1 score when the following parameters vary: (left) Th_w (E_{min} fixed at 3); and (right) E_{min} (Th_w fixed at 18)

Table 1 shows a comparison of the number of burst detected by both methods, the proposed CWT-based method and the TKEO-based one. The optimal parameters of Th_w and E_{min} used in the CWT-based method achieve the highest values of F_1 score (88,64%) in comparison to the TKEO-based method (83,46%). The proposed CWT-based method exhibits a balance between the precision and recall better than TKEO.

Table 1. Counting of true positives (TP), false positives (FP) and false negatives (FN) for the proposed and the TKEO-based methods in the whole dataset. Performance measures achieved with the both methods are shown.

	TP	FP	FN	F1 score	Precision	Recall
CWT-based method	462	46	75	88.64%	90.98%	86.43%
TKEO	340	48	183	83.46%	76.81%	91.4%

Problems with traditional threshold-based methods for detection of muscular activation are widely reported. As the threshold is user selected, it could be specially hard to find the optimal value if the signal has low SNR. This means affectation of precision and recall. If the threshold is too low, the number of false positives increases (low precision), whilst if the threshold is too high, the number of false negatives increases (low recall) [26]. This is specially true in the signals recorded in our work. Two factors come together: the SNR is low (below to 10 dB) and the infrahyoid muscles are highly susceptible to cross-talk. Additionally, amplitude-based methods need previous knowledge of the signal baseline to estimate the threshold [9]. To overcome this limitation, it is necessary to ask the subject not to execute any movement during the first second. By contrast, the proposed time-frequency method does not need an initial background segment.

Merlo et al. proposed a method for onset and offset detection based on CWT [14]. However, their method depends on a scales-energy threshold and does not consider additional information from the CWT scalogram. Our method uses time-frequency analysis and it measures CWT coefficient energies and uses more detailed information from the scalogram. In this way, Th_w is a measure of the energy distribution across the frequency scales for each sample. Based on our observations, noise segments contain less energy across different frequency components and this behavior does not have a strong dependence on the amplitude. Consequently, our method is able to detect onset and offset in signals with low amplitude and low SNR, for instance sEMG signals from infrahyoid muscle.

Figure 3A shows an example of pre-processed sEMG signal with low SNR. Figure 3B shows the same signal after denoising process using DWT (SNR increases). Although three segments with activity are present in this signal, the scalogram (Fig. 3C) shows that only one activity segment has the highest energy components for most scales. After the projection process described in Algorithm 1 only one burst is detected. Figure 3D illustrates a comparison between the reference signal and the burst detection performed by our method. Visual inspection, in comparison to the video recorded during the protocol, confirms that there is only one burst associated with one swallowing.

On the other hand, Fig. 4 shows an example of the burst detection process using TKEO with the same signal used in the Fig. 3 (see Fig. 4B). One threshold applied to RMS signal computed over TKEO time series (Fig. 4C). Figure 4D shows that three bursts are detected using this method, two of them considered as false positives. One of the main problem of this method is its dependence of the selected threshold. This behavior was observed in the whole database.

Several published methods measure the error in time for onset detection [10, 11,22,26,27]. We computed the performance measures for the presence/absence of burst even though our method is able to detect onset and offset times. We have a limitation in our database, because low SNR makes difficult to mark accurately onset and offset times by visual inspection. In future works, simulated sEMG signals and real signals will be used to optimize the method to reduce the error

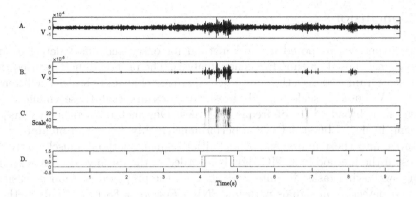

Fig. 3. Example of burst detection by the proposed method: A. Signal filtered with 90–250 Hz bandpass filter, B. Signal after denoising with DWT, C. Scalogram applied to denoised signal, D. Burst detection estimated using the proposed method (blue line) and marks with visual inspection (red dashed line). (Color figure online)

in time. Real sEMG signals will be recorded synchronized with other signals as a reference for mark onset and offset times.

In future works our method will be used for swallowing characterization. For instance, duration of the bursts could be measured. This factor is crucial for the swallowing analysis, because the time required to swallow different kind of boluses varies between grades of compromise in dysphagia [2]. Also, the method can be applied to sEMG signal from different muscles involved in swallowing. In that case, onset and offset times will be used to establish the sequence of activation in healthy and pathological subjects during swallowing.

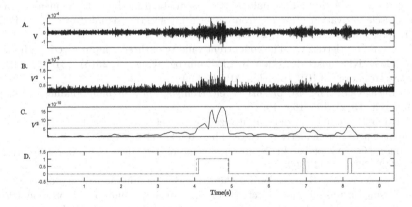

Fig. 4. Example of burst detection by the TKEO based method: A. Filtered sEMG signal with 90–250 Hz bandpass filter, B. TKEO applied to filtered signal, C. $RMS_{TK}(t)$ and thresholds for onset and offset detection, D. Burst detection estimated using the TKEO method (blue line) and marks with visual inspection (red dashed line). (Color figure online)

4   Conclusions

In this paper, we proposed a novel method for onset and offset detection on sEMG signals based on time-frequency analysis. The proposed method used the CWT scalogram to detect the time where there are changes of scales-coefficients energies. We used a scale-related threshold to ensure that those changes are present in a broad range of frequency-scales. Our method avoids two major problems in sEMG burst detection: performance highly dependent on amplitude measures, and the requirement of an initial segment without muscle activity. We tested the method in sEMG signals recorded in the infrahyoid muscle group during swallowing tasks. Results evidence that the proposed method is feasible for burst detection in signals with low SNR - F_1score $= 88,64\%$-. This method is a promissory tool for sEMG segmentation in swallowing analysis.

Acknowledgments. This work has been supported by COLCIENCIAS - República de Colombia, research project No. 115071149746.

References

1. Agostini, V., Knaflitz, M.: An algorithm for the estimation of the signal-to-noise ratio in surface myoelectric signals generated during cyclic movements. IEEE Trans. Biomed. Eng. **59**(1), 219–225 (2012)
2. Aydogdu, I., et al.: Clinical neurophysiology diagnostic value of dysphagia limit for neurogenic dysphagia: 17 years of experience in 1278 adults. Clin. Neurophysiol. J. **126**, 634–643 (2015). https://doi.org/10.1016/j.clinph.2014.06.035
3. Bonato, P., Alessio, T.D., Knaflitz, M.: A statistical method for the measurement of muscle activation intervals from surface myoelectric signal during gait. IEEE Trans. Biomed. Eng. **45**(3), 287–299 (1998)
4. Bonato, P., D'Alessio, T., Knaflitz, M.: A statistical method for the measurement of muscle activation intervals from surface myoelectric signal during gait. IEEE Trans. Biomed. Eng. **45**(3), 287–299 (1998)
5. Carter, S., Gutierrez, G.: The concurrent validity of three computerized methods of muscle activity onset detection. J. Electromyogr. Kinesiol. **25**(5), 731–741 (2015). https://doi.org/10.1016/j.jelekin.2015.07.009
6. De Luca, C.J.: The use of surface electromyography in biomechanics. J. Appl. Biomech. **13**(2), 135–163 (1997)
7. Di Fabio, R.: Reliability of computerized surface electromyography for determining the onsent of muscle activity. Phys. Ther. **67**(1), 43–48 (1987)
8. Ertekin, C., Aydogdu, I.: Neurophysiology of swallowing. Clin. Neurophysiol. **114**(12), 2226–2244 (2003)
9. Liu, J., Ying, D., Rymer, W.Z., Zhou, P.: Robust muscle activity onset detection using an unsupervised electromyogram learning framework. PloS One **10**(6), e0127990 (2015). http://www.pubmedcentral.nih.gov/articlerender.fcgi?artid=4454555&tool=pmcentrez&rendertype=abstract
10. Liu, J., Ying, D., Rymer, W.Z.: EMG burst presence probability: a joint time-frequency representation of muscle activity and its application to onset detection. J. Biomech. **48**(6), 1193–1197 (2015)

11. Magda, M., Martinez-Alvarez, A., Cuenca-Asensi, S.: MOOGA parameter optimization for onset detection in EMG signals. In: Battiato, S., Farinella, G.M., Leo, M., Gallo, G. (eds.) ICIAP 2017. LNCS, vol. 10590, pp. 171–180. Springer, Cham (2017). https://doi.org/10.1007/978-3-319-70742-6_16

12. Maria, P., et al.: Use of surface electromyography in phonation studies: an integrative review. Int. Arch. Otorhinolaryngol. 17(3), 329–339 (2013)

13. Matsuo, K., et al.: Electromyography of swallowing with fine wire intramuscular electrodes in healthy human : activation sequence of selected hyoid muscles. Dysphagia 29(6), 713–721 (2014)

14. Merlo, A., Farina, D., Merletti, R.: A fast and reliable technique for muscle activity detection from surface EMG signals. IEEE Trans. Biomed. Eng. 50(3), 316–323 (2003)

15. Naseem, A., Jabloun, M., Buttelli, O., Ravier, P.: Detection of sEMG muscle activation intervals using gaussian mixture model and ant colony classifier. In: 2016 24th European Signal Processing Conference (EUSIPCO), pp. 1713–1717. IEEE (2016)

16. Poorjavad, M.: Surface electromyographic assessment of swallowing function. Iran. J. Med. Sci. (2016)

17. Restrepo-Agudelo, S., Roldan-Vasco, S., Ramirez-Arbelaez, L., Cadavid-Arboleda, S., Perez-Giraldo, E., Orozco-Duque, A.: Improving surface EMG burst detection in infrahyoid muscles during swallowing using digital filters and discrete wavelet analysis. J. Electromyogr. Kinesiol. 35, 1–8 (2017)

18. Sampaio, M., Argolo, N., Melo, A., Nóbrega, A.C.: Wet voice as a sign of penetration/aspiration in Parkinsons disease: does testing material matter? Dysphagia 29(5), 610–615 (2014)

19. Sasaki, M., et al.: Tongue interface based on surface EMG signals of suprahyoid muscles. ROBOMECH J. 3(1), 9 (2016)

20. Sejdić, E., Steele, C.M., Chau, T.: Classification of penetration-aspiration versus healthy swallows using dual-axis swallowing accelerometry signals in dysphagic subjects. IEEE Trans. Biomed. Eng. 60(7), 1859–1866 (2013)

21. Solnik, S., DeVita, P., Rider, P., Long, B., Hortobágyi, T.: Teager-Kaiser Operator improves the accuracy of EMG onset detection independent of signal-to-noise ratio. Acta Bioeng. Biomech./Wroclaw Univ. Technol. 10(2), 65 (2008)

22. Staude, G., Flachenecker, C., Daumer, M., Wolf, W.: Onset detection in surface electromyographic signals: a systematic comparison of methods. EURASIP J. Appl. Signal Process. 2001(1), 67–81 (2001)

23. Staude, G.H.: Precise onset detection of human motor responses using a whitening filter and the log-likelihood-ratio test. IEEE Trans. Biomed. Eng. 48(11), 1292–1305 (2001)

24. Steele, C.M., et al.: The influence of food texture and liquid consistency modification on swallowing physiology and function: a systematic review. Dysphagia 30(1), 2–26 (2015)

25. Vannozzi, G., Conforto, S., D'Alessio, T.: Automatic detection of surface EMG activation timing using a wavelet transform based method. J. Electromyogr. Kinesiol. 20(4), 767–772 (2010)

26. Xu, Q., Quan, Y., Yang, L., He, J.: An adaptive algorithm for the determination of the onset and offset of muscle contraction by EMG signal processing. IEEE Trans. Neural Syst. Rehabil. Eng. 21(1), 65–73 (2013)

27. Yang, D., Zhang, H., Gu, Y., Liu, H.: Accurate EMG onset detection in pathological, weak and noisy myoelectric signals. Biomed. Signal Process. Control 33, 306–315 (2017)

Hyperthermia Study in Breast Cancer Treatment

Hector Fabian Guarnizo Mendez[1][(✉)],
Mauricio Andrés Polochè Arango[2], and John Jairo Pantoja Acosta[3]

[1] Universidad El Bosque, Bogotá, Colombia
hguarnizo@unbosque.edu.co
[2] Universidad de San Buenaventura - Sede Bogotá, Bogotá, Colombia
mpoloche@usbbog.edu.co
[3] Universidad Nacional de Colombia - Sede Bogotá, Bogotá, Colombia
jjpantojaa@unal.edu.co

Abstract. This paper assesses the initial collateral effects which result from the use of hyperthermia, a technique that elevates the temperature in specific areas of the body to tackle present malignant cells. In this particular case, the focus of study is breast cancer treatment by means of an electromagnetic simulation model. The breast model was created by using the electrical properties of tissues and was radiated by microwaves with a waveguide at 950 MHz, 2.45 GHz and 6 GHz to generate increased temperature and distribute power density inside the breast. In the model, two methods were used to obtain the power density in a tumor and other breast tissues (skin, fat, and muscle). One result shows the general distribution of power density throughout a map on color scale, and the second result shows the normalized power density in the local breast parts. In the same way, results show that the microwave applicator (waveguide) location is a determinant factor.

Keywords: Heat flow · Hyperthermia · Radiation

1 Introduction

Cancer is a disease which largely affects senior population worldwide. Cancerous tumors can affect different tissues and can be located in different parts of the body. In recent years, in order to tackle these diseases, researchers from different areas have developed treatments such as surgery, radiotherapy, chemotherapy, immunotherapy, stem cell transplantation and targeted medicine therapies. Along with these methods, another method known as hyperthermia (or thermal therapy) is being evaluated in clinical studies. Hyperthermia is a method in which body tissues with tumors are exposed to high temperatures in order to destroy the tumor or cancerous cells, but without significantly affecting healthy tissues. This technique is currently under study in human patients [1].

One of the main challenges in the treatment of non-invasive electromagnetic (EM) hyperthermia is to focus the EM energy on the cancerous tissue in order to avoid damaging healthy tissues [2, 3]. In EM hyperthermia, it is essential to reach

J. C. Figueroa-García et al. (Eds.): WEA 2018, CCIS 916, pp. 256–267, 2018.
https://doi.org/10.1007/978-3-030-00353-1_23

temperatures of 35 °C to 45 °C in the affected area [4, 5]. For this reason, it is important to know the temperature and power density distributions in order to obtain a more effective microwave heating and avoid unwanted heating in other tissues. In [6–9], the temperature distribution over 3D breast model is presented. In [9], the use of a radiation frequency of 2.45 GHz is justified, based in the electrical properties of the breast tissues.

This paper analyses the power density distribution dissipated in a breast radiated by microwaves at 950 MHz, 2.45 GHz y 6 GHz to determine overexposure zones and the influence of the position of the applicator. The characteristics used in the electromagnetic simulation are presented in detail. The power density was obtained when the waveguide was located at 90° and 135° over the breast.

2 Methodology

The electromagnetic simulation was carried out by using the ANSYS Electronics® finite element method (FEM) solver, as shown in Fig. 1 only the skin, fat, lobes and muscle of the breast were modeled [8, 10, 11]. The breast model radius was 6.5 cm and the tumor was modeled as a high and large 0.8 cm wide dimension cube. The simulation setup is presented in Table 1.

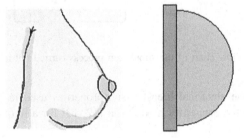

Fig. 1. Normal breast (left) and 3D model (right) implemented in ANSYS Electronics® to represent the breast.

Table 1. HFSS configuration setup

Properties	Values
Maximum number of passes	10
Maximum delta S	0.01
Maximum converged passes	3
Order of basis function	Mixed order

The maximum delta S values and values of maximum converged passes were chosen in order to improve the mesh accuracy and to improve the convergence of the simulation. The mixed order basis function was chosen because the breast has different tissues and different permittivity (ε) and conductivity (σ) electrical properties. Mixed order assigns base function elements based on the need for greater precision in different model parts. Mixed order uses a higher order where more precision is required, and a lower order where fields are weaker.

Figure 2 shows the flow chart of the simulation process carried out in HFSS.

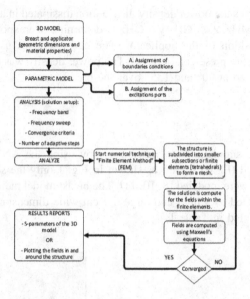

Fig. 2. Flow chart of the simulation process carried out in HFSS.

Table 2 shows the electrical breast tissue properties used in the electromagnetic simulation based on the properties reported in [12, 13] for a frequency of 950 MHz.

Table 2. Electrical properties of the breast tissues

Tissue	Permittivity	Conductivity (S/m)
Muscle	54.9	0.96
Tumor	60	0.5
Fat	5.5	0.05
Skin	41	0.95
Lobes	37	0.3

Table 3 shows the electrical properties of breast tissues used in the electromagnetic simulation based on the properties reported in [12, 13] for a frequency of 2.45 GHz.

Table 3. Electrical properties of the breast tissues

Tissue	Permittivity	Conductivity (S/m)
Muscle	52.7	1.7
Tumor	56	1.8
Fat	5.3	0.3
Skin	38	1.5
Lobes	35	1

Table 4 shows the electrical properties of breast tissues used in the electromagnetic simulation based on the properties reported in [12–14] for a frequency of 6 GHz.

Table 4. Electrical properties of the breast tissues

Tissue	Permittivity	Conductivity (S/m)
Muscle	60	4.7
Tumor	45	7
Fat	10	1.5
Skin	30	5.1
Lobes	30	4

3   Results

Two applicator locations were considered, as shown in Fig. 3 first, the waveguide was placed at 90° to consider a situation in which the tumor location is not aligned with the applicator. Then, the waveguide was placed at 135° over the breast as shown in Fig. 6 to consider alignment between the applicator and the tumor. The WR340 (2.45 GHz), WR770 (950 MHz) and WR159 (6 GHz) waveguides were energized to propagate the TE10 mode and 1 W.

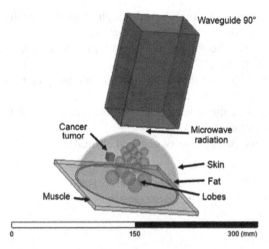

Fig. 3. 3D model for a waveguide at 90° over the breast.

Figure 3 shows the case when the waveguide is 90° over the breast. The highest power density concentration found is presented in Table 5.

Table 5. Power density concentration when the waveguide is 90° over the breast

Frequency (GHz)	Tissue	Power density (KW/m³)
0.950	Skin	~4.3
0.950	Tumor and tissues near the breast center	~0.6
2.45	Skin and lobes	~5.6
2.45	Tumor and tissues near the breast center	~3.5
6	Skin and upper lobes	~20
6	Tumor and tissues near the breast center	~1.0

Figure 4 shows the power density obtained at 950 MHz and 2.45 GHz.

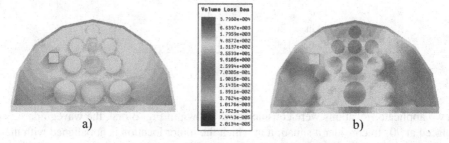

Fig. 4. (a) Power density [W/m³] in the breast model, waveguide (950 MHz) at 90° over the breast. (b) Power density [W/m³] in the breast model, waveguide (2.45 GHz) at 90° over the breast.

As shown in Table 5 and Fig. 4(a), the highest power density concentration is found in the skin located directly below the waveguide.

Both, the tumor and the tissues near the breast center have the second highest power density concentration.

Table 5 and Fig. 4(b) show that the highest power density concentration is found in the lobes located directly below the waveguide.

Both, the tumor and the tissues near the breast center have the highest second power density concentration.

Figure 5 shows the power density obtained at 6 GHz.

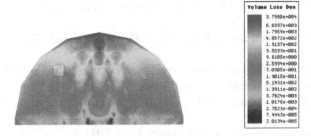

Fig. 5. Power density [W/m³] in the breast model, waveguide (6 GHz) at 90° over the breast.

Table 5 and Fig. 5 show that the highest power density concentration is found in the skin and upper lobes located directly below the waveguide. Both, the tumor and the tissues of the breast's middle part have the second highest power density concentration.

Figure 6 shows the case in which the waveguide is 135° over the breast.

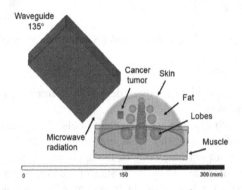

Fig. 6. 3D model for a waveguide at 135° over the breast.

Figure 7 shows the power density obtained at 950 MHz and 2.45 GHz.

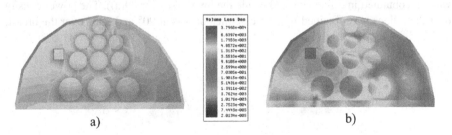

Fig. 7. (a) Power density [W/m³] in the breast model, (a) waveguide (950 MHz) at 135° over the breast. (b) Power density [W/m³] in the breast model, waveguide (2.45 GHz) at 135° over the breast.

Figure 7(a) shows that the highest power density concentration is found in the skin located directly below the waveguide.

Both, the tumor and the tissues near the skin have the second highest concentration power density.

As shown in Fig. 7(b) the highest power density concentration is found in the skin, tumor and lobes of the breast's left half.

The tissues of the breast right half have the second highest power density concentration.

Figure 8 shows the power density obtained at 6 GHz.

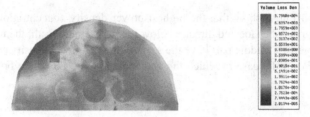

Fig. 8. Power density [W/m^3] in the breast model, (a) waveguide (6 GHz) at 135° over the breast.

Figure 8 shows that the highest power density concentration is found in the skin, tumor and fat near the skin.

The penetration depth of the electromagnetic fields in a hyperthermia treatment is limited by the effect of the skin, that is, at higher frequency, less penetration depth. Therefore, when the operation frequency of the applicator is high, the highest power density is absorbed by the skin and by the tissues of the breast near the skin. Based on the above, in the case of a hyperthermia treatment with microwaves, in which the operation frequency of the applicator is 6 GHz, care must be taken with the radiation time of the breast tissues, since a long time of radiation can produce high temperatures in the tissues and probably causes burns.

Along with the power density shown from Figs. 4, 5, 6, 7 and 8 the power density was also obtained in 3 lines located inside the breast (see Fig. 9(a)). The power density over the 3 lines was obtained when the applicator was at 90° and 135° over the breast.

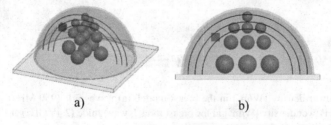

Fig. 9. (a) 3D model and curve lines implemented to analyze the transverse power density over the breast. (b) 3D model and curve lines implemented show a transversal mode

The upper line is located 7 mm below the skin. The middle line is located 14 mm below the skin and intersects the tumor. The lower line is located 21 mm below the skin and intersects the tumor (see Fig. 9(b)).

Figure 10 shows the normalized power density obtained on the upper, middle and lower lines when the waveguide (950 MHz) is used at 90° and 180°.

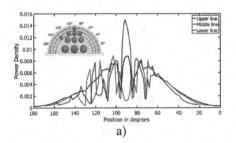
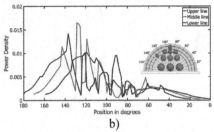

a)   b)

Fig. 10. (a) Result (power density normalized) of 3D model for lines when the waveguide (950 MHz) is used to 90°. (b) Result (power density normalized) of 3D model for lines when the waveguide (950 MHz) is used to 135°.

Figure 10(a) shows that between 100° and 140° and between 50 ° and 80 ° in the middle and lower lines several peaks are obtained. These peaks are due to the presence of the tumor and lobes. Between 80° and 100° on the upper and lower lines the highest peak is observed. This peak is due to the fact that the applicator is located at 90° over the breast.

The differences in the behaviour of the dissipated power presented in the middle line and the lower line at 90° is due to the fact that the middle line only goes through the fat and the lower line goes through a lobe. The differences in the behaviour of the dissipated power presented in the other cases (Fig. 10(a)) is due to different levels of power density absorption, as can also be seen in Fig. 4(a).

In Fig. 10(b) it is observed that between 120° and 150° on the upper line and middle line, the highest power densities are obtained. This is due to the presence of the tumor and the fact that the applicator is at 135° over the breast. The peaks between 80° and 105° on the down line are due to the presence of lobes in this position.

The opposite behaviour presented by the middle line and the lower line at 90° is due to the fact that the middle line only goes through the fat and the lower line goes through a lobe. The opposite behaviour presented in the other cases (Fig. 10(b)) is due to the fact that the highest absorption of power density is obtained in the tissues near the upper-left side of the breast, as can be seen in Fig. 7(a). This opposite behaviour is also due to different levels of power density absorption, as can also be seen in Fig. 7(a).

The normalized power density obtained on the upper line, middle and lower lines when the applicator (2.45 GHz) was at 90° and 135° over the breast is shown in Fig. 11.

In Fig. 11(a) it is observed that between 120° and 135° on the middle line and the lower line a peak is obtained due to the presence of the tumor. Between 70° and 90° and 100° and 110°, peaks are also observed due to the lobes. Finally, it can be observed that the highest power density occurs at 90° due to the fact that the applicator is located at 90° over the breast.

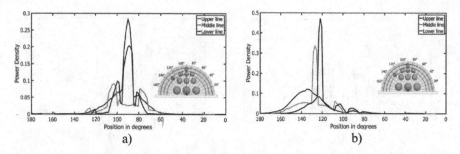

Fig. 11. Result (power density normalized) of 3D model for lines when the waveguide (2.45 GHz) is used to 90°. (b) Result (power density normalized) of 3D model for lines when the waveguide (2.45 GHz) is used to 135°.

The opposite behaviour presented by the middle line and the lower line at 80°, 90° and 100°, is due to the fact that the middle line only goes through the fat and the lower line goes through a lobe.

In Fig. 11(b) it is observed that between 120° and 150° on the upper line, middle line and lower line, the highest power densities are obtained. This is due to the fact that the applicator is 135° over the breast.

Between 120° and 135° on the middle line and the lower line the higher power densities are obtained, this is due to the presence of the tumor in this position.

The peaks presented in the middle line and in the lower line between 90° and 110° are due to lobes presence. The opposite behaviour presented by the middle line and the lower line at 90° is due to the fact that the middle line only goes through the fat and the lower line goes through a lobe. The opposite behaviour presented at 120 ° is due to different levels of power density absorption as can also be seen in Fig. 7(b).

Figure 12 shows the normalized power density obtained on the upper line, middle line and lower line when the waveguide (6 GHz) is used to 90°.

In Fig. 12 it is observed that between 80° and 100° on the upper line, the middle line and the lower line, the peaks of the power densities are obtained because the applicator is at 135° over the breast. The highest power density is obtained in the upper line.

Below, the results obtained in some research works are presented. In these works, some studies on health problems associated with microwave radiation were done. In the case of an electroencephalogram (EEG), slight changes in cerebral metabolism and cerebral blood are observed during exposure; however, these slight changes do not exceed the range of normal physiological variations [15]. At the molecular level, in V79 in vitro and in cultures of human lymphocyte cells, a significant increase in the

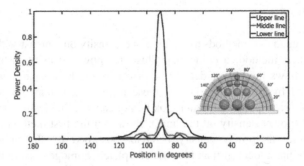

Fig. 12. Result (power density normalized) of 3D model for lines when the waveguide (6 GHz) is used to 90°.

number of specific lesions of the chromosome is observed in the exposed cells [16]. With regard to the heart, it has been observed that due to the location of the heart and the skin effect (poor penetration) the heart is not subject to high microwave fields. It has also been pointed out that an increase in heart rate cannot be related to temperature variations produced by pulsed or continuous electromagnetic waves. On the other hand, it is mentioned that the heartbeat could be regulated with the repetition frequency of the appropriate pulse [17]. In [18] it is mentioned that the organs of the body most susceptible to the thermal effects produced by microwaves are the testicles and the eyes. Nathanson mentions in [19, 20] that treatment with hyperthermia causes changes in the microvascular tumor function, these changes can potentiate the detachment of tumor cells in the heated site. In [21] it is mentioned that local hyperthermia only improves the metastatic rate of melanoma B16. When the treatment with hyperthermia and radiotherapy was implemented, the metastasis decreased.

Based on the above and in other studies, it can be said that there is no conclusive evidence from preclinical models or trials in humans that local-regional hyperthermia causes an increase in metastasis.

With respect to the studies done in the context of the treatment of breast cancer using the hyperthermia technique, in [22] a therapeutic program was implemented combining concurrent taxol, hyperthermia and radiotherapy followed by mastectomy. Within the results obtained, it was observed that hyperthermia may be a strategy to improve tumor reoxygenation. Vujaskovic in [23] presents a neoadjuvant combination treatment of paclitaxel, liposomal doxorubicin, and hyperthermia. In this work it was observed that the treatment is a feasible and well tolerated strategy in patients with locally advanced breast cancer (LABC). In [24] Tamer Refaat shows that hyperthermia and radiation therapy are effective for locally advanced or recurrent breast cancer. In his work he showed that when implementing hyperthermia, an increase of 50% in the effectiveness of the treatment was obtained.

4   Conclusions

This paper presented two methods to obtain power density on a breast with a cancerous tumor. In the first method, a color map illustrates power density distribution. This representation shows the power density absorbed by the breast parts and the power density absorbed by the tumor too, but these results show that the power density absorbed by the breast parts and tumor look homogeneous. The results obtained by the second method (power density on the lines), show that the first method is not entirely accurate, because the power density behavior absorbed by the breast parts and cancerous tumor has a local shift and are not completely homogenous. In the same way, the second method allows for the evaluation of the local shift of the power density in the other tissues presented in the breast model. Additionally, to improve the effectiveness of the treatment with hyperthermia, the location of the applicator is a relevant variable and therefore, it is important to determine the location of the tumor through a previous diagnosis, because a misalignment between the applicator and the tumor can cause unwanted deterioration of nearby cells. With a suitable location of the applicator, the electromagnetic radiation in healthy cells can be avoided. The skin, fat, lobes and tumor absorb the highest power density when the applicator is excited at 2.45 GHz. In the same way, at this frequency, a greater depth of penetration is obtained. When the applicator is excited at 6 GHz, most of the power density is absorbed by the tissue near the place where the applicator is located. The temperature compute is currently being carried out from this result.

References

1. Chicheł, A., Skowronek, J., Kubaszewska, M., Kanikowski, M.: Hyperthermia - description of a method and a review of clinical applications. Rep. Pract. Oncol. Radiother. 12(5), 267–275 (2007)
2. Converse, M., Bond, E.J., Van Veen, B.D., Hagness, S.C.: A computational study of ultra-wideband versus narrowband microwave hyperthermia for breast cancer treatment. IEEE Trans. Microw. Theory Tech. 54(5), 2169–2180 (2006)
3. Neufeld, E., Paulides, M., van Rhoon, G., Kuster, N.: Recent advances in hyperthermia cancer treatment modeling. In: Proceeding and Programme of the EMF Bordeaux Event (EBEA, COST URSI 2010), Bordeaux, France, 26–28 May 2010, pp. 31–32 (2010)
4. Van der Zee, J.: Heating the patient: a promising approach. Ann. Oncol. 13(8), 1173–1184 (2002)
5. Kim, J., Gang, S., Cheon, C., Chung, Y.-S., Kwon, Y.: A study of microwave hyperthermia for breast cancer treatment using cavity applicator. In: 2007 IEEE Antennas and Propagation Society International Symposium, no. 1, pp. 249–252 (2007)
6. Bai, B., Yin, X., Xie, D., Zhang, Y.: FDTD-based temperature distribution computation of microwave hyperthermia for breast cancer. In: Digest of 2010 14th Biennial IEEE Conference on Electromagnetic Field Computation. CEFC 2010, no. 111, p. 7062 (2010)
7. Nguyen, P.T., Abbosh, A.M.: Focusing techniques in breast cancer treatment using non-invasive microwave hyperthermia, pp. 2–4 (2015)

8. Nguyen, P.T., Abbosh, A., Crozier, S.: Realistic simulation environment to test microwave hyperthermia treatment of breast cancer. In: 2014 IEEE Antennas and Propagation Society International Symposium, pp. 1188–1189 (2014)

9. Merunka, I., Fiser, O., Vojackova, L., Vrba, J., Vrba, D.: Utilization potential of balanced antipodal vivaldi antenna for microwave hyperthermia treatment of breast cancer. In: EuCAP 2014 8th European Conference Antennas and Propagation, EuCAP, vol. 6, pp. 706–710 (2014)

10. Korkmaz, E., Isik, O., Sagkol, H.: A directive antenna array applicator for focused electromagnetic hyperthermia treatment of breast cancer. In: 2015 9th European Conference on Antennas and Propagation, vol. 1, pp. 1–4 (2015)

11. Curto, S., Ruvio, G., Ammann, M.J., Prakash, P.: A wearable applicator for microwave hyperthermia of breast cancer: performance evaluation with patient-specific anatomic models. In: Proceedings of 2015 International Conference on Electromagnetics in Advanced Applications. ICEAA 2015, pp. 1159–1162 (2015)

12. Porter, E., Fakhoury, J., Oprisor, R., Coates, M., Popovic, M.: Improved tissue phantoms for experimental validation of microwave breast cancer detection. In: 2010 Proceedings of the Fourth European Conference on Antennas and Propagation (EuCAP), pp. 4–8 (2010)

13. Nikita, K.S. (ed.): Handbook of Biomedical Telemetry, 1st edn. Wiley, Hoboken (2014)

14. Gabriel, C.: Compilation of the dielectric properties of body tissues at RF and microwave frequencies. Report N.AL/OE-TR- 1996-0037, Occupational and environmental health directorate, Radiofrequency Radiation Division, Brooks Air Force Base, TX, USA (1996)

15. Vander Vorst, A., Rosen, A., Kotsuka, Y.: RF/Microwave Interaction with Biological Tissues. Wiley, New Jersey (2006)

16. Garaj-Vrhovac, V., Fucic, A., Horvat, D.: The correlation between the frequency of micronuclei and specific chromosome aberrations in human lymphocytes exposed to microwave radiation in vitro. Mutat. Res. **281**, 181–186 (1992)

17. Tamburello, C.C., Zanforlin, L., Tiné, G., Tamburello, A.E.: Analysis of microwave effects on isolated hearts. In: IEEE MTT-S Microwave International Symposium Digest, Boston, pp. 804–808 (1991)

18. Ely, T.S., Goldman, D.E.: Heating characteristics of laboratory animals exposed to 10 cm microwaves. In: Proceedings of Tri-Service Conference on Biological Hazards of Microwave Radiation (1957)

19. Nathanson, S.D., Cerra, R.F., Hetzel, F.W., et al.: Changes associated with metastasis in B16-F1 melanoma cells surviving heat. Arch. Surg. **125**(2), 216–219 (1990)

20. Nathanson, S.D., Nelson, L., Anaya, P., et al.: Development of lymph node and pulmonary metastases after local irradiation and hyperthermia of footpad melanomas. Clin. Exp. Metastasis **9**(4), 377–392 (1991)

21. Gunderson, L.L., Tepper, J.E.: Clinical Radiation Oncology, 4th edn. Elsevier Inc., New York City (2016)

22. Jones, E.L., et al.: Thermochemoradiotherapy improves oxygenation in locally advanced breast cancer. Clin. Cancer Res. **10**(13), 4287–4293 (2004)

23. Vujaskovic, Z., et al.: A phase I/II study of neoadjuvant liposomal doxorubicin, paclitaxel, and hyperthermia in locally advanced breast cancer. Int. J. Hyperth. **26**(5), 514–521 (2010)

24. Refaat, T., et al.: Hyperthermia and radiation therapy for locally advanced or recurrent breast cancer. Breast **24**(4), 418–425 (2015)

A Non-linear Dynamics Approach to Classify Gait Signals of Patients with Parkinson's Disease

Paula Andrea Pérez-Toro[1]([✉]), Juan Camilo Vásquez-Correa[1,2],
Tomas Arias-Vergara[1,2], Nicanor Garcia-Ospina[1],
Juan Rafael Orozco-Arroyave[1,2], and Elmar Nöth[2]

[1] Faculty of Engineering, University of Antioquia UdeA, Medellín, Colombia
paula.perezt@udea.edu.co
[2] University of Erlangen-Nüremberg, Erlangen, Germany

Abstract. Parkinson's disease is a neuro-degenerative disorder characterized by different motor symptoms, including several gait impairments. Gait analysis is a suitable tool to support the diagnosis and to monitor the state of the disease. This study proposes the use of non-linear dynamics features extracted from gait signals obtained from inertial sensors for the automatic detection of the disease. We classify two groups of healthy controls (Elderly and Young) and Parkinson's patients with several classifiers. Accuracies ranging from 86% to 92% are obtained, depending on the age of the healthy control subjects.

Keywords: Parkinson's disease · Gait assessment · Inertial sensors
Nonlinear dynamics · Classification

1 Introduction

Parkinson's disease (PD) is a neuro-degenerative disorder characterized by the progressive loss of dopaminergic neurons in the mid brain [1], which produces motor and non-motor impairments. Motor symptoms include lack of coordination, tremor, rigidity, and postural instability. Gait impairments appear in most of patients and include freezing, shuffling, and festinating gait. The standard scale to evaluate the neurological state of the patients is the Movement Disorder Society-Unified Parkinson's Disease Rating Scale (MDS-UPDRS-III) [2]. The third section of the scale contains 14 items to evaluate the lower limbs.

Gait analysis of PD patients have been performed commonly with inertial sensors e.g., accelerometers and gyroscopes attached to the shoes of the patients [3,4]. Several studies have described gait impairments of PD patients using kinematics features related to the speed and length of each stride, which are computed from signals captured from the inertial sensors. In [5] several inertial sensors attached to the lower and upper limbs were used to predict the neurological state of PD patients. The authors computed features related to

© Springer Nature Switzerland AG 2018
J. C. Figueroa-García et al. (Eds.): WEA 2018, CCIS 916, pp. 268–278, 2018.
https://doi.org/10.1007/978-3-030-00353-1_24

stance time, length of the stride, and velocity of each step, and reported a Pearson's correlation coefficient of 0.60 between predicted values and real UPDRS score. In [6] the authors classified PD patients and healthy control (HC) subjects with kinematic features computed from inertial sensors attached to the shoes. The features include the stride time, the swing phase, the heel force, the stride length, and others. The authors reported accuracies of up to 90% using a classifier based on Linear discriminant analysis. Recently in [7] the authors proposed new features to assess gait impairments in PD patients. Those new features were the peak forward acceleration in the loading phase and peak vertical acceleration around heel-strike, which encode the engagement in stride initiation and the hardness of the impact at heel-strike, respectively. The results indicated that the proposed features correlate with the disease progression and the loss of postural agility/stability of the patients. In previous studies [8] we computed kinematics features from gait signals captured with the same inertial sensors [9] to evaluate the neurological state of the patients. A Spearman's correlation of up to 0.72 was reported between the MDS-UPDRS-III score of the patients and the predicted values obtained with a support vector regressor.

Although the success of the kinematics features to assess the gait symptoms of PD patients, there are components related with the stability during the walking process that cannot be characterized properly with the classical approach. In order to model those components it is necessary to use Nonlinear dynamics (NLD) features [10,11]. This study considers several NLD features to model the gait process of PD patients and HC subjects. The features include correlation dimension (CD), Largest Lyapunov exponent (LLE), Hurst exponent (HE), Lempel-Ziv Complexity (LZC), and several entropy measures, which have proved to be suitable for the NLD analysis of PD [11,12]. Three classifiers are considered: K-Nearest Neighbors (KNN), Support Vector Machine (SVM) and Random Forest (RF). As aging is an interesting aspect that deserves attention, its effect is considered by the inclusion of two groups of HC subjects: Young HC subjects (YHC) and elderly HC (EHC). The results confirmed that age is an important factor that needs to be addressed when patients with neurodegenerative diseases are considered. In addition, we reported accuracies ranging from 86% to 92%, depending on the age of the HC subjects.

2   Data

Gait signals were captured with the eGaIT system[1], which consists of a 3D-accelerometer (range ±6 g) and a 3D gyroscope (range $\pm500°$/s) attached to the lateral heel of the shoes [4]. Figure 1 shows the eGait system and the inertial sensor attached to the lateral heel of the shoe. The signals are transmitted by bluetooth to a tablet where they are received by an android app.

Data from both foot were captured with a sampling rate of 100 Hz and 12-bit resolution. The tasks performed by the patients include 20 m walking with a stop

---

[1] Embedded Gait analysis using Intelligent Technology, http://www.egait.de/.

at 10 m (Two times 10 m walk, 2 × 10 m), and 40 m walking with a stop every 10 m (Four times 10 m walk, 4 × 10 m).

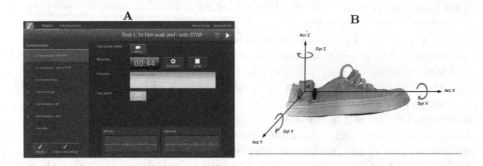

Fig. 1. Interface eGaiT and shoe with its attached inertial sensor.

Data are obtained from 45 PD patients and 89 HC subjects. The HC subjects were divided into two groups: the first one formed with 44 YHC (Young Healthy Controls), and the second one with 45 EHC (Elderly Healthy Controls) subjects. The patients were evaluated by an expert neurologist and labeled according to the MDS-UPDRS-III score. Table 1 shows additional information of the participants of this study.

Table 1. General information of the subjects. **PD** patients: Parkinson's disease patients. **HC**: healthy controls. μ: average. σ: standard deviation. **T**: disease duration.

	PD patients		YHC subjects		EHC subjects	
	Male	Female	Male	Female	Male	Female
Number of subjects	17	28	26	18	23	22
Age ($\mu \pm \sigma$)	65 ± 10.3	58.9 ± 11.0	25.3 ± 4.8	22.8 ± 3.0	66.3 ± 11.5	59.0 ± 9.8
Range of age	41–82	29–75	21–42	19–32	49–84	50–74
T ($\mu \pm \sigma$)	9 ± 4.6	12.6 ± 12.2				
Range of duration of the disease	2–15	0–44				
MDS-UPDRS-III ($\mu \pm \sigma$)	37.6 ± 21.0	33 ± 20.3				
Range of MDS-UPDRS-III	8-82	9-106				

3   Methods

3.1   Nonlinear Dynamics Feature Extraction

Phase Space. The phase space reconstruction is the first step for the NLD analysis. The Takens's Theorem [13] is used for such a purpose. The phase space is represented by Eq. 1 for a time-series s_t. The time-delay τ is computed by the first minimum of the mutual information function, and the embedding dimension m is found using the false neighbor method [14].

$$S_t = \{s_t, s_{t-\tau}, \ldots s_{t-(m-1)\tau}\} \tag{1}$$

Figure 2 shows the phase space obtained from gait signals considering 20 m walking with a stop at 10 m from three subjects: (A) YHC, (B) EHC, and (C) PD patient. Note that the phase space for the YHC exhibits well defined trajectories and a clear recurrence, conversely the trajectories of PD patient attractor are scattered. Several NLD features can be computed from the phase space to assess the complexity and stability of the walking process.

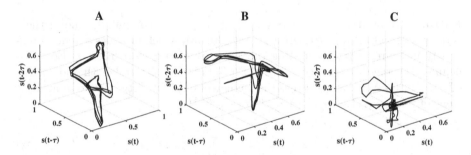

Fig. 2. Phase space from gait signals from 20 m walking with a stop at 10 m of. (A) Female YHC with 22 years old. (B) Female EHC with 52 years old. (C) Female PD patient with 52 years old and MDS-UPDRS = 49.

Correlation Dimension (CD) establishes a measure over the exact space that is occupied by the phase space. The correlation sum $C(\epsilon)$ is defined for a set of points x_n of the phase space according to Eq. 2. Where θ is the Heaviside step function. $C(\epsilon)$ counts the distance between x_i and x_j that are lower than a threshold ϵ and N is the number of embedded points. To compute the CD, a linear regression of $\ln(C(\epsilon))$ vs $\ln(\epsilon)$ is performed. The slope of the resultant line for a small ϵ value corresponds to CD [15].

$$C(\epsilon) = \lim_{n \to \infty} \frac{1}{N(N-1)} \sum_{i=1}^{N} \sum_{j=i+1}^{N} \theta(\epsilon - |x_i - x_j|) \tag{2}$$

Largest Lyapunov Exponent (LLE) measures the sensitivity to initial conditions of the signal, and gives information about the stability properties of the gait signal. LLE quantifies the exponential divergence of the neighbor paths in a phase space, i.e., it measures the degree of non-periodicity of a given signal. After the reconstruction of the phase-space, the nearest neighbor of each embedded point is located. LLE is estimated as the mean separation rate between the nearest neighbor, according to $d(t) = Ae^{\lambda t}$, where λ corresponds to the LLE, $d(t)$ is the mean divergence in an instant t and A is a constant for normalization [15].

Hurst Exponent (HE) evaluates the long-term dependency of the time series. The HE is a smoothness measure of a fractal time series based on an asymptotic behavior of the re-scaled range of the signal. The HE is computed by $T^{\text{HE}} = \frac{R}{S}$, T is the duration of time-series and $\frac{R}{S}$ corresponds to the re-scaled range [15].

Lempel-Ziv Complexity (LZC) correlates the number of different patterns that lie along a sequence. It reflects the order that is retained in a one-dimensional temporal pattern of symbols. The signal is transformed into binary sequences according to the difference between consecutive samples, and the LZC reflects the rate of new patterns in the sequence, and ranges from 0 (deterministic sequence) to 1 (random sequence) [16].

Entropy Measures. Six entropy measurements are computed: One of them corresponds to the Approximate Entropy (ApEn), which provides a general regularity measure. After computing the correlation sum C_i defined by Eq. 2, we define an average version according to Eq. 3. m is the pattern length and r is the effective filter. ApEn is defined as the increment of $\phi^m(r)$ between two immediate steps of m, i.e., $\text{ApEn}(m, r, N) = \phi^m(r) - \phi^{m+1}(r)$.

$$\phi^m(r) = \frac{1}{N - m + 1} \sum_{i=1}^{N-m+1} \log C_i^m(r) \tag{3}$$

Each point in the phase space counts itself when we compute the ApEn. ApEn depends on the length of the time series, causing that short gait signals have a lower estimation than the expected. To avoid this problems the Sample Entropy (SampEn) [17] is also considered in this study. The regularity of the signals computed with ApEn and SampEn is affected by the discontinuity of the Heaviside function in Eq. 2. A proposed solution [18] consists of replacing the Heaviside step function with a Gaussian kernel in the estimation of $C_i^m(r)$. We compute the ApEn and the SampEn with the Gaussian kernel functions.

Another measure considered to analyze the deterministic and chaotic dynamics of gait signals is the Recurrence Probability Density Entropy (RPDE), which is computed using the close returns algorithm [19]. Let's assume there is a small circle $B(S_{n0}, r)$ with radius $r > 0$, which is located close to the data embedded point S_{n0}. Then, the time instant n_1, where the first orbit returns to the circle, is recorded. The difference between two time instants is the recurrence time $T = n_1 - n_0$. The process is repeated for all embedded points S_n, forming an histogram of recurrence times $R(T)$. RPDE is computed according to Eq. 4, where T_{max} is the maximum recurrence time.

$$\text{RPDE} = -\frac{R(i)\ln(R(i))}{\ln(T_{max})} \qquad (4)$$

To compute the stochastic component of the walking process, the Detrended Fluctuation Analysis (DFA) is considered. DFA allows to obtain long-term dependencies of the time-series similar to the HE, except that DFA may be applied to time-series whose underlying statistics are non-stationary.

The above features were extracted from over the entire gait signal. Table 2 shows the number of computed features for each task performed by the patients. Ten NLD features are extracted, which are computed for each of the six signals from the inertial sensors, forming the feature matrix used to classify PD patients and HC subjects.

Table 2. Number of features per task

Foot	Task	Number of axes	Number of features	Total
Left	2x10m	6	10	60
Left	4x10m	6	10	60
Left	Fusion	6	20	120
Right	2x10m	6	10	60
Right	4x10m	6	10	60
Right	Fusion	6	20	120
Both	2x10m	12	10	120
Both	4x10m	12	10	120
Both	Fusion	12	20	240

3.2 Classification

Three classifiers are considered: KNN, SVM with Gaussian kernel, and RF. We ran a 5-fold cross validation, where 3 folds were used for training, one for validation and one for test respectively. The optimization criterion is based on the accuracy on the validation set. The parameter were optimized in a grid search over the train folds, as follows: $\mathbf{K} \in \{3, 5, ...11\}$ for KNN, $\mathbf{C}$ and $\gamma \in \{10^{-4}, 10^{-3}, ... 10^{4}\}$ for SVM and number of trees $(\mathbf{N}) \in \{5, 10, 20, 30, 50, 100\}$ and depth of the decision tress $(\mathbf{D}) \in \{2, 5, 10, 20, 30, 50, 100\}$ for RF.

4   Experiments and Results

Two experiments are performed: (1) classification of PD vs. YHC, and (2) classification of PD vs. EHC. Individual experiments are performed by foot and per task. In addition, the features computed from the two tasks and feet are combined. Table 3 shows the results for the PD vs. YHC subjects. In general the

Table 3. Results to classify PD patients vs. YHC subjects. **ACC:** accuracy in the test set, **AUC:** Area under ROC curve, **K:** number of neighbors in the KNN. **C and γ:** complexity parameter and bandwidth of the kernel in the SVM, **N and D:** Number of trees and depth of the decision trees in the RF.

Foot Task	KNN ACC(%) ($\mu \pm \sigma$)	Sen(%)/Spe(%)	AUC	K	SVM ACC(%)	Sen(%)/Spe(%)	AUC	C	γ	RF ACC(%)	Sen(%)/Spe(%)	AUC	N	D
Left 2x10	85.4%±6.4	75.6/95.3	0.91	5	82.0%±5.0	75.6/88.6	0.92	10^1	10^{-3}	86.5%±7.6	80.0/93.3	0.92	20	20
Left 4x10	84.4%±8.1	73.3/95.6	0.95	9	91.1%±6.3	86.7/95.6	0.96	10^0	10^{-3}	93.3%±7.2	93.3/93.3	0.94	30	20
Left Fusion	88.8%±3.8	77.8/100.0	0.94	5	88.9%±8.8	82.2/95.6	0.94	10^1	10^{-3}	91.1%±7.4	86.7/95.6	0.95	20	100
Right 2x10	85.5%±4.8	71.1/100.0	0.88	9	79.9%±8.3	77.8/81.9	0.91	10^1	10^{-3}	82.0%±4.6	77.8/86.1	0.92	10	5
Right 4x10	78.8%±9.0	60.0/97.8	0.90	7	92.2%±4.9	84.4/100.0	0.92	10^1	10^{-3}	86.6%±6.2	84.4/88.9	0.95	10	100
Right Fusion	82.1%±9.0	68.9/95.6	0.91	7	88.8%±4.9	80.0/61.8	0.93	10^1	10^{-3}	89.9%±6.2	84.4/95.6	0.95	50	5
Both 2x10	86.7%±5.0	73.3/97.8	0.93	7	83.2%±6.7	80.0/86.7	0.94	10^1	10^{-3}	85.5%±11.5	80.0/91.1	0.92	5	2
Both 4x10	84.2%±10.7	71.1/97.8	0.93	5	86.6%±4.8	80.0/93.3	0.90	10^0	10^{-3}	92.2%±6.3	88.9/95.6	0.94	20	2
Both Fusion	86.5%±2.9	73.3/100.0	0.93	5	91.0%±4.9	84.4/97.8	0.96	10^0	10^{-3}	91.1%±4.9	84.4/97.8	0.96	30	10
Average	84.7	71.6/97.7	0.92	-	87.1	81.2/89.0	0.93	-	-	88.7	84.4/92.9	0.94	-	-
STD	2.7	5.1/2.0	0.0	-	4.2	3.5/11.6	0.0	-	-	3.5	4.8/3.7	0.0	-	-

best results are obtained with the RF classifier. The fusion of features from both feet and the two tasks also provides the highest accuracy (91.0% ± 4.9).

The average accuracy in train for Table 3 for the tree classifiers was respectively, KNN = 88.3% ± 2.7, SVM = 95.4% ± 4.0 and RF = 99.1% ± 1.8.

Although the high accuracies of the experiment classifying PD vs. YHC subjects, it does not consider the effect of age in the walking process. The results classifying PD patients vs. EHC subjects with similar age to the patients are shown in Table 4. Note that the results are slightly lower than those obtained in the previous experiment. Although such an impact, relatively high accuracies are obtained, specially when we combine the features from both tasks and both feet. For the separate classification using features computed from each foot, the highest accuracies are obtained for the left foot, which may indicate that the left lower limbs are more affected due to the disease, having in mind that most of the patients are right dominant foot. This fact is known as cross laterality [20].

Table 4. Results to classify PD patients vs. EHC subjects. **ACC:** accuracy in the test set, **AUC:** Area under ROC curve, **K:** number of neighbors in the KNN. **C and γ:** complexity parameter and bandwidth of the kernel in the SVM, **N and D:** Number of trees and depth of the decision trees in the RF.

Foot Task	KNN ACC(%)	Sen(%)/Spe(%)	AUC	K	SVM ACC(%)	Sen(%)/Spe(%)	AUC	C	γ	RF ACC(%)	Sen(%)/Spe(%)	AUC	N	D
Left 2x10	81.1±9.3	80.0/82.2	0.84	5	77.78±13.0	66.7/88.9	0.74	10^{-4}	10^{-4}	83.3±14.2	73.3/93.3	0.89	30	2
Left 4x10	72.2±11.1	68.9/75.6	0.80	5	81.11±12.8	86.7/75.6	0.90	10^0	10^{-3}	84.4±7.2	82.2/86.7	0.89	10	5
Left Fusion	80.0±8.4	73.3/86.7	0.86	5	83.33±6.8	82.2/84.4	0.84	10^{-4}	10^{-4}	83.3±8.8	77.8/88.9	0.89	30	30
Right 2x10	70.0±9.3	60.0/80.0	0.82	5	67.78±7.2	51.1/84.4	0.73	10^{-4}	10^{-4}	78.9±6.1	73.3/84.4	0.79	10	2
Right 4x10	77.8±6.8	73.3/82.2	0.82	3	76.67±7.2	73.3/80.0	0.83	10^1	10^{-3}	80.0±11.5	80.0/80.0	0.87	20	2
Right Fusion	81.1±8.4	73.3/88.9	0.85	3	82.22±4.6	75.6/88.9	0.87	10^1	10^{-3}	85.6±6.3	82.2/88.9	0.91	20	5
Both 2x10	76.7±12.7	68.9/84.4	0.79	5	80.00±8.4	68.9/91.1	0.85	10^1	10^{-4}	78.9±11.4	71.1/86.7	0.86	30	50
Both 4x10	72.2±3.9	75.6/68.9	0.80	3	81.11±6.3	77.8/84.4	0.83	10^{-4}	10^{-4}	82.2±12.7	82.2/82.2	0.91	100	50
Both Fusion	85.6±5.0	77.8/93.3	0.89	3	82.22±4.6	71.1/93.3	0.86	10^{-4}	10^{-4}	85.6±2.5	80.0/91.1	0.91	30	30
Average	77.4	72.3/82.5	0.83	-	79.14	72.6/85.7	0.83	-	-	82.3	78.0/86.9	0.88	-	-
STD	4.8	5.8/7.2	0.0	-	4.5	10.25/5.6	0.1	-	-	2.4	4.4/4.2	0.0	-	-

The average accuracy in train for Table 4 for the tree classifiers was respectively, KNN = 87.8 % ± 4.3, SVM = 91.4% ± 5.9 and RF = 97.9 % ± 3.1.

Figure 3 shows an additional comparison among the best results obtained in the classification of PD patients vs. the two groups of HC subjects. The ROC curves represent the results in a more compact way and it is a standard measure of performance in medical applications. The three classifiers produce similar results for both experiments. The impact of age in the results is also observed.

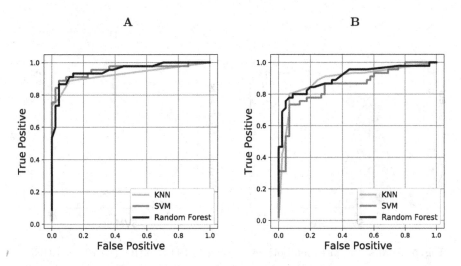

Fig. 3. ROC curve graphics of the best results. (A) PD vs YHC. (B) PD vs EHC. In both cases the fusion of features from both feet and both tasks are considered.

In addition, Figs. 4, 5 and 6 show the scores of each classifier. In KNN and RF, the score is the probability with which sample belongs to the selected class and in SVM is the distance of the hyperplane to the sample.

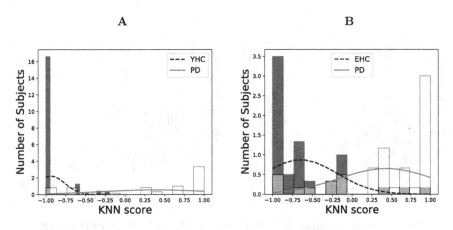

Fig. 4. KNN scores of fusion both feet task. (A) PD vs YHC. (B) PD vs EHC.

In Fig. 4A is observed that YHC subjects are correctly classified, which corresponds to a specificity of 100.0% for this task in Table 3, while in PD patients, the sensitivity is lower (73.3%), playing the age factor an important role. Respect to the Fig. 4B, is obtained a lower specificity, because similar age between both populations, and it tends to get confused between patients and elderly healthy controls.

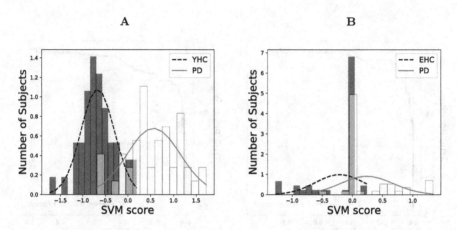

Fig. 5. SVM scores of fusion both feet task. (A) PD vs YHC. (B) PD vs EHC.

In Fig. 5A higher maximization of the hyperplane in comparison with the Fig. 5B can be observed with bigger distances values than in PD vs. EHC being the elderly healthy controls very close to the patients, agreeing also with the higher accuracies (Table 3) in the classification of PD vs. YHC.

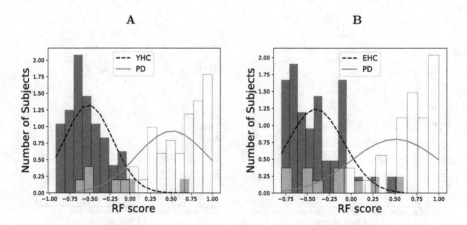

Fig. 6. RF scores of fusion both feet task. (A) PD vs YHC. (B) PD vs EHC.

According to the Fig. 6 a larger separability between the histograms is observed in PD vs. YHC, being easier to classify considering the big difference between the average age (Table 1). In Fig. 6B patients are miss-classified with elderly controls.

Any of the methods is able to find patterns that discriminate to the controls, however, many PD patients are in an early stage of the disease, where the motor capabilities are not too affected yet.

5   Conclusion

An automatic assessment of gait of PD patients is proposed in this study. A NLD approach is considered to evaluate stability, long-term dependency, and complexity of the walking process of the patients. An automatic discrimination between PD patients and two groups of HC subjects is performed to assess the impact of age in the walking process. The set of NLD features included features computed from the phase space and several entropy measures.

The combination of features extracted from different tasks and from both feet is more effective in the classification process, i.e., both tasks and feet provide complementary information to discriminate between PD patients and HC subjects. The results also indicate the presence of the cross laterality effect [20], since higher accuracies are obtained classifying the features computed from the left foot rather than those computed from the right foot, although most of the subjects from this study are right-handed. Further experiments will consider the evaluation of the neurological state of the patients by classifying patients in several stages of the disease according to the MDS-UPDRS-III score. Other NLD based features can also be considered. The proposed features might also be combined with standard kinematics features to improve the results.

Acknowledgments. This work was financed by CODI from University of Antioquia grant #2015–7683. This project has received funding from the European Union's Horizon 2020 research and innovation programme under the Marie Sklodowska-Curie Grant Agreement No. 766287.

References

1. Hornykiewicz, O.: Biochemical aspects of Parkinson's disease. Neurology **51**(2 Suppl 2), S2–S9 (1998)
2. Goetz, C.G., et al.: Movement Disorder Society-sponsored revision of the Unified Parkinson's Disease Rating Scale (MDS-UPDRS): scale presentation and clinimetric testing results. Mov. Disord. **23**(15), 2129–2170 (2008)
3. Oung, Q.W., Muthusamy, H., et al.: Technologies for assessment of motor disorders in Parkinson's disease: a review. Sensors **15**(9), 21710–21745 (2015)
4. Klucken, J., Barth, J., et al.: Unbiased and mobile gait analysis detects motor impairment in Parkinson's disease. PloS One **8**(2), e56956 (2013)

5. Parisi, F., Ferrari, G., et al.: Body-sensor-network-based kinematic characterization and comparative outlook of UPDRS scoring in leg agility, sit-to-stand, and gait tasks in Parkinson's disease. IEEE J. Biomed. Health Inform. **19**(6), 1777–1793 (2015)

6. Perumal, S.V., Sankar, R.: Gait and tremor assessment for patients with Parkinson's disease using wearable sensors. ICT Express **2**(4), 168–174 (2016)

7. Hannink, J., Gaßner, H., et al.: Inertial sensor-based estimation of peak accelerations during heel-strike and loading as markers of impaired gait patterns in PD patients. Basal Ganglia **8**, 1 (2017)

8. Vasquez-Correa, J.C., et al.: Multi-view representation learning via GCCA for multimodal analysis of Parkinson's disease. In: International Conference on Acoustics, Speech and Signal Processing (ICASSP), pp. 2966–2970 (2017)

9. Pérez-Toro, P.A., Vásquez-Correa, J.C., et al.: Análisis motriz en las extremidades inferiores para el monitoreo del estado neurológico de pacientes con enfermedad de parkinson. In: Symposium on Signal Processing, Images and Artificial Vision (STSIVA) (2016)

10. Dingwell, J.B., Cusumano, J.P.: Nonlinear time series analysis of normal and pathological human walking. Chaos: Interdiscip. J. Nonlinear Sci. **10**(4), 848–863 (2000)

11. Sejdic, E., et al.: A comprehensive assessment of gait accelerometry signals in time, frequency and time-frequency domains. IEEE Trans. Neural Syst. Rehabil. Eng. **22**(3), 603–612 (2014)

12. Orozco-Arroyave, J.R., Arias-Londoño, J.D., Vargas-Bonilla, J.F., Nöth, E.: Analysis of speech from people with Parkinson's disease through nonlinear dynamics. In: Drugman, T., Dutoit, T. (eds.) NOLISP 2013. LNCS (LNAI), vol. 7911, pp. 112–119. Springer, Heidelberg (2013). https://doi.org/10.1007/978-3-642-38847-7_15

13. Takens, F.: On the numerical determination of the dimension of an attractor. In: Braaksma, B.L.J., Broer, H.W., Takens, F. (eds.) Dynamical Systems and Bifurcations. LNM, vol. 1125, pp. 99–106. Springer, Heidelberg (1985). https://doi.org/10.1007/BFb0075637

14. Kennel, M.B., et al.: Determining embedding dimension for phase-space reconstruction using a geometrical construction. Phys. Rev. A **45**(6), 3403 (1992)

15. Kantz, H., Schreiber, T.: Nonlinear Time Series Analysis, vol. 7. Cambridge University Press, Cambridge (2004)

16. Lempel, A., Ziv, J.: On the complexity of finite sequences. IEEE Trans. Inf. Theory **22**(1), 75–81 (1976)

17. Richman, J.S., Moorman, J.R.: Physiological time-series analysis using approximate entropy and sample entropy. Am. J. Physiol.-Hear. Circ. Physiol. **278**(6), H2039–H2049 (2000)

18. Xu, L.S., et al.: Gaussian kernel approximate entropy algorithm for analyzing irregularity of time-series. In: International Conference on Machine Learning and Cybernetics, pp. 5605–5608 (2005)

19. Lathrop, D.P., Kostelich, E.J.: Characterization of an experimental strange attractor by periodic orbits. Phys. Rev. A **40**(7), 4028 (1989)

20. Sadeghi, H., Allard, P., Prince, F., Labelle, H.: Symmetry and limb dominance in able-bodied gait: a review. Gait Posture **12**(1), 34–45 (2000)

Changes in Electrocardiographic Signals During Training in Laparoscopic Surgery Simulator: A Preliminary Report

Jazmín Ximena Suárez-Revelo[1]([⊠]) [iD], Any Ruiz-Duque[1] [iD],
Juan Pablo Toro[2], Ana María Mejía-Bueno[3],
and Alher Mauricio Hernández-Valdivieso[1] [iD]

[1] Bioinstrumentation and Clinical Engineering Research Group – GIBIC,
Bioengineering Department, Engineering Faculty,
Universidad de Antioquia UdeA, Calle 70 No. 52-21,
050010 Medellín, Colombia
{jazmin.suarez,alher.hernandez}@udea.edu.co
[2] Trauma and Surgery, General Surgery Department, Universidad de Antioquia,
Carrera 51d # 62-29, Medellín, Colombia
[3] Simulation Center, Medicine Faculty, Universidad de Antioquia,
Carrera 51d # 62-29, Medellín, Colombia

Abstract. The aim of this work is attempting to identify physiological characteristics of the learning process in surgery residents. As an exploratory approach, we are interested in determining statistically significant changes in electrocardiographic (ECG) signals recorded while a group of eleven first year general surgery residents were performing three basic skills tasks from the virtual reality (VR) laparoscopic simulator LapSim®. These signals were processed and heart rate (HR) was calculated to analyze it along with the overall score for each exercise. Statistical analysis was performed by means of analysis of variance showing the effects of training session, difficulty of the task and participants gender on heart rate and performance. Our preliminary experimental results show that the score obtained in the tasks improves with training session, being in the women where significant changes occur. HR analysis showed that it increases with the complexity of the task. Besides, the effect of gender on HR showed that in male group there were the significant changes with the difficulty of the task, and a decrease with the training session in the intermediate level of difficulty task.

Keywords: ECG · HR · Laparoscopic surgery training · Simulation

1 Introduction

Laparoscopic surgery has become the first option to performing surgeries that involve the abdominal cavity [1]. This minimally invasive technique implies a lower incidence of complications such as risk of infection, pain and difficulties in patient recovery [2].

© Springer Nature Switzerland AG 2018
J. C. Figueroa-García et al. (Eds.): WEA 2018, CCIS 916, pp. 279–289, 2018.
https://doi.org/10.1007/978-3-030-00353-1_25

Laparoscopy requires the surgeon to acquire special skills and abilities to operate without tactile and depth perception [3]. In order to preserve patient safety and reduce medical errors, apprentices must receive an adequate training in which they acquire basic skills before arriving in the operating room [4, 5].

It has been shown that skill training such as psychomotor performance, depth perception and spatial judgment does not depend on the operating room and can be done in laboratories with the help of models and simulators [6, 7]. Virtual reality (VR) simulators have become an important part of training for being a safe, ethical and repeatable alternative [8, 9]. Its use produces objective measures of performance, allows feedback to students, and does not require regular supervision [10].

There is a rising interest in the assessment of surgical and performance skills in laparoscopy during the surgeon's training process [11]. Acquisition of surgical competence is a complex and multifactorial process that can take years of experience and training [1]. Having a quantitative evaluation tool that qualifies the performance and progress of the students allows improving the learning experience and reducing failures of the training program [12].

The assessment of residents training involves several aspects including technical skills acquisition through the supervision of an expert [13, 14]; interaction with instrumental using tracking systems of optical, electromagnetic or mechanical monitoring [15]; and behavioral aspects like cognition, stress or fatigue [16, 17]. One of the above aspects, the evolution of cognitive performance throughout learning process, has not been approached in an effective way since it does not include quantitative strategies [18].

Analysis of physiological signals such as electrocardiography (ECG) allows to objectively evaluate the mental state under which the subject is performing an activity [19]. It has been seen that variations in heart rate (HR) can be related to the variation of emotional states. During training in flight simulation tasks, a reduction of the HR was found through the training sessions [20]. It has also been found that heart rate is lower in experts than in novices during the performance of a military training task. Additionally, an increase of HR in both groups has been also reported when going from a resting to task condition. The difficulty of a task also seems to be directly related to an increase in HR [21].

By acquisition of ECG recordings from surgery residents during training sessions in a VR simulator, we attempted to identify physiological features of the learning process. The goal of the current study is to explore changes in residents' ECG signals through training sessions and tasks. The obtained results show effects of training session and participants gender on their tasks performance, and an effect of task difficulty and gender on changes in heart rate.

2 Materials and Methods

2.1 Participants

A total of eleven young healthy adults (5 females, 6 males; 9 right handed; mean age: 28 ± 2.9 years, no significant differences in age between men and women) first year general surgery residents in the Universidad de Antioquia participated in the study. Subjects had no significant prior knowledge in laparoscopic surgery, neither previous contact with the VR simulator. The nature of the study was explained to all subjects prior to enrolment, they gave written informed consent approved by the bioethics committee of the Universidad de Antioquia. In addition, they were asked if they had skills in other domains (arts, music, video games).

In order to maintain uniform conditions for quantitative evaluation training, volunteers were asked to avoid alcohol at least 12 h before each session, as well as to avoid smoking, caffeine, tea, heavy meals right before the experiments; likewise, they were asked to avoid extreme movements over the entire experimental protocol.

2.2 Experimental Protocol

The experimental protocol consisted in four training sessions developed one every week. In each session volunteers performed three basic skills tasks in the VR laparoscopic simulator LapSim® (Surgical Science Ltd., Göteburg, Sweden). Instructions have been provided to each subject on the first day of training. In order to investigate possible trends and changes of the physiological signals across the experimental sessions, heart electrical activity was recorded using a biopotential amplifier. Each session consisted in three repetitions (a total of 12 repetitions at the end of the study) of the same tasks series in which the volunteers also were evaluated with the LapSim® measurements. Nevertheless, physiological signals were recorded only in the second repetition of each session, furthermore before LapSim® exercises recordings, subjects were recorded in resting condition for 2 min. They were in standing position in front of the simulator looking at a blank screen. Figure 1 shows a general schema of the experimental protocol, in which can be observed the repetitions where ECG signals were recorded.

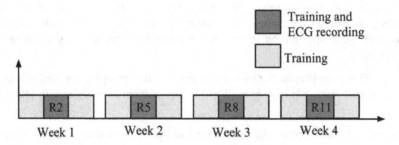

Fig. 1. Experimental protocol. Each square represents a set of three tasks.

2.3 Signals Acquisition

Electrocardiographic signals (ECG) have been recorded by the digital monitoring system Natus® Quantum™ (Natus Neurology Incorporated, Wisconsin, USA) at a sampling frequency of 1024 Hz. Electrodes were placed in Lead II and referenced to the right mastoid bone.

2.4 LapSim Tasks

LapSim® Haptic System is a virtual reality laparoscopic simulator that comprehends a LapCam, a separate laparoscope, a Basic Skills training package containing Basic Skills, Task Training and Camera Anatomy Training modules. Three tasks with incremental difficulty grade were selected according to the LapSim® Basic Skills and Task Training modules. Each assignment was explained and shown to the participants at the beginning of the first session, due to volunteers had no prior contact with the simulator. The default design of each exercise was determined by the software. The overall score (%) for each exercise was evaluated against predefined parameters based on tissue damage, maximum damage, span time, angled or straight navigation, etc. Figure 2 shows three selected exercises that included:

Fig. 2. LapSim® task. A: Task 1: coordination. B: Task 2: grasping. C: Task 3: peg transfer.

Coordination. This task combines the use of the camera and one instrument. It requires the participant to hold the camera with one hand and locate ten randomly appearing objects, pick them up with the instrument and transfer them to a target that appears instantaneously.

Grasping. This is an intermediate-level task that involves grasping six vertical pipes or appendices, pull them from the ground and transport them to a target with alternating hands.

Peg Transfer. In this exercise the workspace consists of a board with 12 pegs (two sets of six pegs each one) and six rings. The task requires the user to lift each ring from a peg, then transfer it between hands and place it in a designated peg on the other set.

2.5   Signals Processing

The first step was decimation of the ECG signals to a sampling frequency of 256 Hz as well as digitally band-pass filtered by a 4th order Butterworth filter (low-pass filter cut-off frequency: 50 Hz, high-pass filter cut-off frequency: 0.8 Hz) [22]. Once the pre-processing stage was achieved, it was applied a peaks-detection algorithm to identify the number of beats per minute, then HR was calculated by the mean beat per minute from each signal on every recording and finally HR obtained values were normalized with reference to the resting condition.

2.6   Statistical Analysis

A statistical analysis was accomplished in order to evaluate changes in heart rate and performance in the simulator tasks through the total score obtained in each one. Data were analyzed with the Statistical Package for the Social Sciences version 25 (SPSS, Chicago, IL).

For HR analysis a mixed design ANOVA was used with gender (2 levels) as inter-subject factor, and training session (4 levels) and task (three levels) as intra-subject factors. Global score was analyzed using a mixed design ANOVA with gender as inter-subject factor and training session as intra-subject factor for each task.

The sphericity assumption was tested with Mauchly's test, and Greenhouse-Geisser correction was used in cases where the assumption was not met. A p-value < .05 was considered statistically significant. Marginal means comparisons were carried out without correcting the p-values due to the exploratory nature of the study.

3   Results

3.1   LapSim® Task Score

Table 1 shows the results of the ANOVA for the global scores obtained in each task. Tasks 1 and 2 had a significant effect of session and the interaction session × gender factors, which indicates that the score obtained in the tasks through the sessions behaves differently in men and women. In the task with the highest level of difficulty (task 3), analysis showed only significant effect of session, indicating that there are not differences in the evolution of task performance according to gender.

Analysis of mean comparisons show significant differences between training sessions for women in tasks 1 and 2, and at a general level in task 3 (see Fig. 3). For easy and intermediate tasks, there are significant differences between session 1 with sessions 2, 3 and 4, and between session 2 and session 4. These differences show an increase in the score from session 2 (compared with session 1) and a subsequent increase in

Table 1. ANOVA results for global score.

Task	Significant effect	F	p-value	η2
Task 1 (Coordination)	Gender	F (1, 9) = 0.593	0.461	0.062
	Session	**F (3, 27) = 15.856**	**0.001**	**0.638**
	Session × gender	**F (3, 27) = 4.452**	**0.048**	**0.331**
Task 2 (Grasping)	Gender	F (1, 9) = 3.195	0.107	0.262
	Session	**F (3, 27) = 17.298**	**0.000**	**0.658**
	Session × gender	**F (3, 27) = 3.376**	**0.033**	**0.273**
Task 3 (Peg transfer)	Gender	F (1, 9) = 0.003	0.958	0.000
	Session	**F (3, 27) = 6.972**	**0.001**	**0.437**
	Session × gender	F (3, 27) = 0.183	0.907	0.020

session 4 (compared with session 2). On the other hand, for the most difficult task, the significant differences are between session 1 with sessions 3 and 4, and session 2 with session 3. The above indicates that the score improves significantly after the third training session. It is important to note that there were no significant differences between men and women in any session for any task.

3.2 Heart Rate

The results of the ANOVA test for the normalized heart rate are shown in Table 2. A significant effect of the task and task x gender was found, no significant effects of session were found. Figure 4 shows HR through the training sessions for the three tasks for each gender group. In male group, task 3 had higher HR compared to the other two tasks (easy and intermediate level) throughout all sessions. When comparing between sessions, no significant differences were found in any task for women group. For men group, there was a significant decrease in HR from session 2 to session 3 in task 2. Comparing means between men and women, there were no significant differences in any session for any task.

Table 2. ANOVA results for HR.

Significant effect	F	p-value	η2
Session	F (3, 27) = 0.182	0.908	0.020
Gender	F (1, 9) = 1.125	0.316	0.111
Session × gender	F (3, 27) = 0.696	0.563	0.072
Task	**F (2, 18) = 7.974**	**0.003**	**0.470**
Task × gender	**F (2, 18) = 4.510**	**0.026**	**0.334**
Session × Task	F (6, 54) = 0.860	0.530	0.087
Session × task × gender	F (6, 54) = 0.933	0.479	0.094

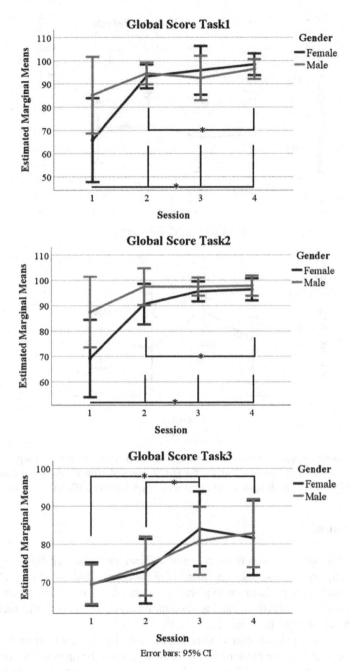

Fig. 3. Estimated marginal means for global score. Significant differences are marked with black lines. In tasks 1 and 2 differences between sessions were in female group. Differences in task 3 occurred at a general level (linking groups of men and women).

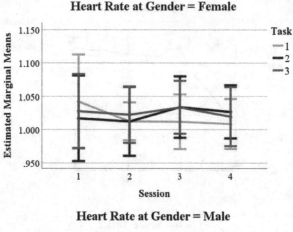

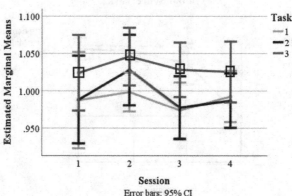

Fig. 4. Estimated marginal means for normalized heart rate. In male group, significant differences were found in sessions 2 and 3 for task 2 (marked with a yellow line), and task 3 showed the highest HR in all sessions (marked with black squares). (Color figure online)

4 Discussion

This paper describes the results of changes in heart rate obtained through training sessions of surgery residents using a laparoscopic surgery simulator. As a preliminary study, we decided to perform an exploration of the data, by means of analysis of variance showing the effects of training session, difficulty of the task and participants gender on heart rate and performance.

The results show that the score obtained in the tasks improves with training session, but that it does not have the same behavior for both genders, being in the women where significant changes occur. Additionally, it is shown that for tasks with easy and intermediate level of difficulty, improvement in performance is achieved since the second session, while for the task of greater difficulty more training sessions could be required to improve.

In the acquisition of surgical skills, male medical students performed better and studies found the greatest gender differences in the visuospatial abilities and speed. However, surgical training eliminated initial gender differences [23]. There may also be a cultural influence, as males may be more likely to have played video and ball games during their childhood, which could help develop their visuospatial abilities [24, 25].

In our study, all male participants have affirmed they played video games sometimes or always, instead of female volunteers, where only two of them have said they play sometimes. Thus, significant differences between training sessions for women global scores in tasks 1 and 2, may be due they were acquiring new visuospatial skills that men had acquired while playing video games.

Grantcharov et al. [26] evaluated the influence of factors such as gender, hand dominance and experience with computer games in surgeons performance using a VR laparoscopic surgery simulator. They found that men take less time to complete tasks and subjects who used computer games had fewer errors than those who did not use them. In addition, they showed that right-handed subjects performed fewer unnecessary movements. In our study we do not consider differences in hand dominance since only two residents (one woman and one man) were left-handed. Likewise, due to the shortage of residents with previous experience using video games, we do not consider the effects of this variable. We hope that for future analysis we can count with more subjects to also analyze the influence of these factors.

Regarding to heart rate analysis, it was found that HR increases with the complexity of the task. The effect of gender on HR showed that in male group there were significant changes, increases in HR with the difficulty of the task, and a decrease with the training session in the grasping task (intermediate level of difficulty). The male participants showed a high level of HR in task 3 compared to the other two tasks (easy and intermediate level) throughout all sessions; while in female participants no significant differences were found in any task.

The increase in HR with the difficulty of the task is consistent with previous studies [21]. A greater difficulty in the task increases participant's effort to deal with the task demands and this leads to an increase in the mental workload [27], and the mental workload can increase the heart rate [28]. However, a decrease in HR was also expected with the training session and the results obtained were not significant, there is not effect of session on HR. This may be due to the great variability observed in the measurements, both for men and for women groups, even though measurements were normalized by the resting condition. Perhaps, analysis of other signal characteristics such as heart rate variability (HRV) may show better indications, since this is an indirect measure of the autonomic nervous system and it has seen its association with stress [29]. Future studies should include this analysis.

5 Conclusion

This work showed an initial exploratory analysis of performance and heart rate data obtained during four training sessions in a laparoscopic surgery simulator of general surgery residents. Our results showed changes in the performance of the task influenced by the training session and gender, indicating that a better performance is achieved in both men and women. The analysis of physiological signals showed an increase in the heart rate associated with the difficulty of the task, but not a decrease with the training session. From these changes, future studies should include analysis of more variables such as HRV, factors such previous experience with video games and hand dominance, as well as other performance features, such as span time and errors, which can be correlated better with the gender differences found here. Our results suggest that it is possible to develop a quantitative surgical training assessment from analysis of performance and physiological signals.

Acknowledgment. This work was supported by Departamento Administrativo de Ciencia, Tecnología e Innovación (COLCIENCIAS), announcement N. 757 Doctorados Nacionales, and Convenio Jóvenes Investigadores e Innovadores N. 761 through the project Fortalecimiento de la plataforma tecnológica para la formación especializada en el área de la salud y el desarrollo de tecnología biomédica/Ruta N 139C.

References

1. Rodríguez-Cañete, A., Pérez-Reyes, T., Álvarez-Alcalde, A., Gallego-Perales, J.L.: La formacion del residente en cirugía laparoscópica. Cirugía Andaluza **18**, 45–48 (2007)
2. Cuschieri, A.: Laparoscopic surgery: current status, issues and future developments. Surgeon **3**, 125–130, 132–133, 135–138 (2005)
3. Choy, I., Okrainec, A.: Simulation in surgery: perfecting the practice. Surg. Clin. N. Am. **90**, 457–473 (2010). https://doi.org/10.1016/j.suc.2010.02.011
4. Buschemeyer, W.C., Cunningham, D.K., Edwards, M.J.: Surgical training and implementation of emerging surgical technologies. Am. J. Surg. **190**, 166–172 (2005). https://doi.org/10.1016/j.amjsurg.2005.05.005
5. León, F., et al.: Simulación en cirugía laparoscópica. Cirugía Española **93**, 4–11 (2015). https://doi.org/10.1016/j.ciresp.2010.08.007
6. Tsuda, S., Scott, D., Doyle, J., Jones, D.B.: Surgical skills training and simulation. Curr. Probl. Surg. **46**, 271–370 (2009). https://doi.org/10.1067/j.cpsurg.2008.12.003
7. Takeda, J., Kikuchi, I., Kono, A., Ozaki, R., Kumakiri, J., Takeda, S.: Efficacy of short-term training for acquisition of basic laparoscopic skills. Gynecol. Minim. Invasive Ther. **5**, 112–115 (2016). https://doi.org/10.1016/j.gmit.2015.06.001
8. Sabench Pereferrer, F., Hernández González, M., Muñoz García, A., Cabrera Vilanova, A., Del Castillo Déjardin, D.: Evaluation of surgical skills in medical students using a virtual simulator. Cirugía Española **91**, 177–183 (2013). https://doi.org/10.1016/j.ciresp.2012.05.019
9. Alaker, M., Wynn, G.R., Arulampalam, T.: Virtual reality training in laparoscopic surgery: a systematic review & meta-analysis. Int. J. Surg. **29**, 85–94 (2016). https://doi.org/10.1016/j.ijsu.2016.03.034
10. Lamata, P., Gómez, E.J., Bello, F., Kneebone, R.L., Lamata, F.: Conceptual framework for laparoscopic VR simulators. IEEE Comput. Graph. Appl. **26**, 69–79 (2006)
11. Lemos, J.D., Hernandez, A.M., Soto-Romero, G.: An instrumented glove to assess manual dexterity in simulation-based neurosurgical education. Sens. (Switz.) **17**, 988 (2017). https://doi.org/10.3390/s17050988
12. Usón-Gargallo, J., Pérez-Merino, E.M., Usón-Casaús, J.M., Sánchez-Fernández, J., Sánchez-Margallo, F.M.: Modelo de formación piramidal para la enseñanza de cirugía laparoscópica. Cir. Cir. **81**, 420–430 (2013)

13. Martin, J.A., et al.: Objective structured assessment of technical skill (OSATS) for surgical residents. Br. J. Surg. **84**, 273–278 (1997)
14. Vassiliou, M.C., et al.: A global assessment tool for evaluation of intraoperative laparoscopic skills. Am. J. Surg. **190**, 107–113 (2005). https://doi.org/10.1016/j.amjsurg.2005.04.004
15. Janeiro, J.M.J.: Sistemas de evaluación de destreza en cirugía endoscópica. Rev. Mex. Cirugía Endoscópica. **8**, 90–96 (2007)
16. Oropesa, I., et al.: Methods and tools for objective assessment of psychomotor skills in laparoscopic surgery. J. Surg. Res. **171**, e81–e95 (2011). https://doi.org/10.1016/j.jss.2011.06.034
17. Vedula, S.S., Ishii, M., Hager, G.D.: Objective assessment of surgical technical skill and competency in the operating room. Annu. Rev. Biomed. Eng. **19**, 301–325 (2017). https://doi.org/10.1146/annurev-bioeng-071516-044435
18. Madani, A., et al.: What are the principles that guide behaviors in the operating room? Ann. Surg. **265**, 255–267 (2017). https://doi.org/10.1097/SLA.0000000000001962
19. Borghini, G., Astolfi, L., Vecchiato, G., Mattia, D., Babiloni, F.: Measuring neurophysiological signals in aircraft pilots and car drivers for the assessment of mental workload, fatigue and drowsiness. Neurosci. Biobehav. Rev. **44**, 58–75 (2014). https://doi.org/10.1016/j.neubiorev.2012.10.003
20. Borghini, G., et al.: Quantitative assessment of the training improvement in a motor-cognitive task by using EEG, ECG and EOG signals. Brain Topogr. **29**, 149–161 (2016). https://doi.org/10.1007/s10548-015-0425-7
21. Johnson, R.R., et al.: Identifying psychophysiological indices of expert vs. novice performance in deadly force judgment and decision making. Front. Hum. Neurosci. **8**, 1–13 (2014). https://doi.org/10.3389/fnhum.2014.00512
22. Blinowska, K.J., Zygierewicz, J.: Application to biomedical signals. In: Practical Biomedical Signal Analysis Using MATLAB®Series in Medical Physics and Biomedical Engineering, pp. 173–176. CRC Press, Taylor & Francis Group (2011)
23. Ali, A., Subhi, Y., Ringsted, C., Konge, L.: Gender differences in the acquisition of surgical skills: a systematic review. Surg. Endosc. Other Interv. Tech. **29**, 3065–3073 (2015). https://doi.org/10.1007/s00464-015-4092-2
24. Enochsson, L., et al.: Visuospatial skills and computer game experience influence the performance of virtual endoscopy. J. Gastrointest. Surg. **8**, 876–882 (2004). https://doi.org/10.1016/j.gassur.2004.06.015. discussion 882
25. Schlickum, M.K., Hedman, L., Enochsson, L., Kjellin, A., Fellander-Tsai, L.: Systematic video game training in surgical novices improves performance in virtual reality endoscopic surgical simulators: a prospective randomized study. World J. Surg. **33**, 2360–2367 (2009). https://doi.org/10.1007/s00268-009-0151-y
26. Grantcharov, T.P., Bardram, L., Funch-Jensen, P., Rosenberg, J.: Impact of hand dominance, gender, and experience with computer games on performance in virtual reality laparoscopy. Surg. Endosc. Other Interv. Tech. **17**, 1082–1085 (2003). https://doi.org/10.1007/s00464-002-9176-0
27. Brookhuis, K.A., de Waard, D.: Monitoring drivers' mental workload in driving simulators using physiological measures. Accid. Anal. Prev. **42**, 898–903 (2010). https://doi.org/10.1016/j.aap.2009.06.001
28. Mulder, T., De Waard, D., Brookhuis, K.A.: Estimating mental effort using heart rate and heart rate variability. In: Stanton, N., Hedge, A., Brookhuis, K., Salas, E., Hendrick, H. (eds.) Handbook of Human Factors and Ergonomics Methods, pp. 1–20. CRC Press (2005)
29. Togo, F., Takahashi, M.: Heart rate variability in occupational health – a systematic review. Ind. Health **47**, 589–602 (2009). https://doi.org/10.2486/indhealth.47.589

Validation of EEG Pre-processing Pipeline by Test-Retest Reliability

Jazmín Ximena Suárez-Revelo[1]([⊠]) (iD), John Fredy Ochoa-Gómez[1] (iD), and Carlos Andrés Tobón-Quintero[2] (iD)

[1] Grupo de investigación en Bioinstrumentación e Ingeniería Clínica – GIBIC, Departamento de Bioingeniería, Facultad de Ingeniería, Universidad de Antioquia UdeA, Calle 70 No. 52-21, Medellín, Colombia
jazmin.suarez@udea.edu.co

[2] Grupo de Neurociencias de Antioquia – GNA, Grupo de Neuropsicología y conducta – GRUNECO, Universidad de Antioquia UdeA, Sede de Investigación Universitaria - SIU, Calle 62 No. 52-59, Medellín, Colombia

Abstract. Artifact removal and validation of pre-processing approaches remain as an open problem in EEG analysis. Cleaning data is a critical step in EEG analysis, per-formed to increase the signal-to-noise ratio and to eliminate unwanted artifacts. Methodologies commonly used for EEG pre-processing are: filtering, interpolation of bad channels, epoch segmentation, re-referencing, and elimination of physiological artifacts such as eye blinking or muscular activity. It is important to consider that the order and application of these steps affect signal quality for further analysis. In order to validate a pre-processing pipeline that can be considered in a clinical follow-up, this paper evaluated test-retest reliability of EEG recordings. EEG signals were acquired during eyes-closed resting state condition in two groups of healthy subjects with a follow-up of one and six months respectively. Signals were pre-processed with five different methodologies commonly used in literature. Test-retest reliability by intraclass correlation coefficient was calculated for power spectrum measures in each pre-processing approach and group. The results showed how test-retest reliability was significantly affected by pre-processing pipeline in both follow-ups. The pre-processing pipeline that com-bines robust reference to average and wavelet ICA improves the test-retest reliability.

Keywords: Artifact removal · EEG · Pre-processing · Test-retest reliability

1 Introduction

The electroencephalography (EEG) provides a non-invasive representation of brain electrophysiological activity, reflecting both global and local activity with high temporal resolution [1]. Different characteristics of waves reflect the current state of brain and help to identify abnormalities associated with brain dysfunction [2]. As brain activity is essentially non-stationary, nonlinear, and noisy, EEG analysis is based primarily on signal processing based treatments to obtain stable and reliable signal characteristics [3].

© Springer Nature Switzerland AG 2018
J. C. Figueroa-García et al. (Eds.): WEA 2018, CCIS 916, pp. 290–299, 2018.
https://doi.org/10.1007/978-3-030-00353-1_26

Quantitative EEG (qEEG) refers to mathematical treatment of EEG data in order to quantify specific signal parameters [4]. The qEEG processing techniques have identified phase, amplitude, and power characteristics which reflect unique aspects of brain function. Five main groups of oscillations are distinguished and defined according their frequency ranges: delta (1–4 Hz), theta (4–8 Hz), alpha (8–13 Hz), beta (13–30 Hz) and gamma (30–50 Hz) [5], being the alpha rhythm the most prominent and with the main functional significance [6]. Posterior alpha rhythms reflect the activity of dominant oscillatory neural networks at resting and represent a global functional feature of brain [7]. Alpha rhythms are mainly modulated by thalamo-cortical and cortico-cortical interactions that facilitate/inhibit the transmission of sensorimotor information between subcortical and cortical pathways, and the retrieval of semantic cortical storage information [8]. Power of low-frequency alpha rhythms is related to IQ, memory and the state of global cognition. High-frequency alpha rhythms reflect the oscillation of more selective neuronal systems for the development of sensorimotor and semantic information [9].

A crucial step in the analysis of electrophysiological data is to improve the signal-to-noise ratio under the restrictions given by the low amplitude of biosignals [10]. The electrical field generated by neural activity and measurable by EEG is small, implying neural signals recorded on range of microvolts that can easily be masked by artefactual sources technical and physiological [11]. Technical artifacts correspond to interference of power supply (60 Hz), fluctuation of the electrode impedance, defects in cables and electrical noise of electronic components [12]. Among physiological artefacts, the most common types include blinking, eye movements, muscle activity and heartbeat. During signals acquisition is possible, and necessary, to reduce the artifacts using different techniques, as ensuring a low impedance between the electrodes and the scalp, but is impossible to avoid all kind of artifacts being more critical the situation when the work is done with clinical populations.

Due to all these sources of artifacts, several pre-processing steps should be considered for EEG analysis such as: low-pass and high-pass filtering, to eliminate breathing component and high frequency noise respectively; detection and interpolation of bad channels to avoid introducing errors in statistical analysis; epoch segmentation to assurance the assumption of quasi-stationarity; re-referencing data to average which is the closest to zero voltage; and removing of physiological artifacts by techniques such as independent component analysis (ICA) and regression to electrooculographic (EOG) or electrocardiographic (ECG) signals [13–15].

However, several issues must be considered when applying these pre-processing steps since they can have a negative effect over the EEG signal quality. Filtering can result in significant distortions of time course and amplitude of signal [10]. Referencing data, either to single channel or to average, can be affected by atypical channels [16]. Removal of artifacts using ICA can lead to loss of brain signal mixed with noisy signal [17]. In addition, these methods are generally based on the intervention of an expert and in the visual search for artifacts, something subjective and difficult to standardize.

In order to describe a disease stages and its progression, EEG measurements should be characterized by having low variability between subjects and high reliability between longitudinal tests [18]. With the aim to validate a protocol for EEG pre-processing which can be used in a clinical follow-up, this study assess the test-retest reliability of power spectrum measures calculated in EEG recordings with different preprocessing methodologies commonly applied [16, 17, 19, 20]. In previous works [21, 22], we have evaluated other frequency bands and pre-processing pipelines, obtaining good test-retest reliability for theta and alpha bands. Furthermore, we have improved the signal pre-processing in order to obtain a more automatic methodology as the proposal in this paper. With this work, unlike the previous ones, we want to evaluate test-retest reliability in two different time intervals over alpha band given its functional relevance [6]. If EEG features continue to be preserved at a longer time interval in healthy subjects, it will allow us to perform a longitudinal study in clinical populations, ensuring that what we are going to observe is due to physio pathological changes characteristic of a disease and not because of the methodology of analysis.

EEG signals were recorded during eyes-closed resting state condition in two groups of healthy subjects, with a follow-up of one and six months respectively. The intraclass correlation coefficient (ICC) was used as a measure of reliability for relative power in alpha band (8–13 Hz). Our findings indicate that the pre-processing approach affects significantly test-retest reliability of qEEG measures, and that this reliability can be improved with an adequate pre-processing flow, that for the current paper is the workflow that uses robust reference to average and wavelet ICA.

The remaining of the paper is divided as follows: Sect. 2 provides a detailed description of EEG datasets, pre-processing approaches, extraction of power spectrum measurements and test-retest reliability evaluation. Section 3 shows the reliability values obtained for the different methodologies and statistical analysis. Section 4 presents a discussion of the results and their applications. Finally, conclusions are presented in Sect. 5.

2 Experimentation

2.1 Subjects and EEG Recordings

Two groups of healthy subjects were used for this analysis. The first group (G1) consisted of 18 young people aged between 20 and 30 years (Mean = 23.29; SD = 2.82), who were recorded twice with one-month interval. The second group (G2) consisted of 10 older subjects aged between 40 and 60 years (Mean = 46; SD = 8.45) with six months interval between recording sessions. EEG recordings were performed at awake resting state with eyes closed for 5 min. EEG signals were acquired with 58 tin electrodes (positioned according to the international system 10–10) using the software and amplifiers Neuroscan (Scan 4.5, SynAmps2). Signals were digitized at a sampling rate of 1000 Hz and filtered online (bandpass filter: 0.05 to 200 Hz, and band reject filter of 60 Hz to eliminate noise from the power supply). The reference acquisition consisted of an electrode located on the right earlobe, and an electrode located between Cz and Fz was used as ground. Recordings were made in an isolated cabin of audio and external electromagnetic signals (Faraday cage). Informed consent, approved by the Human Subjects Committee of the Universidad de Antioquia, was obtained from all subject's participation.

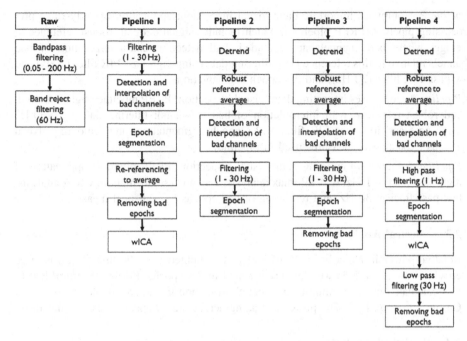

Fig. 1. EEG pre-processing pipelines. 4 pre-processing pipelines were applied using the EEGLAB and standardized early-stage EEG processing pipeline (PREP) MATLAB toolbox.

2.2 EEG Data Pre-processing Pipelines

We applied four semi-automated pre-processing pipelines using functions of two MATLAB toolbox: EEGLAB [19] and the standardized early-stage EEG processing pipeline (PREP) [16]. In addition to these approaches, raw records were included in the analysis. Pre-processing approaches are described below (see Fig. 1):

Raw. Records taken directly from the amplifier without any further pre-processing step. The signals were in a frequency range of 0.05 to 200 Hz, and filtered by a notch filter at 60 Hz.

Pipeline 1. This approach has been used in the previous works to evaluate test-retest reliability in other frequency bands and over one month interval [21, 22]. The methodology consist of importing data; visual inspection to eliminate segments that represent abrupt movements of the patient; high-pass filtering at 1 Hz and low-pass filtering at 30 Hz using FIR filters zero phase sinc, with Hamming window (Order = 3300, Transition bandwidth = 1 Hz); detection of atypical noisy channels using kurtosis, probability, and spectrum measures; interpolation of bad channels by spherical splines; data segmentation into 2 s epochs; re-referencing data to average; removing artefactual epochs using linear trend, joint probability and kurtosis measures [20]; and ICA enhanced by wavelet (wICA) to correct remaining eye blinks [17].

Pipeline 2. Comprises importing data; visual inspection; application of early-stage pre-processing pipeline (PREP pipeline), which includes signal detrend, robust reference to average, where bad channels are excluded, and detection and interpolation of bad channels relative to this reference [16]; filtering data using high-pass FIR filter (1 Hz) and low-pass FIR filter (30 Hz); and 2 s epoch segmentation.

Pipeline 3. Comprises importing data; visual inspection; PREP pipeline (signal detrend, and robust reference with interpolation of bad channels); filtering data at 1–30 Hz (high-pass and low-pass FIR filters); 2 s epoch segmentation; and removing of bad epochs by statistical measures used in pipeline1.

Pipeline 4. Includes importing data; visual inspection; PREP pipeline; application of high-pass filter at 1 Hz; ICA infomax analysis; 2 s epoch segmentation; wICA analysis; low-pass filter at 30 Hz; and removing of bad epochs by statistical measures.

2.3   Spectral Analysis

Relative power in alpha band (8–13 Hz) was computed over the first 50 artifact-free epochs. Raw recordings were also segmented in 2 s epochs. Power spectrum density was calculated using the multitaper spectral estimation method available in MATLAB Chronux toolbox [23]. The power averaging across the 50 epochs was calculated.

2.4   Statistical Analysis

Intraclass correlation coefficient (ICC) was used to quantify the test–retest reliability of alpha power in each group. Specifically, we used a two way mixed model with an absolute agreement definition between two sessions [24]. ICC values were reported descriptively and with a one-way ANOVA analysis to test the hypothesis about the effect of pre-processing approach on reliability. Statistical significance of 5% was used for all tests. All statistical comparisons, and the validation of statistical assumptions, were implemented in MATLAB.

3   Results

Table 1 shows the number of channels interpolated, epochs removed, and epochs remaining in each pre-processing pipeline. With pipeline 1, a smaller number of channels were interpolated. Pipelines 2, 3, and 4, which include the use of PREP toolbox, interpolated a larger number of channels. Also, it is observed that pipelines 1 and 3 removed a similar number of epochs. In contrast, pipeline 4 removed less epochs.

Mean ICC values calculated over all channels for raw recordings and each pre-processing pipeline are shown in Fig. 2. Average ICC values were the lowest (mean values < 0.1) in raw data for both groups. Pre-processed recordings with approaches 2, 3 and 4 showed generally good reliability (mean values > 0.5) in both groups. ANOVA analysis showed a significant effect of pre-processing pipeline for G1 $(F(4) = 240, p < 0.001)$, where pipelines 2, 3 and 4 are more reliable than pipeline1 and raw data. For G2 group, there was also a significant effect of pre-processing approach (F(4) = 108, p < 0.001), and pre-processed data with any pipeline are more reliable than raw data.

Mean ICC values for each electrode are represented in Fig. 3 over a surface rendered of the scalp. For raw data test-retest reliability is the lowest over all scalp. For pipeline 1, reliability is lower in G1 group, but increases in G2. The other pipelines have similar reliability in the two follow-ups.

Table 1. Resulting number of epochs and interpolated channels

Pipeline	Group	Number of interpolated channels Mean ± SD		Number of removed epochs Mean ± SD		Number of remaining epochs Mean ± SD	
		S1	S2	S1	S2	S1	S2
P1	G1|	1.3 ± 0.7	1.3 ± 0.9	13.1 ± 5.2	19.3 ± 6	123.1 ± 23.9	136.1 ± 6.6
	G2	1.1 ± 0.7	1.1 ± 0.6	18.4 ± 7.9	26.1 ± 12	146.4 ± 14.6	135.5 ± 19.3
P2	G1	5.9 ± 3.6	8.0 ± 3.2	–	–	136.2 ± 27.3	155.4 ± 4.6
	G2	5.9 ± 4.9	6.1 ± 4.3	–	–	164.8 ± 13.2	161.6 ± 14.6
P3	G1	5.9 ± 3.6	8.0 ± 3.2	13.3 ± 5.5	19.2 ± 5.5	122.9 ± 23.8	136.2 ± 6.1
	G2	5.9 ± 4.9	6.1 ± 4.3	18.7 ± 8.2	25.2 ± 11.7	146.1 ± 14.8	136.4 ± 18.6
P4	G1	5.9 ± 3.6	8.0 ± 3.2	5.8 ± 2.2	7.8 ± 1.9	130.3 ± 26.3	147.6 ± 4.7
	G2	5.9 ± 4.9	6.1 ± 4.3'	8.5 ± 3.8	8.9 ± 3.1	156.3 ± 13.1	152.7 ± 14.2

P1: Pipeline 1, P2: Pipeline 2, P3: Pipeline 3, P4: Pipeline 4.
S1: session 1, S2: session 2, G1: one-month follow-up.
G2: six months follow-up.

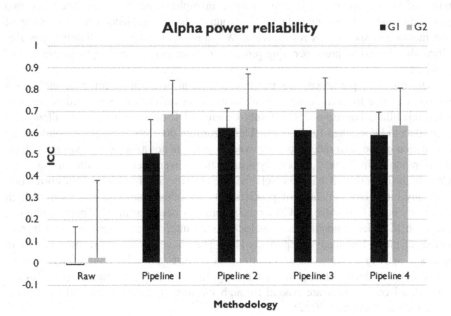

Fig. 2. Mean ICC values (ICC: intraclass correlation coefficient. Vertical bars show the standard deviation).

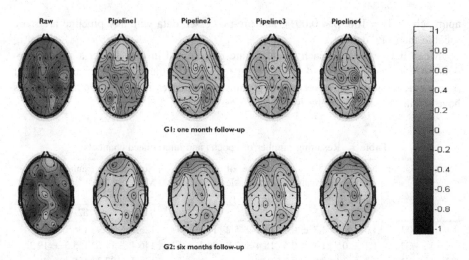

Fig. 3. Scalp map representations of test-retest reliability (measured by ICC) of alpha power. Results for the two follow-ups are given from top to bottom and are categorized according to pre-processing pipeline from left to right.

4 Discussion

In order to validate an EEG pre-processing protocol that can be used in a clinical follow-up, this study evaluated the effect of signal pre-processing on test-retest reliability of power spectrum. Relative power in alpha band was calculated for two recording sessions in resting state, in two groups of healthy subjects with a follow-up of one month and six months respectively. We found that test-retest reliability was significantly affected by pre-processing pipeline for both groups, leading to an increase of reliability.

The use of a pre-processing pipeline, which in addition to filtering, includes a robust reference to average and wICA analysis for artifacts removal, improves test-retest reliability. The use of PREP toolbox corrects DC offset in signals and allows that more data to be retained for analysis. This algorithm does not consider the outliers for calculation of the reference; thus, the average value is not affected by extreme values. As is reported in Table 1, more atypical channels were detected with this toolbox. Criteria for detection of bad channels include extreme amplitudes, lack of correlation with any other channel, lack of predictability by other channels, and unusual high frequency noise [16]. Also, wICA analysis removes ocular artifacts. This technique is based on ICA decomposition and includes as an intermediate step a wavelet thresholding of the independent components [17]. The above enables to recover persistent neuronal activity in components identified as artifacts. An advantage of wICA is its automation, it does not require visual inspection of the independent components. Instead, all components are passed through the threshold procedure and only high-magnitude artifacts are filtered.

Several studies have reported good test-retest reliability of qEEG measurements during resting state, mainly for theta and alpha bands. High reliability values have been found at short intervals of time or days [25], for one month [18], nine months [26] and for one year [27]. Although in literature there are higher average values (0.8) than those obtained in this paper (~ 0.65), in previous studies the test-retest reliability of power spectrum was calculated only on some channels. In this work, we evaluated reliability over whole scalp, providing a more complete analysis. In addition, unlike the previous works, a more automatic pre-processing pipeline was developed, which facilitates the analysis and excludes subjectivity in artefactual epochs and components removal, which allows standardizing the process for evaluators and studies. This pipeline is not fully automated because we include the visual inspection of the signals as a first step, aimed to remove abrupt subject movements that may affect the subsequent treatment of signals and lead to identifying a greater number of channels or atypical components. However, when a large amount of data is handled, the processing times can be increased excessively, and will be needed try to automate the process in the future.

It is necessary to consider that since the test-retest repeatability is being evaluated on two groups, which differ in age as well as in time intervals, the groups can not be correlated, thus the analyzes were carried out in each group separately. A future study that keeps only one variable to analyze, will allow to extract more information and perform correlations between time interval between records and reliability. It is also needed to take into account the gender differences for future analysis.

5 Conclusions

The qEEG measurements offer significant and stable results over time, which give them relevance and clinical usefulness. Resting state EEG represents an easy and fast procedure to be performed in clinical setting. Its use does not require devices to stimulate or record subject behavior, and is not susceptible to fatigue and anxiety typically associated with task execution. This makes it more suitable for recordings in elderly subjects and clinical populations such as mild cognitive impairment or Alzheimer's disease. In this work we validate a semi-automatic pre-processing pipeline that allows test-retest reliability of qEEG measurements.

Acknowledgments. This work was supported by Vicerrectoría de Investigación of Universidad de Antioquia (CODI), Project "Neurofisiología y Neuropsicología en Enfermedad Ganglio Basal", code PRG2014-768, Departamento Administrativo de Ciencia, Tecnología e Innovación (COLCIENCIAS), announcement N. 757 Doctorados Nacionales, and the project "Identificación de Biomarcadores Preclínicos en Enfermedad de Alzheimer a través de un Seguimiento Longitudinal de la Actividad Eléctrica Cerebral en Poblaciones con Riesgo Genético", code 111577757635, announcement 777-2017 of COLCIENCIAS.

References

1. MacDonald, D.B.: Electroencephalography: Basic Principles and Applications. Elsevier, New York City (2015)
2. Millett, D., Coutin-Churchman, P., Stern, J.M.: Basic principles of electroencephalography. In: Brain Mapping, pp. 75–80. Elsevier (2015)
3. Indic, P., Pratap, R., Nampoori, V.P., Pradhan, N.: Significance of time scales in nonlinear dynamical analysis of electroencephalogram signals. Int. J. Neurosci. **99**, 181–194 (1999)
4. Medeiros, A.P., Anghinah, R., Smidth, M.T., Silva, J.M.: The clinical use of quantitative EEG in cognitive disorders. Dement Neuropsychol. **3**, 195–203 (2009)
5. Sanei, S., Chambers, J.A.: EEG Signal Processing. Wiley, Hoboken (2007)
6. Başar, E., Güntekin, B.: A short review of alpha activity in cognitive processes and in cognitive impairment. Int. J. Psychophysiol. **86**, 25–38 (2012). https://doi.org/10.1016/j.ijpsycho.2012.07.001
7. Babiloni, C., et al.: Sources of cortical rhythms in adults during physiological aging: a multicentric EEG study. Hum. Brain Mapp. **27**, 162–172 (2006). https://doi.org/10.1002/hbm.20175
8. Başar, E.: A review of alpha activity in integrative brain function: fundamental physiology, sensory coding, cognition and pathology. Int. J. Psychophysiol. **86**, 1–24 (2012). https://doi.org/10.1016/j.ijpsycho.2012.07.002
9. Lizio, R., Vecchio, F., Frisoni, G.B., Ferri, R., Rodriguez, G., Babiloni, C.: Electroencephalographic rhythms in alzheimer's disease. Int. J. Alzheimers. Dis. **2011**, 1–11 (2011). https://doi.org/10.4061/2011/927573
10. Widmann, A., Schröger, E.: Filter effects and filter artifacts in the analysis of electrophysiological data. Front Psychol. **3**, 233 (2012)
11. Winkler, I., Haufe, S., Tangermann, M.: Automatic classification of artifactual ICA-components for artifact removal in EEG signals. Behav. Brain Funct. **7**, 30 (2011). https://doi.org/10.1186/1744-9081-7-30
12. Tavakoli, P., Campbell, K.: The recording and quantification of event-related potentials: II. Signal processing and analysis. Quant. Methods Psychol. **11**, 98–112 (2015)
13. Gross, J., et al.: Good practice for conducting and reporting MEG research. Neuroimage **65**, 349–363 (2013). https://doi.org/10.1016/j.neuroimage.2012.10.001
14. Tavakoli, P., Campbell, K.: The recording and quantification of event-related potentials: I. Stimulus presentation and data acquisition. Quant. Methods Psychol **11**, 89–97 (2015)
15. Wallstrom, G.L., Kass, R.E., Miller, A., Cohn, J.F., Fox, N.A.: Automatic correction of ocular artifacts in the EEG: a comparison of regression-based and component-based methods. Int. J. Psychophysiol. **53**, 105–119 (2004). https://doi.org/10.1016/j.ijpsycho.2004.03.007
16. Bigdely-Shamlo, N., Mullen, T., Kothe, C., Su, K.-M., Robbins, K.A.: The PREP pipeline: standardized preprocessing for large-scale EEG analysis. Front. Neuroinform. **9**, 1–20 (2015). https://doi.org/10.3389/fninf.2015.00016
17. Castellanos, N.P., Makarov, V.A.: Recovering EEG brain signals: artifact suppression with wavelet enhanced independent component analysis. J. Neurosci. Methods. **158**, 300–312 (2006). https://doi.org/10.1016/j.jneumeth.2006.05.033
18. Cannon, R.L., et al.: Reliability of quantitative EEG (qEEG) measures and LORETA current source density at 30 days. Neurosci. Lett. **518**, 27–31 (2012). https://doi.org/10.1016/j.neulet.2012.04.035

19. Delorme, A., Makeig, S.: EEGLAB: an open source toolbox for analysis of single-trial EEG dynamics including independent component analysis. J. Neurosci. Methods **134**, 9–21 (2004). https://doi.org/10.1016/j.jneumeth.2003.10.009
20. Delorme, A., Sejnowski, T.J., Makeig, S.: Enhanced detection of artifacts in EEG data using higher-order statistics and independent component analysis. Neuroimaging. **34**, 1443–1449 (2007). https://doi.org/10.1016/j.neuroimage.2006.11.004
21. Suárez-Revelo, J., Ochoa-Gomez, J., Duque-Grajales, J., Montoya-Betancur, A., Sanchez-Lopez, S.: Test – retest reliability in electroencephalographic recordings. In: 2015 20th Symposium on Signal Processing, Images and Computer Vision (STSIVA), pp. 1–5 (2015). https://doi.org/10.1109/stsiva.2015.7330412
22. Suarez-Revelo, J., Ochoa-Gomez, J., Duque-Grajales, J.: Improving test-retest reliability of quantitative electroencephalography using different preprocessing approaches. In: 2016 IEEE 38th Annual International Conference of the Engineering in Medicine and Biology Society (EMBC), pp. 961–964. IEEE (2016)
23. Mitra, P., Bokil, H.: Observed Brain Dynamics. Oxford University Press, New York (2008)
24. McGraw, K.O., Wong, S.P.: Forming inferences about some intraclass correlations coefficients: Correction. Psychol. Methods **1**, 390 (1996). https://doi.org/10.1037/1082-989x.1.4.390
25. McEvoy, L., Smith, M., Gevins, A.: Test–retest reliability of cognitive EEG. Clin. Neurophysiol. **111**, 457–463 (2000). https://doi.org/10.1016/S1388-2457(99)00258-8
26. Corsi-Cabrera, M., Galindo-Vilchis, L., del-Río-Portilla, Y., Arce, C., Ramos-Loyo, J.: Within-subject reliability and inter-session stability of EEG power and coherent activity in women evaluated monthly over nine months. Clin. Neurophysiol. **118**, 9–21 (2007). https://doi.org/10.1016/j.clinph.2006.08.013
27. Hatz, F., Hardmeier, M., Bousleiman, H., Rüegg, S., Schindler, C., Fuhr, P.: Reliability of fully automated versus visually controlled pre- and post-processing of resting-state EEG. Clin. Neurophysiol. **126**, 268–274 (2015). https://doi.org/10.1016/j.clinph.2014.05.014

Bioacoustic Signals Denoising Using the Undecimated Discrete Wavelet Transform

Alejandro Gómez, Juan P. Ugarte$^{(\boxtimes)}$, and Diego Mauricio Murillo Gómez

Facultad de Ingenierías, Universidad de San Buenaventura, Medellín, Colombia
juan.ugarte@usbmed.edu.co

Abstract. Biological populations can be monitored through acoustic signal processing. This approach allows to sense biological populations without a direct interaction between humans and species required. In order to extract relevant acoustic features, signals must be processed through a noise reduction stage in which target data is enhanced for a better analysis. Due to the nature of the biological acoustic signals, the denoising strategy must consider the non-stationarity of the records and minimize the lost of significant information. In this work, a Last Approximation standard deviation algorithm (*LAstd*) for the processing of bioacoustic signals based on wavelet analysis is presented. The performance of the proposed algorithm is evaluated using a database of owls, which have been modified with different rates of coloured noise. Furthermore, the approach is compared to a standard denoising method from the Matlab Wavelet Toolbox. The results show that the proposed algorithm is able to improve the signal-to-noise ratio of the owl's registers within a wide frequency range and different noise conditions. Furthermore, the algorithm can be adapted to process different biological species, thus it can be an useful tool for characterizing avian ecosystems.

Keywords: Wavelet transform · Threshold denoising
Bioacoustic signals

1 Introduction

The analysis of acoustic signals is a relevant approach for monitoring biological populations because it allows an automatic classification of species without having direct contact with them [1]. The acquisition of information by directional microphones is a common practice when different sources, interacting within the ecosystem, need to be registered [2,3]. Nevertheless, some of these sources may be understood as noise if an extraction of information for a specific specie is desired.

Denoising strategies are intended to improve the signal-to-noise ratio (SNR) of biological acoustic sources in the soundscape. This process retains the quality of a desired signal while reducing the influence of undesired components [4]. The traditional approach is based on the application of filters, which are effective

© Springer Nature Switzerland AG 2018
J. C. Figueroa-García et al. (Eds.): WEA 2018, CCIS 916, pp. 300–308, 2018.
https://doi.org/10.1007/978-3-030-00353-1_27

when the signal and noise are in different frequency bands. However, this method is unable of preserving the desired signal when spectral content is overlapped. Furthermore, denoising methods based on exclusive spectral analysis impose important limitations when the signal has non-stationary characteristics [5].

The Wavelet transform has been widely used in the digital signal processing field [6–10] due to its capability to process time-frequency characteristics, which outperforms the traditional Fourier analysis of transient or non-stationary signals. From the work of Donoho and Johnstone [11], the Wavelet transform has been applied to denoise signals by thresholding a set of wavelet coefficients obtained through an orthogonal wavelet transform using a nonlinear rule.

Some studies have shown the versatility of wavelets for denoising bioacoustic signals [5,12–15]. Taking into consideration these previous implementations and with the aim of potential applications in the characterization of colombian avian ecosystems, this paper presents the denoising strategy Last Approximation standard deviation ($LAstd$), which is based on the Undecimated Discrete Wavelet Transform (UDWT) for processing birds songs.

The proposed method has been focused on owls having a wide spectral content. It has been assessed under distinct noise conditions and compare it to a standard algorithm from the Wavelet Toolbox of Matlab.

2 Materials and Methods

2.1 Last Approximation Standard Deviation Denoising Strategy

The proposed method is based on the UDWT, which yields a multilevel decomposition of the signal by obtaining *detail* and *approximation* coefficients. This process is equivalent to apply a filter bank with high-pass and low-pass filters [16]. Figure 1 illustrates the $LAstd$ strategy where the input signal S is decomposed in L levels by applying the wavelet filters $H_j(\omega)$ and $L_j(\omega)$ which provide the details cD_j and approximations cA_j, respectively ($j = 1, 2, \ldots, L$). Subsequently, the detail coefficients cD_j are soft thresholded applying a threshold $\lambda = q \times \lambda_u$ where λ_u is estimated from the last approximation cA_L, which is then set to zero to eliminate noisy components predominant at this level (i.e. q controls the denoising level). The wavelet reconstruction is performed by using the reconstruction filters $\widehat{H_j}(\omega)$ and $\widehat{L_j}(\omega)$, resulting in a denoised version $\widehat{S}$ of the input signal. Figure 1 illustrates an example for $L = 2$ levels of decomposition. In the following sections, a description of the characteristics of the proposed method is presented.

Wavelet Selection and Decomposition Level Estimation. The selection of the wavelet is made by considering the minimum aliasing effects produced when a reference bioacoustic signal is processed using the traditional Discrete Wavelet Transform (DWT) with different wavelets (Haar, Daubechies 8, Daubechies 10, Symlet 8, Coiflet 5 and Discrete Meyer). Due to the aliasing inhering in the DWT algorithm, a suitable wavelet need to be chosen [17]. Similar to the $LAstd$

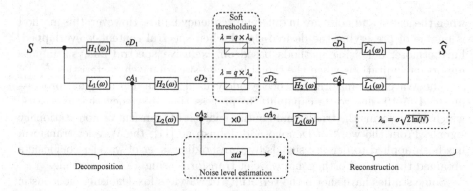

Fig. 1. *LAstd* denoising strategy using the UDWT.

strategy, the last approximation coefficients obtained in the DWT decomposition are set to zero to later reconstruct the signal. For the current work, the selection of the wavelet was carried out by a visual inspection of the spectrogram and choosing the most accurate reconstruction. Some of the tested wavelets are shown in Fig. 2.

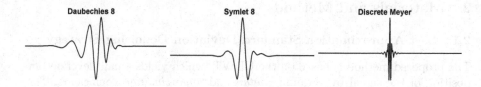

Fig. 2. Some of the compared wavelets.

A Shannon entropy criteria was implemented to define the appropriate number of decomposition levels [5]. The latter provides a standard measure of uncertainty or disorder in a system and it is defined as [18]:

$$ShEn = -\sum_i s_i^2 \ln(s_i^2), \tag{1}$$

where s_i is the ith sample of the signal [19,20] and assuming the convention $0 \times \ln(0) = 0$.

The decomposition level L is estimated by analyzing the approximation coefficients because they retain the coarser information of the original signal. Starting from $L = 1$, the decomposition is performed until *ShEn* at level L is greater than the *ShEn* at level $L - 1$, setting L as the decomposition level. Figure 3 shows a levels vs. Shannon Entropy plot that illustrates an example where the level is estimated as $L = 6$.

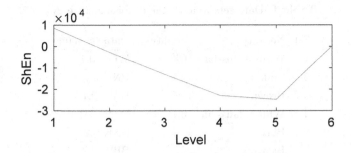

Fig. 3. Wavelet decomposition levels vs. Shannon entropy.

Thresholding. The threshold level is computed as [21]

$$\lambda = q \times \lambda_u = q \times \sigma \sqrt{2\ln(N)}, \tag{2}$$

in which N is the length of the signal, σ is the standard deviation of cA_L [10] and q is a control parameter that can be adjusted to smooth the threshold level and is set between 0 and 1.

Wavelet denoising eliminates the small coefficients assuming that the noise components have high frequency content, thus, it is usually applied on cD_j. In order to avoid discontinuity distortions, a *soft thresholding* function δ_{so} is applied as:

$$\delta_{so} : \begin{cases} \widehat{cD_j} = 0 & \text{if } |cD_j| \leq \lambda, \\ \widehat{cD_j} = cD_j - \lambda & \text{if } cD_j > \lambda, \\ \widehat{cD_j} = cD_j + \lambda & \text{if } cD_j < -\lambda. \end{cases} \tag{3}$$

2.2 Test Database

A sample of 10 owls audio recordings from www.owling.com are considered to assess the *LAstd* algorithm. The frequency range varies depending on the specie, ranging from 350 Hz to 15 kHz with a sampling frequency of 44.1 kHz. It has been shown that a wide range of environmental acoustic variability can be modeled trough colored noise [22,23]. Therefore, white Gaussian, Pink and Brown additive noise are introduced into the owls signals to simulate distinct environmental noise conditions. The noisy signal is designed by considering 10%, 20% and 30% of the free-noise signal amplitude. This leads to a database of 90 noisy signals distributed in 9 datasets. The characteristics of the datasets are summarized in Table 1.

2.3 Performance Measure

The signal to noise ratio (SNR) has been selected as a metric to evaluate the performance of the *LAstd* denoising method. The SNR is defined as:

$$SNR = 20\log_{10}\left(\frac{||S_{ref}||}{||S_{noise}||}\right), \tag{4}$$

Table 1. Data sets to asses the denoising strategy

Set	Noise type	Amplitude	Data set name
1	White Gaussian	10%	WGN 0.1
2	Pink	10%	PNK 0.1
3	Brown	10%	BRW 0.1
4	White Gaussian	20%	WGN 0.2
5	Pink	20%	PNK 0.2
6	Brownian	20%	BRW 0.2
7	White Gaussian	30%	WGN 0.3
8	Pink	30%	PNK 0.3
9	Brownian	30%	BRW 0.3

where S_{ref} and S_{noise} are the free-noise and noisy signal, respectively. $\| \cdot \|$ corresponds to the Euclidean norm operator. *LAstd* strategy is also compared to the Matlab wavelet denoising function *wden*. This function computes an automatic wavelet denoising algorithm with different thresholding selection rules. An universal threshold argument (*sqtwolog*) with a soft thresholding technique and a level dependent estimation of noise level (*mln*) has been used for the analysis.

3   Results and Discussion

Figure 4 shows the effect of different wavelets on a reference signal. It can be seen that, for this specific case, Meyer approach provides the better performance. Therefore, the *LAstd* method uses this wavelet to denoise the owls' audio files.

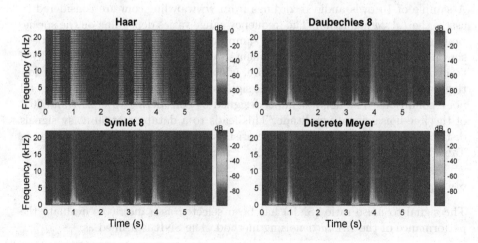

Fig. 4. Aliasing effect induced by different wavelets

Figure 5 shows the median bar graphs of the SNR obtained after applying the *LAstd* and *wden* denoising strategies to each dataset (red and yellow bars, respectively). Three variations of the threshold control parameter q were tested ($q = 1$, 0.5 and 0.25). The median SNR values of the noisy data are also shown (blue bars).

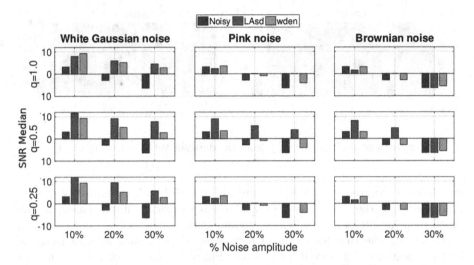

Fig. 5. Median SNR values of the noisy and denoised signals using the *LAstd* and *wden* algorithms. The results for four q values are shown under different noise conditions. (Color figure online)

Regarding the threshold control parameter q, results of SNR suggest that in the case of $q = 1$, *LAstd* outplays *wden* in 55.56% of datasets (5/9). When $q = 0.5$, *LAstd* outplays *wden* in 88.89% of datasets (8/9). Finally, for $q = 0.25$, *LAstd* outplays *wden* in 66.67% of datasets (6/9).

When noise concentrates most of its power in low frequency bands (colored noise cases), the *LAstd* strategy estimates a high noise level that surpass some wavelet coefficients with coarse information. This may lead to a lost of important signal features in the thresholding process. However, this can be controlled with an appropriate value for q, which yields better performance compared to the *wden* function (e.g. when $q = 0.5$).

Important spectral distortion was found for cases where *wden* yielded to better results than *LAstd* according to SNR measure. Figure 6 shows a representative example where aliasing effects are present, which were introduced by the *wden* function. Figure 7 shows another example where the *wden* function performs a strong denoising. However, spectral information is lost, while the *LAstd* method is capable to preserve frequency content by adjusting its parameter $q = 0.25$.

Both strategies present limitations in the case of Brown noise. However, the *LAstd* strategy is tolerant to the noise amplitude (20% and 30%) when the

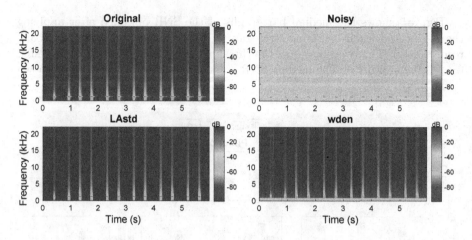

Fig. 6. Denoising over a signal from the data set WGN 0.1 using $q = 1$

signals are corrupted with White Gaussian and Pink noise. Figure 8 shows an example where the *LAstd* strategy achieves a significant improvement in the signal reducing high amplitude noise components.

Regarding the threshold control parameter q, the results suggest that the best performance is achieved for $q = 0.5$ (Fig. 5). In this case, *LAstd* outplays *wden* in 88.89% of datasets (8/9), which supports better performance of *LAstd* even in the presence of Brownian noise. The *LAstd* strategy can be tuned to analyze other avian species. It is important to achieve a strong correlation between the signal and the chosen wavelet, besides the criteria of avoiding aliasing. This method of wavelet selection was also used in [5], where the *dmey* wavelet is suitable for analyzing bioacoustic signals. The threshold q is estimated by vary-

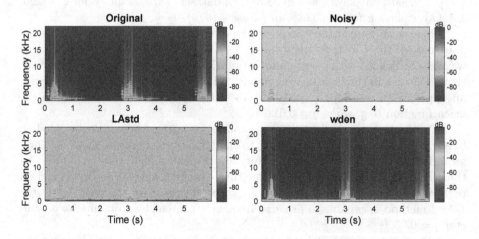

Fig. 7. Denoising over a signal from the data set WGN 0.1 using $q = 0.25$

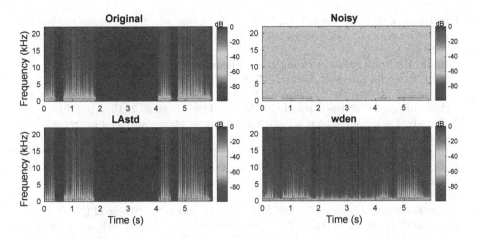

Fig. 8. Denoising over a signal from the data set WGN 0.3 using $q = 1$

ing the parameter q and by assessing the SNR measure under distinct noise configurations.

4   Conclusions

The *LAstd* denoising approach has been proposed based on the wavelet transform. The method is focused on the characterization of avian ecosystems through their acoustic features. The algorithm is capable to improve the SNR of avian audio registers with a wide frequency range and under different noise conditions. A specific setup for the *LAstd* algorithm applied to owl's registers has been presented. Future research will be oriented on enhancing the threshold estimation and reducing the degrees of freedom of the algorithm.

References

1. Alonso, J.B., et al.: Automatic anuran identification using noise removal and audio activity detection. Expert Syst. Appl. **72**, 83–92 (2017)
2. Wielgat, R., Zielinski, T.P., Potempa, T., Lisowska-Lis, A., Król, D.: HFCC based recognition of bird species. In: Signal Processing: Algorithms, Architectures, Arrangements, and Applications, SPA 2007 - Workshop Proceedings, pp. 129–134 (2007)
3. Bedoya, C., Isaza, C., Daza, J.M., López, J.D.: Automatic recognition of anuran species based on syllable identification. Ecol. Inform. **24**, 200–209 (2014)
4. Chen, G., Bui, T.: Multiwavelets denoising using neighboring coefficients. IEEE Signal Process. Lett. **10**, 211–214 (2003)
5. Priyadarshani, N., Marsland, S., Castro, I., Punchihewa, A.: Birdsong denoising using wavelets. PLoS ONE **11**, e0146790 (2016)
6. Jing-Yi, L., Hong, L., Dong, Y., Yan-Sheng, Z.: A new wavelet threshold function and denoising application. Math. Probl. Eng. **2016**, 8 p. (2016)

7. Srivastava, M., Anderson, C.L., Freed, J.H.: A new wavelet denoising method for selecting decomposition levels and noise thresholds. IEEE Access **4**, 3862–3877 (2016)
8. Patil, R.: Noise reduction using wavelet transform and singular vector decomposition. Procedia Comput. Sci. **54**, 849–853 (2015)
9. Blanco, S., Garay, A., Coulombie, D.: Comparison of frequency bands using spectral entropy for epileptic seizure prediction. ISRN Neurol. **2013**, 5 p. (2013)
10. Varady, P.: Wavelet-based adaptive denoising of phonocardiographic records. In: 2001 Conference Proceedings of the 23rd Annual International Conference of the IEEE Engineering in Medicine and Biology Society, vol. 2, pp. 1846–1849 (2001)
11. Donoho, D.L., Johnstone, J.M.: Ideal spatial adaptation by wavelet shrinkage. Biometrika **81**, 425–455 (1994)
12. Brown, A., Garg, S., Montgomery, J.: Automatic and efficient denoising of bioacoustics recordings using MMSE STSA. IEEE Access **6**, 5010–5022 (2017)
13. Ranjard, L., et al.: MatlabHTK: a simple interface for bioacoustic analyses using hidden Markov models. Methods Ecol. Evol. **8**, 615–621 (2017). Cited By 1
14. Gur, B.M., Niezrecki, C.: Autocorrelation based denoising of manatee vocalizations using the undecimated discrete wavelet transform. J. Acoust. Soc. Am. **122**, 188–199 (2007)
15. Ren, Y., Johnson, M.T., Tao, J.: Perceptually motivated wavelet packet transform for bioacoustic signal enhancement. J. Acoust. Soc. Am. **124**, 316–327 (2008)
16. Mallat, S.: A theory for multiresolution signal decomposition: the wavelet representation. IEEE Trans. Pattern Anal. Mach. Intell. **11**, 674–693 (1989)
17. Yang, J., Park, S.-T.: An anti-aliasing algorithm for discrete wavelet transform. Mech. Syst. Signal Process. **17**, 945954 (2003)
18. Shannon, C.E.: A mathematical theory of communication. Bell Syst. Tech. J. **27**, 379–423 (1948)
19. Wang, D., Miao, D., Xie, C.: Best basis-based wavelet packet entropy feature extraction and hierarchical EEG classification for epileptic detection. Expert. Syst. Appl. **38**, 14314–14320 (2011)
20. Ma, H., Dang, J., Liu, X.: Research of the optimal wavelet selection on entropy function. In: Deng, W. (ed.) Future Control and Automation. LNEE, vol. 173, pp. 35–42. Springer, Berlin (2012). https://doi.org/10.1007/978-3-642-31003-4_5
21. Donoho, D.: De-noising by soft-thresholding. IEEE Trans. Inf. Theory **41**, 613–627 (1995)
22. Halley, J., Inchausti, P.: The increasing importance of 1/f-noises as models of ecological variability. Fluct. Noise Lett. **4**, 1–26 (2004). Cited By 43
23. Vasseur, D., Yodzis, P.: The color of environmental noise. Ecology **85**, 1146–1152 (2004). Cited By 177

Automatic Calculation of Body Mass Index Using Digital Image Processing

Juan D. J. Amador[1], Josué Espejel Cabrera[1], Jared Cervantes[2(✉)],
Laura D. Jalili[1], and José S. Ruiz Castilla[1]

[1] Posgrado e Investigación, UAEMEX (Autonomous University of Mexico State),
56259 Texcoco, Mexico
juandjamador@uaemex.mx, jec0309@hotmail.com, lauradojali2@gmail.com,
jsergioruizc@gmail.com

[2] Instituto Politécnico Nacional, Escuela Superior de Ingeniería Mecánica y Eléctrica,
C.P. 07738 Mexico City, Mexico
cercaja@hotmail.com

Abstract. In this paper we present a vision system to detect BMI from images. The proposed system segments the image and extracts the most important features, from these features a classifier is trained. An analysis of the results with different classification techniques is presented in the experimental results. The results show that the system can obtain good classification accuracies using images under controlled conditions.

1 Introduction

The vision algorithms have been implemented in many fields of application. The fields of application cover almost any aspect of daily duties/aspects that we can imagine, but can also be seen in areas such as health, providing support with some physical studies, such as estimates of body mass index (BMI). The BMI is a visible signal that can be used to infer a person's health status. It has been shown that having a large BMI is linked to an increased risk of cardiovascular disease and diabetes.

The BMI indicates weight and size relation of any individual, thus the BMI can indicates the weight condition of the person whose being evaluated. According to the World Health Organization, the overweight and obesity can be defined as the excessive or abnormal accumulation of fat in the body, this condition can trigger several health issues. Therefore in healths so many disciplines based their approaches according with the any individual BMI and subsequent treatment if it is necessary. The BMI can being classified in three different categories, underweigth, normal weigth, overweight, obesity 1, obesity 2, obesity 3. The BMI range of each category is shown in Table 1.

In Order to calculate the BMI is necessary to obtain the size (m) and the weight $(kg$. Whit the size and weight the BMI is calculated with the next formula:

$$BMI = \frac{Kg}{m^2} \tag{1}$$

© Springer Nature Switzerland AG 2018
J. C. Figueroa-García et al. (Eds.): WEA 2018, CCIS 916, pp. 309–319, 2018.
https://doi.org/10.1007/978-3-030-00353-1_28

Table 1. BMI categories.

Categories	BMI
Underweight	<18.5
Normal weight	18.6–24.9
Overweight	25.5–29.9
Obesity 1	30–34.9
Obesity 2	35–39.9
Obesity 3	≥40

The manual and most common BMI calculating method is no the best and only way to obtained it. Another method is by using a body composition analyzer by electrical bio impedance that brings a higher reliability, nevertheless the high process costs and the very thorough steps during the BMI calculation are all a though disadvantage for this method. Counting on this so as to obtain the best BMI estimation is necessary to develop a system whom can make the process easier to anyone.

By means of a digital image processing the estimation of the BMI could be easier and faster for everyone. In order to develop the system it's necessary to get and manage representative images for every category of BMI to performance a geometrical pattern recognition system without alterations in samples.

In this research, the volunteers passed for a detailing process in order to obtain a very accurate anthropometric data set, specific corporal composition instruments were used to reach this objective. The pictures acquisition was made under controlled conditions, this aspect is crucial for reducing the time processing.

2   Related Work

The mean physical descriptors for a visual health analysis of any person are the skin color semblance, the tonality of the sclerotic in the eyes and mainly the Quetelet index or Body Mass Index(BMI), this factor is used in order to determine the nutritional condition of the person/subject. The BMI is the relationship between weight and tall. The medical statutes says that the BMI let us to identify if a person is healthy or he or she has nutritional deficiencies, which not only the doctors could determine if the person needs nutritional assistance but also decide some kind of extra medical study.

The BMI is a very helpful tool used through the years supporting the specialists to identify weight troubles, this aspect has become a reason for investigation, not only in heaths but also in areas like math [2–5], sport sciences [6–9], computing sciences [10–13], whose focuses their researches trying to automate the BMI estimates by a robust system, like WEB calculators, which users insert their weight and tall so as to receive the BMI and the proportional BMI rank/class.

The technology is the final step of the science, where the researches create the basics afterwards everybody enjoys in any kind of aspect in the daily lifestyle. The technology is the final step of the science and research, here it's applying all the knowledge acquired through the years to give a comfortable life style, Artificial vision is a new and outstanding computational tool, which is used in face recognition and detection, object detection and their classification, quality control of different kind of products, and something else, nevertheless in the field of computing sciences there is lack of any kind of literature about artificial vision based researches about BMI. The computer vision object detection study based on images with several pattern recognition techniques supporting by digital image processing (DIP) and classification, all have been increased together. The great progress of automatic image recognition algorithms allows us achieve a develop of a robust system, that through a previous person images acquisition in a controlled environment whit some DIP and segmentation techniques the obtainment of the BMI.

In [5] it is proposed a 3D manikin generation, all of them with different characteristics, after that RGB images are generated from the 3D manikin, and whit the implementation of neuronal networks, all the images are classified whit an oscillation of 0.34 and 0.50 between the estimated value and the real BMI value.

In this way, Bipemdu et al. [1], propose a mathematical complement for the original formula in order to complement the volumetric estimation of the patient, based on segmented images, reporting a 4.04 variance with the traditional method. Madariaga and Linsangan [14] perform the tall and weight estimation calculating the leakage point in a group of cells, all of then setting up with the relation of the appearance of the camera.

Another study make the calculus of the BMI based on face images [11], here there is used an algorithm similar/alike to face recognition algorithms, here the algorithm detects the volunteer eyes in order to calculate the coordinates of the face principle components using support vector machines (SVM), although all the processes used in the research the results shown have no correlation with the traditional method.

In [15], by means of the description of heart sounds in relation with the age, gender and the body mass index (BMI), they were obtained results to determinate the cardiac health condition in men and women. The correlation between BMI and the cardiac sounds show significant results for further research.

Nahavandi come up with a kinect based system [16] in order to estimate the body mass index (BMI) of human body. This system is shown as innovator, because of the absence of a weight scale, the observed weight in the subjects is estimated using a corporal surface regression technique. Deep learning is implemented so as to extract significant features and to be able to estimate the BMI whit an 95% of precision.

3   Proposed Method

In this Section, the steps of the proposed methodology are described in detail. Methodology of proposed system is shown in Fig. 1. First the images are pre-processed and segmented, A step of feature extraction is implemented after of segmentation. After of features extraction the proposed methodology uses different techniques to select the best features of the data set. This step allows to reduce the dimensionality of the data set, reduce the training time and in some cases improve the performance of the system, this due to the elimination of features that introduce noise to the classifier.

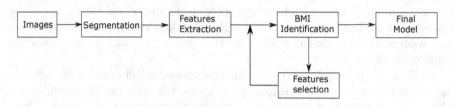

Fig. 1. Proposed methodology diagram

3.1   Segmentation Techniques

Firstly the images are preprocessed and segmented. The images often are surrounded by objects in the background. However, the images used in the experiments are images in a controlled environment (images with only the subject and white background). In all the experiments Otsu algorithm was used for segmentation. Several segmentation techniques were tried. However, because the image was obtained in a semi controlled environment, the results were very similar and it is not necessary to use a more robust technique (Fig. 2).

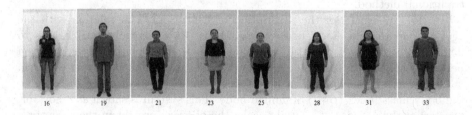

Fig. 2. Initial images

In order to obtain a good segmentation even when there are changes in global brightness conditions, the region of the leave in each image was segmented using the following steps (1) Computation of high-contrast gray scale from optimal linear combination of RGB color components [30,31]; (2) Estimate optimal border using cumulative moments of zero order and first order (Otsu method) [30,31]. (3) Morphological operations to fill possible gaps in the segmented image [30–32]. By segmenting the image, the proposed system can use only the region of the leaf, determine its edges and calculate properties by extracting features (Fig. 3).

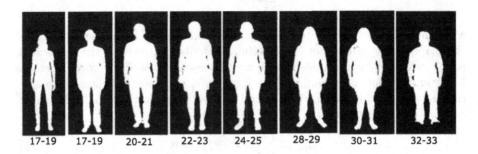

17-19   17-19   20-21   22-23   24-25   28-29   30-31   32-33

Fig. 3. Segmented images

3.2   Features Extractors

Feature extraction is a critical process in any pattern recognition system. The feature extraction has a big influence on the final identification. Feature extraction allows us to represent the image using a set of numerical and/or categorical values. In order to improve the performance the features obtained must be invariant to scaling, rotation and translation, enabling the classifier to recognize objects despite having different size, position and orientation. All these features play an important role in the algorithm performance and allow the classifier to discriminate between different classes in an appropriate manner. Deeper information on the subject can be found in [33–35]. In our experiments shape features were obtained.

Shape Features. The geometric features are one of the most important visual properties used to classify an object. The geometric features provide information on the size and shape of the previously segmented region. Elementary geometric features provide intuitive information of the basic properties of the region to be recognized, such as area of the region, roundness, length of the edge, elongation defined by the length and width, the coordinates x and y of gravity center, rectangularity, projection (on the components x, y), eccentricity, center of gravity (components x, y), Danielson factor, equivalent diameter, axis length (x, y), orientation, solidity, extencion, area convex, filled area, ellipse (variance, orientation, eccentricity, area, major axis, minor axis, ellipse center x, and). However, an efficient classification system should be able to recognize objects regardless of their orientation, location and size, i.e. it must be invariant to scaling, rotation and position.

Moments are commonly used in image recognition, they can recognize these images regardless of their rotation, translation or inversion. Invariant moments were initially introduced by Hu [34]. Both Hu moments of order $(p + q)$ of an intensity function $f(x, y)$ are defined as:

The moments of order $(p + q)$ are defined as:

$$m_{pq} = \sum_x \sum_y x^p y^q \rho(x, y).$$

where $\rho(x, y)$ is defined by the segmented region. Low order moments describe the shape of the region. For example, m_{00} describes the area of the segmented region, while m_{01} and m_{10} define the x and y coordinates of the gravity center. However, moments $m_{02}, m_{03}, m_{11}, m_{12}, m_{20}, m_{21}$ y m_{30} are invariant to translation, rotation and inversion. The central moments are invariant to displacement and can be calculated by

$$\mu_{pq} = \sum_{i,j \in R} (i - \bar{i})^p (j - \bar{j})^q \tag{2}$$

where p, q belongs to segmented region and the gravity center of the region is defined by:

$$\bar{i} = \frac{m_{10}}{m_{00}}, \bar{j} = \frac{m_{01}}{m_{00}} \tag{3}$$

Hu moments can be obtained as follows:

$$\phi_1 = \eta_{20} + \eta_{02} \tag{4}$$
$$\phi_2 = (\eta_{20} - \eta_{02})^2 + 4\eta_{11}^2$$
$$\phi_3 = (\eta_{30} - 3\eta_{12})^2 + (3\eta_{21} - \eta_{03})^2$$
$$\phi_4 = (\eta_{30} - 3\eta_{12})^2 + (\eta_{21} + \eta_{03})^2$$
$$\phi_5 = (\eta_{30} - 3\eta_{12})(\eta_{30} + \eta_{12})[(\eta_{30} + \eta_{12})^2 - 3(\eta_{21} + \eta_{03})^2] +$$
$$(3\eta_{21} - \eta_{03})(\eta_{21} + \eta_{03})[3(\eta_{30} + \eta_{12})^2 - (\eta_{21} + \eta_{03})^2]$$
$$\phi_6 = (\eta_{20} - \eta_{02})[(\eta_{30} + \eta_{12})^2 - (\eta_{21} + \eta_{03})^2] +$$
$$4(\eta_{11}(\eta_{30} + \eta{12})(\eta_{21} + \eta_{03})$$
$$\phi_7 = (3\eta_{21} - \eta_{03})(\eta_{30} + \eta_{12})[(\eta_{30} + \eta_{12})^2 - 3(\eta_{21} + \eta_{03})^2] -$$
$$(\eta_{30} - 3\eta_{12})(\eta_{21} + \eta_{03})[3(\eta_{30} + \eta_{12})^2 - (\eta_{21} + \eta_{03})^2]$$

where $\eta_{pq} = \frac{\mu_{rs}}{\mu_{00}^t}$, $t = \frac{p+q}{2} + 1$.

Other used features were ellipse descriptors, region convexity, Flusser moments $(F_1, \ldots F_4)$ [36,37], R Moments $(R_1, \ldots, R_{10})$, Fourier descriptors (first 8 descriptors) [32,37].

57 geometric features were extracted from each image. The geometric feature vector X_g obtained can be represented as:

$$Xg = [x_1, x_2, \ldots, x_{57}] \tag{5}$$
$$Xg = [x_{gb}, x_{Hu}, x_F, x_R, x_{DF}] \tag{6}$$

where x_{gb} represents the elemental geometric features ($x_{gb} = [x_1, \ldots, x_{28}]$), x_{Hu} represents the Hu invariant features ($x_{Hu} = [x_{29}, \ldots, x_{35}]$), x_F represents the Flusser invariant moments ($x_F = [x_{36}, \ldots, x_{39}]$), x_R represents the invariant moments to changes in ilumination ($x_R = [x_{40}, \ldots, x_{49}]$), x_{DF} represents the first 8 Fourier descriptors ($x_{DF} = [x_{50}, \ldots, x_{57}]$). Description in detail about Fourier descriptors can be founded in [32,37].

3.3 Classification Techniques

Classification, consist is detect or recognize a pattern in terms of properties or features. Pattern recognition is one of the most important tasks. However, it is also one of the most complex tasks. In experiments the results were compared with some classification techniques, logistic regression [17–19], Bayesian classifier [20,21], the Backpropagation learning algorithm [22,23] and support vector machine (SVM) [24].

4 Experimental Results

4.1 Data Acquisition

The sample included 122 people with an age range of 18 to 27 years (71 women and 51 men), all of them inhabitants of the State of Mexico. The instruments used in the research are a body composition analyzer by Inbody (Mod. 230), wall mounted height meter by Seca. Muslin fabric(1.50 m width, 3 m large), an aluminium tripod, digital camera (16.1 Mega Pixels) Nikon Coolpix P510 (Table 2) (Fig. 4).

To obtain the dataset it was used the body composition analyzer and the wall mounted height meter with $1mm$ accuracy, gathering the best BMI possible dataset.

Initially the people were invited to participate in the research, each one received an agreement to sign whit the specifications of the research on it, then they were separated in groups, every group had between 15 to 20 volunteers each in a closed area, after that all the people take off their shoes and all kind of fancy object or extra clothes. (*e.g.*, jackets, sweters, belts, keys, cellphones). The pictures was taken under controlled conditions, like the distance of the camera and the font color, the focal angle in each volunteer, so as to avoid bad behavior in the BMI estimation.

About the volunteers it was asked for a vertical position, feet alignment with the shoulders and the arms in the side position.

4.2 Results

In the experiments, all data sets were normalized and in order to validate the results cross validation technique was used with $k = 10$

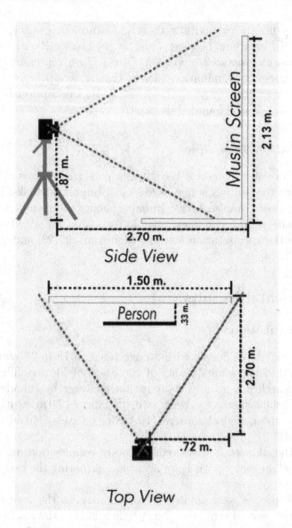

Fig. 4. Position of the participant with respect to the camera

Table 3 shows the results obtained *Bayes* represents the results obtained using the Naive Bayes algorithm, *BP* represents the performances using the backpropagation learning algorithm, *LR* logistic regression, while SVM_{RBF}, represent the results obtained with SVM using the RBF kernel. The metric used to evaluate the performance of the classifier was precision and this is obtained from the guesses of the classifier among the total of the data set.

Table 2. Dataset used in experiments.

Datasets

BMI	Avg. height	Avg. weight	Avg. age	Men	Women	Size
17–19	164	49	22	7	11	18
20–21	166	56	20	10	10	20
22–23	165	61	22	16	12	28
24–25	160	62	21	5	19	24
26–27	165	70	22	8	11	19
28–29	158	69	30	1	4	5
30–31	167	86	27	2	2	4
32–33	170	88	21	2	2	4

Table 3. Performance of the classifiers to calculate the BMI

	Bayes			SVM_{RBF}			BP			LR		
Subset	Acc	F-measure	AUC	Acc	F-measure	AUC	Acc	F-measure	AUC	Acc	F-measure	AUC
17–19	87.13	0.87	0.86	89.47	0.893	0.873	86.2	0.83	0.85	85.3	0.82	0.85
20–21	75.9	0.83	0.89	77.34	0.838	0.920	76.6	0.82	0.87	76.7	0.79	0.83
22–23	71.8	0.77	0.62	75.1	0.821	0.671	72.7	0.78	0.58	73.5	0.78	0.59
24–25	77.3	0.80	0.91	79.4	0.835	0.947	78.5	0.81	0.89	77.9	0.80	0.88
26–27	82.7	0.72	0.90	85.7	0.857	0.924	83.2	0.79	0.87	81.7	0.78	0.81
28–29	64.7	0.75	0.83	65.7	0.789	0.835	65.3	0.76	0.81	61.3	0.71	0.79
30–31	55.9	0.73	0.79	58.4	0.735	0.826	56.3	0.71	0.79	51.9	0.67	0.78
32–33	43.8	0.51	0.74	46.2	0.610	0.815	42.7	0.56	0.75	40.3	0.51	0.73
Average	69.90	0.7475	0.81	72.16	0.79725	0.851	70.18	0.7575	0.80	68.57	0.7325	0.78

5   Conclusions

In this paper we present a new algorithm to calculate the Body Mass Index and compare the results with some classifiers. The system extracts a set of features based on shape properties. In the proposed algorithm is used a features selection algorithm in order to reduce the training time and obtain the best features to obtain a good classification accuracy. In the results obtained, it is shown that in some subsets the performance is very low, this is possibly due to the size of the subset of data. Subsequent studies aim to improve the classification accuracy by adding information about the edge or silhouette of people.

References

1. Bipemdu, H., Hayfron-Acquah, J.B., Panford, J.K., Appiah, O.: Calculation of body mass index using image processing techniques. Int. J. Artif. Intell. Mech. **4**, 1 (2015)
2. Trefethen, N.: Calculate your new BMI. University of Oxford (2013)

3. Ares, G.: Mathematical and Statistical Methods in Food Science and Technology. Wiley, Hoboken (2013)
4. Mamat, M., Deraman, S.K., Noor, N.M.M., Zulkifli, N.F.: Relationship between body mass index and healthy food with a balanced diet. Appl. Math. Sci. **7**(4), 153–159 (2013)
5. Wiam, B., Abdesslam, B., Mohamed, L., Mohamed, D.: A mathematical model of overweight/obesity in Morocco using human biomass. Int. J. Latest Res. Sci. Technol. **3**(6), 65–67 (2014)
6. Duncan, M.J., Nevill, A., Woodfield, L., Al-Nakeeb, Y.: The relationship between pedometer-determined physical activity, body mass index and lean body mass index in children. Int. J. Pediatr. Obes. **5**, 445–450 (2010)
7. Pontaga, I., Zidens, J.: Estimation of body mass index in team sports athletes. LASE J. Sport Sci. **2**, 33–44 (2011)
8. Franz, D.D., Feresu, S.A.: The relationship between physical activity, body mass index, and academic performance and college-age students. Open J. Epidemiol. **3**, 4–11 (2013)
9. Mwangi, F.M., Rintaugu, E.G.: Physical activity and health related physical fitness attributes of staff university members in a Kenyan Public University. Int. J. Sports Sci. **7**(2), 81–86 (2017)
10. Karnyanszky, T.M., Musuri, C., Karnyanszky, C.A.: Expert software for determination of Juvenil's people obesity. Annals Computer Sciencie Series 6: Tome 1 (2008)
11. Wen, L., Guo, G.: A computational approach to body mass index prediction from face images. Image Vis. Comput. **31**(2013), 392–400 (2013)
12. Mardolkar, M.: Body mass index (BMI) data analysis and classification. J. Comput. Sci. Inf. Technol. **6**(2), 8–16 (2017)
13. Millard, L.A.C., Davies, N.M., Tilling, K., Gaunt, T.R., Smith, G.D.: Searching for the causal effects of BMI in over 300 000 individuals, using Mendelian randomization. bioRxiv preprint (2017). First posted online 19 Dec 2017
14. Madariaga, N.E., Linsangan, N.B.: Application of artificial neural network and background subtraction for determining BMI in Android devices using Bluetooth. Int. J. Eng. Technol. **8**(5), 366 (2016)
15. Larsen, B.S., Winther, S., Buttcher, M., Nissen, L., Struijk, J., Samuel, S.: Correlations of first and second heart sounds with age, sex, and body mass index. IEEE Comput. Cardiol., 4 (2017). https://doi.org/10.22489/CinC.2017.141-408
16. Nahavandi, D., Abobakr, A., Haggag, H., Hossny, M., Nahavandi, S., Filippidis, D.: A skeleton-free kinect system for body mass index assessment using deep neural networks, pp. 1–6 (2017). https://doi.org/10.1109/SysEng.2017.8088252
17. Borges, J., Bioucas, D.J., Maral, A.: Bayesian hyperspectral image segmentation with a discriminative class learning. IEEE Trans. Geosci. Remote Sens. **49**(6), 2151–2164 (2011)
18. Bernardo, J., Smith, A.: Bayesian Theory. Wiley, Hoboken (1994)
19. Dempster, A., Laird, N., Rubin, D.: Maximum likelihood from incomplete data via the EM algorithm. J. R. Stat. Soc. **1**(39), 1–38 (1977)
20. Ng, A.Y., Jordan, M.I.: On discriminative vs. generative classifiers: a comparison of logistic regression and naive Bayes. In: Advances in Neural Information Processing Systems 14, pp. 841–848. MIT-Press (2002)
21. Russell, S., Norvig, P.: Artificial Intelligence: A Modern Approach, 2nd edn. Prentice Hall, Upper Saddle River (2003)
22. Rumelhart, D.E., Hinton, G.E., Williams, R.J.: Learning representations by back-propagating errors. Nature **323**(6088), 533–536 (1986)

23. Werbos, P.J.: The Roots of Backpropagation. From Ordered Derivatives to Neural Networks and Political Forecasting. Wiley, New York (1994)
24. Vapnik, V.: The Nature of Statistical Learning Theory. Springer, New York (1995). https://doi.org/10.1007/978-1-4757-3264-1
25. Wang, Z.: Body mass index and all-cause mortality. JAMA **316**(9), 991–992 (2016)
26. Perera, S.: Body mass index is an important predictor for suicide: results from a systematic review and meta-analysis. Psychoneuroendocrinology **65**, 76–83 (2016)
27. Cohen, A., Baker, J., Ardern, C.I.: Association between body mass index, physical activity, and health-related quality of life in Canadian adults. Hum. Kinet. J. **24**(1) (2016)
28. Curtis, D.S., Fuller-Rowell, T.E., Doan, S.N., Zgierska, A.E., Ryff, C.D.: Racial and socioeconomic disparities in body mass index among college students: understanding the role of early life adversity. J. Behav. Med. **39**(5), 866–875 (2016)
29. D. Nahavandi, A. Abobakr?, H. Haggag, M. Hossny, S. Nahavandi and D. Filippidis A Skeleton-Free Kinect System for Body Mass Index Assessment using Deep Neural Networks. IEEEXPLORE (2016)
30. Sonka, M., Hlavac, V., Boyle, R.: Image Processing, Analysis and Machine Vision. Springer, Heidelberg (1993). https://doi.org/10.1007/978-1-4899-3216-7
31. Gonzalez, R.C., Woods, R.E.: Digital Image Processing Using MATLAB. Pearson, Upper Saddle River (2010)
32. Nixon, M., Aguado, A.: Feature Extraction and Image Processing. Academic Press, Cambridge (2002)
33. Zhang, S., Lei, Y.K.: Modified locally linear discriminant embedding for plant leaf recognition. Neurocomputing **74**(14), 2284–2290 (2011)
34. Hu, M.K.: Visual pattern recognition by moment invariants. IRE Trans. Inform. Theory **8**, 179–187 (1962)
35. Hu, R., Collomosse, J.: A performance evaluation of gradient field HOG descriptor for sketch based image retrieval. Comput. Vis. Image Underst. **117**(7), 790–806 (2013)
36. Flusser, J., Suk, T.: Pattern recognition by affine moment invariants. Pattern Recognit. **26**(1), 167–174 (1993)
37. Yang, M., Kpalma, K., Ronsin, J.: A Survey of Shape Feature Extraction Techniques, Pattern Recognition Techniques. INTECH Open Access Publisher (2008)
38. Liu, N., Kan, J.: Improved deep belief networks and multi-feature fusion for leaf identification. Neurocomputing **216**, 460–467 (2016). ISSN 0925-2312

Network Applications

Improving Early Attack Detection
in Networks with sFlow and SDN

Alexander Leal[1]([⊠]), Juan Felipe Botero[1], and Eduardo Jacob[2]

[1] Universidad de Antioquia, Calle 67 # 53 - 108, Medellín, Colombia
{erwin.leal,juanf.botero}@udea.edu.co
[2] Dpto. de Ingeniería de Comunicaciones, Escuela de Ingeniería de Bilbao,
UPV/EHU, Pza. Ingeniero Torres Quevedo 1, 48013 Bilbao, Spain
eduardo.jacob@ehu.eus

Abstract. Network monitoring is a paramount aspect for the detection
of abnormal and malicious activity. However, this feature must go hand
by hand with mitigation techniques. On SDN environments, control techniques may be easily developed as a result of its ability for programming
the network. In this work, we take advantage of this fact to improve the
network security using the sFlow monitoring tool along with the SDN
controller. We present an architecture where sFlow is in charge of detecting network anomalies defined by user rules, while the SDN technology is
responsible to mitigate the intrusion. Our testbed has been implemented
on Mininet and the SDN environment is governed by Opendaylight controller and the OpenFlow southbound protocol. Experimental validation
demonstrate that our system can effectively report various types of intrusion associated with the reconnaissance phase of an attack.

Keywords: Intrusion · Reconnaissance · Attack · Security · sFlow
SDN

1 Introduction

Network security is in charge to prevent information theft as well as guarantee privacy communications and service availability. Therefore, it has become a
inherent network feature as important as the connectivity itself. In this paper,
we consider the problem of detecting intrusions in a communication network
running under the Software Defined Networking environment (SDN). This technology provides a network architecture in which the network control plane is
decoupled from the data plane. This fact enables the network control to become
directly programmable and the underlying infrastructure to be abstracted for
applications and network services [20].

The SDN environment provides several alternatives to implement network
anomalies detection: (1) Put the entire onus on the SDN controller, providing
it with mechanisms for traffic pattern analysis. To achieve this purpose, it will
be necessary for each switch to install flow rules to redirect all ingress traffic

© Springer Nature Switzerland AG 2018
J. C. Figueroa-García et al. (Eds.): WEA 2018, CCIS 916, pp. 323–335, 2018.
https://doi.org/10.1007/978-3-030-00353-1_29

from edge devices to the controller. However, this behavior overloads the centralized control plane, forcing the SDN controller to deteriorate its performance over other tasks [14], and overloading the link to the controller; (2) Incorporate a NIDS (Network Intrusion Detection System) into the network. This option implies the implementation of port mirroring mechanisms in the switches to forward the traffic from edge devices to the NIDS, even incorporating an overlaying network. Even so, mirroring the whole network traffic to another device may result in significant resource consumption, especially in high traffic environments [13]; (3) Use of OpenFlow flow statistics counters. In this scenario OpenFlow is responsible of communicating control messages to the switches and monitoring traffic as well. This scheme does not come without major consequences. The number of flow-entries in the flow table of the edge switch may grow extensively (counted in tenths of thousands of flows per time-window), thus affecting the switching performance [14].

In this context, although alternatives mentioned above offer good results, they register scalability issues with the increase in traffic. In order to provide an alternative solution to the detection and mitigation of network intrusions, we take advantage of packet sampling capability of sFlow [22] along with the SDN technology. In our approach, sFlow will be in charge of detecting network anomalies defined by user rules, while the SDN controller will be responsible of mitigating the intrusion. Summarizing, the main contribution of this paper is the design of an Intrusion Detection System (IDS) prototype with a mitigation technique SDN based, and its validation with effective scalability improvements.

The paper is structured as follows. In Sect. 2, we present the related work, while in Sect. 3 we bring an overview of sFlow technologies. Section 4 illustrates the architecture proposal and its operation scheme. Next, in Sect. 5, the implementation details of the proposed system along with the steps in a reconnaissance process are explained. Section 6 shows the experimental validation performed and Sect. 7 presents a discussion of the functionalities achieved. Finally, Sect. 8 concludes the paper and presents future work.

2   Related Work

In this section, we examine several approaches that propose solutions around network security field with sFlow under SDN approach.

In [14], authors implement a system that can detect DDoS (Distributed Denial of Service), Worm propagation and Portscan attacks using an Entropy-based algorithm. Moreover, they present experimental results that demonstrate the effectiveness of the sFlow mechanism compared with the use of OpenFlow flow statistics counters, in terms of overhead imposed on the usage of system resources. The evaluation of this proposal is carried out in a NOX Controller [15] and, according to the traffic condition analyzed, they use a hardware-based switch NEC-IP8800/S3640 or a software-based OpenvSwitch [2] hosted on Dual-Core 3 GHz with 8 GB RAM server.

Mitigation of SYN Flooding Attack under a DDoS scenario is proposed in [19]. The methodology used to detect the attack relies on monitoring a threshold value of the sum cumulative of TCP-SYN packets reported by each sFlow switch agent. The evaluation of this technique was implemented on Mininet [4] using four OpenvSwitch [2] and controlled by a Floodlight controller [3].

An information security defense mechanism (ISDM) was deployed to perform anomaly detection, mitigation and reduce the loss caused by the DDoS attack [16]. ISDM uses attack signatures to provide security on Internet of Things environments (smart living appliances). The experimental platform employs OpenvSwitches hosted on a Raspberry Pi 2 using a Ryu Controller [6].

In [25], OrchSec, an architecture oriented to detect and mitigate ARP Spoofing/Cache Poising, DoS/DDoS was developed. OrchSec functionalities were validated utilizing Mininet [4] and Floodlight [3]/POX [5] controllers.

In [13], authors propose a modular and scalable architecture to enhance the Remote Triggered Black-Hole functionality, a routing approach towards Distributed Denial of Service (DDoS) attack mitigation. To test their solution, they implement a POX Controller [5], a software-switch (OpenvSwitch) [2] and a software-router (Vyatta Core), each of them hosted on individual Dual-Core 3 GHz with 8 GB RAM server.

An SDN controller can be a victim of a DDoS attack too. In [12], authors study how to improve the controller security in this scenario. The method not only considers the malicious packet to detect a DDoS attack, but it also takes into account the time properties of DDoS attack such as duration and time to detection, in order to prevent the future attack. To demonstrate the operation of their method, they use the Opendaylight controller [8] and Mininet [4].

FlowTrApp [11] provides an architecture for DDoS attack detection and mitigation in Data Centers. The proposed mechanism first matches an incoming flow with a legitimate sample of traffic and then installs mitigation actions (e.g. a flow is found not lying in the bounds of legitimate traffic pattern i.e., flow rate and flow duration). FlowTrApp was tested using Mininet emulator [4] and the Floodlight controller [3].

Unlike the approaches mentioned in this section, which are mostly oriented to detect and mitigate DDoS attacks, our proposed work aims to detect and control an attack in its reconnaissance phase.

3   sFlow

Sflow is a sampling technology for monitoring and collecting data from a wide range of equipment: physical and virtual network devices (switches and routers), physical and virtual hosts (FreeBSD, Linux, Windows; Containers; Hyper-V, KVM, and Xen hypervisors) and software applications (Apache/PHP, JAVA) [22]. A couple of major aspects of sFlow consist of taking advantage of the statistical properties of packet sampling to produce statistically quantifiable measurements, and having its own RFC 3176 specification [21]. Also, sFlow provides REST and JavaScript APIs making easy to configure customized measurements, retrieve metrics, set thresholds, and receive notifications. These features transform sFlow in an open-source network tool with a huge capacity to interact with other components: SDN controllers, Orchestrators or DevOps (see Fig. 1).

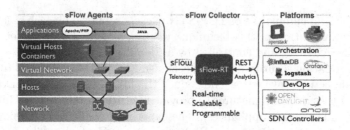

Fig. 1. sFlow-RT environment

3.1 sFlow Components and Operation Scheme

A sFlow based monitoring system is integrated by three elements (see Fig. 2):

- *sFlow Collector:* A software application, running on a workstation or server, that collects and analyses traffic data sent to it by the sFlow agents in the network. Through sFlow collector, the information collected can be analyzed and presented to network administrators in a variety of ways, such as traffic rates charts, dashboards, and thresholds events [10].
- *sFlow Agent:* On the network devices context, an agent corresponds to a switch or router that gathers information about traffic on its interfaces and sends it to the sFlow collector. sFlow Agents operate by regularly polling interface statistics registers (counters) such as: [In/Out]UcastPkts, [In/Out]MulticastPkts, [In/Out]BroadcastPkts, [In/Out]Errors; and packet sampling information if the packet sampling is also configured on the agent. Currently, a wide network equipment support sFlow Agents: Alcatel, Cisco, Dell, HP, Huawei, Juniper, OpenvSwitch, Pica8, among others [10,22].
- *sFlow datagrams:* datagrams sent by the sFlow agent to the host where the sFlow Collector through UDP port 6343 is running. They include statistics and packet sampling information [22].

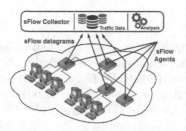

Fig. 2. sFlow components

3.2 sFlow Applications

SFlow applications can be developed externally using the sFlow-RT REST API or embedded using sFlow-RT's internal JavaScript API. This paper is focused on the last option. Detailed information about how to write a sFlow-RT application can be found on [9].

Typically, applications implement a number of the following steps. Nevertheless, there are other functions to improve the applications.

- *Define flows:* Flows have to be specified in order to detect and mark accordingly the traffic of interest. A flow is defined using a name, keys (usually Ethernet, IP, TCP or UDP headers), value (bytes, frames) and optionally filter attributes. When the flow definition is done, it is possible to identify a set of packets that share common attributes within a period of time.
- *Handle flow records:* It allows the user to register a flow handler to be notified of each new match flow, according with the flows definition. Flows will only be logged if log:true is specified in the flow specification. In this work, we use that option to generate alarm messages in the system.
- *Define Threshold:* Thresholds are applied to flows defined above and they can be used to generate a notification when the rate value associated with a flow exceeds the threshold. We use this option to identify ARP network discovering, TCP-SYN service discovering and Deny of Service intrusions.
- *Handle threshold events:* Register an event handler function to be notified of each new event.

We list below a snippet code to identify a DoS attack using sFlow-RT's internal JavaScript API (see Listing 1.1).

```
// Flow Definition
setFlow('dos_attack',{keys:'ipdestination,stack',value:'frames',filter:'link:outputifindex=null'});
// Threshold setting
setThreshold('dos_threshold',{'metric':'dos_attack',value:10000,'byFlow':true,'timeout':1});
// Event Handler
setEventHandler(function(evt) {
  switch(evt.thresholdID) {
    case 'dos_threshold':
    let ddosKeys = {};
    ddosKeys[evt.flowKey] = evt.value;
    logWarning("DDoS Alert: ", JSON.stringify(ddosKeys));
    break; } },['dos_threshold']);
```

Listing 1.1. Snippet code to identify a DoS attack using sFlow

4 Architecture Proposal

This work is oriented to detect and control the reconnaissance process -the initial step of any intrusion operation. For this purpose, we implement an architecture composed by two domains called Monitoring and Countermeasure (see Fig. 3).

- *Monitoring domain,* in charge to detect the initial steps of an attack. In this domain identifies three elements: (1) the sFlow agent who resides inside the network device with sFlow support, (2) the sFlow Collector locate on the server and (3) a supervision element to visualize the behavior of the network and the alert messages (supervision PC).

– *Countermeasure domain,* responsible to mitigate the intrusion. This area is governed by and SDN environment with its respective control plane (controller) and data plane (switches). These planes interact using a southbound protocol (e.g., Open Flow [18]).

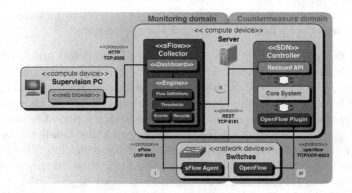

Fig. 3. Architecture proposal

4.1 Operation

When the sFlow agent is enabled in the OpenvSwitch, sample packets' header is encapsulated along with metadata to be sent to the sFlow Collector (Step I in Fig. 3). The metadata includes sampling ratio, a timestamp at the time of capture, switch ID, and forwarding information such as the input and output port numbers. Here, it is important to mention that the rate of samples sFlow produces is not constant; this depends on the rate of packet arrivals.

Then, the real-time analytics engine of the sFlow Collector processes the gathered information. If any sampled packet's header matches with some flow definition in the monitoring script, this sample is processed to determine if an event should be triggered. In that case, a REST request is sent to the other component of our architecture, the SDN controller, responsible for the mitigation of anomalous operations (Step II in Fig. 3). That request contains the information necessary to neutralize the attack (switch ID, port, and MAC address). So, at this point, the controller is able to make adjustments to the network employing a southbound protocol. It means, to add a DROP flow action in the forwarding device table to block the intruder (Step III in Fig. 3). This flow-entry have higher priority than any other in the flow table and its life-time is 30 s.

5   Testbed

5.1   Environment

The machine used for this testbed runs Ubuntu 16.04 LTS, with an Intel Core i7 @3.40 GHz x 8 CPU, and 16 GiB of RAM. To generate network topologies we use

Mininet [4], a network emulator used in the SDN research field which includes OpenvSwitch [2] (a virtual switch that supports OpenFlow and the sFlow agent). The control plane of the testbed is governed by the Opendaylight Controller [8] and the collecting process is in charge of the sFlow-RT collector [9].

The testbed topology consists of a tree topology where each virtual switch is connected to the Opendaylight Controller and the sFlow-RT collector, which are hosted on the same server. At the beginning, the testbed implements a scenario with a tree topology of depth 2 and fanout 2 (Fig. 4a). Later, to verify if the approach is scalable, we modify the parameters of the topology in this manner: depth 3 and fanout 4 (Fig. 4b).

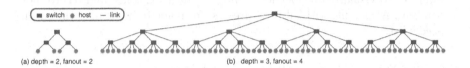

(a) depth = 2, fanout = 2   (b) depth = 3, fanout = 4

Fig. 4. Testbed topologies

5.2 Setup

- *Mininet:* For generating network topologies we just run the command *sudo mn–custom sflowtestbed.py –topo tree, depth = 3, fanout = 4 –link tc, bw = 100 –controller remote, ip = 127.0.0.1:6633*. The script file *sflowtestbed.py* includes several functions to execute over mininet topology, such as:
  - To enable sFlow agent on each OpenvSwitch that belongs to the topology and set the sampling and polling parameters. In this testbed the sampling rate was defined: 1:100. A sampling rate of 1:100 means that among every 100 packets captured by sFlow agent, only the header information related to one will be sent to the collector.
  - To post a JSON representation of the Mininet topology to sFlow collector using REST API.
  - To generate pseudo-randomly ICMP, TCP and UDP background traffic. ICMP traffic is generated at random intervals between all hosts for the first scenario (Fig. 4a), and between 8 hosts groups in the other case (Fig. 4b). TCP and UDP flows are established among all hosts, in pairs, using Iperf [1]. We take advantage of the Iperf command to set randomly the port [1024–65535], the duration [50–100 s] and the bandwidth [1–10 Mbps] parameters within the aforementioned ranges. We define whether the flow will be TCP or UDP by the port value (odd or even).
  - To control the execution of the intrusion process.

Finally, in all scenarios the link bandwidth was set to 100 Mbps *(tc, bw = 100)*, to guarantee a reasonable workload of the local system resources when all hosts are transmitting background traffic.

– *OpenDaylight Controller:* the controller is configured to discover the topology and to set rules via OpenFlow with the purpose of guaranteeing basic connectivity between all stations. It means, managing broadcast (ARP) and unicast (IP, TCP, UDP) traffic. We assign a low priority to the flows in charge of forwarding tasks, thus the controller could use high priorities to install the flows to mitigate the intrusion and guarantee the primacy of these rules over the others.

– *sFlow Collector:* sFlow-RT manages several script files in order to process and visualize information. In this testbed, we define JavaScript functions to indicate to the sFlow-RT real-time analytics engine how to detect reconnaissance attacks discussed in the previous section. Moreover, we built a dashboard interface to visualize our metrics of interest, set thresholds, and receive notifications. Also, a file with all IP addresses was made to implement the control access list.

5.3   The Reconnaissance Phase in an Attack

Intrusion in networks takes many forms including denial of service, man-in-the-middle, viruses propagation, etc. Typically, in an intrusion situation, the intruder attempts to gain access to a particular resource (data or host). However, any kind of intrusion is preceded by a reconnaissance process. Reconnaissance is the unauthorized discovery and mapping of systems, services, or vulnerabilities [24].

In the initial stage of an intrusion, the intruder eavesdrops the network for the auto-assigning of an IP address in the compromised network segment. For this step, we build an access control list with all IP addresses allowed in our system. If the IP source address of any packet sampled does not match with that list, an event will be triggered. This access control list can be built by the network administrator or in automatic way with the information collected from the topology by the controller. Also, eavesdropping process could be detected polling periodically hosts to detect NIC (Network Interface Card) in promiscuous mode [23]. This task could be programmed in the controller. But, since our testbed performs over a emulation platform, this functionality was not implemented.

Next, to determine which hosts are available, the intruder will start a network discovery process. In our work, we implement a countermeasure for hosts discovery based on an ARP Request sweep. To detect this process we define a rule to count the ARP Request frames by second. If the frames' number exceeds a predefined threshold an event is generated.

Later, the intruder scans TCP and/or UDP ports in the discovered hosts to determine what network services are available. At this point, TCP-SYN scan technique is used for this purpose. For this type of intrusion we define two rules. For TCP scan, we count the number of TCP-SYN segments sent in one second from the same IP address. If the number of segments exceeds a predefined threshold, an event is generated. For UDP scan, we detect any ICMP unreachable messages in the network. This type of messages is produced when the intruder tries to access to UDP ports that do not have any service configured.

Subsequently, the intruder queries the ports to determine the application type and version, even the type and version of the operating system. Based on this information, the intruder can determine whether a possible vulnerability exists that can be exploited. And with this, the reconnaissance process ends.

In order to evaluate the effectiveness of our approach we replicate each reconnaissance step as follow:

- To emulate the moment when the attacker allocated an IP address inside the network segment, we just set the IP address of a random machine outside of the range defined in the access control list.
- Network discovery process could be done through the NMAP tool [17] with the modifiers "-sP -PR [target IP address]". This instruction causes an Arp Request Scan on the network segment defined by the user.
- TCP and UDP service discovery processes are achieved using the NMAP tool too. For the TCP case, we use the modifier "-sS [IP address target]". This command triggers a port-scan process using TCP SYN segments. For the UDP case we use the modifier "-p [ports] -sU [IP address target]".
- In order to emulate a DoS attack to conclude the intrusion process, we used the tool NPING (a NMAP complement) with the following sintaxis "nping – udp –source-port 53 –data-length 1400 –rate 2000 –count 200000 –no-capture –quiet [IP address target]".

6   Validation

To visualize and analyze the behavior of our system a dashboard was designed on sFlow-RT (http://IP_sflow_collector:8008). There, see Fig. 5, we present three charts in order to identify the reconnaissance process suggested in Sect. 5.3: hosts discovery with ARP scan, service discovery with TCP-SYN scan and a DoS attack; on a scenario with a tree topology of depth 2 and fanout 2 (Fig. 4a).

ARP activity chart, TCP-SYN activity chart, and DoS monitoring chart represent the number of ARP Request frames, TCP-SYN segments, and IP packets gathered for all sFlow agents on every second. Moreover, threshold values for each chart can be changed for the network manager through Settings tab.

On the left side of the Fig. 5 (disabled control), we can observe how the network discovery process (timeline 11:38:00 to 11:39:00), the exploration of possible services (timeline 11:39:00 to 11:39:20) and a denial of service attack (timeline 11:39:20 to 11:40:00) were performed. The following list details the log console of the sFlow collector for this part of the procedure (see Listing 1.2).

```
11:38:00 INFO: Listening, sFlow port 6343
11:38:01 INFO: Listening, HTTP port 8008
11:38:01 INFO: Scripts s3n_stats.js and s3n_alarms.js started
11:38:37 WARNING: ARP_SCAN Alert {MAC:Frames} -> {"DA5C3216AE0B":103.26693339459928} , on device -> {"port
         ":"1","dpid":"0000000000000003"}
11:39:05 WARNING: TCPSYN_SCAN Alert {srcIP,dstIP:Frames} -> {"10.0.0.1,10.0.0.4":100.4977565214356} , on
         device -> {"port":"1","dpid":"0000000000000002"}
11:39:23 WARNING: DoS Alert {srcIP,dstIP,protocol:Frames} -> {"10.0.0.2,10.0.0.3,eth.ip.udp.dns"
         :10001.445090767767} , on device -> {"port":"2","dpid":"0000000000000002"}
11:39:36 WARNING: Unreachable port operation between: 10.0.0.3->10.0.0.2 on udp_40125
```

Listing 1.2. Alert messages on sFlow console log

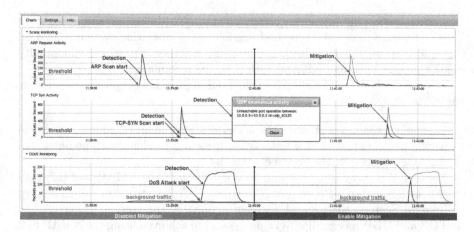

Fig. 5. Reconnaissance stage

On the right part of the graph, the same reconnaissance process is executed with the mitigation condition enabled. To improve the evidence about the mitigation process achieved, traffic shapes in gray (which are replicas of the traffic behavior on the left), were added. Finally, the dialog box shown in the figure, it is a consequence of the DoS attack performed since in the testbed there is no service running on UDP port 53 (DNS service), hence ICMP unreachable messages are generated as evidence of an anomalous network condition.

To evidence the scalability of sampling technology such as sFlow, the same procedure described above was implemented on a scenario with a tree topology of depth 3 and fanout 4 (Fig. 4b). The results are presented in the Fig. 6 using a sampling rate of 1:100 (left side) and 1:10 (right side), in order to verify the

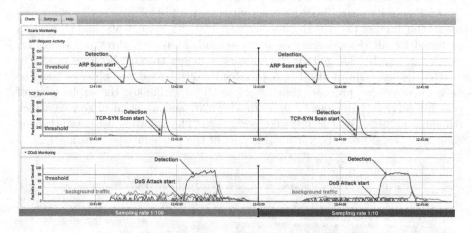

Fig. 6. Sampling comparison

behavior of the intrusion process under these conditions. The reader can verify that all parts of the reconnaissance process were detected effectively, regardless of the network size or the sampling rate defined.

7   Discussion

The tests carried out show that sFlow is a scalable sampling technology for measuring, collecting, and analyzing network traffic data. This fact enables the technology for different purposes, in our case the capacity to detect a reconnaissance process in order to improve the network security. From the obtained outcomes, we can conclude that:

- The process of host discovering, through the use of the ARP Request scan technique, is a process that is carried out in a highly efficient way. The required time for this procedure depends directly on the size of the network to be scanned, but generally, hundreds of hosts can be scanned in few seconds. As it is a brief type of intrusion, it does not generate any type of stress within the network, hence its detection becomes less important. However, as we mentioned before, this procedure precedes attacks of another magnitude.
- The exploration of available services is a procedure that will depend on the number of hosts to be scanned and the number of ports of interest. In the tests performed, the identification of services was oriented to a single host in the network, where the TCP-SYN process was focused on only 2000 specific ports (NMAP default operation mode). Hence, the action registered in the chart was very short. However, if this task is executed simultaneously for all discovered stations, the outcome can significantly disturb the behavior of network traffic, even emulating the presence of a DoS attack.
- Regarding the DoS attack, the mitigation technique acquires greater prominence in comparison with the aforementioned discovery processes, which have a shorter action in the timeline. However, it is important to mention that when a control is implemented in a discovery processes, we do not only prevent the network flooding with ARP or TCP-SYN packets —on the contrary, we have identified the location of the intruder (switch and associated port) and his network identifier (MAC or IP address) and, therefore, all traffic originating from that device has been blocked, which will cancel the advance of the other steps in the intrusion process—.
- With respect to the values of sampling rate, 1:10 and 1:100, they were defined around of the recommendations offered by sFlow for the large flow detection (1:10 for links speed of 10 Mbps, 1:100 for 100 Mbps and 1:1000 for 1 Gbps) [7]. The sampling rate values affected the resolution of the traffic shape, but it did not influence the detection process in the testbed.
- Finally, for the two scenarios proposed: the first one integrated by 3 switches, 4 hosts and 8 ports-witch, and the second one composed of 21 switches, 64 hosts and 104 ports-switch; the results achieved were identical.

8 Conclusion

In this paper, we evaluated the applicability of using sampling technology, under SDN environment, to detect and mitigate reconnaissance anomalous activity, which is the initial step of any kind of attack. For this purpose, we proposed an architecture and built a testbed to demonstrate the effectiveness of our approach even in large scenarios. Results show that our prototype can effectively detect and control the anomalous activities described in Sect. 5.3, and can be extended to identify other ones. Also, we illustrate a system that can be easily replicated in other scenarios with similar needs.

As future work, in order to continue improving the security network, we will use the statistical information provided by sFlow to implement entropy analysis. Also, we will continue the construction of new flow definitions to increase the robustness of the system.

Acknowledgments. This work has been partially funded by the CODI project 2015-7793 of the University of Antioquia (Colombia) and the research project TEC2016-76795-C6-5-R *"Adaptive Management of 5G Services to Support Critical Events in Cities"* of the Ministry of Economy, Industry and Competitiveness (Spain).

References

1. What is iPerf/iPerf3? (2003). https://iperf.fr/
2. OpenvSwitch (2009). http://www.openvswitch.org
3. Floodlight Controller (2012). http://www.projectfloodlight.org
4. Mininet: An instant virtual network on your laptop (2012). http://mininet.org
5. POX controller (2012). https://github.com/noxrepo/pox/
6. Ryu controller (2012). https://osrg.github.io/ryu/
7. Large flow (2013). http://blog.sflow.com/2013/06/large-flow-detection-script.html
8. OpenDaylight controller (2013). https://www.opendaylight.org
9. Writing sFlow applications (2015). https://sflow-rt.com/writing_applications.php
10. Allied Telesis: how to — use sFlow in a network (2013). https://www.alliedtelesis.com/sites/default/files/aw-_use_sflow_in_a_network_revb1.pdf
11. Buragohain, C., Medhi, N.: FlowTrApp: an SDN based architecture for DDoS attack detection and mitigation in data centers. In: 2016 3rd International Conference on Signal Processing and Integrated Networks (SPIN), pp. 519–524. IEEE (2016)
12. Dharma, N.G., Muthohar, M.F., Prayuda, J.A., Priagung, K., Choi, D.: Time-based DDoS detection and mitigation for SDN controller. In: Network Operations and Management Symposium (APNOMS), pp. 550–553. IEEE (2015)
13. Giotis, K., Androulidakis, G., Maglaris, V.: Leveraging SDN for efficient anomaly detection and mitigation on legacy networks. In: 2014 Third European Workshop on Software Defined Networks (EWSDN), pp. 85–90. IEEE (2014)
14. Giotis, K., Argyropoulos, C., Androulidakis, G., Kalogeras, D., Maglaris, V.: Combining OpenFlow and sFlow for an effective and scalable anomaly detection and mitigation mechanism on SDN environments. Comput. Netw. **62**, 122–136 (2014)
15. Gude, N., et al.: NOX: towards an operating system for networks. ACM SIGCOMM Comput. Commun. Rev. **38**(3), 105–110 (2008)

16. Hsiao-Chung, L., Ping, W.: Implementation of an SDN-based security defense mechanism against DDoS attacks. In: DEStech Transactions on Economics, Business and Management (ICEME-EBM) (2016)
17. Lyon, G.: Nmap: The Network Mapper (1997). https://nmap.org/
18. McKeown, N., et al.: OpenFlow: enabling innovation in campus networks. ACM SIGCOMM Comput. Commun. Rev. 38(2), 69–74 (2008)
19. Nugraha, M., Paramita, I., Musa, A., Choi, D., Cho, B.: Utilizing openFlow and sFlow to detect and mitigate SYN flooding attack. J. Korea Multimed. Soc. 17(8), 988–994 (2014)
20. Open Networking Foundation: Software-Defined Networking (SDN) Definition (2018). https://www.opennetworking.org/sdn-resources/sdn-definition
21. Panchen, S., McKee, N., Phaal, P.: InMon corporations sFlow: a method for monitoring traffic in switched and routed networks. RFC 3176, September 2001. https://doi.org/10.17487/rfc3176, https://rfc-editor.org/rfc/rfc3176.txt
22. Phaal, P., Lavine, M.: sFlow protocol specification version 5 (2004)
23. Sanai, D.: Detection of promiscuous nodes using ARP packets (2001). http://www.securityfriday.com/promiscuous_detection_01.pdf
24. Uma, M., Padmavathi, G.: A survey on various cyber attacks and their classification. IJ Netw. Secur. 15(5), 390–396 (2013)
25. Zaalouk, A., Khondoker, R., Marx, R.: An orchestrator-based architecture for enhancing network-security using network monitoring and SDN control functions. In: Network Operations and Management Symposium (NOMS), pp. 1–9. IEEE (2014)

Design and Implementation of a Controlled and Monitored Multipurpose Exploratory Device Through a Wi-Fi Connection Using MatchPort

Arnaldo Andres González[(✉)], Luis Eduardo Pallares,
Roberto Ferro Escobar, and Jorge Enrique Portella

Corporación Unificada Nacional de Educación Superior CUN, Bogotá, Colombia
arnaldogonzalez@gmail.com,
{luis_pallares, roberto_ferro, jorge_portella}@cun.edu.co

Abstract. Currently, the use of remotely controlled and monitored devices that perform high-risk exploration activities is increasing. The design and implementation of a robot type device for exploration that allows real-time data capture of different conditions depending on the sensors that are configured, using one of the serial ports available in the MatchPort which in turn supports the connection using Wi-Fi technology the device has a camera that performs visual recognition of the environment.

Keywords: Wi-Fi · MatchPort · Serial port

1 Introduction

In the search for a satisfactory solution at the hardware level, a circuit is implemented that allows: first, the wireless connection with Wi-fi that performs the transducer function between a TCP/IP wireless network connection to the serial port, facilitating the use of a microcontroller for the management of the device and the acquisition of data from the sensors, second, the necessary electrical power supply, both for loco-motion of the device that would have differential traction to facilitate its displacement in places with irregular terrain and the movement of the camera allows the movement in two degrees of freedom, in order to explore the environment [1, 6].

The document has the sections describing the problem, design and modeling, implementation, results, conclusions and future work [2].

The results obtained show as a device with traccion differential raises the power of all system, but maintenance the nivels appropriate the same (see Fig. 11) the total current consumed by the device during initialization of the system to its stable state, maintain 13 W power it is something very assertive.

In the description of the problem, it is proposed what characteristics the result-oriented device should have, in design and modeling the technical characteristics that define the prototype based on the functionality are described and finally Sects. 4 and 5 respectively collect quantitative measurements and the conclusions of the work.

© Springer Nature Switzerland AG 2018
J. C. Figueroa-García et al. (Eds.): WEA 2018, CCIS 916, pp. 336–347, 2018.
https://doi.org/10.1007/978-3-030-00353-1_30

2   Problem Description

The actions of the search and location of people affected by emergencies or disasters until access to them, their clinical and operative assessment, stabilization and evacuation of the impact zone, involving specialized, intermediate and basic relief groups. The attention of an emergency requires technical preparation, planning and coordination capacity among those who participate in it; otherwise, improvisation, disorder, omission of functions, increase of time in the rescue of survivors, high costs, loss of lives and risks of operation may be incurred [7].

Taking into account this items, the device must provide support in the recognition works, the search and recovery of the location in high risk places, it must comply with the following characteristics:

- Must be a portable device with a camera controlled and remotely monitored through a wireless connection.
- The device must allow easy adaptation of any type of sensors according to the task to be performed.

These conditions suggest obtaining information of the necessary electronic characteristics that allow a correct response of the device in extreme conditions, that can give support the following search techniques:

- Lifeguards: They are an organized group of people selected and trained to support one or more areas of operation in an emergency; They have specialized equipment, according to the place and type of accident.
- Salvation dogs: They are used in various rescue specialties in catastrophes that consists of training them to search for people buried in landslides caused by explosions, earthquakes, structural failures thanks to their sensory attributes, agility and versatility that are superior to humans and even to technological solutions.

3   Design and Modeling

Based on the functionality, the device is defined as a mobile that moves in the direction determined by a user who is remotely located and who can perceive the movements of the same and its surroundings, with a camera that adheres to the robot. the architecture of the hardware can adapt different types of sensors according to the task to be performed, the device has dimensions and weight that make it easily transportable inside a suitcase, then in the (see Fig. 1), you can see the diagram of blocks of the different stages of the hardware.

Here is a brief explanation of the stages that make up the project:

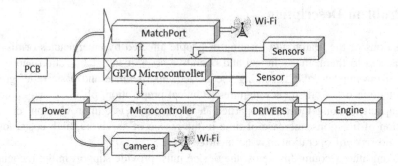

Fig. 1. Block diagram of the different hardware stages that make up the robot device.

3.1 Power

Its function is to provide power for the different stages of the circuit; the power source is a battery. The stage must perform voltage conversion to provide TTL and CMOS levels, we can appreciate the power requirements of each of the components in Table 1.

Table 1. Power requirements for each stage.

Component/phase	Voltage	Current	Power
Half-H driver and engines	12 V	2A	24 W
Microcontroller	5 V	6 mA	0.03 W
Camera	5 V	680 mA	3.4 W
total output 5 V		686 mA	3.47 W
MatchPort	3.6 V	300 mA	1.08 W

3.2 MatchPort

It is the key component of the communication, it performs the conversion of information that comes via TCP/IP to serial port, before the start-up, the device must configure the network conditions, which is, indicate an SSID with its respective password Network, an IP address and a TCP port number where the application socket is identified. In this stage the MatchPort Demo Board circuit was implemented, the block consists of a base plate where the MatchPort device is housed, ensuring that it provides all the connections and functionalities available.

The scheme of the connection of the stage (see Fig. 2), can be seen as the MatchPort communicates with the PCB through a serial port in which a bidirectional communication has been implemented, under serial standard; additionally there is a connector that leaves the PCB and arrives at the reset pin, which is used in case the device goes into error status and continues in that state for more than 15 s at the end of which it is sent a signal that I restart, releasing all the connections that have been established. Because the technology implemented in the PCB is TTL and the Match-Port works under CMOS technology, for the connection of the reset pin, it was necessary to implement the coupling stage in the PCB, which receives the signal from the microcontroller, and reduce it to 3.6 V[1].

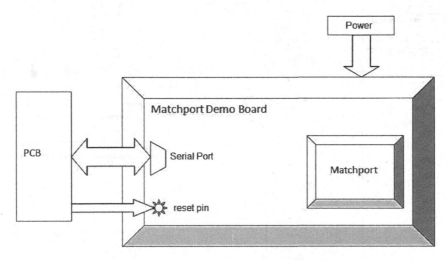

Fig. 2. Block diagram of the MatchPort stage, with its internal logical connections and power stage.

3.3   Microcontroller

It receives the signal from the MatchPort stage and, according to the instruction sent by the user, generates the signals that are transmitted to the Drivers. The microcontroller selected for the project was the MC68HC908GP32, it has modules SCI, TIM, IRQ and PLL, essential to achieve the project's objectives[2].

The program of the microcontroller performs the tasks sequentially; the timers are controlled by means of a subroutine generated by the module TIM2, the TIM1 is reserved for the PWM signals (see Eqs. 1 and 2). The interruption of the IRQ pin is used to count the rotor cycles, the counter every second is reset and the resulting value is put in a register that will be consulted in the data sending subroutine (Fig. 3 and Table 2).

$$T = \frac{4.Preescaler.(TH{:}TL)}{f_{oscilador}} \tag{1}$$

---

[1] Lantronix Corporation. MatchPort b/g Integration Guide. Part number 900-485 July 2007.
[2] Freescale Semiconductor Inc. MC68HC908GP32 Technical Data. rev. 6 2002.

340   A. A. González et al.

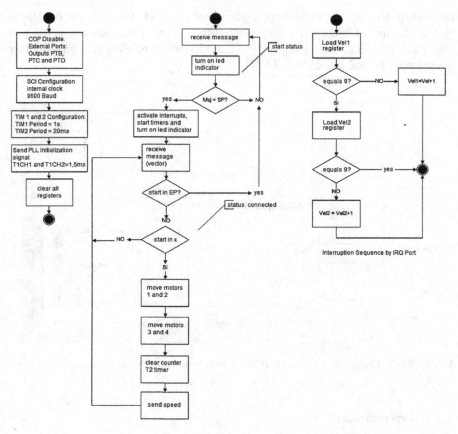

Fig. 3. Flow of the main program of the microcontroller.

Table 2. According to the MC68HC908GP32 microcontroller's datasheet, the value of the period to be counted by the TIM module to generate the signal is given by Eq. 2, where $T_H{:}T_L$ corresponds to the internal record of the channel, with which the comparison is made, it *Preescaler* is a register of the module and $f_{oscilador}$ is the frequency of the external crystal (4.915200 Hz), the table presents the values of the PWM module registers needed to generate the square signals.

Period	Preescaler	$T_H{:}T_L$
20 ms	1	24576
1 ms	1	1229
2 ms	1	2458

$$T_H{:}T_L = \frac{1}{4}\frac{(T)(f_{oscilador})}{Preescaler} \tag{2}$$

3.4   Camera

The Linksys model WVC80N camera was chosen within the design. The camera obtains the power supply voltage of the main PCB, where a socket with 5 V and a capacity of 1 A is reserved; the configuration is done through the network.

3.5   Sensor

For monitoring purposes we want to measure the speed of displacement, for this the robot was implemented a quick switch magnetic switch; which is nothing more than a contact that closes when passing close to a magnetic field, said sensor is coupled to the chassis of the left traction track and reacts to a small magnet coupled to the traction motor shaft of the left track.

The conditioning and reading of the sensor must be processed by the microcontroller and/or the application to inform the user, Fig. 6 shows the scheme of connection of the sensor to the microcontroller, the most convenient unit of measure is cm/s since the displacements are very short.

3.6   Drivers

They receive the output signals of the microcontroller and transmit them to the actuators; they are used for two purposes: one as protection of the microcontroller and two for the current management in the actuators. The drivers are the stages of electrical coupling between the microcontroller and the actuators. Two types of driver are implemented, one for the D.C. and another for the servomotors, in both cases the drivers provide high impedance inputs that help protect the outputs of the microcontroller and help deliver the output signal needed by the actuator for its operation.

Drivers D.C Motors

To meet the requirements of displacement, we thought of a differential traction system that would allow the device to move forward, back and rotate both to the right and to the left according to the user's commands; to achieve this it is clear that both motors change their direction of rotation independently, this means frequent change of polarity in the power supply.

To solve this problem, two H-bridges are implemented, one for each motor. The L298N integrated circuit is added to the project, which provides two integrated bridges in the same package and meets the need for current and voltage. It is also compatible with TTL level control signals from the microcontroller ports (Fig. 4).

Servomotor Driver

The actuators responsible for carrying out the movement of the camera are servomotors controlled by PWM, although in theory the microcontroller can supply the necessary energy to drive the motors, due to experiments that prove it was not enough, since

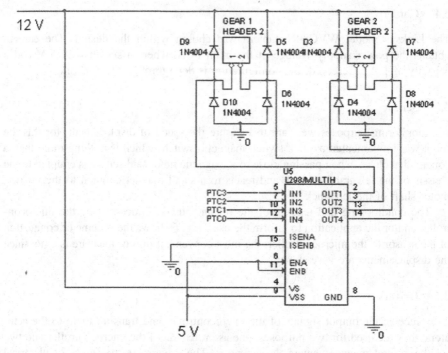

Fig. 4. Electrical diagram of the L298N connection.

when putting the motors to test with their respective inertial load did not meet the torque requirement necessary for proper operation, so it was necessary to implement a driver capable of supporting an even greater current. A pair of TIP41C transistors connected to the output of each PWM channel was implemented, one for each servomotor.

3.7 Actuators

These are the devices in charge of converting the electrical signals coming from the microcontroller into physical movement, in this case they are motors that generate all the movements of the robot, convert the electrical signal coming from the drivers, in mechanical movement that will be transmitted to the caterpillars and to the mechanical arm that moves the camera, two kinds of engines were used.

DC Motors

These are responsible for providing the power of movement of the device, two identical 12 V motors with gearbox were implemented in order to give the mobile a powerful differential traction that allows it to perform without any problem the translation thereof. They are electrically connected to the L298N and physically by means of toothed wheels to a caterpillar of 5.1 cm, which provide sufficient traction to the device to travel terrains with different degrees of inclination.

Servomotors Controlled by PWM
Their function is to provide the camera with the movement to explore the surroundings of its location without moving the entire body of the robot. Two servomotors are implemented model SG5010 of Towerpro, widely used in aeromodelling due to its performance and low cost, are controlled by a PWM signal.

4 Measurements

In this section we present the results of the different measurements made in the device which allows us to analyze the results of the work done, and helps answer the questions posed at the beginning of the document in the approach to the problem.

4.1 Tests or Measurements on Hardware

The measurements made on the hardware seek to obtain information that allows determining factors such as the power consumption used, in each of the stages of greatest consumption. The stages of:

- Camera.
- MatchPort.
- Servomotors.
- D.C Motors.

Measurement of Current Consumption in the Camera
The camera works with a power supply of 5 V D.C, the current consumption varies over time. When the camera is turned on there is an initial consumption that oscillates between 280 mA and 300 mA, this happens when the operating system of the camera is started, then when it starts to connect to the network and the first echo tests are made, the consumption increases to values close to 680 mA and varies when there are strong changes in the image, reaching peak values that reach 800 mA (see Fig. 5).

Measurement of Current Consumption in the MatchPort
The power and current values are presented (see Fig. 6), the first is obtained by multiplying the data obtained in the measurement of the current by 3.6 V. When the system is initialized, the current consumption in the device reaches values around 275 mA, and then when the initialization tasks are finished, it descends around 170 mA, when the data transmission is started through the WI-FI network. at its nominal consumption level of 338 mA.

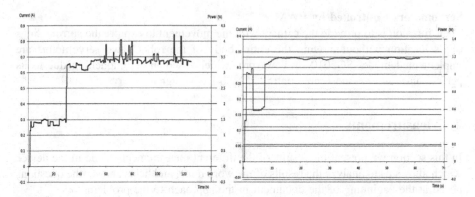

Fig. 5. Power and current consumed by the camera and the MatchPort device from left to right respectively.

Table 3. Current measurement in servomotors

Angle (Degrees)	Current (mA)
0	158.5
30	156.7
45	134.4
60	92
90	5.09

Measurement of the Current in the Servomotors that Drive the Movement of the Camera

The current is measured according to the torque that is exerted, starts at an angle of 0 grados and goes gently turning until it reaches 180°, the results are shown in Table 3. The current consumption of the servomotors is not something significant, since in the position of maximum torque this hardly consumes 158.5 mA; 90° being the vertical position without any inclination and 0 degrees the position of maximum inclination towards the front of the camera.

Measurement of the Current in the Motors D.C.

The current consumption in one of the D.C. motors is shown. that provide the differential traction of the device (see Fig. 5), when starting, the current consumption is higher because enough power must be provided to the motors to overcome the inertial state of the device, the current consumption is stabilized around −700 mA with small deviations caused by imperfections in the mechanical gear couplings of the device.

Measurement of Total Current

The total current consumption of the device is presented (see Fig. 7); where it is shown that it is the result of the sum of the graphs of the power consumption of the camera, the

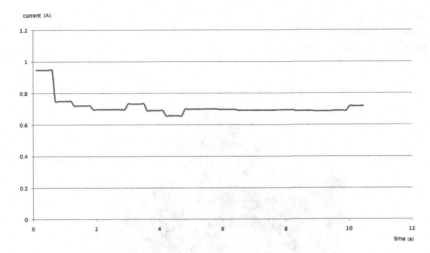

Fig. 6. Measurement of the current in the D.C.

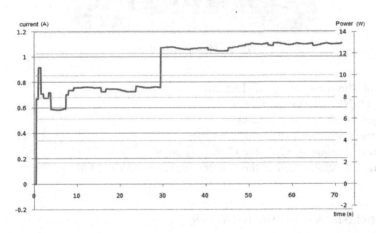

Fig. 7. Total current consumed by the device during initialization of the system to its stable state.

MatchPort and of course also the PCB. In summary, it is noticeable that the power consumption and/or current of the device at rest stabilize around 13 W and 1.1A for a nominal power supply of 12 V, if a 12 V VRLA battery is used that supplies 7A per hour (84 W) and a consumption of 13 W, an approximate average of 6.5 h of auton-omy is obtained, without counting the weight of the device and the extra attachments required in the exploration.

Mechanical Specifications

Below are the physical dimensions of the device, weight, average speed of movement and rotation of the camera [5] (Fig. 8).

- Long: 30 cm.
- Width: 32 cm.
- Height Max (up camera): 25.5 cm.

Fig. 8. Photography device

- Height Min (down camera): 15.5 cm.
- Weight (No battery): 2.15 kg
- Weight (With battery): 3.82 kg
- Average Displacement Speed: 2.3 km/h.
- Average rotation speed of the Camera (acimut 180°): 14.55°/s.
- Average rotation speed of the Camera (elevation 135°): 14.48°/s.

5   Conclusions and Future Work

In general, the implemented device constitutes a proposal for a basic platform, search and exploration, this quality allows you to mutate into a variety that is almost unlimited, depending on the sensors that are installed according to the task, although this affects the energy consumption a considerably, but allows it to differentiate itself from other proposals, which as main idea would an acquire plug and play as a design modular style that will undoubtedly be able to take better advantage of the device is design [6, 7].

It will allow developing diverse functions; The design already proposed can be further optimized based on the specific task to be carried out, which can range from the detection of landmines, the support system for conducting surveillance rounds, the structural verification of buildings at risk of collapse, and the scouting of sites with biological risk [3, 4, 6].

References

1. Murphy, R.R., et al.: Search and rescue robotics. In: Siciliano, B., Khatib, O. (eds.) Springer Handbook of Robotics, pp. 1151–1173. Springer, Heidelberg (2008). https://doi.org/10.1007/978-3-540-30301-5_51
2. Takahashi, T.: Hinomiyagura: Comparison Simulation Results to Data of Local Government. Robocup Rescue Simulation League 2006 Team Description Paper, Bremen, Germany, 14–20 June 2006 (2006)
3. Barrientos, A., Peñín, L.F., Balaguer, C., Aracil, R.: Fundamentos de Robótica. McGrawHill, New York (2007). ISBN 8448156366
4. Maki, K.H., Yvan, B.: Robot-assisted risky intervention, search, rescue and environmental surveillance. Int. J. Adv. Robot. Syst. **7**, 001–008 (2010). ISSN 1729-8806
5. Stormont, D.P., Allan, V.H.: Managing risk in disaster scenarios with autonomous robots. Syst. Cybern. Inform. **7**, 66–71 (2009). ISSN 1690-4524
6. Tadokoro, S.: Special project on development of advanced robots for disaster response (DDT Project). In: Proceedings of IEEE Workshop on Advanced Robotics and its Social Impacts (ARSO 2005), Nagoya, Japan, 12–15 June 2005 (2005)
7. Bermudez, G., Novoa, S., Infante, W.: Robotics in search and urban rescue activities Origin, present time and perspectives. Tecnura **8**, 98–108 (2004). https://doi.org/10.14483/issn.2248-7638

A Fast Reliability Analysis Approach for Colombian Natural Gas Subnetworks

Wilson González-Vanegas[(✉)], Andrés Álvarez-Meza,
and Álvaro Orozco-Gutiérrez

Faculty of Engineerings, Universidad Tecnológica de Pereira,
Automatic Research Group, Pereira, Colombia
wilgonzalez@utp.edu.co

Abstract. The Colombian natural gas sector is going through a challenging stage concerning the management of available reserves. Recently, some weather conditions have shown drawbacks in security and reliability regarding supply and transportation. Regasification technology has been installed in the system as a solution for leading the unbalance between demand and supply. However, the inadequate pipeline infrastructure for transporting large natural gas flows in the short and long-term is demanding an expansion for enhancing the system reliability. Here, we develop a Markov chain-based isolation method for performing fast reliability analysis in subnetworks of the Colombian natural gas system, based on the optimal operational cost. We assess our methodology on a real data set concerning a simplified Colombian natural gas system. Obtained results show that our proposal remarkably improves the computation time employed for computing the reliability of subnetworks and preserves the accuracy in the calculation of the optimal operational cost.

Keywords: Colombian natural gas system · Linear optimization
Markov chain · Reliability

1 Introduction

In the last decades, natural gas has become a valuable worldwide energy resource due to its low environmental impact and competitive cost compared to other fossil fuels. In particular, natural gas combustion leads to fewer CO_2 emissions per generated unit than coal and oil, reflecting potential advantages towards a sustainable low-carbon society [5]. In the near-medium term, the role of natural gas will be closely linked to the power sector since gas can be used to improve the reliability of electricity systems that rely on intermittent renewable resources, because gas-fired power plants can be ramped up quickly and provide flexible generation schedules. On the other hand, global electricity demand is expected to double by 2060 and the power sector offers the highest growth for the gas sector [11]. According to the Energy Information Administration (EIA), the

© Springer Nature Switzerland AG 2018
J. C. Figueroa-García et al. (Eds.): WEA 2018, CCIS 916, pp. 348–356, 2018.
https://doi.org/10.1007/978-3-030-00353-1_31

proved worldwide reserves of natural gas have increased rapidly in the last ten year, reaching around 6922 trillion cubic feet in 2017 [3]. In the Middle East, Asia, and North America, the natural gas markets concern about exportations and developments regarding the pipeline infrastructure [1]. However, in Central and South America, although the gas is relatively abundant, investment delays and inadequate infrastructure have led to situations that compromised the system security [4]. In Colombia, for instance, the weather conditions have recently affected the natural gas system as a consequence of extreme droughts that drastically reduced the hydroelectric power generation, demanding for the maximum natural gas supply to support the electric sector [10]. In particular, this situation revealed some drawbacks in the Colombian system concerning the delayed installation of regasification points in the Caribean, not to mention the need for a pipeline system expansion for enhancing the system reliability.

Some studies have been proposed for analyzing the Colombian natural gas system. Authors in [6] provided a gas market vision concluding that the Colombian system is not able to supply its demand under several contingency conditions due to inappropriate pipeline infrastructure. Villada et al. in [10] proposed to use a simulation-based approach to analyze the security of natural gas supply in Colombia, using different linear programming-based modules to maximize the profit of producers in order to evaluate whether an increase in flexibility contracts led to an overall increase in the security of supply. Regarding the system reliability, authors in [8] proposed a simulation model for analyzing the risks associated with the continuity in wells, including the financial effects of non-served gas produced by different weather conditions. On the other hand, the Mining and Energy Planning Unit (UPME in Spanish), provides annual plans concerning the evaluation of investment and expansion alternatives. However, they considere simulations models rather than optimal flow analysis, which is crucial for setting the best system conditions that produce minimal cost [9]. Although these approaches have introduced potential advances for the Colombian gas sector, any of them have contemplated sectorized studies that allow fast analysis and highlight relevant information in subnetworks.

In this work, we introduce a novel simulation-based model for performing fast reliability analysis in subnetworks of the Colombian natural gas system. In this sense, our approach facilitates the analysis of investment alternatives such as the construction of new pipelines in sections or small regions of the system based on the optimal operational cost. Attained results on a real data set concerning a simplified Colombian natural gas systems show that our proposal remarkably reduces the computation time.

The remainder of this paper is organized as follows: Sect. 2 shows the optimization model for the Colombian natural gas system. Section 3 describes the mathematical foundations of our proposal. Section 4 describes the experimental set-up and the obtained result. Finally, the conclusions are outlined in Sect. 5.

2   Optimization Model for Reliability Analysis in the Colombian Natural Gas System

To analyze the reliability of the Colombian natural gas system, we consider the following optimization problem based on the network operational cost [8]:

$$
\tilde{g}^t, \tilde{h}^t, \tilde{f}^t = \underset{g^t, h^t, f^t}{\mathrm{argmin}} \quad \sum_{n=1}^{N}\sum_{u=1}^{U} \beta_{u,n} g_{u,n}^t + \sum_{w=1}^{W} \alpha_w h_w^t + \sum_{p=1}^{P} \gamma_p f_p^t
$$

$$
\text{s.t.} \quad \sum_{\phi \in \Phi_n^t} \phi - \sum_{u=1}^{U} g_{u,n}^t = \xi_n^t, \quad \forall n \in \{1,2,\dots,N\}
$$

$$
0 \le g_{u,n}^t \le \epsilon_{u,n}^t, \quad \forall u \in \{1,2,\dots,U\};\ n \in \{1,2,\dots,N\}
$$

$$
0 \le h_w^t \le \overline{h_w^t}, \quad \forall h_w^t \in \mathcal{W}
$$

$$
-\overline{f_p^t} \le f_p^t \le \overline{f_p^t}, \quad \forall f_p^t \in \mathcal{P},
$$

(1)

where $N, U, W, P \in \mathbb{N}$ are the number of nodes, users, wells, and, pipelines, respectively, $\mathcal{W} = \{h_w^t \in \mathbb{R}^+\}_{w=1}^{W}$ is the set of well flows and $\mathcal{P} = \{f_p^t \in \mathbb{R}^+\}_{p=1}^{P}$ is the set of pipeline flows. Moreover, $\beta_{u,n}, \alpha_w, \gamma_p \in \mathbb{R}^+$ are the costs associated with the non-supplied gas of the u-th user at the n-th node, the injection cost of the w-th well, and the transportation cost of the p-th pipeline, respectively. The equality constraint represents the mass balance equation, where $\Phi_n^t \subset (\mathcal{P} \cup \mathcal{W})$ is the set of incoming (negative reference) and outcoming (positive reference) flows in the n-th node, and $\xi_n^t = \sum_{u=1}^{U} \epsilon_{u,n}^t$ is the total demand at each node, where $\epsilon_{u,n}^t \in \mathbb{R}^+$ is the demand of the u-th user at the n-th node. Regarding the inequality constraints, the nodal non-supplied gas per user, $g_{u,n}^t \in \mathbb{R}^+$, cannot exceed its corresponding demand. Furthermore, the flow at each well and pipeline is bounded by $\overline{h_w^t}, \overline{f_p^t} \in \mathbb{R}^+$, respectively, allowing bidirectional flows in pipelines. Besides, t represents an index time.

In a real-world natural gas system, several optimization problems arise, not only due to changes in demand but also concerning supply and transportation failures. For leading such uncertainty, we set a Gaussian distribution to model the demand of the u-th user at the n-th node as $\epsilon_{u,n}^t \sim \mathcal{N}(\mu_{u,n}, \sigma_{u,n}^2)$, where $\mu_{u,n}, \sigma_{u,n} \in \mathbb{R}^+$. For wells and pipelines failures, the uncertainty is set through a reduction in the capacities $\overline{h_w^t}, \overline{f_p^t}$ by using profiles over time, obtained by modelling the number of interruptions as a Poisson event $\zeta_x^t \sim \mathscr{P}(\lambda_x)$, where $\lambda_x \in \mathbb{R}^+$. Besides, the duration of such interruptions follows a log-normal distribution as $\delta_x^t \sim lognormal(\nu_x, \psi_x^2)$, where $\nu_x, \psi_x \in \mathbb{R}^+$, and the percentage of volume reduction follows a uniform distribution as $\vartheta_x^t \sim \mathscr{U}(a_x, b_x)$, where $a_x, b_x \in [0,1]$, and $x \in \{w, p\}$. Here, the parameters of the distributions are found towards a Maximum Likelihood Estimation (MLE)-based approach over historical data.

In turn, given a natural gas system, we draw from the proposed distributions to find the optimal network flows by solving the model in Eq. (1) for $t \in \{1, 2, \cdots, T\}$. Moreover, for enhancing the uncertainty treatment, we use a Monte Carlo simulation for a fixed number of iterations I. Finally, we compute the expected value of the optimal flows and the reliability for each well and pipeline.

3   Subnetwork Isolation for Fast Approximated Analysis

Let us assume a situation where we want to evaluate an alternative to improve the reliability in a subnetwork of the Colombian natural gas system, e.g., the construction of a loop in a specific pipeline. Instead of analyzing such an alternative directly over the whole original natural gas network, we propose to isolate the corresponding subnetwork as an intermediate step, and then evaluate any alternative over the isolated network using the model in Eq. (1). Namely, we run the optimization procedure in Sect. 2 over the original system to use the obtained results for isolating the subnetwork, by means of a *Virtual Equivalent Well* (VEW) $\widehat{w}$ connected in the *Isolation Node* (IN) $\widehat{n}$, as shown in Fig. 1.

Regarding the failure VEW parameters, we employ a continuous Markov chain to model each state of the repairable system formed by the elements in the set $\mathcal{X} = \{x \in \{w, p\} | h_x^\dagger, f_x^\dagger \in \mathcal{I}\}$, where $h_x^\dagger, f_x^\dagger \in \mathbb{R}^+$ are the expected value over time and Monte Carlo iterations of $\widetilde{h_x}, \widetilde{f_x}$, respectively, and $\mathcal{I}$ is the set holding only incoming flows in the IN. To the best of our knowledge about the Colombian natural gas system, the probability of residing in a state where two or more units in $\mathcal{X}$ fail at the same time is negligible, leading to a chain of $X+1$ states, where $X = |\mathcal{X}| \in \mathbb{N}$ is the number of units. In particular, we compute the *Mean Residence Time* (MRT) in each state as [2]:

$$m_0 = \frac{1}{\sum\limits_{x \in \mathcal{X}} \rho_x}; \quad m_k = \frac{1}{\theta_k + \sum\limits_{\substack{x \in \mathcal{X} \\ x \neq k}} \rho_x}, \quad \forall k \in \mathcal{X}, \tag{2}$$

where $m_0 \in \mathbb{R}$ is the MRT of the state holding operative units, and $m_k \in \mathbb{R}$ is the MRT of the state where the k-th unit is failed and the rest are operative. Furthermore, $\rho_x = \lambda_x/(T - \lambda_x \nu_x)$ and $\theta_x = 1/\nu_x$ are the failure rate and the repair rate of the x-th unit in $\mathcal{X}$, respectively. From Eq. (2), it is easy to note that the VEW mean time in failure yields $\tau = T(1 - m_0/\sum_{x \in \mathcal{X}} m_x)$. In this paper, we set $\lambda_{\widehat{w}} = \lceil \tau \rceil$ and $\nu_{\widehat{w}} = \tau/\lambda_{\widehat{w}}$. Besides, we set $\psi_{\widehat{w}}^2 = 0$ to fix $\delta_{\widehat{w}}^t = \nu_{\widehat{w}}$, modelling the VEW uncertainty only through $\zeta_{\widehat{w}}^t$. Regarding the percentage of volume reduction, we define $\varphi = 1 - \mu_{\widehat{n}}/L$ as the failure depth, where $\mu_{\widehat{n}} \in \mathbb{R}$ is the total IN mean demand and $L = \sum_{y \in \mathcal{Y}, y \neq \widehat{p}} \ell_y^\dagger$, $L \in \mathbb{R}$, is the VEW mean injection, where $\widehat{p}$ is the *Feeder Pipeline* and $\mathcal{Y}$ is an index set holding all the elements connected to the IN, where $\ell_y^\dagger \in \{f_y^\dagger, h_y^\dagger\}$. Here we set $a_{\widehat{w}} = \varphi - \Delta$ and $b_{\widehat{w}} = \varphi + \Delta$, where $\Delta \in \mathbb{R}^+$ is a small threshold. On the other hand, the VEW capacity is calculated as $\overline{h_{\widehat{w}}} = \kappa L$, where $\kappa = T/(T - \lambda_{\widehat{w}} \nu_{\widehat{w}} \varphi)$. Lastly, $\alpha_{\widehat{w}} = (1/L) \sum_{y \in \mathcal{Y}, y \neq \widehat{p}} \Omega_y \ell_y^\dagger$, stands for the VEW injection cost, where $\Omega_y \in \{\alpha_y, \gamma_y\}$.

Fig. 1. A simplified sketch for the proposed methodology.

4   Experiments and Results

To evaluate the performance of the proposed methodology, we considered the simplified natural gas system of the Colombian network shown in Fig. 2[1]. Seven different users ($U = 7$) associated with the main sectors were considered per node sorted as follows: residential, industrial, commercial, vehicular, refinery, petrochemical and thermoelectric. The costs of non-supplied gas in USD per Million Cubic Feet per Day (MCFD) were 100 for users (1)&(3), 21 for users (4)&(5), and 16.4 for the rest. A 12-node subnetwork was connected in the CQR node where the load for each user at every node follows a Gaussian distribution with mean according to Table 1 and a coefficient of variation fixed to 0.07; users (5)–(7) were set to have zero demand. Table 1 also shows the capacity, the transportation costs, and the fitted historical failure data for the subnetwork pipeline system.

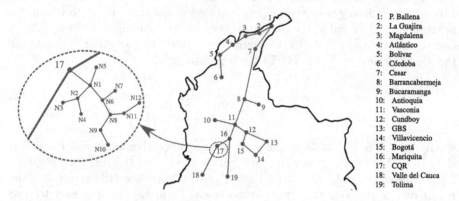

1:	P. Ballena
2:	La Guajira
3:	Magdalena
4:	Atlántico
5:	Bolivar
6:	Córdoba
7:	Cesar
8:	Barrancabermeja
9:	Bucaramanga
10:	Antioquia
11:	Vasconia
12:	Cundboy
13:	GBS
14:	Villavicencio
15:	Bogotá
16:	Mariquita
17:	CQR
18:	Valle del Cauca
19:	Tolima

Fig. 2. 19-node Colombian natural gas network.

We considered two different scenarios for specific testing. In the first one, we compared the 12-node system results using the whole natural gas system (Colombian system+subnetwork) and the isolated subnetwork. In the second scenario, we tested the robustness of the proposed methodology by evaluating an investment alternative associated to the construction of a *Loop* in the pipeline N1–N6 for both cases, the whole natural gas system and the isolated subnetwork. Moreover, we used three different comparison methodologies as quantitative assessment: the average absolute value of the non-served

---

[1] Available online in: https://github.com/WilsonGV/FRAACNGS.git.

Table 1. 12-node subnetwork information. Pipeline system information (left), nodal mean demand for each user in MCFD (right).

Pipeline	$\overline{f_p}$ (MCFD)	γ_p ($\frac{\text{USD}}{\text{MCFD}}$)	λ_p (-)	ν_p (Days)	τ_p (Days)	a_p (-)	b_p (-)	Node	$\epsilon_{1,n}$	$\epsilon_{2,n}$	$\epsilon_{3,n}$	$\epsilon_{4,n}$
CQR–N1	29.250	0.030	0.000	0.000	0.000	0.000	0.000	N1	0.990	0.960	0.390	1.020
N1–N2	5.145	0.020	2.410	0.660	0.200	0.000	1.000	N2	0.870	0.860	0.340	0.890
N1–N5	0.039	0.015	1.300	0.700	0.030	0.000	1.000	N3	0.530	0.530	0.210	0.540
N1–N6	17.729	0.012	3.800	4.460	1.300	0.600	1.000	N4	0.980	0.970	0.380	1.000
N2–N3	1.809	0.019	0.000	0.000	0.000	0.000	0.000	N5	0.010	0.010	0.010	0.010
N2–N4	3.336	0.011	0.000	0.000	0.000	0.000	0.000	N6	0.980	0.970	0.380	1.010
N6–N7	3.171	0.020	0.000	0.000	0.000	0.000	0.000	N7	0.930	0.920	0.360	0.950
N6–N8	11.215	0.023	2.410	0.300	0.050	0.000	1.000	N8	0.990	0.980	0.380	1.010
N8–N9	3.596	0.013	1.230	0.900	0.050	0.000	1.000	N9	0.280	0.273	0.107	0.280
N8–N11	4.263	0.014	1.200	0.650	0.010	0.400	1.000	N10	0.780	0.774	0.304	0.800
N9–N10	2.659	0.014	1.100	0.900	0.100	0.000	1.000	N11	0.820	0.813	0.319	0.840
N11–N12	1.468	0.016	1.200	0.200	0.060	0.300	1.000	N12	0.430	0.427	0.168	0.440

gas differences in each node, the average absolute value of the transported gas differences in each pipeline and a non-parametric density estimation of the average operational cost, using a Parzen window-based approach of the form $q(z^{(i)}) = (1/I) \sum_{j=1}^{I} \kappa_G(d_e(z^{(i)}, z^{(j)}); \sigma_z)$, where $z^{(i)} \in \mathbb{R}^+$ is the i-th sample of the subnetwork operational cost and $q(z^{(i)}) \in [0, 1]$ corresponds to the estimated probability; $\kappa_G(d_e(z^{(i)}, z^{(j)}); \sigma_z) = \exp(-d_e(z^{(i)}, z^{(j)})/2\sigma_z^2)$ stands for the Gaussian kernel, where d_e represents the Euclidean distance and $\sigma_z \in \mathbb{R}^+$ is the kernel width [7]. We considered $T = 365$, $I = 200$, and $\Delta = 0.01$ for both scenarios. Finally, all the experiments were performed using the linear programming solver included in the Matlab R2016a Optimization Toolbox.

Scenario 1 Results. Based on the sketch in Fig. 1, we start running the optimization program over the whole natural gas system and then use the obtained results to perform the isolation methodology with $\widehat{w} = \{17\}$ and $\widehat{p} = \{17-N1\}$, leading to the VEW parameters: $\overline{h_{\widehat{w}}} = 53.620[\text{MCFD}]$, $\gamma_{\widehat{w}} = 2.241[\text{USD/MCFD}]$, $\lambda_{\widehat{w}} = 1$, $\nu_{\widehat{w}} = 0.450[\text{days}]$, $\psi_{\widehat{w}} = 0[\text{days}]$, $a_{\widehat{w}} = 0.444$, and $b_{\widehat{w}} = 0.454$. Each optimal non-served and pipeline flow is averaged over Monte Carlo iterations for both the whole system and the isolated subnetwork. Figure 3(a) shows the difference between the average optimal non-served gas of both systems over time. As seen, small differences are obtained in those nodes that are close to the IN, showing an appropriate performance of the proposed methodology. On the other hand, as expected in a radial configuration, more markable differences can be seen in those nodes that are farther to the IN, as a consequence of the uncertainty propagation produced by failures in the pipelines that serve them as feeders. Regarding the subnetwork pipeline system, Fig. 3(c) shows the difference between the average optimal flows, where the pipelines 17–N1, N1–N6, and N6-N8 present the highest differences since they comprise larger capacities highlighting small flow changes, not to mention their longer failure information that introduce more uncertainty into the optimization

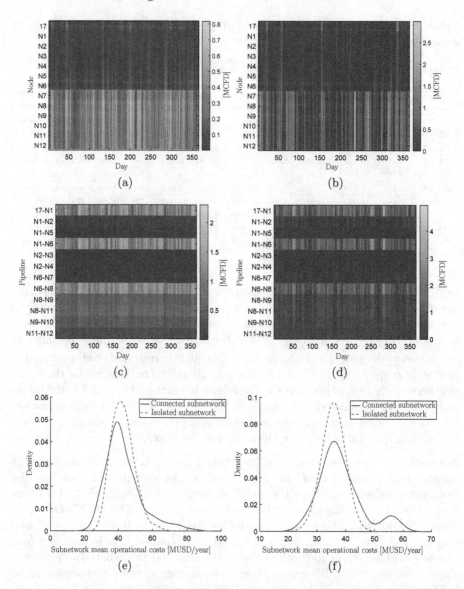

Fig. 3. Scenario 1 (left column) and scenario 2 (right column) results. (a)–(b) Absolute value of the difference regarding the average optimal non-served gas at each subnetwork node. (c)–(d) Absolute value of the difference regarding the average optimal flow through each subnetwork pipeline. (e)–(f) Kernel density estimation of the average optimal subnetwork operational cost.

procedure. However, notice from Figs. 3(a) and (c) that the differences belong to a sufficiently small variation range compared with the flow values in Table 1 for demand and transportation. Finally, according to the results in Fig. 3(e), the probability density function of the operational cost estimated for the isolated subnetwork is similar to the one computed for the whole system. In particular, the relative error for the estimated expected value of the operational cost is 0.95% taking the whole system results as reference.

Scenario 2 Results. According to the failure information shown in Table 1, the pipeline N1-N6 is the one with the longer time in failure, leading to a low reliability. For enhancing this pipeline reliability, and so the overall subnetwork one, we install an additional pipeline connected between nodes N1 and N6 (loop), with the same capacity to the actual one and a reduction of 60% regarding its failure information, for both the whole system and the isolated subnetwork. Obtained results after running the optimization program reveal in Figs. 3(b) and (d) how the loop reduces the differences for the average optimal non-served gas and the average optimal flows, respectively, since there is an alternative path for gas transportation when the pipeline N1-N6 is in failure. Regarding the subnetwork operational cost, Fig. 3(f) shows that the estimated densities for both the whole system and the isolated subnetwork take higher probabilities around similar values. In fact, notice that these values are smaller that those in Fig. 3(e), due to lower costs associated with the non-served gas.

Concerning the computation time, all the experiments were performed on an HP600-G1TWR machine with an Intel Core i7-4770 3.4 GHz processor. For scenario 1, the whole system took 1758.2 s while the isolated subnetwork took 595.1 s, leading to an improvement of 66.15%. In turn, for scenario 2, the whole system took 1771.0 s and the isolated subnetwork 582.9 s for an improvement of 67.08%. These remarkable differences regarding accuracy and computation time show the efficiency of our proposal.

5   Conclusions

We introduced a novel Markov chain-based isolation method to analyze the reliability in subnetworks of the Colombian natural gas system. Remarkably, our approach seeks for the parameters of a Virtual Equivalent Well (VEW) to perform approximated reliability analysis based on the optimal operational cost. We tested our method on a real data set concerning a simplified 19-node Colombian natural gas system. Obtained results demonstrated how our proposal drastically improves the computation time while preserves the accuracy in the calculation of the optimal operational cost. Indeed, our isolation method allows a fast and accurate evaluation of investment alternatives for enhancing the subnetwork reliability. Although a particular case concerning the Colombian case was tested, our method can be employed to analyze subnetworks in any natural gas system with any topology, including the cyclic one. As future work, authors plan to introduce non-parametric techniques for modeling the system uncertainty. Moreover, using Bayesian inference to support the computation of the VEW parameters is a future line of research.

Acknowledgments. Research under grants provided by the project "Desarrollo de una plataforma para el cálculo de confiabilidad en la operación interdependiente de los sistemas de gas natural y sector eléctrico de Colombia que permita evaluar alternativas de inversión y regulación para optimizar los costos de operación", with code: 1110-745-58696, funded by Colciencias. Moreover, author W. González-Vanegas was supported under the project with code: E6-18-2, funded by Universidad Tecnológica de Pereira, Colombia.

References

1. Alam, M.S., Paramati, S.R., Shahbaz, M., Bhattacharya, M.: Natural gas, trade and sustainable growth: empirical evidence from the top gas consumers of the developing world. Appl. Econ. **49**(7), 635–649 (2017)
2. Billinton, R., Allan, N.: Reliability Evaluation of Engineering Systems. Springer, Boston (1992). https://doi.org/10.1007/978-1-4899-0685-4
3. EIA (Energy Information Administration): International Energy Statistics (2018). https://www.eia.gov/naturalgas/. Accessed 25 Apr 2018
4. Fan, M.W., Gong, J., Wu, Y., Kong, W.H.: The gas supply reliability analysis of natural gas pipeline network based on simplified topological structure. J. Renew. Sustain. Energy **9**(4), 045503 (2017)
5. Holz, F., Richter, P.M., Egging, R.: A global perspective on the future of natural gas: resources, trade, and climate constraints. Rev. Environ. Econ. Policy **9**(1), 85–106 (2015). https://doi.org/10.1093/reep/reu016
6. Meneses, L.A.E., Piamba, A.F.C.: Gas market vision in Colombia. In: 2012 IEEE International Symposium on Alternative Energies and Energy Quality (SIFAE), pp. 1–6. IEEE (2012)
7. Silverman, B.: Density Estimation for Statistics and Data Analysis. Routledge, London (2018)
8. SNC-Lavalin Itansuca, Freyre: Reliability study and risk analysis for production wells capacities (2012). (in Spanish). http://apolo.creg.gov.co/Publicac.nsf/52188526a7290f8505256eee0072eba7/ed90092e974f3bb3052579b9006af5c2/$FILE/CIRCULAR011-2012. Accessed 21 Apr 2018
9. UPME (Unidad de Planeación Minero Energética): Indicative plan for natural gas supply (2016). (in Spanish). http://www1.upme.gov.co/Hidrocarburos/Estudios%202014-_2016/Plan_Transitorio_Absatecimiento_Gas_Natural_Abril_2016.pdf. Accessed 21 Apr 2018
10. Villada, J., Olaya, Y.: A simulation approach for analysis of short-term security of natural gas supply in Colombia. Energy Policy **53**, 11–26 (2013)
11. Word Energy Council: The Role of Natural Gas (Perspective from the 2016 World Energy Scenarios). https://www.worldenergy.org/publications?year=2017&s. Accessed 21 Apr 2018

Implementation of the AODV Routing Protocol for Message Notification in a Wireless Sensor Microgrid

Elvis Gaona-García[1]($\boxtimes$), Sergio Palechor-Mopán[2], Laura Murcia-Sierra[2], and Paulo Gaona-García[2]

[1] Electronic Engineering, Universidad Distrital Francisco José de Caldas, Bogotá D.C., Colombia
egaona@udistrital.edu.co
[2] Computer Engineering, Universidad Distrital Francisco José de Caldas, Bogotá D.C., Colombia
{sdpalechorm,lmmurcias}@correo.udistrital.edu.co,
pagaonag@udistrital.edu.co

Abstract. This paper analyzes the behavior of the AODV routing protocol applied in a telecommunication network that transmits information for the management of the energy resources of an electric microgrid. Each node represents a sensor that captures primary data on voltage, current, phase, and frequency to be sent to a central node; in the opposite direction it receives instructions to activate or deactivate loads or sources. The implementation was performed with Raspberry Pi3 devices, encoding the routing protocol in Python 2.7. The network tests involve two topologies (trees and mesh). Through the tests, service quality metrics such as delay, throughput, and PDR were compared.

Keywords: AODV · Microgrid · Raspberry Pi3 · Python · Delay Throughput · PDR

1 Introduction

Wireless networks are currently used in a variety of applications, and this technology is spreading rapidly. However, most depend on infrastructures such as access points and routers; this makes communication in dynamic topologies difficult. As a result, ad-hoc networks have emerged, that is, decentralized networks that allow better communication even when there is mobility at the nodes; they provide flexibility and autonomy as there is no need for central management.

With the emergence of these networks, there is a need to implement routing protocols that can easily adapt to changes that may occur. The choice of these routing protocol to be implemented on communication networks on microgrids is fundamental, as it is necessary to satisfy the network system requirements for Neighborhood Area Networks (NAN) applications on microgrids, such as low

J. C. Figueroa-García et al. (Eds.): WEA 2018, CCIS 916, pp. 357–369, 2018.
https://doi.org/10.1007/978-3-030-00353-1_32

latency and high reliability. The distribution of information in these networks depends principally on node quantity and the network topology, by which it is necessary to analyze the most appropriate routing protocol that ensures compliance of communication requirements for smart grids and microgrids. To achieve this goal there are two types of routing protocols, on the one hand, proactive protocols are proposed; each node maintains routes to the other nodes available on the network, and the creation and maintenance of these routes is carried out through periodic updates. On the other hand, there are reactive protocols, which calculate the routes as they are needed and in their tables store only information on the active communications.

This paper shows the analysis of the time delay and the throughput obtained in the implementation of the reactive AODV protocol in two communication network topologies such as tree and mesh topologies, in order to analyze the performance of the data routing protocol applied to the operating conditions in an isolated rural microgrid. These results are compared with the latency parameters acceptable to data transfer in a microgrid and with the values obtained when simulating the routing protocol with the NS2 tool.

To this end, the paper is divided into six sections distributed as described below: Sect. 2 shows the characteristics of isolated rural microgrids and their operating parameters as a function of the time of data collection for their control. Section 3 details the operation of the reactive protocol to be analyzed. Section 4 presents the parameters and configurations of the implementation. Section 5 presents an analysis of the results obtained. Finally, Sect. 6 presents the conclusions of the study.

2   Rural Microgrids

An electric microgrid is a system composed of loads and generators that works independently of the electrical distribution network, created in order to supply energy to a certain local area.

The main elements of microgrids are loads, distributed generators, and storage devices or controllable loads that allow them to operate in a coordinated manner [1]. The objective is to save energy, to minimize costs, and to increase reliability through the use of digital technology and the integration of renewable sources [2].

Due to the high economic and technical costs of traditional electricity networks in the electrification of hard-to-reach areas, rural microgrids are emerging [3]. These are a good alternative when what is required is greater reliability and quality of energy, also allowing these small communities to control energy use [4].

2.1   Operation Parameters in Rural Microgrids

Factors such as the quality, size, characteristics of the electrical distribution, number of generating sources, and power demand define the technical principles and architecture of a microgrid. To define the type of current to be operated by the system (direct or alternating), the technology used and the energy management strategy must be considered; for example, while batteries and photovoltaic generation provide direct current (DC), others such as generators and hydroelectric power stations provide alternating current (AC). There are also hybrid microgrids, in which a bidirectional inverter is installed to control the power supply between the alternating current bars and the battery [5].

The routing protocols to be implemented in this type of wireless network must coincide with the latency requirements according to the application to be used in the microgrid. Table 1 shows the applications and their latency.

Table 1. Latency requirements in the operation of a communication network on a microgrid (Source: [6])

Application	Latency
AMI (Advanced Meter Infrastructure)	2–15 s
Demand response	500 ms–few minutes
Knowledge of behavior on wide area	20–200 ms
Storage and distributed energy resources	20 ms–15 s
Power transmission	2 s–5 min
Distributed management	100 ms–2 s

3   Reactive Wireless Routing Protocols

There are currently numerous routing protocols for wireless networks [7]. Depending on the topology, the scenario in which that topology is proposed, and the information to be transmitted, the appropriate protocol to be implemented is chosen.

The grid proposed in this paper, a microgrid capable of obtaining information on the power generated, the state of the batteries, and the consumption of the loads were analyzed in order to notify a coordinating node for the subsequent management of the energy resources of that grid, a reactive protocol is chosen to be used considering that there is data transfering on real time, it is necessary the calculation of routes on demand, that is, the route establishing will only be accomplished with a request sent from a sensor node.

With the use of this type of protocol, network resources are optimized, avoiding the sending of unnecessary packets [8]. This kind of scenario has been simulated previously, however as of today, it has not been implemented on a real-case rural microgrid. The AODV reactive protocol implemented for the communication of the nodes of this microgrid is described below.

3.1   AODV Routing Protocol

AODV is one of the most commonly used protocols in mobile ad-hoc networks. It is reactive, works on demand, and generates only a routing table when it is necessary to transmit a message to a particular destination. Therefore, it reduces control messages and regulates the energy consumption of the devices that use the protocol; the routing table is stored on each node to reduce the use of bandwidth [9] (Table 2).

The fields stored on the routing tables are described below [10].

Table 2. Routing table (Source: own elaboration)

Destination IP address	It is the IP address of the node to which information will be sent
Next hop	This entry identifies the next node necessary to reach the destination node
Destination sequence number	It refers to the sequence number of the destination node, obtained from the control information
Hop count	It represents the number of hops required to arrive from the source node to the destination node
Status	It identifies whether the route is active or inactive, by determining whether a new route can be used or should be discovered
Lifetime	Through this attribute, routes are discarded and deleted from the table once their useful life has expired, in order to avoid network overloads

This algorithm has two main phases: route discovery and route maintenance. Both phases are represented globally in Figs. 1 and 2 respectively.

3.1.1   Route Discovery

This phase occurs when a node needs to send a message to a destination node and does not have any valid route in its routing table. Then it broadcasts a route request packet (RREQ) to the destination node via broadcast; the neighbors of the originator node will receive this RREQ message. If there is no route to the destination, the number of hops must be increased and this packet must be also broadcasted. At the same time, they must store a route to the node that caused the request on their routing table, taking into account the information they receive in the packet. If it does have a route to the destination, it generates a route response packet (RREP) [11]. Table 3 shows the structure of the RREQ message.

In order to avoid repeated information, each RREQ will be identified with an unique number (which increases each time a node issues a new packet) and with

Table 3. RREQ message format (Source: own elaboration)

Message type
Sender
Originator IP address
Originator sequence number
Unique identifier
Destination IP address
Destination sequence number
Hop count

the sequence number of the originator of the request. Thus, when an intermediate node processes this packet, it will discard it if it notices that it has already analyzed the same request from the same sender [12].

If an RREQ packet arrives at the destination node, it must create or update the route as appropriate and diffuse an RREP via unicast. When an intermediate node receives this RREP, it also diffuses the packet via unicast, considering the reverse routes stored on the routing tables through which the RREQ was transmitted. Table 4 shows the structure of the RREP message.

The protocol uses two sequence numbers: the sequence number of the source keeps information updated for the route contrary to the source, and the sequence number of the destination helps determine whether the route submitted can be accepted by the source or whether a more recent route exists [13].

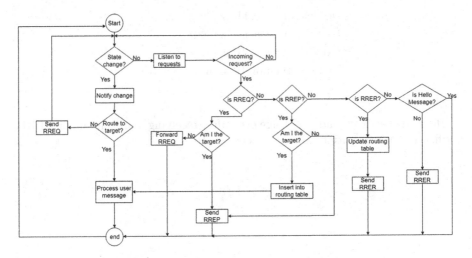

Fig. 1. Flowchart: route discovery (Source: own elaboration)

Table 4. RREP message format (Source: own elaboration)

Message type
Sender
Originator IP address
Hop count
Destination IP address
Destination sequence number

3.1.2   Route Maintenance

In this phase periodic messages called hello messages are used. These are transmitted to the neighboring nodes in order to notify that a node is still present in the network. When after a while a "hello" is not received from a neighbor, a route error packet (RERR) is generated to the source node: the RERR contains the IP address of the node that has become inaccessible. Each intermediate node that processes the RERR will update the routes used by the node that is now inaccessible and continue to propagate the packet until the broken link notification has been communicated to all nodes in the network [14,15]. Table 5 shows the structure of the RRER message.

Table 5. RRER message format (Source: own elaboration)

Message type
Sender
Destination IP Address
Destination sequence number
Extra destination IP address
Extra destination IP sequence number

If a node needs to send a message even after receiving a broken link or RERR notification, it can initiate a route discovery [16].

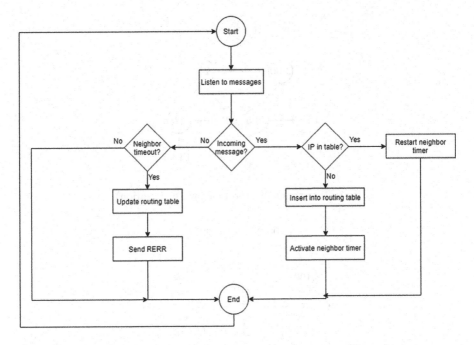

Fig. 2. Flowchart: route maintenance (Source: own elaboration)

4 Methodology

The network topologies used correspond to the configuration of an isolated micro-grid, where a sensor node needs to communicate a change of state in its energy source to the others, so that each one can store this information and make decisions that affect the supply from the microgrid. Figure 3 shows the tree topology and Fig. 4 shows the mesh topology. In both topologies, nodes are tagged with the last byte of their static address corresponding to the network address 192.168.0.0. Both scenarios include static nodes with static IP addresses, that is, the topology is not modified unless a node is shut down or external conditions prevent connection to it; in either case, inactive routes will only change state (RRER) but will not be deleted. For this purpose, a SQLite database was used; it stores the routing tables in order to maintain the routes to the different nodes.

Additionally, the separation of the nodes is six meters, configured at low power, in order to facilitate the implementation and obtaining of results in open field.

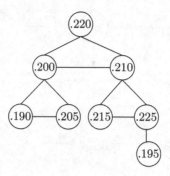

Fig. 3. Tree topology (Source: own elaboration)

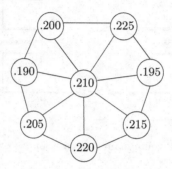

Fig. 4. Mesh topology (Source: own elaboration)

The sending of messages is performed by a single originator (.220) that constantly plays a fixed size message of 100 bytes every 30 s. This message represents a change of state at the originator node.

The algorithm is implemented and run on Raspberry Pi3 B devices, with Wi-Fi transmitters in ad-hoc mode and their power (Txpower) at 3 dBm to limit the range of coverage. For the operation of the program, different modules were developed, coded in Python 2.7.13 only. These are the modules:

– Neighbors and network node discovery script: *find_neighbors.py*, which lists the IP addresses of all the nodes found on the network through flooding (see Fig. 5).
– AODV Protocol script: *aodv_protocol.py*. It comprises the routines and subroutines for sending, receiving, and processing request messages (see Fig. 6).
– Main script: *main.py*. It is the one in charge of instantiating and integrating the functionalities of the two modules described above.

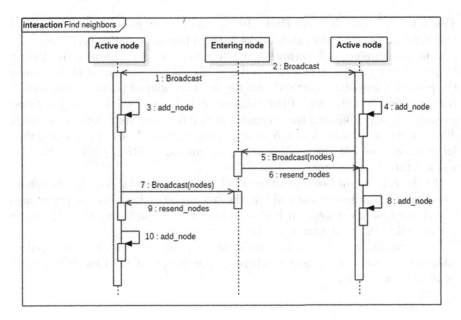

Fig. 5. Sequence diagram: find_neighbors.py (Source: own elaboration)

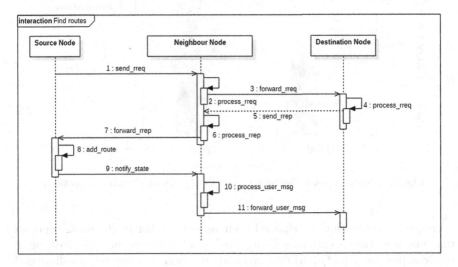

Fig. 6. Sequence diagram: aodv_protocol.py (route finding) (Source: own elaboration)

5 Results

This section presents a comparison between the results of simulations in the NS-2 tool and the implementations performed with the Raspberries Pi3 B devices.

Throughput, Packet Delivery Ratio (PDR), and latency metrics were considered to determine how the algorithm works in the different scenarios proposed.

The measurement of network reliability is performed through the Packet Delivery Ratio (PDR); this metric is defined as the percentage relation between the packets successfully received and the total number of packets transmitted. Network testing begins with PDR measurement. A set of five tests is performed on each topology, allowing the originator device to notify its status to the seven different nodes, for a total of 175 messages transmitted. It should be noted that for this measurement the sending of request messages (RREQ, RREP, RERR) was not taken into account.

Figure 7 shows the behavior of the PDR in the proposed topologies. As can be seen, in both simulation and real life, the tree topology has a higher percentage of successful packet delivery. It is also evident that in real life a lower percentage is obtained than in the simulation for the two topologies.

Additionally, it is evident that reliability requirement described by Saputro, Akkaya and Uludag in [6] is met, where it's specified that PDR for AODV must be higher than 91.4%.

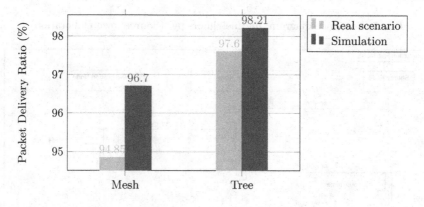

Fig. 7. Average Packet Delivery Ratio (PDR) (Source: own elaboration)

Figure 8 shows that the channel occupancy is higher in the mesh topology; this is because the central node, being directly related to seven nodes (see Fig. 4), receives, processes, and distributes more information than any intermediate node in tree topology.

Figure 9 shows that the mesh topology has lower latency than the tree topology, both in the simulation and in the tests performed on Raspberry devices, that is, less time in the transmission of messages from the originator node to the other sensor nodes. Given the latency requirements for the operation of a communication network over a microgrid described in Table 1, both topologies are in the range of applications: knowledge of wide area behavior, distributed energy resources, and distributed storage and management. In contrast, for

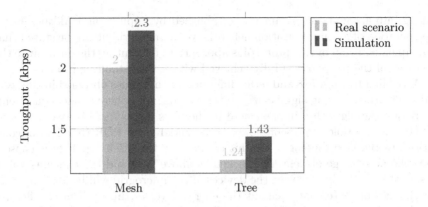

Fig. 8. Average throughput per topology (Source: own elaboration)

"AMI applications, demand response and power transmission" the topologies are in a lower range than those described.

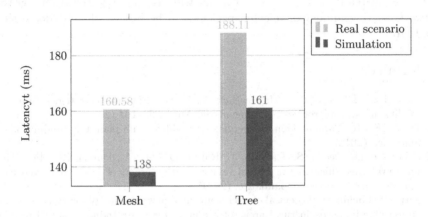

Fig. 9. Average latency per topology (Source: own elaboration)

6 Conclusions

In addition to the protocol script, it was implemented a module that let nodes know every single node within the network by broadcasting messages (flooding), in order to obtain a list with destination nodes for which a route must be found and send a message using AODV protocol. This module was proven and used together with the protocol to carry out the tests and obtain the results described below.

The AODV routing protocol presents stable latency (see Fig. 9), PDR (see Fig. 7) and throughput (see Fig. 8) metrics for both the mesh and tree topology.

Taking into account the parameters established by Saputro and Akkaya [6] for the operation of a communication network over a microgrid, it can be stated that the implementation of this protocol is appropriate for routing the data, since the objective of the microgrid is fully achieved within the established ranges.

According to Figs. 7, 8 and 9 the difference of the values obtained in the tests and simulations is not significant, so the results are coherent and equivalent. Therefore, the algorithm implemented in the tests meets its objective.

The mesh topology presents lower latency and lower PDR (94.85%) in comparison to the tree topology. For this case study, the mesh topology is chosen, since the percentage of delivered packets is above 94% and the transmission of messages is faster. In this way, the devices of the microgrid will be able to notify the changes of state that occur at the energy level in time and in an effective way. It is important to clarify that the difference between these topologies is not significant for this case, since there are few nodes and the difference in number of hops from the originator node to the other sensor nodes is minimal.

Although the tests presented represent a microgrid of eight nodes, it is expected that both the throughput in the network and the latency will increase by increasing the number of sensor nodes in the isolated microgrid. As for the PDR, the increase in the number of nodes will also increase the traffic on the network, so the number of rejected packets will be higher, thereby decreasing the PDR.

References

1. González, N., Cusgüen, C., Mojica-Nava, E., Pavas, A.: Control strategies for power quality in rural microgrids. UIS Ingenierías 16(2), 93–104 (2017)
2. Ducoy, F.J.R.: implantación de energías renovables en un planta de producción de amoniaco (2012)
3. Schnitzer, D., Deepa, S., Carvalo, J., Ranjit, D., Jay, A., Daniel, K.: Microgrids for Rural Electrification: a critical review of best practices based on seven case studies. United Nations Foundation (2014)
4. Raju, B., Sachin, B.: Potential of microsources, renewable energy sources and application of microgrids in rural areas of Maharashtra state India. Energy Procedia 14, 2012–2018 (2012)
5. De Alaminos, J., et al.: Estudio sobre las microrredes y su aplicaciÓn a proyectos de electrificacion de zonas rurales (2014)
6. Saputro, N., Akkaya, K., Uludag, S.: Survey a survey of routing protocols for smart grid communications. Comput. Netw. 56(11), 2742–2771 (2012). https://doi.org/10.1016/j.comnet.2012.03.027
7. Capella Hernández, J.V.: Redes inalámbricas de sensores: una nueva arquitectura eficiente y robusta basada en jerarquía dinámica de grupos. Ph.D. thesis, Universidad Politécnica de Valencia (2010)
8. Ding, Z., Liu, M., Lee, W., Wetz, D.: An autonomous operation microgrid for rural electrification. In: IEEE Industry Applications Society Annual Meeting, pp. 1–8 (2013)
9. Rocabado, S.H.: Caso de estudio de comunicaciones seguras sobre redes móviles. In: 3rd International Conference on Electrical Engineering and Information Communication Technology (ICEEICT), pp. 1–5 (2016)

10. Rojas Rivera, D.P.: Estudio comparativo basado en la simulación de escenarios entre los protocolos de encaminamiento saodv y aodv utilizados en redes ad-hoc. thesis (2015)
11. Dearle Jon, S.: Diseño y evaluación de un protocolo de encaminamiento para redes ad hoc basado en la congestión de red. thesis (2015)
12. Perkins, C., Roger, E.: Ad-hoc on-demand distance vector routing. In: Mobile Computing Systems and Applications (1999)
13. Holter, K.: Comparing AODV and OLSR. Essay (2005)
14. Bartolomé Arquillo, D.: Análisis de la distribución del tráfico en redes móviles ad-hoc conectadas a internet. thesis (2006)
15. Aguilar, D., León, P., Rojas, D.: Estudio comparativo sobre simulación de escenarios de protocolos saodv y aodv. Revista Tecnológica ESPOL - RTE **29**(1), 88–105 (2016)
16. Santos, A.M.: Comparativa de los protocolos aodv y olsr con un emulador de redes ad hoc. thesis (2006)

SNMP Converter and the Forward Data Collection as Management Method in Dynamic Distributed Networks

Mauricio Tamayo$^{(\boxtimes)}$, Henry Zarate$^{(\boxtimes)}$, and Jorge Ortíz Triviño$^{(\boxtimes)}$

Universidad Nacional de Colombia, Faculty of Engineering,
Av Carrera 30 No 45 - 03, Bogotá 111321, Colombia
{emtamayog,hzaratec,jeortizt}@unal.edu.co

Abstract. A method of network management based on the protocol conversion SNMP to others, like serial or UDP, to manage small
devices in a wireless sensor network is shown, whose reference framework combines the hierarchical network management with the dynamic,
distributed and heterogeneous characteristics of an Ad Hoc network and
how the SNMP protocol accomplish its habitual devices management
functions, and at the same time, some of its messages are used to build a
forward data collector that expands and contracts dynamically the storage capacity of the SNMP tables of the agent, adapting to the amount
of devices in the network.

Keywords: Network management · SNMP · Protocol conversion
Finite-state converter · Ad hoc · Distributed processes
Forward data collection

1 Introduction

This work is part the research project TLÖN, where a computational scheme
inspired in social models is proposed, considering justice, immanence, paradigm,
government, existence and essence concepts [1] and supported in a multiagent
system [2] which requires a management system. The results of the implementation of a protocol converter to include devices with administration restriction [3]
like small sensors, are shown in this paper. In the Sect. 2, it explains briefly the
methods to address some challenges in the network administration in Ad Hoc
networks. In the Sect. 3, the SNMP architecture is analyzed to understand the
protocol and use it to build the protocol converter. In the Sect. 4, it gives the
protocol design, how some challenges are faced, the message mapping and the
forward data collection concept. Finally, part of the results and conclusions of
the implementation are detailed.

2 Management Systems in Ad Hoc Networks

The researches about management systems for Ad Hoc networks are centered
in the protocol development as ANMP [4], GUERRILLA [5] or LiveNCM [6],

© Springer Nature Switzerland AG 2018
J. C. Figueroa-García et al. (Eds.): WEA 2018, CCIS 916, pp. 370–381, 2018.
https://doi.org/10.1007/978-3-030-00353-1_33

which are trying to mitigate the impact of the inherent to the operation of these networks as the energy limited usage, the wireless medium restrictions, the nodes heterogeneity, the autoconfiguration and automanagent. In addition, the continuous technology and scientific develops give tools to respond that challenges in turn new efforts and concepts appear like the use of a mathematical architecture named STEPS (Step Rate Storage) to model the collaborative management storage and data rate control in Wireless Sensor Networks (WSN) [7], the blockchain usage to develop distributed management systems in MANET [8] (Mobile Ad Hoc Networks), or the design of architectures based on SDN (Software Defined Networks) y NFV (Network Function Virtualization) to monitor the UAVs (Unmanned Aerial Vehicles) telemetries [9]. When we found such varied works about the network management in a lot of environments, it means that information is relevant and vital to the network operation and its services.

In general, the sensors are configured through serial connections, where they can be managed and programmed to capture and show the sensed information. If you want to obtain such information through a management protocol such as those mentioned above, we will find an incompatibility of protocols. LAM [10] mentions that this situation can be seen as a problem of interoperability of processes and could be solved using common protocol images and designing a protocol converter of finite state machines.

In this way and considering the challenges of managing small devices with management limitations, that is, they do not support management protocols, and processing restriction, it is proposed to use protocol conversion by combining a finite state converter with the functions of a proxy agent SNMP through serial ports [3] and extending its use to wireless interfaces.

This work is not focus to evaluate various management protocols or investigate if SNMP is the ideal protocol for managing the WSN. We are exploring for a method of administration through a standard protocol in telecommunications (SNMP has emerged as the most widely used and deployed network management framework [11]), integrating the Ad Hoc network management with other existed systems, perhaps in hierarchical topologies.

3   SNMP Architecture

SNMP is an application protocol by means of which the variables defined in the MIB (management information base) of the managed device can be inspected or altered [12]. The SNMP-based management systems use the client-server paradigm, composed of a manager, an agent, managed resources and SNMP messages [13].

The implementation of the SNMP architecture is called SNMP entity (see Fig. 1). It consists of an engine and one or more associated applications. The engine provides all the services of sending and receiving messages through the dispatcher, with the processing model supports and treats messages in all its versions, executes authentication and coding with the security model and access control to the managed objects [14]. The SNMP applications, which are defined in RFC3413 [15], make use of the services provided by the engine. They include the command generator (monitor and manipulate management data), command responder (provides access to management data), originator of notifications (initiates asynchronous messages), receiver of notifications (processes asynchronous messages) and proxy forwarder (forwarding of messages between entities) [13].

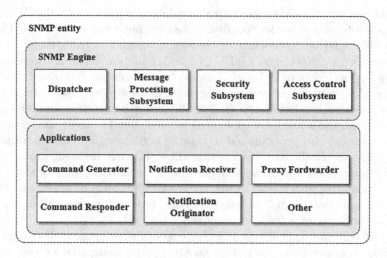

Fig. 1. SNMP entity architecture. Source: [14]

Abstract service interfaces are defined by primitives that determine the services and data elements when the service is invoked [14]. They describe the communication between each SNMP engine component, and between them and the applications modules. Some primitives are used to design the protocol: *sendPdu, processPdu, returnResponsePdu, processResponsePdu* and *errorIndication*.

4   Protocol Designed

Since the protocol conversion can be seen as a problem of interoperability of processes [10], the protocol design considers each protocol with its corresponded messages as an independent process that communicates with an intermediate entity. This design allows the execution of each process in a distributed way and permits to increase the range of protocols that could be converted to SNMP. In this work, the protocols serial and UDP were tested. An example is displayed in the Fig. 2, the process J (SNMP) sends messages to I (converter), which treats the packets, in case it has the information to answer, it will send the respective message to the source or in other cases a message is forward to the S process (serial) and when it sends back the responses, I puts the information in the MIB to answer to J. In this instance, the converter has SNMP agent functions to response SNMP requests or generating events and notifications, and a DTE (data terminal equipment) device generating serial communication commands.

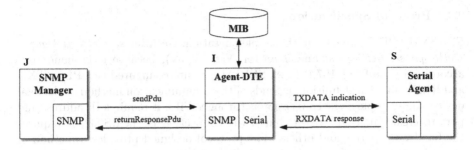

Fig. 2. Interoperability of JIS processes. Source: Own

Based on this, an operation scheme was designed so that non-SNMP devices could be managed. Finite state machines of each protocol were built independently using the service primitives that are necessary from each one to leave their protocol image. Then a relational finite state machine was integrated to establish the communication process between the two protocols. The final state machine shown in the Fig. 3 represents the flow of messages and their states.

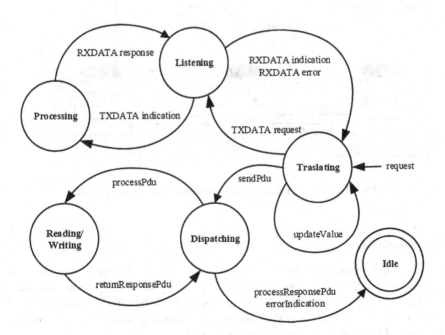

Fig. 3. Finite state machine. Source: Own

4.1   Protocol Specification

Five SNMP PDUs are used in this implementation: *GetRequest, GetNextRequest, GetResponse, SetRequest* and *Trap* (or *Notification*), because it is mandatory according to the RFC1157 [12]. At SERIAL site are configured two PDU: TXD and RXD; but their definition depends of the communication method of the final device, for example if the connection is through WiFi, it requires IP address and port to create an UDP socket, but if the connection is via RS232, it requires the baud rate, parity and others. The protocol designed provides a method of managing variables of operation of non-SNMP devices through the exchange of PDUs asymmetrically between SNMP and SERIAL entities (Fig. 4 shows the exchange of REQUEST, RESPONSE, TRAP, TXD and RXD PDUs) which have several procedures and mechanisms that are detailed in the functions of the protocol like timers, codification, auto-configuration, sequence and flow control.

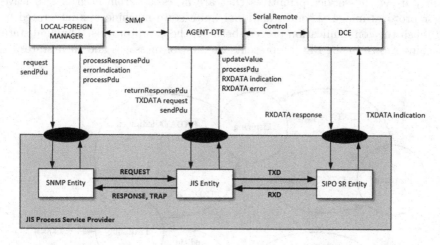

Fig. 4. Service and protocol communication. Source: Own

4.2   Challenges

Based on the experience during this development, we consider that the main challenges for a SNMP converter protocol (or even pure SNMP) to be used in an Ad Hoc network are heterogeneity, dynamism and distributed operations. Next, we explain how each of these challenges was addressed, which finally constitute the basis of the protocol architecture proposed.

Heterogeneity. Network management through SNMP requires the definition of objects in the MIB management information base, which is designed and built knowing the device, its functions and the things that can be measured. In this sense and when a network is heterogeneous, the complicated issue is not to manage a great diversity of devices, the difficult thing is to cover the management of equipment that are not known since they are not included in the MIB. One of the characteristics of Ad Hoc networks is self-configuration, so creating and/or modifying the MIBs autonomously is ideal, but it is a challenge that becomes, by itself, a rather complex job that is out of reach from this project.

The construction of the MIB was done employing the MIB Smithy software[1] whose design follows some recommendations of Walsh [16] like it must be syntactically correct, without mixing SMIv1 and SMIv2, validating the MIB in various compilers, etc. Thereby, with each object MIB, which are scalars, a conceptual table is created, using a tabular structure as mentioned in RFC2578 [17], generating an ordered collection of objects. For example, the OID 1.3.6.1.4.1.49843.1.1.1.2.1[2] is a table that represents a sensor that measures pressure and temperature like the BMP180 (see the MIB tree in the Fig. 7). Each object is configured as a table based on the dynamism of Ad Hoc networks.

Dynamism. WSNs undergo dynamic topology changes due to the entry or exit of a node from the network, although compared to MANETs these changes are made to a lesser extent [18]. To make dynamic connections through SNMP, the use of fixed OIDs for each object is omitted, since the number of hosts that are going to operate within the network is not known, while it is important to manage the reuse of physical and logical resources. For this reason tables are configured that have conceptual rows that allow the creation or elimination of instances of objects [17] through a columnar object called *RowStatus* whose value represents the state of its row in the SNMP table. There are six possible values that define this state: *active* (1), *notInService* (2), *notReady* (3), *createAndGo* (4), *createAndWait* (5), *destroy* (6) [19]. The value of *RowStatus* can be changed through *setRequest* commands, either with a string value or an integer value.

When a new device enters the network, an available row is searched to be assigned though a *setRequest* command, modifying the value of *RowStatus* with 4 or *createAndGo*. With this new row, a new OID is assigned adding a branch in its structure, e.g. the sensor BMP180 has the OID 1.3.6.1.4.1.49843.1.1.1.2.1, a new device of this type will be assigned to 1.3.6.1.4.1.49843.1.1.1.2.1.1 (add a branch) and if additional sensor is connected to the network, it will have the next OID 1.3.6.1.4.1.49843.1.1.1.2.1.2. When the device leaves the network, the row is deleted placing the value 6 or *destroy* in the *RowStatus* field, freeing the resource that can be used with new accesses to the network.

Distribution. Usually SNMP runs in centralized networks under the client-server model. In this work a part of this concept is kept in relation to the manager's queries to the agent and storage of the MIB. However, all processes of

---

[1] http://www.muonics.com/Products/MIBSmithy/.

[2] The object identification tree OID has numbering assigned by the IANA to the Universidad Nacional de Colombia. https://www.iana.org/assignments/enterprise-numbers/enterprise-numbers.

info request, data storage in the base of information management and detection of input/output of devices in the network, are done splitting them in multiple instances that can be executed in different devices with their own local resources interconnected into the network as a distributed computing system [20].

4.3   Architecture

The JIS entity architecture (see Fig. 5) is compound for various modules, each one executes complementary processes that could run in one or more devices on the network. **SNMP Agent** contains the necessary software to build the SNMP base tables defined in the MIB and it has the command responder and notifications originator functions, using a dispatcher as communication interface for the external applications and internal services. **Monitor** is a function to verify the topology changes and send commands to create or destroy rows in the SNMP table through the **modifyRow** module, which contains another methods to exchange data with the SNMP agent. The **updateData** module updates the management information in the SNMP tables, being the entity that interact with the SNMP and SERIAL protocols. Finally, **dataRequest** is responsible for the communication against non-SNMP devices, using their medium, protocol and specific format (serializing the information to send it through a TTY port or creating a UDP socket for wireless communications) to execute information requests whose answers they are collected and formatted and then stored in the SNMP tables of the agent using *setRequest* commands. When *getRequest* messages are sent from the SNMP manager, the agent already has the management information and responds in a typical SNMP process. All was programmed with Python language using already existing libraries such as pysnmp [21] and pyserial [22], both facilitate the developments in SNMP services and serial communications respectively.

Forward Data Collection. The automatic detection of a new device generates a new row within the table according to the type of device. A responsible process of validating the hosts registered in the tables, makes periodic request of each management object in each device, updating the fields in the table to maintain its consistency with the management information. So when the SNMP manager makes a query through a specific OID, the agent will be able to respond immediately. This process is named forward data collection (FDC), the stored information may or may not be used, but the process allows to increase the effectiveness in the delivery of the management information as well as its response time. Although there is some generation of traffic to obtain the information previously, this modality allows the development of distributed management processes and automatic detection of topology changes (input/output of host in the network) that could be executed by different devices within of the Ad Hoc network, for example one device can take the role of responder agent and another can be the forward collector, and in case the first mentioned leaves the network, another can assume its functions, even the same collector.

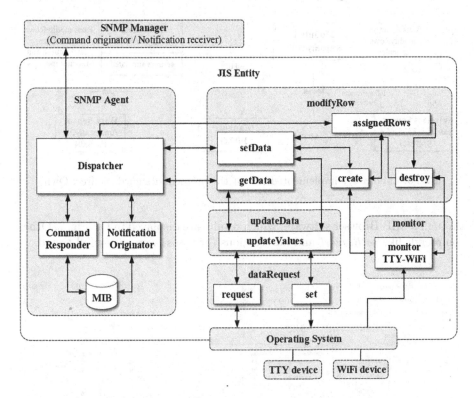

Fig. 5. Architecture of protocol converter SNMP to Serial or UDP. Source: Own

4.4   Implementation

The implementation of the protocol was done on a small network of sensors trying to cover different types of physical connections, virtualization, topologies and formats. This implementation design allows test the environment where the protocol is going to work, where three items were considered [23]: operating system, application and protocol-specific execution. The laboratory topology used is shown in the Fig. 6. Two Raspberry Pi B3 with Raspbian operating system were used to create an Ad Hoc network, where the modules shown in the architecture were charged in each device to operate in a distributed way. One of them was working as agent SNMP and the another one simulated various sensors for testing UDP protocol. Additionally, an Arduino UNO with ultrasound proximity sensor HC-SR04 was connected via USB to one Raspberry to test wired serial communication. Despite the project covers Ad Hoc networks, a BMP180 temperature and pressure sensor connected to a Nodemcu ESP8266 was also used with a WiFi connection in infrastructure mode. An external machine runs a SNMP network management application, fulfilling the functions of manager.

The tests include some habitual SNMP operations like get subtree information which generates a *getRequest* message for each object created in the MIB

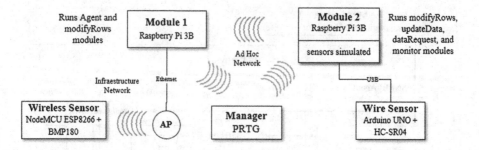

Fig. 6. Laboratory implemented to test the protocol designed. Source: Own

through a MIB Browser software, which results are displayed in the Fig. 7. Other commands like *setRequest* and notifications (or traps) were sucessfull tested.

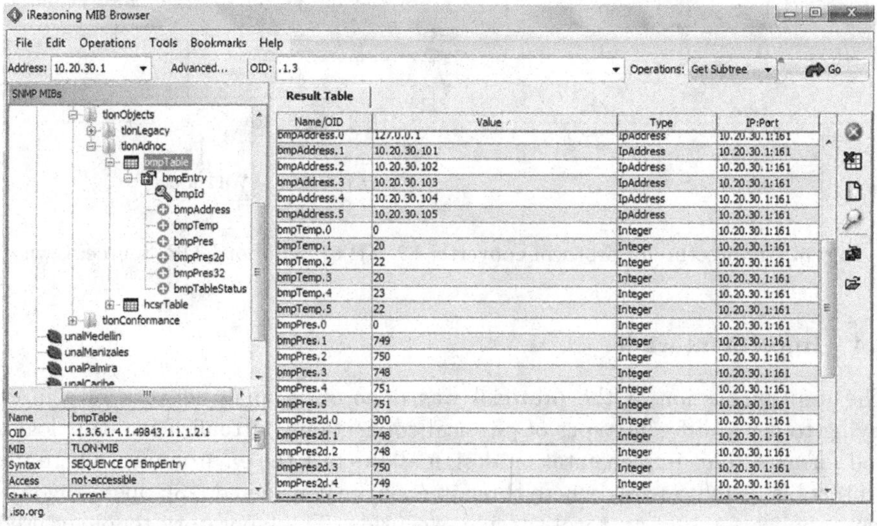

Fig. 7. Results of get subtree command: Own

The devices and their objects were created in the manager software to monitor periodically the sensors mentioned above, one of the historical graph is shown int the Fig. 8. While the manager sensed the devices, the exchange packets were capture with a sniffer as it is shown in the Fig. 9).

The checking procedure gave good results in both topologies, Ad Hoc and Infrastructure, and the SNMP manager was able to capture the data from all devices with their correspond connections and protocols. The monitor service detected topology changes creating a row in the SNMP table when the device access to the network and destroying when the device leaves the network.

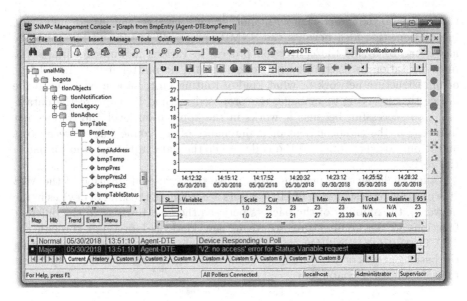

Fig. 8. Historical graph of a sensor Source: Own

```
⊿ Simple Network Management Protocol
    version: v2c (1)
    community: public
  ⊿ data: get-request (0)
    ⊿ get-request
        request-id: 9814
        error-status: noError (0)
        error-index: 0
      ⊿ variable-bindings: 1 item
        ⊿ 1.3.6.1.4.1.49843.1.1.1.2.1.1.4.4: Value (Null)
            Object Name: 1.3.6.1.4.1.49843.1.1.1.2.1.1.4.4 (iso.3.6.1.4.1.49843.1.1.1.2.1.1.4.4)
            Value (Null)

⊿ Simple Network Management Protocol
    version: v2c (1)
    community: public
  ⊿ data: get-response (2)
    ⊿ get-response
        request-id: 9814
        error-status: noError (0)
        error-index: 0
      ⊿ variable-bindings: 1 item
        ⊿ 1.3.6.1.4.1.49843.1.1.1.2.1.1.4.4: 748
            Object Name: 1.3.6.1.4.1.49843.1.1.1.2.1.1.4.4 (iso.3.6.1.4.1.49843.1.1.1.2.1.1.4.4)
            Value (Integer32): 748
```

Fig. 9. Get and get-response packets capture with sniffer. Source: Own

5   Conclusions and Future Work

The service architecture designed permits the conversion from multi-protocols
to SNMP, because the messages exchange between them is not done directly.
The concept of FDC is a method that uses the MIB tables as main data base of

the service, so the integration with another data bases schemes is not necessary, in addition, this idea permits the SNMP operations faster and minimize the lost data. To divide the conversion process in various modules facilitates the implementation in distributed networks. Finally, no matter if it is an Ad Hoc or infrastructure network or what kind of routing protocol is used, or even the device that is trying to manage, the proposed method for capture the data is executed successful, because it works in the application level and it does not intervene in the establishment or maintenance of the connexion between hosts and it only needs to include the code to get the data in the specific format of the device.

Some challenges are pending to face like the auto-configuration of the MIB (the creation or destruction of MIB objects according to the kind of devices in the network), the mobility of the packets between the host to reassign the different functions in the architecture, to create new kind of data types through the TEXTUAL-CONVENTION (for example the feelings of an agent) for associating the basic concepts of a social model in the multi-agent system and to implement the solution using containers.

Acknowledgments. We appreciate the contributions of the research group TLÖN's members from Universidad Nacional de Colombia as well as Michael Kirkham from Muonics, Inc. who gave us a free academical license of MIB Smithy software to develop the MIB used in this project.

References

1. TLÖN - Grupo de Investigación en Redes de Telecomunicaciones Dinámicas y Lenguajes de Programación Distribuidos and Universidad Nacional de Colombia. Proyecto TLÖN (2017). http://www.tlon.unal.edu.co
2. Zárate-Ceballos, H., Sanchez-Cifuentes, J.F., Ospina-López, J.P., Ortiz-Triviño, J.E.: 44. Sistema de Telecomunicaciones Social-Inspirado mediante Comunidades de Agentes, p. 1. Cicom (2015)
3. García, M.T., Zarate, H., Ortíz Triviño, J.: Protocol conversion approach to include devices with administration restriction on a framework of reference of management network. In: Figueroa-García, J.C., López-Santana, E.R., Villa-Ramírez, J.L., Ferro-Escobar, R. (eds.) WEA 2017. CCIS, vol. 742, pp. 72–83. Springer, Cham (2017). https://doi.org/10.1007/978-3-319-66963-2_8
4. Chen, W., Jain, N., Singh, S.: ANMP: ad hoc network management protocol. IEEE J. Sel. Areas Commun. **17**(8), 1506–1531 (1999)
5. Shen, C.C., Jaikaeo, C., Srisathapornphat, C., Huang, Z.: The Guerrilla management architecture for ad hoc networks. In: Proceedings of IEEE MILCOM, pp. 1–6 (2002)
6. Jacquot, A., Chanet, J.P., Hou, K.M., De Sousa, G., Monier, A.: A new management method for wireless sensor networks. 2010 The 9th IFIP Annual Mediterranean Ad Hoc Networking Workshop (Med-Hoc-Net), pp. 1–8 (2010)
7. Kabashi, A.H., Elmirghani, J.M.H.: Adaptive rate control & collaborative storage management for challenged ad hoc & sensor networks employing static & dynamic heterogeneity. IEEE International Symposium on Personal, Indoor and Mobile Radio Communications, PIMRC (3) (2010)

8. Goka, S., Shigeno, H.: Distributed management system for trust and reward in mobile ad hoc networks. In: 2018 15th IEEE Annual Consumer Communications & Networking Conference (CCNC), pp. 1–6 (2018)

9. White, K.J.S., Pezaros, D.P., Knudson, M.D.: A programmable resilient high-mobility SDN + NFV architecture for UAV telemetry monitoring, pp. 2–7, June 2016

10. Lam, S.S.: Protocol conversion. IEEE Trans. Softw. Eng. **14**(3), 353–362 (1988)

11. Kurose, J.F., Ross, K.W.: Computer Ntworking: A Top-Down Approach, 6th edn. Pearson, London (2013)

12. Case, J., Davin, J., Fedor, M., Schoffstall, M.: RFC 1157 - A Simple Network Management Protocol (SNMP) (1990)

13. Miller, M.A.: Managing Internetworks with SNMP, 3rd edn. Wiley, Foster City (1999)

14. Harrington, D., Presuhn, R., Wijnen, B.: RFC 3411 - An Architecture for Describing Simple Network Management Protocol (SNMP) Management Frameworks (2002)

15. Levi, D., Meyer, P., Stewart, B.: RFC 3413 - Simple Network Management Protocol (SNMP) Applications (2002)

16. Walsh, L.: SNMP MIB Handbook, 2nd edn. Wyndham Press, Stanwood (2008)

17. McCloghrie, K., Perkins, D., Case, J., Rose, M., Waldbusser, S.: RFC2578 - Structure of Management Information Version 2 (SMIv2) (1999)

18. Benhaddou, D., Al-Fuqaha, A. (eds.): Wireless Sensor and Mobile Ad-Hoc Networks. Springer, New York (2015). https://doi.org/10.1007/978-1-4939-2468-4

19. McCloghrie, K., Perkins, D., Case, J., Rose, M., Waldbusser, S.: RFC2579 - Textual Conventions for SMIv2 Status (1999)

20. Sinha, P.K.: Fundamentals. In: Distributed Operating Systems: Concepts and Design, vol. 1, chap. 1, 1st edn, p. 764. Wiley-IEEE Press (1997)

21. Etingof, I.: Python SNMP library for Python (2017). http://pysnmp.sourceforge.net/

22. Liechti, C.: Welcome to pySerial's documentation (2015). https://pythonhosted.org/pyserial/

23. König, H.: Protocol Engineering. Springer, Heidelberg (2012). https://doi.org/10.1007/978-3-642-29145-6

Miscellaneous Applications

Miscellaneous Applications

How Does the Toolbox Choice Affect ERP Analysis?

Andrés Quintero-Zea[1]([⊠]) [iD], Mónica Rodríguez[1], María Isabel Cano[1],
Karen Melisa Pava[1], Manuela Suaza[1], Natalia Trujillo[2,3],
and José David López[1] [iD]

[1] SISTEMIC, Engineering Faculty, Universidad de Antioquia UDEA,
Calle 70, No. 52-21, Medellín, Colombia
`andres.quintero@udea.edu.co`
[2] GISAME, Facultad Nacional de Salud Pública, Universidad de Antioquia UDEA,
Calle 62 No. 52-59, Medellín, Colombia
[3] Neuroscience Group, Universidad de Antioquia UDEA,
Calle 62 No. 52-59, Medellín, Colombia

Abstract. Event-related potentials (ERP) help understanding neural activity related to both sensory and cognitive processes. But due to their low SNR, EEG signals must be processed to obtain the ERP waveform. Such a processing can be carried using a number of toolboxes that may provide different results on further analyses. Here, we present an experimental design that quantitatively evaluates the effect of choosing a particular toolbox in the further ERP analysis. We select three widely used toolboxes: EEGLAB, SPM12, and Fieldtrip to process EEG data acquired from a Flanker-like task with a Biosemi Active-Two device. Results show that although there is not a significant difference between ERP obtained from each toolbox, the choice of a specific toolbox may have subtle effects in the resulting ERP waveforms.

Keywords: EEG · ERP · Flanker task · Toolbox · EEGLAB
SPM12 · Fieldtrip

1 Introduction

Electroencephalography (EEG) is a noninvasive technique that records the electrical activity of the brain [1]. EEG provides an excellent medium to understand cognition and brain function. Furthermore, time-locked EEG activity or event-related potential (ERP) allow researchers to analyze human brain activity associated with presentation of specific stimuli [2].

ERP records neural responses of task-related events with high temporal resolution, and constitutes a convenient method to explore dynamics of brain behavior. ERP technique has been used for decades to answer questions about sensory,

---

A. Quintero-Zea and M. Rodríguez—These authors contributed equally to the work.

© Springer Nature Switzerland AG 2018
J. C. Figueroa-García et al. (Eds.): WEA 2018, CCIS 916, pp. 385–394, 2018.
https://doi.org/10.1007/978-3-030-00353-1_34

cognitive, motor, and emotion-related processes in clinical disorders such as mild cognitive impairment [3], dementia [4], or emotional processing [5,6].

An ERP waveform is described according to latency and amplitude [2], and it can be split in two categories: the early exogenous components peaking within the first 100 ms after stimulus; and the later endogenous components that reflect how the subject evaluates the stimulus. Among these later components is the N200 (or N2), which is associated with conflict detection. N2 is the negative deflection peaking at about 200 ms after stimulus presentation. It is evoked during tasks in which two or more incompatible response tendencies are activated simultaneously, such as go/no-go or Flanker tasks [5].

To obtain the ERP waveform, the recorded EEG activity has to be processed off-line by means of a computational program. There are a number of freely available software packages, commonly known as toolboxes, to analyze these data. Despite the large number of studies investigating brain function by means of ERP, there is not a systematic effort to examine how different software packages can affect the findings and their associated neurophysiological interpretation. It is reasonable to expect that the results obtained with different toolboxes may differ, but it would be necessary a proper statistical analysis to determine if they are significant.

The aim of this paper is to evaluate the impact of the toolbox choice on the ERP components. To this end, we selected three widely used toolboxes to obtain the ERP waveforms for a Flanker task: EEGLAB [7], SPM12 [8,9], and Fieldtrip [10]. Further, we applied a repeated measures experimental design on the N2 component latencies and peak amplitudes to quantitatively evaluate differences among them.

2   Experimental Data

EEG data were acquired by the mental health (GISAME) research group of Universidad de Antioquia (Medellín, Colombia). Participants were 20 adults with mean age of 35 years and standard deviation of 9 years. This convenience sample was 100% Colombian, and included 15 men and five women. Volunteers that informed having psychiatric and neurological disorders were excluded from the study. All subjects participated voluntarily and signed an informed consent in agreement with the Helsinki declaration. The research protocol was approved by ethical committee of University of Antioquia (Medellín, Colombia).

EEG registers were acquired with a 64-electrode BIOSEMI EEG ActiveTwo system [11] at a sampling rate of 2048 Hz and 24-bit resolution. The electrodes were placed according to the international 10–20 system [12].

ERPs were recorded using a Flanker task [13]. Participants were seated in a comfortable chair in front of a computer monitor at a distance of 60 cm. Participants were asked to try not to blink, move, nor speak while performing the task. The impedances were maintained below 10 kΩ to obtain an adequate conductivity between scalp and electrodes.

The Flanker attentional emotional task involves violent and neutral situations. The stimuli were 60 real violent images, 60 neutral real images and as distraction 60 drawings of animate and inanimate objects. The participants were specifically instructed that the monitor would screen a central stimulus that could contain either a real picture or a black and white drawing. When a real image appeared on the center should be classified between a violent or neutral image, or if a drawing appeared in the center position should be classified as animate or inanimate. Four events result per each stimuli: threatening periphery (TP), threatening center (TC), neutral periphery (NP), and neutral center (NC) depending on the position of the real images. Further details about the experiment protocol have been previously described in [13].

3 Methods

We selected three toolboxes to process the Flanker-task related EEG data: EEGLAB[1] [7], FieldTrip[2] [10], and SPM12[3] [8,9]. We have performed a similar data processing with each toolbox and obtained their respective ERPs. The differences on data processing obey to actual differences on the software packages, as they not always offer the same methods for specific stages. Once we obtain the ERPs with each software, we perform two analyses aiming to find variations on typical ERP parameters: latency and peak intensity of N2, and an ANOVA test over the same component.

3.1 Data Processing

The stages of data processing are not standard but procedures do not largely vary from those depicted in [14,15]. Most variations on these stages are due to specific requirements of the task or due to the acquisition device characteristics. For the task and device used for experimentation, we perform off-line the following stages: Downsampling, filtering, bad channels rejection, re-referencing, artifact rejection, epoching, baseline correction, and visual noise rejection. These stages are presented below:

Downsampling: The high temporal resolution of most EEG devices is not necessary for most studies, but it may cause high computational burden; then, most authors reduce the frequency sample to around 200–500 Hz. The term downsampling refers to the process of reducing the sampling rate of a signal. In this case from 2048 Hz to 500 Hz. This stage was equally implemented in the three toolboxes.

---

[1] http://sccn.ucsd.edu/eeglab/.

[2] http://fieldtrip.fcdonders.nl/.

[3] http://www.fil.ion.ucl.ac.uk/spm/.

Filtering: To reduce environmental artifacts (such as power line noise) in the EEG data and to extract specific frequency bands associated with human cognition, it is necessary to filter the signals. A band-pass IIR digital filter was applied in all toolboxes. The cutoff frequencies were 0.5 and 30 Hz to elicit the typical frequency band of interest for ERP studies.

Bad Channels Rejection: Once the signal is filtered, it is desired to remove and interpolate those channels with low recording SNR. For EEGLAB case, bad channels are detected using `findNoisyChannels()` function from PREP pipeline library [16] and further interpolated using the spherical interpolation function `eeg_interp()`. In FieldTrip, this step is performed with `ft_channelrepair()` function, which finds the time series of the missing or damaged channel using a weighted average of its neighbors. SPM12 only offers the option of setting a channel as bad without interpolation for further processing. For such a reason, interpolation was not performed in SPM12.

Off-line Re-referencing: Next step consists on re-referencing the signals using a common reference for all channels. In this case, EEG data was re-referenced to the average of all electrodes.

Artifact Rejection: EEG signals are known to be contaminated with noise artifacts. The most common physiological artifacts are perhaps those generated by muscles. This includes eyes blinking, eye movements (EOG), muscular contractions (EMG), cardiac signals (ECG), and pulsations [17]. In addition, breathing and body movement can cause alterations in EEG signals. There are additional artifacts caused by the skin-electrode connection; if there are deformities, such as scars, they can change the impedance. Each toolbox offers different algorithms to reduce the impact of artifacts.

In SPM12, we used visual artifact rejection `spm_eeg_ft_artefact_visual()`. This tool is a FieldTrip function which is included in the SPM12 toolbox. This function allows browsing through the large amount of data in a MATLAB GUI by showing a summary of all channels and trials. The user visually identifies the trials or data segments that are contaminated, and selects those to be removed from the data.

In EEGLAB and FieldTrip, we used the Independent Component Analysis (ICA) [18] algorithm for artifact rejection. This methodology is widely used in EEG because ICA allows decomposing the signals into different independent components (in terms of variance). Some of these components are expected to be sources of artifacts. In this case, all components are presented as images to the user, whose must manually remove those considered as noise based.

Epoching, Baseline Correction and Visual Noise Rejection: After identifying and removing artifacts, the registers are segmented from 200 ms and 800 ms prior and after the stimulus, respectively. Each type of stimulus described in Sect. 2 is known as condition and constitutes a kind of epoch or trial. In our experimental design, we have four conditions leading to four epoched data types: threatening periphery (TP), threatening center (TC), neutral periphery (NP), and neutral center (NC).

Once epoched, we are able to remove very low frequency noise that may affect the zero level among trials. Trials are then baseline corrected by determining the trend of the baseline before the stimulus (time window -200 to 0 ms, being 0 ms the stimulus trigger time), and then removing this trend of the rest of the window (0 to 800 ms). Each trial is inspected for leftover noise to make sure that only clean segments go forward for later analysis. Finally, epoched averaged data per condition of all participants are combined in a 3D matrix (channels × time points × trials) which forms the basis for all further ERP analysis.

3.2 Data Analysis

To evaluate differences in ERPs, we focused data analysis within a time window of 180 to 240 ms to obtain the peak amplitude and latency of the N2 component. This time window is adopted after a visual inspection of the grand averages, and it is similar to those reported in previous studies (e.g. [19]). Only two electrodes (F3, PO3) are used for the successive statistical analysis.

The statistical analysis consists on a one-way repeated-measures ANOVA aimed to compare variations due to the toolbox used on amplitude and latency of the ERP-N2 component. This analysis is performed using the Statistical Package for Social Sciences (IBM SPSS version 23.0 for Windows).

4 Results

In this section, we present differences on peak amplitudes and latencies of N2 component between the waveforms obtained with the three toolboxes. From the topographic maps shown in Fig. 1 maps seem roughly similar. Such likelihood is not present in the map obtained with EEGLAB for the threatening center stimulus. Smaller differences were observed between FieldTrip and SPM12.

The grand average ERPs at selected electrodes are depicted in Figs. 2 and 3. Note that waveforms obtained from EEGLAB exhibited lower N2 peak amplitudes, being more notorious at the central condition. Figure 2 also shows visual differences on the EEGLAB ERP in the late positive potential (LPP) component for latencies above 300 ms. This difference is extended to the three toolboxes in the central condition of Fig. 3. Although these differences in LPP are not part of the window of interest and are consistent among conditions and sensors (i.e., they should not affect posterior analysis within single software), these results demonstrate that there exist confidence issues for performing analyses on this window. No latency variations are observable.

Descriptive statistics for peak amplitudes and latencies are summarized in Table 1. In terms of amplitude, a consistent trend is observed: in all cases EEGLAB presented the lower amplitudes, followed by FieldTrip and then by SPM12. However, the variance was close among toolboxes and in all cases larger than mean variations. PO3 presented larger variance than F3, which is expected as the sensor is farther from the source of neural activity.

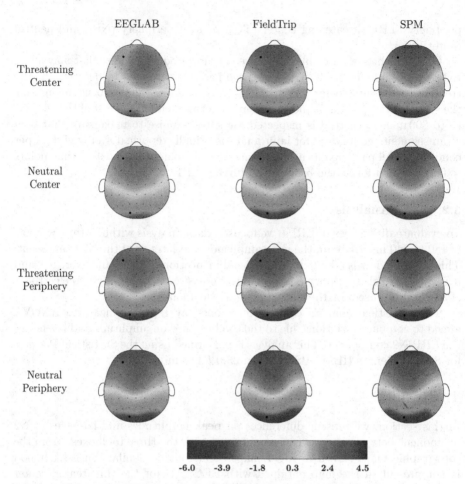

Fig. 1. Topographic maps of the averaged EEG amplitude (in µV) within the 180 to 240 ms window. Big black dots represent the selected electrodes F3 and PO3.

Regarding latency there are not clear trends among toolboxes. They are indeed close to each other, being 6.9 ms the largest variation for a single condition (between FieldTrip and EEGLAB on TP-PO3). Their variance is consistent too.

Table 2 shows results of the one-way repeated-measures ANOVA. These results show that there was not a significant main effect of the toolbox on the average peak amplitude nor latency in any of the conditions (TC, TP, NC, NP). This result is expected because as observed in Figs. 2 and 3 the separation of the ERP obtained with EEGLAB was not outside the confidence region. Besides, as presented in Table 1, these smaller amplitude values were consistent among conditions and sensors, and there were not observable latency variations.

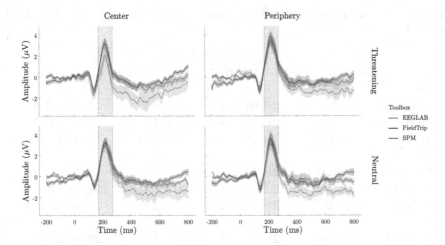

Fig. 2. Grand average ERPs recorded at F3 electrode. The waveforms obtained with the different toolboxes are overlaid for the threatening center stimuli (left-top), the threatening periphery stimuli (right-top), the neutral center stimuli (left-bottom), and the neutral periphery stimuli (right-bottom). Solid lines depict the mean value, and the shaded backgrounds show the standard error of the mean. Yellow-shaded areas show the 180 to 240 ms window used to calculate the N2 component.

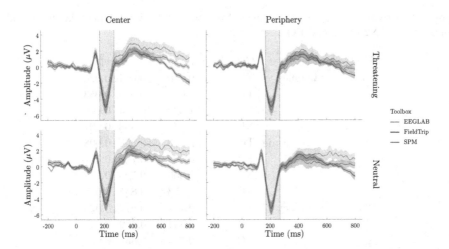

Fig. 3. Grand average ERPs recorded at PO3 electrode. Same conditions of Fig. 2. N2 activity was closer on all toolboxes than at F3. However, LPP presented larger differences on all of them at Center condition.

Table 1. Mean and standard deviation for peak latencies and amplitudes of N2 at F3 and PO3.

	F3		PO3	
	Amplitude (μV)	Latency (ms)	Amplitude (μV)	Latency (ms)
TC				
EEGLAB	3.59 ± 2.54	210.66 ± 21.11	5.30 ± 3.89	205.26 ± 20.58
FieldTrip	3.85 ± 2.01	212.46 ± 19.76	5.68 ± 3.06	208.86 ± 16.32
SPM12	3.89 ± 2.23	216.16 ± 18.81	5.99 ± 3.10	210.86 ± 15.90
TP				
EEGLAB	4.03 ± 2.25	210.16 ± 17.50	5.48 ± 3.07	209.06 ± 21.96
FieldTrip	4.44 ± 2.41	209.06 ± 19.80	6.00 ± 3.41	202.16 ± 20.22
SPM12	4.39 ± 2.24	214.36 ± 19.13	6.42 ± 3.29	206.66 ± 17.80
NC				
EEGLAB	3.52 ± 1.95	210.76 ± 18.75	4.57 ± 2.91	203.96 ± 20.05
FieldTrip	3.75 ± 1.84	212.56 ± 18.80	5.60 ± 3.16	206.56 ± 18.56
SPM12	3.97 ± 2.04	217.56 ± 17.98	5.75 ± 3.16	206.86 ± 17.92
NP				
EEGLAB	3.84 ± 2.48	212.96 ± 18.13	5.89 ± 4.02	205.26 ± 17.63
FieldTrip	4.13 ± 2.82	213.46 ± 17.19	5.84 ± 3.62	204.36 ± 17.58
SPM12	4.16 ± 2.32	215.36 ± 19.01	6.14 ± 3.11	204.96 ± 16.94

Table 2. Results of the one-way repeated-measures ANOVA for peak latencies and amplitudes of N2 at F3 and PO3.

Electrode	Metric	Condition	$F(2,38)$	p	η_p^2
F3	Latency	TC	0.510	0.604	0.026
		TP	1.064	0.355	0.053
		NC	1.338	0.274	0.066
		NP	0.142	0.868	0.007
	Amplitude	TC	0.150	0.861	0.008
		TP	0.338	0.715	0.017
		NC	0.356	0.703	0.018
		NP	0.153	0.858	0.008
PO3	Latency	TC	0.497	0.612	0.025
		TP	0.841	0.439	0.042
		NC	0.154	0.857	0.008
		NP	0.019	0.981	0.001
	Amplitude	TC	0.277	0.760	0.014
		TP	0.638	0.534	0.032
		NC	1.284	0.289	0.063
		NP	0.061	0.941	0.003

5   Conclusion

The present study investigated the effect of using a specific toolbox to process EEG data intended to ERP analysis. In summary, regarding to the N2 component we did not find significant differences between data extracted with the three tested toolboxes: EEGLAB, FieldTrip and SPM12. Although there are not significant differences, results showed that peak amplitude data extracted using EEGLAB exhibited lower average values, but these were consistent among conditions. Then, we do not expect differences in contrasts tests due to this issue. Further work could include a detailed investigation of which steps in the processing contribute most to this variation.

There are visual differences between the ERP waveforms for later potentials (LPP). This could be inconvenient for emotion regulation research, given that LPP reflects facilitated attention to emotional stimuli. Further investigation must be carried to establish how a particular toolbox can affect contrasts among conditions and later group analysis.

Acknowledgement. This work was partially supported by Colciencias Grant 111577757638. AQ was supported by Colciencias doctoral fellowship call 647 (year 2014).

References

1. Gevins, A., Leong, H., Smith, M.E., Le, J., Du, R.: Mapping cognitive brain function with modern high-resolution electroencephalography. Trends Neurosci. **18**(10), 429–436 (1995). https://doi.org/10.1016/0166-2236(95)94489-R
2. Sur, S., Sinha, V.: Event-related potential: an overview. Ind. Psychiatry J. **18**(1), 70–73 (2009). https://doi.org/10.4103/0972-6748.57865
3. Gozke, E., Tomrukcu, S., Erdal, N.: Visual event-related potentials in patients with mild cognitive impairment. Int. J. Gerontol. **10**(4), 190–192 (2016). https://doi.org/10.1016/j.ijge.2013.03.006
4. Hirata, K., et al.: Abnormal information processing in dementia of alzheimer type. A study using the event-related potential's field. Eur. Arch. Psychiatry Clin. Neurosci. **250**(3), 152–155 (2000). https://doi.org/10.1007/s004060070033
5. Wauthia, E., Rossignol, M.: Emotional processing and attention control impairments in children with anxiety: an integrative review of event-related potentials findings. Front. Psychol. **7**, 562 (2016). https://doi.org/10.3389/fpsyg.2016.00562. https://www.frontiersin.org/article/10.3389/fpsyg.2016.00562
6. Trujillo, S.P., et al.: Atypical modulations of N170 component during emotional processing and their links to social behaviors in ex-combatants. Front. Human Neurosci. **11**(May), 1–12 (2017). https://doi.org/10.3389/fnhum.2017.00244
7. Delorme, A., Makeig, S.: EEGLAB: an open source toolbox for analysis of single-trial EEG dynamics including independent component analysis. J. Neurosci. Methods **134**(1), 9–21 (2004). https://doi.org/10.1016/j.jneumeth.2003.10.009
8. Friston, K., Ashburner, J., Kiebel, S., Nichols, T., Penny, W.: Statistical Parametric Mapping (1994)
9. Litvak, V., et al.: EEG and MEG data analysis in SPM8. Comput. Intell. Neurosci. **2011**, 32 (2011)

10. Oostenveld, R., Fries, P., Maris, E., Schoffelen, J.M.: FieldTrip: open source software for advanced analysis of MEG, EEG, and invasive electrophysiological data. Comput. Intell. Neurosci. **2011**, 156,869 (2011). https://doi.org/10.1155/2011/156869

11. BioSemi, B.: BioSemi ActiveTwo [EEG system]. BioSemi, Amsterdam (2011)

12. Jurcak, V., Tsuzuki, D., Dan, I.: 10/20, 10/10, and 10/5 systems revisited: their validity as relative head-surface-based positioning systems. Neuroimage **34**(4), 1600–1611 (2007)

13. Parra Rodríguez, M., Sánchez Cuéllar, M., Valencia, S., Trujillo, N.: Attentional bias during emotional processing: evidence from an emotional flanker task using IAPS. Cogn. Emotion 1–11 (2017). https://doi.org/10.1080/02699931.2017.1298994

14. Picton, T., Lins, O., Scherg, M.: The recording and analysis of event-related potentials. In: Handbook of Neurophysiology, pp. 4–73. Elsevier Science (1995)

15. Picton, T., et al.: Guidelines for using human event-related potentials to study cognition: recording standards and publication criteria. Psychophysiology **37**, 127–152 (2000)

16. Bigdely-Shamlo, N., Mullen, T., Kothe, C., Su, K.M., Robbins, K.A.: The prep pipeline: standardized preprocessing for large-scale eeg analysis. Front. Neuroinform. **9**, 16 (2015). https://doi.org/10.3389/fninf.2015.00016

17. Teplan, M.: Fundamentals of EEG measurement. Measur. Sci. Rev. **2**(2), 1–11 (2002)

18. Hyviirinen, A., Karhunen, J., Oja, E.: Independent Component Analysis. Wiley, Hoboken (2001)

19. Balconi, M., Pozzoli, U.: Event-related oscillations (ERO) and event-related potentials (ERP) in emotional face recognition. Int. J. Neurosci. **118**(10), 1412–1424 (2008). https://doi.org/10.1080/00207450601047119

A Test Bed to Measure Transverse Deflection of a Flexible Link Manipulator

Cecilia Murrugarra[1]([✉])(ⓘ), Osberth De Castro[2](ⓘ), and Angel Terrones[3]

[1] El Bosque University, Bogota D.C. 110111, Colombia
cmurrugarra@unbosque.edu.co
[2] De San Buenaventura University, Bogota D.C. 110111, Colombia
odecastro@usbbog.edu.co
[3] Simon Bolivar University, Caracas, Venezuela
aterrones@usb.ve
http://www.unbosque.edu.co
http://www.usbbog.edu.co
http://www.usb.ve

Abstract. In this paper, we present a test bed to measure transverse deflection in different parts of a link of a manipulator of flexible links. For the mathematical modeling of the link, the *Euler-Bernoulli* beam theory has been used as a simplification of the linear elasticity theory, which allows calculating the load and the deflection characteristics of a beam. In order to measure the transverse deflection of the beam, we have used strain gauge arrangements that have been placed at three points of the flexible link, the test bed, allowing to reconstruct the position of the beam taking into account the actual position of the *end-effector*, the motion controller, and real-time interface PC. In addition to knowing with certainty the position of the manipulator arm, it has also been considered in the calculation of the manipulator dynamics using Euler-Lagrange and assumed modes for modeling the transverse deflection and the vibrations of the beam. This information will be used in modern control schemes to perform transverse deflection compensation, vibration suppression and ensure that the *end-effector*, reaches the set point set in the control system in a finite time.

Keywords: Flexible · Transverse deflection · Dynamics · Vibrations
Robot · Manipulator

1 Introduction

The robot manipulators have great use and performance in the industrial area, in the assembly of vehicles, packaging, storage, palletized, etc. With the intention of building light robots in terms of reducing their geometric dimensions,

This work is supported by a grant with the project number PFI-2018-014, Electronic Engineering Program of the Faculty of Engineering of El Bosque University.

© Springer Nature Switzerland AG 2018
J. C. Figueroa-García et al. (Eds.): WEA 2018, CCIS 916, pp. 395–407, 2018.
https://doi.org/10.1007/978-3-030-00353-1_35

it is possible to use actuators that consume less energy, transform into non-holonomic robotic systems, being necessary not only to sense the position of the *end-effector*, but also the deformation of the links so that this information is used to correct the position of the robot-manipulator and it can perform the tasks specified in its workspace. In [1] performed the mathematical modeling of a flexible two-link manipulator robot for space applications using the *assumed modes* method to model the transverse deflection of the flexible links. In [2] a mathematical model, position control, and test bed of a planar manipulator for aerospace applications, based on the results obtained in [1]. The mathematical model of the dynamics of a manipulator robot of a flexible link is explained in [3], the equations of the planar robot-manipulator for ν vibration modes, that allows to calculate the transverse deflection in any point of a cantilever beam and also takes into account the friction at the junction of the robot-manipulator. In [4] present the results of simulating mathematical modeling and a virtual sensor to measure the deformation of a robot-manipulator of flexible link and is used to compensate the deformation of the link. In [5], present experimental results for the measurement of the deformation of a planar manipulator of two degrees of freedom (d.o.f), without effects of the gravitational force.

In this paper, we show the mathematical development to include the transverse deflection of a cantilever Euler-Bernoulli beam with three points of the link. This robot manipulator is a planar X-Y, and is under the effect of the force of gravity, and we explained all the development for the implementation of the experimental platform. We present experiments by performing a position control of the *end-effector*, a particular position and sensing transverse deflection at three points of the beam, and an analysis of the results obtained by this robot manipulator is a planar X-Y, and is under the effect of the force of gravity, and we explained all the development for the implementation of the experimental platform the Test-Bed implemented.

2   Mathematical Model

The theory of Euler-Bernoulli beams [6], is a simplification of the linear theory of elasticity, which provides a type to calculate the load and the deflection of a beam. For the study of beams, a system of rectangular coordinates is considered in which the axis x, is tangent to the barycenter axis of the beam, and the axes y, and z, coincide with the principal axes of inertia [7].

2.1   Assumptions

The basic assumptions of the beam theory for the simple bending in the X-Y plane are:

1. The material of the beam is elastically linear, with Young's modulus E. and Poisson's coefficient negligible.
2. At each point of the beam, the vertical displacement only depends on x : $u_y(x, y) = \omega(x)$, where $\omega(x)$ is the curvature of the beam.

3. The neutral fiber points only suffer vertical displacement and rotation with respect to the axis $Z : u_x(x, 0) = 0$.
4. The tension perpendicular to the neutral fiber is zero: $\sigma_{yy} = 0$.
5. The planar sections initially perpendicular to the axis of the beam, remain perpendicular to the axis of the beam once curved.

From item 1 to 4, define Timoshenko's beam [8]. The Euler-Bernoulli theory is a simplification of the previous theory by accepting assumption 5 as true, then in real beams, it is only an approximation, provided that the magnitude of $u_y(x, y)$ is very small. Obtaining the following kinematic equations on the displacements [9], $u_x(x, y) = y\theta_z(x) = y\frac{d\omega}{dx}$, and $u_y(x, y) = \omega(x)$.

2.2   Beam Equation

For the determination of the beam equation, it is necessary to first develop the equations for the deformation (*strain*) and the mechanical stress (*stress*) for the case of a beam. **Strain:** is the relation between the variation of length of a material and its initial length: $\varepsilon = \Delta L / L$. The strain ($\varepsilon_x$), is defined by [10]:

$$\varepsilon_x = \frac{\Delta s' - \Delta x}{\Delta x} = \frac{(\rho - y)\Delta\phi - \rho\Delta\phi}{\rho\Delta\phi} = \frac{-y}{\rho} \tag{1}$$

The maximum strain is $\varepsilon_{max} = -c/\rho = \varepsilon_c$, where $c = \overline{A'B'}$, and replacement in Eq. (1).

$$\varepsilon_x = \frac{y}{c}\varepsilon_{max} = \frac{y}{c}\varepsilon_c \tag{2}$$

Stress: is the distribution of a force per unit area, is expressed as $\sigma = F/A$, where σ, is the average stress and F, is the applied force at an area A. The stress in the x, direction can be calculated in the same way as it was done with then *strain*:

$$\sigma_x = \frac{y}{c}\sigma_c \tag{3}$$

The components of the coordinate system y, z are considered zero, according to the assumptions previously explained.

For the static equilibrium, the resistive moment of material is M_r is equal to the applied moment M, such as $\sum M_i = 0$ [9]. Using of *Hooke Law* $\sigma_x = E\varepsilon_x$, where E, is the coefficient of Young of material, and the Eq. (3), obtained $\sigma_x = \frac{y}{c}E\varepsilon_c$, and replacing the last expression in $M_r = \int_A y dF = \int_A y\sigma_x dA$. The integral is the second moment of inertia I of the solid, substituting and obtained σ_x:

$$\sigma_x = \frac{My}{I} \tag{4}$$

Deflections of the beams depend on the stiffness of the material and the dimensions of the beams as well as the more obvious applied loads and supports [9]. Using the Euler-Bernoulli assumption obtained:

$$\phi = \frac{L}{\rho} = \frac{L+\delta}{\rho+c} \tag{5}$$

and writing the Eq. (5)

$$\frac{c}{\rho} = \frac{\delta}{L} = \varepsilon = \frac{\sigma}{E} = \frac{Mc}{EI}; \quad then, \quad \frac{1}{\rho} = \frac{M}{EI} \tag{6}$$

The radius of curvature of a function is given by:

$$\rho = \frac{\left[1 + (dy/dx)^2\right]^{3/2}}{d^2y/dx^2} = \frac{\left[1 + (\partial u_y/\partial x)^2\right]^{3/2}}{\partial^2 u_y/\partial x^2} \tag{7}$$

because the vertical displacements are small and $\partial w/\partial x \approx 0$, obtained:

$$\frac{1}{\rho} = \frac{\partial^2 u_y}{\partial x^2} \tag{8}$$

replace Eq. (8) in Eq. (6) is obtained:

$$EI\frac{\partial^2 u_y}{\partial x^2} = M \tag{9}$$

The general deflection equation of a beam, based on the Euler-Bernoulli assumptions and **Deflection of the Cantilever-Beam** to determine the transverse deflection at a point x of the beam, it is assumed that a force is applied at the free end of the beam, which means that the resistive moment M_r of the beam is $F(x-L)$. Using the Eq. (9) obtained: $EI\frac{\partial^2 u_y}{\partial x^2} = F(x-L)$, integrating and using the boundary conditions: $u|_{x=0} = 0$, $\frac{\partial u_y}{\partial x}|_{x=0} = 0$, the equation of the vertical deflection of the beam in function of x is obtained: $u_y(x.y) = w(x) = \frac{Fx^2}{6EI}(x-3L)$.

2.3   Dynamics Equation of Robot-Manipulator

We have considered the flexible manipulator with rotational joint under gravity. Fig. 1, shows the flexible manipulator in the X-Y plane, the dynamics of the system will be obtained from *Euler-Lagrange* Eq. (10), with: $q_j = [\theta, q_i]$, where q_j, is generalized coordinates of the system, θ, rotational angle of link in the plane X-Y, and q_i, temporal generalized coordinates associated at Eq. (17), i, number d.o.f. of the system flexible beam or vibration modes and j, number of generalized coordinate of the system.

$$\frac{d}{dt}\frac{\partial L}{\partial \dot{q}_j} - \frac{\partial L}{\partial q_j} = \tau_j \tag{10}$$

The Eq. (11), is the kinetic energy, the Eq. (12), potential and potential elastic energy of the system. The position matrix of the manipulator $P(\hat{x})$ shows in the Eq. (13), this matrix considers elastic deformation contributions in the frame (x_0, y_0) of a dm beam differential in the frame (x_1, y_1). Deriving with respect to the time to $P(\hat{x})$, and replacing $dm = \rho A d\hat{x}$, in expressions Eqs. (11) and (12) obtain the extended expressions Eqs. (14) and (15), where A, ρ, I_b and l, are

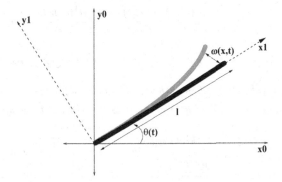

Fig. 1. Flexible manipulator planar X-Y workspace.

cross-sectional transverse area, uniform mass density, inertia and the length of the link respectively.

$$K = \frac{1}{2}\int_0^l r^2 dm = \frac{1}{2}\int_0^l \dot{P}^T \dot{P} dm \qquad (11)$$

$$V_g = \int_0^l g^T r dm = \int_0^l g^T P dm, \quad V_f = \frac{1}{2}EI\int_0^l [w''(\hat{x},t)]^2 d\hat{x} \qquad (12)$$

$$\mathbf{P}(\hat{\mathbf{x}}) = \begin{bmatrix} \hat{x}cos(\theta(t)) - w(\hat{x},t)sin(\theta(t)) \\ \hat{x}sin(\theta(t)) + w(\hat{x},t)cos(\theta(t)) \end{bmatrix} \qquad (13)$$

$$K = \frac{1}{2}\dot{\theta}^2 I_b + \frac{1}{2}\rho A\left[\dot{\theta}^2\int_0^l w^2(\hat{x},t)d\hat{x} + \int_0^l \dot{w}^2(\hat{x},t)d\hat{x} + 2\dot{\theta}\int_0^l \hat{x}\dot{w}(\hat{x},t)d\hat{x}\right] (14)$$

$$V = \frac{1}{2}\left\{\rho A\left[gl^2 sin(\theta) + 2gcos(\theta)\int_0^l w(\hat{x},t)d\hat{x}\right] + EI\int_0^l [w''(\hat{x},t)]^2 d\hat{x}\right\} (15)$$

The dynamic equations of motion of the robot-manipulator show in the Eq. (10) is obtained from the *Lagrangian* $L = K - V$, from Eqs. (14) and (15) we get a function: $f(\theta, \dot{\theta}, w, \dot{w}, \ddot{w}, w'') = \tau$, where $w(\hat{x},t)$, is the transverse deflection in a point $\hat{x}$ of the beam, $\dot{w} = \partial w(\hat{x},t)/\partial t$, $\ddot{w} = \partial w^2(\hat{x},t)/\partial t^2$, and $w'' = \partial w^2(\hat{x},t)/\partial \hat{x}^2$. For model of the beam the torsion effect and damping have been neglected [11]. The dynamics equation of the beam can be described by *Euler-Bernoulli* beam Eq. (16), and as solution to this differential equation, we have Eq. (17), where $\phi_i(\hat{x})$ is the spatial component and its solution Eq. (18) and $q_i(t)$ the temporal component and its solution Eq. (19) [12], where $k^2 = \sqrt{\frac{\rho\omega^2}{EI}}$, and $\omega = (\beta_n l)^2 \sqrt{\frac{EI}{\rho l^4}}$, is the angular frequency of the ν_{th} modes. We assume that boundary conditions of the beam have been taken *clamped-free* [8].

$$\rho\frac{\partial^2 w(\hat{x},t)}{\partial t^2} + EI\frac{\partial^4 w(\hat{x},t)}{\partial x^4} = p(\hat{x},t) \qquad (16)$$

$$w(\hat{x},t) = \sum_{i=1}^{\nu}\phi_{i(\hat{x})}q_{i(t)} \qquad (17)$$

$$\phi(\hat{x}) = C_1 sin(k\hat{x}) + C_2 cos(k\hat{x}) + C_3 sinh(k\hat{x}) + C_4 cosh(k\hat{x}) \qquad (18)$$

$$q(t) = Acos(\omega t) + Bsin(\omega t) = q_0 e^{j\omega t} \qquad (19)$$

$$w(\hat{x},t)\Big\|_{x=0} = 0 \qquad \frac{\partial w(\hat{x},t)}{\partial x}\Big\|_{x=0} = 0$$

$$\frac{\partial^2 w(\hat{x},t)}{\partial x^2}\Big\|_{x=l} = 0 \qquad \frac{\partial^3 w(\hat{x},t)}{\partial x^3}\Big\|_{x=l} = 0 \qquad (20)$$

To calculate the constants C_1, C_2, C_3 and C_4 of the system, was expressed with Eq. (18), the first, second and third derivative, to obtain a solution Eq. (21), non-trivial. Replacing these constants in Eq. (18), its obtained Eq. (22), where i represent the subscript associate the natural frequency oscillation of *Euler-Bernoulli* beam.

$$C_1 = -C_3, \quad C_2 = -C_4, \quad and \quad C = -\left[\frac{cosh(k_i l) + cos(k_i l)}{sinh(k_i l) + sin(k_i l)}\right] \qquad (21)$$

$$\phi_i(\hat{x}) = [cos(k_i\hat{x}) - cosh(k_i\hat{x})] - C[sin(k_i\hat{x}) - sinh(k_i\hat{x})] \qquad (22)$$

The Lagrangian (L) was calculated from Eqs. (14) and (15), the solution of the *Euler-Bernoulli* beam Eq. (17), using the separability principle [12], the

orthogonality principle: $\phi_i\phi_j = \begin{cases} \phi_i\phi_j; & i = j \\ 0; & i \neq j \end{cases}$, and the following constants:

$a_{0i} = \int_0^l \phi_i^2(\hat{x})d\hat{x}, \ a_{1i} = \int_0^l \phi_i(\hat{x})\hat{x}d\hat{x}, \ a_{2i} = \int_0^l \phi_i(\hat{x})d\hat{x}, \ a_{3i} = \int_0^l \left[\frac{d\phi_i^2(\hat{x})}{d\hat{x}^2}\right]^2 d\hat{x},$
with $i = [1, 2, \ldots, \nu]$, obtaining the Eq. (23).

$$L = \frac{1}{2}\rho A\dot{\theta}^2(a_{01}q_1(t)^2 + \ldots + a_{0\nu}q_{\nu(t)}^2) - \rho Ag\frac{l^2}{2}sin\theta + \frac{1}{2}\rho A(a_{01}\dot{q}_{1(t)}^2 + \ldots + a_{0\nu}\dot{q}_{\nu(t)}^2)$$

$$+ \frac{1}{2}\dot{\theta}^2 I_b + \rho A\dot{\theta} * (a_{11}\dot{q}_{1(t)} + \ldots + a_{1\nu}\dot{q}_{\nu(t)}) - \rho Agcos\theta(a_{21}q_{1(t)} + \ldots + a_{2\nu}q_{\nu(t)})$$

$$- \frac{1}{2}EI(a_{31}q_{1(t)}^2 + \ldots + a_{3\nu}q_{\nu(t)}^2) \qquad (23)$$

The equation of motion the flexible manipulator has been calculated with Eq. (23), expressed in state variables $\dot{x} = f(x) + g(x)u$, and $y = h(x)$, for ν frequencies of vibration, where $x = [\theta, \ \dot{\theta}, \ q_1 \ \dot{q}_1, \cdots, q_\nu \ \dot{q}_\nu]^T$, is the state vector, u is the input control (τ), $y = I_{nxn} * x$, is the output of the system, $b_{0\nu} = \rho Aa_{0\nu}, \ b_{1\nu} = \rho A(a_{1\nu}^2/a_{0\nu}), \ b_{2\nu} = \rho Aa_{1\nu}, \ b_{3\nu} = \rho A(a_{1\nu}/a_{0\nu}), \ b_4 = \rho Al^2/2,$ $b_{5\nu} = a_{2\nu}\rho A, \ b_{6\nu} = EIa_{3\nu}, \ b_{7\nu} = (a_{2\nu}/a_{0\nu}),$ and $b_8 = I_b$, to obtained Eq. (24), as equations of the dynamics of the flexible manipulator with ν modes of vibrations.

$$\dot{x}_1 = x_2$$
$$\dot{x}_2 = [\tau - b_4 g cos(x_1) - 2x_2 b_{0(i)} [x_{(2i+1)} x_{(2i+2)}]^T - x_2^2 b_{2(i)} x_{(2i+1)}^T$$
$$+ g cos(x_1) b_{2(i)} b_{7(i)}^T + x_{(2i+1)} b_{3(i)} b_{6(i)}^T + g sin(x_1) b_{5(i)} x_{(2i+1)}^T]$$
$$* [b_{0(i)} * [x_{(2i+1)}^2]^T + b_{1(i)} [ones_{(i)}]^T + b_8]^{-1}$$
$$\dot{x}_{(2i+1)} = x_{(2i+2)}$$
$$\dot{x}_{(2i+2)} = [x_2^2 x_{(2i+1)} - b_{3(i)} \dot{x}_2 - b_{7(i)} g cos(x_1) - \frac{b_{6(i)}}{b_{0(i)}} x_{(2i+1)}] \qquad (24)$$

3 Experimental Platform

The Test-Bed developed is a system designed for the implementation of control algorithms and the identification of the transverse deflection parameters for the manipulator of the flexible-link. In the Fig. 2a, can see a general scheme of three modules developed in conjunction with the manipulator interaction: (1)

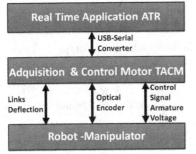

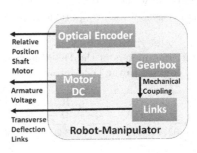

(a) The general scheme of the electronics system developed.

(b) Development scheme of the robot-manipulator modules.

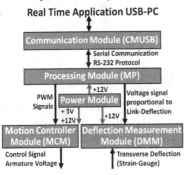

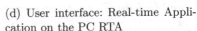

(c) Acquisition and Control Motor (TACM) modules.

(d) User interface: Real-time Application on the PC RTA

Fig. 2. Diagrams of the development system

Robot-Manipulator, which consists of the physical structure and coupling of DC motors. (2) Acquisition and Control Motor (TACM), which is responsible for the handling of the DC motors of the joints of the Robot-Manipulator, and measures of the transverse deflections of the links of the Robot-Manipulator. (3) Real-Time Application (RTA), which is using as an interface with the user for handling the Robot-Manipulator-TACM system and PC.

3.1 Robot-Manipulator

The Robot-Manipulator consists of two brush DC-motors *Faulhaber*, with gearbox metal, gear in planetary configuration, and incremental optical encoders in quadrature HEDS5500 A14 (2K-500L5mm). From Table 1, the parameters of each DC-Motor, and the parameters of the planetary gears coupled to the motors. The kinematic configuration of the manipulator for one or two d.o.f. is such that the axes of motion of the joints are parallel to each other and perpendicular to the gravity vector, the workspace of the manipulator is the vertical X-Y plane. In addition, the links are constructed by the aluminium beam, with a circular cross-section of the $0.01m$. of diameter, $0.6135m$. of length, and $0.1285Kg$. mass. Figure 2b, shows the interaction between the robot-manipulator modules and the signals necessary for its operation.

Table 1. Parameters of the DC-Motors of the manipulator prototype and planetary gearbox coupled to the DC-Motors.

Motor	U_N (V)	R Ω	L (μH)	K_n (rpm/V)	K_E (mV/rpm)	τ_m (ms)	J (gcm^2)
2657W024CR	24	3.20	380	275	3.64	3.9	15
3042W012C	12	1.7	165	456	2.19	7	18

Motor	Code GearBox	Reduction	$In_{vel-max}$ (rpm)	Efficiency (%)	$Torque_{max}$ (N)
2657W024CR	30/1	134:1	3000	60	4.5
3042W012C	30/1	66:1	3000	70	4.5

3.2 Acquisition and Control Motor (TACM)

The **TACM** module is an electronic card that measures of the transverse deflection of robot-manipulator and position control of the DC-motor. Figure 2c, shows the modular architecture, and internally have five submodules that described below:

1. **Power Module**. This module provided the regulated power voltages required by the TACM, have a 5 independent voltage sources, which are: (a) +5V, to digital circuits as LCD screen, H-bridge, and optical encoders. (b) +12V, to analog circuits and power supply to $DEMO9S12XEP100$. (c) +5V, power

supply to H-bridge of the second motor. (d) $+12V$, power supply to H-bridge of the first motor and (e) $-12V$, for analog circuits. Each power supply using the voltage regulators of the $LM78XX$ and $LM79XX$, family for positive and negative voltages respectively. This module allows currents of up to 1A, in continuous mode in each of the sources, peak currents of up to 2A, and protection against inverse voltages in the input power.

2. **Transverse Deflection Measurement Module (DMM).** To determine the final position of the *end-effector* is necessary to know which are the transverse deflection. To measure the transverse deflection, axial strain gauges placed at three points along with the link. The variation of the electrical resistance of the gauges, which is done by means of a *Wheatstone bridge*. Figure 3a and b, shows the configuration used, it allowed compensated the measurement errors due to temperature and axial deflections using only two gauges, in addition, to allow the output to be linear, with respect to the deflection of the beam.

3. **Motion Controller Module (MCM).** For the handling of the DC-motors, an integrated H-bridge was used, specifically, the MC33886 (*Freescale Semiconductor*), the configuration implemented is shown in the Fig. 4b.

4. **Communications module (CMUSB).** USB-Serial converter module, which allows data transmission rates of up to $1Mbps$, which is 8.7 times faster than the maximum transmission rate of the *RS-232* interface of a PC, which is $115.200bps$. The module used was developed by *SparkFun* Electronics, based on the integrated circuit CP2102 (*Silicon Labs*).

5. **Processing Module (PM).** This module is responsible for digitizing the voltage signals that indicate the deflection in the links; to control and drive the motors; to read the optical encoders in order to determine the position of the motor shaft and send the acquired data to the PC. This module is made up of the development card $DEMO9S12XEP100$.

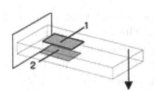 

(a) StrainGauge: Configuration to compensated for axial deflection and temperature.   (b) Amplification circuit and strain gauge.

Fig. 3. Transverse deflection measurement circuits.

3.3   Real-Time Application of the PC Module (RTA)

Real-Time software implemented on the PC, which is responsible for providing an interface between the TACM Motor Acquisition and Control Card and user interface. Figure 2d, shows the general diagram of the system PC, and the Fig. 4a, shows the panel control of the application in the PC. This software has been implemented in two completely independent programs or modules for the processing load that involves performing the following tasks: (a) Acquisition and processing of the data obtained from the TACM. (b) Generation of graphs in real time. Figure 4b, shows the architecture and modules interact with the robot-manipulator and acquisition system implemented.

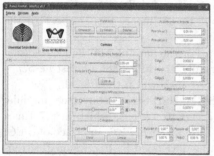

(a) Main window of the Control Panel   (b) Robot-Manipulator and data acquisition module

Fig. 4. Control Panel and data acquisition robot-manipulator.

4   Results and Analysis

To measure the transverse deflection of the beam, an object with a mass of $151.8g.$, was placed on the *end-effector* of the link. The measurements were made for different angles of a position of the axis of the articulation of the base or reference system of the manipulator and without appreciable vibrations in the link. The theoretical value of the transverse deflection $\delta_{theorical} = (\frac{FL^3}{3EI} + \frac{\omega L^4}{8EI})cos(\theta)$, where $\frac{FL^3}{3EI}$, is the deflection in the beam due to the mass placed at the end-effector of the robot-manipulator and $\frac{\omega L^4}{8EI}$, it is the deflection caused by the mass of the beam. From Table 2a, theoretical and experimental measures from the transverse deflection *end-effector*. From Table 2b and c, can see the results of the measurements X and Y coordinates, and compare between RTA system (experimental), and the measure of the *end-effector* theory value and error calculated between these values. The values of the position in the axis Y, through the processing of the deflections in the link, presents a difference of up to $3mm$ respect to the measurements directly on the link, which can be attributed to the following factors: (a) Offset present on the DMM of the TACM. (b) The noise present in the prototype. (c) Vibrations of the beam. (d) Mechanical disturbances between the final shaft of the motor and the part where the link is attached. (e) Mechanical disturbances in the gearbox train. (f) Discretization error in the angular position of the motor shaft due to the optical encoders. Respect to the error, in the measurement of the position on the axis X, it was observed that the value of the error is lower compared to that observed in the measurements in position on the axis Y, which is attributable to its dependence with respect to the rotation angle of the joint of the base, as can be seen in the Eq. 13, with $\hat{x} = L$, is the length of the link and $w(L, t)$, is the transverse deflection of the *end-effector* of the link. Figure 5a, shows the X-Y position of the *end-effector* of the robot-manipulator, for an angular trajectory type step to $0°$, $5°$, $10°$, $15°$ and $20°$. Figure 5b, shows the voltage signal by the DMM of the TACM, and that is proportional to the deformation of the link at that point. Deformation measured in strain-gauge1, near the joint. Figure 5c shows the actuator response to a step in the angular reference, with a mass of $151.8g$ at the *end-effector* of the robot-manipulator and Fig. 5d, shows transverse deflection measured at three points of the robot-manipulator.

Table 2. Measures transverse deflections of the end-effector robot-manipulator.

θ (degree position)	$\delta_{RTA}(mm)$	$\delta_{theo}(mm)$	Error %
$5°$	4,185977	4,020958	4,1%
$10°$	4,095375	3,974996	3,02%
$15°$	4,022549	3,898783	3,17%

(a) Measures from the transverse deflection end-effector.

θ (degree)	$Y_{ATR}(mm)$	$Y_{real}(cm)$	$Y_{theo}(mm)$	$Error_{ATR-theo}$ %	$Error_{real-theo}$%
$5°$	4,98	4,7	4,94	0,81%	4,86%
$10°$	10,25	10,1	10,26	0,097%	01,56%
$15°$	15,47	15,4	15,50	0,193%	0,645%
$20°$	20,61	20,6	20,62	0,049%	0,097%

(b) Measures of the X coordinate of the end-effector.

θ (degree)	$Y_{ATR}(mm)$	$Y_{real}(cm)$	$Y_{theo}(mm)$	$Error_{ATR-theo}$ %	$Error_{real-theo}$%
$5°$	4,98	4,7	4,94	0,81%	4,86%
$10°$	10,25	10,1	10,26	0,097%	01,56%
$15°$	15,47	15,4	15,50	0,193%	0,645%
$20°$	20,61	20,6	20,62	0,049%	0,097%

(c) Measures of the Y coordinate of the end-effector.

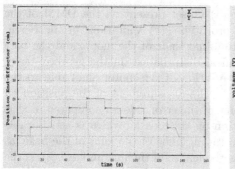

(a) X-Y position of the end-effector of the robot-manipulator.

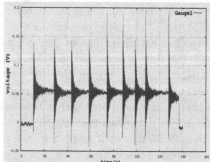

(b) Transverse deflection measured in strain-gauge 1, near the joint.

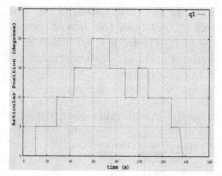

(c) Actuator response to a step in the angular reference.

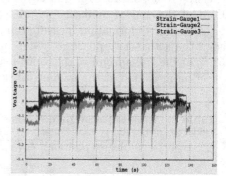

(d) Transverse deflection measured at three points of the robot-manipulator.

Fig. 5. Measurements made to the robot-manipulator from joint and the end-effector positions.

5   Conclusions

A data acquisition system was developed to measure the transverse deflection of the links of a flexible robot manipulator, the measurement of the spatial location of the *end-effector* of the manipulator. A control and management system for DC-motors was also implemented, consisting of two integrated H-bridges; and a digital position PID controller with configurable parameters. An application was also developed in real time on the PC, in order to implement the algorithms for manipulator control. A modular program was made using C++ language and allows in the future, add more functionalities and facilitates the modification of existing functions. This application was implemented in the Linux operating system, in real-time and can be used in integrated systems and in any application that requires a high-speed response.

References

1. Oakley, C.: Experiments in modelling and end-point control of two-link flexible manipulators. Ph.D. thesis, Standford University, Standford, USA (1991)
2. Lertpiritasuwat, V.: Development of a mathematical model for the control of flexible electromechanical systems test bed. Ph.D. thesis, Universidad of Washington, Seattle, Seattle, WA, USA (1994)
3. Murrugarra, C., Grieco, J.C., Fernandez, G., De Castro, O.: A generalized mathematical model for flexible link manipulators with n vibration frequencies and friction in the joint. In: IEEE 5th International Symposium on Robotics and Automation 2006, ISRA 2006, Mexico, pp. 23–28 (2006)
4. Volech, J., Mráz, L., Šika, Z., Valášek, M.: Model of flexible robot with deformation detection. Procedia Eng. **96**(Complete), 510–516 (2014)
5. Esfandiar, H., Korayem, M.H., Haghpanahi, M.: Large deformation modeling of flexible manipulators to determine allowable load. Struct. Eng. Mech. **62**(5), 619–629 (2017)
6. Timoshenko, S.: History of Strength of Materials. McGraw-Hill, New York (1953)
7. Han, S.M., Benaroya, H., Wei, T.: Dynamics of trnaversely vibrating beamns using four engineering theories. J. Sound Vibr. **225**(5), 935–988 (1999)
8. Thomson, W.: Theory of Vibration with Applications, 5th edn. Prentice Hall, Upper Saddle River (1993)
9. Bucciarelli, L.: Stresses: beams in bending. In: Dover-Publications (eds.) Engineering Mechanics for Structures, 1st edn., chap. 9, pp. 235–261. Dover Publications (2009)
10. Terrones, A.: Diseño e implementación de un banco de pruebas para el control de un manipulador flexible, 1 edn. Simon Bolivar University (2009)
11. Plummer, A.R., Sutton, R.P., Wilson, D.A., Halikias, G.D.: Experimental results in the vibration control of a highly flexible manipulator. Ph.D. thesis, University of Waterloo, Waterloo, Leeds, UK (1998)
12. Moorehead, S.: Position and force control of flexible manipulators. Ph.D. thesis, University of Waterloo, Waterloo, Ontario, Canada (1996)

Work of Breathing Dynamics Under Changes of PEEP and Pressure Support in Non-invasive Mechanical Ventilation

Yessika María Ortega[✉][iD], Isabel Cristina Muñoz[iD],
and Alher Mauricio Hernández[iD]

Bioinstrumentation and Clinical Engineering Research Group - GIBIC,
Bioengineering Department, Engineering Faculty, Universidad de Antioquia
UdeA, Calle 70 No. 52-21, 050010 Medellín, Colombia
{yessika.ortega,isabelc.munoz,
alher.hernandez}@udea.edu.co

Abstract. In spontaneous ventilation patient governs his breaths and the correct configuration of the mechanical ventilator is indispensable to avoid extra load in the ventilation process. Parameters like PEEP and pressure support (PS) affects directly the ventilatory comfort of the patient, therefore, they should be adjustable to improve oxygenation and reduce work of breathing (WOB). The objective of this study is to assess the WOB dynamics during incremental stimuli of PEEP and PS as additional information to the absolute WOB value. Variations of 2 cmH2O for 3 min up to 10 cmH2O for PEEP and PS separately were carried out in healthy subjects to analyze the changes in the WOB dynamics. 31 male adults were enrolled in this study, the absolute WOB, and three indexes of WOB dynamics (inspiratory slope, expiratory slope and ΔPeak) were calculated from ventilatory signals. Inspiratory slope shows a linear trend with the absolute WOB, nevertheless after the threshold of 0.8 J/L has a high dispersion, which suggests that high values of WOB could be obtained under different breathing pattern. In conclusion, the inspiratory slope like an index of WOB dynamics provides extra information that in future works could be compared with muscular and ventilator variables to identify positive or negative increases of WOB which clinicians could analyze to make decision about the optimum treatment of the patient.

Keywords: Work of breathing · Mechanical ventilation · PEEP
Pressure support

1 Introduction

In spontaneous ventilation the breathing is governed by the patient and the correct configuration is indispensable to avoid producing extra load in the respiratory process. Furthermore, generally in this mode the clinicians make decisions about if it is necessary to continue with treatment or if is possible to try extubation and withdraw the mechanical ventilation [1]. Parameters like PEEP and pressure support affects directly the ventilatory comfort of the patient, therefore, they should be carefully configured [1].

© Springer Nature Switzerland AG 2018
J. C. Figueroa-García et al. (Eds.): WEA 2018, CCIS 916, pp. 408–417, 2018.
https://doi.org/10.1007/978-3-030-00353-1_36

The PEEP is the positive pressure of the airway at the end of expiration. It is an adjustable parameter to improve oxygenation, alveolar recruitment and reduction of work of breathing (WOB). In many cases, the PEEP is used as compensation for autoPEEP. However, the configuration of this parameter must be carefully controlled since an increase in this parameter can produce unnecessary load for the patient [2, 3]. Also, PEEP values at 20 cmH$_2$O might impair tissue oxygen delivery significantly because of reduced cardiac output, for this reason clinical guides suggests the PEEP should be between 5 and 10 cmH$_2$O, looking to maximize alveolar protection while minimizing the reduction in global oxygen delivery [4].

The pressure support (PS) consists of adding a positive pressure when the patient makes a spontaneous inspiratory effort. This parameter is used to reduce the work of breathing in the ventilation process, decreasing the respiratory muscle effort. It is usually set between 5 and 10 cmH2O, with continuous monitoring, because it may not be enough for the patient's clinical condition, resulting in insufficient support. In contrast, high levels of pressure support ventilation can produce complications like arrhythmias in some patients [1] and increments in work of breathing (WOB). In patients with airflow limitation diseases, such as asthma or COPD, late termination of the breath could be very harmful. Considering this, less time will be available for expiration, leading to dynamic hyperinflation and patient-ventilator asynchrony [5]. Nowadays, the changes in the configuration of PEEP and PS are made according to the patient's condition, based on dyspnea, clinical signs such as oxygen saturation, and arterial blood gases [6, 7].

Knowledge about WOB have contributed to the understanding of the pathophysiology of weaning failure and have also contributed to the progress made in the field of mechanical ventilation [8]. However, to calculate the WOB in spontaneous ventilation is necessary to measure esophageal pressure with a balloon catheter, but this technique is not used frequently in the ICU because is an invasive, expensive and complex procedure [9].

Other studies have shown that WOB can predict the success or failure of extubation [10]. Due to PEEP and PS are parameters used during weaning of mechanical ventilation, it is important to know the effect of these in WOB to optimize the configuration of the ventilator and decrease patient discomfort. Additionally, the respiratory mechanics is highly dynamic during a breathing cycle, which induces the interest to study the behavior of WOB during the patient's respiratory cycle and to search for indexes with capacity to describe in a better way the state of the patient.

The objective of this study is to assess the WOB dynamics during incremental stimuli of PEEP and PS, looking for transient behaviors that describe how the WOB varies at different respiratory efforts demanded by changes in PEEP and PS, as additional information to the WOB value reported by Campbell and other authors [8, 10, 11]

2 Methods

2.1 Experimental Design

Two experiments were designed to analyze the changes in the dynamic work of breathing (WOBdyn) under different settings of PEEP and PS in spontaneous ventilation. In both experiments, the participants were connected to non-invasive ventilation with ventilator Hamilton G5 (Hamilton Medical, Bonaduz, Switzerland). The initial ventilator settings were: spontaneous mode, PEEP = 0 cmH$_2$O, PS = 0 cmH$_2$O, and FiO$_2$ = 21%

The first experiment consisted in PEEP variations from 0 to 10 cmH$_2$O with increments of 2 cmH$_2$O for 3 min each one [11]. The second experiment with PEEP in 0 cmH$_2$O consisted in PS variations from 0 to 10 cmH$_2$O with increments of 2 cmH$_2$O for 3 min each one. The first minute of the record was considered as stimulus adaptation, therefore, the analysis was made using the last two minutes.

2.2 Subjects

After Ethics Committee approval (University of Antioquia, Approval report 15-59-664) of the experimental design, informed consent, and inclusion and exclusion criteria (Inclusion: Male adult subjects. Exclusion: Subjects with a body mass index higher than 30, under medical treatment, thoracic trauma, or with implanted electronic devices, who have consumed alcohol 48 h before, who use hallucinogens, and who practiced yoga or pilates) were included 31 subjects (age: 26.55 ± 5.26 years old, height: 1.72 ± 0.04 m, weight: 74.16 ± 9.57 kg).

2.3 Measurements

Respiratory Mechanics and Muscular Pressure Estimation. To know compliance values of the system (C), an expiratory pause was performed for each record. This maneuver allows to eliminate the airflow for a few seconds generating a plateau in the volume and pressure signals. With the value of the plateau pressure (Ppl) it was possible to calculate the compliance of each subject by means of Eq. (1) [12].

$$C = \frac{V_t}{P_{Pl} - PEEP} \tag{1}$$

where Vt is the maximum value of the tidal volume and PEEP is the positive pressure at the end of the total expiration configured in the mechanical ventilator.

The airway resistance (R) and the muscular pressure (Pmus) were calculated with an optimization algorithm from the equation of motion (2), see details in [12].

$$P_{aw} + P_{mus} = \frac{1}{C} * V_t + R * Q + PEEP_{total} \tag{2}$$

Where Paw is the airway pressure, Pmus is the muscular pressure, C is the compliance, Vt is the tidal volume, R is the resistance, Q is the airflow and PEEP total is the sum of configured PEEP on the mechanical ventilator and intrinsic PEEP of the subject. Due to in this study all included subjects are healthy the last term was considered equal to 0 cmH$_2$O.

Work of Breathing (WOB) Estimation. Using the *Pmus* signal obtained from Eq. (2), the Work of Breathing (WOB) was calculated using the next expression [8]:

$$WOB = \frac{1}{V_t} \int_0^t P_{mus} * Q \, dt \tag{3}$$

where *Vt* is tidal volume and *Q* is the airflow signal.

In the estimation of numerical *WOB* value, t is defined in three ways: a total respiratory cycle time, WOB_t, an inspiratory cycle time, WOB_i and an expiratory cycle time, WOB_e. While in the case of dynamic *WOB (WOBdyn)* the indefinite integral was solved obtaining the curve that indicates the changes of *WOB* throughout respiratory cycle (see Fig. 1).

WOB Signal Processing. With the purpose of characterizing the dynamics of *WOB*, three indexes were calculated from the curve (see Fig. 1), maximum inspiratory slope (Slope$_i$), maximum expiratory slope (Slope$_e$) and delta between maximum and minimum *WOB* (Δpeak).

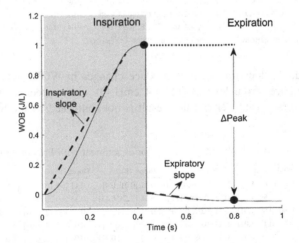

Fig. 1. Indexes obtained from the curve of work of breathing (WOBdyn). Inspiratory slope (Slope$_i$), expiratory slope (Slope$_e$), and delta between maximum and minimum WOB (Δ peak).

2.4 Statistical Analysis

The data were presented as the median and interquartile range after proving the non-normal distribution of the data with the Kolmogorov-Smirnov test. To identify if there were statistically significant differences between the data in each stimulus level respect to the basal, the Kruskal-Wallis test with a post-hoc Tukey-Kramer test for multiple comparisons was used.

3 Results

Table 1 shows the values of WOB obtained for total breathing cycle, inspiratory and expiratory phases, as well as the indexes calculated from the WOBdyn for the incremental PEEP experiment. As shown, the WOB increases respect to the PEEP increments according to all indexes, but the obtained values during the inspiratory phase have significant differences from level 4 (PEEP = 6 cmH$_2$O) respect to basal data (PEEP = 0 cmH$_2$O), while for the expiratory phase, only the information obtained from WOBdyn presents statistically significant differences from PEEP equal to 8 cmH$_2$O respect to the basal level. In contrast, for the expiratory phase, where WOB does not show any change when high values of PEEP are applied, the Slope$_e$ identifies small increases in WOB (see Table 1).

Table 1. WOB and WOBdyn indexes for experiment with PEEP.

PEEP	WOB$_t$ (J/L)	WOB$_i$ (J/L)	WOB$_e$ (J/L)	Slope$_i$ (J/L/s)	Slope$_e$ (J/L/s)	Δ peak (J/L)
0	1.05 [0.77, 1.34]	1.05 [0.76, 1.22]	0.02 [−0.001, 0.06]	0.4 [0.31, 0.51]	−0.15 [−0.2, −0.06]	1.19 [0.87, 1.39]
2	1.32 [0.83, 1.48]	1.26 [0.82, 1.46]	0.01 [0.002, 0.03]	0.45 [0.37, 0.64]	−0.09 [−0.15, −0.05]	1.33 [0.87, 1.57]
4	1.31 [1.13, 1.52]	1.25 [1.12, 1.5]	0.01 [0.003, 0.02]	0.55 [0.34, 0.71]	−0.08 [−0.12, −0.03]	1.33 [1.17, 1.61]
6	1.48 [1.19, 1.78]*	1.46 [1.15, 1.72]*	0.02 [0.003, 0.03]	0.66 [0.44, 0.82]*	−0.08 [−0.11, −0.03]	1.55 [1.17, 1.78]*
8	1.68 [1.51, 2.01]*	1.65 [1.5, 2.01]*	0.01 [0.002, 0.02]	0.72 [0.53, 1.0]*	−0.04 [−0.09, −0.03]*	1.71 [1.52, 2.05]*
10	1.89 [1.58, 2.17]*	1.83 [1.56, 2.13]*	0.01 [0.004, 0.02]	0.81 [0.59, 1.0]*	−0.04 [−0.06, −0.01]*	1.82 [1.52, 2.16]*

*p < 0.01: Statistically significant difference respect to the basal values (PEEP = 0 cmH2O)

As expected, PS does not seem to produce changes in WOB, only WOBe have significant differences from level 3 (PS = 4 cmH$_2$O) with respect to the basal data (PS = 0 cmH$_2$O) (see Table 2), but this result is not confirmed by the Slope$_e$ index.

Table 2. WOB and WOBdyn indexes for experiment with Pressure Support.

PS	WOB$_t$ (J/L)	WOB$_i$ (J/L)	WOB$_e$ (J/L)	Slope$_i$ (J/L/s)	Slope$_e$ (J/L/s)	Δ peak (J/L)
0	0.83 [0.72, 1.05]	0.83 [0.69, 1.02]	0.02 [0.006, 0.034]	0.31 [0.21, 0.4]	−0.11 [−0.16, −0.07]	0.89 [0.76, 1.12]
2	0.86 [0.64, 1.15]	0.82 [0.59, 1.13]	0.05 [0.018, 0.12]	0.35 [0.18, 0.53]	−0.13 [−0.2, −0.03]	0.91 [0.67, 1.25]
4	0.96 [0.59, 1.11]	0.80 [0.56, 1.01]	0.11 [0.07, 0.16]*	0.34 [0.2, 0.49]	−0.02 [−0.12, 0.04]	0.87 [0.6, 1.06]
6	0.8 [0.58, 1.16]	0.67 [0.45, 1.01]	0.13 [0.06, 0.16]*	0.27 [0.2, 0.48]	−0.05 [−0.14, 0.03]	0.68 [0.47, 1.1]
8	0.74 [0.44, 1.04]	0.62 [0.39, 0.91]	0.13 [0.08, 0.17]*	0.24 [0.17, 0.45]	−0.06 [−0.15, 0.03]	0.69 [0.42, 1.0]
10	0.85 [0.36, 1.05]	0.74 [0.25, 0.95]	0.12 [0.08, 0.17]*	0.27 [0.07, 0.53]	−0.05 [−0.13, 0.01]	0.73 [0.28, 0.96]

*p < 0.01: Statistically significant difference respect to the basal level values (PS = 0 cmH2O)

Figure 2 shows WOBdyn indexes associated with the inspiratory phase versus WOB calculated during inspiration (WOB$_i$). A linear trend with a Pearson correlation coefficient of 99% between Δpeak and WOB$_i$ in both PEEP and PS is shown, in contrast, with a Pearson correlation coefficient less than 67%, the slope$_i$ (plots A and C) shows a linear trend before the WOB threshold of 0.8 J/L, slope values located after the threshold show an increased dispersion. Clinicians affirm that values less than 0.8 J/L indicate low WOB in mechanical ventilation, that during a weaning test is associated with successful extubation [10].

Figure 3 shows the relationship between WOBdyn indexes that contain information about expiratory phase and the WOB during expiration (WOB$_e$). None of the graphs of this figure present a definite trend, this is corroborated with the Pearson correlation coefficient (ρ) less than 40% and the regression coefficient (r^2) less than 0.02. Nevertheless, the Slope$_e$ was more negative at low PEEP and particularly PS stimulus, which shows that when any of the stimulus increases, the WOB decreases during expiration, this behavior is not easy to identify with the absolute values of WOB, which is confirmed by the low correlation between Slope$_e$ and WOB$_e$ and p-values showed in Table 2. Finally, Fig. 4 shows the relationship between WOBdyn indexes and the WOB calculated during a total respiratory cycle (WOBt). In these graphs, the dispersion of Slope$_i$ for WOB higher than 0.8 J/L can be observed more clearly than in Fig. 2.

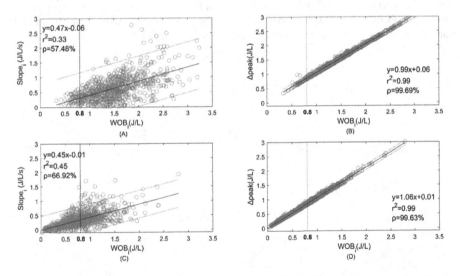

Fig. 2. The WOB Dynamic indexes, inspiratory slope (Slope$_i$) and delta peak (Δpeak) are presented respect to inspiratory WOB (WOBi). A and B show the indexes for the experiment 1 (incremental PEEP). C and D show the indexes for the experiment 2 (Incremental PS). In each figure the linear trend, the square r and Pearson correlation coefficient (ρ) are presented.

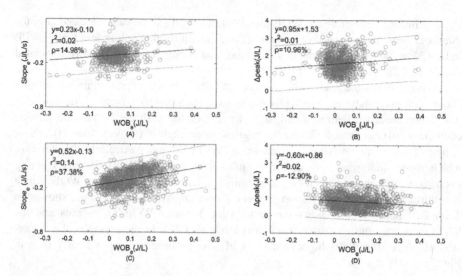

Fig. 3. The WOB Dynamic indexes, expiratory slope (Slope$_e$) and delta peak (Δpeak) are presented respect to expiratory WOB (WOB$_e$). A and B show the indexes for the experiment 1 (incremental PEEP). C and D show the indexes for the experiment 2 (Incremental PS). In each figure the linear trend, the square r and Pearson correlation coefficient (ρ) are presented.

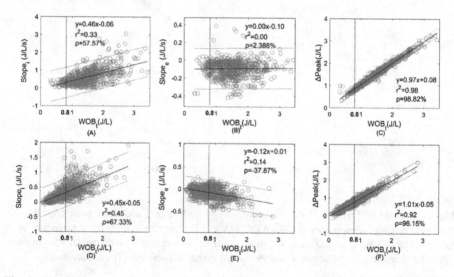

Fig. 4. The WOB Dynamic indexes, inspiratory slope (Slope$_i$), expiratory slope (Slope$_e$) and delta peak (Δpeak) are presented respect to WOB. A, B, and C show the indexes for the experiment 1 (incremental PEEP). D, E, and F show the indexes for the experiment 2 (Incremental PS). In each figure the linear trend, the square r and Pearson correlation coefficient (ρ) are presented.

4 Discussion

The WOB values presented in Table 1 show that PEEP levels higher than 6 cmH_2O produce high respiratory efforts with median values of WOB_i and WOB_t higher than 1.4 J/L, which are considered elevated by other studies [10] that have demonstrated that WOB values greater than 1.4 J/L are associated with unsuccessful extubations. When seeing the significant difference between the last 3 levels respect to basal condition and considering that the subjects in this study were clinically healthy, it can be concluded that the high WOB values were the result of high levels of PEEP and not due to pathologies related to the respiratory system. This shows the importance of monitoring the WOB during spontaneous ventilation to take it into account in the configuration of the PEEP and not only the other characteristics such as dyspnea and autoPEEP [6, 7], because an inadequate configuration of PEEP can produce high WOB, which added to the efforts associated to each respiratory pathology could cause delays in patients treatment. As expected, the expiratory WOB values during PEEP experiment are negligible respect to WOB_e and WOB_t and do not present significant differences respect to the basal condition, because the expiration is a passive phase, where the respiratory muscles are relaxed [13].

The WOB values associated with the incremental PS experiment (Table 2) are mostly concentrated in values less than 1.4 J/L, this is because the objective of pressure support ventilation is to help the patients to overcome the resistive load in the airway and facilitate the entry of the air, reducing the respiratory muscles effort and work of breathing [1, 7]. It is important to highlight that in WOB_e values higher than 4 cmH2O present significant differences respect to the basal level, although the values are not associated with high PS, this difference may have relationship with Alotaibi [5] who expresses that high levels of PS are associated with delayed breath termination that can get to contract active expiratory muscles. Although, in healthy subjects, WOB_e is not increased excessively, it is possible that in patients with pathologies such as COPD in whom it is difficult to modify the inspiratory time, the PS increases the WOB. Nevertheless, the finding of WOBe for high levels of PS is not confirmed by the $Slope_e$ or any other index, which leaves the research topic open to future works.

Because the ventilatory process is dynamic and the ventilatory mechanics changes during each respiratory cycle [14], it is important to know the behavior of the WOB transiently, for this purpose indexes were proposed from the curve WOBdyn to look for information complementary to the WOB. The linear trend between Δpeak and WOB allows to appreciate that there are no evident differences between indexes, which indicates that any of those could be used for the same porpose of previous studies [8, 9, 15]. In contrast, $Slope_i$ before the threshold of 0.8 J/L has a lower dispersion in comparison with the dispersion after the threshold, which suggests that higher values of WOB could be obtained in different ways, for instance, changing the breathing pattern. It can be noted that when the WOBi and WOBt increases, the $Slope_i$ dispersion increases too, that is, to reach the same value of WOB different slopes are presented.

The units of the $Slope_i$ indicate that the respiratory effort is normalized both by the volume like the WOB as for the time, this index indicates how quickly the maximum level of WOB is reached, it gives information about the morphology of the curve in terms of the initial inclination, but it is possible that the area under the curve does not vary (see Figs. 2 and 4). This may indicate that there are different ventilatory or muscular patterns to achieve high WOB values. Studies like the presented by Serna et al. [16] compares several models that present different patterns to compensate pulmonary ventilation during exercise, modifying either their respiratory rate, their tidal volume, or the respiratory muscles engagement as a response of chemoreceptors of the cardiorespiratory system or motor neurons such as phrenic. These results found in exercise may indicate that different patterns can also be found for patients. Hernandez et al. [2] show that different muscle patterns can be presented in healthy subjects for the same level of PEEP, changing the response regarding the coupling of the respiratory muscles. The above corroborates that different muscle patterns can be presented at the same level of WOB among subjects.

In conclusion, the inspiratory slope like an index of WOB dynamics can suggest the ventilatory pattern of the patient, which offers an extra information to the clinicians to make decision about the optimum treatment to be applied. These results open a window of research that allows to explore the ways that may exist to achieve high WOB values. One of them is to contrast the results of this study with the activity of the respiratory muscles in response to increases in PEEP and PS looking for answers that complement the results obtained in this paper.

Acknowledgements. Research supported by Universidad de Antioquia through the Project code PRG-2015-7851 "Análisis de la actividad muscular respiratoria en ventilación mecánica no invasiva y su relación con la configuración del ventilador".

References

1. Ladeira, M.T., Vital, F.M.R., Andriolo, R.B., Andriolo, B.N.G., Atallah, A.N., Peccin, M.S.: Pressure support versus T tube for weaning from mechanical ventilation in adults (Review). Cochrane Database Syst. Rev. **5**, 1–67 (2014). https://doi.org/10.1002/14651858.CD006056.pub2
2. Hernández, A.M., Salazar, M.B., Muñoz, I.C.: Efecto del incremento del PEEP en la actividad muscular respiratoria en sujetos sanos bajo ventilación espontánea. IATREIA **29** (3), 280–291 (2016). https://doi.org/10.17533/udea.iatreia.v29n3a03
3. Peces-Barba, G.: Fisiopatología del atrapamiento aéreo en la EPOC. Rev. Patol. Respir. Patol. Respir. **8**(2), 255–261 (2005)
4. Chikhani, M., Das, A., Haque, M., Wang, W., Bates, D.G., Hardman, J.G.: High PEEP in acute respiratory distress syndrome: Quantitative evaluation between improved arterial oxygenation and decreased oxygen delivery. Br. J. Anaesth. **117**(5), 650–658 (2016). https://doi.org/10.1093/bja/aew314
5. Alotaibi, G.A.: Effect of pressure support level, patient's effort, and lung mechanics on phase synchrony during pressure support ventilation. Middle East J Anaesthesiol. **22**(6), 573–582 (2014)
6. Montaño, E.A., et al.: Utilidad del índice CROP como marcador pronóstico de extubación exitosa. Med. Interna Mex. **31**(2), 164–173 (2015)
7. Figueroa, R.S., Hernández, F.A.: Ventilación mecánica en paciente con enfermedad pulmonar obstructiva crónica. Rev. Chil. Med. Intensiva. **27**(1), 23–33 (2012)

8. Cabello, B., Mancebo, J.: Work of breathing. Intensive Care Med. **32**(9), 1311–1314 (2006). https://doi.org/10.1007/s00134-006-0278-3

9. Akoumianaki, E., et al.: The application of esophageal pressure measurement in patients with respiratory failure. Am. J. Respir. Crit. Care Med. **189**(5), 520–531 (2014). https://doi.org/10.1164/rccm.201312-2193CI

10. Kirton, O.C., DeHaven, C.B., Morgan, J.P., Windsor, J., Civetta, J.M.: Elevated imposed work of breathing masquerading as ventilator weaning intolerance. Chest **108**(4), 1021–1025 (1995)

11. Teixeira, C., Zimermann, P.J., Pickersgill, P., Oliveira, E.S.: Work of breathing during successful spontaneous breathing trial. J. Crit. Care **24**(4), 508–514 (2009). https://doi.org/10.1016/j.jcrc.2008.10.013

12. Bellani, G., et al.: Clinical assessment of auto-positive end-expiratory pressure by diaphragmatic electrical activity during pressure support and neurally adjusted ventilatory assist. Anesthesiology **121**(3), 563–571 (2014)

13. Muñoz, I.C., Hernández, A.M.: Cambios en la mecánica ventilatoria debidos a variaciones de la PEEP y la presión soporte: estudio en sujetos sanos bajo ventilación mecánica no invasiva. Rev. Fac. Med. **65**(2), 459–466 (2017). https://doi.org/10.15446.v65n2.60938

14. Fishman, C.L., Rodriguez, N.E.: The respiratory system. In: Egan's Fundamentals of Respiratory Care, pp. 158–208 (2017)

15. Shen, D., Zhang, Q., Shi, Y.: Dynamic characteristics of mechanical ventilation system of double lungs with bi-level positive airway pressure model. Comput. Math. Methods Med. **2016**, 1–13 (2016). https://doi.org/10.1155/2016/9234537

16. Serna, L.Y., Mañanas, M.A., Hernández, A.M., Rabinovich, R.A.: An improved dynamic model for the respiratory response to exercise. Front. Physiol. **9**(69), 1–16 (2018). https://doi.org/10.3389/fphys.2018.00069

Design and Implementation of a Sliding Mode Observer-Based Controller for a Mass-Spring System

Carlos M. Florez R.[1], Hector Botero Castro[1],
and Esteban Jiménez-Rodríguez[2(✉)]

[1] Facultad de Minas, Universidad Nacional de Colombia,
Sede Medellin, Carrera 80 No. 65-223, Medellín, Colombia
{cmflorezr,habotero}@unal.edu.co
[2] Department of Electrical Engineering, Cinvestav Guadalajara,
Av. del Bosque 1145 Col. El Bajío, Zapopan, Mexico
ejimenezr@gdl.cinvestav.mx

Abstract. This work presents the implementation of a sliding mode observer-based controller on a mass-spring experimental platform. The controller is based on the super-twisting algorithm and the observer is based on a high order sliding mode algorithm, to obtain continuous control signal. The simulations and practical results show a good performance of the complete structure.

Keywords: Sliding mode · Super-twisting algorithm
Observer-based control

1 Introduction

Nonlinear control is currently a trending research topic in a wide spectrum of academic programs around the world. A large amount of works in this topic have been published in specialized journals and books [6,12,14]. Among nonlinear control research, the sliding mode control algorithms have attracted a lot of attention because of its desirable properties of insensitivity to bounded disturbances, robustness and finite-time convergence [4,9,11], especially in electromechanical systems [14]. Generally, sliding mode controllers require the whole state vector knowledge, making necessary the implementation of observer-based controllers.

The sliding mode observer-based controller problem have been highly studied [2,7,8]. However, most of these works deeply explain theoretical concepts and advanced mathematical tools, while few of them focus their attention on the implementation of such techniques. Therefore, for educative purposes, there is an essential gap between theory and practice, especially in advanced topics such as sliding mode algorithms. Some causes of this gap are the complexity of control engineering practice, produced by the fundamental limitation of control theory to

© Springer Nature Switzerland AG 2018
J. C. Figueroa-García et al. (Eds.): WEA 2018, CCIS 916, pp. 418–427, 2018.
https://doi.org/10.1007/978-3-030-00353-1_37

consider all the decision space in real problems [13]; the lack of control engineers and researchers which jointly look for solutions to practical control problems where assumptions and constraints are consistent with real-world problems [5], and also the lack of projects and seminars in close contact with the industry problematic and issues concerning control engineering [10]. Nevertheless, some authors have shown applications of sliding mode observer based control in real plants using specialized software [2,3], but this software is not still available in all industrial environments.

Hence, the design of an experimental platform and implementation of a super-twisting controller (STC) based on a high order sliding mode observer (HOSMO) for a low cost mass-spring system is studied in this paper. The experimental platform allows the programming of different observer-based control strategies on a low cost platform in order to verify the real performance of these strategies in the electromechanical system. In this system it is also possible to test advanced techniques of control and to verify the performance in presence of noise in sensor and limitations in actuators.

The rest of the paper is organized as follows. Section 2 presents the model of the experimental plant. Section 3 summarizes the selection of observer-based controller structures and explains some disadvantages of each structure. Section 4 shows and analyzes the simulation and implementation results. Finally, in Sect. 5 the conclusions are summarized.

2 System Description and Modeling

2.1 System Description

A low cost mass-spring system was designed and constructed due to its simplicity and nonlinear dynamics. The system consists of a mass, a spring, an electromagnet (generally used in building doors), an ultrasonic sensor and a low cost processor. The picture of the system is shown in Fig. 1.

The mass is suspended by means of the spring. The electromagnet, which exerts a force over the mass, is located in the bottom. The position of the mass is measured with an ultrasonic sensor placed in the bottom of the system. Such sensor has an transmitter that sends a short pulse whose duration is proportional to the time traveled by the ultrasonic wave which arrives to the receiver. So the time is proportional to the wave travel distance and therefore is proportional to the position of the mass with respect to the floor. The processor consists in a low cost board Arduino-UNO [TM] [1].

2.2 System Modeling

To develop a mathematical model of the experimental platform in Fig. 1, the Newton's second law was applied over the mass, it yields:

$$m\ddot{x} = -kx + f_u, \tag{1}$$

Fig. 1. Experimental platform.

where m is the suspended weight, k represents the elastic spring constant, x is the position of the mass with respect to the reference axis, and f_u represents the external force provided by the electromagnet. The reference axis is taken positive downwards. The electromagnet force f_u in Eq. (1) can be calculated by the Lorentz law, as follows:

$$f_u = \frac{B^2 A}{2\mu}, \tag{2}$$

where B represents the induced magnetic field by the flux current through the copper wire, A is the transversal area of the coil, and μ represents the medium permeability. Now, the magnetic field B is calculated as:

$$B = \frac{Ni\mu}{l - x}, \tag{3}$$

where N indicates the the number of turns around the iron core, i represents the current flowing through the coil, and l is the distance between the electromagnet and the reference axis. Replacing (3) into (2), considering that $e = Ri$, with e the source voltage and R the electrical resistance of the winding, Eq. (2) can be written as:

$$f_u = \frac{\mu N^2 A e^2}{2R^2(l - x)^2}. \tag{4}$$

Finally, replacing (4) into (1), a model of the experimental platform described in Subsect. 2.1 is:

$$m\ddot{x} = -kx + \frac{\mu N^2 A e^2}{2R^2(l-x)^2}. \tag{5}$$

2.3   State Space Representation

The second-order system (5) can be expressed as a first-order two-dimensional system of nonlinear ordinary differential equations, by means of the introduction of the velocity variable $v = \dot{x}$, as follows:

$$\dot{x} = v$$
$$\dot{v} = \frac{-kx}{m} + \frac{\mu N^2 A e^2}{2mR^2(l-x)^2}. \tag{6}$$

Thus, defining $x_1 = x$ and $x_2 = v = \dot{x}$, the nonlinear system (6) can be rewritten of the form:

$$\dot{x}_1 = x_2$$
$$\dot{x}_2 = b(x)u + \rho_1 \tag{7}$$
$$y = x_1,$$

where $b(x) = \frac{\mu N^2 A}{2mR^2(l-x)^2}$ is a bounded nonlinear function with known bound of the form $b(x) \geq \delta > 0$, since the limits of the position x are previously defined, $u = e^2$ is a term that encompasses the control action and $\rho_1 = \frac{-kx}{m}$ is an unknown but bounded perturbation (the mass position is always finite), whose time derivative is also bounded (the mass velocity is always finite). Note that the voltage e is between a strong nonlinearity, which requires a robust control strategy that ensures a strong control action what a traditional control can not handle.

3   Sliding-Mode Observer-Based Controllers

As previously noted, the system (7) represents a mass-spring dynamic system. The next step is to select a sliding mode-based control strategy given the structure proposed in [2,3]. However, the model used in the cited reference is a double integrator, but in this case the model has a term $b(x)$ instead of 1. Therefore, in this work we assume the term $b(x)$ as if it were an additional disturbance and we simply use the same algorithms of the double integrator. In addition, note that it is not possible to design a STC of the form $u = -k_1 |x_1|^{\frac{1}{2}} \operatorname{sig}(x_1) - \int_0^t k_2 \operatorname{sig}(x_1) d\tau$, or the form $u = -k_1 |\hat{x}_2|^{\frac{1}{2}} \operatorname{sig}(\hat{x}_2) - \int_0^t k_2 \operatorname{sig}(\hat{x}_2) d\tau$, since system (7) has relative degree two with respect to the output $y = x_1$. Hence, the three strategies proposed in [2,3] are compared and summarized in Table 1, comments regarding each strategy are included below.

Table 1. Structure of controller and observer (Based in [3])

Algorithm	Observer	Controller
STC+STO	$\dot{\hat{x}}_1 = \hat{x}_2 + k_1 \|e_1\|^{\frac{1}{2}} \text{sig}(e_1),$ $\dot{\hat{x}}_2 = u + k_2\text{sig}(e_1),$ $e_1 = x_1 - \hat{x}_1$	$u = -k_2\text{sig}(e_1) - c_1\hat{x}_2 -$ $\quad \lambda_1 \|s\|^{\frac{1}{2}} \text{sig}(s) - \int_0^t \lambda_2\text{sig}(s)d\tau,$ $s = c_1x_1 + \hat{x}_2$
STC+STOF	$\dot{\hat{x}}_1 = \hat{x}_2 + k_1 \|e_1\|^{\frac{1}{2}} \text{sig}(e_1),$ $\dot{\hat{x}}_2 = u + k_2\text{sig}(e_1),$ $e_1 = x_1 - \hat{x}_1$	$u = -c_1\hat{x}_2 - \lambda_1 \|s\|^{\frac{1}{2}} \text{sig}(s) -$ $\quad \int_0^t \lambda_2\text{sig}(s)d\tau,$ $s = c_1\hat{x}_1 + \hat{x}_2$
STC+HOSMO	$\dot{\hat{x}}_1 = \hat{x}_2 + k_1 \|e_1\|^{\frac{2}{3}} \text{sig}(e_1),$ $\dot{\hat{x}}_2 = \hat{x}_3 + u + k_2 \|e_1\|^{\frac{1}{3}} \text{sig}(e_1),$ $\dot{\hat{x}}_3 = k_3\text{sig}(e_1),$ $e_1 = x_1 - \hat{x}_1$	$u = -c_1\hat{x}_2 - \int_0^t k_3\text{sig}(e_1)d\tau -$ $\quad \lambda_1 \|s\|^{\frac{1}{2}} \text{sig}(s) - \int_0^t \lambda_2\text{sig}(s)d\tau,$ $s = c_1x_1 + \hat{x}_2$

3.1   STC - Super-Twisting Observer (STO)

If the sliding variable $s = c_1x_1 + \hat{x}_2$ is considered, then the undesirable discontinuous (and consequently non-differentiable) term $k_2\text{sig}(e_1)$, with $e_1 = x_1 - \hat{x}_1$, appears in the dynamics of s, making impossible to induce a sliding mode on the manifold $s = \dot{s} = 0$ with a conventional super-twisting algorithm. If the term $k_2\text{sig}(e_1)$ is canceled by the control signal [14], then it is possible to induce a sliding mode on the manifold $s = \dot{s} = 0$ but the control signal ceases to be continuous (see Table 1).

3.2   STC - Super-Twisting Output Feedback (STOF)

A second strategy was derived in [8] considering the sliding variable $s = c_1\hat{x}_1 + \hat{x}_2$. This selection yields a continuous controller, however it neglects some effects explained in the STC-STO comments, producing some chattering.

3.3   STC-HOSMO

In [2] the observer-based controller proposal is based on a traditional STC while a HOSMO is used to estimate the state of the system (7). This work considers $s = c_1x_1 + \hat{x}_2$. The dynamics of s is free of discontinuous terms, at the price of increasing the complexity of the state observer.

4   Results

In this section, both simulation and implementation results are presented. The simulations were tested with the three structures presented in Table 1, while the implementation was carried out only with the STC+HOSMO strategy, which was programmed in the processor.

4.1 Simulation Results

The initial condition of the integrators and the parameters of the tested strategies are shown in Table 2.

Table 2. Simulation parameters parameters

Control settings	Value
Initial condition of plant	$x(0) = [0.1, 0]^T$
Initial condition of observers	$\hat{x}(0) = [0.15, 0.05]^T$
Set point value	0.3 cm for $t < 1$ s, 1 cm for $t > 1$ s
STC-STO and STC-STOF gain values	$k_1 = \lambda_1 = 9$, $k_2 = \lambda_2 = 1.5$
STC-HOSM gain values	$k_1 = 5$, $k_2 = 15$, $k_3 = 15$, $\lambda_1 = 9$, $\lambda_2 = 1.5$

On the other hand, the plant parameters are listed in Table 3.

Table 3. Plant parameters

Parameter	Value
Number of turns around the core	762
Electromagnet cross sectional area	$0.0031 \, \text{m}^2$
Coil resistance	5.5 ohm
Electromagnet reference distance	0.02 m
Permeability of free space	$4\pi 10^{-7} \, \text{NA}^{-1}$
Magnetic permeability of steel	$1000 \, \text{NA}^{-1}$
Elastic spring constant	$90.4367 \, \text{Nm}^{-1}$
Weight of the mass	0.648 kg

In the first case (STC+STO) the controller has the disadvantage of discontinuous control action, producing the well-known chattering effect as shown in Fig. 2 and with more detail in Fig. 3. However, an acceptable time-response is obtained (see Fig. 2).

In the second case (STC-STOF) the time-response of the closed-loop system is similar to previous case, but a slight reduction of the chattering effect is obtained, as can be seen in Figs. 4 and 5.

Finally, in the third case (STC-HOSMO) the chattering effect is apparently eliminated, and the time-response is better with respect to the settling time. The results as shown in Figs. 6 and 7.

It is worth to notice that the gains of STC based on STO and STOF are the same because the controlled dynamic system has the same mathematical model. The difference lies in the variables used for closing the loop. In Figs. 3 and 5, it

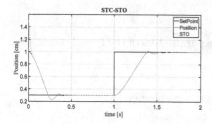

Fig. 2. STC-STO mass position.

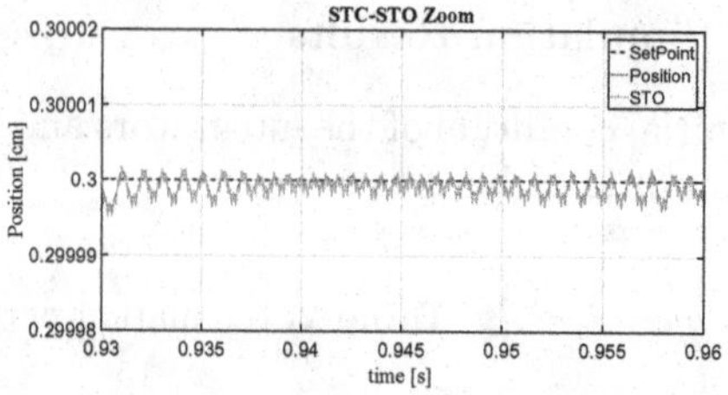

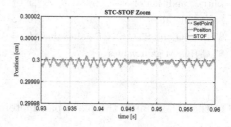

Fig. 3. Zoom in STC-STO mass position.

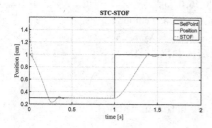

Fig. 4. STC-STOF mass position.

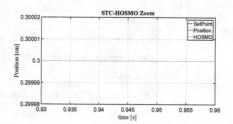

Fig. 5. Zoom in STC-STOF mass position.

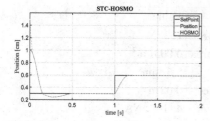

Fig. 6. STC-HOSMO mass position.

Fig. 7. Zoom in STC-HOSMO mass position.

is noticeable that the chattering effect is low, however it is high recommended to reduce it as much as possible in order to avoid fast changes in actuators, to prevent fails, damages, among others.

In order to quantitatively compare the performance of the controllers, the integral of the absolute error (IAE) index is calculated in each case over the control tracking error. The results can be seen in Table 4, where the STC-HOSMO is the structure which presents the best performance with respect to this index.

4.2 Implementation Results

Based on the results of the previous subsection, it was concluded that the observer-based control strategy which provided best performance is the STC-HOSMO combination. Therefore, this subsection describes the practical implementation in the real experimental platform shown in Fig. 1. The control action

Table 4. Performance indexes

Case	IAE
STC-STO	0.02521
STC-STOF	0.0193
STC-HOSMO	0.0030

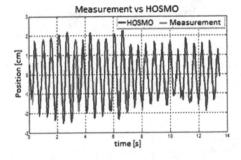

Fig. 8. Position estimation.   **Fig. 9.** Velocity estimation.

is carried out by a PWM, due to the difficulty in having an analog output by processor. Thus, the control task is to automatically adjust the duty cycle of the PWM.

In order to protect the electronic circuit, the low power signal generated by the processor was separated of the high-power signal applied to the electromagnet and supplied by an external source. The implementation of the observer and controller algorithms were carried out by means of the low-cost processor. Therefore, the implementation of the system does not require specialized equipment or software. The sample time used for implementation of controllers and observers was 0.03 s and the Euler integration method was also used.

Initially, the HOSMO was tested without control. The results are shown in Figs. 8 (position estimation) and 9 (velocity estimation), where the noise attenuation capability can be noticed.

From Figs. 8 and 9, it is possible to see a good observer performance, still in presence of sensor noise. The velocity estimation is accurate and suitable for observer-based controller strategies.

Finally, the whole STC-HOSMO strategy was implemented in the platform. The results are shown in Fig. 10.

Figure 10 shows that the performance of the STC-HOSMO strategy is appropriate since the set point signal is tracked with a settling time of 0.5 s, and no overshoot when the set point is increased. However, a remarkable undershoot can be seen when the set point signal is decreased, because the set point in 0 cm is farther than 1 cm setpoint with respect to the electromagnet and the exerted force is less. In addition, when the mass moves upwards, controllability is lost due to the electromagnet reduces the magnetic field and the spring force is the

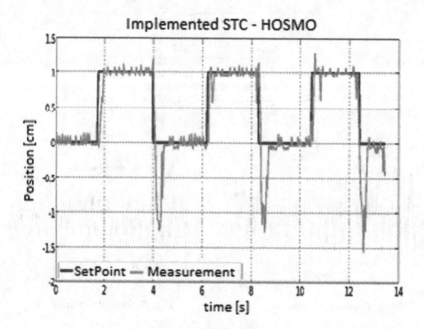

Fig. 10. Implementation results

restorative input. Nevertheless, the performance of the sliding mode observer-based controller strategy is satisfactory despite the modeling uncertainties and measurement noise, showing its robustness.

5   Conclusions

A comparative study between different sliding mode observer-based controller strategies was carried out in this paper. The comparison was done through the IAE index, over the tracking error, using numerical simulations. The STC-HOSMO was the structure which presented the best performance with respect to this index. Then, this strategy was implemented in a low-cost processor and tested over a real low-cost mass-spring system, whose model (which was also developed in this paper) matches a perturbed double integrator system.

It is worth to mention that the electromagnet can only exert an attraction force. Thus, the practical results showed a remarkable performance when the mass was to be attracted (positive changes in the reference), while a poor performance was observed in the opposite case. Therefore in this example was possible to analyze a practical problem of loss of controllability. On the other hand, implementation results also suggest that it is still necessary to consider several issues in real plant implementations like measurement noise, limitations in the actuators, among others. In this sense, the need of more real implementation studies is still open.

References

1. Arduino-UNO: Getting Started with Arduino and Genuino products (2018). https://www.arduino.cc/en/Guide/HomePage
2. Chalanga, A., Kamal, S., Fridman, L., Bandyopadhyay, B., Moreno, J.A.: How to implement super-twisting controller based on sliding mode observer? In: 2014 13th International Workshop on Variable Structure Systems (VSS), pp. 1–6, June 2014. https://doi.org/10.1109/VSS.2014.6881145
3. Chalanga, A., Kamal, S., Fridman, L.M., Bandyopadhyay, B., Moreno, J.A.: Implementation of super-twisting control: super-twisting and higher order sliding-mode observer-based approaches. IEEE Trans. Ind. Electron. **63**(6), 3677–3685 (2016). https://doi.org/10.1109/TIE.2016.2523913
4. Edwards, C., Colet, E., Fridman, L.: Advances in Variable Structure and Sliding Mode Control. Springer, Berlin (2009)
5. Gao, Z., Rhinehart, R.R.: Theory vs. practice: the challenges from industry. In: Proceedings of the 2004 American Control Conference, pp. 1341–1349, June 2004
6. Khalil, H.: Nonlinear Systems, 3rd edn. Pearson Education Limited, London (2013)
7. Levant, A.: Sliding order and sliding accuracy in sliding mode control. Int. J. Control **58**(6), 1247–1263 (1993). https://doi.org/10.1080/00207179308923053
8. Levant, A.: Higher-order sliding modes, differentiation and output-feedback control. Int. J. Control **76**(9–10), 924–941 (2003). https://doi.org/10.1080/0020717031000099029
9. Perruquetti, W., Barbot, J.: Sliding Mode Control in Engineering. Automation and Control Engineering. CRC Press, Boca Raton (2002)
10. Piechottka, U., Hagenmeyer, V.: A discussion of the actual status of process control in theory and practice: a personal view from german process industry. Automatisierungstechnik **62**(2), 67–77 (2014). https://doi.org/10.1515/auto-2014-1018
11. Shtessel, Y., Edwards, C., Fridman, L., Levant, A.: Sliding Mode Control and Observation. Control Engineering. Springer, New York (2013)
12. Smith, C.A., Corripio, A.B.: Principles and Practices of Automatic Process Control, 3rd edn (2005)
13. Strmnik, S., Juricic, D.: Case Studies in Control. Advances in Industrial Control. Springer, London (2013). https://doi.org/10.1007/978-1-4471-5176-0
14. Utkin, V.I., Guldner, J., Shi, J.: Sliding Mode Control in Electro-Mechanical Systems. Automation and Control Engineering, 2nd edn. CRC Press, Boca Raton (2009)

Design of a Device for Recording Bioelectric Signals with Surface Electrodes, in the Evaluation of the Effect of Ultraviolet Radiation on a Tissue

Fabian Garay[1,2] ⓘ, Aura Hernández[1], Hans López[2], Helber Barbosa[1], and Bibiana Vallejo[1(✉)] ⓘ

[1] Grupo de Investigación en Procesos de Transformación de Materiales para la Industria Farmacéutica (PTM), Universidad Nacional de Colombia, Bogotá, Colombia
{fsgarayr,arhernandezc,hdbarbosab, bmvallejod}@unal.edu.co
[2] Grupo de Investigación, Desarrollo y Aplicaciones en Señales (IDEAS), Universidad Distrital Francisco José de Caldas, Bogotá, Colombia
hilopezc@udistrital.edu.co

Abstract. The accepted methodology by regulatory agencies to determine the efficacy of sunscreen products makes use of healthy human volunteers who are exposed to radiation. In order to find an alternative to these types of evaluations, the effect of exposure to *UV* radiation was investigated in an *ex vivo* pig skin model on the bioelectrical signals of the tissue in terms of energy and impedance. A system was implemented using the measurements configuration of 4 electrodes (Two electrostimulation electrodes and two electrodes for the signals acquisition all of them were silver cup electrodes) and a mathematical model was established in relation to electrical change as a function of exposure time. As a result, an attenuation of the energy response signal relative to the non-irradiated tissue was obtained, as well as impedance values after irradiation. This behavior is directly related to damage in the tissue structure. The results allow to conclude that the device can quantify the effect caused by radiation on the electrical properties of an *ex vivo* tissue and are promising in the understanding of the phenomena associated with the electrical response of a tissue to ultraviolet radiation.

Keywords: Electrical energy · Biomedical device · *UV* radiation Signals · Tissue

1 Introduction

The dielectric properties of biological tissues are affected when exposed it to an electric field, generating chemical and physical processes [1]. Each one of the structures and regions of the biological tissues have a particular properties and electrical phenomena that depend on their nature and state as well as the applied frequency [2]. Some researchers have identified relaxation or dispersion factors related to tissue response to current and frequency. Tissues exhibit dispersions due to physical processes that

J. C. Figueroa-García et al. (Eds.): WEA 2018, CCIS 916, pp. 428–441, 2018.
https://doi.org/10.1007/978-3-030-00353-1_38

include polarization along the membrane boundary structure [3]. The study of changes on the electrical characteristics of tissues has been previously studied [4]. However, variations in the electrical response of tissues because of a stimulus such as ultraviolet (*UV*) radiation are unknown. This radiation is located at wavelengths from 200 nm to 400 nm and it has been proven that prolonged exposure to it can cause damage to human skin such as burns, pigmentation change, texture, and even long-term carcinogenic effects [5].

As a strategy to evaluate the effect of *UV* radiation on electrical properties of tissues the use of low complexity biomedical equipment and Digital Signal Processing (DSP) techniques is proposed. This research presents the evaluation of electrical changes on an *ex vivo* tissue exposed to radiation as well as the efficacy of the proposed device for detecting changes in the samples.

2 Conceptualization

As a starting point it is necessary to identify the data acquisition systems and primary elements according to the application, since it is desired to obtain records of precise bioelectric signals, which subsequently will be processed analogically and digitally.

2.1 Electrical Behavior of Biological Tissues

The response of tissues to current and frequency has shown that for frequencies below 1 kHz, the conductivity of tissues is dominated by the conduction of electrolytes in the extracellular space. Tissues exhibit the alpha (α) dispersion due to physical processes that include polarization along the membrane boundary structure [3]; in the case of frequencies higher than 100 kHz, displacement currents are presented through the cell wall, which produce dielectric relaxation phenomena due to the polarization of several dipoles and the movement of the induced charges [6].

2.2 Electrodes

They are the primary element of the measurement chain and are put in contact to biological samples. The bad conduction of the cells shield part of the electrode, hence the electrode material is fundamental to determine the polarization impedance. The inductance of the test and the connection wires add another series of components that interfere with the measurement. The size and type of electrode are also important in determining that impedance; the larger ones (surface electrodes) tend to have smaller impedances, while the smaller ones such a needle electrodes or micro-electrodes, have much greater values of impedance [7].

2.3 Signal Conditioning

During the processing of the biological signals, especially if it is related to bioelectric potentials, the isolation of the noise (either thermal or induced by the electrical network) and the optimal filtering conditions are very important issues for avoiding affectations in the signal integrity. In particular, the electrical network induces selective noise in spectral components of interest. The harmonics, which are frequencies multiples of the fundamental working frequency, for the case of 60 Hz networks, can appear at 120 Hz and 240 Hz. These harmonics are the most relevant noises because its magnitudes are comparable with the bioelectric potential captured. Therefore, electric filters type notch, which can reduce these components, must be implemented [8].

2.4   Energy of a Signal (Parseval Function)

Expressed in terms of power × time, in the context of the Theory of Signals and Systems, in engineering, the normalized energy of a real function f(t), in a time interval (a, b) can be obtained with the Eq. 1.

$$E = \int_a^b \|f(t)\|^2 dt \tag{1}$$

2.5   Electrostimulator (TENS)

TENS stimulates tissue by using monopolar or bipolar direct current pulses. These non-lethal current levels are achieved by generating a high voltage. These pulses have a current that can range from 1 mA to 120 mA, working frequency from 1 to 250 Hz and pulse duration from 50 μs to 400 μs. This frequency is controlled by three modes (Fixed frequency, Burst and modulated) [9].

3   Materials and Methods

Firstly, the criteria for the selection and processing of the tissue samples as well as the construction of the modules for recording the bioelectric signals and the responses in voltage and current of the tissue will be described. Likewise, the design of the electrostimulator for the injection of current to the samples will be outlined. Then, the selection of the module for storage and digital processing of the data obtained for computer visualization will be included, which allowed the analysis and evaluation of the mathematical model obtained. Finally, the procedure for conducting the experimental tests will be presented.

3.1   Selection of the Test Tissue

Pig skin was used as a study model, taking into account its recognized similarity with human skin, especially in its outer layers [10]. The age of the animal was not relevant in this case, but it was important that it had not been blanched or flamed after being slaughtered, since this type of pre-treatment completely destroys the integrity of the epidermis [11].

3.2 Selection of Electrodes

The silver cup surface electrodes were selected to obtain measurements of the bio-electric signals generated in the tissue and to examine the response to the electro-stimulation impulses, due to their low impedance. Needle electrodes were used for the implementation of the electro-stimulator; the concentric needle electrode type was selected.

3.3 Acquisition Module

The 4-electrode or tetra-polar method (Fig. 1) was fixed. I this case, a current is applied by two electrodes and the potential value can be visualized from two other electrodes located on the region of interest. With this method it is possible to minimize the effect of the impedance of the electrodes, since the impedance of these is lower than the input impedance of the voltage acquisition module [12].

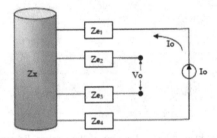

Fig. 1. Schematic 4-electrodes configuration for measuring impedance [12].

3.4 Conditioning Module

A band pass filter from 10 Hz to 300 Hz was designed, which rejects all signals outside this range, with a quality factor $Q = 0.188$ and a central frequency $f0 = 54.77$ Hz. In addition, a Notch filter with a state variable of 60 Hz and 100 Hz with quality factor $Q = 15$ and 20 respectively, to mitigate the effect of the appearance of harmonics induced by the electrical network.

3.5 Electro-Stimulator (TENS)

For the design, the criteria of a bipolar Burst signal were taken into account and Eqs. 2 and 3, were used, where the envelope frequency values were established taking into account the PTD (Pulse Time Duration), PSD (Pulseless Duration) and working pulses.

$$T = PTD + PSD \tag{2}$$

$$Fp = \frac{1}{T} \tag{3}$$

where number of pulses: 6 and working frequency of the pulses: 21 Hz which leads to $T = 0.2501 + 0.266 = 0.5161$.

The signal obtained from TENS has a fundamental frequency of 1.93 Hz and a current peak of ± 0.025 mA, each train of pulses is characterized by a frequency of 20.87 Hz.

3.6   DAC Module (Digital Analog Conversion)/Oscilloscope

For the implementation of the ADC/oscilloscope module, a device Analog Discovery provided by DIGILENT and Analog Devices Inc., was used in a connection with a computer, see Fig. 2.

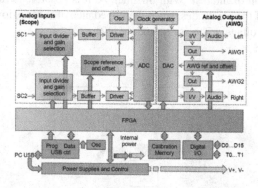

Fig. 2. Hardware blocks diagram of the analog discovery [13].

3.7   Digital Signal Processing- IIR Filter

The final processing of the signal was realized using a digital filter IIR to 60 Hz, suitably to work in real time and visualization from the computer. Equation 4 shows the mathematical modeling for the filter.

$$y[n] = x[n] - (2cos\,\theta)x[n-1] + x[n-1] + (2r)(cos\,\theta)y[n-1] - (r^2)y[n-1] \quad (4)$$

3.8   Experimental Development

Testing Chamber. Was used a chamber of irradiation constructed in metal, with dimensions of 40 cm × 45 cm × 30 cm, inside this one a tray with maximum capacity of four samples. It was used a lamp of mercury with UV range between 200 and 300 nm and irradiance of the 2.5 mW/cm^2, they guaranteed a uniform exposition for each sample of tissue.

Samples of Tissue. There were used pig skin samples extracted from the ventral region; this zone was selected due to the characteristics of the tissue like low exposition to the UV radiation that could have had the living animal. The tissue samples were obtained from a slaughter and 8 samples were acquired of healthy different pork. The samples were classified (mn) like this: m1, m2, m3, m4, m5, m6, m7 and m8. Every sample was cut in four portions, of which three were assigned to the group of testing (pmn), where (m) is the sample of origin and (n) the number of portion and another one to the group of tissue of reference or control (rn). Four more samples were left for the later validation of the device. Thereby, 36 samples were completed. To prepare and preserve the tissue it was immersed in glycerin and it was kept on an icebox at 4 ° C ± 0.5. The dimensions of the samples were 5.4 cm of length and 10.9 cm of width and the thickness of 2 cm ± 0.4 (preserving the adiposity).

Electrodes Positioning. The position of the electrodes of stimulation was done in order to perceive the applied signal in the whole tissue and to facilitate the potentials detection on the sensors of acquisition. From the tetrapolar method there were positioned two electrodes of needle of injection of current in the ends of the tissue and two silver cup electrodes, to obtain the value of the voltage or current of response in the middle of the sample, see Fig. 3. The value of the depth of the puncture of the needle electrodes was established in 5.5 mm ± 0.5.

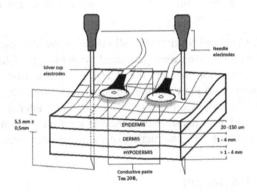

Fig. 3. Location of the 4 electrodes in the samples.

In order to improve the conductivity between the tissue and the electrodes and to facilitate the signals capturing, without interferences from the stratum corneum, enough conductive paste Ten20® was used.

Parameters for Accomplishment Testing. The tissues were divided in two groups: the first one corresponded to those samples of reference, those that were not exposed to the radiation and that used as control, in order to discriminate against external factors as the decomposition that could alter the measurements. The second group corresponded to the samples that were radiated in the testing chamber. In the experimentation the tissues of the second group were radiated for 4 h. Every sample was positioned to 6 cm of the source of UV radiation, see Fig. 4. The samples of the first group were in rest to temperature set (19 °C ± 1).

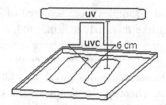

Fig. 4. Hook up system: distance between group 2 and UV radiation source.

For both groups the electrical response of the tissues was monitored by measurements of voltage and current every hour until 4 h. For that measurement, an indirect method was employed evaluating the voltage on a resistance equal to 1Ω and then by using Ohm's law was possible to obtain the value of the current.

For both groups 1 and 2, needle electrodes were positioned in connection with the electro-stimulator and immediately the silver cup electrodes were located in the module of conditioning and in direct connection with the channel 1 of the module ADC/oscilloscope, which had allowed the real time visualization of the signal with the computer and recording the information in an extension files .csv for its digital processing and statistical analysis.

Mathematical Modeling and Statistical Validation. From the results obtained in the previous stage, different analyses were generated by the aim to obtain a mathematical model, to describe the relation between the electrical characteristics of the tissues and the time of the exposition to the radiation. In order to assure a high reliability of the results, by Minitab 12® software the resultant information after digital processing of the signal and through check mathematical models up with experimental information that they did not do part of the construction of the same ones (cross validation).

4   Results and Discussion

4.1   Energetic Analysis

As proved from the calculations of energies across Parseval's theorem and by means of the Eq. 1, it was found a set of information of energy of the signal proceeding from both groups irradiated tissues (pmn) and reference tissues (rn), where a wide differentiation was demonstrated between the signals of energy of both groups. The behavior and trends were similar in the energetic response between members of the same group of samples (mn). In order to estimate the behavior of the information, the average of the energies was calculated for the set of the samples of the groups of tissues of reference (rn) by means of the Eqs. 5 and 6, there were obtained only two sets of information of energy named ER1 and ER2:

$$E_{R1} = \frac{\sum_{n=1}^{4} r_n}{4} \tag{5}$$

$$E_{R2} = \frac{\sum_{n=5}^{8} r_n}{4} \tag{6}$$

In the same way, for the information of the set of irradiated tissues (pmn), there was calculated the average of the energies, with the Eqs. 7, 8, 9 and 10 and obtained only 4 sets of information of energy named EP1, EP2, EP3 and EP4:

$$E_{P1} = \frac{\sum_{m=1}^{2} \sum_{n=1}^{3} P_{mn}}{6} \tag{7}$$

$$E_{P2} = \frac{\sum_{m=3}^{4} \sum_{n=1}^{3} P_{mn}}{6} \tag{8}$$

$$E_{P3} = \frac{\sum_{m=5}^{6} \sum_{n=1}^{3} P_{mn}}{6} \tag{9}$$

$$E_{P4} = \frac{\sum_{m=7}^{8} \sum_{n=1}^{3} P_{mn}}{6} \tag{10}$$

where (n) is the number of portion and m the number of sample of origin.

Despite of the fact that the evaluations were done for periods of 4 h, the behavior between samples was distinguishable and estimable until 3 h, see Fig. 5, where one shows the trend lines for the irradiation time from 0 to 3 h.

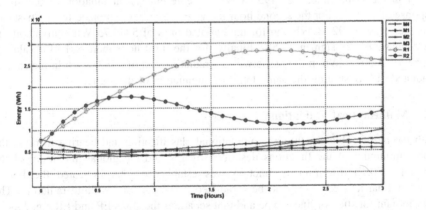

Fig. 5. Average energy of the irradiated samples EP (M1, M2, M3, M4) and reference ER (R1, R2) vs time from 0 to 3 h

To obtain the final mathematical model of the energy depending on the time, the average of the previous averages was calculated and the most identical line of trend to the information was chosen for obtaining two expressions: the first one, a polynomial function of order 3 that describes the behavior of the energy for not radiated samples and the second one, a polynomial function of order 2 that there characterizes the behavior of the energy of the radiated samples from 0 to 3 h, as appears in Fig. 6.

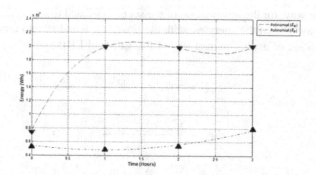

Fig. 6. Average energy of the irradiated samples EP ▲ and reference ER ▼ vs time from 0 to 3 h, final model.

The mathematical are: $E_R = 2133.9t^3 - 12626t^2 + 22800t + 7624.8$ and $E_P = 684.16t^2 - 1276.9 + 5407.2$. It is necessary to emphasize the percentage of the attenuation of the signal of energetic response from the radiated samples, evaluated in the three times. In the first hour the value of the energy obtained with the presented results which represents to the set of averages of energy of the reference samples was 19932.6 Wh, whereas the energy for the set of radiated samples calculated with the model in the same time, was 4959.8 Wh, it represents an attenuation of the signal response of 75.11%. For the second hour the value of energy estimated for the tissue of reference was 19792.31 Wh and for the radiated ones of 5444.75 Wh equivalently to the decrease of the sign in 72.5%. Finally, for the third hour there is had a value of energy of 20007.3 Wh in the tissue without radiating and of 7782.4 Wh in the sample irradiated, demonstrating the same trend of attenuation of the signal.

4.2 Mathematical Validation

With the aim to obtain a future computational classification and bearing in mind the global minimum of the functions described by ER and the global maximum of the functions EP, a discriminant function was established, that indicated the border between what it is considered to be a radiated tissue and one without radiating. The discriminant function of linear type and that separates the signs EP and ER e.g. $E_{DIS} = 162.93t + 12690$ shown in Fig. 7.

Then, the discriminant function leads to the following conditions:

$$\begin{cases} E \leq E_{DIS}, & IRRADITED\ TISSUE \\ E > E_{DIS}, & NON-IRRADITED\ TISSUE \end{cases}$$

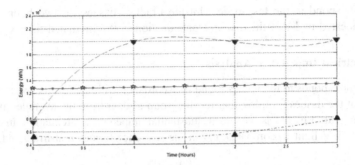

Fig. 7. Discriminant function -✳- separating the irradiated tissues area ▲ from the reference tissue area ▼.

The above indicates that the bioelectrical signal of the irradiated tissues with light UV weakens regarding to reference samples that were never irradiated. From the discriminant function, it is possible to say that the values of average energy obtained for a certain samples which are above of the line described by the discriminant function, can be classified as response of energy of not irradiated tissue or reference samples; but if the value of energy is minor and remains located below the function, it will be said that the values of energy obtained are the response of a radiated tissue. To clarify that part previously described, it is show in Fig. 8, it is the resulting graphic from two tissues mean energy, one of the samples was irradiated for two hours (test 1 UV) and other one was used as a reference at the same time (test 1 ref), it is important stand out that the samples used for to test the model, was not part of mathematic model construction and were separated for established a cross-validation.

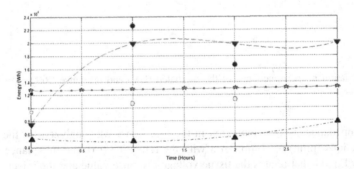

Fig. 8. Test 1 ref ◆ located up of the discriminant function in the non-irradiated tissues zone ▼. Test 1 UV ○ located down of the discriminant function in the irradiated tissues zone ▲.

Is noticeable how the data of the (test 1 ref) are located in the non-irradiated tissues zone or of reference with exception of the first point, because this represent a zero hour value energy, and whose value must be similar in all tests. Conversely, the data of (test

1 UV) correspond to the test made whit the irradiate tissues for two hours, and are correctly located under of the discriminant function in the irradiated tissues zone.

4.3 Electrical Impedance Analysis

Figure 9 corresponds to the values found in accordance with the results about energetic response of the tissues samples, that for the group of data from the average impedance calculation with Eq. 11, is visible a substantial impedance attenuation in irradiate tissues with UV light in comparison with the reference tissues non-irradiated.

$$Z_X = \frac{V_O}{I_O} [\Omega] \tag{11}$$

where Z_X is the tissue impedance of interest, "Vo" is the voltage coming from the sample and Io the electro-stimulation current in connection with the tissue.

The electrical impedance measure is used how confirmation method of the integrity and condition of the skin, to determine the irritation and potential corrosion caused by chemical and personal care products [14]. This change on the impedance can be explain how result of damage on the tissue; it is known that the UV radiation produce tissues alterations, this has been evidenced in the histological tests results of exposed skin to UVA and UVB radiation where is presented physiologic alterations, that would explain the variations found in the impedance values [15].

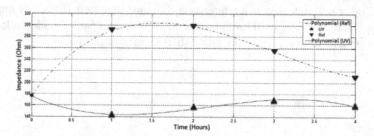

Fig. 9. Variation in the impedance of the irradiated (UV) and reference (Ref.) samples in the course of 0 to 4 h.

The impedance signal attenuation in the four hours was analyzed for the irradiate tissues sections (pmn) in comparison with the reference (rn), the impedance was calculated by Eq. 11 that relates the tissue voltage response value and the injected current which value was obtained as indirect measure on a 1Ω resistance.

In the first hour the average impedance value is 291.6 Ω, against the average impedance of the irradiate samples group in the same time was 140.3 Ω, this value represent a 51.9% signal attenuation. For the second hour the average impedance value for the non-irradiate tissues was 295.5 Ω and for the irradiates was 158.9 Ω, in this case the attenuation value is approximately 46.23% and the third hour the average impedance value for the reference tissues was 255.9 Ω and 166.8 Ω respective, with 32.81%

attenuation. Finally, for the four hour evaluation was obtained values of 210.3 Ω and 159.5 Ω hold the signal attenuation comportment, in this case of 24.16% of the irradiate tissues impedance during the test.

4.4 Statistical Analysis

The statistical analysis was used to describe the nature of the data obtained and to valid the model creation. For the voltage data obtained and from which the previous analyzes were derived, they were subjected to normality tests and goodness of fit tests to determine the most appropriate statistical distribution, under hypothesis test analysis. For that we used Minitab 12® software whose algorithms involve the hypothesis tests for verification of goodness of fit.

A probability Graph obtained for the references data, with a CI (Confidence Interval) of 95% allows verifying if the points distributed within the curves obtained or they approach these. The Correlation Coefficient was 0.954, which indicates that the variables are approximately 95.4% related and the Anderson-Darling Coefficient (AD) was 1.609, which is not small enough to ensure a good fit. For the UV irradiation data as in the previous case, some data go out of the probability curve, the AD coefficient had a value of 2.669, while the Correlation Coefficient was 0.921, and these data did not fit as a normal distribution. Was necessary to carry out other goodness of fit tests, for the experimental data.

The analysis of the correlation coefficient and Anderson-Darling values obtained, it allowed to establish the best indices for the Lognormal and Loglogistics distributions, for the reference data and of UV irradiated tissues. It was determined the Loglogistics distribution as the distribution model for the two data sets. To check the selection, were evaluated the Graphical overview of distribution and probability graph for the Loglogistics distribution for both sets of data.

The data are coupling to the Loglogistics distribution, for the two data sets, the correlation coefficient is higher than 0.95, which implies a good correlation between the data. The Anderson-Darling index that should be a low value in none of the two data sets exceeds the value of 1.4; this value indicates that the data is distributed very close to the line PP characteristic of the selected distribution.

5 Conclusions

It was visible the energetic changes of the tissue exposed to UV radiation (pmn) in comparison with the tissue that was not exposed (rn) giving indications of an alteration of the electrical balance due to exposition, these data are relevant in the energy values for the irradiated tissues compared to the reference values for the three hours of evaluation. However, at four hours the energy data of the different tissue groups are often scattered and are difficult to differentiate so it took three hours at the optimal time to perform the evaluations.

The mathematical models obtained, as in the case of the average energy for the tissues irradiated with UV light, showed a behavior easily separable by a discriminant function. This will facilitate a data classification processes through methods that use computational intelligence algorithms, such as neural networks or diffuse systems training by genetic algorithms.

The statistical analysis of the tissues evaluated data (reference and irradiated), showed that with a Confidence Index (CI) of 95% the behavior of the data is correctly described under the statistical model of a Loglogistics probability distribution. This as a result from the observation and analysis of the Anderson-Darling coefficient that was 1.36 and 1.06 for irradiated and reference samples respectively, and by the correlation coefficient that was 0.96 for both samples.

This study opens the possibility of deepening the implications of prolonged exposure to UV radiation in living beings, mainly in alterations in the electrical behavior of their tissues and the implications that these would have. Contributes to the field of research in the pharmaceutical sciences, biology, electrophysiology, medicine and materials science among others.

References

1. Rigaud, B., Morucci, J.P., Chauveau, N.: Bioelectrical impedance techniques in medicine. Part I: bioimpedance measurement. Second section: impedance spectrometry. Crit. Rev. Biomed. Eng. **24**, 257–351 (1996)
2. Schwan, H.P.: Dielectric properties of biological tissue and biophysical mechanisms of electromagnetic-field interaction. In: Illinger, K. (ed.) Biological Effects of Nonionizing Radiation, pp. 109–131. American Chemical Society, Washington, D.C. (1981). https://doi.org/10.1021/bk-1981-0157.ch008
3. Grimnes, S., Martinsen, Ø.G.: Chapter 3 - Dielectrics. In: Grimnes, S., Martinsen, Ø.G. (eds.) Bioimpedance and Bioelectricity Basics, 3rd edn, pp. 37–75. Academic Press, Oxford (2015). https://doi.org/10.1016/b978-0-12-411470-8.00003-9
4. Moncada, M.E., Saldarriaga, M.D.P., Bravo, A.F., Pinedo, C.R.: Medición de impedancia eléctrica en tejido biológico – revisión. TecnoLógicas **25**, 51–76 (2010). https://doi.org/10.22430/22565337.113
5. Sarkany, R.P.E.: Ultraviolet radiation and the skin (2018). http://linkinghub.elsevier.com/retrieve/pii/B9780124095489109315, https://doi.org/10.1016/b978-0-12-409548-9.10931-5
6. Foster, K.R., Schwan, H.P.: Dielectric properties of tissues. In: Polk, C., Postow, E (eds.) Handbook of Biological Effects of Electromagnetic Fields, pp. 25–102. CRC Press Inc., Boca Raton (1996)
7. Geddes, L.A.: Historical evolution of circuit models for the electrode-electrolyte interface. Ann. Biomed. Eng. **25**, 1–14 (1997). https://doi.org/10.1007/BF02738534
8. Vaseghi, S.V.: Noise and distortion. In: Advanced Digital Signal Processing and Noise Reduction, pp. 35–50. Wiley, Chichester (2008). https://doi.org/10.1002/9780470740156
9. Tashani, O., Johnson, M.: Transcutaneous electrical nerve stimulation (TENS) a possible aid for pain relief in developing countries. Libyan J. Med. **4**, 62–65 (2009). https://doi.org/10.4176/090119
10. Flaten, G.E., Palac, Z., Engesland, A., Filipović-Grčić, J., Vanić, Ž., Škalko-Basnet, N.: In vitro skin models as a tool in optimization of drug formulation. Eur. J. Pharm. Sci. **75**, 10–24 (2015). https://doi.org/10.1016/j.ejps.2015.02.018
11. Meyer, W., Schonnagel, B., Fleischer, L.-G.: A note on integumental $(1 \rightarrow 3)(1 \rightarrow 6)\beta$-D-glucan permeation, using the porcine ear skin model. J. Cosmet. Dermatol. **5**, 130–134 (2006). https://doi.org/10.1111/j.1473-2165.2006.00239.x

12. Salazar Muñoz, Y.: Caracterización de tejidos cardíacos mediante métodos mínimamente invasivos y no invasivos basados en espectroscopia de impedancia eléctrica. TDX (Tesis Dr. en Xarxa) (2004)
13. DIGILENT & Analog Devices Inc.: Analog Discovery Technical Reference Manual. https://reference.digilentinc.com/reference/instrumentation/analog-discovery/start
14. Davies, D.J., Heylings, J.R., McCarthy, T.J., Correa, C.M.: Development of an in vitro model for studying the penetration of chemicals through compromised skin. Toxicol. Vitr. **29**, 176–181 (2015). https://doi.org/10.1016/j.tiv.2014.09.012
15. Bernerd, F., Asselineau, D.: An organotypic model of skin to study photodamage and photoprotection in vitro. J. Am. Acad. Dermatol. **58**, S155–S159 (2008). https://doi.org/10.1016/j.jaad.2007.08.050

Bioinformatics Approach to Analyze
Influenza Viruses

Karina Salvatierra[1] and Hector Florez[2(✉)]

[1] Universidad Nacional de Misiones, Posadas, Argentina
karinasalvatierra@fceqyn.unam.edu.ar
[2] Universidad Distrital Francisco Jose de Caldas, Bogotá, Colombia
haflorezf@udistrital.edu.co

Abstract. Influenza viruses are highly contagious respiratory illness and responsible for the severe annual morbidity and mortality worldwide. They are classified into types, influenza A, B and C. Influenza viruses accumulate point mutations during replication, especially in three proteins: matrix-membrane, hemagglutinin, and neuraminidase. Nucleotide and amino acid variations may produce selective advantages for viral strains, in the matrix-membrane and neuraminidase may be related to eluding host immunity, while variations in the hemagglutinin are responsible for the appearance of antigenic drift that evade preexisting host immunity and cause reinfections. In this paper, we present a bioinformatics study for detecting mutations implicated in variability in the hemagglutinin, neuraminidase and matrix-membrane of influenza strains using our bioinformatics tool *BMA*. In this study, we calculate, compare, and analyze genetic variations associated with antigenic drift in hemagglutinin protein from influenza A H1N1. *BMA* allows users to identify mutations in sequences quickly and efficiently for the detection of antigenic drift.

Keywords: Bioinformatics · Hemagglutinin · Neuraminidase
Influenza viruses

1 Introduction

Influenza viruses are significant for human respiratory infections disease. They belong to the family Orthomyxoviridae and the genome has seven or eight segments of single-stranded antisense RiboNucleic Acid (RNA) [1]. The Influenza viruses are classified into three types A, B, and C. They are further subdivided based on the antigenic properties of their envelope glycoproteins: the hemagglutinin (HA) and the neuraminidase (NA) [2]. On the one hand, in most cases, influenza B and C viruses affect humans. On the other hand, influenza A viruses infect some avian and mammalian species [3–5]. Influenza A and B viruses are the most frequent causes of respiratory illness, which occur in throughout the year, usually in winter for tempered weather areas and rainy seasons in tropical weather areas [6].

© Springer Nature Switzerland AG 2018
J. C. Figueroa-García et al. (Eds.): WEA 2018, CCIS 916, pp. 442–452, 2018.
https://doi.org/10.1007/978-3-030-00353-1_39

Humans can be very susceptible to this viral infection. Outbreaks of respiratory diseases may be possible due to the combination of weathers factors such as cold temperature and low humidity. Social behavior also facilitates the transmission from person to person through the respiratory airways, being in public places or closed environments [7].

The genome of Influenza A and B viruses are similar, but Influenza C is more divergent, because genome consists of seven RNA segments. The enveloped Influenza viruses have three membrane proteins: HA, NA, and matrix-membrane (M) [1]. HA, which is the main antigen and major surface glycoprotein of the Influenza viruses, is responsible for binding the virus to cells during the process of infection. The HA glycoprotein is a homotrimer (three identical monomers), with each monomer formed of sub-units HA1 and a HA2 [8]. NA, is another antigenic surface glycoprotein envelope of the Influenza virions [9,10]. The M gene has multiple functions and is intriguing because it encodes two proteins: matrix and membrane [11].

Consequently, the aim of this study was to use a bioinformatics tool, which has been designed and developed in one of our previous works, to demonstrate that users can identify changes in nucleotide and amino acid sequences of hemagglutinin, neuraminidase and matrix-membrane protein in a efficient manner.

The paper has the following structure. Section 2 explains the main characteristics of mutations, which corresponds to the context of the work. In Sect. 3, we inform the main reasons of the importance of bioinformatics analysis. In Sect. 4, our approach for analyzing Influenza viruses sequences is presented. Section 5 provides the results obtained through our approach using Influenza viruses. Finally, in Sect. 5, we provide our conclusions.

2 Mutation

Similar to many RNA viruses, Influenza virus suffers high rate mutations during replication, leading to variability in HA, NA and M proteins. Mutations (also known as substitutions or variants) that modify amino acids in antigenic sites of proteins structure (HA and NA) may evade host immunity. The viruses evades host immune responses caused Influenza outbreaks, because minor changes in the surface glycoproteins occur frequently, these strategies that viruses have needed is called "antigenic drift", and occurs in all types of Influenza viruses. However, major changes in the proteins structure is called "antigenic shift", when two different virus strains (human, avian or other mammalians) recombine to form a new virus, and occurs only in Influenza A viruses (responsible of pandemic outbreaks) [1,5]. Nevertheless, minor changes in the M protein may cause a critical deficiency in virus replication, and may be related to host immune responses and tropism [12].

There are three influenza antiviral drugs recommended for treatment. However, recent emergence of antiviral resistance Influenza variants is a matter of great concern [13]. Similar to others drugs, replication of viruses in contact of antiviral drug intensify the selection for variations in the viral target proteins, which leads to the mechanisms of virus antiviral resistance.

Some mutations in NA confer resistance to antivirals [14]. But it is also known that certain amino acid substitutions in NA are compensated with amino acid substitutions in HA to restore viral fitness [15–17]. Some of these amino acid substitutions can alter the binding of HA with host cells (receptors for sialic acids) [18].

Furthermore, there are many influenza viruses and they are constantly changing so it is not unusual for new Influenza strains to appear each year. The composition of influenza vaccines is changed annually. Depending on the manufacture of the vaccine, it can protect for three or four strains of the viruses [7]. Influenza vaccines confer considerable but incomplete protection and are recommended for everyone.

3   Importance of Bioinformatic Analysis

When 100 years of the first influenza pandemic (1918) were commemorated, the appearance of a new Influenza virus could be the result of different events that happen in nature [19]. Having knowledge of some of these events (nucleotide or amino acid substitutions) through bioinformatics tools, several researchers will be able to understand the epidemiology and will help to define the appearance of a new viral strain that could affect the human being.

In endemics or epidemics, Influenza viruses remain being the biggest health problem. Thus, vaccine development and planning strategies remain a challenge because of the rapid, continuous, and unpredictable viral evolution. Careful analysis of the nucleotide and amino acid changes will contribute to our understanding of the variable genetic of Influenza viruses.

Different computer tools have been developed in our research to facilitate the analysis and identification of mutations [20,21], and there is no doubt that in the future they will continue to design bioinformatics tools that facilitate the analysis and interpretation of data. In addition, we have used these tools to provide important results regarding desired microorganisms analyses based on novel computing approaches [22–25].

4   Tool for Analyzing Sequences

In this work, we used our bioinformatics tool named Biomedical Mutation Analysis (BMA)[1] [20]. By using this tool, it is possible to analyze several sequences giving as result, a full description of nucleotides and amino acid changes of each analyzed sequence. BMA is able to present such results through different visualizations techniques in order to make results easily understandable.

BMA enables users to make analysis of several sequences from plain text files in FASTA format, which is very useful due to it is compatible with results provided by most bioinformatics tools that use nucleotides sequences as input or output.

---

[1] http://bma.itiud.org/.

Algorithm 1. *BMA*

---

for all ω in Ω **do**
  $\Theta_\omega \leftarrow split(\omega)$
  for all δ in Δ **do**
    $\Gamma_\delta \leftarrow split(\delta)$
    $position \leftarrow 0$
    for all θ in Θ_ω, α in A_δ **do**
      if $\theta \mathrel{!=} \alpha$ **then**
        $\Phi \leftarrow group(\theta, \alpha, position)$
      end if
      $increment(position)$
    end for
  end for
end for

The algorithm of *BMA* iterates all text files. For each text file, it iterates all sequences. Later on, for each sequence, it compares every amino acid and nucleotide of such sequence to the corresponding amino acid and nucleotide in the reference sequence of the selected virus and gene, which has been taken from GenBank[2] database and stored in *BMA*. The algorithm has been tested with several case studies. Those studies have included up to 30 plain text files in FASTA format, where each file has included in average up to 40 sequences. Then, based on the tests, *BMA* ensures accurate analysis results, independently the amount of data to be analyzed.

Algorithm 1 presents the *BMA* Algorithm, where Ω is the set of patient sequences to be analyzed, Θ_ω corresponds to the group of nucleotides taken from the sequence ω, Δ is the group of reference sequences that belong to a specific microorganism gene of the influenza A H1N1 virus (e.g., HA1), Γ_δ identifies the group of nucleotides that belong to the reference sequence δ, Φ is the set of changes of nucleotides that belongs to ω, and *pos* is the position of the nucleotide change found in the analysis.

In this study, for performing mutation analyses, we used 28 nucleotide sequences of the HA glycoprotein from influenza A H1N1 virus, representative of different countries of Europe, which have been obtained from the GISAID database[3].

BMA has been supported by different components such as frameworks and libraries. Figure 1 presents the corresponding component diagram. The language used to develop *BMA* was PHP. The front end, which is responsive, was supported by Bootstrap. Moreover, JQuery was used to provide some JavaScript services. Furthermore, *BMA* is able to provide its analyses results through a pdf file. For this, *BMA* uses the component EZPDF. In addition, to deploy results, *BMA* uses Data-Driven Documents (D3JS). Finally, the persistence is done by using a MySQL database.

---

[2] https://www.ncbi.nlm.nih.gov/genbank/.
[3] http://platform.gisaid.org/.

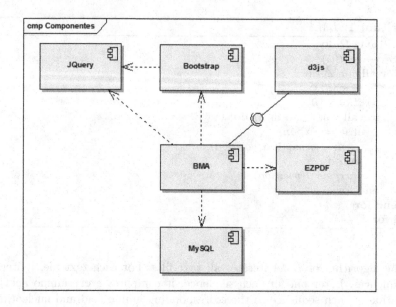

Fig. 1. Component diagram.

In addition, amino acid substitutions were modeled in the three-dimensional structure of HA protein from the influenza A/H1N1/2009 virus (Protein Data Bank [PDB] code 3LZG) using the *PyMOL Molecular Graphics System*[4].

5   Results

A data set with 28 HA sequences was constructed, including Belgium (2 sequences), Czech republic (1 sequence), England (2 sequences), France (2 sequences), Germany (3 sequences), Greece (1 sequence), Italy (1 sequence), Norway (5 sequences), Portugal (1 sequence), Russia (4 sequences), Slovenia(1 sequence), Spain (1 sequence), Switzerland (1 sequence), Sweden (1 sequence), and Ukraine (2 sequences), obtained from the GISAID database.

Nucleotides and amino acid substitutions of 28 HA sequences were compared with reference sequence (vaccine strain A/California/7/2009) using *BMA*. The analysis process consists in performing the following activities:

Initially, the user needs to access *BMA* and selects from *Mutation Analysis* menu, the sub-menu *Influenza A (H1N1)*. The user also can select other kinds of influenza such as A (H3N2) among others, which are presented in Fig. 2.

Later on, the user can select one of the genes to be analyzed. Figure 3 shows the list of available genes for influenza A (H1N1) virus, which are HA, M and NA that include names, brief description, and reference sequences, which can be displayed by clicking on the zoom icon.

---

[4] https://pymol.org/2/.

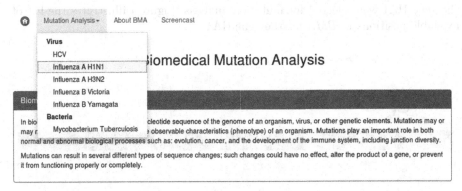

Fig. 2. List of available influenza viruses.

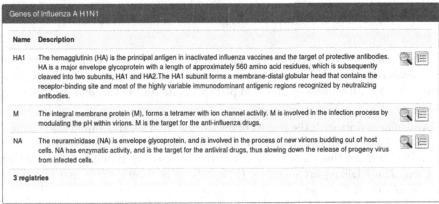

Fig. 3. List of available genes of influenza A(H1N1).

Afterwards, the user can select the positions to be analyzed. In this case the gene HA1 was selected for mutation analysis. Figure 4 illustrates the list of available positions in *BMA* for the gene HA1.

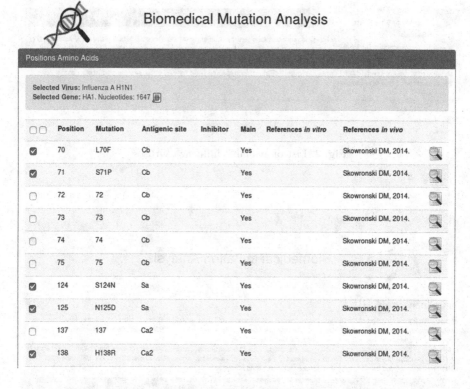

Fig. 4. List of positions for the gene HA1 of influenza A (H1N1).

Then, once the user provide the plain text files with the sequences intended to be analyzed, the *BMA* algorithm described above is executed. The *BMA* algorithm analyzes all sequences provided presenting its results through the following ways:

1. An online report with the results of nucleotide changes and amino acid change, which generates antigenic drift or shift. This report is presented in Fig. 5.
2. A PDF report that is sent by email to the user by filling a basic contact form. The PDF report includes: (a) synthesis of changes (i.e., mutations) of nucleotides and amino acids detected for each analyzed sequence and (b) an itemized report, which includes all information related to the analysis.
3. A graph that groups nodes, where each node corresponds to a nucleotide change of the analyzed sequences. This graph is characterized as *force-directed*, which implies that the nodes from the same color corresponds to the

Biomedical Mutation Analysis

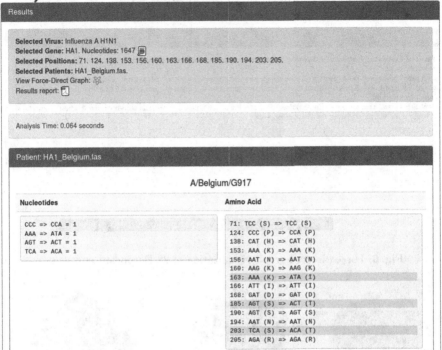

Fig. 5. Results through online visualization for the changes observed in a Belgium sequence.

same source. In this study, nodes are grouped by sequences from countries as well as grouped by the amount of amino acid changes. Figure 6 presents the results through the corresponding graph.

We used *BMA* to analyze the nucleotide sequences of the HA1 gene compared with the reference sequence to show nucleotide and amino acid changes at positions related to antigenic sites. Then, the information obtained was used on the dimeric tridimensional structure of HA1 protein in order to visualize the localization of variable amino acids. HA1 is a more variable subunit, which contains the receptor binding sites (host cell), while HA2 is a relatively conserved subunit.

The amino acid substitutions located in globular head region of HA1 (antigenic site) are T72A, H138Q/R, A141T, G155E, S162N, K163Q/I/T, S185T, A186T, D187Y, S203T, and R205K (See Fig. 7).

The location of these amino acid substitutions indicated that they have a very important role in antigenic drift due to they are located on the structure and

Biomedical Mutation Analysis

Force-Direct Graph

The Force-Directed Graph allows to visualize the distribution of secuences regarding the reference sequence, which is represented by the central blue node.

Each patient corresponds to the collection of nodes with the same color. However, some nodes from the same patient might have different groups. Each group of each patient indicates that the sequences represented by the gruped nodes contain the same amount of mutations (Amino Acid changes).

By placing the mouse pointer over a node, the following information is shown: 1) patient file name, 2) sequence name, 3) amount of mutations, 4) positions and mutations regarding the reference sequence.

HA1_noruega.fas. A/Norway/2620 (2). 185: AGT (S) => ACT (T). 203: TCA (S) => ACA (T).

Fig. 6. Force directed graph visualization of 28 European sequences.

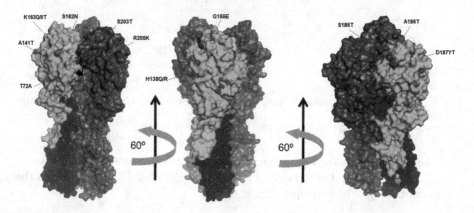

Fig. 7. Location of the amino acid substitutions in the structure of the HA from influenza A (H1N1)

function of the HA molecule in known antigenic sites (T72A in Cb, H138Q/R and A141T in Ca2, G155E, S162N, and K163Q/I/T in Sa, S185T, A186T, and D187Y in Sb, S203T, and R205K Ca1 respectively). These mutations probably decrease receptor-binding avidity of HA.

In this study, based on the use of *BMA*, we quickly and efficiently detected mutations in antigenic sites of HA, which can cause antigenic drift in the virus and evade the immune response of the host. To improve the protection of the population against influenza, new methods are needed to predict and evaluate the effectiveness of the vaccine. Therefore, our developed method, compared to "ISM-based phylogenetic algorithm ISTREE analysis" [26], is more complete because it provides information necessary to determine the mutations that occur in the sequences of the influenza virus.

6 Conclusions

The advance of technologies allow new research tools, opportunities to dissect and use new software for the analysis of complex biological data.

Developing software for the detection of variants associated with antigenic drift or shift and resistance to antivirals is very important, because they guaranty accurate and reliable results. This work provided a software tool called *BMA* for the detection of minor or major mutations in patients' sequences with influenza infection.

BMA offers the advantage of sequences analysis obtained by conventional direct sequencing. Furthermore, it accepts many sequences that facilitate the characterization of substitutions. In addition, the analysis for each sequence is done in less than one second. *BMA* deploys the results through different means in order to ease their interpretation.

The results generated for *BMA* are adequate for the epidemiological surveillance of influenza viruses. *BMA* may be used by health professional and researchers, and may help public health in preventing new strains of influenza virus, and helping to determine whether existing vaccines and antiviral drugs will work against new influenza strains circulated.

Acknowledgment. Authors are grateful for the support received from the Information Technologies Innovation Research Group.

References

1. Lamb, R.A.: Orthomyxoviridae: the viruses and their replication. In: Fields Virology (2001)
2. Obenauer, J.C., et al.: Large-scale sequence analysis of avian influenza isolates. Science **311**(5767), 1576–1580 (2006)
3. Osterhaus, A., Rimmelzwaan, G., Martina, B., Bestebroer, T., Fouchier, R.: Influenza B virus in seals. Science **288**(5468), 1051–1053 (2000)
4. Youzbashi, E., Marschall, M., Chaloupka, I., Meier-Ewert, H.: Distribution of influenza C virus infection in dogs and pigs in Bavaria. Tierarztl. Prax. **24**(4), 337–342 (1996)
5. Webster, R.G., Bean, W.J., Gorman, O.T., Chambers, T.M., Kawaoka, Y.: Evolution and ecology of influenza A viruses. Microbiol. Rev. **56**(1), 152–179 (1992)
6. Centers for Disease Control and Prevention (CDC), et al.: Update: influenza activity-united states and worldwide, 1999–2000 season, and composition of the 2000–01 influenza vaccine. MMWR Morb. Mortal. Wkly. Rep. **49**(17), 375 (2000)
7. Treanor, J.J.: Influenza vaccination. N. Engl. J. Med. **375**(13), 1261–1268 (2016). PMID: 27682035

8. Barbey-Martin, C., et al.: An antibody that prevents the hemagglutinin low pH fusogenic transition. Virology **294**(1), 70–74 (2002)
9. Matrosovich, M.N., Matrosovich, T.Y., Gray, T., Roberts, N.A., Klenk, H.D.: Neuraminidase is important for the initiation of influenza virus infection in human airway epithelium. J. Virol. **78**(22), 12665–12667 (2004)
10. Yen, H.L., et al.: Importance of neuraminidase active-site residues to the neuraminidase inhibitor resistance of influenza viruses. J. Virol. **80**(17), 8787–8795 (2006)
11. Lamb, R.A., Lai, C.J., Choppin, P.W.: Sequences of mRNAs derived from genome RNA segment 7 of influenza virus: colinear and interrupted mRNAs code for overlapping proteins. Proc. Natl. Acad. Sci. **78**(7), 4170–4174 (1981)
12. Furuse, Y., Suzuki, A., Kamigaki, T., Oshitani, H.: Evolution of the M gene of the influenza A virus in different host species: large-scale sequence analysis. Virol. J. **6**(1), 67 (2009)
13. Eyer, L., Hruska, K., et al.: Antiviral agents targeting the influenza virus: a review and publication analysis. Vet. Med. **58**(3), 113–185 (2013)
14. Bloom, J.D., Gong, L.I., Baltimore, D.: Permissive secondary mutations enable the evolution of influenza oseltamivir resistance. Science **328**(5983), 1272–1275 (2010)
15. McKimm-Breschkin, J.L., et al.: Generation and characterization of variants of NWS/G70C influenza virus after in vitro passage in 4-amino-Neu5Ac2en and 4-guanidino-Neu5Ac2en. Antimicrob. Agents Chemother. **40**(1), 40–46 (1996)
16. Yang, P., Bansal, A., Liu, C., Air, G.M.: Hemagglutinin specificity and neuraminidase coding capacity of neuraminidase-deficient influenza viruses. Virology **229**(1), 155–165 (1997)
17. Blick, T.J., et al.: The interaction of neuraminidase and hemagglutinin mutations in influenza virus in resistance to 4-guanidino-Neu5Ac2en. Virology **246**(1), 95–103 (1998)
18. Hensley, S.E., et al.: Hemagglutinin receptor binding avidity drives influenza A virus antigenic drift. Science **326**(5953), 734–736 (2009)
19. Medina, R.A.: 1918 influenza virus: 100 years on, are we prepared against the next influenza pandemic? Nat. Rev. Microbiol. **16**(2), 61–62 (2018)
20. Salvatierra, K., Florez, H.: Biomedical mutation analysis (BMA): a software tool for analyzing mutations associated with antiviral resistance. F1000Research **5** (2016)
21. Salvatierra, K., Florez, H.: Pathogen sequence signature analysis (PSSA): a software tool for analyzing sequences to identify microorganism genotypes. F1000Research **6** (2017)
22. Salvatierra, K., Florez, H.: Analysis of hepatitis C virus in hemodialysis patients. Infectio **20**(3), 130–137 (2016)
23. Salvatierra, K., Florez, H.: Prevalence of hepatitis B and C infections in hemodialysis patients. F1000Research **5** (2016)
24. Florez, H., Salvatierra, K.: A web-based approach for analyzing microorganism sequences. In: Figueroa-García, J.C., López-Santana, E.R., Villa-Ramírez, J.L., Ferro-Escobar, R. (eds.) WEA 2017. CCIS, vol. 742, pp. 96–107. Springer, Cham (2017). https://doi.org/10.1007/978-3-319-66963-2_10
25. Florez, H., Salvatierra, K.: Bioinformatics study of mutations of resistance to antivirals in the NS5A Gen of HCV. Information **20**(9), 6665–6672 (2017)
26. Paessler, S., Veljkovic, V.: Using electronic biology based platform to predict flu vaccine efficacy for 2018/2019. F1000Research **7** (2018)

3D Object Pose Estimation for Robotic Packing Applications

C. H. Rodriguez-Garavito[1], Guillermo Camacho-Munoz[1(✉)],
David Álvarez-Martínez[2], Karol Viviana Cardenas[1], David Mateo Rojas[1],
and Andrés Grimaldos[2]

[1] Faculty of Engineering, La Salle University, Cra 2 No 10-70, Bogotá, Colombia
`gacamacho@unisalle.edu.co`
[2] Department of Industrial Engineering, School of Engineering,
Universidad de Los Andes, Cra 1 East No. 19A - 40, Bogotá, Colombia

Abstract. Given the growth of internet-based trading on a global level, there are several expected logistic challenges regarding the optimal transportation of large volumes of merchandise. With this in mind, the application of technologies such as computer vision and industrial robotics in facing these challenges presents significant advantages regarding the speed and reliability with which palletization tasks, a critical point in the merchandise transportation chain, can be performed. This paper presents a computer vision strategy for the localization and recognition of boxes in the context of a palletization process carried out by a robotic manipulator. The system operates using a Kinect 2.0 depth camera to capture a scene and processing the resulting point cloud. Obtained results permit the simultaneous recognition of up to 15 boxes, their position in space and their size characteristics within the workspace of the robot, with an average error of approximately 3 cm.

Keywords: Box detection · Bin packing problem · Convex hull
Point cloud · Mean-Shift

1 Introduction

The growth in the online retail market and the diversification of the customer demands has increased the number of high-mix and low volume warehouses around the world. Research show that 80% of current warehouses are manually operated with no supporting automation [3]. These manual warehouses are experimenting problems associated with the packing operations: exposure of the operators to physical risks as a consequence of manual loading of the container, exposure of the company to reintegration costs as a consequence of damage, mistakes in packing or disappearance of goods, and high costs of operation as a consequence of elevated times and resources involved in the packing operation. Therefore, the automation in the Warehouse is required to reduce the effects of those problems. As a solution, we find the robotic packing system [10,15,19],

© Springer Nature Switzerland AG 2018
J. C. Figueroa-García et al. (Eds.): WEA 2018, CCIS 916, pp. 453–463, 2018.
https://doi.org/10.1007/978-3-030-00353-1_40

which allows to compute optimal solutions to the packing problem and to implement those solutions (loading/unloading task) with robotic platforms. Those systems depends on a vision module that gives to the machine the knowledge of the environment to take decisions related with the packing task.

The vision module represents one of the challenging problems since multiple issues need to be addressed, such as low illumination conditions, clutter, texture-less, variable orientation of the objects and reflective objects. Different approaches have been proposed to compute resolve those problems [1, 2, 12, 17]: some of them are based on object color and histogram data. Others make the extraction based on geometrical features from 3D information. Other works present a technique based on the matching of image features to those stored in a model. Alternative methods try matched 3D perception data to a stored 3D model.

However, those proposals have not been adapted to the specific application of packing with robotics. For this application, the goal is to extract a set of features of the items to be pack, guaranteeing specific tolerances. The relevant features of each object are three: (1) size (width, length and height), (2) position of the grasp point and (3) orientation of the object with respect to the base-frame of the robot.

This paper proposes a new base-line to resolve 3D-object pose estimation in the robotic packing systems. We assume that all the items to be pack are boxes and, the boxes and the base of the robot are supported on the same plane. Those assumptions have two consequences: (1) the grasping position of each box in z axis (p_{i_z}) and the height of the box (h_i) are equivalent, (2) the orientation is represented by a single angle α_i. Therefore, the main problem consists in compute three features for each box: (1) size (width w_i, length l_i and height h_i), (2) grasping-position represented as a vector of two dimensions $p_i = [p_{i_x}, p_{i_y}]$ located at the centroid of the top-side of the box, and (3) orientation α_i. Those features are computed from a single RGB-D image which represents a scene.

Each scene is composed by a set if I boxes with different sizes. For each scene we have collected K RGB-D images from a known position of the camera O_c. The parameters of our database are: number of boxes fixed at each scene $I = 5$, twenty RGB-D images per scene $K = 20$ and six scenes $N = 6$.

The obtained results allow to conclude low errors of estimation for the target features. Those errors are suitable to resolve the packing pattern and to execute a packing operation without collisions.

2   Related Works

Pose and size estimation of objects are the focus tasks of the vision module treated in this paper. The range of techniques proposed for these purposes is vast, however, most of the approaches assume unsuitable conditions for the packing application: deal with different shapes [6], allow free body orientations [6, 7, 12], requires repeated objects in scene [1] deal with a single object [5] or do not resolve size estimation. We have classified the existing techniques in two categories: (1) single-image and (2) multiple images.

The single-image alternative use a single RGB-D image to make the estimation of parameters and is suitable for systems with high production rates (i.e. 100 objects/min). In this group we found the work of [6] which presents a supervised approach that builds 3D models of objects during the training stage. Then, in the test phase they compare descriptors of the test image with those associated to the 3D models and estimate pose and orientation. Another proposal of this group is presented in [7] with the MOPED (Multiple Object Pose Estimation and Detection) framework. The MOPED framework integrates an ICE (Iterative Clustering-Estimation) algorithm that allows to solve the correspondence and pose estimation through an iterative procedure. This proposal is integrated with HERB project [8] and have reported grasping success of 91% and 98% using single-image setup and three-camera setup, respectively. In [12] they propose a method to reduce the computational complexity arguing that the ICE algorithm consumes $O(MN)$ time where N and M represent the number of features in a model and the numbers of models, respectively. Their results allow to reduce the computing time in four orders of magnitude but they do not conclude about the accuracy. Those techniques are interesting for picking applications but not suitable for packing where the variability of boxes is undefined and the orientation is limited to one degree of freedom.

The work in [1] present a method for unsupervised 3D object discovery, reconstruction and localization under scenes with multiple instances of an identical object contained in a single RGB-D image. The method seeks recurrent patterns in an RGB-D image by utilizing appearance and geometry of the salient regions. The validation is computed in a subset of images of the Amazon Picking Challenge [11] and includes a robotic arm in four picking scenarios: scenes containing a single or multiple object types, and scenes with or without clutter and occlusion. The quantitative results allow to conclude an F1-score of 0.966 for pairwise matches and a value of 0.974 for n-instances with $n \geq 3$. This method is interesting but depends on the existence of multiple instances of one object in the scene, that assumption could be broken in a packing scenario.

By the other side, the multiple images methods relies on 3D scanning systems. One of the founding proposals in this group is the Kinect Fusion [18] which allows to create a 3D model of a scene tacking a sequence of depth maps streamed from a Kinect Sensor. There are variants from this proposal that increase the robustness of geometric alignment of ICP stage [14], enhance the memory consumption in high sized rooms applications [20] and resolve the detection of loop closures [21]. But the main limitation for our application consists in the deformation for concave zones of the objects [16]. This limitations prevents the reconstructions of high-frequency details such as the sharp edges of a box. This problem has been addressed in [5] with a proposal called CuFusion. The proposal requires a known reference in the scene to enhance camera localization and substitute the classical moving average processing with a prediction-corrected TSD data fusion strategy. They use the cloud-to-mesh-distance metric to validate their proposal, on a public dataset. The results allow to conclude lower errors for the CuFusion approach compared with the classical Kinect Fusion [18] and a recent proposal

[22]. As limitations, the authors highlighted the small-sized scenes reconstruction as a consequence of the 16 bytes representation per voxel, the steadily moving required during the acquisition of images and the memory efficiency (use of four times as much memory as Kinect Fusion).

Databases used by the authors considered in related-works and the reported in [13] are not suitable for our problem: deal with different shapes, allow free body orientations, prioritize picking applications and don't register the size of the objects. We have build an own database as presented in the next section.

3 Database

Our database satisfies conditions for bin-packing applications: (1) all objects are regular boxes, (2) each object is located over a flat surface, (3) there is not stacked objects, (4) the existence of repeated boxes is not necessary, (5) there exists annotations for position, orientation and size of each item and (6) is composed of scenes with multiple boxes. With this requirements we have collected 6 scenes, each one composed by five boxes with different sizes. The boxes at each scene have been distributed with random position and orientation within the field of view of the camera. For each scene we have collected twenty RGB-D images. The Fig. 1 presents one of the scenes in two-dimensions. The schematic annotations for position and orientation are presented in Fig. 2. The annotations for size, position and orientation of each box were registered by humans with help of conventional measurement tools.

id	p_x	p_y	p_z	α	w	l
36	590	412	149	87	199	251
20	911	360	300	224	150	199
12	1130	322	251	221	100	148
5	392	357	250	289	99	251
43	208	334	200	206	99	100

Fig. 1. Collected image for scene 1 and annotations. Dimensions are in mm and grades are in degrees. The height h and the p_z coordinate are equivalent.

The evaluation methodology consists in compute three indicators: (1) difference between the predicted and the ground-truth position at each axis, (2) difference between the predicted angle and the ground-truth angle and (3) difference between the predicted size and the ground truth, at each dimension.

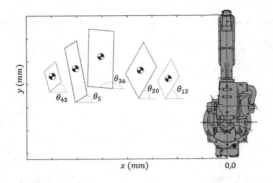

Fig. 2. Annotation for position and orientation in scene 1

4   Methodology

The proposed method is composed by six stages as depicted in Fig. 4. The first stage makes the acquisition of the image with an RGB-D sensor. The result is point-cloud PC_{raw} which represents the scene.

4.1   Pre-processing

The purpose is to adjust the raw point cloud (PC_{raw}) until obtain an aligned and ground-referenced $PC_{grounded}$ and then delete the ground plane of the scene. This is accomplished in three sub-stages: (a) gross adjust which rotates and translates the zero reference of the PC to a point near to the ground, (b) fine adjust which computes the ground-plane by applying the RANSAC algorithm and align its normal vector with the gravity vector direction, and (c) remove ground, where the points coincident with the ground-plane are removed from the scene; we have defined a threshold of two centimeters to remove those points. Results are depicted in Figs. 3a to 3c.

4.2   Clustering

In this stage, we have selected the Mean-Shift classifier with descriptors composed by position of each point in the cloud. The Mean-Shift classifier was selected by its capacity of find variable number of modes or boxes and for having presented good results as an unsupervised classification method [9]. At the output we obtain a set of point-clouds PC_j as depicted in Fig. 3d; with $\{j \in \mathbb{Z}, j = 1, \ldots, J\}$, where J is the number of detected clusters.

4.3   Filtering

For each point-cloud PC_j we apply a sequence of filtering criteria based on thresholds of size (th_{size}), angle (th_{ang}) and height (th_h). Those criteria are

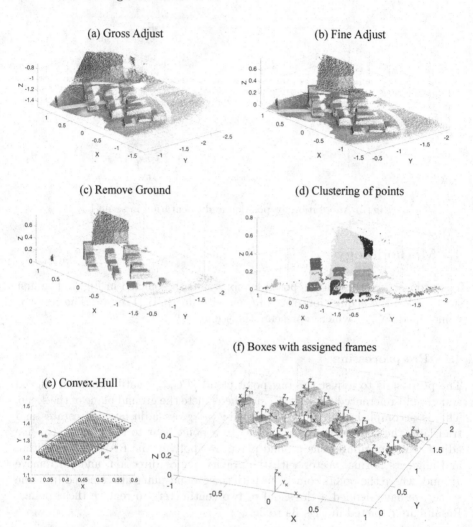

Fig. 3. Outputs at each stage of the methodology

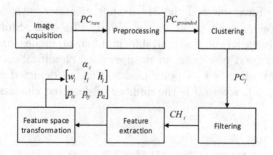

Fig. 4. Processing line

applied after converting each cluster that is co-planar to ground-plane, into a Convex-Hull CH_i; where $CH_i = [n_i, h_i]$ and n_i is the perpendicular vector to the plane CH_i. This conversion is based on the computing of the smallest convex set that contains a bounded set of points in a plane. In Fig. 3e we present this convex for the points associated to a single box. The edges and vertex of the convex are presented in blue and red color, respectively.

Once we have computed the top-planes for each cluster, the filtering criteria are applied in the next sequence: 1. If $|PC_i| < \frac{max(|PC_1|,....,|PC_I|)}{th_{size}}$, then delete the point-cloud PC_i. 2. If $n_i \cdot g < th_{ang}$, then delete the point-cloud PC_i; g is the gravity vector. 3. If $h_i < th_h$, then, delete the point-cloud PC_i; where h_i is the height of each top-plane.

At the end of this stage we obtain the set CH_i with $\{i \in \mathbb{Z}, i = 1, \ldots, I\}$, where I is the number of detected boxes.

4.4   Feature Extraction

At this stage we compute two last features: (a) the length l_i and width w_i of each box and (b) the rotation of the top side of the box α_i with respect to the camera frame. Both are computed by processing each Convex-Hull built in the previous step.

Initially, we compute a signature for the Convex-Hull CH_i. This computing consists in plotting a line $Lx_i(\alpha)$ centered at the centroid of each plane CH_i and with the orientation α, as depicted in Fig. 3e. Then, we identify the intersection point between $Lx_i(\alpha)$ and the edges of the Convex-Hull borders $P_{wbi}(\alpha)$ and $P_{wfi}(\alpha)$. The evolution of the distance $Dist(P_{wbi}, P_{wfi})$ in function of α is presented in Fig. 5. This evolution allow us to compute the width of the box as $w_i = min(Dist(P_{wbi}(\alpha^*), P_{wfi}(\alpha^*))$. The orientation of the length will correspond to $\alpha^l = \alpha^* + \frac{\pi}{2}$ so, the length can be computed as $l_i = Dist(P_{lbi}(\alpha^l), P_{lfi}(\alpha^l))$.

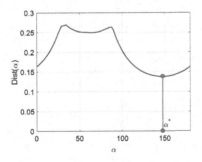

Fig. 5. Signature of each Convex-Hull CH_i.

4.5   Feature Space-Transformation

In this stage we compute a transformation matrix from the frame of the camera $O_{C_{grounded}}$ to the base frame of the robot O_b. This computation is based on the direct kinematic model of the manipulator as presented in [4]. With the matrix $T_b^{C_{grounded}}$ we compute the transformation of position and orientation of each box.

To conclude this stage, we assign a framework to each box with the origin in the center of the Convex-Hull CH_i and x axis orientation in α_i^* degrees as depicted in Fig. 3f.

5   Results

The results are presented in terms of three indicators: (1) position error (e_x, e_y), (2) angle error (e_α) and (3) size error $(e_{length}, e_{width}, e_{heigth})$. Each error was computed as the difference between the ground-truth value and the estimated value.

Figures 6 and 7 present the trend of errors for the twenty observations at a single scene and with a single box. Figure 6 focus on the evolution of errors for scene dependent features: position and angle. The presented trend allow us to conclude a good behaviour for estimation of position and orientation of the box. Figure 7 presents the evolution of errors for independent scenery features: length, width and height. Note that these errors are one order or magnitude greater than those presented in Fig. 6.

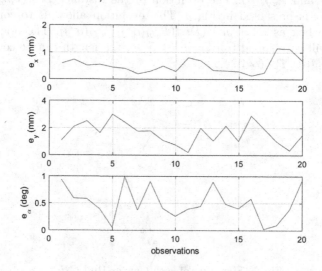

Fig. 6. Error evolution in the scene 1, box 36 - Part 1. Mean values are $\overline{e_x} = 0.50\,\text{mm}$, $\overline{e_y} = 1.5984\,\text{mm}$, $\overline{e_\alpha} = 0.50°$

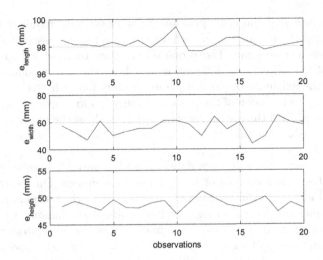

Fig. 7. Error evolution in the scene 1, box 36 - Part 2. Mean values are $\overline{e_{length}}$ = 98.22 mm, $\overline{e_{width}}$ = 55.75 mm, $\overline{e_{heigth}}$ = 48.72 mm

The overall results are presented in Table 1. This Table presents mean errors of the estimated features. The first half of the Table focus on the error reached at each scene and along all the boxes. The data allow to identify a superior behavior of the algorithm when computing position for the first three scenes. The higher error is reached in the estimation of size. The second half of the Table focus on the error of each box along all the scenes. The trends are consequent with the first half, were the lower errors are obtained with position and higher errors are related to size. The box 20 was the one with the highest errors.

Table 1. Mean errors for each scene along all boxes and for each box along all scenes

Scene	e_x	e_y	e_α	e_{length}	e_{width}	e_{height}	Box	e_x	e_y	e_α	e_{length}	e_{width}	e_{height}
1	1.07	1.69	0.91	59.74	57.83	123.33	36	9.29	13.89	6.59	56.13	6.27	49.39
2	3.70	9.86	9.61	61.42	59.03	137.55	20	16.30	30.76	2.34	51.53	90.08	166.15
3	5.14	1.61	1.71	60.64	57.39	122.62	12	16.66	11.96	3.93	48.00	95.75	150.16
4	25.38	51.85	4.65	54.56	55.69	122.44	5	11.05	35.76	1.97	130.52	9.65	151.17
5	28.17	35.78	0.94	49.70	60.11	120.20	43	16.08	19.14	5.05	5.02	93.84	103.20
6	18.77	31.78	3.25	63.63	64.75	117.90							

6   Conclusions and Future Works

Detection and recognition of boxes inside the workspace of an HP20D robotic manipulator can be performed by using a Kinect 2.0 camera and the application of the computer vision-based strategy proposed in this paper.

The processing of the color-position point cloud only required the spatial information for the estimation of each system of reference associated with segmented boxes in the scene. The proposed strategy took advantage of several properties of the objects to differentiate, such as the direct contact with the ground and the existence of parallel planes in pairs for each box.

Regarding the precision of the position estimation for a given box, this result varies as a function of the proximity of an object in the scene to the camera, with measurement values fluctuating from 1.97 mm to 35.76 mm, as can be observed in the Table 1.

For future works we will use a database with a variable number of boxes at each scene. Use different type of boxes between scenarios. On the other hand, the precision in the measurement of the location and orientation of the boxes is expected to increase by capturing the cloud point from different viewpoints in the scene. Additionally, we propose the improvement of descriptors used in the point clustering process for each box through features like surface-normal vectors for captured points, enhancing the differentiation of close and/or occluded boxes.

References

1. Abbeloos, W., Ataer-Cansizoglu, E., Caccamo, S., Taguchi, Y., Domae, Y.: 3D Object Discovery and Modeling Using Single RGB-D Images Containing Multiple Object Instances (2017)
2. Logoglu, K.B., Kalkan, S., Temizel, A.: CoSPAIR: colored histograms of spatial concentric surflet-pairs for 3D object recognition. Robot. Auton. Syst. **75**, 558–570 (2016)
3. Bonkenburt, T.: Robotics in logistics. A DPDHL perspective on implications and use cases for the logistics industry (2016)
4. Camacho-Muñoz, G.A., Rodriguez, C., Alvarez-Martinez, D.: Modelling the kinematic properties of an industrial manipulator in packing applications. In: Proceedings of the 14th IEEE International Conference on Control and Automation, Washington, DC, USA. IEEE Control Systems Society (2018)
5. Cheng, Z., Cufusion, H.Y.: Accurate real-time camera tracking and volumetric scene reconstruction with a cuboid. Sensors **17**, 1–21 (2017)
6. Collet, A., Berenson, D., Srinivasa, S.S., Ferguson, D.: Object recognition and full pose registration from a single image for robotic manipulation. In: 2009 IEEE International Conference on Robotics and Automation, pp. 48–55, May 2009
7. Collet, A., Martinez, M., Srinivasa, S.S.: The moped framework: object recognition and pose estimation for manipulation. I. J. Robot. Res. **30**(10), 1284–1306 (2011)
8. Collet, A., Srinivasa, S.S.: Efficient multi-view object recognition and full pose estimation. In: 2010 IEEE International Conference on Robotics and Automation, pp. 2050–2055, May 2010
9. Comaniciu, D., Meer, P.: Mean shift: a robust approach toward feature space analysis. IEEE Trans. Pattern Anal. Mach. Intell. **24**(5), 603–619 (2002)
10. Copal: Container stripper and palletizer (2013)
11. Correll, N., et al.: Analysis and observations from the first Amazon picking challenge. IEEE Trans. Autom. Sci. Eng. **15**(1), 172–188 (2018)
12. Feng, R., Zhang, H.: Efficient monocular coarse-to-fine object pose estimation. In: 2016 IEEE International Conference on Mechatronics and Automation, ICMA 2016, pp. 1617–1622. IEEE (2016)

13. Firman, M.: RGBD datasets: past, present and future. IEEE Computer Society Conference on Computer Vision and Pattern Recognition Workshops, Section **3**, 661–673 (2016)
14. Henry, P., Krainin, M., Herbst, E., Ren, X., Fox, D.: RGB-D mapping: using Kinect-style depth cameras for dense 3D modeling of indoor environments. Int. J. Robot. Res. **31**(5), 647–663 (2012)
15. Institut für Technische Logistik: Parcel Robot (2013)
16. Meister, S., Izadi, S., Kohli, P., Hämmerle, M., Rother, C., Kondermann, D.: When can we use kinectfusion for ground truth acquisition. In: Workshop on Color-Depth Camera Fusion in Robotics, vol. 2, October 2012
17. Narayanan, V., Likhachev, M.: Deliberative object pose estimation in clutter. In: Proceedings - IEEE International Conference on Robotics and Automation, pp. 3125–3130 (2017)
18. Newcombe, R.A., et al.: Kinectfusion: real-time dense surface mapping and tracking. In: Proceedings of the 2011 10th IEEE International Symposium on Mixed and Augmented Reality, ISMAR 2011, pp. 127–136, Washington, DC, USA. IEEE Computer Society (2011)
19. TEUN: TEUN takes a load off your hands (2012)
20. Whelan, T., et al.: Kintinuous: spatially extended kinectfusion. Technical report, Massachusetts Institute of Technology, Cambridge, USA (2012)
21. Whelan, T., Leutenegger, S., Salas Moreno, R., Glocker, B., Davison, A.: Elastic-Fusion: dense SLAM without a pose graph. Robot.: Sci. Syst. **11**, 1–9 (2015)
22. Zhou, Q.-Y., Koltun, V.: Depth camera tracking with contour cues. In: 2015 IEEE Conference on Computer Vision and Pattern Recognition (CVPR), pp. 632–638, June 2015

Development of a Line-Follower Robot for Robotic Competition Purposes

Harold Murcia[(✉)], Juan David Valenciano, and Yeison Tapiero

Facultad de Ingeniería, Grupo de Investigación D+TEC, Programa de Electrónica, Universidad Ibagué, Carrera 22 calle 67, Ibagué 730001, Colombia
`harold.murcia@unibague.edu.co`

Abstract. A fast line follower is an intelligent robot that must detect and follow a line drawn on a surface with possible changes of inclination. The robotics competitions demand that the robot go over a racetrack in the shortest possible time. The purpose of this paper is to study the line follower robot from the Control Engineering point of view to optimize its performance in standard races. In this paper we propose a SISO angle control scheme based on the relation between estimated line position and yaw robot angle. A sensitive position estimation respect to the line was implemented to improve the provided information interpretation from infrared array sensors respect to the conventional robots. Finally a suction turbine engine and a guarantee action algorithm were added to improve the angle controller response at high speeds and loss of grip on the wheels.

Keywords: Robotic competitions · Line follower robot
Embedded control

1 Introduction

Mobile robotics is one of the fields of robotics with more progress in recent decades. New mechanical configurations, control structures, unmanned vehicles developments and low-cost platforms have changed the way we knew about robotic systems. At university level, exist academic encounters which invite minds from around the world to compete in different events and have gained considerable popularity in recent years e.g.: RoboCup, Robot-challenge, all Japan Sumo, Mercury challenge and Robot-games. Colombia presents the same trend and the robotic competitions like Runibot and Robo-Matrix are increasing the number of participants each year. These spaces also compare efforts among universities allowing that participants to share experiences that not only help them strengthen their knowledge of the branches of engineering involved such as: Mechanical analytical properties of materials, electronic, instrumentation,

---

Our source implementation is freely available online and can be obtained from https://github.com/HaroldMurcia/LineFollower.git.

© Springer Nature Switzerland AG 2018
J. C. Figueroa-García et al. (Eds.): WEA 2018, CCIS 916, pp. 464–474, 2018.
https://doi.org/10.1007/978-3-030-00353-1_41

handling engine and automatic control among others; but also promote investigative skills such as observation, hypothesis testing approach and innovative development reflected in their different prototypes each year. Line follower robot LFR has very rich history [1] and is the most popular robot among competition robots with a specific and simple task: Follow a black path in a white color background (or vice versa) with the fastest speed possible. A large number of authors have addressed the issue of line followers; especially in its design [2,3], implementation [4] and possible applications [5,6]. However, less research have studied its control strategies and much less the mathematical models, most of the time people tune their controllers based on its practical experience [7] or use fuzzy control [8] where the need for a model are not significant.

2   The Line-Follower Robot LFR

The main problem of this platforms is how to smoothly and accurately follow the line and complete the circuit in the shortest possible time. To perform this goal, we consider three important aspects: (1) The more knowledge the LFR has about the position of the line with respect to its own center, the better it will follow the reference; (2) an appropriate controller generate correct the actions on the motors to keep the robot centered on the line and to go fast without getting off the race track; (3) a drifts effects compensation the due to the centrifugal and centripetal forces on the curves of the racing circuit. The following subsections detail the proposed elements to accomplish the goals based on modeling, parameter estimation, automatic control and perception system to estimate the robot speeds and line position estimation respect to the line.

2.1   Modeling and Control

A LFR is an autonomous system which usually uses differential topology, where two DC gear motors located symmetrically to ensure the center of mass generate the traction and direction movements by combinations of the angular velocities. In this subsection, a differential drive mobile robot is described by a kinematic model. The main purpose of kinematic modeling is to represents the robot velocities as a function of the driving wheels velocities along with the geometric parameters of the robot. Then, a corresponding open loop scheme is proposed including the motor dynamic response and a close loop is presented in order to stabilize the robot. Differential robots (see Fig. 1a) have a non-holonomic constraints [9,10] and its kinematic equations are normally referenced in the inertial frame:

$$\dot{q} = \begin{bmatrix} \dot{x} \\ \dot{y} \\ \dot{\theta} \end{bmatrix} = \begin{bmatrix} \frac{R}{2}cos(\theta) & \frac{R}{2}cos(\theta) \\ \frac{R}{2}sin(\theta) & \frac{R}{2}sin(\theta) \\ \frac{R}{L} & -\frac{R}{L} \end{bmatrix} \begin{bmatrix} \dot{\varphi}_R \\ \dot{\varphi}_L \end{bmatrix} \tag{1}$$

where $\dot{\varphi}_R$ and $\dot{\varphi}_L$ are the wheel angular speeds: ω_R and ω_L respectively, R is the wheel radio and L is the distance between the wheels.

The kinetic model presented in Eq. (1) has two problems when applied directly to a line follower: First, the robot does not have an inertial frame system, and second the robot don't measure the angle "θ''" directly. Therefore the model presented in Eq. (1) can be expressed as Eq. (2) in function of the line reference:

$$q = \begin{bmatrix} \dot{x}_t \\ \dot{\theta} \end{bmatrix} = \begin{bmatrix} \frac{R}{2} & \frac{R}{2} \\ \frac{R}{L} & -\frac{R}{L} \end{bmatrix} \begin{bmatrix} \dot{\varphi}_R \\ \dot{\varphi}_L \end{bmatrix} \tag{2}$$

Where X_t is the distance traveled by the LFR

Dynamics is the study of the motion of a mechanical system taking into consideration the diferent forces that affect its motion unlike kinematics where the forces are not taken into consideration. The dynamic model of the system is essential for simulation analysis of the motion and for the design of control algorithms. Figure 1b shows a simple proposed model basic in Eq. (2) to control the LFR angle by reading the line sensor-array and includes the dynamic of the DC motors as a angular velocity "ω" in function of the input voltage "V_{in}" and the centered reference (3500) given the sensor range: $0 < d < 7000 \ x10^{-5}$ m.

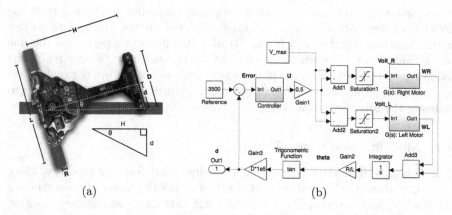

Fig. 1. (a) Proposed control chart of a SISO strategy for a LFR; (b) LFR in a differential drive mobile configuration

The proposed closed loop structure of the system is a conventional feedback structure, a PD controller is defined by two actions, proportional and derivative which have different effects on the error $e_{(s)}$. The integral action is discarded since in a position control, the system includes an integral action. This simple controller is proposed to regulate the LFR angle given its easy implementation and low computational cost. The PD controller is represented by the following equations:

$$\frac{U_{(s)}}{e_{(s)}} = K_p \Big[1 + s * T_d \Big] = K(s - z_1) \tag{3}$$

Equation (3) express a PD controller as a transfer function and its tune consist in define the values for a gain K and a zero z_1. An initial PD controller was implemented in discrete time and tuned from experimental tests on different race tracks. Then after data acquisition and parameter estimation a new PD controller was tuned based on FRTool [11], a design method previously successfully used on similar platforms [12].

2.2   Guaranty of Control Action

The control strategy focuses on an angle control estimated from the distance to the line-array and manipulates the difference between angular velocities or between the applied voltages assuming that both motors are identical. Similar applied control effort can be found in: [7,13]. Control the differential robot as a SISO system implies the following relations between the control effort, the applied voltages on the motors, the robot velocity and robot angle:

$$U = U_R - U_L \tag{4}$$

$$U_R = U_{base} + \frac{U}{2}; U_L = U_{base} - \frac{U}{2} \tag{5}$$

$$\nu = \frac{(U_R + U_L)R}{2}C \tag{6}$$

where "U" is the control effort, "U_{base}" is the control effort when the LFR is at null error; "U_R''" and "U_L" represent the duty cycle for the applied voltage on the motors respectively, "ν" is a LFR velocity indicator and "C" is a constant from the close loop system "$H_{(s)}$" in steady state.

However, this method only works with a base velocity "U_{base}" and control effort "U" around zero; in other words: in straight line or soft curves due to the energy limits: "U_{Lim}" (See Eq. (7)). When "U" or "U_{base}" increase its value, the condition expressed in Eq. (4) is not guaranteed, given the input limits described by:

$$-U_{Lim} \leq U_{R,L} \leq U_{Lim} \tag{7}$$

Thereby, a big control effort implies a saturation on applied voltage on motors, which could affect the voltage difference on motors and generate a false control action. To automatically eliminate the effect is necessary to decrease "U_{base}" without slowing too much the robot and in this way ensure the proper control signal. A solution to this problem is proposed in the following equations:

$$U_{base} = U_{Bref} - \Delta_1 - \Delta_2 \tag{8}$$

$$\Delta_1 = (U_R - U_{Lim})(1 - sign(U_{Lim} - U_R)) * 0.5; \tag{9}$$

$$\Delta_2 = (U_L - U_{Lim})(1 - sign(U_{Lim} - U_L)) * 0.5 \tag{10}$$

where U_{Bref} is a constant reference value for U_{base}, δ represent the robot speed decreasing necessary to ensure difference voltage applied on motors without a saturation.

Where U_{Bref} is the initial constant base velocity which is modificated to ensure the velocities difference in U_{base}.

Algorithm 1. Implementation of algorithm to guarantee the control action

$\triangleright$ %comment: Finding ideal U_R and U_L values %

% Calculate $U[k]$ from PD controller

$U_{base} = U_{Bref}$

$U_{R[k]} = U_{base} + U_{[k]}/2$

$U_{L[k]} = U_{base} - U_{[k]}/2$

if $(U_{R[k]} > U_{Lim})$ or $(U_{R[k]} < -U_{Lim})$ **then**

$\quad \Delta_1 = U_{Lim} - U_{R[k]}$

$\quad U_{base} = U_{base} + \Delta_1$

end if

if $(U_{L[k]} > U_{Lim})$ or $(U_{L[k]} < -U_{Lim})$ **then**

$\quad \Delta_2 = U_{Lim} - U_{L[k]}$

$\quad U_{base} = U_{base} + \Delta_2$

end if

% Update motor actions

$U_{R[k]} = U_{base} + U_{[k]}/2$

$U_{L[k]} = U_{base} - U_{[k]}/2$

2.3 Perception

To follow the line reference on the speedway the robot uses infrared IR sensors on the frontal part to measure the distance from the nose-robot to the line. Although sometimes the position information is complemented with additional sensors such as Inertial Measurements Units IMU, encoders or digital cameras, the line follower robots for speed competencies usually have only Infrared (IR) sensors given it's fast response. The IR Line-sensors consist of an IR emitter and an IR photo-transistor pair to detect the line strip, such that the robot steers itself with respect to data coming from sensors. The photo-transistor is connected to a pull-up resistor to form a voltage divider that produces an analog voltage output between zero volts and input voltage Vin as a function of the reflected IR where a lower output voltage is an indication of greater reflection (white background) [14]. Figure 2b illustrates the electronical sensor configuration for each IR sensor and Figs. 2c and 2d show the output voltage signals for black and white background with two different measurement distances on a spinning disk at 3000 Revolutions Per Minute RPM. The used disk had a half part in white and the other one in black color for a fifty percent duty cycle on the output voltage signal. The high time of the signal corresponds with the black part detection and the low time corresponds with the white part detection. Therefore, the voltage response for each sensor depends on both the distance from the sensor to the surface and the color of the surface.

In the most of works done on the estimation of the position for line follower robots, the sensor responses are binarized to obtain boolean values for true-positive and true-false line detection. Thus, the resolution of the position measurement is equal to the distance between each sensor. However, this poor estimation reflects an oscillation effect around the line strip and cant not operate with high speeds given it's low resolution on the control output. In previous

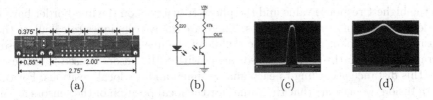

Fig. 2. Line sensor configuration: (a) QTR-8A reflectance sensor array from Pololu; (b) schematic diagram for the IR-line sensor; (c) sensor-output response 3 mm away from a spinning disk; (d) sensor-output response 10 mm away from a spinning disk.

stages, the analog value between a pure black and a pure white was considered as noise and people removed it in order to refined the boolean detection; but at last, it was realized over time that within that "noise" was valuable information about distance to the line. The approach of this section is to use that information and combine each photo-transistor output to increases the measurement resolution and in this way improve the line-following performance.

Sensors Adaptation. In the most common case, an array of eight sensors with analog responses per each IR is used for this purpose, the output of this sensor array is digitized by 10- bit Analog-to-Digital converter (ADC) on the micro-controllers for a total of eight digital values with a range from 0 to 1023. The measurement of sensors vector is denoted as $m = [m1, m2, ..., m8]$ and the position is denoted as $P = [p1, p2, ..., p8]$; the leftmost sensor $p1$ is located to approximately 35 mm from the center of the sensor array and the distance between each sensor is 10 mm such as $P = [-35, -25, -15, -5, 5, 15, 25, 35]$. The width of the line strip is 19±1 mm and the reference for the array is the middle of the line strip to ensure the line following. The first problem with the sensor array is the difference between the photo-transistor responses for the same surface given robot inclinations or electronic devices tolerance. A practical solution to reduce this difference is a calibration process before the position estimation based on minimal response (white background) and maximum response (black background) for each photo-transistor. By using the Eq. 11, the normalized responses are obtained with values from 0 to 1000.

$$S = (m - m_{min})./(m_{max} - m_{min}) * 1000 \tag{11}$$

where S is the normalized sensor vector, the minimum and maximum vectors are denoted by: $m_{min} = [min_1, min_2, ...min_8]$, $m_{max} = [max_1, max_2, ..., max_8]$.

Measurement and Estimation. According to [15] with an uniform illuminated surface the discrete output of sensor array on line can be fitting as a normal distribution, in an ideal case, where the center of the robot corresponds with the middle of the line strip, the extreme photo-transistors on the array trend to a null response, on the other hand, the centered photo-transistors trend to the highest response value and the photo-transistors on the line-border have a widely range of intermediate values. There are many techniques to calculate the position of the robot respect to the middle of the line strip by fussing the sensor array outputs. In this work, a sensor array with 8 IR sensors is used to estimating this distance according to each analog signal and it's local positions. For the data fusion, we assume that the values for the local position of the sensors are in an interval [−35,35]. Moreover, we consider positive weights within the following weighted averaging function based on Bajraktarevic mean (Called mixture function) [On some properties of weighted averaging with variable weights],[Data Fusion: Theory, Methods and applications]:

$$D_{S[P]} = \frac{\sum_{i=1}^{n} S(P_i)P_i}{\sum_{i=1}^{n} S(P_i)} \qquad (12)$$

where n is the number of sensor on the array, the vector of weights is the normalized sensor signals S, P represents the position of the sensors and D is the calculated distance from the center of the sensor array to the middle of the line strip. The Fig. 3a shows an experimental validation of the position estimation respect to 72 manually measurements with a total of 72×8 digital samples in a range evaluation [−35,35] mm, the mean square error obtained presented an acceptable value for the application around 6.5 mm which includes both, the measurement and estimation error, a second graphical validation of LFR angle estimation from line IR-array is showed in Fig. 3b, where the angle estimation is compared with an angle obtained from a magnetometer on-board of the LFR at different positions evaluation.

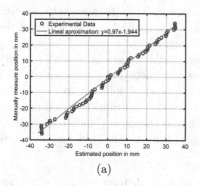 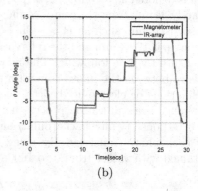

(a)   (b)

Fig. 3. (a) Calibrated distance of LFR respect to the line; (b) Graphical validation of LFR angle estimation from line IR-array with a second sensor signal

3   Experimental Evaluation

3.1   The Prototype

Figure 4a illustrates the pictorial shematic from the prototype that was built to examine the feasibility and develop control algorithms for the competences in

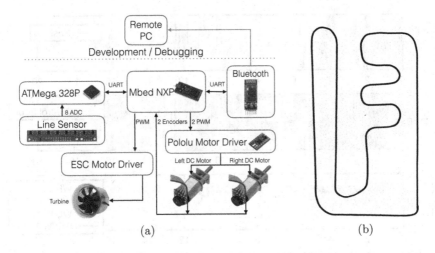

Fig. 4. (a) The schematic diagram of the electronics, (b) the race track tests

LFR category. The prototype consists of a Printed Circuit Board (PCB) plate that holds battery, the microcontroller, the infrared sensors, the motor driver and the wheels through the DC micro motors with a total weight of 125 g.

The overall electronics setup except for the power, which was provided by a constant voltage battery Li-Po of 2 cells with a boost converter tunned at 12 VDC. We selected the an ATMEGA328P-AU clocked at 20 MHz from ATMEL as the slave controller given its small size, rapid prototyping and readily available community support. On the other hand a mbed LPC1768 microcontroller performs the master controller tasks such as: communications data recording and control algorithm. In these applications, the used micro motors, speed control unit and sensors are generally from Pololu company. The motors 10:1 Micro Metal Gearmotor HPCB 12 V are brushed DC motor with a metal gearbox, 3000 RPM and 100 mA with no load, 4 oz-in (0.3 kg-cm) and 0.8 A at stall. The encoders use a magnetic disc and hall effect sensors to provide 12 counts per revolution of the motor shaft. The Dual Motor Driver Carrier DRV8833, can deliver 1.2 A per channel continuously (2 A peak) to a pair of DC motors. With an operating voltage range from 2.7 V to 10.8 V and built-in protection against reverse-voltage, under-voltage, over-current, and over-temperature, this driver is a great solution for powering small, low-voltage motors. The line sensor used was the QTR-8A Reflectance Sensor Array from Pololu, which has 8 IR LED/phototransistor pairs mounted. Finally in order to decrease the slip effects generated by at high speeds, agressive curves and friction reduction by dust, a suction EDF27 turbine was implemented on the robot. Although this turbine can reach 0.7 N of pushing force to improve the performance in curves, also the current consumption has a big increase reaching the 5.2 A, which has big negative impact on battery and the LFR autonomy. In this sense, a power activation equation in function of the LFR speed was tuned from experimental data:

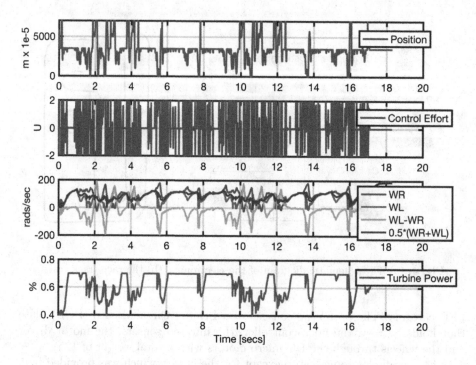

Fig. 5. Close loop responses for PD controller on a test race track.

$$Turbine_{Power} = 1400 + K_T * V_{LFR}^2 \tag{13}$$

where $Turbine_{Power}$ is the applied power on the turbine engine with a range: $1000 < Turbine_{Power} < 1700$ and K_T is an empirical constant and V_{LFR} is the LFR speed calculated from: $0.5 * R(W_R - W_L)$.

Experimental Data. Figure 4b shows the used race track to test the LFR, it consists of a black line on a withe surface with 10 m of travel approximately. Once the controller was tunned with the PD constants $Kp = 0.001091$ $[\frac{duty_{cycle}}{meters x 10^{-5}}]$, $Kd = 0.000055$ $[\frac{duty_{cycle}}{meters x 10^{-5}}]$ with a sample time $Ts = 8 \times 10^{-3}$ s. The Fig. 5 illustrates the obtained signals of the LFR in a race cycle for sensor line distance. The upper chart shows the position response with a reference of 3500 $x10^{-5}$ m and a Mean Squared Error $MSE = 0.17680 \times 10^{-3}$ m^2. Next chart presents the control effort according to subsect. 2.2 with $U_{base} = 0.78$ at 12 VDC. The third chart from top to bottom show the adapted encoders response corresponding to the right motor angular speed W_R in rad/s, left motor angular speed W_R in rad/s, LFR speed calculated from angular speeds $0.5 * R * (W_R + W_L)$ and the difference between the angular speeds $(W_R - W_L)$ which is an LFR angle estimation. The bottom chart show the Turbine effort calculated according to the Eq. 13.

4   Conclusions

A LFR robot was designed and implemented in this paper. Thanks to the position estimation implemented in the Eq. 12, it is possible to implement classic control schemes such as Fuzzy or PID. In this work, a simple mathematical model was proposed using a SISO control scheme, then a PD controller with a guarantee control action given the constrained outputs was implemented and tested in an experimental prototype and race track by adding a third actuator to improve the LFR performance in presence of aggressive curves at high speeds. The control actions guarantee that the LFR follows the trajectory of the race track and that it travels in approximately 17 s. The Mean Squared Error $MSE = 0.17680 \times 10^{-3} m^2$, which implies a good path following even at high speeds and agressive disturbances. The motion control was successful but improvements need to be made, such as a new mathematical model which includes the Turbine effect and the center of mass, where a state space representation, to compare MIMO vs MISO schemes would show a more complete approach.

Acknowledgments. This research is being developed with the partial support of the "Gobernación del Tolima" under "Convenios de cooperacion 1026–2013" - Research Culture and "Convenio No 055-17". The results presented in this paper have been obtained with the assistance of students from the Research Hotbed on Robotics (SIRUI), Research Group D+TEC, Universidad de Ibagué, Ibagué-Colombia.

References

1. Mehrl, D., Parten, M., Vines, D.: Robots enhance engineering education. In: 27th Annual Conference on Proceedings Frontiers in Education 1997. Teaching and Learning in an Era of Change, vol. 2, pp. 613–618. Stipes Publishing
2. Pakdaman, M., Sanaatiyan, M.M.: Design and implementation of line follower robot. In: 2009 Second International Conference on Computer and Electrical Engineering, pp. 585–590. IEEE (2009)
3. Pakdaman, M., Sanaatiyan, M.M., Ghahroudi, M.R.: A line follower robot from design to implementation: technical issues and problems. In: 2010 The 2nd International Conference on Computer and Automation Engineering (ICCAE), pp. 5–9, IEEE, February 2010
4. Hasan, K.M., Al Mamun. A.: Implementation of autonomous line follower robot. In: 2012 International Conference on Informatics, Electronics & Vision (ICIEV), pp. 865–869. IEEE, May 2012
5. Rafi, R.H., Das, S., Ahmed, N., Hossain, I., Reza, S.T.: Design & implementation of a line following robot for irrigation based application. In: 2016 19th International Conference on Computer and Information Technology (ICCIT), pp. 480–483. IEEE, December 2016
6. Binugroho, E.H., Pratama, D., Syahputra, A.Z.R., Pramadihanto, D.: Control for balancing line follower robot using discrete cascaded PID algorithm on ADROIT V1 education robot. In: 2015 International Electronics Symposium (IES), pp. 245–250. IEEE, September 2015

7. Engin, M., Engin, D.: Path planning of line follower robot. In: 2012 5th European DSP Education and Research Conference (EDERC), pp. 1–5. IEEE, September 2012
8. Głowicki, M., Butkiewicz, B.S.: Autonomous line-follower with fuzzy control. In: 2013 Signal Processing Symposium (SPS), pp. 1–6. IEEE, June 2013
9. Fukao, T., Nakagawa, H., Adachi, N.: Adaptive tracking control of a nonholonomic mobile robot. IEEE Trans. Robot. Autom. **16**(5), 609–615 (2000)
10. Gomes, M., Bassora, L., Morandin, O., Vivaldini, K.: PID control applied on a line-follower AGV using a RGB camera. In: 2016 IEEE 19th International Conference on Intelligent Transportation Systems (ITSC), pp. 194–198. IEEE, November 2016
11. De Keyser, R., Ionescu, C.: FRtool: a frequency response tool for CACSD in Matlab®. In: 2006 IEEE Conference on Computer Aided Control System Design, 2006 IEEE International Conference on Control Applications, 2006 IEEE International Symposium on Intelligent Control, pp. 2275–2280. IEEE, October 2006
12. Murcia, H.F., Gonzalez, A.E.: Performance comparison between PID and LQR control on a 2-wheel inverted pendulum robot. In: 2016 IEEE Colombian Conference on Robotics and Automation (CCRA), pp. 1–6. IEEE, September 2016
13. Balaji, V., Balaji, M., Chandrasekaran, M., Khan, M.A., Elamvazuthi, I.: Optimization of PID control for high speed line tracking robots. Procedia Comput. Sci. **76**, 147–154 (2015)
14. Pololu: QTR-8A and QTR-8RC Reflectance Sensor Array User's Guide
15. Yufka, A., Aybar, A.: Line estimation for a line-following mobile robot. In: 2015 9th International Conference on Electrical and Electronics Engineering (ELECO), pp. 890–893, IEEE, November 2015

Author Index

Printed in the United States
By Bookmasters